sasol
reaching new frontiers

SOUTHERN AFRICAN BIRDFINDER

D0807357

Where to find 1 400 bird species in southern Africa and Madagascar

Callan Cohen • Claire Spottiswoode • Jonathan Rossouw

In memory of Kirsten Louw (1979-2005), exceptional naturalist and birder, field companion and beloved friend

With special thanks to
Etienne Marais • Anthony Cizek • Pete Leonard
for major contributions to the text.

Struik Publishers
(A division of New Holland Publishing
(South Africa) (Pty) Ltd)
Cornelis Struik House
80 McKenzie Street
Cape Town
8001
New Holland Publishing is a member
of the Johnnic Publishing Group.
Visit us at
www.struik.co.za
Log on to our photographic website
www.imagesofafrica.co.za
for an African experience.

www.imagesofafrica.co.za
IMAGES OF AFRICA
PHOTO LIBRARY

First published in 2006

10 9 8 7 6 5 4 3 2 1

Copyright © in text, 2006: Callan Cohen and Claire Spottiswoode
Copyright © in maps, 2006: Struik Publishers
Copyright © in photographs, 2006: individual photographers as credited alongside images (Note: IOA = Images of Africa)
Copyright © in published edition, 2006: Struik Publishers

Publishing manager: Pippa Parker
Managing editor: Lynda Ingham-Brown
Editorial team: Brenda Brickman, Helen de Villiers
Proofreader: Tessa Kennedy
Indexer: Cora Ovens
Design concept: Janice Evans
Designer: Robin Cox
Cover design: Robin Cox
Cartography: Carl Germishuys and Claire Spottiswoode (site maps)
Reproduction by Hirt & Carter Cape (Pty) Ltd
Printed and bound by Kyodo Printing Co (S'pore) Pte Ltd, Singapore

All rights reserved. No part of this publication may be reproduced, stored in a retrieval system, or transmitted, in any form or by any means, electronic, mechanical, photocopying, recording, or otherwise, without the prior permission of the copyright owners and publishers.

ISBN 1 868 72 725 4

The authors and publisher of this book accept no resposibility for any loss, injury or death sustained while using this book as a guide.

Title page: Lesser Seedcracker (Johann Grobbelaar)

IBA
BirdLife
IMPORTANT BIRD AREA

BirdLife International's Important Bird Area Programme aims to conserve bird species by identifying, protecting and managing sites throughout their ranges, which are used in the development of national and regional protected area networks.

To order extra pull-out maps of the region, contact **sabfmap@birdingafrica.com**

SPONSOR'S FOREWORD

Birding has become one of the world's fastest-growing pastimes. But, in the fast-paced world we live in, birding enthusiasts now increasingly seek 'productive birding' – in other words, they are no longer prepared to waste time trying to find that desirable but elusive species in the wrong locale.

Democracy in South Africa has also made it possible for birders on the African sub-continent to cross borders into neighbouring countries' birding sites with a minimum of formalities. The time, therefore, is doubly right for *Southern African Birdfinder: Where to find 1 400 bird species in southern Africa and Madagascar.*

In this informative volume, the authors pinpoint more than 300 top birding sites – and the species you are likely to find there – right across southern Africa. Not only are South Africa, Namibia, Botswana, Zimbabwe and Madagascar covered, but also the relatively undiscovered and undocumented birding treasures of Angola, Mozambique, Zambia and Malawi.

The authors have been to explore all these sites, having travelled southern Africa extensively in pursuit of its best birding treasures. Experience is the best tutor when it comes to birding!

So, for those keen on finding the sub-continent's top 150 birds and its many 'specials' and endemics on 39 exciting routes, this guide will prove as indispensable as a road map on a brand-new journey. As sponsors, Sasol is also delighted that this publication – in line with our corporate policy – will assist birders in 'reaching new frontiers'.

Enjoy.

PAT DAVIES
Chief Executive Sasol Limited

sasol
reaching new frontiers

ACKNOWLEDGEMENTS

Callan Cohen and Claire Spottiswoode

This project is the product of the shared experience and goodwill of very many birding colleagues and friends, to all of whom we are tremendously grateful. This book would not exist without their contributions, comments and field testing, and their wonderful hospitality during our travels in preparation for this book.

First and foremost, we would like to thank Etienne Marais, Anthony Cizek and Peter Leonard for their major contributions to the Eastern South Africa, Zimbabwe and Zambia chapters, respectively.

The names of the legion of people who very kindly helped in many ways are listed below, according to the geographical region where they made the largest contribution. Our sincerest thanks to them all, and to anyone we may inadvertently have missed. We would like particularly warmly to thank the following among them who provided especially extensive assistance and comments: David Allan, Duan Biggs, Françoise Dowsett-Lemaire, Andrew Hester, Phil Hockey, Kirsten Louw, Warren McCleland, Michael Mills, Vincent Parker, Faansie Peacock, Peter Ryan, Ian Sinclair, Stephanie Tyler, Colin Valentine and David Winter. Many thanks to Martin Benadie for proofing the checklist.

The many people who have at various stages shared, encouraged or endured our lifelong obsessions with birds are indirectly responsible for this project. Among them we would like gratefully to single out the following: David Allan, Tim Boucher, Edward and Marilyn Burn, Nigel Collar, Elaine Cook, Malcolm Fair, Lincoln Fishpool, Mike and Liz Fraser, John Graham, Marc and Diane Herremans, Phil Hockey, Jan Hofmeyr, Rob Leslie, Geoff Lockwood, Kirsten Louw, Michael Mills, Anders Møller, Giselle Murison, Morné du Plessis, Raju Raman, Jonathan Rossouw, Peter Ryan, Ian Sinclair, Peter Steyn, Mel Tripp, Les Underhill, Ross Wanless, David Winter, Phil Whittington, and all at the Cape Bird Club, Percy FitzPatrick Institute of African Ornithology and Avian Demography Unit at the University of Cape Town, and the bird group at the Department of Zoology in Cambridge. We are also grateful to our research supervisors, Tim Crowe and Morné du Plessis at the University of Cape Town and Nick Davies at the University of Cambridge, for their trust and forbearance during a project which has overlapped with, and occasionally threatened to overwhelm, both of our doctoral studies. We owe perhaps the largest debt of all to our parents, Mark and Alice Cohen and Christopher and Cécile Spottiswoode for encouraging our birding interest from an early age.

We are also grateful for the financial support we have received during this period from the South African National Research Foundation, the University of Cape Town, and St John's College, Cambridge, as well as to the many reconnaissance trips sponsored by Birding Africa.

For her confidence in and support of the project, which was not always easy, we would like to thank Pippa Parker, and her excellent backup team: Brenda Brickman, Robin Cox, Carl Germishuys, Colette Stott, Janice Evans, Helen de Villiers, Tessa Kennedy, Cora Ovens and Steve Connolly.

SOUTH AFRICA

Mark Anderson, Naas du Preez, Mel Tripp, Pat Cardwell, Cliff Dorse, Dalton Gibbs, Rynhard Kok, Chris Spengler, Ron Searle, Esther Burger, Brian van der Walt, Per Lor, Keith Harrison, Willy Pike, Margaret McIver, Adam Weltz, Mike Buckham, Eric Herrmann, Ross Wanless, Anne Gray, Mariana Delport, Trevor Hardaker, Japie Claasen, Nigel Anderson, David Bishop, Dave Brown, Andre Botha, Jonathan Boucher, Mark Brown, Peter Carnall, Hugh Chittenden, Murray Christian, Roy Cowgill, Greg Davies, Steve Davis, Dawie de Swart, Ryan Ebedes, Ehren & Johan Eksteen, Roger Fieldwick, Dale Forbes, Rob Geddes, Malcolm Gemmell, Rihann Geyser, Ashwell Glasson, Ken Gordon, Rob Gradwell, Joe Grosel, Robin Guy, Dave Hoddinott, Peter Holt, Pete Irons, John Isom, Jon Jackson, Wayne Jones, Mostert Kriek, Geoff Lockwood, Athol Marchant, Paul Martin, Andre Marx, John McAllister, Cameron McMaster, Ara Mondjem, Richard Montinaro, Dalena Mostert, Jenny Norman, Rick Nuttall, Pete Outhwaite, Chris Patton, Barry

Porter, Duncan Pritchard, Selwyn Rautenbach, Adam Riley, Chris Roche, Dominic Rollinson, Robert Rotteveel, Jimmy Saunders, Keith Seaton, Murrie Slotar, Andrew Sutherland, Déwald Swanepoel, Warwick Tarboton, Alf Taylor, Colin Valentine, Rudi Van Staden, Sarah Venter, Dave Weaver, Johnny Wilson, Graham Winch, Peter Wragg and Ross Zietsman.

NAMIBIA AND BOTSWANA

Ulrik Andersen, Mark Boorman, Tim Boucher, Steve Braine, Renee Braithwaite, Patrick and Marie-Lousie Cardwell, George Cox, James Currie, Digby Cyrus, Chris de Vries, Wayne Delpoort, Eckart Demasius, Cliff Dorse, Mike Ford, Paul Funston, Guy Gibbon, Tertius Gous, Chris Hines, Alan and Meg Kemp, Greg Lock, Tim & Laurel Osborne, Mark Paxton, Shaun Peard, Barry Reed, Nancy Robson, Colin Rodgers, Rob Simmons, John Suart, Wessel Swanepoel, Mike Taylor, Keith Wearne, John van der Woude, Wendy and Remi Borello, Chris Brewster, Richard Randall, Dragan Simic, Alison Flatt, Marc Herremans, Ruud and Kitty Kampf, Hans Meevis, Mark Muller, and especially Stephanie Tyler.

ZIMBABWE AND MOZAMBIQUE

Ferdi & Tracey Couto, Ken Dixon, Gruff Dodd, Gary Douglas, Peter Ginn, Peter Jordi, Chris Pollard, Ian Ridell, Martin Smith, Derek Solomon, Julia and Dorothy Wakeling, Lesley Cizek, Darryl Tiran, Alex Masterson (ably assisted by his hound Shava), Michael Mason, Grant Nealon, Stephen James, Carl Beel, Colin Baker, Carlos Bento, Rod Cassidy, Rita Covas, Morné de la Rey, Martim Pinheiro de Melo, Alastair Kilpin, Jean-Louis Kromer, Helen Biram, Clayton Burne, Sam de Beer, Dave Deighton, Paul Funston, David Kelly, Ken Logan, Peter Thompson, Rudi van Staden, Fred Berrington and Clayton Burne. The Zimbabwe first draft was edited by Anthony Cizek.

MALAWI, ZAMBIA AND ANGOLA

Klaas-Douwe Dijkstra, Bob Dowsett, Françoise Dowsett-Lemaire, Jens Haugaard, Warren McClelland, Bob Medland, Mark Sprong, John Wilson, Geoff Lockwood, Elaine Cook, Peter Steyn, Nick Cobb, Henk Hendriks, Robert Langhendries, Valéry Schollaert, Ian and Emma Bruce-Miller, Mark Harvey, Derek Solomon, Dan Sonnenberg, Louise Warburton, Giles Mullholland, Pedro vaz Pinto, Henk Visser, John Jones and Mimi of Rio Longo and Wings over Africa.

MADAGASCAR

Brian Finch, Olivier Langrand, Pete Morris, Nathalie Seddon, Derek Schuurman, Jonathan Ekstrom, Julia Jones and Lyn Mair.

Jonathan Rossouw

A work of this nature builds upon the combined birding experience of innumerable people. Much of my information was gleaned, either through mutual experience or through conversation, on birding trips with David Allan, Bruce and Penny Biccard, Richard and Wilma Boon, Christian Boix, Timothy Boucher, Callan Cohen, Malcolm Fair, Erik Forsyth, David Kaplan, Claire Spottiswoode, Andrew Sutherland and David Weaver. I am especially grateful to my birding buddies and business partners in Rockjumper Birding Tours, Adam Riley and David Hoddinott, for sharing their extensive knowledge of KZN's birds. For generously proof-reading and commenting on portions of the text, I am grateful to David Allan, Brian Finch, Pete Morris, Pieter de Kock, Malcolm Gemmel, David Johnson, Allan Kirby, Lyn Mair, Keith Wearne, Tim Wood, the innumerable bird guides in Madagascar, especially Maurice and Patrice Ratsisakanana, Andrew Sutherland, David and Gill Weaver, Ian Michler and Gavin and Bridget Dickson. For their support and encouragement over the years, I am grateful to David Allan, Hamish Campbell, Pat Cardwell, Phil Hockey, Barrie Rose, Peter Ryan, Warwick Tarboton and Hardy Wilson.

Special thanks for the phenomenal encouragement of my parents, Denis and Annette, and my step-father, Martin, who endured my fledgling obsession. And last, but not least, to my partner, Holly Faithfull, for her endless sense of humour in the early hours of the morning.

QUICK GUIDE TO BIRDING ROUTES

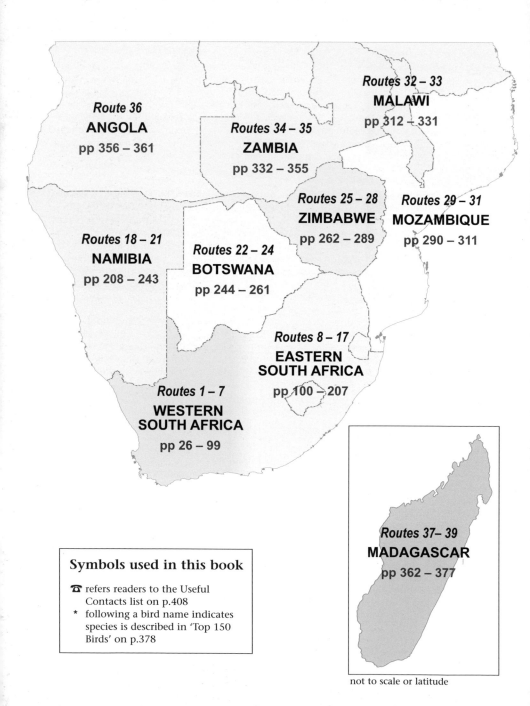

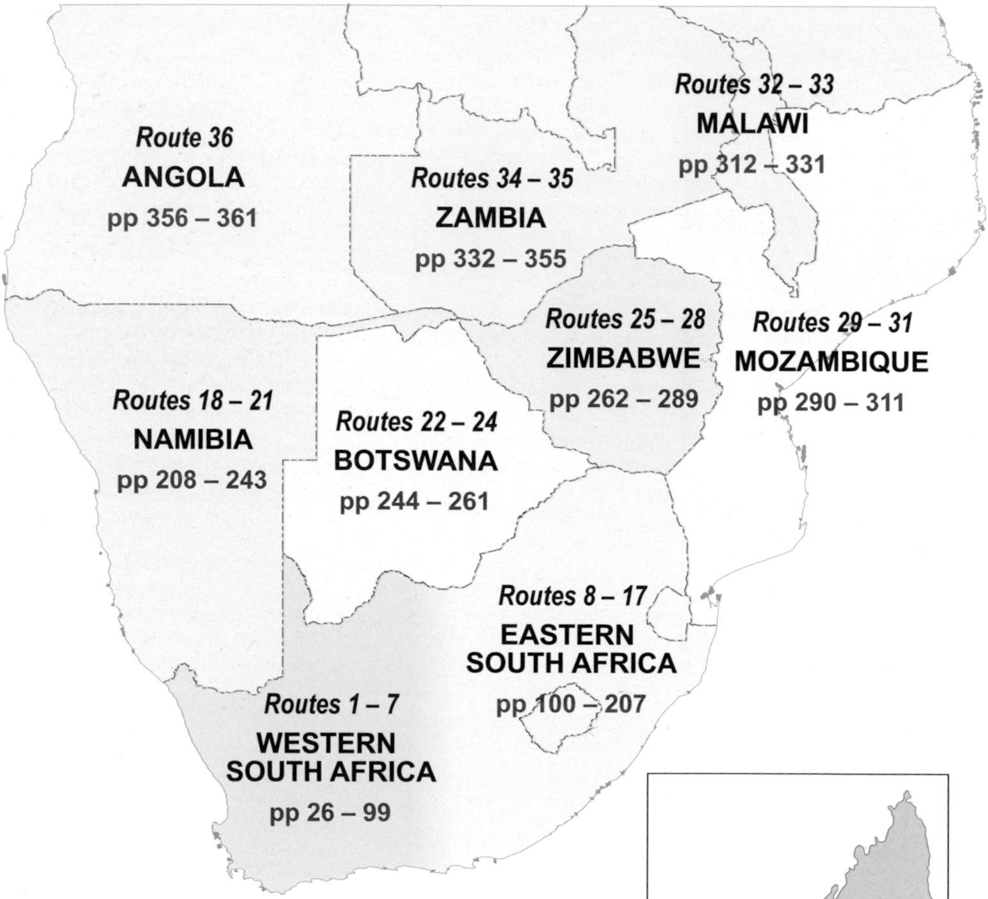

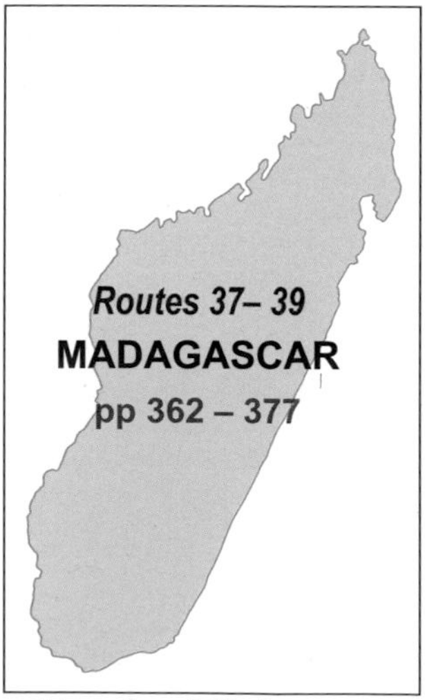

not to scale or latitude

Symbols used in this book

☎ refers readers to the Useful Contacts list on p.408

* following a bird name indicates species is described in 'Top 150 Birds' on p.378

CONTENTS

INTRODUCTION

WORLD CLASS BIRDING

South Africa and Madagascar, widely acknowledged as two of the world's top 10 birding areas, form the main focus of this guide that also extends to many lesser-known birding hot spots in the southern third of Africa. The well-defined birding region of southern Africa – south of the Zambezi and Kunene rivers – is well covered by local field guides and forms the basis of this book's coverage. However, the adjacent but lesser-known regions of northern Mozambique, Angola, Zambia and Malawi also offer highly diverse and endemic-rich birding, and for this reason we include these countries in this book. Madagascar, inexorably linked to the African continent, is one of the world's great ornithological treasure troves.

Callan Cohen

Southern Africa offers diverse birding opportunities.

The sites introduced in this book are grouped into 39 practical birding routes that can be explored by international and local birders alike, and provide detailed directions to finding over 1 400 species (60% of Africa's bird species), with an emphasis on seeing the more than 350 species endemic to this region. Throughout this book, we refer to 'endemics' as those birds restricted to greater southern Africa, unless stated otherwise. Near-endemics are those birds with ranges extending only marginally beyond the borders of this region, but which are unlikely to be seen by birders outside of the region.

The region covered by this book extends beyond the traditionally accepted definition of southern Africa (Africa south of the Kunene and Zambezi rivers) and also encompasses Zambia, Malawi, the whole of Mozambique, Angola and the island of Madagascar. For ease of recognition, this region is described here as the greater southern African region as opposed to the traditional southern African region (as represented in the field guide *Sasol Birds of Southern Africa*).

Plans are afoot to break the world 'one day' birding record in the region: already a small team of birders has recorded over 325 species in a single 24-hour period in South Africa, and a total of 360 seems quite possible.

There is special emphasis, too, on the growing number of pelagic birding opportunities in the region, which present some of the world's greatest birding spectacles.

Both experienced and novice birdwatchers are inevitably drawn to the region by its scenic

UNIQUE FAMILIES

Of the over 20 bird families endemic to Africa and the Indian Ocean islands, all but one may be found by using this book. Indeed, no fewer than seven families are found only within the regions discussed here. Sugarbirds and Rock-jumpers are confined to the Cape and montane regions of southern Africa, while Vangas, Asities, Ground-Rollers, Mesites and Cuckoo-Rollers are endemic to the Malagasy region. Two localised families extend beyond our borders to East Africa – the bizarre Shoebill (Zambia) and the elusive Dapplethroat and Spot-throat (N Mozambique and N Malawi). Widespread endemic African families include Ostrich, Hamerkop, Guineafowl, Secretarybird, Mousebirds, Turacos, Woodhoopoes, Ground Hornbills, Oxpeckers, Bush-Shrikes, Batises and Wattle-eyes and African Barbets.

and cultural diversity and, especially in South Africa, by its well-developed infrastructure, high standard of accommodation and excellent network of national parks and nature reserves. In addition, information on ecotourism attractions, such as the region's big game species, whale-watching opportunities, botanical diversity and unusual animals such as lemurs, is also included in the birding routes.

PLANNING YOUR TRIP

The majority of this book is devoted to South Africa, largely because it has a vast resident birding community, but also because it receives by far the most visitors. Indeed, South Africa offers the best combination of features for a new birder to southern Africa (see table below). Also, independent travel in a hired car in South Africa (and Namibia too) is very easy.

CHOOSING YOUR DESTINATION

It can be seen from the table below that South Africa, Namibia, Angola and Madagascar have the most endemic birds, with South Africa and Namibia being logistically the easiest and Angola the most difficult and the most expensive. The tropical areas with the highest diversity also have the most shared species (low level of endemism), but offer the best opportunities for exploration and adventure. They are the most logistically difficult areas to visit, with the exception of Eastern South Africa, which does not present a challange. South Africa and Namibia are both easily visited by independent birders, while countries such as Angola and Madagascar are best visited as part of a structured birding tour.

WHEN TO VISIT

Because this guide covers such a large area, each route and site in the text offers advice on the best time to visit. Generally speaking, birding is good throughout the year as most of the species are resident. Summer migrants are present from Oct-Mar. Birds are most active across most of the summer-rainfall areas from Oct-Mar (peak Dec-Feb), although this is not true for the extensive miombo woodlands, which have a Sept peak. The winter-rainfall Western Cape is at its best from Sept-Nov, with pelagic birding most rewarding from Aug-Oct. Having said this, there are few times in southern Africa when the birding is poor. For Madagascar, the best months are Sep-Nov.

Choosing your country

Region	Endemism hot spot	Total number of species	Infrastructure and ease of travel	Health and safety	Wildlife viewing	Pelagic birding	Cost	Exploration options
Western SA	1	2	1	1	1	1	1	3
Eastern SA	1	1	1	1	1	2	1	3
Namibia	1	2	1	1	1	2	1	2
Botswana	3	1	2	2	1	-	2	2
Zimbabwe	3	1	2	2	1	-	1	2
Mozambique	3	1	3	2	2	2	1	1
Zambia	3	1	2	2	1	-	2	1
Malawi	2	1	2	2	2	-	1	2
Angola	1	1	3	3	2	3	3	1
Madagascar	1	2	3	2	1	3	2	2

1 = excellent; 2 = good; 3 = moderate to poor

HEALTH, SAFETY & TRAVEL

Conditions can change rapidly, so always consult local tourist information offices for further information before you set off on a birding trip. Foreign office advisories often stress excessive caution; advice from these organisations should be considered in balance with local knowledge.

HEALTH

Malaria is present throughout the low-lying northern and eastern areas of the region, and is especially prevalent during the rainy summers. Malaria is not present in the Cape and the high-lying areas of South Africa, but becomes more prevalent as one moves further north in the region. We recommend that you discuss prophylaxis options with your doctor and always take precautions against being bitten. Malaria is transmitted by *Anopheles* mosquitoes that are nocturnal and are almost silent.

Some ticks carry a non-lethal 'tick-bite fever', and measures should be taken to prevent being bitten. HIV is common in the region, and it is a good idea to take a set of sterile syringes with you in case you need emergency medical treatment in remote areas. Discuss other inoculations, such as that for yellow fever, with your foreign travel clinic.

SAFETY

None of the sites covered in this book are unusually dangerous, although we do urge visitors to be cautious and alert, particularly in or near the larger cities, as birders inevitably need to carry conspicuously valuable equipment, making them potential targets for casual muggings. The majority of the reported birder muggings, which are remarkably rare compared to those in places like South America, have been in the Durban (KwaZulu-Natal) and Johannesburg (Gauteng) areas. Urban birding sites are perhaps best not visited alone, although years of birding activities at these sites have yet to result in serious incidents. Petty theft is common throughout; never leave bags or birding equipment unattended on car seats. Public transport is often limited, frequently unsafe, and best avoided.

Only experienced African travellers should visit Angola as certain areas in this country are highly unsafe.

WHERE ARE THE LANDMINES?

Landmines are a potential problem in Mozambique, and a particularly serious problem in certain areas in Angola. In Mozambique, mapping and clearing of mines is an ongoing process, and many hundreds of birders have birded many of the sites described in this book without incident. Naturally, we cannot guarantee that you will not encounter mines, but observing the following simple precautions will reduce risk:

- do not use roads that are overgrown and look like they have not been driven in a long time;
- when stopping for 'comfort stops' do not leave the road, as the road edge is a high risk area;
- do not leave the road near old, overgrown buildings and especially along railway lines;
- follow only recently used footpaths in the vicinity of these birding sites;
- employ the services of local guides; they often have a good idea of which areas are safe and which are unsafe.

DANGEROUS ANIMALS

The big game that occurs in much of southern Africa is one of the region's greatest attractions. While dangerous game animals are mostly restricted to protected areas, especially in South Africa, intrepid birders exploring northern Namibia, the Kalahari in Botswana, parts of Zambia and Mozambique and the Zambezi River Valley in Zimbabwe need to be especially vigilant. It is very likely that a small number of birders using this book will, at some stage or other, encounter some of these creatures on foot. On our last standard birding tour to Namibia, we were quite unlucky in this regard, and encountered (on foot) two Elephant, one Hippo at night at close range in our tented camp, and a pride of nine Lion while walking in a river valley west of Etosha. In light of this, we recommend that birders do not leave their cars in game reserves, and do not walk in such areas without an armed guide.

Leopard occur in most of the sites in this book, even in the mountains on the outskirts of the greater Cape Town area. They are largely nocturnal, shy and, as they slip away in the distance, are seen by only the most fortunate. Leopards only rarely attack people, but should never be approached. Lion are generally restricted to reserves in South Africa but also occur widely in the Kalahari and the Zambezi River Valley outside of formal reserves. Lion sightings on foot are rare but should you encounter Lion on foot, freeze, and then slowly walk backwards to safety; do not be tempted to run. Elephant are becoming increasingly common outside of reserves north of South Africa, from Northern Namibia across northern Botswana and to the Zambezi River Valley. Although superficially docile, Elephant can quickly become aggressive and should NEVER be approached closely.

Callan Cohen

Dangerous animals alert

Adriaadne van Zandbergen/IOA

Although superficially docile, elephants should always be treated with respect.

Lone Buffalo and Black Rhinoceros (and to a lesser extent White Rhinoceros) can be especially temperamental, and extremely dangerous when surprised (always make sure you have a nearby tree to climb). Make sure that you *never* position yourself between a Hippopotamus and the water! Crocodiles are widespread in most of the more tropical areas (roughly in all areas where malaria occurs). Never swim in water bodies in such areas; and, in fact, stay away from the water's edge as crocodiles can move very quickly when snatching prey from the banks.

If you are fortunate enough to see a snake or scorpion, please be cautious as some species are potentially dangerous. In particular, be aware of the superbly camouflaged Puffadder, which lies lethargically across paths and is found fairly commonly over the entire region. Deadly cobras and mambas are very shy and rarely seen.

INDEPENDENT TRAVEL

As mentioned, southern Africa, especially South Africa and Namibia, is an excellent destination for independent birders wishing to hire a car and explore the region at their own pace. The road infrastructure in these areas is excellent, and a wide range of accommodation is available across most of the region, especially in the coastal areas; consult tourist information for further details. Accommodation in the national parks and most nature reserves is superb and provides great value for money.

Most small rural towns have service stations and offer accommodation at basic, inexpensive hotels, and many also have municipal camp sites. Tap water in towns is potable in South Africa and southern and central Namibia only. As one moves further north, more planning is required for independent travel, especially in Zambia and Mozambique. Madagascar, and particularly Angola, are logistically very challenging for the independent traveller.

DRIVING

Although the road infrastructure in southern Africa is generally very good, there might be potential driving hazards in rural areas for those unaccustomed to 'gravel' roads. Avoid the temptation to drive fast on good quality gravel roads, as it is remarkably easy to lose control on corners and when braking – 60 km/h is a good maximum. Never brake hard, even if there is a bustard standing at the roadside! Also, avoid driving at night as wild animals and livestock are serious hazards. If you need to travel long distances in desert areas, even those relatively close to Cape Town, be sure to carry a good water supply in case of breakdowns. In the latter respect, be aware that mobile phone coverage in more remote areas is far from complete. Make sure your spare wheel is in working condition, and ideally carry several inflating cartridges (such as TyreWeld).

Claire Spottiswoode

Driving off-road requires experience.

If you are venturing off the beaten track, especially in the north of the region, and are unaccustomed to these conditions, consult a book on advanced 4WD driving as road conditions approaching birding sites are frequently challenging, especially during the rainy season. When travelling in remote areas, try to travel in two cars if possible. One or more jerry cans of fuel can save an enormous amount of trouble. For extricating yourself from mud or sand, make sure you have a spade and at least one tow rope of good length (most are too short for this purpose). For travelling on minor roads in the rainy season, a high-lift jack is highly recommended (an ordinary scissor jack is generally useless in these circumstances), together with a large can of oil spray to keep it functional, and a block of wood to keep it from sinking. Rubber or, ideally, metal 'track mats' can also be helpful. A footpump or electric compressor is useful for reinflating tyres that have been deflated for easier travel on sand (deflate to about 1.2 bars). Take suitable spares such as fan belts, radiator hoses, brake and transmission fluid, and air, fuel and oil filters, and fill your radiator with plenty of antifreeze (also acts as a coolant).

In summer, glance at your temperature gauge regularly while driving, and keep your radiator clear of grass seeds and insects, especially where there is a grassy middle track. If you have a 4WD with a metal plate protecting the underside of your engine, frequently clear any accumulated grass from this potential tinderbox.

At police roadblocks, be courteous and polite at all times. Obey the speed limit when entering any towns or settlements, regardless of whether or not you feel it is appropriate. Carry all your car documentation. Make sure that if you are not the owner of the car you are driving, you have multiple copies of a signed and police-authorised letter from the owner with his and your identity/passport numbers, and car engine and chassis numbers. Certain countries (e.g. Mozambique and Zambia) have legislation regarding particular reflective signs that must be exhibited on the rear of your vehicle; this is heavily enforced, so make sure you are all 'legal'.

BIRDING ETIQUETTE

With the ever-increasing popularity of birding in southern Africa, there is inevitably pressure on certain well-visited sites. While the roadside often provides excellent birding in rural areas, ask permission at the nearest farmhouse or village if you would like to enter private land.

Playback of bird calls is a very helpful birding tool, and limited tape playing is unlikely to have a detrimental effect in most cases. However, we urge birders to refrain from excessive playback, especially during the breeding season and at popular sites near the major cities, and in rest camps in national parks.

THE BIRDING COMMUNITY

BIRD CLUBS

There is a very active birding community in southern Africa and local birders are encouraged to join their local branch of BirdLife South Africa (see ☎, p.408). These clubs offer activities that include a monthly evening meeting and numerous monthly half-day outings and other events. By supporting BirdLife South Africa you are contributing to the conservation of birds and their habitats.

INTERNET BIRDING

Regular updates to information in *Southern African BirdFinder* will be published online at http://www.birdingafrica.com. Please contact us at sabf@birdingafrica.com with any updates you might have and these will be posted on the website. For further details visit the website, or write to sabf@birdingafrica.com.

The South African e-mail list, SABirdNet, provides an active forum of over 700 birders for local observations, rarity updates, trip reports and local birding events (to find out more and to join, contact norman@nu.ac.za). E-mail lists provide the birder with all sorts of helpful tit-bits for trip preparation. You may also wish to join one of the other South African active local e-mail lists: Pretoriabirds (Pretoria area), CapeBirdNet (western South Africa), SA Rare Bird Alert (rarities), Zulubird (Zululand) or AfricanBirding (continent wide). These can be joined by sending a blank e-mail to, for example, capebirdnet-subscribe@yahoogroups.com; or consult www.birdingafrica.com for a complete listing and subscription details.

RARE BIRDS AND REPORTING

If you see any species that are either very rare or not recorded for the region, please urgently contact the local or national rare bird committees via www.birdingafrica.com (see also SABirdNet above). Any sightings of rare birds should be mailed immediately to sararebirdalert@yahoogroups.com, to enable local birders to view and verify the records. Further details are available on http://www.birdingafrica.com.

Birders can also contribute to other valuable bird monitoring projects such as those run by the Avian Demography Unit ☎. Please report any ring recoveries or sightings of colour-ringed birds to SAFRING ☎.

Claire Spottiswoode

Many of southern Africa's endemic birds are found on the desolate plains of the Karoo.

CHANGING BIRD NAMES

Southern Africa's birds have long had distinctive indigenous names. These common names are often derived from Afrikaans, and many of them have filtered into official English usage. These include 'korhaan' for small bustards, 'dikkop' ('thick-head') for thick-knees, and 'lourie' for turacos. Others have become internationally accepted, such as 'Hamerkop' ('hammer-head'). However, in the interests of global consistency, all common names have recently been made to conform to international nomenclature. For ease of reference, a list of the new and old names can be found in the annotated checklist on p.408.

TAXONOMY FOR BIRDERS

Our perception of the relationships between the birds of the southern African region is currently fraught with controversy and confusion. Not only have many of the common names undergone change, but there is the added complication of 'new' species that have emerged in field guides over the past few years. These include the discovery of totally undescribed forms, such as Long-tailed Pipit (p.93) that was recently discovered near Kimberley, although most of these 'new' species represent subspecies that have been 'split' and elevated to full species status, such as Agulhas Long-billed Lark.

The 'species', a unit integral to science, conservation and indeed birding, may not be as absolute as we would imagine it should be. The way scientists view species ('species concepts') has always been subject to much debate, and whether similar forms should be designated as species or subspecies is, in practice, frequently a matter of opinion.

The once dominant and undoubtedly valuable Biological Species Concept places emphasis on the ability of individuals to interbreed: forms that can interbreed and produce fertile offspring are regarded as members of the same species. One weakness of this concept is that it fails to deal effectively with isolated populations that would never naturally come into contact and interbreed. It also fails to deal objectively with natural hybridisation, and strict supporters suggest that hybridising groups must belong to the same species. It is thus often associated with 'lumping', which is the 'downgrading' of similar species into subspecies of a single species. A local example of a situation where application of the Biological Species Concept might be misleading is that of the narrow hybrid zone between Karoo Lark and Barlow's Lark (p.85). These two distinctly different species are not even each other's closest relatives, and their inappropriate 'lumping' into one species would obscure the myriad fascinating differences shown between these forms.

The relatively recent Phylogenetic Species Concept is gaining popularity among ornithologists. It places emphasis on consistent differences (even if small) between forms, and is applied within the framework of a phylogeny (a family tree of evolutionary relationships). It is based on the indirect argument that if forms show distinct differences, then they must be separate, because interbreeding results in shared features, not distinct ones. Because the Phylogenetic Species Concept recognises small differences between forms, it is often linked with 'splitting', which is the process of elevating subspecies to full species status. Both concepts have their drawbacks, and are currently causing much debate among scientists.

Changing species concepts are only part of the reason for the recent appearance of 'new' species. Thorough new research spearheaded by ornithologists at the Percy FitzPatrick Institute of African Ornithology at the University of Cape Town has revealed previously undetected differences among closely similar groups of southern African birds. Central to these studies are genetic techniques that probe deep into the birds' evolutionary histories to obtain estimates of their uniqueness, as part of a multifaceted approach that also includes evidence from plumage, size, calls and behaviour, resulting in taxonomic decisions that are likely to stand the test of time.

Peter Steyn

Orange River White-eye is a recent split.

TAXONOMIC PENDULUM:
RECENT SPLITS IN SOUTHERN AFRICA

'Old' Status	New Status = Split
Royal Albatross	Northern/South Royal Albatross
Wandering Albatross	Wandering/Tristan Albatross
Shy Albatross	Shy/Salvin's Albatross
Yellow-nosed Albatross	Atlantic/Indian Yellow-nosed Albatross
Broad-billed Prion	Broad-billed/Antarctic Prion
White-chinned Petrel	White-chinned/Spectacled Petrel
Black Kite	Black/Yellow-billed Kite
Black-rumped Buttonquail	Black-rumped/Hottentot Buttonquail
White-bellied Korhaan	White-bellied (northern Namibia)/Barrow's Korhaan
Black Korhaan	Southern/Northern Black Korhaan
Kelp Gull	Kelp (vagrant)/Cape Gull
Lesser Black-backed Gull	Lesser Black-backed/Heuglin's Gull
Knysna Turaco	Knysna/Livingsone's/Schalow's Turaco
Cape Parrot	Cape/Grey-headed Parrot
Lesser Cuckoo	Lesser/Madagascar Cuckoo
Burchell's Coucal	Burchell's/White-browed Coucal
Red-billed Hornbill	Southern Red-billed/Damara Red-billed Hornbill
Karoo/Dune Lark	Karoo/Barlow's/Dune Lark
Long-billed Lark	Cape/Agulhas/Karoo/Eastern/Benguela Long-billed Lark
Clapper Lark	Cape/Agulhas/Eastern Clapper Lark
Rufous-bellied Tit	Rufous-bellied/Cinnamon-breasted Tit
Yellow-streaked Greenbul	Yellow-streaked/Sharpe's Greenbul
Stripe-cheeked Greenbul	Stripe-cheeked/Olive-headed Greenbul
Olive Thrush	Olive/Karoo/Mountain Thrush
Bleating Warbler	Green-backed/Grey-backed Camaroptera
Black-backed Cisticola	Luapula/Rufous-winged/Winding Cisticola
Bar-throated Apalis	Bar-throated/Yellow-throated/Namuli Apalis
Spotted Prinia	Karoo/Drakensberg Prinia
Gorgeous Bush Shrike	Gorgeous/Perrin's Bush-Shrike
Cape White-eye	Cape/Orange River White-eye
Grey-headed Sparrow	Southern Grey-headed/Northern Grey-headed/ Swahili Sparrow
Cape Canary	Cape/Yellow-crowned Canary
Black-headed Canary	Black-headed/Damara Canary
Black Widowfinch	Black/Twinspot Widowfinch

Controversial and pending decisions (not split in this book)

Green Barbet	Green (Malawi)/Woodwards' (KwaZulu-Natal) Barbet
Sabota Lark	Sabota/Bradfield's Lark
Cloud Cisticola	Cape Cloud/Eastern Cloud Cisticola
Barred Owlet	Cape/Ngami Barred Owlet
Short-toed Rock-Thrush	Short-toed/Pretoria Rock-Thrush

Visit the 'African Bird Taxonomy' website at http://www.birdingafrica.com for news of updates.

BIRDING HABITATS

SOUTHERN AFRICA

The search for any bird species is simplified by an understanding of the habitat or habitats that it occupies. While some species are highly habitat specific, many occur in more than one biome or vegetation type. Relative to most of the rest of continental Africa, habitat diversity in southern Africa is high. Below, we have summarised the major habitat types and the features that characterise them, as well as some of the region's habitat-specific birds. The habitats and birds of Madagascar are described separately (see p.19).

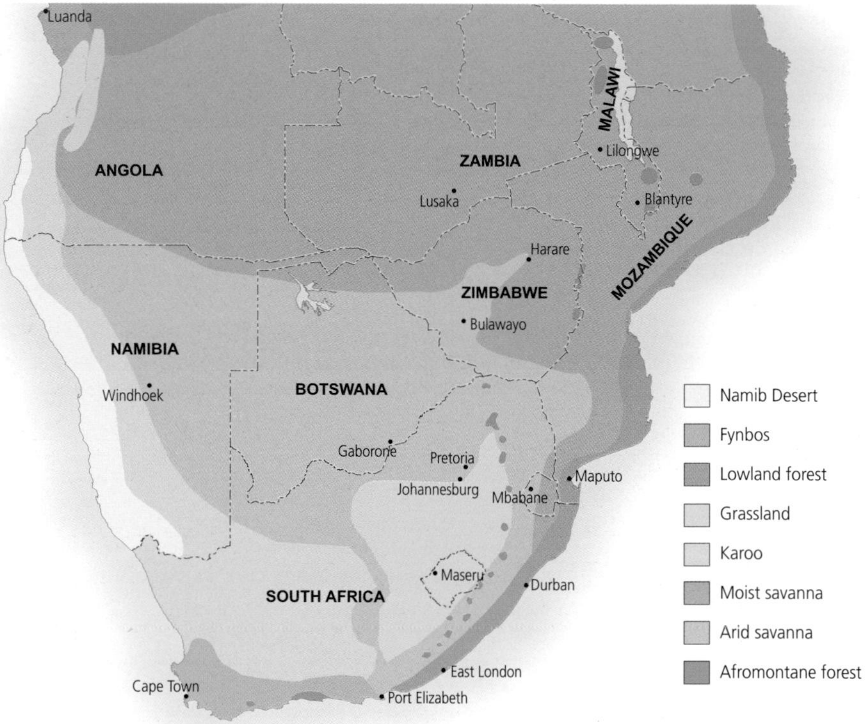

VEGETATION MAP OF THE GREATER SOUTHERN AFRICAN REGION

Karoo

The Karoo is a vast semi-desert, botanically divided into two very different regions. It dominates the arid western half of South Africa and large areas of southern Namibia. It is a sparsely inhabited open area of stony plains, scattered with small plants, and punctuated by low dunes and small hills (koppies).

The winter-rainfall Succulent Karoo (Tanqua Karoo and Namaqualand) region is characterised by small succulent plants, whereas the summer-rainfall Nama Karoo (most of the Karoo interior, including Bushmanland) is dominated by grasses and low, woody shrubs.

Despite these fundamental climatic and vegetation differences, most Karoo specials occur in both regions. Endemics and near-endemics include **Karoo Korhaan**, **Ludwig's Bustard***, **Red***, **Karoo**, **Barlow's**, **Karoo Long-billed** and **Sclater's* Larks**, **Black-eared Sparrowlark***, **Karoo** and **Tractrac Chats**, **Karoo Eremomela***, **Cinnamon-breasted***, **Namaqua*** and **Rufous-eared Warblers**, **Pale-winged Starling** and **Black-headed Canary***.

Fynbos (Cape Floral Kingdom)

Fynbos, the dominant vegetation of the smallest of the world's six floral kingdoms, is largely confined to the mountains and coastal lowlands of the winter-rainfall Western Cape. Fynbos is a shrubby vegetation type characterised by proteas, ericas and reed-like restios, which thrive in nutrient-poor soils. Fynbos supports a low diversity of birds, but compensates with a high level of endemism. True fynbos endemics, namely **Hottentot Buttonquail***, **Cape Rock-jumper***, **Victorin's Scrub-Warbler***, **Cape Sugarbird***, **Orange-breasted Sunbird**, **Cape Siskin*** and **Protea Seed-eater***, are largely confined to mountain fynbos. Lowland fynbos specials such as **Agulhas Long-billed** and **Agulhas Clapper Larks** also occur in the surrounding renosterveld, a drier vegetation type that occurs on richer soils and has thus been largely converted to agriculture.

Gerhard Dreyer/IOA

Fynbos vegetation

Namib Desert and Escarpment

The Namib Desert is the most extreme of southern Africa's habitats and is characterised by almost unvegetated expanses of stony open plains and dunes. Namib endemics are **Dune Lark** (dunes) and **Gray's Lark*** (open plains). At the eastern edge of the Namib is the Namibian escarpment (which extends north into Angola), a rugged, rocky and much more vegetated habitat. Escarpment endemics and near-endemics include **Rüppell's Korhaan**, **Herero Chat***, **Hartlaub's Francolin***, **Benguela Long-billed Lark***, **Damara Rockrunner**, **Monteiro's Hornbill**, **White-tailed Shrike** and **Cinderella Waxbill***.

Arid and moist savanna

Perhaps Africa's most characteristic vegetation type, savannas are characterised by a mix of grasses and trees and may range from open habitats to closed woodlands. They can broadly be divided into two main categories.

Arid savanna, or thornveld, is dominated by acacia species. It is characteristic of the western areas of southern Africa (although it occurs patchily in the east as well) and is isolated from the arid savannas of East Africa by a broad belt of moist savanna. The isolation of the western arid savannas has resulted in the occurrence of many endemics, including **Short-clawed Lark***, **Kalahari Scrub-Robin**, **Ashy Tit**, **Southern Pied Babbler**, **Chestnut-vented Tit-Babbler**, **Black-chested Prinia**, **Marico Flycatcher**, **Burnt-necked Eremomela**, **Crimson-breasted Shrike** and **Black-faced Waxbill**.

Moister, broad-leaved savannas and woodlands dominate the northern and eastern parts of the region, and many different variations occur. In South Africa, 'bushveld' is a general term given to this vegetation type. From a birding perspective, the moist savanna type that occurs across Angola, Zambia, Malawi, Zimbabwe and Mozambique (almost restricted to the area covered by this book) is miombo, a broad-leaved woodland type rich in endemics, described in detail on p.267.

Forest

This biome can be divided into Afromontane forest, where most of the endemics occur, and lowland forest, which stretches along the eastern coastal regions.

Patches of Afromontane forest and associated vegetation types, such as montane grassland, are found in an archipelago of 'forest islands' from the southern Cape through the Drakensberg, the Eastern Highlands of Zimbabwe and Mozambique, in Malawi, and on the western escarpment of Angola. While some of the species occur at sea level in the south of their range, further north they are only found at high altitudes. Species endemic to these forests (and forest edges) include **Forest Buzzard***, **Knysna Woodpecker***, **Knysna Turaco**, **Chorister**

Robin-Chat, **Brown Scrub-Robin**, **Cape Batis**, **Knysna*** and **Barratt's Warblers**, **Chirinda Apalis***, **Roberts' Warbler***, **Bush Blackcap***, **Olive Bush-Shrike** and **Forest Canary**. Afromontane forest endemics restricted to Angola are discussed on p.356.

Other forest specials include **Green Barbet***, **Swynnerton's Robin***, **African Crowned Eagle**, **Narina Trogon*** and **Green-headed Oriole***, while **Spot-throat***, **Dappled Mountain Robin***, **White-winged Apalis*** and **Sharpe's Akalat** are restricted in the region to Malawi and northern Mozambique.

Several species are endemic to the belt of lowland evergreen forest and associated thickets occurring in the extreme eastern areas of southern Africa northwards. **Rudd's Apalis**, **Woodwards' Batis**, **Neergard's Sunbird*** and **Pink-throated Twinspot*** are endemic to southern Africa, while **Southern Banded Snake-Eagle**, **Tiny Greenbul**, **Gorgeous Bush-Shrike**, **Chestnut-fronted Helmet-Shrike***, **Black-bellied Starling** and **Grey** and **Plain-backed Sunbird** are more generally distributed along the East African coast. **Mangrove Kingfisher*** is restricted to mangroves along the east coast of Africa.

Mushitu forest, which occurs in north-western Zambia, is discussed in detail on p.341.

Grasslands

Grasslands cover much of the central and eastern highveld area of South Africa, the Mashonaland Plateau in Zimbabwe, and small patches in mountains across the region. Many of southern Africa's most endangered species cling onto ever-decreasing patches of medium-altitude grassland, threatened by habitat transformation. The numerous grassland endemics include **Southern Bald Ibis***, **Blue Korhaan**, **Rudd's***, **Botha's***, **Eastern Long-billed** and **Melodious*** **Larks**, **Yellow-breasted Pipit***, **Buff-streaked Chat**, **Blue Crane**, **Gurney's Sugarbird*** and **Drakensberg Prinia**. Species endemic to high montane grasslands include **Drakensberg Rock-jumper**, **Mountain Pipit** and **Drakensberg Siskin**. Other characteristic grassland specials include **Blue Swallow***, **Long-tailed Widowbird**, **Denham's Bustard***, **Barrow's Korhaan*** and **Wattled*** and **Grey Crowned Cranes**.

Freshwater wetlands

Dambos, vleis, swamps, flood plains and marshes are wetlands with emergent vegetation; they are typically rich in birds. The largest such area is the Okavango Swamps. Wetland endemics include **Slaty Egret***, **Coppery-tailed Coucal**, **Hartlaub's Babbler**, **Swamp Boubou** and **Chirping Cisticola**. Dambos (p.264) and vleis support a characteristic assemblage of species, many of which are migrants. The largest rivers in the region have few endemics but are host to many sought-after specials, such as **African Skimmer***, **White-crowned Lapwing**, **Rock Pratincole***, **Pel's Fishing-Owl*** and **White-backed Night-Heron***.

The coast and sea

The Atlantic and Indian oceans meet at Africa's southernmost point, Cape Agulhas. The Benguela Current moves up the Atlantic coast, bringing chilly, nutrient-rich waters from Antarctica, while the warmer Agulhas Current moves south and west down the east coast of Africa from the tropics. The birds endemic or near-endemic to the southern African Atlantic coast and nearshore islands are **African Penguin**, **Cape Gannet**, **Cape**, **Bank*** and **Crowned Cormorants**, **African Black Oystercatcher***, **Hartlaub's** and **Cape Gulls** and **Damara Tern***. Offshore waters and their associated fishing fleets attract impressive numbers of migrant pelagic seabirds (see p.20), from albatrosses to storm-petrels.

Callan Cohen

Benguela Current endemics

Huge numbers of Palearctic-breeding waders crowd coastal mudflats in the summer, and are best viewed at the larger lagoons and estuaries on the West Coast, including Walvis Bay Lagoon and Langebaan Lagoon. **Crab Plover*** is a special of the eastern coast.

MADAGASCAR

Evergreen humid forest (rainforest) is home to most of the island's endemic birds. It once blanketed eastern Madagascar from Vohemar in the north to Tolagnaro in the south, with an isolated northern pocket on Amber Mountain. The most extensive indigenous habitat, covering an area of almost 25 000 km², this forest type is found only in areas receiving more than 2 500 mm of year-round annual rainfall. It is broadly subdivided into lowland (0-600 m asl), mid-altitude (600-1 400 m) and montane (above 1 400 m) forest, with many birds restricted to just one or two altitude band(s).

Red-breasted Coua, **Scaly Ground-Roller***, **Red-tailed Newtonia***, and **Bernier's** and **Helmet Vangas*** occur in the lowlands, **Common Sunbird-Asity** at mid-altitudes, and **Rufous-headed Ground-Roller***, **Yellow-browed Oxylabe**, **Brown Emutail***, **Cryptic Warbler** and **Pollen's Vanga** in mid- and high-altitude forests. **Yellow-bellied Sunbird-Asity*** occurs only in ridgetop forests at the highest altitudes. Madagascar's forests have been and are still being severely reduced by slash-and-burn agriculture (called *tavy* in Madagascar), firewood collection and timber extraction. The only remaining large tract of lowland forest is on the Masoala Peninsula.

The *western deciduous forests* are scattered between about Isalo in the south and Cap d'Ambre in the north. They differ from the evergreen humid forest in having a high proportion of deciduous trees (up to 80%), although this habitat shares many birds with its moister eastern counterpart. Birds largely restricted to western deciduous forest include such scarce and sought-after species as **White-breasted Mesite**, **Coquerel's Coua**, **Schlegel's Asity***, **Appert's Greenbul** and **Van Dam's Vanga**. Western deciduous forests have been even more severely impacted upon than eastern forests, with only relict patches remaining (collectively covering about 15 000 km²).

The *southern deciduous dry forest*, or *Spiny Forest* (sometimes called Spiny Desert), extends from just west of Tolagnaro in the south-east to the Mangoky River, some 400 km north of Toliara, in the south-west. Perhaps Madagascar's most extraordinary habitat, the Spiny Forest is dominated by bizarre 'Octopus Plants' in the endemic genera *Didierea* and *Alluaudia*, and numerous, often prickly, cactus-like euphorbias. Bottle-shaped baobab trees are common in places. Gems such as **Long-tailed Ground-Roller*** and **Sub-desert Mesite*** are restricted to the taller Spiny Forest north of Toliara, while **Verreaux's Coua**, **Littoral Rock-Thrush** and the newly described **Red-shouldered Vanga** are found only in the dense, euphorbia dominated coral rag scrub south of Toliara. More widespread species, nonetheless confined to this habitat, include **Running Coua**, **Archbold's Newtonia**, **Sub-desert Brush-Warbler** as well as **Lafresnaye's Vanga**.

Malagasy savanna is a highly man-modified habitat (comprising mostly a few grass and very few tree species) that covers much of the High Plateau, mainly in the west and the south. It supports a depauperate avifauna, though **Madagascar Lark** and **Madagascar Cisticola** are often numerous, and **Réunion Harrier**, **Madagascar Partridge**, **Madagascar Buttonquail** and **Madagascar Sandgrouse** are also present.

In the east, Madagascar's *wetlands* comprise mostly lakes, marshes and rivers; western lakes are typically shallower and more saline. The wetlands are home to a host of rare endemics, almost all of which are threatened by a combination of drainage for rice paddies, introduction of alien fish, siltation, and insecticide contamination. In the eastern part of Madagascar, **Alaotra Little Grebe** and **Madagascar Pochard** are in all likelihood already extinct, while **Slender-billed Flufftail*** is known only from a very few, scattered localities. **Meller's Duck**, although still fairly common in some remote wetlands, is decreasing in the face of severe hunting pressure. **Madagascar Rail**, **Madagascar Snipe** and **Grey Emutail** are also essentially restricted to the highland marshes of the east, but these birds are still reasonably widespread and common.

Western wetlands support such specials as **Madagascar Fish-Eagle** (about 100 pairs remain), **Bernier's Teal*** (also threatened, although recent sightings of more than 100 birds in the Betsiboka Delta suggest that it may be more common than previously thought) and the elusive **Sakalava Rail***. The impressively large **Humblot's Heron** is another inhabitant of western wetlands, but is also found along the coast.

PELAGIC BIRDING

OFF THE CAPE COAST

The Cape's amazing seabird abundance and diversity is the product of the Benguela Current that originates in the icy waters of Antarctica. Surging up the West Coast of southern Africa, the nutrient-rich waters cause an upwelling along the continental shelf, nurturing a profusion of ocean life that supports both a lively fishing industry and vast numbers of seabirds. Pelagic species – those which breed on land but otherwise remain at sea – congregate around the trawlers, making them easy to locate and approach.

The high point of a pelagic birding trip is sure to be that of wallowing behind a trawler with up to 5 000 birds squabbling for scraps in its wake.

In winter, day trippers regularly see over 10 000 seabirds of up to 30 species, making it arguably the world's most memorable yet easily accessible seabirding experience.

The diversity of seabirds is highly seasonal, so consult the monthly table (opposite), compiled from over 300 pelagic birding trip lists from the past 10 years.

Winter seabird-watching

Winter (May-Sept) is the most spectacular time at sea. Huge numbers of albatrosses and other pelagic seabirds migrate northwards from their breeding sites as far south as Antarctica, moving into Cape waters to escape the harsh polar winter. **Shy** and **Black-browed Albatrosses** are abundant, and both **Indian** and **Atlantic Yellow-nosed Albatrosses** are regular in small numbers. The great prize of a winter trip must be a **Wandering Albatross***, although it has become very scarce in recent years. There is also always a chance of seeing the rare **Northern Royal** and **Grey-headed Albatrosses**.

White-chinned Petrel, **Sooty Shearwater** and **Cape Gannet** are joined by huge numbers of flashy **Pintado Petrel**, **Antarctic Prion** and **Wilson's Storm-Petrel**. Both **Northern** and **Southern Giant Petrels** are present in small numbers, and **Antarctic Fulmar** and **Spectacled Petrel*** make an occasional appearance, as does fast-flying **Soft-plumaged Petrel**. **Subantarctic Skua** is usually present, and **Antarctic Tern** is sometimes seen close inshore.

Summer seabird-watching

From Oct-Apr, North Atlantic seabirds migrate south. Although seabird numbers are generally smaller at this time of the year, summer trips are nonetheless spectacular, and provide an opportunity to see several other species.

Black-browed and **Shy Albatrosses**, **Northern** and **Southern Giant Petrels**, **White-chinned Petrel** and **Sooty Shearwater** are joined in summer by **Cory's** (mainly the *diomedea* subspecies, also known as **Scopoli's Shearwater**) and **Great Shearwaters**, along with smaller numbers of **Soft-plumaged Petrel** (early summer), the occasional **Spectacled Petrel***, and **Manx** and **Flesh-footed Shearwaters**.

Claire Spottiswoode

Following a trawler off Cape Town

Great-winged Petrel is fairly common at this time, and good numbers of **European Storm-Petrel** join **Wilson's Storm-Petrel**; the rare **Leach's Storm Petrel** is mainly seen beyond the continental shelf. The migratory **Black-bellied Storm-Petrel** is present in small numbers on passage in late Sept/Oct and again in April.

Closer inshore, **Subantarctic Skua**, **Pomarine** and **Long-tailed** (very scarce) **Jaegers** patrol the skies. **Arctic Tern** is a passage migrant, but a few are present, along with **Sabine's Gull**, throughout summer. Lucky observers may see small flocks of **Grey Phalarope**.

SEASONAL TABLE FOR SEABIRDS OFF THE CAPE

Key (percentage chance of seeing bird): 5–25% 25–50% 50–75% 75–100%

	JAN	FEB	MAR	APR	MAY	JUN	JUL	AUG	SEP	OCT	NOV	DEC
Northern Royal Albatross					5–25%	25–50%	25–50%	25–50%	5–25%	5–25%	5–25%	
Wandering Albatross			5–25%	5–25%	25–50%	25–50%	25–50%	25–50%	25–50%	25–50%	5–25%	
Shy Albatross	75–100%	75–100%	75–100%	75–100%	75–100%	75–100%	75–100%	75–100%	75–100%	75–100%	75–100%	75–100%
Black-browed Albatross	75–100%	75–100%	75–100%	75–100%	75–100%	75–100%	75–100%	75–100%	75–100%	75–100%	75–100%	75–100%
Grey-headed Albatross					5–25%	5–25%	5–25%	5–25%	5–25%	5–25%		
Atlantic Yellow-nosed Alb.	75–100%	50–75%	50–75%	50–75%	25–50%	25–50%	50–75%	75–100%	75–100%	75–100%	75–100%	50–75%
Indian Yellow-nosed Alb.	50–75%	75–100%	75–100%	75–100%	75–100%	50–75%	25–50%	75–100%	75–100%	50–75%	50–75%	50–75%
Southern Giant Petrel	50–75%	25–50%	5–25%	5–25%	50–75%	75–100%	75–100%	75–100%	75–100%	75–100%	50–75%	50–75%
Northern Giant Petrel	50–75%	25–50%	5–25%	25–50%	50–75%	75–100%	75–100%	75–100%	75–100%	75–100%	50–75%	50–75%
Antarctic Fulmar				5–25%		5–25%	5–25%	25–50%	5–25%	5–25%	5–25%	
Pintado Petrel				5–25%	50–75%	75–100%	75–100%	75–100%	75–100%	75–100%	50–75%	5–25%
Great-winged Petrel	50–75%	50–75%	50–75%	25–50%	25–50%	5–25%	5–25%	25–50%	25–50%	25–50%	75–100%	50–75%
Soft-plumaged Petrel					25–50%	25–50%	25–50%	75–100%	75–100%	50–75%	25–50%	
Antarctic Prion (desolata)				5–25%	25–50%	75–100%	75–100%	50–75%				
White-chinned Petrel	75–100%	75–100%	75–100%	75–100%	75–100%	75–100%	75–100%	75–100%	75–100%	75–100%	75–100%	75–100%
Spectacled Petrel	5–25%	5–25%	5–25%	5–25%	5–25%	5–25%	5–25%	5–25%	5–25%	5–25%	5–25%	5–25%
Cory's Shearwater	75–100%	75–100%	75–100%	75–100%	75–100%	5–25%					75–100%	75–100%
Great Shearwater	75–100%	75–100%	75–100%	75–100%	75–100%	25–50%		25–50%	75–100%	75–100%	75–100%	75–100%
Flesh-footed Shearwater	5–25%	5–25%	5–25%	5–25%	5–25%					5–25%	5–25%	5–25%
Sooty Shearwater	75–100%	75–100%	75–100%	75–100%	75–100%	75–100%	75–100%	75–100%	75–100%	75–100%	75–100%	75–100%
Manx Shearwater	50–75%	50–75%	25–50%	25–50%	5–25%					25–50%	25–50%	50–75%
European Storm-Petrel	75–100%	75–100%	75–100%	75–100%	75–100%				25–50%	25–50%	75–100%	75–100%
Leach's Storm-Petrel	5–25%	5–25%	5–25%	25–50%							25–50%	5–25%
Wilson's Storm-Petrel	75–100%	75–100%	75–100%	75–100%	75–100%	75–100%	75–100%	75–100%	75–100%	75–100%	75–100%	75–100%
Black-bellied Storm-Petrel					25–50%				25–50%	50–75%	5–25%	
Cape Gannet	75–100%	75–100%	75–100%	75–100%	75–100%	75–100%	75–100%	75–100%	75–100%	75–100%	75–100%	75–100%
Arctic Skua	75–100%	75–100%	75–100%	50–75%	25–50%				25–50%	75–100%	75–100%	75–100%
Long-tailed Skua	25–50%	5–25%	5–25%	25–50%	5–25%					5–25%	5–25%	5–25%
Pomarine Skua	50–75%	25–50%	50–75%	25–50%	5–25%					5–25%	50–75%	50–75%
Subantarctic Skua	75–100%	75–100%	75–100%	75–100%	75–100%	75–100%	75–100%	75–100%	75–100%	75–100%	75–100%	75–100%
Sabine's Gull	75–100%	75–100%	50–75%	25–50%					25–50%	50–75%	75–100%	75–100%
Arctic Tern	75–100%	75–100%	75–100%	75–100%	25–50%	5–25%	5–25%	25–50%	25–50%	25–50%	75–100%	75–100%

LAND-BASED SEABIRD-WATCHING FROM THE CAPE PENINSULA

In winter, for land-bound seabirdwatchers, the most rewarding conditions are on the west side of the Peninsula when a strong north-westerly is blowing. The best spots are on the cliffs above the parking area at the Cape of Good Hope, Cape Point (take the path from the old lighthouse to the new one; pp.32-33) and Kommetjie (from the shore near the lighthouse). **Cape Cormorant, Cape Gannet, White-chinned Petrel** and **Sooty Shearwater** are usually present close inshore. If there is a strong wind, **Shy** and **Black-browed Albatrosses** may also be seen, with regular sightings of **Subantarctic Skua, Northern** and **Southern Giant Petrels, Wilson's Storm-Petrel** and **Antarctic Prion**.

Callan Cohen

Cape Point offers good seabird-watching.

In spring, summer and autumn, persistent south-easterly winds produce good sea-watching, and the best vantage points are Glencairn and Cape Point. At Glencairn, stand next to the railway station, or at the whale-watching site 1 km north of the railway station. The most rewarding sea-watching is in Oct, and Feb-Mar, on the first or second day of the south-easter. Birds are blown into False Bay and are best viewed in the late afternoon as they move south, out of the bay. Most common are **Cape Gannet, Parasitic Jaeger, Sooty Shearwater** and **White-chinned Petrel**. Less common, but regular, are **Pomarine Jaeger** and **Cory's Shearwater**. **Soft-plumaged Petrel, Great Shearwater** and **Long-tailed Jaeger** are rare.

In summer, scan from the Mouille Point lighthouse for distant flocks of **Sabine's Gull** (Oct-Apr), as well as **Cape Gannet, White-chinned Petrel, Arctic Jaeger** and **Swift Tern**.

VAGRANT SEABIRDS OFF THE CAPE

For local birders, it is the lure of rarities that makes a pelagic trip so exciting. Almost anything can turn up. The following are vagrant species recorded in the Western Cape, characteristically in winter: **Southern Royal Albatross** (5 records at sea), **Buller's Albatross** (2 records at sea), **Sooty Albatross** (4 confirmed records at sea, 2 on land, 10 washed up dead on beaches) and **Light-mantled Albatross** (2 confirmed records at sea, 3 beached), **Antarctic Petrel** (2 beached), **White-headed Petrel** (3 at sea, 1 beached), **Atlantic Petrel** (very scarce, no figures available), **Kerguelen Petrel** (very scarce), **Blue Petrel** (very scarce), **Slender-billed Prion** (very scarce, although irruptive in some years, and easily overlooked), **Fairy Prion** (1 beached), **Grey Petrel** (very scarce), **Little Shearwater** (scarce), **Black-legged Kittiwake** (2 at sea, 1 on land) and **South Polar Skua** (scarce). Rarities seen in summer include **White-bellied Storm-Petrel** (very scarce) and **Laysan Albatross** (1 at sea).

In July 1984, a remarkable northward seabird irruption occurred in South Africa, extending as far east as Australia and New Zealand, possibly linked to El Niño weather conditions during the previous season. There were many sightings of birds ordinarily very rare at sea, including **Kerguelen Petrel**, **Blue Petrel** and **Slender-billed Prion**. The most bizarre record was surely that of a dazed **Sooty Albatross** found atop an apartment block in suburban Cape Town!

OFF THE EAST COAST OF SOUTH AFRICA

Although it lacks the enormous numbers and predictability of species of the cold Benguela Current, the warm Agulhas Current still supports an excellent selection of pelagic seabirds. Irregular pelagic trips are offered from Port Elizabeth, East London, Durban and Richards Bay.

More than half of all pelagics known from southern African waters have been seen on trips from Durban, including 17 Southern Ocean species and a handful of tropical vagrants not recorded further south. A trip in winter, especially when the sardines are running (Jun/Jul) or after the passage of a cold front in Sept/Oct, is likely to produce reasonable numbers of **Atlantic Yellow-nosed Albatross, White-chinned Petrel, Sooty Shearwater, Wilson's Storm-Petrel, Subantarctic Skua** and **Cape Gannet**, along with smaller numbers of **Shy** and **Black-browed Albatrosses, Soft-plumaged Petrel** and **Flesh-footed Shearwater**. Rarities recorded include **Wandering*** and **Grey-headed Albatrosses, Black-bellied** and **White-bellied Storm-Petrels, White-headed Petrel** and **Streaked Shearwater**.

Geoff McIlleron: Firefly Images

Pintado Petrel

Summer trips tend to be less productive, except after a cyclone in the Mozambique Channel, when vagrants from tropical waters may include **Sooty** and **Bridled Terns, Red-tailed Tropicbird, Brown Booby, Audubon's Shearwater**, and **Matsudaira's Storm-Petrel**.

OFF MOZAMBIQUE

In recent years there has been much interest in pelagic birding from Vilankulo (p.296), and reports have ranged from spectacularly productive to almost birdless! Small fishing boats can be chartered, or boats can be hired from one of the hotels, and taken through the channel between Bazaruto and Benguerra islands and up to 25 nautical miles into the Indian Ocean.

Prize tropical species such as **Greater Frigatebird, Wedge-tailed Shearwater, Red-tailed Tropicbird**, and **Bridled** and **Black-naped Terns** have been recorded, as have small numbers of more widespread species such as **Pintado** and **White-chinned Petrels**, and **Wilson's Storm-Petrels**.

Large flocks (ca 500 birds) of **Sooty Tern** have been seen >10 km offshore, but small groups are occasionally seen close to Bazaruto. Apparently, the much sought-after **Red-footed Booby** only makes an appearance some distance out, towards the middle of the Mozambique Channel, although vagrants have come ashore on Bazaruto.

ORGANISING A PELAGIC TRIP

Reasonably priced day trips, led by experienced local leaders, depart from Simon's Town harbour, about an hour's drive south of Cape Town, at least twice a month and every weekend in peak season. Most trips off the Peninsula leave at dawn, and head for the trawling grounds about 25 miles south of Cape Point.

For a full, up-to-date listing of all pelagic trips in Cape Town, Port Elizabeth, East London, Richards Bay and Durban, including booking details, contact Cape Town Pelagics ☎ or check on the web at www.capetownpelagics.com.

Callan Cohen

Pelagic trips are organised almost every weekend in season off Cape Town.

HOW TO USE THIS BOOK

The book is divided up into the individual countries of the greater southern African region (see p.8). Each chapter presents a new country or region, each with its own set of **bird routes**. These routes form the essential structuring element of the book, and are numbered sequentially from 1 to 39. Routes cover large areas and are made up of several **sites**; these are of a much more local scale and are often (in the case of the more important sites) accompanied by a detailed **site map**. Sites are also numbered, from 1 to 335.

- Each site is given a rating that ranges from essential ✔✔✔ to excellent ✔✔ or regional ✔. *Essential* sites are the very best and most strategic in terms of 'top' species to be seen. Visiting only these sites will provide almost all endemics and much of the diversity on offer in the region. These sites are also well placed logistically. *Excellent* sites offer tremendous diversity, many endemics and many specials. *Regional* sites offer great local birding and serve as back-up sites for nearby essential and excellent sites.
- Sites marked 4X4 are logistically challenging but offer potential for interesting discoveries and vast wilderness areas.
- Those marked with R are hotspots where many rarities have been found.
- Sites carrying the IBA logo are Important Bird Areas, as defined by BirdLife International (see imprint page or visit www.birdlife.org).

PAGE LAYOUT

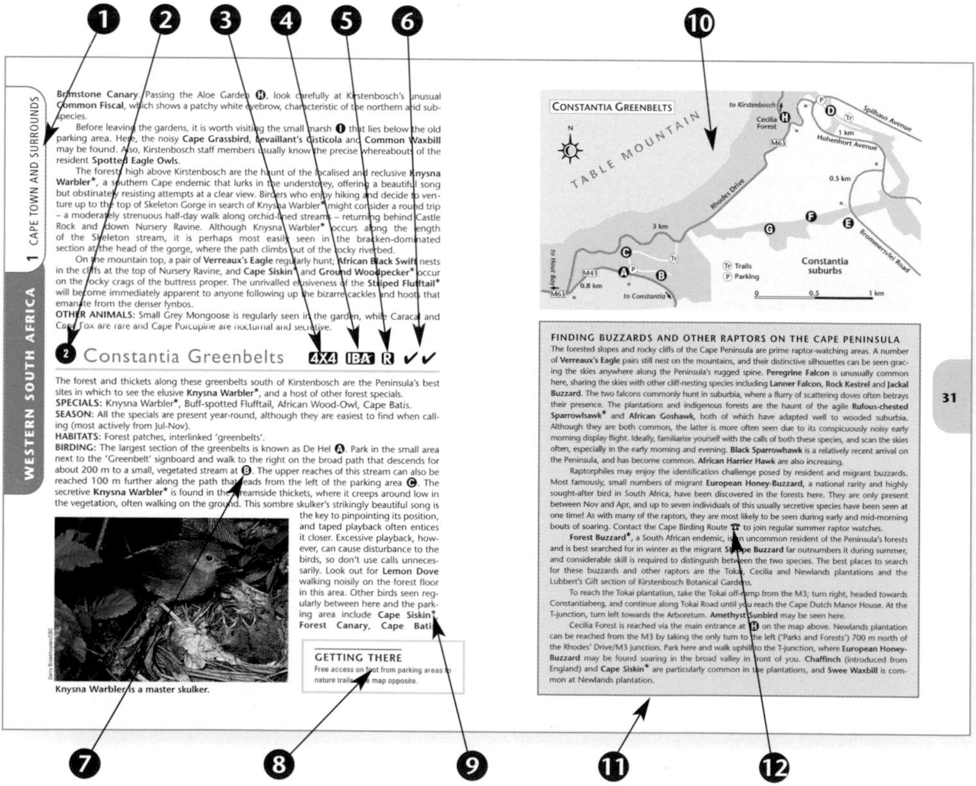

KEY TO PAGE LAYOUT

1. Route tab for quick reference
2. Site number and name (cross-referenced on pull-out map)
3. 4-wheel-drive vehicle required for exploring parts of the site
4. Important Bird Area as defined by BirdLife international
5. Rarity site
6. Site rating: indicates significance of site in terms of birding experience (see p.24)
7. Locator symbols (e.g. Ⓓ) in text refer to places on the accompanying site map
8. Summarises access to the site
9. An asterisk (*) follows the name of a bird featured in the region's 'top 150 birds' (p.378) or 'top 20 birds' of Madagascar (p.404)
10. Site maps with lettered locations that are cross-referenced in the text. These maps accompany the most important sites
11. Feature boxes provide further insight within that region
12. ☎ = useful contact, cross-referenced to contact details at the back of the book (p.408)

STRUCTURE OF THE BOOK

The book is arranged in chapters that correspond to the countries of southern Africa; South Africa itself is treated in two chapters, Eastern and Western South Africa. Countries are delineated with a colour-coded tab at the edge of pages. A detailed map of the region under discussion is provided at the start of chapters, together with a locator map of the continent. Within the chapters are routes, numbered sequentially from the start of the book, and the routes are divided into a number of sites. At the start of each route is a table of the top 10 birds – the most sought-after species occurring within that route.

THE REGION'S TOP 150 BIRDS

The section 'Top 150' represents a selection of bird species (out of more than 1 400 within the region covered) that are both highly sought-after and can be difficult to locate without some extra help. Each entry discusses the most reliable sites and the most fruitful techniques for finding these birds. This section will appeal to those wanting to locate an elusive species that, once found, would provide the highlight of a birding trip (Pel's Fishing-Owl, African Pitta or Sclater's Lark, for example). Within the routes, an * following a bird's name signals that the bird is featured in the 'Top 150' (of southern Africa) or 'Top 20' (of Madagascar) sections.

PULL-OUT MAP OF THE REGION

The large pull-out map inside the back cover is an invaluable tool. It presents the entire region covered by this book and features all routes and their associated sites, offering an overall perspective of the region and how all the routes lie. Countries are colour-coded and tie up with the coding used inside the book. Sites are numbered and labelled and are cross-referenced to their route in the book. The map will help you to orientate yourself and tailor birding itineraries to your particular needs and time constraints. Extra maps can be ordered from **sabfmap@birdingafrica.com**, or contact Birding Africa ☎.

CHECKLIST AND INDEX

A checklist that doubles as an index to all birds discussed in the guide appears on p.410 at the back of the book. Arranged in traditional order by common name, this also offers 'old' common names where relevant, scientific name, and gives details on whether the bird is endemic to the region or not.

WESTERN SOUTH AFRICA

The western half of South Africa is a unique African destination. Dramatic mountain ranges, epicentre of the unique Cape Floral Kingdom, contrast with the vast semi-desert plains of the Karoo. This uniqueness is reflected in the birds: no other areas in Africa offer such a high concentration of endemics in so accessible a setting: over 80% of the birds restricted to South Africa occur here.

In addition, international and local birders are drawn to the region by the tourism gem of Cape Town, and by the region's scenic and cultural diversity, well-developed infrastructure, high standard of accommodation, and excellent network of national parks and provincial and private nature reserves. A total of 450 bird species have been recorded here, and a two-week trip could expect to yield in excess of 350 species. Indeed, more than 220 species have been seen around Cape Town in a single day!

Western South Africa encompasses the Western and Northern Cape provinces. The first route includes the mountains and coast around Cape Town (R1), where one can find fynbos endemics (p.17) such as Cape Sugarbird, and Benguela marine endemics (p.18) such as African Penguin. The West Coast Route (R2) includes important estuaries for migrant water birds. The accessible Tanqua Karoo Route (R3) is home to Karoo endemic desert birds (p.16), while the Bushmanland & Namaqualand Route (R5) leads one deeper into remote areas in search of arid specialities. The Overberg & Garden Route (R4) follows the southern Cape coast, through forests (Knysna Turaco) and open plains (Blue Crane). In the far north of western South Africa, the Southern Kalahari Route (R6) offers excellent game-watching. The final route, the N1 Route (R7), follows South Africa's main national road and spans the entire country; it features many sites in the Free State not covered elsewhere. We've included it here because it begins in Cape Town.

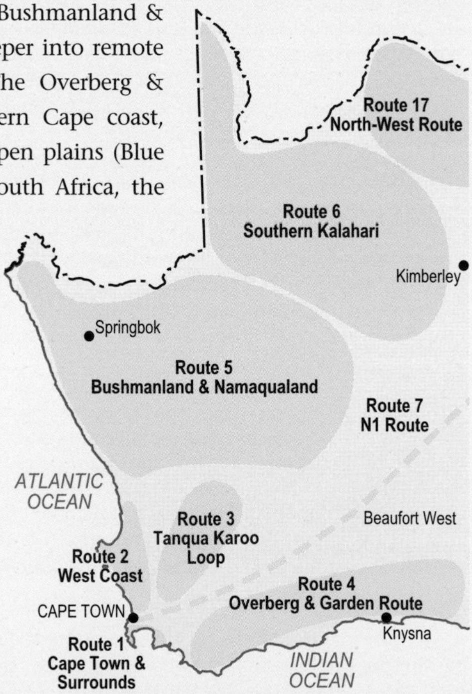

Western South Africa also offers world-famous pelagic birding trips from Cape Town (pp.20-23). The Cape Birding Route ☎, an internet-based booking service, provides birders with free trip-planning advice for western South Africa.

ROUTE 1

CAPE TOWN & SURROUNDS

Often considered one of the most scenic stretches of landscape in the world, the Cape Peninsula ranks among Africa's premier tourism destinations. For birders, the Peninsula itself and the mountains that lie to the east provide easy access to a good selection of coastal and mountain specials, and some of the world's best sites for such highly localised endemics as Cape Rock-jumper*, Victorin's Scrub-Warbler*, Cape Siskin* and Knysna Warbler*, and seabirds such as African Penguin and Bank Cormorant*. It is also the departure point for world-famous pelagic trips (see p.20).

TOP 10 BIRDS

- African Penguin
- Bank Cormorant
- Cape Rock-jumper
- Rufous-chested Sparrowhawk
- African Black Oystercatcher
- Hottentot Buttonquail
- Antarctic Tern
- Knysna Warbler
- Cape Sugarbird
- Cape Siskin

A narrow, 75 km-long strip of land separating the cold Atlantic upwelling from the waters of False Bay, the Peninsula's landscape is dominated by a rugged mountain chain, culminating at its northern end in the famously geometrical massif of Table Mountain.

Rising to 1 086 m and sculpted from delicately coloured sandstone, the mountains of the Peninsula are clad in the extraordinarily diverse fynbos vegetation that is unique to the southern Cape region. Table Mountain alone supports a staggering 2 600 plant species, more than the entire British Isles. Much of the Peninsula's pristine mountain landscape is protected in the newly proclaimed Table Mountain National Park that runs, discontinuously, from Table Mountain to the Peninsula's tip at the Cape of Good Hope. Dedicated birders with limited time can fit in an excellent day's birding across the Peninsula by starting at Kirstenbosch National Botanical Garden and Constantia Greenbelts, and taking in a scenic drive to the Cape of Good Hope Nature Reserve (via Kommetjie) and nearby Boulders Beach. Kirstenbosch requires an early start as, by mid-morning, birds are less visible and the gardens become quite crowded with tourists. A visit to Strandfontein Sewage Works, Rondevlei, Blouvlei, Paarl Bird Sanctuary and Rietvlei (West Coast, p.45) is a must for those with an interest in water birds. Paarl Mountain Reserve offers fynbos species and is especially good for sunbirds.

The Hottentots Holland range, traversed by Sir Lowry's Pass, interrupts the sandy, low-lying flats east of Cape Town. Sir Lowry's is legendary in birding circles for its numerous fynbos specials, which are easily accessible only a short walk from the national road. Just to the south is a spectacular drive winding along the eastern coast of False Bay and through the coastal villages of Rooi Els and Betty's Bay, where further fynbos and coastal specials are on offer.

The Cape Birding Route organisation ☎, based in Cape Town, arranges local accommodation in birder-friendly establishments, pelagic trips and guiding, and offers free birding advice.

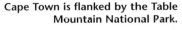

Walter Knirr/IOA

Cape Town is flanked by the Table Mountain National Park.

❶ Kirstenbosch Botanical Garden ✔✔✔

Widely recognised as one of the world's finest botanical gardens, Kirstenbosch National Botanical Garden would be an essential destination for its pleasing landscapes and spectacular floral displays alone. Here, it is possible to approach a number of Cape endemics at close quarters, including such desirable species as **Cape Sugarbird***, **Orange-breasted Sunbird** and **Cape Spurfowl**.

SPECIALS: Cape Sugarbird*, Orange-breasted Sunbird, Cape Spurfowl, Forest Canary, Red-chested Cuckoo, Cape Batis, African Olive-Pigeon, Lemon Dove, African Goshawk, Rufous-chested Sparrowhawk*, Knysna Warbler* (scarce).

SEASON: Birding is good year-round.

HABITATS: Indigenous gardens, adjacent indigenous forest and fynbos, small wetland.

BIRDING: Castle Rock stands sentinel over the gardens, flanked by Skeleton Gorge and Nursery Ravine. These are two of numerous gorges that cut through the steep and moist eastern face of Table Mountain. In the ravines, two metres of annual rainfall (mainly in mid-winter) maintains pockets of pristine Afromontane forest, through which acidic, fast-flowing streams course over moss-swathed boulders and decaying trunks festooned with ferns. The most accessible forest is along the Braille Trail Ⓓ, an easy walk that loops gently through the trees. It begins on a broad gravel path opposite the Fragrance Garden, which is just a short stroll across the lower lawns from the main entrance and Visitors' Centre. **Knysna Warbler*** sometimes lurks along the streams and thickets here, but the Constantia Greenbelts (p.30) are more reliable for this species.

Lemon Dove is a true forest species that is often found shuffling through the leaf litter in the dappled shade of the understorey; chances of seeing it are increased if you make an early start up the gravel track from where the Braille Trail starts at Ⓓ, concentrating your search beyond the sharp corner after about 300 m Ⓔ.

Other forest birds found here and along the Braille Trail also extend down into the formal gardens. These include **African Olive-Pigeon**, **Sombre Greenbul**, **Olive Thrush**, **Cape Batis**, **African Paradise** and **African Dusky Flycatchers**, and **Forest Canary** – the latter a relatively recent arrival on the Peninsula. The whole of Kirstenbosch is also a fine area for raptors: early mornings and evenings are when forest hawks, such as **Rufous-chested*** and **Black Sparrowhawks** and **African Goshawk**, are most likely to be seen. **European Honey-Buzzard** may be seen anywhere in the gardens from Dec-Mar, especially in the Lubbert's Gift area on the northern border of Kirstenbosch (see box, p.31).

A small, tranquil forest patch known as the Dell Ⓕ surrounds Colonel Bird's Bath, a clear spring welling up in the middle of the gardens. Here, huge trees overlooking the spring invariably hold perched **African Olive-Pigeons**. From the Dell, you can ascend through the Cycad Garden into the upper reaches of Kirstenbosch Ⓖ, where protea and erica plants abound. Their flowerheads are adorned with approachable **Cape Sugarbirds*** and **Orange-breasted Sunbirds**. Fynbos vegetation is globally renowned for its remarkable diversity of bird-pollinated plants, and Kirstenbosch is a perfect place to observe this mutualism in action.

GETTING THERE

Kirstenbosch is well signposted from Rhodes Drive in Cape Town's Southern Suburbs. The main entrance leads to the Visitors' Centre Ⓐ, while Ⓑ and Ⓒ offer alternative access points. The gardens (which boast well-stocked gift shops, coffee shops and restaurants) are accessible from sunrise to 19h00 in summer and from sunrise to 18h00 in winter.

Shaen Adey/IOA

The eastern slopes of Table Mountain loom over the gardens.

Make your way downhill from the protea section, along the right-hand edge of the Dell, following one of the myriad paths that eventually lead to the lower gardens. Common and conspicuous birds of the cultivated gardens are **Cape Spurfowl, Helmeted Guineafowl, Cape Robin-Chat**, **Karoo Prinia**, **Southern Boubou** and **Southern Double-collared Sunbird**. Species found here that are characteristic of more wooded environments in the Cape are **Red-chested Cuckoo** (calling Sept-Dec), **Black Saw-wing** (summer), **Speckled Mousebird** and

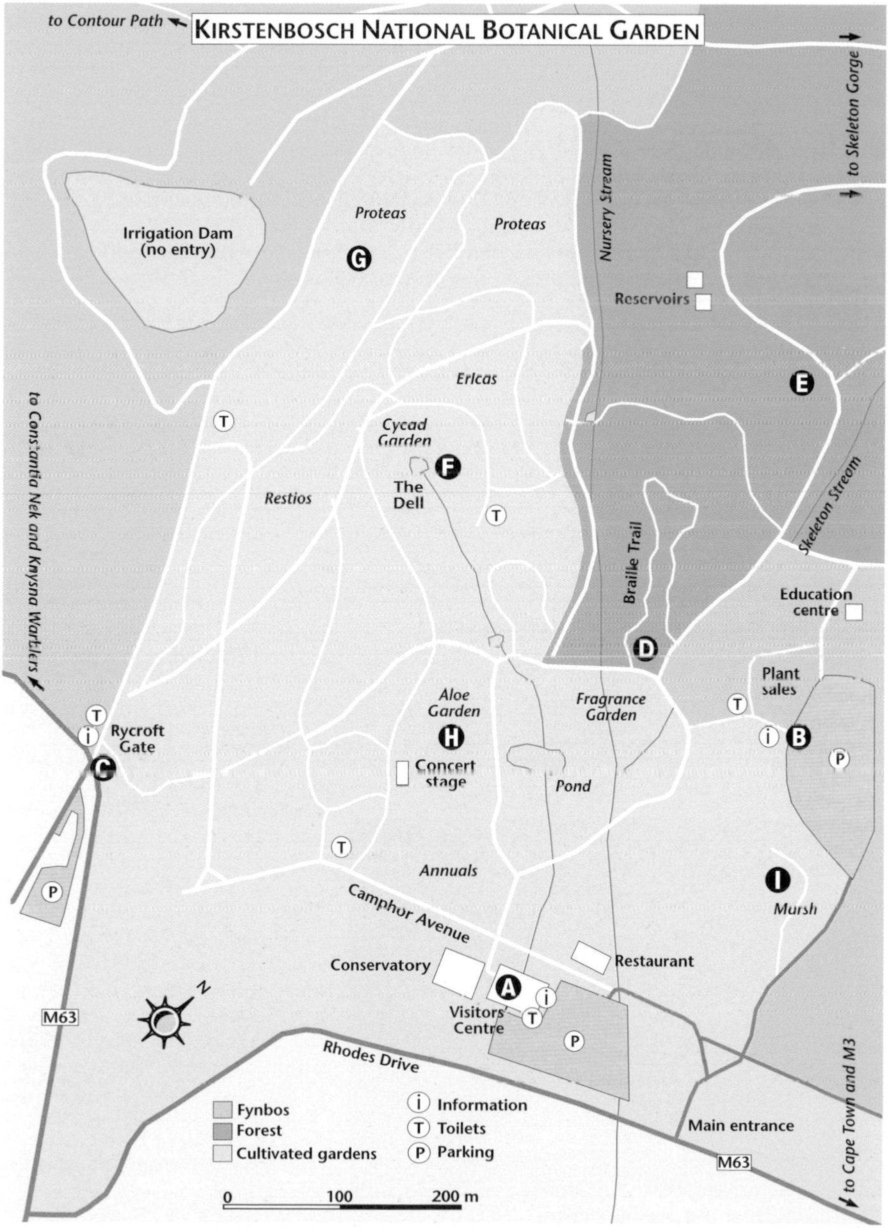

Brimstone Canary. Passing the Aloe Garden (H), look carefully at Kirstenbosch's unusual **Common Fiscal**, which shows a patchy white eyebrow, characteristic of the northern arid subspecies.

Before leaving the gardens, it is worth visiting the small marsh (I) that lies below the old parking area. Here, the noisy **Cape Grassbird**, **Levaillant's Cisticola** and **Common Waxbill** may be found. Also, Kirstenbosch staff members usually know the precise whereabouts of the resident **Spotted Eagle Owls**.

The forests high above Kirstenbosch are the haunt of the localised and reclusive **Knysna Warbler***, a southern Cape endemic that lurks in the understorey, offering a beautiful song but obstinately resisting attempts at a clear view. Birders who enjoy hiking and decide to venture up to the top of Skeleton Gorge in search of Knysna Warbler* might consider a round trip – a moderately strenuous half-day walk along orchid-lined streams – returning behind Castle Rock and down Nursery Ravine. Although Knysna Warbler* occurs along the length of the Skeleton stream, it is perhaps most easily seen in the bracken-dominated section at the head of the gorge, where the path climbs out of the rocky riverbed.

On the mountain top, a pair of **Verreaux's Eagle** regularly hunt; **African Black Swift** nests in the cliffs at the top of Nursery Ravine, and **Cape Siskin*** and **Ground Woodpecker*** occur on the rocky crags of the buttress proper. The unrivalled elusiveness of the **Striped Flufftail*** will become immediately apparent to anyone following up the bizarre cackles and hoots that emanate from the denser fynbos.

OTHER ANIMALS: Cape Grey Mongoose is regularly seen in the garden, while Caracal and Cape Fox are rare and Cape Porcupine is nocturnal and secretive.

2 Constantia Greenbelts ✔✔

The forest and thickets along these greenbelts south of Kirstenbosch are the Peninsula's best sites in which to see the elusive **Knysna Warbler***, and a host of other forest specials.

SPECIALS: Knysna Warbler*, Buff-spotted Flufftail, African Wood-Owl, Cape Batis.

SEASON: All the specials are present year-round, although they are easiest to find when calling (most actively from Jul-Nov).

HABITATS: Forest patches, interlinked 'greenbelts'.

BIRDING: The largest section of the greenbelts is known as De Hel (A). Park in the small area next to the 'Greenbelt' signboard and walk to the right on the broad path that descends for about 200 m to a small, vegetated stream at (B). The upper reaches of this stream (C) can also be reached 100 m further along the path that leads from the left of the parking area. The secretive **Knysna Warbler*** is found in the streamside thickets, where it creeps around low in the vegetation, often walking on the ground. This sombre skulker's strikingly beautiful song is the key to pinpointing its position, and taped playback often entices it closer. Excessive playback, however, can cause disturbance to the birds, so don't use calls unnecessarily. Look out for **Lemon Dove** walking noisily on the forest floor in this area. Other birds that are seen regularly between here and the parking area include **Cape Siskin***, **Forest Canary**, **Cape**

Gerry Broekhuysen/CBC

Knysna Warbler is a master skulker.

GETTING THERE

Free access on foot from parking areas to nature trails. See map opposite.

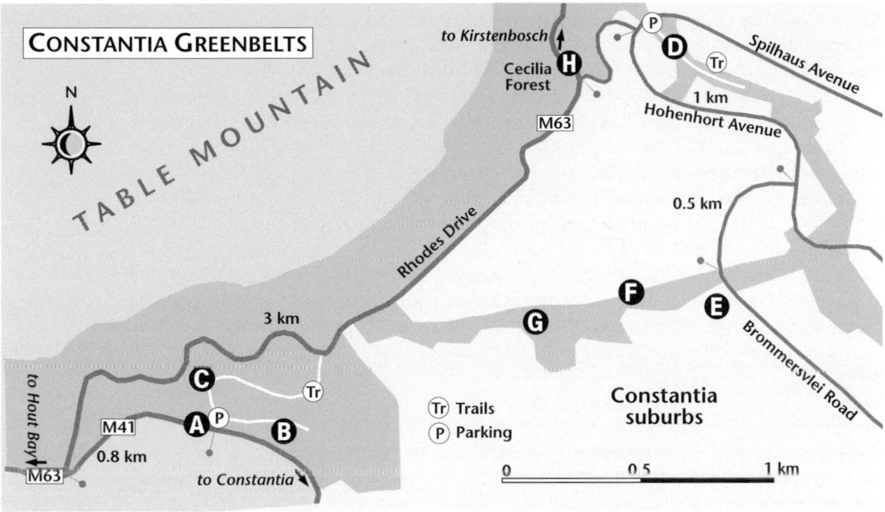

FINDING BUZZARDS AND OTHER RAPTORS ON THE CAPE PENINSULA

The forested slopes and rocky cliffs of the Cape Peninsula are prime raptor-watching areas. A number of **Verreaux's Eagle** pairs still nest on the mountains, and their distinctive silhouettes can be seen gracing the skies anywhere along the Peninsula's rugged spine. **Peregrine Falcon** is unusually common here, sharing the skies with other cliff nesting species including **Lanner Falcon, Rock Kestrel** and **Jackal Buzzard.** The two falcons commonly hunt in suburbia, where a flurry of scattering doves often betrays their presence. The plantations and indigenous forests are the haunt of the agile **Rufous-chested Sparrowhawk*** and **African Goshawk**, both of which have adapted well to wooded suburbia. Although they are both common, the latter is more often seen due to its conspicuously noisy early morning display flight. Ideally, familiarise yourself with the calls of both these species, and scan the skies often, especially in the early morning and evening. **Black Sparrowhawk** is a relatively recent arrival on the Peninsula, and has become common. **African Harrier Hawk** is also increasing.

Raptorphiles may enjoy the identification challenge posed by resident and migrant buzzards. Most famously, small numbers of migrant **European Honey-Buzzard**, a national rarity and highly sought-after bird in South Africa, have been discovered in the forests here. They are only present between Nov and Apr, and up to seven individuals of this usually secretive species have been seen at one time! As with many of the raptors, they are most likely to be seen during early and mid-morning bouts of soaring. Contact the Cape Birding Route ☎ to join regular summer raptor watches.

Forest Buzzard*, a South African endemic, is an uncommon resident of the Peninsula's forests and is best searched for in winter as the migrant **Steppe Buzzard** far outnumbers it during summer, and considerable skill is required to distinguish between the two species. The best places to search for these buzzards and other raptors are the Tokai, Cecilia and Newlands plantations and the Lubbert's Gift section of Kirstenbosch Botanical Garden.

To reach the Tokai plantation, take the Tokai off-ramp from the M3; turn right, headed towards Constantiaberg, and continue along Tokai Road until you reach the Cape Dutch Manor House. At the T-junction, turn left towards the Arboretum. **Amethyst Sunbird** may be seen here.

Cecilia Forest is reached via the main entrance at **H** on the map above. Newlands plantation can be reached from the M3 by taking the only turn to the left ('Parks and Forests') 700 m north of the Rhodes Drive/M3 junction. Park here and walk uphill to the T-junction, where **European Honey-Buzzard** may be found soaring in the broad valley in front of you. **Chaffinch** (introduced from England) and **Cape Siskin*** are particularly common in the plantations, and **Swee Waxbill** is common at Newlands plantation.

Batis, Sombre Greenbul, African Dusky and **African Paradise Flycatchers, African Olive-Pigeon, Red-chested Cuckoo** (vocal from Sept-Dec), **Southern Double-collared Sunbird, Bar-throated Apalis, Swee Waxbill** and the introduced **Chaffinch.**

Knysna Warbler* can also be found at **D**, a footpath that leads down the densely vegetated stream, along which the birds lurk. Park at the 'Greenbelt' signboard nearby.

Buff-spotted Flufftail is another star bird of the Constantia Greenbelts. A legendary skulker, the flufftail is among the hardest to find of Africa's birds. Males should be searched for on summer nights, when their ventriloquial, hooting call emanates from dense tangles of vegetation, often from a position of up to 3 m above ground. Park at the point where the Greenbelt crosses Brommersvlei Road **E** and walk west for 300 m to the wooden bridge that spans the small wetland **F**. In the evenings, Buff-spotted Flufftail can sometimes be heard calling along a stretch from here up to the tar road that crosses the Greenbelt **G**, although they are perhaps more reliable at **D**. **African Wood-Owl** and **Spotted Eagle-Owl** can be heard at night.

3 Table Mountain ✔

Cape Town's most famous landmark is easily accessible in an impeccably modern cable car, or via an excellent network of hiking paths of every level of severity. The wind-buffeted plateau can be explored by following the well-marked surfaced paths that lead from the upper cableway station. The fynbos here holds a remarkably low density of birds, although **Orange-breasted Sunbird, Neddicky** and **Cape Grassbird** are usually reasonably common, and **Cape Siskin*** and **Ground Woodpecker*** are best located by their calls.

Red-winged Starling, Speckled Pigeon and Rock Hyrax (Dassie) compete for food scraps from tourists. **Rock Martin** and **African Black** and **Alpine Swifts** fly overhead. Visitors to the plateau should also keep alert for raptors: **Verreaux's Eagle, Peregrine Falcon** and **Rock Kestrel**, along with **White-necked Raven**, all nest on cliff faces in this vicinity and are regularly seen in flight.

4 Kommetjie ✔✔

Kommetjie is a small seaside village situated on a rocky promontory on the west coast of the Peninsula, and provides convenient access to a number of endemic or localised coastal species, notably **Bank Cormorant*** and **Antarctic Tern*** (winter).

SPECIALS: Bank* and Crowned Cormorants, Antarctic Tern*, African Black Oystercatcher*, and White-fronted Plover.

SEASON: Antarctic Tern* is present Apr-Oct.

HABITATS: Boulders, beach.

BIRDING: The bird for which Kommetjie is best known is the distinctively stocky, subtly coloured **Antarctic Tern***, which can reliably be found here in small numbers in winter. By early spring, shortly before undertaking their return flight across the southern oceans, the birds have often already attained their superb white, grey and deep red breeding plumage.

The tern roost here includes **Swift Terns** year-round; **Common Tern** dominates during the summer. A handful of threatened **Bank Cormorant*** can usually be found on the rocks throughout the year, alongside more common **Cape, Crowned** and **White-breasted Cormorants.**

An assortment of waders, including resident **White-fronted Plover** and **African Black Oystercatcher***, as well as migrant **Ruddy Turnstone, Common Sandpiper, Common Ringed Plover** and **Common Whimbrel**, is usually found pottering among the interesting technicolour rock pools.

Kommetjie is also a well-known sea-watching (see p.34) vantage point during the winter months.

GETTING THERE

Entering Kommetjie from the east on the M65, turn right down Van Imhoff Road (at the sharp bend opposite the hotel). Continue to a prominent parking area on the left, where a path leads onto the rocky promontory.

OTHER ANIMALS: Cape Clawless Otter may be seen by early risers.
NEARBY SITES: Wildevoëlvlei, a largish lake nearby, is easily accessible from the Imhoff's Gift housing development (take the signposted road north from the M65, a few kilometres east of Kommetjie). **Great Crested Grebe** and **Yellow-billed Egret** still occur here. In recent years, however, the lake has suffered heavily from blooms of toxic blue-green algae, resulting in a dramatic drop in bird numbers. Another excellent site for **Cape Siskin*** (as well as **Cape Rock-Thrush**) is the rocky cliffs at Jonkersdam. The parking lot is signposted from the Glencairn Expressway, a southerly extension of Ou Kaapse Weg, about 2 km before you reach Glencairn.

Callan Cohen
Coastal birds roosting at Kommetjie

5 Cape of Good Hope NR

R ✔✔

The rugged coastline and windswept moorlands of this spectacular reserve at the south-westernmost tip of Africa have been incorporated into the Table Mountain National Park. The reserve is most famous for its striking landscapes, rich history, and botanical diversity; this is in sharp contrast to the low density of bird life – a scarcity which is, fortunately, more than compensated for by the quality of a few of the local specials.
SPECIALS: Hottentot Buttonquail*, Cape Siskin*, Peregrine Falcon, Cape Sugarbird* and Plain-backed Pipit.
SEASON: All the specials are present year round.
HABITATS: Sea cliffs, pelagic shoreline, fynbos-covered plains and slopes, coastal thicket, beach.
BIRDING: The dramatic sea cliffs at Cape Point form the focus of most visits to the reserve. There is a shop and restaurant here, and visitors can take a short funicular ride up to South Africa's oldest lighthouse, which offers sweeping views of the ocean, the cliffs, and the craggy length of the Cape Peninsula.

Experienced birders will be consoled with the fact that, while fulfilling this essential tourist activity, they are also optimally positioned to see the endemic **Cape Siskin***. This rather inconspicuous canary can be seen anywhere in the scrub around Cape Point, the best areas being along the paths to the sea-cliff view sites (starting below the toilets on the Cape of Good Hope side of the parking lot) and along the precarious path to the lower lighthouse. Common birds here are **African Black Swift**, **Cape Robin-Chat**, **Grey-backed Cisticola** (curiously localised on the Peninsula and not even recorded at Kirstenbosch), **Karoo Prinia, Southern Boubou, Red-winged Starling** and **Cape Bunting**. Keep a look out for **Peregrine Falcon** in this vicinity, although it can turn up anywhere in the reserve. The Cape Point and Cape of Good Hope promontories must rank among the best sea-watching (see p.22) sites in the world.

The open plains of the reserve, as mentioned, are one of the few sites in the world to see the localised **Hottentot Buttonquail***, although finding this bird usually poses a considerable challenge, and there are more reliable sites in the Overberg (pp.42 & 67). Take the second tar road to the right (opposite Kanonkop on the map provided at the entrance) when driving south from the entrance gate, and continue for about 2 km until you reach the only road to the left. Park at the gate just past this junction, and walk north to the broad, shallow valley dominating the landscape to the west of Sirkelsvlei. Concentrate your search on the plains dominated by low plants. It will soon become distressingly evident that there is a vast amount of habitat here, and the dedicated birding group may have to spend a few hours on these windswept plains, with no guarantee of success! Birds are

GETTING THERE

Opening times are 06h00-18h00 from Oct-Mar and 07h00-17h00 from Apr-Sep; a map is provided at the entrance gate.

The Cape of Good Hope Nature Reserve is an excellent place to see Cape Siskin.

curiously scarce here, although **Cloud Cisticola*, Grey-backed Cisticola, Cape Grassbird, Cape Clapper Lark*, Grey-winged Francolin** and **Cape Longclaw** may be seen.

The scenic Atlantic beaches and rocky shores near Olifantsbos lie off the main tourist itinerary and are ideal for a stroll. A trail leads south to the rock-perched hull of the *Thomas T. Tucker*. The small beach just north of the parking area is an excellent spot for **Plain-backed Pipit,** and several are usually seen foraging just above the high-water mark – rather an atypical habitat for this species! **African Black Oystercatcher*, White-fronted Plover** and **Little Egret** also forage on these shores, and they are joined in summer by **Common Whimbrel, Ruddy Turnstone, Sanderling,** and **Swift, Sandwich** and **Common Terns**. **Cape, White-breasted** and **Crowned Cormorants** roost on the rocks. Numerous rarities, including **Little Blue Heron, Baird's, Pectoral** and **White-rumped Sandpipers** and **American Golden Plover,** have been recorded from this stretch of shoreline.

The coastal thicket adjacent to the parking area supports **Fiscal Flycatcher, Cape Bulbul, Southern Boubou** and **Speckled Mousebird**. **Common Ostrich** and Bontebok – a once critically endangered antelope endemic to the Cape – graze in the open near the parking area. Flowering patches here and elsewhere in the reserve attract large numbers of nectarivorous species, such as **Cape Sugarbird*, Orange-breasted Sunbird, Malachite Sunbird** and **Southern Double-collared Sunbird**. Rocky places in the reserve are worth searching for the likes of **Ground Woodpecker*, Jackal Buzzard, Cape Rock-Thrush, Cape Siskin*, Familiar Chat** and the much rarer **Sentinel Rock-Thrush**.

OTHER ANIMALS: Watch out for cheeky Chacma Baboon in the reserve; bolder individuals will enthusiastically jump onto or even into cars and steal food and other parcels from unsuspecting visitors. Habituated baboons often become dangerous and need to be destroyed, and it is against the law to feed them. Eland, Cape Grysbok and Cape Mountain Zebra may also be seen.

WHALE-WATCHING

The south-western coast of Africa is the favoured calving ground of Southern Right Whale seeking more temperate waters during the harsh Antarctic winter. During the winter and springtime months (Jul-Nov, but especially Aug-Sept), they can be observed close inshore all along the Western Cape coast. Good whale-watching sites are to be found along the Atlantic coast from Postberg in Route 2 (p.48), to the western side of False Bay (Boyes Drive, above Muizenberg, is an excellent vantage point) and, most famously, Hermanus on the south coast. Witsand, at the mouth of the Breede River (opposite Infanta), is also one of the world's top whale-watching sites.

❻ Boulders Beach, Simonstown IBA ✔✔

This area, site of the larger of the two mainland colonies of the endearing and globally threatened **African Penguin**, is home to over 1 000 pairs of penguins, peering suspiciously from their shallow, sheltered burrows at a now considerable following of tourists.
SPECIALS: African Penguin.
SEASON: Year-round.
HABITATS: Sandy beaches, boulders, dense coastal thicket.
BIRDING: The penguins seem so much at home at Boulders Beach that it is difficult to believe that they are relatively recent arrivals. A pioneering pair first nested here in 1985, launching a colonisation process that has seen rapid expansion. It is bolstered each year mainly by immigrant birds who desert their natal colonies for this secluded haven, free from natural predators (owing to human disturbance), and with good feeding grounds nearby (there is no large-scale commercial fishing in the adjacent bay). Breeding occurs throughout the year, with a distinct peak in the winter months. The eggs, usually two, are laid in protected environments – in burrows or under bushes – although ruthless competition for space forces many birds at Boulders Beach to nest in exposed sites.

Additionally, **Cape** and **Crowned Cormorants** roost on the offshore boulders, while **White-backed Mousebird**, **Southern Boubou** and **Brimstone Canary** inhabit the thickets through which the footpath to the colony passes.

Callan Cohen

African Penguin is easily seen at Boulders.

GETTING THERE
Boulders Beach is on the southern edge of Simon's Town, and is well signposted from Main Road: turn down along the northern edge of the golf course. Take a camera, and don't forget to check under your car for lurking penguins before driving off! Simon's Town harbour is a popular departure point for pelagic birding trips (pp.20-23).

❼ Strandfontein Sewage Works IBA R ✔✔

The extensive Strandfontein Sewage Works provides the best water-bird locality close to Cape Town. The abundant and diverse bird life makes it an ideal destination for the beginner and serious twitcher alike, and it is possible to see more than 80 species here on a summer day: our record currently stands at 118 species in a morning. Sadly, the existence of the sewage works is under threat from a new motorway.
SPECIALS: Greater Flamingo, Great White Pelican, Maccoa Duck, Black-necked Grebe, and African Marsh-Harrier.
SEASON: Birding is good year-round, although summer brings the migrants.
HABITATS: Reed-fringed pans, open water.
BIRDING: The poorly marked entrance to the works is adjacent to a derelict building at the south end of Zeekoevlei Ⓑ, where **African Fish-Eagle** is often seen roosting in the trees to the west. Bird numbers and water levels at Strandfontein vary widely depending on the year and season, and the following suggested route is intended as a general guide to the most productive areas. From the entrance, continue along the tar road towards the plant

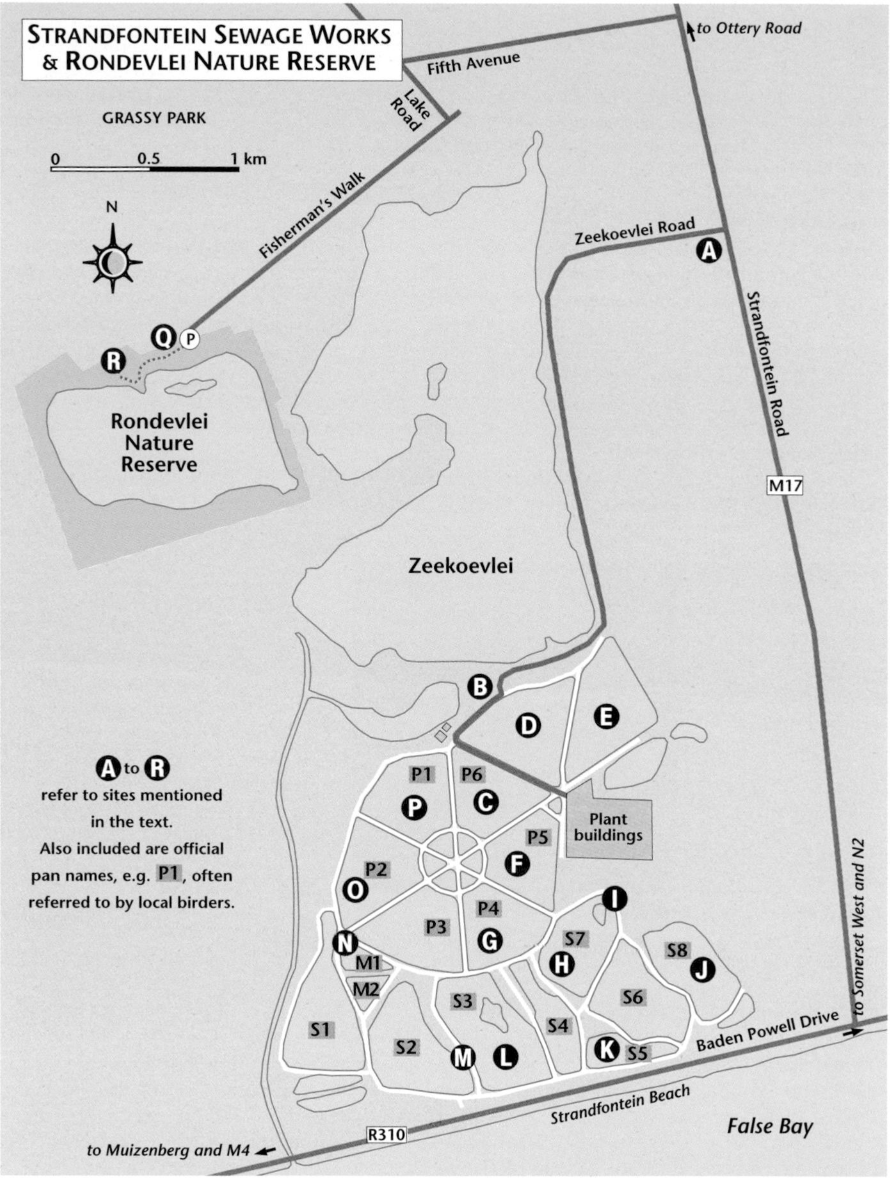

buildings, and check the deep pans C and D on both sides of the road for **Black-necked Grebe**, **Maccoa Duck**, **Southern Pochard**, and **Cape Teal**. Here too you will see the first of various other waterfowl species that are common throughout the sewage works, such as **Cape Shoveler**, **Yellow-billed Duck** and **Red-billed Teal**, while **African Purple Swamphen** stalk along the reed-lined edges. **Levaillant's Cisticola** is very common in the long grass fringing the pans, and agitated birds draw attention to themselves with their characteristically frenetic calls. **White-throated** and **Barn Swallows** (summer) and **Brown-throated Martin** often dart low overhead.

Where the road meets the sewage plant itself, scan the pan at Ⓔ for a good variety of waterfowl.

Continue to the pan at Ⓕ. This pan, and the small, reed-enclosed pond at its northern end, are usually also productive. At the 'hub' of the wheel of large pans, turn left. Pan Ⓖ, on your right, often holds **Black-necked Grebe, Great White Pelican, Maccoa Duck** and **Greater Flamingo**.

The western and northern corners of pan Ⓗ are always worth investigating. The former often has an exposed beach frequented by waders (including **Pied Avocet**); the latter is good for scarcer ducks such as **Cape Teal** and **South African Shelduck**, and occasionally **Hottentot Teal**. Continue around the northern apex of the pan at Ⓘ and head south to pan Ⓙ. The reeds in this vicinity are particularly good for **Little Rush Warbler, Lesser Swamp-Warbler** and, in summer, **African Reed-Warbler**. Very much more evident in the alien thicket are **Cape Spurfowl** and **Cape Bulbul**. Pan Ⓙ itself usually offers great birding, providing a good selection of waterfowl and wading birds in its northern reaches.

GETTING THERE

A major advantage on this route is the opportunity to bird from the comfort and security of your car, which can be used as a moving hide. The vast network of reed-fringed pans that radiates from the sewage plant buildings is connected by good gravel roads, but beware of occasionally treacherous sandy patches, especially along the southern coastal road.

To enter the Strandfontein Sewage Works from the Cape Town side, take the M5 freeway south from Cape Town, and turn left into Ottery Road at the Ottery turn-off; continue for 4.5 km until the junction with Strandfontein Road (M17); turn right here, and continue (southwards) along Strandfontein Road for 4 km; turn right again at the 'Zeekoevlei' sign Ⓐ within a stand of gum trees just after a petrol station, opposite 15th Avenue.

To enter the works from the False Bay side, turn north onto Strandfontein Road from Baden Powell Drive (R310), 6.8 km east of the Muizenberg traffic circle, and you'll reach the Zeekoevlei turn-off after 4.1 km. Baden Powell Drive follows the False Bay coast westwards to Muizenberg and Simon's Town, and eastwards to the N2 highway near Somerset West.

Further options are limited by sandy roads, so retrace your route and turn left along the southern border of pan Ⓗ. This is an especially good area for **African Marsh-Harrier** – the sight of this bird flying low over the alien thicket and adjacent reedbeds is virtually guaranteed.

Head south again, and cast a glance over pan Ⓚ for **African Black Oystercatcher***. Turn right where the road meets the coastal dunes, where **Swift** and **Sandwich Terns** and **Little Stint** (summer) often roost. Spare a moment to look up from your binoculars and enjoy the splendid view over False Bay and its embracing mountains.

Callan Cohen

Strandfontein offers excellent wetland birding.

Good numbers of water birds can reliably be found on pan Ⓛ. **Cape** and **White-breasted Cormorants, Great White Pelican** and miscellaneous waterfowl roost at Ⓜ, while rafts of assorted ducks bob on the usually choppy water.

Having absorbed all that pan Ⓛ has to offer, continue past a series of relatively unexceptional pans before re-entering the central wheel at Ⓝ. The small pan at Ⓝ is often productive, as is Ⓞ. Recently, lower water levels in Ⓞ have attracted large numbers of **Greater Flamingo, South African Shelduck, Pied Avocet** and Palearctic migrant waders. Before leaving, you might find it worthwhile to check pan Ⓟ for **Great Crested Grebe**.

OTHER ANIMALS: Cape Grey and Water Mongoose may be seen.

8 Rondevlei Nature Reserve ✔

The vlei and its surrounding reedbeds are protected in this cosy, well-maintained reserve, where Hippopotamus has been reintroduced.

The wide selection of common bird species, the excellent series of hides along a short, pleasant footpath, and the small museum make Rondevlei especially suited to the novice birder. Scan the reedbeds from hides at Ⓠ and Ⓡ (see map on p.36) for interesting species such as **African Darter, African Spoonbill, Little Bittern, Purple Heron, African Purple Swamphen, Malachite Kingfisher, African Snipe, Caspian Tern** and a selection of waders (when water levels are low).

Shaen Adey/IOA

Bird hide at Rondevlei

Boat trips ☎ provide an excellent opportunity to see a high diversity of species and breeding colonies. Rondevlei's entrance is situated at the western end of Fisherman's Walk, and can be reached by following the signs from the M5 in Grassy Park. The nearby Zandvlei Estuary Nature Reserve offers good water birds and is situated at the end of Coniston Road, signposted from Military Road.

9 Robben Island to Bakoven IBA ✔

For birders, Robben Island is renowned not only for its sinister political history: the island supports significant seabird breeding colonies, including a substantial population of the endemic **African Penguin**, and is of additional local interest in that it plays host to two introduced species found nowhere else in South Africa. While small coveys of **Chukar Partridges** are usually seen on the prescribed bus tour of the island, **Common Peafowl** lurks in the denser thicket, especially behind the prison, and is seldom seen.

Of rather higher significance in a global context are the substantial breeding colonies of **African Penguin**, **Bank Cormorant***, which breed on the harbour breakwater, **Crowned Cormorant**, **African Black Oystercatcher***, **Hartlaub's Gull** and **Swift Tern**. These are all easily seen along the island's coastline. A boardwalk offers access to the penguin colony. There can also be interesting seabirding en route to and from the island, and **Sabine's Gulls** may be seen lifting off the waves on tri-coloured wings as the ferry ploughs its way across Table Bay in summer. **Parasitic** and **Pomarine Jaegers** can also be seen in summer, while in winter, **Subantarctic Skua** mercilessly harry the other seabirds for their hard-won meals.

For those with limited time, or less of a stomach for the choppy ride across the bay, there is plenty to see along the city's western seaboard. The alternately rocky and sandy shoreline from the Waterfront westwards to the suburbs of Mouille Point and Sea Point supports small numbers of roosting **African Black Oystercatcher*** and **Cape** and **Crowned Cormorants,** as well as **Swift** and **Common Terns**. Scan opposite the Mouille Point Lighthouse for **Sabine's Gull** in summer. At nearby Bakoven, the globally threatened **Bank Cormorant*** breeds on the elephant-like boulders that lie just offshore, and is best observed by telescope.

10 Blouvlei (Intaka Island) ✔

This newly rehabilitated wetland offers convenient birding adjacent to one of Cape Town's largest shopping malls, Canal Walk. In addition to a good selection of common water-bird species, Blouvlei is one of the best places in the Cape to see **Greater Painted Snipe, African Snipe** and **Little Bittern**. **African Purple Swamphen** and **Black-crowned Night-Heron** are easily seen, and **Hottentot Teal** is recorded regularly.

Take the Sable Road/Century City off-ramp from the N1, and at the first traffic lights, turn right. After 1 km, take a left turn at the traffic circle; the parking lot for Intaka Island is at the end of this road. Also close to the N1 is the Tygerberg Nature Reserve, which offers a good diversity of birds in an urban setting. From the N1, take the Jip de Jager turn-off (Exit 20) and head northwards for 2 km to the Kommissaris Road traffic lights, where you turn left and follow the signboards.

11 Sir Lowry's Pass ✔✔✔

This is a classic Cape birding spot in the Hottentots Holland Mountains, and provides easy access to two fynbos endemics (**Cape Rock-jumper*** and **Victorin's Scrub-Warbler***) that, inexplicably, do not occur on the Cape Peninsula, despite an abundance of apparently ideal habitat.

SPECIALS: Cape Rock-jumper*, Victorin's Scrub-Warbler*, Ground Woodpecker*, Striped Flufftail*, Hottentot Buttonquail*, Neddicky and Cape Siskin*.

SEASON: All the specials are present year-round.

HABITATS: Rocky mountain fynbos with seeps.

BIRDING: Running north of the road is a rocky ridge of minor outcrops leading up to the summit of Kanonkop peak at B. Winding along its eastern contour is a broad track C leading north towards a neck in the mountains at Gantouw Pass D. Close by lies a pair of antique signal cannons. The rocky slopes here are the domain of the **Cape Rock-jumper***. The entire length of the ridge between the N2 viewsite and the summit of Kanonkop is, in fact, prime Cape Rock-jumper* country, and birders alert to its loud, piping call will be sure to locate a group of these fine birds. **Hottentot Buttonquail*** is also occasionally flushed from the slopes here.

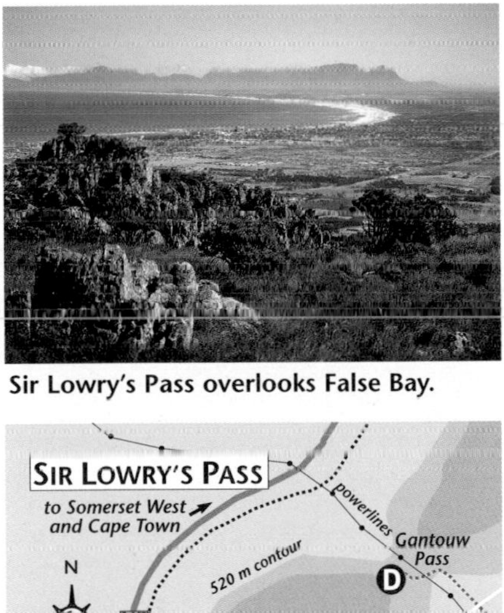

Claire Spottiswoode

Sir Lowry's Pass overlooks False Bay.

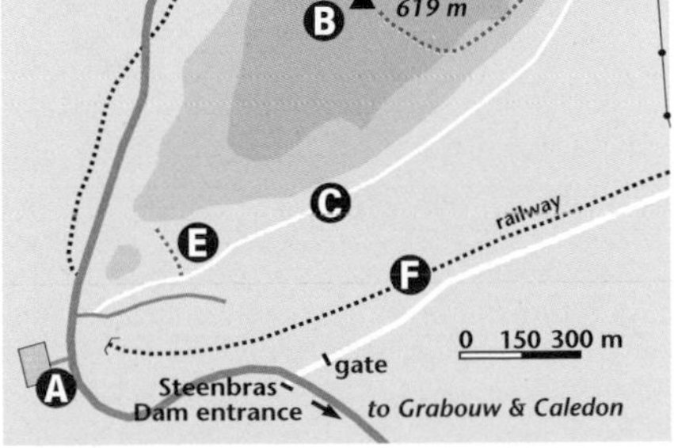

Birds are scarce in this landscape, but the area does have its rewards. The series of rocky outcrops along the path and the ridges above also hold low densities of **Ground Woodpecker***, **Familiar Chat**, **Cape Siskin***, **Cape Rock-Thrush** and, more rarely, **Sentinel Rock-Thrush**. Common birds of the dense fynbos between the ridge and gravel track are **Neddicky, Cape Grassbird**, **Karoo Prinia** and **Orange-breasted Sunbird**. **Cape Sugarbird*** and **Yellow Bishop** occur more scarcely in denser vegetation, such as that growing along the stream under the powerlines.

GETTING THERE

Excellent fynbos birding may be had minutes from the viewsite next to the N2 at the summit of the pass, just 50 minutes' drive from the city. The first hurdle lying between visiting birders and their quarry is a blind corner on the N2; this needs to be crossed on foot with considerable caution after parking at the viewsite on the southern side of the road A. Strictly, a permit needs to be obtained in advance (free of charge via the Cape Birding Route ☎).

FINDING CAPE ROCK-JUMPER

Cape Rock-jumper

At Sir Lowry's Pass the most accessible area to search for rock-jumpers is the rock-strewn slope at Ⓓ (map p.39) to the south of Gantouw Pass. To reach this slope, follow the gravel track until it intersects with some powerlines, and turn left onto a small, inconspicuously marked footpath leading up to Gantouw Pass. Walk up to the signal cannons, and work your way to the left (southwards) up the slope, keeping an eye out for rapidly scurrying silhouettes on the clusters of boulders. Note that searching for rock-jumpers typically involves scrambling along rocky outcrops and is only recommended for birders confident of their agility! You can also gain access to the ridge at its southern end, just north of the N2, although this is not an easy walk. An inconspicuous footpath at Ⓔ leads up the slope from the gravel track. At the ridge, the path peters out and you will need to work your way northwards along the series of outcrops.

Victorin's Scrub-Warbler* can be heard singing from the slightly denser vegetation of the hill slopes. Its call is difficult to distinguish from the superficially similar, but less repetitive song of the more conspicuous **Cape Grassbird**. Victorin's Scrub-Warbler* is far more readily lured from cover in this relatively open habitat than it is from habitat more typical of this species, such as impenetrable streamside thicket found beneath the powerlines at Gantouw Pass, where it is common. Another good area for the warblers is in the dense vegetation along the railway track at the bottom of the mountain at Ⓕ. To reach this spot, drive past the viewsite, turn left opposite the entrance to Steenbras Dam, and park at the gate. This area also supports **Striped Flufftail***, although this species is near impossible to see during the day.

Jackal Buzzard (including at least one potentially confusing white-breasted individual), **Rock Kestrel** and **Peregrine Falcon** are the most frequently seen raptor species at Sir Lowry's Pass, although numerous other birds of prey occasionally pass through the area; these include **Verreaux's** and **Martial Eagles**, **Black Harrier*** and **Rufous-chested Sparrowhawk***. The rewarding birding walk at Sir Lowry's Pass can be completed in just two to three hours – longer if you're waylaid by the remarkable plant diversity of these mountain slopes.

OTHER ANIMALS: Klipspringer may be seen on the slopes, while Smith's Red Rock Rabbit and Leopard are rarely seen.

NEARBY SITES: Along the way, look out for Cape Town's steadily increasing **House Crow** population in the vicinity of the N2 airport off-ramp. On the Cape Town side of the pass, Helderberg Nature Reserve in Somerset West offers a mix of fynbos and forest birding in a scenic setting. Specials in the lower part of the gardens include **Cape Sugarbird***, **Fiscal Flycatcher**, **Olive Woodpecker** and **Amethyst Sunbird** (scarce). The nearby Dick Dent Bird Sanctuary in Strand holds a good selection of water birds and directions can be obtained from the local bird club ☎.

⓬ Rooi Els ✔✔

East of False Bay, the contours of the Hottentots Holland plunge precipitously into the sea, creating a spectacular stretch of coastline where mountain fynbos and marine specials can be seen virtually alongside each other. Heading east of Cape Town on the N2, pass through Somerset West and turn right onto the R44 (signposted 'Gordon's Bay/Kleinmond'). Continue to the T-junction at the edge of the town of Gordon's Bay, and turn left onto the scenic and dramatically sinuous coastal road that meanders southwards to the holiday village of Rooi Els. At the edge of the village, the road crosses the Rooi Els River before veering to the left and heading steeply uphill towards Betty's Bay. To look for **Cape Rock-jumper***, take the second turn-off to the right (an unsurfaced road), just as the R44 begins its ascent. Park at the gate about 1 km further on, and continue on foot. Look out for rock-jumpers on the left-hand side for the next 2 km, and for **Verreaux's Eagle**, **Ground Woodpecker***, **Cape Siskin***, **Orange-breasted Sunbird**, **Cape Sugarbird*** and **Cape Rock-Thrush**.

13 Betty's Bay ✔✔

Stony Point is the site of one of only two mainland colonies of **African Penguin**, while on the lower mountain slopes of the dramatic Kogelberg range is the Harold Porter Botanical Garden, offering good fynbos and forest birding.

SPECIALS: African Penguin, Bank Cormorant*, Victorin's Scrub-Warbler*, Cape Siskin*, Blue-mantled Crested Flycatcher, Olive Woodpecker, Cape Rock-Thrush, Ground Woodpecker*.

SEASON: All the specials are present year-round.

HABITATS: Extensive fynbos, Afromontane forest, rocky coastline.

BIRDING: The **African Penguin** colony at Stony Point is smaller than that at Boulders Beach on the Cape Peninsula (p.35). **Bank Cormorant*** also breeds here, alongside the more common **Crowned**, **Cape** and **White-breasted Cormorants**.

The cultivated gardens at Harold Porter are quite small, but surrounded by moist mountain fynbos dissected by two forested ravines, Disa Kloof (to your left) and Leopard Kloof (to your right). From the entrance gate, head up through the cultivated gardens to the bridge over the Disa Kloof stream, and continue along the path up the kloof itself. Common birds of the lower gardens are **Black Saw-wing**, **Cape Bulbul**, **Karoo Prinia**, **Southern Boubou**, **Malachite**, **Orange-breasted** and **Southern Double-collared Sunbirds**, **Yellow Bishop**, **Brimstone Canary** and conveniently accessible **Cape Siskin***. Swifts and swallows (including **Rock Martin** and **African Black** and **Alpine Swifts**) usually forage overhead, alongside soaring raptors (most commonly **Verreaux's Eagle** and **Jackal Buzzard**).

The forested path up Disa Kloof leads to a small, bitterly black dam, and ends a few hundred metres further on where a waterfall interrupts the stream. The forest along this path provides **Bar-throated Apalis**, **Cape Batis**, **African Paradise** (summer) and **African Dusky Flycatchers**, **Swee Waxbill** and, occasionally, **Brown-backed Honeybird**. During late summer, spectacular Red Disa orchids can be seen clinging to the dripping and slippery cliffs adjoining the waterfall. Make your way back to the dam and cross the bridge over its wall. A pair of **African Black Duck** is often present on the dam, if not elsewhere along the stream. A gentle path then leads out of the kloof and around the buttress between the two kloofs, before dropping back down into the gardens. **Cape Siskin***, **Neddicky**, **Orange-breasted Sunbird**, **Victorin's Scrub-Warbler***, **Cape Grassbird**, **Cape Rock-Thrush** and **Ground Woodpecker*** occur along this path. To visit Leopard Kloof, ask for a key at the entrance to the gardens. The forest conceals a series of pleasant waterfalls and, in addition to the forest species mentioned above, hosts **Olive Woodpecker** and the Cape's westernmost and regularly occurring **Blue-mantled Crested Flycatcher**, which sometimes flit down into the cultivated gardens. With luck, **Cape Eagle-Owl*** may be seen in the gardens at dusk. Listen for its deep call, especially in winter.

Nico Myburgh

Victorin's Scrub-Warbler

GETTING THERE

To reach Stony Point, take the signposted right turn off the R44 towards the coast, just before the series of lakes on your right as you enter the rambling village of Betty's Bay. A boardwalk and viewing platform provide convenient access. The Harold Porter Botanical Garden (signposted), which has a restaurant and small shop, lies on your left on the R44 just past the commercial centre of Betty's Bay.

OTHER ANIMALS: The Stony Point **African Penguin** colony has been preyed upon by a Leopard that descended from the adjacent mountains, and the big cat is seen occasionally in the Betty's Bay area. Cape Clawless Otter is present along the rocky coastline. Rock Hyrax can be seen at close range at Stony Point.
NEARBY SITES: Low fynbos at a site near Arabella Country Estate, outside Kleinmond, is proving one of the best sites for **Hottentot Buttonquail***. Contact the Cape Birding Route ☎ for access details.

14 Paarl Mountain & Bird Sanctuary R ✔✔

The winelands town of Paarl has two excellent birding sites associated with it, offering localised fynbos species and water birds. These sites can easily be tackled as a relaxed day trip from Cape Town or included in a Karoo excursion.
SPECIALS: Maccoa Duck, Malachite Kingfisher, and Protea Seed-eater*.
SEASON: Year-round.
HABITATS: Fynbos, thicket, sandbanks, wetlands/pans.
BIRDING: The oak- and jacaranda-lined streets of Paarl lie along the banks of the Berg River, at the eastern foot of the low, sprawling massif of Paarl Mountain. The massif offers good fynbos birding and is a well-known site for the inconspicuous and elusive **Protea Seed-eater***. A few kilometres north of the town centre is the Paarl Bird Sanctuary, a picturesque and productive sewage works that attracts an excellent diversity of water birds. These include several species that are otherwise fairly scarce close to Cape Town, such as **Little Bittern, African Black Duck, Water Thick-knee** and **Malachite Kingfisher**.

The Wildflower Reserve (B) is a small, pleasant botanical garden that often holds large numbers of confiding **Cape Sugarbird*** and **Orange-breasted Sunbird**. Other common species to be found here are **Black Saw-wing, Cape Bulbul, Bar-throated Apalis, Fiscal Flycatcher, Cape Batis, Malachite Sunbird** and an assortment of canaries, including **Streaky-headed Seed-eater** and, towards the top of the garden, the occasional **Protea Seed-eater***.

The friendly, manageable character of the Paarl Bird Sanctuary (map p.43) contrasts strongly with the stark, windy nature of its Cape Town counterpart, the Strandfontein Sewage Works. Paarl offers well-positioned hides, a good diversity of habitats within a modest area, and almost guaranteed sightings of several tricky species.

Malachite Kingfisher is invariably present in secluded, reed-fringed inlets, such as the hides at (A) and (H). These areas are also

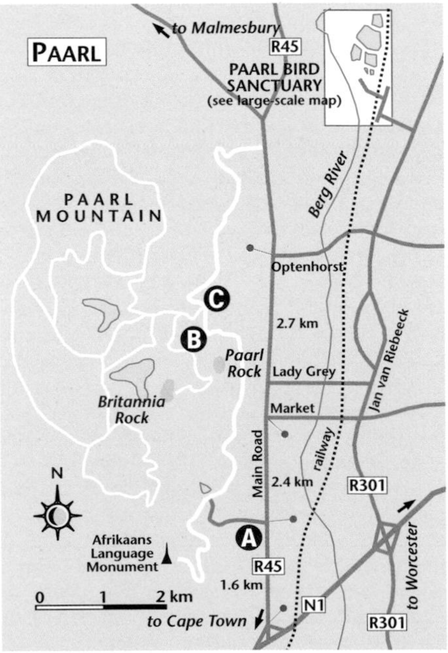

GETTING THERE

Take the first, rather inconspicuously marked 'R45: Main Road' turn-off to Paarl from the N1 from Cape Town. The soaring monument to your left honours the Afrikaans language. The Paarl Mountain Nature Reserve, incorporating a small wildflower garden in one of its wooded valleys, is easily reached from Main Road. Turn left (1.6 km north of the off-ramp) onto Jan Phillips Mountain Drive (A). The drive winds up through vineyards, then contours northwards, passing the wildflower garden (B), and the turn-off to the mountain reserve (C). See map for directions to nearby bird sanctuary.

Rita Meyer

A morning spent at Paarl Bird Sanctuary is likely to turn up many water birds.

good for **African Purple Swamphen**, and, in summer, **White-throated Swallow** and **Southern Red Bishop** are much in evidence. The reedbed edges provide perhaps the best place in the Cape to see **Little Bittern**.

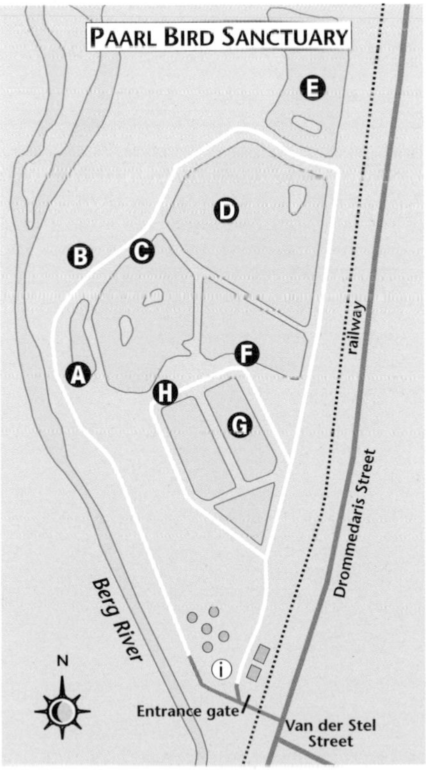

The alien thicket at Ⓑ is overrun with **African Reed-Warbler** and **African Paradise-Flycatcher** during summer. The hide at Ⓒ usually produces an excellent diversity of ducks, which should also be looked for in Ⓓ. In addition to the more common waterbirds, several interesting species can be seen here, among them **Southern Pochard**, **Maccoa Duck**, the occasional **White-faced Duck** (scarce in the Cape) and, usually more typical of mountain streams, **African Black Duck**, which visits from the adjacent Berg River.

In pan Ⓔ, an island supports a heronry where, among others, **Black-crowned Night-Heron** breed. **African Fish-Eagle** often roosts in the gum trees at the far side, and **Common Sandpiper** and **African Snipe** feed in the road-side ditch between pans Ⓓ and Ⓔ. Returning towards the entrance gate, turn right to the hide at Ⓕ. The sandbank in front of this hide usually lures a good diversity of migrant waders, including the localised **Common Sandpiper**, as well as roosting waterfowl. The reeds here hold **Black Crake** and **African Rail**. Before leaving, take a look around the sewage mixing enclosures at Ⓖ, where a loose group of **Water Thick-knee** usually eye one disap-provingly from somewhere in this vicinity. In summer, keep a look out for the large flocks of fluttering **White-winged Tern**. **Grey-headed Gull** may also be seen here.

ROUTE 2

WEST COAST

The West Coast, stretching along the Atlantic shore from Cape Town northwards to the Olifants River mouth, is best known for its superb beaches, bountiful sea life, internationally recognised coastal wetlands, and spring wild flower displays that are nothing short of spectacular. Birding here is excellent: there is an abundance of migrant waders and other water birds, and rewarding strandveld birding. Highlights range from the quietly elegant Black Harrier* quartering low over the scrublands of the West Coast National Park, to the frenzied Cape Gannet colony at Lambert's Bay.

TOP 10 BIRDS

- Black Harrier
- Grey-winged Francolin
- Southern Black Korhaan
- Chestnut-banded Plover
- Cape Long-billed Lark
- Cape Clapper Lark
- Sickle-winged Chat
- Cape Penduline-Tit
- Cloud Cisticola
- Protea Seed-eater

This topographically unassuming region is dominated by a coastal plain, covered in low, scrubby strandveld vegetation and studded in many areas with picturesque granite outcrops. Distinctly different in character from the Cape's southern seaboard, the West Coast is decidedly more arid and exposed. The rich waters of the Benguela Current not only make this region the heart of the country's fishing industry, but the associated sea life supports massive breeding seabird colonies on the scattered offshore islands. The coastline consists largely of endless lonely beaches, punctuated by salty, white-washed fishing villages and an ever-increasing number of holiday retreats.

The West Coast is best birded in spring and early summer (from about Aug-Oct), when most of the resident birds are breeding and the wild flowers are at their peak, although Oct-March is best for migrant waders. The region is particularly dry in late summer. The southern areas of the West Coast, extending northwards to the West Coast National Park and even the Berg River estuary, can be comfortably explored in a day trip from Cape Town. However, a two- to three-day loop would allow for more relaxed exploration of the region, including the Lambert's Bay area. Birding is best in the mornings as it is usually persistently windy later in the day.

Claire Spottiswoode

The West Coast is an excellent place to find the region's nine coastal endemics.

15 Rietvlei

IBA ✔

The main arterial road running up most of the western shoreline is the R27, which can be reached from the N1 just north of Cape Town. If you're headed from the city, take the Paarden Eiland turn-off onto Marine Drive, which, as you enter the coastal suburb of Milnerton, becomes known as Otto du Plessis Drive (R27).

As you pass through Milnerton, scan the lagoon that lies between the R27 and the conspicuous Woodbridge Island lighthouse on your left. A number of widespread water-bird species are often found here, most notably **Little Egret**, **Caspian** and **Swift Terns**, and **Pied Kingfisher**.

A few kilometres further north, the road swings to the left. Here, a number of large water bodies are visible on your right. Initially, the non-perennial pan of Rietvlei (dry and dusty in late summer) can be seen in the distance. During winter and spring, the pan supports an excellent diversity and abundance of water birds, and these can be viewed from the bird hide on the opposite side of the pan (see below for directions). Birders visiting at the right time of year and with time to spare will find a visit to Rietvlei rewarding.

A short distance further along the R27, the deep waters of Flamingo Vlei come into view on your right. This lake is used mainly for watersports and bird life is less diverse, although **Great White Pelican** and **African Darter** can often be seen here.

At the third set of traffic lights beyond the lighthouse (after 6.4 km), there is a series of pans surrounding the road: one lies to the left, another to the right, and one to the left beyond the traffic lights. These 'Dolphin Beach' pans can be birded from the roadside (watch out for passing traffic), and support a remarkable diversity of water-bird species, including **Little Grebe**, **Yellow-billed Egret**, **Glossy Ibis**, **Cape Shoveler**, **Yellow-billed Duck**, **Red-knobbed Coot**, **Common Moorhen**, **African Purple Swamphen**, **African Snipe**, **Three-banded Plover**, **Black-winged Stilt** and, in summer, **Little Stint**, **Wood Sandpiper**, **Ruff** and **White-winged Tern**. The localised **White-backed Duck** is often present on the pan beyond the traffic lights. Scan the reedbeds for **Little Rush Warbler**, and the vegetation along the edges of the pans for the conspicuous **Levaillant's Cisticola** and **Common Waxbill**. **Brown-throated Martin** and **White-throated Swallow** hawk insects overhead, and **African Marsh-Harrier** can often be seen over the reedbeds.

Returning to the R27, continue northwards. Should you wish to visit Rietvlei, turn right at the first set of traffic lights (after 0.7 km) beyond the roadside pans; take first right again (Pentz Drive) and continue for just over 1 km until you reach the SANCCOB seabird rehabilitation centre on your right. This very worthwhile organisation deserves a quick visit as there are always recovering seabirds on site. From SANCCOB, turn right at the first four-way stop and enquire at the Aquatic Club for access to the bird hide. There is a 15-minute walk to the hide, and a small fee is payable.

16 Koeberg Nature Reserve

✔

Uniform thickets comprising alien Port Jackson line the road as you head north along the R27. These trees, introduced from Australia in the 19th century to stabilise the dunes, continue to spread and smother the indigenous plants. Resisting most attempts to root them from the landscape, they currently pose one of the greatest threats to South Africa's natural vegetation.

However, as you proceed further north, the low, scrubby plant cover native to the area becomes more evident. Here referred to broadly as 'strandveld', it occurs on very sandy soils and is characterised by low, dense, thicket vegetation (with many fruit-bearing shrubs) interspersed with stands of restios (brown, reed-like plants), and supports a rich bird community.

On the left, only 30 km from the centre of Cape Town, loom the controversial reactor domes of South Africa's only nuclear power station, Koeberg. A number of trails lead through the strandveld in the adjacent nature reserve (turn off the R27 at the Koeberg sign and continue to the information centre), which offers good birding.

The thicker vegetation harbours species such as the **White-backed Mousebird, Cape Penduline-Tit, Cape Bulbul, Cape Robin-Chat, Karoo Scrub-Robin, Chestnut-vented Tit-Babbler, Layard's Tit-Babbler, Grey-backed Cisticola, Long-billed Crombec, Bar-throated Apalis, Cape Grassbird, Bokmakierie, Southern Double-collared** and **Malachite Sunbirds, Cape Weaver**, and **Yellow** and **White-throated Canaries** and **Cape Bunting**. Look overhead for **Peregrine Falcon**.

Black-shouldered Kite, Pied Crow and **Common Fiscal** are regular roadside birds along the R27, and they are joined in summer by **Steppe Buzzard** and **Yellow-billed Kite**.

17 Darling Wildflower Route ✔✔

Continue for a further 42 km from the 'Dolphin Beach' pans on the R27 before turning right onto a gravel road marked 'Darling Hills Road' (opposite the conspicuous 'Grotto Bay' sign); look for the yellow flags at Ⓐ. **Cape Clapper Lark*** and **Southern Black Korhaan**, both very vocal in spring, occur in the patch of vegetation at the junction of these two roads.

Continue along the Darling Hills gravel road for 0.6 km until you reach a small pond (dry in late summer) on the left, where **Three-banded Plover** can often be seen. **African Pied Starlings** have burrowed their breeding tunnels into a sandy bank here, and a male **Pin-tailed Whydah** often displays overhead. This area is most active in winter and spring, when the surrounding wheatlands are filled with birds; after the summer harvest it becomes progressively drier and less active. Small numbers of **Blue Crane** may be found in the adjacent fields Ⓑ, especially in summer. **Red-capped Lark, Capped Wheatear, Familiar Chat, African Pipit** and **Cape Sparrow** are common in this vicinity. In spring and summer, look overhead for **Banded Martin** and **Pearl-breasted Swallow** among the more numerous **Greater Striped** and **Barn Swallows**.

Continue along the Darling Hills road, and look out for the small stream passing under the road at Ⓒ. A **Southern Masked Weaver** colony is present in the large tree on your right at this point and, in spring, a parasitic **Diederik Cuckoo** lurks near the colony. All three mousebird species have been seen perched in a single bush here!

The road continues along a winding, overgrown river course until you reach a bridge at Ⓓ. **White-throated Swallow** breeds under the bridge, and alien vegetation in this vicinity holds **Fiscal Flycatcher, Acacia Pied Barbet** and **Cardinal Woodpecker**. **Chestnut-vented Tit-Babbler** and **Long-billed Crombec** may be found in the remnant natural scrub. In

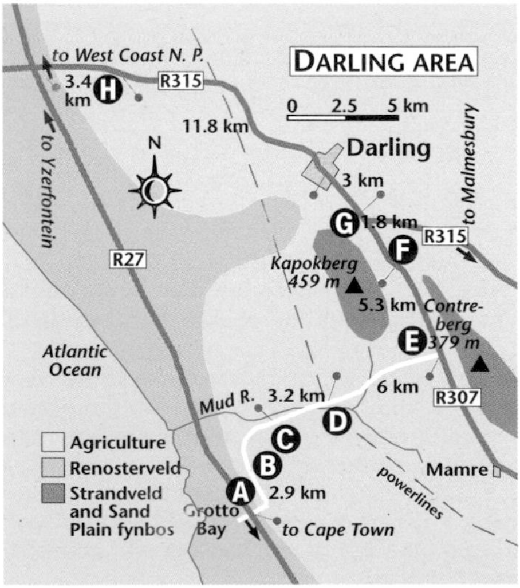

Derek Longrigg

Cloud Cisticola near Darling

the stands of exotic trees in this area, listen carefully for **Klaas's Cuckoo**, **African Hoopoe** and **Greater Honeyguide** (scarce). **Secretarybird** is sometimes seen stalking the open fields along the road, and **Namaqua Dove** may be seen in summer. The route intersects a tar road (the R307 Ⓔ); just before turning left towards Darling, scan for **Jackal Buzzard**, which often perches in this area.

If you're passing through these parts at any time during Aug-Oct, pay a visit to the Waylands Wild Flower Reserve Ⓕ, where renosterveld vegetation occurs. The vivid colours and massive diversity of flowering bulbs are truly spectacular. This is also an excellent place to see **Cape Clapper Lark***.

A male Southern Black Korhaan

Continuing towards Darling, the tiny Oudepos Wild Flower Reserve Ⓖ provides further great birding as well as flower-viewing, which can be enjoyed from the comfort of your car. You'll see the white gateway to the reserve on your left, directly opposite the R315 turn-off to Malmesbury. A few pairs of **Cloud Cisticola*** breed here, and **Cape Longclaw**, **Large-billed Lark**, **African Pipit** and **Yellow Canary** are also common in this reserve.

Continue through Darling along the R315 towards Yzerfontein (poorly signposted). The unassuming Tienie Versveld Nature Reserve lies on the left at Ⓗ. There are no facilities here – its presence is betrayed by a small sign and a stile over the fence. For most of the year, it resembles an ordinary, abandoned field, but in spring it undergoes a spectacular transformation, becoming a vast mosaic of flowers. It is best known among birders as an excellent site for **Cloud Cisticola***, which is common in the tall grass areas. **Common Quail** (summer), **Large-billed** and **Red-capped Larks**, **Capped Wheatear**, **Cape Longclaw** and **African Pipit** are also found here. The seasonally flooded marsh often holds **African Snipe**, and **Blue Crane** is an occasional visitor to the reserve.

18 Yzerfontein ✔

This is a scenically attractive coastal village that holds a number of quality species. However, it is probably only worth visiting if you are not going any further north. To find **Chestnut-banded Plover**, take the R315 towards Yzerfontein for 4 km from its junction with the R27. Turn right here towards the 'Gypsum Mine' (often locked on weekends), and continue for a further 1.8 km (the first 1 km of this track is good for strandveld birding) until you get to the mine at the edge of the vast Yzerfontein saltpan. Ask permission at the office before checking the edges of the pan for the plovers. Although water levels fluctuate greatly throughout the year, there are almost always Chestnut-banded Plover here.

Returning to the R315 (look out for **European Bee-eater** here in spring and summer), continue along the main road into Yzerfontein village, and search the rocks along the shore for **Crowned Cormorant** and **African Black Oystercatcher***. The rocky island beyond the harbour is home to breeding **Bank Cormorant***. The nests on the top right of the island belong to this species, and should preferably be viewed through a telescope. Heaviside's Dolphin can often be seen offshore.

19 West Coast National Park IBA R ✔✔✔

The West Coast National Park is best known for the large numbers of migrant waders that crowd the mudflats during summer. These can easily be observed from the well-positioned bird hides, offering local birders an excellent chance of finding rarities. The top-class strandveld birding, spring flowers and proximity to Cape Town all make the West Coast National Park a most productive, pleasant, and accessible birding destination.

SPECIALS: Black Harrier*, Southern Black Korhaan, Cape Penduline-Tit, African Rail and a host of waders.

SEASON: Aug-Oct is best for resident species, while Oct-Mar is best for migrant waders.

HABITATS: Granite inselbergs, seashore, salt-marsh, mudflats, strandveld vegetation.

BIRDING: Roadside birding in the park is highly rewarding. **Common Ostrich** is readily seen, and **Cape Spurfowl** is very common throughout the reserve. Coveys of the smaller and scarcer **Grey-winged Francolin** should be carefully searched for on the road edges in the early morning and evening. **Black Harrier*** may be seen quartering low over the vegetation anywhere in the park. **Black-shouldered Kite**, however, prefers roadside perches, and many roost communally at night in the large reedbeds on the eastern side of the lagoon, after gathering in one of the lonely palm trees in this area. Flocks of **African Pied** and **Wattled Starlings** occur throughout the park. **Southern Black Korhaan** is regularly seen at the roadside, especially between Geelbek and the park's northern exit near Langebaan village.

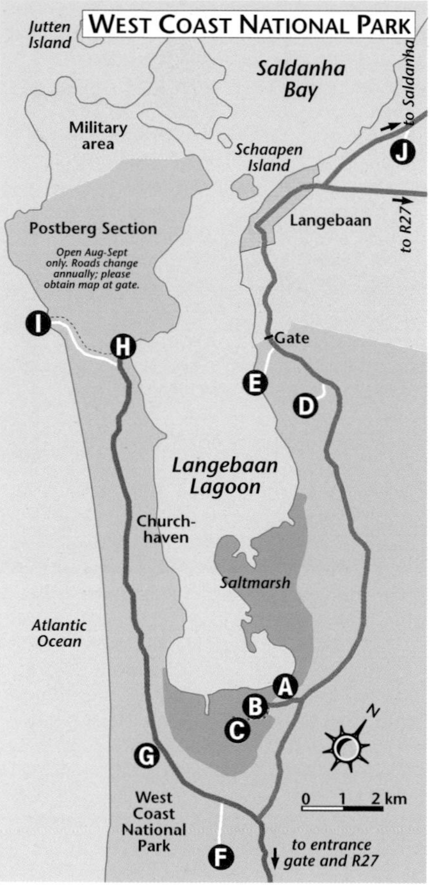

The strandveld vegetation throughout the park harbours species such as **White-backed Mousebird**, **Karoo Lark**, **Cape Penduline-Tit**, **Cape Bulbul**, **Cape Robin-Chat**, **Karoo Scrub-Robin**, **Chestnut-vented Tit-Babbler**, **Layard's Tit-babbler** (rare), **Grey-backed Cisticola**, **Long-billed Crombec**, **Bar-throated Apalis**, **Cape Grassbird**, **Bokmakierie**, **Southern Double-collared** as well as **Malachite Sunbirds**, **Cape Weaver**, **White-throated** and **Yellow Canaries** and **Cape Bunting**. Check for **Pearl-breasted Swallow** among the flocks of more common **Barn** and **White-throated Swallows**.

The Geelbek mudflat bird hide **A** allows for superb wader watching in summer, and is arguably South Africa's best water-bird hide. The array of desirable vagrant waders that has been found here over the last few years renders it the favoured haunt of dedicated twitchers, who make the pilgrimage here with fanatical regularity. It allows for close-up views of a large diversity of

GETTING THERE

Approaching from the south along the R27, the well-marked turn-off to the West Coast National Park is 10.9 km beyond the R315 Yzerfontein/Darling junction. The direct route along the R27 from Cape Town takes less than an hour. An entrance fee, which includes a map and bird list, is payable at the gate. Accommodation is available in Langebaan.

wading species: common summer migrants include **Curlew Sandpiper, Little Stint, Sanderling, Red Knot, Ruddy Turnstone, Common Greenshank, Marsh Sandpiper, Common Whimbrel, Grey** and **Common Ringed Plovers, Bar-tailed Godwit,** and a smaller number of resident **White-fronted** and **Chestnut-banded Plovers**. A few of the localised **Eurasian Curlew** are always present, and it usually takes some careful scanning to pick up the scarce but regular **Terek Sandpiper** and, with some luck, **Greater Sand Plover** and **Common Redshank. Broad-billed Sandpiper, White-rumped Sandpiper, Pectoral Sandpiper, Hudsonian Godwit,** as well as **Mongolian Plover** have all been recorded here.

Nigel J. Dennis/IOA

The secretive African Rail may be seen at Abrahamskraal (Ⓕ on map).

Timing is very important: the area is at its most rewarding on the correct part of the tidal cycle. This is notoriously difficult to predict, although the best viewing usually begins about 4.5 hours after the 'High tide in Table Bay' as listed in Cape Town newspapers. At this time, the water drops and slowly begins to expose the mud and its invertebrates on the surface. The longer-legged waders land first, soon to be joined by the smaller species as the water recedes further still. If you get the timing wrong, try the Seeberg hide Ⓔ, which is good at high tide.

A wide variety of other water birds may be seen from the hide, including **South African Shelduck. African Rail** may be seen darting in and out of the sedges, especially to the right of the hide in the early morning. **African Marsh-Harrier** breeds in the adjacent reedbeds, and **Osprey** passes overhead in summer. The approach to the hide is by way of a wooden boardwalk that serves to protect a splendid tract of multicoloured saltmarsh. This endangered vegetation type is very sensitive to disturbance and takes many years to recover from damage from trampling, so please stick to the boardwalk. Check the small pools here for **Kittlitz's Plover, Black-winged Stilt, Blacksmith Lapwing** and **Cape Wagtail**. Noisy **Levaillant's Cisticola, Little Rush Warbler** and **Lesser Swamp-Warbler** occur in the adjacent reedbeds.

Geelbek Manor House Ⓑ, restored in typical Cape Dutch style, has a small restaurant with tame **Cape Spurfowl** and **Cape Weaver** in attendance. **Acacia Pied Barbet, Chestnut-vented Tit-Babbler** and the occasional **Cardinal Woodpecker** frequent the stands of largely alien trees. A further two bird hides are located at a pan on the edge of a vast saltmarsh Ⓒ, a 20-minute walk from the manor house. Starting at the parking area, the walk passes through old farmlands where **Large-billed Lark, Levaillant's** (near water) and **Grey-backed Cisticolas, Common Stonechat** and **Cape Sparrow** are common. The number of birds on this saltpan depends on the water level, and on the state of the tide; high tide is best, as many birds roost here when forced off their mudflat feeding grounds. Mainly smaller waders occur here, including large numbers of **Little Stint**. When water levels are low, **White-fronted, Chestnut-banded** and **Kittlitz's Plovers** are often common. Small groups of **Caspian Plover**, a species unknown elsewhere in the Cape, have regularly been seen in this vicinity. Keep a lookout overhead for **Peregrine Falcon**, which frequently harass the waders.

On the road to Langebaan village, the Seeberg lookout Ⓓ can be seen perched on a granite hillock. The lookout provides a panoramic view of the lagoon, and it is worth scanning from here for **Black Harrier***. The granite boulders below are home to a group of Rock Hyrax (Dassie). The viewsite is reached by a short, unsurfaced road that is probably the best place in the park to look for **Southern Black Korhaan**. This small bustard is often seen at close quarters in the open areas near the viewsite parking area, especially in the morning and evening. A covey of **Grey-winged Francolin** can be found in this vicinity.

The short road down to the Seeberg hide Ⓔ offers good strandveld birding. Most of the strandveld species can be seen at the parking area near the hide, including **Cape Penduline-Tit**.

Although the Seeberg hide is not as well situated as that at Geelbek, it offers a good selection of waders and terns, especially at high tide. Large numbers of **Bar-tailed Godwit** may be seen here, and **Little Tern** often roosts on the closest sandbank.

Abrahamskraal waterhole **F** is one of the only sources of fresh water in the park, and many birds come here to drink, including **Namaqua Dove** (summer), **Wattled Starling**, **White-throated** and **Yellow Canaries**, and **Cape Bunting**. **Lesser Swamp Warbler**, **Little Rush Warbler** and **Levaillant's Cisticola** are common and easily seen in the reeds, while **Black Crake** and **African Rail** skulk lower down at the reed bases. A variety of widespread water birds also occur, including **African Spoonbill**, **Common Moorhen** and **Three-banded Plover**. **Brown-throated Martin** hunts overhead.

West Coast National Park in spring

The viewsite at **G** offers not only panoramic views over the lagoon and sea, but is a good spot to look for **Karoo Lark**. The north-western Postberg **H** section of the park is open only during the flower season (Aug-Oct). Dominated by sloping meadows strewn with granite boulders, this part of the reserve offers spectacular scenery, excellent flower-viewing, pleasant birding and a variety of introduced game species, including Gemsbok and Springbok.

There is year-round access to the sea at Tsaarsbank **I**, where **African Black Oystercatcher*** and **Cape**, **White-breasted** and **Crowned Cormorants**, as well as **Antarctic Tern*** (winter), occur on the rocks. **Cape Gannet** and **White-chinned Petrel** can often be seen offshore.

Cape Weaver, endemic to South Africa

OTHER ANIMALS: Because the vegetation is so dense, visitors are unlikely to see many of the mammals (including Eland, Red Hartebeest, Bontebok, Plains Zebra) that occur here. Two small antelope, Common Duiker and Steenbok, are often startled at the road edges (especially in the early morning). The peculiar tortoise roadsigns along this route refer to Angulate Tortoise, which is commonly seen crossing the park roads.

20 Langebaan Quarry ✔

The greatest attraction here is a pair of **Verreaux's Eagle**, which usually breed between May-Nov, although they may be seen in the general vicinity throughout the year. At the northern edge of Langebaan village, turn left towards Club Mykonos. After a few kilometres along this road, turn sharply to the right opposite the horseshoe-shaped 'Long Acres' sign. Follow the main track for about half a kilometre, veering right wherever it splits **J** (see map, p.48). This will take you to the section of quarry where the well-known eagles' nest is situated. **Rock Kestrel** and **African Black Swift** also breed on the cliff faces. The alien thicket at the quarry edges is a reliable site for **Grey Tit** and **Acacia Pied Barbet**. Permission may be required in the future. The eagles have also attempted breeding at a nearby site and may not always be present.

21 Vredenburg to Paternoster ✔✔

The granite outcrops, agricultural lands and scrubby vegetation of the Columbine Peninsula provide access to a suite of species not easily available elsewhere in this region.

Vredenburg can be conveniently reached from the R27, or from Langebaan. Take the Paternoster road west of Vredenburg, and scan along the fence posts for **Sickle-winged Chat** (remarkably common), **Ant-eating Chat** and **Yellow Canary**. Regularly seen roadside raptors include **Jackal Buzzard** and **Lanner Falcon**. Continue westwards to the picturesque fishing village of Paternoster, before heading north towards Stompneusbaai and St Helena Bay.

Check the fallow lands along this road for **Cape Long-billed Lark***, as well as **Large-billed Lark**, **Red-capped Lark** and **Grey-backed Sparrowlark** (late summer). Small patches of natural vegetation harbour the regular strandveld species in addition to the scarcer **Grey Tit**, **Cape Penduline-Tit** and, rarely, **Yellow-bellied Eremomela**. Inspect small patches of water for **South African Shelduck**, and the occasional drinking **Namaqua Sandgrouse**. From Stompneusbaai, the road runs along the rocky shoreline of St Helena Bay before reaching the Berg River Estuary at Velddrif.

22 Berg River Estuary (Velddrif) IBA R ✔✔

Situated at Velddrif, the estuary and flood plain cover a vast area, extending 40 km inland along one of the Cape's biggest rivers. The flood plain is very seasonal and difficult to access, and holds few birds that cannot be seen nearer the mouth, although **Palm-nut Vulture*** is sometimes seen here. Rather, it is the mudflats and saltpans that provide the most rewarding birding; in fact, these mudflats support the highest density of waders along the entire east Atlantic seaboard.

SPECIALS: Chestnut-banded Plover, Greater and Lesser Flamingos, Great White Pelican, and a host of waders.

SEASON: Summer is best as the waders are present.

HABITATS: Beaches, mudflats, reedbeds, riverine channels, strandveld, flood plain.

BIRDING: The pans Ⓑ closest to the offices of the saltworks (see map on p.52) are the most reliable for **Chestnut-banded Plover**. The bulk of South Africa's population of this localised species occurs on the saline pans of the West Coast. **Kittlitz's Plover** is also common here, and often nests on the edges of the roads that skirt the pans. During summer, large numbers of waders feed along the pan margins; the most common species include **Little Stint**, **Ruff**, **Common Ringed Plover** and **Curlew Sandpiper**. Other birds here, especially in the vicinity of Ⓒ, include **Black-necked Grebe**, **Greater** and **Lesser Flamingos**, **Cape Teal** and **Caspian Tern**. It is also worth scanning the pans on the east side of the R27 at Ⓓ, which hold a selection of small waders, **Black-winged Stilt**, **Pied Avocet** and **South African Shelduck**. **Black Tern** and **Red-necked Phalarope** are recorded here infrequently. Also look out for **Large-billed Lark** and **Capped Wheatear** in the saltworks.

To reach the back entrance of the saltworks, take the R399 Vredenburg road and follow the Flaminkvlei right turn Ⓔ. This road initially passes some farmland: **Large-billed Lark** and **Common Stonechat** occur here and **Jackal Buzzard** is often seen in this vicinity (note that juveniles can resemble **Steppe Buzzard**).

A number of rarities – most famously the first African record of the American **Little Blue Heron** – have been seen at the Riviera mudflat in Velddrif. The bird hide is situated at Ⓕ (ask at the Riviera Hotel for the key). The best viewing from the hide begins about 1.5 hours after the 'High tide in Table Bay', as listed in Cape Town newspapers. A diverse selection of water birds may be observed from here, including **Great White Pelican**, **African Spoonbill**, **Greater** and **Lesser Flamingos**,

GETTING THERE

Just before the road crosses the river Ⓐ, the Cerebos saltworks Ⓑ lie to the left. The evaporation pans of this conveniently non-tidal locality are particularly good for roosting waders. Permission must be obtained in advance ☎.

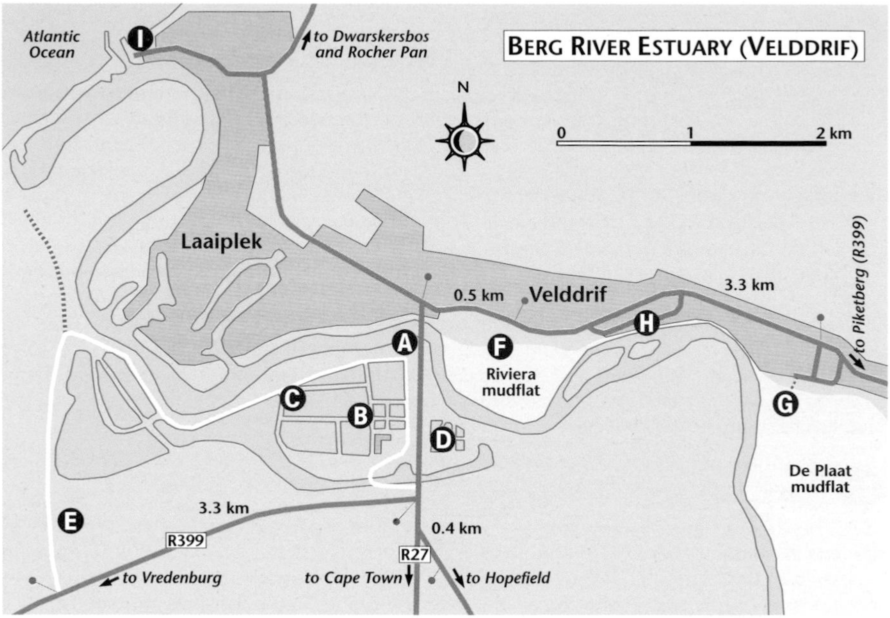

Purple Heron, **Little Egret**, and a wide selection of terns including **Caspian** and **Little Terns**. The mudflats are excellent in summer for migrant waders that include **Curlew Sandpiper**, **Little Stint**, **Sanderling**, **Ruddy Turnstone**, **Common Greenshank**, **Marsh Sandpiper**, **Common Whimbrel**, **Grey** and **Common Ringed Plovers** and **Bar-tailed Godwit**. Confiding **Levaillant's Cisticola** calls from the nearby sedges.

The De Plaat mudflat **G** holds similar birds, and **Eurasian Curlew** and **Bar-tailed Godwit** are easier to see here, although it is not as easy to approach them closely. De Plaat can be reached by taking the R399 to Piketberg and turning right into Vrede Road (opposite the Spreewal Kafee building). Turn right again, follow this road to its end, and walk down past the eucalyptus trees to the wooden jetty. Again, be sure to visit on the correct tide: the best viewing begins about 3.5 hours after the 'High tide in Table Bay'.

To reach an area of riverine channels and reedbeds **H**, where a variety of herons, warblers and other water birds may be found, take the main road east past the bird hide, and turn right into the road signposted 'Bokkoms Industry' (bokkoms are a West Coast speciality of small, dried fish) and continue to the banks of the river. Wooded residential areas of Velddrif, such as those in this vicinity, usually provide **Red-faced Mousebird** and **Acacia Pied Barbet**. At the harbour on the river mouth in Laaiplek **I**, a selection of cormorants, gulls (a good site for **Grey-headed Gull**) and terns roost. The latter are harried offshore in summer by **Parasitic Jaeger**.

Callan Cohen

Velddrif bird hide at F on map above

NEARBY SITES: The ephemeral Rocher Pan, a large water body protected in a nature reserve 24 km north of Velddrif, can be reached via the hamlet of Dwarskersbos. The pan often supports an interesting selection of water birds, and is flanked by very productive strandveld vegetation and a lonely coastline. A desolate beach stretches towards the seemingly limitless horizon, populated only by the occasional pair of **African Black Oystercatcher***.

23 Lambert's Bay

IBA R ✔✔

The **Cape Gannet** colony at Lambert's Bay is a spectacle not to be missed, and must rank as one of the birding highlights of the West Coast. Nearby strandveld and wetland birding offers a diversity of species.

SPECIALS: Cape Gannet, Cape Long-billed Lark*, Cape Clapper Lark*, Cape Penduline-Tit.

SEASON: Year-round, especially spring.

HABITATS: Gannet colony, beaches, strandveld, saline wetlands.

BIRDING: Nearly 14 000 pairs of **Cape Gannet** breed on the bay's Bird Island, now connected to the mainland by a wide concrete breakwater extending from the harbour. Small numbers of **African Penguin**, and **Cape** and **Crowned Cormorants**, can also be seen here. A host of gulls and terns, including **Swift Tern**, are also present. A good selection of waterfowl and waders usually inhabit Jakkalsvlei, a lake on the northern edge of town (reached from the caravan park). Note, however, that it can be dry for the most part in summer. Regular species here are **Greater Flamingo**, **South African Shelduck**, and **Cape** and **Red-billed Teals**.

The strandveld vegetation south and east of the town holds, among other species usually found in this habitat, **Cape Clapper*** and **Karoo Larks**, **Pearl-breasted Swallow**, **Yellow-bellied Eremomela** and **Rufous-eared Warbler**. Follow the coastal road south from Lambert's Bay towards Elands Bay (look out for the uncommon **Chat Flycatcher**) and, after 11.8 km (just before the railway bridge), turn right to follow the railway line until you reach Wadrifsoutpan ('wagon drift saltpan') after about 1 km. This is a private road, and you are not permitted to proceed past the toll station adjacent to the pan. Wadrifsoutpan is split in two by the railway line, and the smaller seaward section is worth searching for a selection of water-bird and wader species, including **South African Shelduck**, **Cape Teal** and **Greater Flamingo**. However, it can be predominantly dry in summer. A wide variety of strandveld birds occurs here, most notably **Cape Long-billed** and **Cape Clapper Larks***.

OTHER ANIMALS: The handsome and localised Heaviside's Dolphin, a small cetacean endemic to the western coast of South Africa and Namibia, may sometimes be seen inshore here, and boat trips can be arranged to view them. Cape Fur Seals also breed on Bird Island.

Callan Cohen

Crowned Cormorant is endemic to South Africa.

GETTING THERE

Lambert's Bay can be reached by following the N7 national road from Cape Town to Clanwilliam, and then taking the tarred R364 towards the coast (look out for **Ant-eating Chat** along the way). It can thus be easily visited as a detour from the N7 while en route to Namaqualand or Bushmanland, and is well combined with a visit to Kransvleipoort.

CAPE GANNET COLONY

The Lambert's Bay colony is the most accessible of the six **Cape Gannet** colonies in existence. Huge numbers of gannets are present throughout the year, and can be viewed at point-blank range from a modern, newly constructed hide. A panel of one-way glass forms one side of the hide, allowing undisturbed observation of the gannets' curious behavioural interactions. A few individuals of the vagrant **Australian Gannet** annually linger in an offshore **Cape Gannet** colony further south.

Callan Cohen

24 Verlorenvlei   IBA ✔

Elands Bay is situated at the mouth of the bird-rich Verlorenvlei ('lost lake'). At Elands Bay, turn southwards along the road that crosses the vlei, and turn to the left at the T-junction on the southern bank. Scan the reedbed edges (such as those in the vicinity of the road bridge) for **Little Bittern**, **African Rail**, **Red-chested Flufftail**, **African Purple Swamphen**, **Purple Heron**, **Malachite Kingfisher** and **African Marsh-Harrier**. The rocky slopes lying south of the T-junction hold a host of scrub birds, including **Grey Tit**. A pair of **Verreaux's Eagle** breed on the nearby cliffs and are often seen overhead.

You may wish to continue along the southern edge of the lake for a few more kilometres, as a wide diversity of water-bird species may be seen from the road. These include **Great Crested Grebe**, **Great White Pelican**, **Greater** and **Lesser Flamingos**, **South African Shelduck**, **African Fish Eagle**, **Goliath Heron** (rare), **Caspian Tern** and a variety of waders.

Retrace your steps to Elands Bay, then turn right onto the R366. This follows the 40 km length of Verlorenvlei inland towards Redelinghuys (please ask the landowners' permission should you wish to reach the lake itself at any point), before heading south to Aurora. The mountains to the east of Aurora, including the Mountain Mist property ☎, hold a number of interesting species, including **Protea Seed-eater***, and **Verreaux's** and **Booted Eagles**. The tarred road resumes from Aurora southwards, and ultimately intersects with the R399, 41 km to the east of Velddrif.

25 Kransvleipoort, Clanwilliam   ✔✔✔

Tucked away close to the N7, just over 200 km north of Cape Town en route to Lambert's Bay, Namaqualand and/or Bushmanland, Kransvleipoort is a highly accessible and reliable site at which to see the often-elusive **Protea Seed-eater***. From the N7, exactly 10 km south of Clanwilliam, turn left onto the gravel road marked 'Paleisheuwel'. Just over 2 km further, the road enters the cliffs and follows a reed-lined stream through a steep valley.

Search for **Protea Seed-eater*** in the taller streamside vegetation fringing the roadside and the lower cliffs, especially near the prominent bend in the road towards the end of the poort. The protea stands that line the route as it rises out of the poort are, oddly, not the best place to look for this bird. Other seed-eaters found in the poort include **White-throated**, **Brimstone** and **Cape Canaries** and **Streaky-headed Seed-eater**. **Little Rush Warbler** and **Yellow Bishop** are found along the stream, and **Verreaux's Eagle** as well as **Ground Woodpecker*** frequent the cliffs and rocky outcrops. **Layard's Tit-Babbler**, **Long-billed Crombec** and **Fairy Flycatcher** occur in the hillside scrub.

John Harvey/CBC

Fairy Flycatcher is a handsome southern African endemic.

ROUTE 3

TANQUA KAROO LOOP

Just two southern African regions have been bestowed the honour of designation as Biodiversity Hotspots by Conservation International. One is, of course, the Cape Floral Kingdom, and the other is the Succulent Karoo. For those whose image of the south-western Karoo is a shimmering wasteland to be endured as briefly as possible en route to Cape Town or Johannesburg, this may come as a surprise. Though the remarkable endemism and diversity of the Succulent Karoo flora is its most renowned aspect, the Karoo as a whole has much to offer the birder. With no less than 18 endemics almost wholly restricted to it, it is an essential birding destination.

TOP 10 BIRDS

- Karoo Eremomela
- Namaqua Warbler
- Fairy Flycatcher
- Cinnamon-breasted Warbler
- Ludwig's Bustard
- Burchell's Courser
- Black-headed Canary
- Layard's Tit-Babbler
- Rufous-eared Warbler
- Black-eared Sparrowlark

Consequently, the south-western corner of the Karoo – a low-lying, mountain-bound section of the Succulent Karoo biome known as the Tanqua Karoo, has received a great deal of birding attention. Here, in sparsely populated semi-desert landscapes just two and a half hours' drive from Cape Town, the majority of the Karoo specials are accessible in a (rather long) day's outing from the city. Although the region merits one full day's exploration at the very least, two days are preferable. The parched brown expanses, aloe-lined escarpments and lonely isolated hills of the Tanqua Karoo provide an apt setting for such fine and sought-after dry western endemics as Karoo Eremomela* and Cinnamon-breasted and Namaqua Warblers*, among many others.

The town of Ceres is a good starting point from which to explore the Tanqua Karoo, although one should ideally try to stay at one of the small B&B establishments in the Karoo itself, as a round trip from Cape Town entails a total drive of about 500 km. All the Karoo birding spots can be reached from the desolate gravel R355 from Karoopoort to Calvinia, and it is also worth exploring the series of scenic and productive passes that lie between Ceres and Cape Town for fynbos species. The Tanqua Karoo also makes an excellent start to a Bushmanland trip, as the R355 can be followed north all the way to Calvinia.

Spring is best for birding, and a dawn start is optimal: birding is at its peak from Aug-Oct, when the region may also burst into flower. However, the majority of the specials (with the possible exception of Black-headed Canary*, Ludwig's Bustard* and Black-eared Sparrowlark*) are accessible year-round.

Please take care when driving in the remote reaches of this region. The road gravel is sharp and often loose, and much caution needs to be taken with corners and sudden stops. Give some thought to your fuel and water requirements, bearing in mind that there are no towns in the Tanqua Karoo proper, and that the closest refuelling points are Ceres, Sutherland and Calvinia. The Cape Birding Route ☎ organises day-trips from Cape Town.

Callan Cohen

Birding in the Tanqua Karoo

26 Karoopoort ✔✔

The most direct route from Cape Town to the Tanqua Karoo along the N1 leads you through everything from the majestic peaks of the Du Toit's Kloof Mountains (burrowed through by the 4 km Huguenot Tunnel) to the pleasingly geometric vineyard mosaic of the Hex River Valley. Fynbos grades into progressively drier scrub and, at Karoopoort, one ultimately emerges through a gap in the mountains onto the arid, scrubby plains of the Tanqua Karoo.

This gateway to the Karoo offers an excellent introduction to the area. To reach Karoopoort, take the N1 from Cape Town and, 10 km before Touws River, turn left (north) onto the R46 (signposted 'Ceres'). At the T-junction 33 km further on, turn right (east) onto the R355. Along the R46, and particularly in the vicinity of this T-junction, jittery coveys of **Grey-winged Francolin** are regularly seen feeding on the roadside in the early morning. From here, the R355 follows a reed- and thicket-lined riverbed, which passes though a gap in the mountains before reaching the open Karoo.

The essential Karoopoort species for many visitors will be **Namaqua Warbler***, which is a common and noisy bird of the *Phragmites* reedbeds and adjacent acacia thicket. Look for the warbler opposite the oak-shaded farmhouse **A**. Though noisy, it sometimes requires a little effort to find it.

Among other typically dry western species of the acacia thicket are **White-backed Mousebird**, **Chestnut-vented Tit-Babbler**, **Fairy Flycatcher** and **White-throated Canary**. **Mountain Wheatear** occurs on the rocky hillsides flanking the road and a pair resides along the first kilometre of gravel road. Flocks of **Red-winged** and, notably, **Pale-winged Starlings** fly purposefully overhead, and balance on cliff faces or feed on fruiting fig trees next to the farmhouse. While **Cinnamon-breasted Warbler*** has been recorded here (especially at the picnic site at **B**), it is more reliably found at Skitterykloof, a little further north.

27 Eierkop ✔✔

Emerging from the Koue Bokkeveld Mountains and onto the semi-desert plains of the Tanqua Karoo, one soon reaches a fork in the road **B**. In contrast with their unassuming appearance, each of these roads is associated with a South African record: the R356 to the right leads to the town of Sutherland which, thanks to its crisp, pollution-free desert skies, is the site of a world-renowned astronomical observatory. To the left is the R355 to Calvinia, the longest road in South Africa uninterrupted by a town (250 km in all). The surface is of good quality gravel, but travellers driving all the way to Calvinia should nonetheless come well prepared with fuel and emergency water supplies. Birders should be particularly aware that braking suddenly on these roads could well result in a damaged tyre, as the gravel in this region is iniquitously sharp.

Common birds of the relatively moist scrublands just north of the road fork **B** are **Pale Chanting Goshawk**, **Karoo Lark**, **Karoo Chat**, **Yellow Canary** and, more scarcely, **Southern Black Korhaan**. At **C**, the road is crossed by an acacia-lined river course, where **Pririt Batis** and **Chestnut-vented Tit-Babbler** occur.

Nico Myburgh
Karoo Eremomela

At **D** is a large dam, visible some distance to the east of the road. More often than not, the water level is low and the associated water birds are distant, reduced to amorphous shimmering blobs in the telescope. Nonetheless, it is worth the 200 m stroll down from the road to the farm fence to scan the water, as the adjacent scrub is, in any case, always good for a number of bird species. **South African Shelduck** and **Greater Flamingo** are often present on the dam, and **Namaqua Sandgrouse** occasionally fly in to drink. The dam is situated on the game reserve Inverdoorn; please respect the fence – there are rhino to enforce the law!

One kilometre further on, at **E**, there is a prominent sandy intrusion on the landscape. A small group of **Ant-eating Chat** is usually present on these low, vegetated dunes. These most peculiar birds nest in burrows, hence their association with a soft substrate. Aardvark is sometimes seen along this stretch of the R355 at night.

An excellent spot to look for several key Karoo specials is the distinctive pair of tillite hills straddling the road at **F**. An inconspicuous gravel track, easily negotiable by 2WD, leads

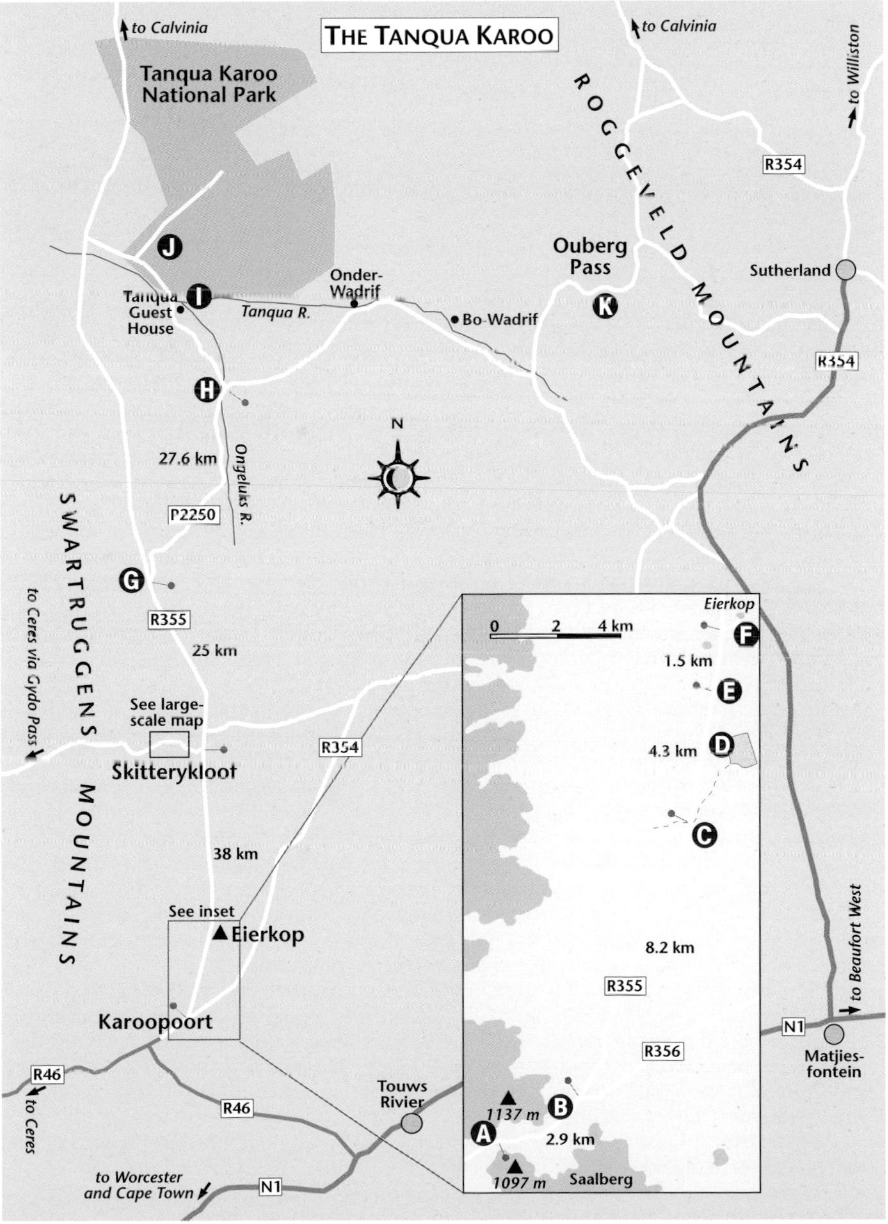

The plains below Eierkop are among the best sites globally for Karoo Eremomela.

500 m east from the R355 to the base of Eierkop, the right-hand hill. Eierkop ('egg-hill', pronounced 'ay-yir kop') possibly owes its name to the tiny, smoothed pieces of ostrich eggshells found on the summit; these were probably left by the early San hunter-gatherers, whose paintings are found in nearby rock shelters. Eierkop is arguably the most accessible site worldwide for **Karoo Eremomela***. A small party is more often than not present on the plains surrounding this hill, moving quickly and inconspicuously from bush to bush, usually keeping an infuriatingly fixed distance ahead of observers. Other common and typical birds of this habitat are **Karoo Lark**, **Karoo Chat**, **Rufous-eared Warbler** and **Grey-backed Cisticola**. The slightly denser scrub around the base of Eierkop supports **Grey Tit**, **Fairy Flycatcher**, **Layard's Tit-Babbler**, **White-throated Canary**, **Malachite Sunbird** and, in spring during years of good rainfall, **Black-headed Canary*** and **Lark-like Bunting**.

The short scramble up to the top of Eierkop is well worth the effort: the summit is bedecked with an intriguing diversity of succulents, and provides stunning panoramic views over the surrounding expanse of brown desert plains and shimmering purple mountains.

As you head north from Eierkop along the R355, the landscape becomes progressively more arid until, approaching Skitterykloof, bushes are few and far between and the ground gleams with the mineral patina of desert pebbles. This is classic **Tractrac Chat** country: birds are most often spotted, 10-15 km north of Eierkop, as they flush near the road, and display their white rumps as they fly a short distance to perch again on a fence or low bush. The chats of the Karoo appear, at first glance, dauntingly alike. However, Tractrac Chat's much-discussed resemblance to **Karoo Chat** is only superficial: Tractrac is a smaller, paler and more compact bird, shorter-tailed and with a characteristically pale rump.

The most common larks of this stretch of road are **Large-billed** and **Red-capped Larks**. **Spike-heeled Lark** is also regularly seen. It is worth keeping an eye out for pairs of **Karoo Korhaan**, although they are very well camouflaged in their natural habitat. Listen for their frog-like calls at dawn, and check in the shade of the occasional roadside tree at midday. Drainage lines with slightly denser scrub are good areas to search for small, restless flocks of **Cape Penduline-Tit**, best detected by their soft, inconspicuous call.

Pale Chanting Goshawk is reasonably common throughout the Tanqua Karoo, and **Greater Kestrel** frequently wanders into the area. If you visit after recent rain, you will see that pools forming close to the road invariably attract **South African Shelduck**, drinking flocks of **Namaqua Sandgrouse** and irruptive seed-eaters such as **Lark-like Bunting**.

28 Skitterykloof ✔✔✔

A small picnic spot and birding site situated at the edge of the Tanqua Karoo, Skitterykloof offers easy access to numerous tricky Karoo specials, and provides an excellent selection of species typical of the Karoo's arid, rocky gorges and acacia thickets, all within a three-hour drive from Cape Town. It is the classic site to find **Cinnamon-breasted Warbler***, a peculiar and often evasive warbler of hill slopes and cliffs. Skitterykloof is often erroneously referred to by birders as Katbakkies; the real Katbakkies Pass lies 20 km to the west (see p.60).

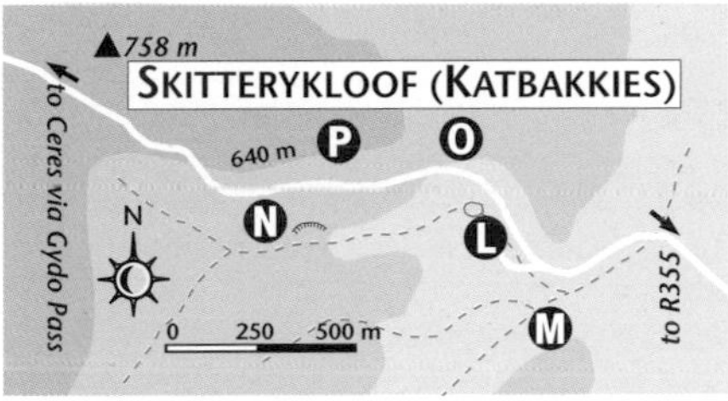

SPECIALS: Cinnamon-breasted Warbler*, Layard's Tit-Babbler, Fairy Flycatcher, Pririt Batis, Grey Tit, Black-headed Canary* and Ground Woodpecker*.

SEASON: Breeding occurs in Aug-Oct, but all the specials are present and obtainable year-round (with the exception of **Black-headed Canary***, which is only present in spring).

HABITATS: Aloe stands, acacia thicket, rocky slopes, small reed-fringed dam.

BIRDING: Skitterykloof picnic site is situated in an aloe lined 'gap' in the mountains, where a small pass winds steeply up into the moister, fynbos-like scrub of the Swartruggens. Impenetrable acacia thicket lines the riverbed leading into the top of the picnic site, where there is also a tiny, reed-bordered dam. Below, the valley broadens and there is a small seep Ⓜ feeding a dense reedbed. The rock-strewn valley sides and precipitous, red-cliffed escarpments presiding over the picnic site are covered with a remarkable density of Clanwilliam Aloe, an unusually tall aloe restricted to a tiny area of this part of the Karoo.

The rock-strewn slopes around the Skitterykloof picnic site are legendary as the most accessible site in the world to see **Cinnamon-breasted Warbler***. Familiarity with this species' call is essential, as it is otherwise almost impossible to locate. The pair on the slopes adjacent to the band of red cliffs at Ⓝ, a short walk up the riverbed from the picnic site, are arguably South Africa's most tape-pressured birds, yet still nest here annually and still regularly respond to provocation. However, please be very sparing with playback at this site in order to keep disturbance to a minimum. The birds tend to call loudly in short bursts, even without playback, usually from exposed sites on a rock or aloe, then remain silent for another 10 or 15 minutes – so don't despair. They are constantly on the move, delving around the bases of bushes and scurrying, rodent-like, between rock jumbles. You are most likely to be successful if you scan the area in which the birds can be heard, as playback at this site does not draw the birds closer, but often makes them call slightly more frequently.

There are several pairs of birds within a few hundred metres of the picnic site. Birds are often present on the cliffs as one enters the Skitterykloof gorge. Another good area to investigate is the steep ridge that runs parallel to the right-hand side of the road.

Claire Spottiswoode

Skitterykloof

GETTING THERE

Take the R355 north of Karoopoort and 21 km after Eierkop turn left (west) at the 'Kagga Kamma, Swartrugpad' sign. After 3.5 km, a small track Ⓛ leads left and immediately into the picnic site, just past the road's initial passage into the mountains. Picnic tables, a rustic toilet and a tap with potable water are provided.

Begin at the bend in the road, at **O**, 150 m from the picnic site turn-off. Climb straight up the slope and onto the top of the ridge, aiming to skirt the right-hand edge of the cliff at **P**. It is well worth the scramble, as this ridge has the advantage of height, making birds much easier to locate as they call intermittently among the rocks below.

On the slopes, **Grey Tit**, **Layard's Tit-Babbler**, **Mountain Wheatear** and **Grey-backed Cisticola** can also be seen. **Pale-winged Starling** and **Black-headed Canary*** regularly overfly the valley, and **Ground Woodpecker*** sometimes hurls invective from the ridges. **Dusky Sunbird** occasionally moves into the area if the rains have been plentiful. Keep an eye skyward for the likes of **Verreaux's** and **Booted Eagles**, and **Rock Kestrel**.

Cinnamon-breasted Warbler

The acacia thicket in the picnic site is usually alive with birds, even at midday. The essentials here are **Fairy Flycatcher** and **Pririt Batis**. Other interesting birds of this habitat are **Acacia Pied Barbet**, **White-backed Mousebird**, **African Reed-Warbler** (summer), **Long-billed Crombec**, **White-throated Canary** and **Cape Bunting**.

Three-banded Plover frequents the boggy lower seep, while the adjacent reedbeds hold resident **Levaillant's Cisticola** and **Lesser Swamp-Warbler**.

OTHER ANIMALS: Leopard (rarely), Chacma Baboon, Cape Rock Elephant-Shrew, and Klipspringer.

29 Swartruggens ✔✔

The Swartruggens, one of the most accessible places close to Cape Town for **Cape Eagle-Owl***, is a high plateau best explored from the road (largely gravel) that links Skitterykloof and the small town of Op-die-Berg. A focal point of this drive is the true Katbakkies Pass that plunges dramatically down towards the Riet River, 20 km west of Skitterykloof. The rocky slopes of the pass itself hold **Ground Woodpecker***, **Layard's Tit-Babbler**, **Black-headed Canary*** and **Cape Siskin***, while **Protea Seed-eater*** is scarce in proteas in the vicinity. Night drives in the area offer a moderate chance of **Cape Eagle-Owl*** (scan the roadside telephone poles and large roadside boulders) but note that similar **Spotted Eagle-Owl** is also regular here, and frequently ventures out of its favoured copses of exotic trees. Also look out for Smith's Red Rock Rabbit, Klipspringer, Grey Rhebok and the occasional Leopard. Contact the Cape Birding Route ☎ for accommodation options.

30 The P2250 ✔✔✔

This unassuming regional road is perhaps one of the finest for birding in the south-western Karoo, particularly in spring, when the scrub is alive with displaying, nest-building and chick-provisioning birds. It passes through a desolate and beautiful stretch of semi-desert, bounded in the west by the Cederberg range.

SPECIALS: Black-eared Sparrowlark*, Ludwig's Bustard*, Karoo Eremomela*, Karoo Korhaan, Burchell's Courser*, Namaqua Sandgrouse.

SEASON: The best birding is between Aug-Oct, when one stands the best chance of **Black-eared Sparrowlark***.

HABITATS: Open Karoo plains.

BIRDING: Perhaps the most conspicuous species along these arid stretches is **Tractrac Chat**, a gravel-plains specialist with a short-tailed, dumpy jizz. The most common bird of the adjacent scrub is usually **Rufous-eared Warbler**, a noisy and beautifully marked endemic of southern

Africa's arid west. **Spike-heeled Lark** is also common here, as are **Thick-billed, Karoo** and **Red-capped Larks**. **Karoo Lark** is particularly easy to find in spring, when its rattling call is heard everywhere. The most common seed-eater in the area is usually **Yellow Canary**; however, nomadic species such as **Black-headed Canary*** and **Lark-like Bunting** periodically invade the area. The latter can be abundant at times, and is generally more regularly present here than it is in the far south of the Tanqua Karoo.

Coveys of **Namaqua Sandgrouse**, another erratic visitor further south, flush up at intervals from the roadside. **Ludwig's Bustard*** may be present in some numbers, and is best spotted in flight, especially in winter and spring, while **Karoo Korhaan** occurs year-round. Pairs or small parties are occasionally seen within sight of the road, although their true density is only revealed at dawn, when their atmospheric frog-like duets drift across the scrub.

Callan Cohen

Karoo Korhaan

Greater Kestrel, a scarce bird further south in the Tanqua, is fairly regularly seen along the P2250, as are the more common **Pale Chanting Goshawk, Rock Kestrel** and the occasional **Black-breasted Snake-Eagle** and **Martial Eagle**.

Karoo Eremomela*, a sometimes tricky Karoo endemic, is common along here. Look especially along the shallow drainage lines 4-7 km from the R355, always remaining alert for its calls (a high-pitched, pulsating whine, somewhat like the tightening of a rusty bolt, and a Spike-heeled Lark-like krrr-krrr). Small groups of this social and cooperative-breeding species follow each other through the scrub, popping up at intervals to let forth a volley of whines. Approximately 8–9 km from the R355, scan the open plains for **Burchell's Courser***.

The highly nomadic **Black-eared Sparrowlark***, considered a Bushmanland special, may well be a regular visitor to this region. In exceptional seasons, it occurs and probably breeds right down to Eierkop at the Tanqua's southern edge; however, it occurs at highest densities along the P2250, and patchily in the Tanqua Karoo National Park (see overleaf). When breeding, aerially displaying males are easy to locate, looking more like giant, floppy black butterflies than birds. In flight, only their dangling white legs break the pure black of their underwings and bodies. Landing groups tend to be frustratingly concealed in the scrub; the best technique is to walk slowly up to the spot, and wait quietly until a foraging bird potters into view.

As the day heats up or once you have exhausted the possibilities of the gravel plains and scrub, you may wish to make a stop at the first or especially the second acacia-lined watercourse (the latter crosses the P2250 exactly 27.6 km from the R355). These watercourses supply all the expected Karoo thicket species, such as **Pririt Batis, Cape Penduline-Tit** (also in the adjacent lower scrub), **Chestnut-vented Tit-Babbler** and **White-backed Mousebird**. Just beyond the second watercourse, a turn-off to the left, signposted 'Tanqua' (H) (see map p.57), leads to the Tanqua River and Guest House (I) after 12 km. However, the river does lie on private land, so if you wish to visit for the day please obtain prior permission from the farm owner

GETTING THERE

Twenty-five kilometres north of the Skitterykloof turn-off, a minor road, the P2250 (G), heads off north-eastwards towards the distant towns of Middelpos and Sutherland. The initial stretches are relatively heavily vegetated and resemble the familiar R355; however, before long the bushes grow further and further apart and stretches of gleaming gravel appear. Approaching the junction marked (H) on the map, two watercourses en route to the larger Tanqua River, not far to the north, cross the road and break the monotony of the barren landscape with their dense sweet-thorn thickets.

(see Cape Birding Route ☎). **Namaqua Warbler*** is very common and fairly easily seen in the mixture of reeds and acacia thicket that densely lines the Tanqua River. This riparian strip is also one of the more reliable sites in the area in which to look for **Dusky Sunbird**, a highly nomadic desert sunbird that occasionally ventures south to the Eierkop-Skitterykloof area.

The Tanqua River is dammed just beyond the guest house, creating a rather startling and substantial water body, which hosts varying numbers of waterfowl and waders, perhaps most characteristically **South African Shelduck** and **Pied Avocet**.

31 Tanqua Karoo National Park ✔✔

The Tanqua Karoo National Park is now open to the public but offers few visitor facilities. The park protects one of the most starkly beautiful tracts of the Tanqua Karoo and is well worth visiting for several reasons, among them its koppie-studded, lunar-like landscape, diversity of succulent plants, and fine Karoo birding – perhaps most notably, the above-average chance of finding the enigmatic **Burchell's Courser***. The park is criss-crossed by a number of vehicle tracks, most of which are easily negotiable in a 2WD.

Birders will probably want to concentrate their efforts along the track running parallel to the park's southern boundary Ⓙ, which is easily accessible from the Tanqua Guest House Ⓘ. **Burchell's Courser*** is seen fairly regularly on the patches of bare, burnished gravel along this road, and has even been seen with chicks along here. It is a poorly known and notoriously tricky bird: it may be absent altogether in some years, and even when present requires considerable effort to spot. The best technique is to drive along slowly, stopping now and then to scan promising-looking expanses of gravel, and to keep a very sharp eye out for odd-shaped birds flying over. **Double-banded Courser** and **Karoo Long-billed Lark** (near the southern limit of its range) also occur here.

The guest house is very conveniently situated on the southern bank of the Tanqua River, a stone's throw from the national park. Built somewhat like a desert fort, it offers a range of accommodation and the owners are also able to arrange access to the park; contact the Cape Birding Route ☎ for more information.

Callan Cohen

Burchell's Courser

Callan Cohen

Scan desolate plains in the Tanqua Karoo National Park for Burchell's Courser.

32 Ouberg Pass to Sutherland ✔

Ouberg Pass Ⓚ rises precipitously up through 600 m of Roggeveld escarpment in a series of dramatic switchbacks. The rewards are superb views of the great, hazy basin of the Tanqua Karoo below, and excellent birding. Ouberg Pass is possibly the most reliable place within striking distance of Cape Town to see **African Rock Pipit*** (knowledge of its call is essential), and it is also a good site for other Karoo escarpment birds such as **Sickle-winged Chat**, **Pale-winged Starling** and, together with the plateau beyond, **Cape Eagle-Owl***.

Ouberg Pass, which is best reached by heading eastwards from the Tanqua Karoo National Park via a potentially confusing network of roads (see map p.57), works its way over the Roggeveld escarpment and on to the town of Sutherland. (Note, however, that there is petrol available only in Ceres and Sutherland, and you might need a jerry can to complete the journey.) If you approach the Tanqua Karoo from the east, an attractive option is to work your way over the pass, having first taken the tarred R354 from the N1 towards Sutherland.

Callan Cohen

African Rock Pipit occurs at Ouberg Pass.

33-35 Theronsberg, Mitchell's & Bain's Kloof Passes ✔

For a more relaxed trip to the Tanqua from Cape Town, one that avoids the busy N1, there is a very scenic alternative route via Ceres and Wellington. This takes in three superb mountain passes, all of which supply interesting birding in addition to marvellous mountain landscapes.

Theronsberg Pass, between Karoopoort and Ceres, has the gentlest landscape of the three, with grassy slopes frequented by **White-necked Raven**, **Grey-winged Francolin**, **Cape Clapper Lark*** and **Black Harrier***. At the base of this pass, 10 km east of Ceres, is a roadside dam that holds large numbers of waterfowl, including **South African Shelduck**.

In Mitchell's Pass, west of Ceres, a good area to bird is the slope behind the conspicuous Tolhuis restaurant and pub. A footpath leads up from the shade of the Tolhuis oaks to a railway line on a protea-dense slope, where **Protea Seed-eater*** may be found. However, an even better site for Protea Seed-eater* is on Gydo Pass, to the north of Ceres on the R303. It may be found by searching the stands of grey-leaved proteas at the higher viewpoints.

Bain's Kloof Pass, traversing the mountains above Wellington, takes in 30 km of dramatic curves through spectacularly rugged, boulder-strewn terrain laced with icy streams. These streams, stained a deep tea colour by humic acid leached from herbivore-deterring plants, support the dense vegetation in which **Victorin's Scrub-Warbler*** is commonly found along the entire length of the pass.

At the summit of Bain's Kloof Pass there is a small settlement shaded by alien trees frequented by **Fiscal Flycatcher**. **Cape Rock-Thrush**, often scarce elsewhere, regularly perches on the houses here. The ridges in this vicinity are good for **Cape Rock-jumper*** and **Cape Siskin***. **Victorin's Scrub-Warbler*** also occurs in the denser vegetation on the slopes. Scan overhead for **Verreaux's Eagle**. Birders still out at nightfall would do well to carefully check all outcrops and telephone poles for the distinctive, bulky silhouette of the (admittedly ever-scarce) **Cape Eagle-Owl***.

ROUTE **4**

OVERBERG & GARDEN ROUTE

On the far side of the Hottentots Holland Mountains that lie east of Cape Town, between the Langeberg range and the ocean, is the fertile Agulhas Plain (Overberg), a gently undulating coastal plain that today lies predominantly under wheat. This region provides a large diversity of much-coveted open-country species including Blue Crane and Cape Vulture*. Futher to the east, the Garden Route region, which stretches roughly from Mossel Bay to the Tsitsikamma area, is a paradisiacal stretch of coastal belt, backed by the dramatic peaks. Mountain and sea are separated by extensive tracts of canopy forest, providing a remarkable diversity of habitats that offer rewarding birding, where species such as Knysna Turaco and Narina Trogon* abound.

TOP 10 BIRDS

- Cape Vulture
- Blue Crane
- Denham's Bustard
- Damara Tern
- Narina Trogon
- Knysna Woodpecker
- Agulhas Long-billed Lark
- Southern Tchagra
- Forest Buzzard
- Knysna Turaco

To the north, the fynbos-cloaked Swartberg Pass (where six of the fynbos endemic birds may be readily found close to the road) is also the last outpost of moist landscape before the vast and arid Karoo.

To explore the Overberg and the southern coastal regions of the Cape, head out of Cape Town on the N2 and over Sir Lowry's Pass. Continue eastwards, towards Swellendam, which lies at the foot of the Langeberg, and at the heart of the Agulhas Plain. De Hoop Nature Reserve and the adjacent farmlands offer excellent birding, and Grootvadersbos provides the closest exciting forest birding to Cape Town. However, if it's forest and wetland birds you are after, then continue further along the N2 to Wilderness and Nature's Valley, the latter site offering arguably the best forest birding in the region.

Colin Paterson-Jones

The Overberg is the stronghold of the Blue Crane.

36 Agulhas Plain Loops

IBA ✔✔✔

The superficially sterile monoculture of the Overberg wheatlands harbours a surprising diversity of birds, including such sought-after species as **Black Harrier***, **Blue Crane**, **Denham's Bustard***, **Karoo Korhaan**, **Agulhas Long-billed Lark** and the endemic **Agulhas Clapper Lark**. The area is also pleasantly scenic, with only the scatter of fiery red aloes across the winter hillsides destroying the illusion of a restful southern European landscape.

Agulhas Long-billed Lark

One of the best birding areas to explore is that between Swellendam and De Hoop Nature Reserve. Three good gravel roads run between the two, flanked by a mosaic of wheatfields, fallow lands, and, on the steeper hillsides and valleys, islands of natural renosterveld. A rewarding loop that offers access to all the important birds is the following: take the N2 to the hamlet of Buffeljagsrivier, just 7 km east of Swellendam. Just beyond the BP service station, turn right onto the gravel road (signposted 'Malagas'); turn left after 3.3 km and continue for a further 4.3 km before pulling off. Search the scrub along the road edge for **Agulhas Long-billed Lark** and **Agulhas Clapper Lark**. Both are common here and are especially conspicuous when aerially displaying in spring. This road is also good for the scarce **Denham's Bustard***, **Karoo Korhaan** (rather atypically in such moist habitat), **Grey-winged Francolin** (seen feeding on the road verges in the mornings and late afternoons) and **Long-billed Pipit**. The road crosses the Breede River at Malagas; here, you can experience having your car inched across the river on one of the country's last working ponts.

Just past Malagas, the route joins the gravel road that leads to Potberg and the De Hoop Nature Reserve, and ultimately to the town of Bredasdorp. The remnant patches of indigenous scrub near this junction are good for **Agulhas Clapper Lark**, and the stretch from here to Bredasdorp (especially around the De Hoop turn-off from this road) is excellent for **Denham's Bustard***. If you wish to return to the N2, you can turn right at the fork 1 km later and follow another gravel road to Swellendam, along which there are also good numbers of **Agulhas Long-billed Lark**, **Karoo Korhaan** and **Blue Crane**. The latter is a fairly common sight throughout the plain.

The Overberg region is good raptor country; species that are regularly seen here include **Secretarybird**, **Martial Eagle**, **Lesser Kestrel** and **Black Harrier***. Common and characteristic species of the agricultural lands are **White Stork**, **Cape Crow**, **Large-billed** and **Red-capped Larks**, **Capped Wheatear**, **Cape Longclaw**, **African Pied Starling**, **Pin-tailed Whydah**, **Yellow Canary** and, particularly in old fields, **Cloud Cisticola***.

37 De Hoop Nature Reserve

IBA ✔✔

Potberg's southern cliff face hosts the Western Cape's last breeding colony of **Cape Vulture***, while the coastal thickets of the reserve's lowlands offer access to such desirable endemics as **Southern Tchagra*** and **Knysna Woodpecker***. The 14 km-long vlei can be a haven for migrant waders and water birds when the water levels are right.

SPECIALS: Cape Vulture*, Knysna Woodpecker*, Southern Tchagra*, Agulhas Clapper Lark, Hottentot Buttonquail*.

SEASON: All the specials are present year-round.

HABITATS: Lowland fynbos, fynbos-clad mountain, vlei/wetland.

BIRDING: The parking area at Potberg is an excellent vantage point from which to look for **Cape Vulture*** soaring over the nearby slopes, and a half-hour's scan overhead is bound to

Cape Mountain Zebra

Nigel J. Dennis

turn up birds wandering from the nearby colony.

The eucalyptus plantation and mixed alien and indigenous thicket along the stream adjacent to the parking area host a surprising number of interesting species. **Knysna Woodpecker*** occurs in the riverine strip of woodland, but is unobtrusive and difficult to locate. These alien trees have also hosted all three of the south-western Cape's honey-guide species (**Greater** and **Lesser Honeyguides** and **Brown-backed Honeybird**), along with a contingent of forest raptors, including **Black Sparrowhawk**, **African Goshawk** and **African Harrier Hawk**. **Swee Waxbill** and **Southern Tchagra*** lurk in the thicket between the parking area and the eucalyptus stand.

The pleasant Klipspringer Trail ascends to the summit of the Potberg (4 km each way), offering some good fynbos birding (**Cape Rock-jumper***, **Orange-breasted Sunbird**, **Cape Siskin***) in addition to guaranteed sightings of overflying **Cape Vulture***. The colony itself is not accessible to visitors. **Hottentot Buttonquail*** and **Striped Flufftail*** occur on the southern slopes of the mountain, but, as ever, it is very difficult to see these ground dwellers.

De Hoop's main entrance gate is located on a range of limestone hills, from which the road winds down onto the lowland fynbos-swathed plains below. **Common Ostrich** favours these pastures and is bound to be seen in good numbers in the vicinity of the turn-off to the reserve headquarters and rest camp (on the right, 4 km from the entrance). **Capped Wheatear** also inhabits these short-grass areas. In the open fynbos, look out for striding **Secretarybird** and **Southern Black Korhaan**, and quartering **Black Harrier***.

The reserve office and rest camp are set among dense, gnarled milkwood thickets adjacent to De Hoop Vlei. This large, irregularly shaped lake attracts a huge number and an excellent diversity of waterfowl and waders, although this varies greatly from season to season. **Great Crested Grebe** is regular here, and occasionally breeds in large numbers. **Southern Tchagra*** is shy, but reasonably easy to find in the thickets around the camping area – its call is loud and conspicuous (De Hoop is one of the more westerly sites where it may be found). **Knysna Woodpecker*** is frequent around the vlei, but is characteristically tricky to find: look in the thickets partitioning the camping sites. Common residents of the vlei-side thicket are **Bar-throated Apalis**, **Sombre** and **Cape Bulbuls**, **Southern Boubou** and, rarely, **Black Cuckooshrike**. The area around the vlei and reserve buildings is also one of the best places in the south-western Cape to see **Pearl-breasted Swallow**, which often feeds alongside other hirundines such as **White-throated Swallow** and **Brown-throated Martin**.

De Hoop is one of the few places in the Western Cape where **Horus Swift** is regularly seen, most often in the vicinity of the vlei or flying low over the vegetated coastal dunes – for instance, those around Koppie Alleen. The parking area at Koppie Alleen

GETTING THERE

From Cape Town, De Hoop Nature Reserve is most easily reached by taking the N2 as far as Caledon, where you turn right onto the R316 to Bredasdorp. In Bredasdorp, turn left (north) onto the R319, and turn right, 6 km later, onto the signposted gravel road. The turn-off to the reserve entrance (also signposted) is 30 km along this road (a particularly good one for seeing **Denham's Bustard***), and the reserve gate another 6 km further on. Allow at least three hours to reach the reserve from Cape Town. An alternative route is via Swellendam, along the birding loops described on p.65.

Access to Potberg mountain is not, as one might expect, through the reserve's main entrance. Instead, continue along the gravel road from Bredasdorp, drive past the turn-off to the main entrance, and follow the signs for about 10 km to the parking area and environmental centre below Potberg's southern slopes.

Accommodation can be had in the form of self-catering cottages and camp sites. The adjacent Buchu Bush Camp offers superb lodge accommodation and a restaurant.

38 The Damara Tern colony

De Mond is the site of one of only two Western Cape breeding colonies of **Damara Tern***. Currently, only a handful of pairs of this species breed here. At the estuary mouth, small numbers of these terns occasionally roost or feed, primarily between the months of November and March.

The colony is 9 km west of the estuary and is best reached by road. From the reserve gate, retrace your route for 11 km, turn left at the crossroads and continue until you join the tarred R319 to Struisbaai. About 5 km before Struisbaai, take an inconspicuous turn-off to the left, signposted 'Struisbaai Plaat'. A gravel track runs through dune thicket (where **Southern Tchagra*** occurs) and forks twice. At the first fork, turn right; at the second, turn left. Park in the small parking area at the edge of the beach, and walk to your left (northwards). The colony is usually within 200 m of the parking spot, on the flat, shell-covered dune slacks where the dunes meet the beach. Please keep your distance, so as not to disturb the breeding birds. The birds are easiest seen by scanning along the shoreline.

Claire Spottiswoode

Damara Tern

(follow the signs on the main road from the entrance gate) is at the eastern edge of a vast sand-sea of pure white coastal dunes. The rockier coastline to the east of Koppie Alleen is frequented by good numbers of **African Black Oystercatcher***, together with more widespread coastal birds such as **White-fronted Plover**, and a selection of migrant waders including **Sanderling** and **Ruddy Turnstone**.

OTHER ANIMALS: From Jul-Nov, many mating and calving Southern Right Whales make their appearance along this stretch of coast. Chacma Baboon, Bontebok, Eland, Cape Mountain Zebra, and Angulate Tortoise favour the old pasture areas.

NEARBY SITES: The adjacent Buchu Bush Camp, which is signposted from the De Hoop entrance gate, offers excellent birding, superb lodge accommodation and a restaurant. **Agulhas Clapper Lark** is common in the low fynbos here, while **Southern Tchagra*** prefers the denser vegetation. **Hottentot Buttonquail*** also occurs here, and walks to search for this species can be arranged via the Cape Birding Route ☎.

39 De Mond Nature Reserve IBA R ✔

This reserve is greatly underrated as a birding site. Quite apart from the fact that it hosts a breeding colony of **Damara Tern*** (see box), a highly threatened, diminutive and attractive species endemic to the South African and Namibian coasts, the reserve is a beautiful spot, centred on the broad and placid estuary of the Heuningnes River and flanked by battlements of white dunes.

To reach De Mond, take the R316 southwards from Bredasdorp and, after 10 km, turn right onto the 16-km-long signposted gravel road to the reserve entrance. Park at the reserve gate, and take a look around the adjacent milkwood thicket for **Southern Tchagra***, as well as more widespread coastal-thicket birds such as **Fiscal Flycatcher** and **Acacia Pied Barbet**. Take the footpath that leads from the reserve buildings and across a suspension bridge over the river, before following the western bank of the estuary to its outlet into the Indian Ocean. In addition to common wader species, one can pick out scarcer and more localised birds such as **Bar-tailed Godwit**, **Eurasian Curlew** and, occasionally, **Terek Sandpiper** and **Mongolian** and **Greater Sand Plovers**, as well as a number of national rarities. **African Black Oystercatcher***, **Damara Tern*** and **Caspian Tern** (the reserve protects important breeding colonies of the latter two) feed at the estuary mouth.

40 Swellendam ✔

Swellendam, straddling the N2 some 250 km east of Cape Town, marks the westernmost occurrence of several bird species. In addition to offering agreeable camping and affordable cottage accommodation, the municipal camp site in town is a good site for several scarce species. The small path that leads through the dense riparian vegetation lining the flanking stream may yield **Tambourine Dove**, **Brown-hooded Kingfisher** and **Olive Woodpecker**. Flocks of **Swee Waxbill** scatter autumn-leaf-like at the camp site edges. **Southern Grey-headed Sparrow** can be found in the trees around the cottages, where a pair of **African Wood-Owl** call nightly.

41 Bontebok National Park ✔

On the plains to the south-east of Swellendam, along the Breede River, lies the Bontebok National Park. The signposted turn-off is on the N2 just east of the town, and the park entrance is a further 3 km along this untarred road.

Quail Finch, a scarce bird in the Cape, occurs in moist depressions between the N2 and the park gate. Much of the park consists of low, fynbos-clad plains, enlivened by grazing Bontebok, Grey Rhebok and Cape Mountain Zebra. Driving the few kilometres across the plains to the rest camp along the Breede River at the park's southern boundary, you might be disappointed by the apparent paucity of birds. It is well worth scanning the plains, however, for **Secretarybird** and **Southern Black Korhaan**. Look for the occasional distant white dot, which is likely to be a displaying male **Denham's Bustard***.

An early start and a thorough search through the roadside scrub between the park entrance and the rest camp should produce **Agulhas Clapper Lark** and **Grey-winged Francolin**, the latter feeding nervously at the road edges. This is also one of the better areas in the Overberg for **Martial Eagle** and **Black Harrier***.

There is excellent birding close to the rest camp, which offers both camping facilities and caravans for hire. A short trail starts behind the information centre and winds westwards through acacia thicket. Another begins at the bottom of the camp site, on the river bank, and leads to an aloe-clad hillside bedecked with sunbirds in the winter flowering season.

Other notable species (in Cape terms) are **Klaas's Cuckoo**, **Cardinal Woodpecker**, **Lesser Honeyguide**, **Southern Tchagra***, **Southern Grey-headed Sparrow** as well as **Streaky-headed Seed-eater**. **Pearl-breasted Swallow** nests annually in the camp buildings, and is easily seen during summer; other common birds of the camp site area are **Cape Bulbul**, **Bar-throated Apalis**, **Fiscal Flycatcher**, **Southern Boubou**, **Malachite Sunbird** and, feeding on the lawn edges, flocks of **Swee Waxbill**. You are bound to hear **Fiery-necked Nightjar** calling in the camp site at night, and are likely to see such river-loving species as **African Black Duck** and **Giant Kingfisher** along the Breede.

Richard du Toit

Bontebok are endemic to the southern Cape.

42 Grootvadersbosch NR

IBA ✔✔

The extensive wilderness area of the Grootvadersbosch Nature Reserve incorporates a 250-hectare indigenous forest, the largest in the south-western Cape and certainly the region's richest in bird diversity. A number of more characteristically eastern species reach their western limit here.

SPECIALS: Narina Trogon*, Knysna Woodpecker*, Knysna Warbler* and Victorin's Scrub-Warbler*, Forest Canary, Forest Buzzard*, African Crowned Eagle, Blue-mantled Crested Flycatcher, Terrestrial Brownbul, Yellow-throated Woodland-Warbler, Olive Bush-Shrike.

SEASON: All the specials are present year-round, although spring (Sept–Nov) is when they are at their most vocal.

HABITATS: Forest, forest edges, moist mountain fynbos.

GETTING THERE

Take the N2 east of Swellendam for 11 km; turn left onto the R324 (signposted 'Suurbraak/Barrydale'). Continue along this road, perhaps stopping to scan the lily- and reed-fringed pond on the left, which sometimes hosts **Giant Kingfisher**, **African Rail** and **White-backed Duck**. **Pearl-breasted Swallow** is also very often seen along this road. Pass through the picturesque village of Suurbraak, checking any flowering coral trees for feeding sunbirds, notably **Amethyst Sunbird**. The road from Suurbraak to the reserve passes over a series of hills, over which **Black Harrier*** regularly hunts. Where the road forks (the first fork is 26 km from the N2), follow the signposts to Grootvadersbosch (or 'Boosmansbos Wilderness Area'). The reserve entrance Ⓐ is on a ridge overlooking the forested valleys and the Langeberg range. Next to the entrance is a parking area, an information centre and a beautifully situated camp site. The adjacent Honeywood Guest Farm offers great value accommodation in a sweeping setting ☎.

BIRDING: Greater Double-collared Sunbird feeds in the office garden, where you need to obtain a day permit to enter the forest. From here it is a short, steep walk down a bracken-covered slope known as Bosbokrand Ⓑ before you enter the forest on an excellent network of paths. West of the ridge, the forest is predominantly slightly drier and lower than that to the east of the ridge. A gentle walk of roughly three hours (allowing time for lots of birding) follows a 1.7 km loop through the eastern valley, described below. However, you might also want to make a short foray into the western portion of the forest, or into the moist, fynbos-clad slopes above.

Disturbed areas, such as those on the descent from the camp site to the forest edge at Bosbokrand, are the favoured feeding habitat of several seed-eaters, including small flocks of **Swee Waxbill, Forest Canary** and **Cape Siskin***. This is also a good place to look for foraging **Black Saw-wing**, and for raptors. **African Crowned Eagle** reaches its western limit at Grootvadersbosch, and is sometimes seen overflying this ridge. More common forest raptors

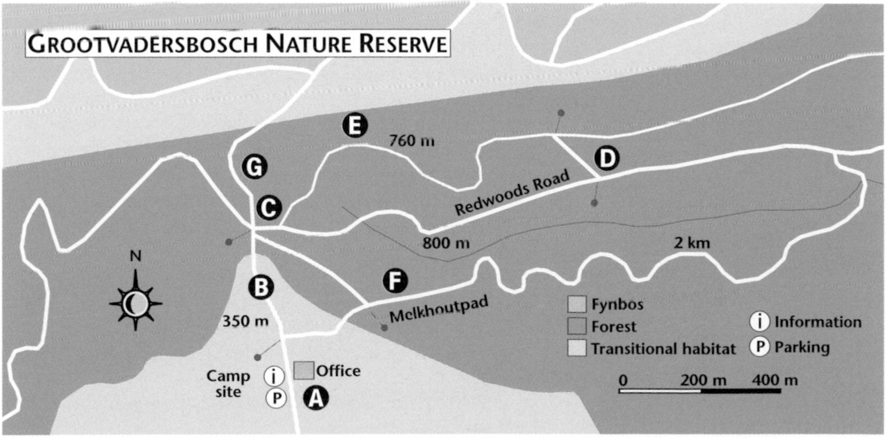

are **Forest Buzzard***, **Black Sparrowhawk** and **African Goshawk**, which are often seen perching on the skeletons of the introduced Giant Redwoods that protrude through the indigenous forest canopy at various places in the forest. **African Cuckoo Hawk** has also been seen here in recent years.

Grootvadersbosch Forest

From Bosbokrand, turn right at (C) onto the signposted 'Redwoods Road', a gravel track winding down the slope's lower contour. Walking down this track early in the morning, you may catch glimpses of the Cape's westernmost **Red-necked Spurfowl**, scurrying off the path edge or calling ahead. The most common and conspicuous birds in the forest are **Sombre Greenbul, Cape Batis** and **Bar-throated Apalis**. Before long, however, you will intercept a mixed-species foraging flock, among which you are likely to find **Olive Woodpecker, Terrestrial Brownbul, African Paradise-Flycatcher, Blue-mantled Crested Flycatcher, Yellow-throated Woodland-Warbler** and **Greater Double-collared Sunbird**. While all of these are very vocal birds, some, such as **Terrestrial Brownbul** and **Olive Bush-Shrike**, are inconspicuous lurkers, and you will need to invest a little time before obtaining good views.

The streamside undergrowth holds typically vocal yet skulking **Knysna Warbler***. This area is also a good spot for **Knysna Woodpecker***, which is not uncommon in the forest, as evidenced by its very distinctive, shrieking call. The challenge to birders lies in that this species only calls at 10–15 minute intervals, although it can often be located by following its soft but more regular tapping. **Olive Woodpecker**, conversely, is both vocal and conspicuous.

Ignore the continuation of the broad gravel track at (D), and turn left along the footpath back up the northern slope of the valley, where the forest is taller and moister. The forest clearing a few hundred metres up this path is a good spot to look for over-flying raptors. Also look out for **Grey Cuckooshrike**, a subtly beautiful canopy species that, although fairly common, requires a little alertness to its peculiarly sibilant call, vaguely reminiscent of that of **African Dusky Flycatcher**. Another stunning bird that reaches its western limit at Grootvadersbosch is **Narina Trogon***. It is surprisingly easy to locate once you become familiar with its repetitive, hoarse hooting call. Listen for it in the vicinity of the canopy hide at (E), as well as elsewhere in the forest. Returning to Bosbokrand, you might want to make a short detour to the other canopy hide – 500 m down the signposted 'Melkhoutpad' that follows a higher contour down the same valley as the Redwoods Road – at (F). This hide provides an excellent vantage point from which to scan for raptors, which often perch on the skeletons of the redwoods across the valley.

Albert Froneman

Narina Trogon

North of Bosbokrand, a gravel track (G) soon leads into moist fynbos to become the beginning of the Boosmansbos Hiking Trail, a route that leads the rugged on a two-day loop among the Langeberg peaks. **Victorin's Scrub-Warbler*** is very common here, even a few hundred metres from the forest edge. **Red-winged Francolin** occurs on the slopes, but is decidedly scarce.

OTHER ANIMALS: Throughout the forest, look out for South Africa's most westerly Bushbuck, which bark startlingly as they make a crashing escape through the dense undergrowth ahead.

NEARBY SITES: Tradouw Pass on the road to Barrydale offers a selection of fynbos (including **Victorin's Scrub-Warbler***) and rocky-slope specials.

43 The Wilderness Region IBA ✔✔

At the western end of the Garden Route, the Wilderness National Park encloses a system of reed-fringed coastal lakes that are sandwiched between a beach and an escarpment cloaked with lush coastal forest. A number of tranquil paths lead through the forest, offering easy and pleasant access to an excellent selection of forest birds, including **Knysna Turaco**.

En route from George, the N2 passes through the dramatic Kaaimans River gorge and over the river itself. Shortly after the N2 bridge over the Kaaimans, take the first turning to your right. This gravel track immediately doubles back, leading towards the N2 bridge and to a low concrete causeway over the river. This site is good for **African Finfoot***, which may be seen swimming inconspicuously below overhanging vegetation at the river's edge.

The park's rest camp is at Ebb and Flow **A**, a 1 km drive north of the N2 (turn inland at the signs just east of Wilderness village). The hutted camp and camp site, particularly at Ebb and Flow north (adjacent to Ebb and Flow south), offers good birding that includes **African Wood-Owl** (night time) and is a rewarding place to base your explorations into the surrounding forests.

Leading from Ebb and Flow are four trails, all named after local kingfishers. Good forest birding is to be had along the Giant Kingfisher Trail, which begins at the northern end of the north camp site. It runs alongside the eastern bank of the Touw River, ascending its forested valley and ultimately reaching a waterfall at **B**, 3.5 km from the camp site. The most conspicuous species in the forest are usually **Bar-throated Apalis** and **Green-backed Camaroptera**. **Terrestrial Brownbul** and **Chorister Robin-Chat** lurk in the lower strata, while common species of the mid-canopy are **Cape Batis**, **African Dusky Flycatcher**, **Sombre Greenbul**, **Yellow-throated Woodland-Warbler**, **Blue-mantled Crested Flycatcher**, **Olive Woodpecker** and, less conspicuously, **Olive Bush-Shrike**. It is especially important to familiarise yourself with the calls of otherwise cryptic canopy species such as **Eastern Black-headed Oriole**, **Narina Trogon***, **Grey Cuckooshrike**, **Scaly-throated Honeyguide**, **Black-bellied Starling**, **Knysna Turaco**, and **Green Woodhoopoe**. The latter two birds often venture into the rest camp edges. Look out for **Red-necked Spurfowl** feeding cautiously in open areas near the forest edge, especially in the early morning and in the evening. Listen for the deep hoot of **Buff-**

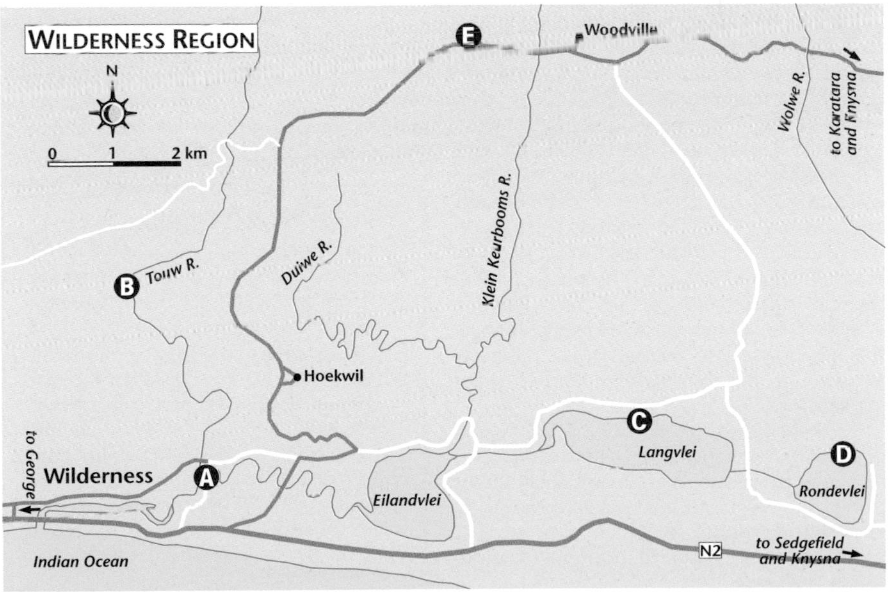

Forest and lake at Wilderness

spotted Flufftail at night. **African Crowned Eagle** and **African Goshawk** may be seen overhead here, as indeed in any of the Garden Route forests. **Lemon Dove** (the most common) and **Tambourine Dove** are birds of the forest floor, and are most often seen when flushed.

Also providing good access to these forest species is the Half-collared Kingfisher Trail, running along the other side of the Touw River for 2.5 km. It offers a good view of the river edges, and thus better access to its scarce and inconspicuous namesake, which is resident along its length. The reeds along the Touw River at the camp site edges have hosted **Great Reed-Warbler**, which may be a scarce visitor here, despite being almost unknown in the Cape.

In the Wilderness system, the best lakes for birding are Langvlei and Rondevlei, largely because both have well-positioned hides (at Ⓒ and Ⓓ respectively), which are accessed along boardwalks cut through dense reedbeds. These hides, especially the one at Rondevlei, are excellent places from which to search for stubborn skulkers such as **Red-chested Flufftail** and **African Rail**. The best way to see these birds is to lure them across the gap in the reeds formed by the boardwalk. **Baillon's Crake** also occurs here, but is less likely to be enticed into view, and is best searched for at the reed edges in the early morning. Rallids aside, the lakes offer a pleasant selection of more conspicuous species, including **Yellow-billed Egret**, **Purple Heron**, **African Fish-Eagle**, **Osprey** (summer), **African Marsh-Harrier**, **Malachite Kingfisher**, **Lesser Swamp-Warbler** and **Little Rush Warbler**.

Excellent forest birding (possibly even superior to that at Wilderness) may also be enjoyed in Woodville Forest, just to the north of the lakes (follow the signs to the 'Big Tree' at Ⓔ). A few minutes' walk from the parking area leads you to the aptly named tree – a gargantuan Outeniqua Yellowwood – from which a 2 km footpath loops gently through the forest. All the birds listed for the Wilderness forests occur here. Furthermore, Woodville is probably a better site for **White-starred Robin**, **Knysna Woodpecker*** (albeit scarce) and, in streamside undergrowth and scrubby forest edge habitats, **Knysna Warbler***. Secondary growth at forest edges – such as that along the short section of road leading to the parking area – is worth checking for **Forest Canary**, **Swee Waxbill** and **Greater Double-collared Sunbird**.

Another good site for **Knysna Warbler*** is Victoria Bay, situated between Wilderness and George. Take the signposted turn-off south from the N2 and follow this winding road all the way down to the beach, where there is a gate and parking area. **Knysna Warbler*** is common in the undergrowth of the adjacent dense coastal thicket (for example, near the boardwalk on the left of the parking area).

Forest Buzzard* occurs in forests and plantations throughout the Garden Route, and regularly perches on roadside telephone poles along the N2 from Wilderness through to Knysna and Nature's Valley. In summer, it is joined by **Steppe Buzzard**, posing an identification challenge.

TIPS ON FOREST BIRDING

Despite their often vivid colours, forest birds are adept at remaining cunningly concealed in the foliage. The key to successful forest birding is familiarity with the bird calls, and a little preparation will be of great help in locating many of the more inconspicuous species. An unobtrusive, patient approach is often very successful: try remaining still occasionally and birds will come alive around you. Another good strategy is to try to locate a noisy mixed-species foraging flock, or bird party, and to remain with it until you have seen all the participants.

44 Knysna ✔

The town of Knysna, immortalised in several bird names and perched at the edge of the Knysna Lagoon, lies midway between Wilderness and Nature's Valley. The N2 crosses the northern end of the lagoon, providing a vantage point from which to scan for the sometimes large numbers of water birds. You may wish to visit the famous Knysna Heads, guarding the lagoon mouth, as much for their scenic attraction as for **Knysna Warbler***, which is resident in the coastal undergrowth between the parking area and the sea. The signposted turn-off to the Heads is in the commercial centre of Knysna, 8.5 km east of the bridge over the lagoon. Check the nearby Woodbourne Lagoon for an excellent selection of waders and other water birds. Typical forest and forest edge birding is available close to town, and a wide variety of options is available, including the Pledge Nature Reserve and Diepwalle Forest Walk. Consult Knysna Tourism for further information on the forest walks.

Rita Meyer

Knysna Turaco

45 Robberg Nature Reserve ✔

This coastal reserve offers easily accessible fynbos specials. Robberg is situated on the point at Cape Seal, south of Plettenberg Bay (well signposted from the town). **Orange-breasted Sunbird** is best seen among the ericas near the car park, while **Cape Sugarbird*** frequents the flowering proteas. Skulking **Victorin's Scrub-Warbler*** is common on the southern fynbos-covered slopes, while **Cape Siskin*** occurs on the northern slopes, particularly during the winter months.

46 Keurbooms Estuary ✔✔

Boat trips up this extensively forested system have yielded some of the Western Cape's most exciting river birding.

SPECIALS: White-backed Night-Heron*, African Finfoot*, Half-collared Kingfisher, Narina Trogon*.

HABITATS: Intertidal banks, marine environment, riverine and coastal thicket, forest.

SEASON: Birding is good throughout the year, although the summer months (Oct-Mar) are best for Palearctic waders.

BIRDING: Canoeing birders heading inland may see **Half-collared Kingfisher** and possibly even the scarce **African Finfoot*** by carefully scanning under overhanging vegetation on the river edges. The highlight of this stretch of river must be the resident pair of **White-backed Night-Heron***, here at the western edge of their range, which roost during the day in dense riverside tangles. The best way to find them is to take a boat cruise upriver with the local operator ☎.

The picnic site alongside the N2 bridge that crosses the Keurbooms River is a convenient place to look for **Knysna Turaco** among a host of forest species.

Migrant waders such as **Curlew Sandpiper**, **Grey Plover**, **Common Whimbrel**, **Common Greenshank** and sometimes **Bar-tailed Godwit** feed at the estuary, where **Caspian Tern**, **African Fish-Eagle** and occasionally **Osprey** are also seen.

NEARBY SITES: Good birding can also be enjoyed along the nearby Bitou River, either from a vehicle or along the nature trails starting at Wittedrif and Rietvlei Dam.

GETTING THERE

Keurbooms Estuary marks Plettenberg Bay's northern boundary. Park at Lookout Beach and follow one of the pathways down to the beach. Walk (northwards) to the estuary. River cruises/boat trips can be arranged.

47 Nature's Valley

IBA ✔✔

View from the Groot River bridge

Callan Cohen

At the eastern end of the Garden Route lies the Tsitsikamma National Park, incorporating a stretch of coastline altogether more rugged than that of the Wilderness region. Excellent forest birding is easily accessible in the national park's western De Vasselot section. Here, large tracts of pristine forest surround the strikingly picturesque coastal village of Nature's Valley. To reach the latter, follow the N2 east of Plettenberg Bay for 28 km, and turn south onto the R102 just before the tollgate. Immediately before the road begins its sharp descent, search the scrub around the viewpoint for **Lazy Cisticola**. The road winds down the densely forested Grootrivier Pass for 12 km before reaching the coast and Nature's Valley. Continue for a few hundred metres past the village, and park at the De Vasselot camp site, where you need to obtain a permit at the office.

The Grootrivier Trail meanders in a gentle, 4.5 km loop around the forested Groot River lagoon. The marked trail begins on the eastern side of the Groot River bridge, a minute's walk further along the tar road. **African Finfoot*** (scarce) occurs along this stretch of river: from the bridge, carefully scan overhanging vegetation at the river edges, and check the series of pools between the river and the camp site. **Half-collared Kingfisher** is also occasionally seen here. Understorey and middle-stratum species that commonly occur close to this bridge include **Bar-throated Apalis, Green-backed Camaroptera, Terrestrial Brownbul, Chorister Robin-Chat, Cape Batis, African Dusky Flycatcher, Sombre Greenbul, Yellow-throated Woodland-Warbler, Blue-mantled Crested Flycatcher, Olive Woodpecker** and **Olive Bush-shrike**, while canopy-dwellers include **Eastern Black-headed Oriole, Narina Trogon*, Grey Cuckooshrike, Scaly-throated Honeyguide, Black-bellied Starling, Knysna Turaco**, and **Green Woodhoopoe**. Additionally, at Nature's Valley there is an increased likelihood of

RDPL/AI

Nature's Valley is idyllically situated and offers fantastic forest birding.

encountering **African Crowned Eagle, Little Sparrowhawk, African Emerald Cuckoo** (summer), **Scaly-throated Honeyguide, Knysna Woodpecker*** and **White-starred Robin**. At night, you are likely to hear **African Wood-Owl** and **Buff-spotted Flufftail**, although the latter is notoriously difficult to see (see p.122 for tips).

Beyond De Vasselot and east of Nature's Valley, the R102 winds up the spectacular Bloukrans Pass, providing a good vantage point from which to scan for **African Crowned Eagle. Victorin's Scrub-Warbler*** occurs in the dense fynbos at the roadside.

Shortly before the R102 rejoins the N2 there is a sawmill, adjacent to the road, where **Black-winged Lapwing** is occasionally seen on the lawns.

48 Swartberg Pass

IBA ✔✔

As you head north from Oudtshoorn, the road begins to climb, and there is a sudden switch from arid scrub and ravine-side thicket to moist, mist-wreathed mountain fynbos. The 24-km-long pass that links Oudtshoorn and Prince Albert crests the Swartberg at an altitude of 1 436 m before dropping precipitously through a series of dramatic switchbacks supported by dry-stone walls. As the landscape becomes progressively more arid, the road emerges into the Karoo proper through a kloof presided over by agonizingly contorted rock layers folded by massive geological upheavals.

To reach the pass, take the R328 from Oudtshoorn, and follow the signs. By the time the pass proper begins (where the road surface changes to gravel, 43 km north of Oudtshoorn), the altitude has rapidly transformed the parched scrub into mountain fynbos.

The distances given are measured from the end of the tarred road at this point; those in brackets are measured from the beginning of the tarred road on the other side of the pass, 2 km from Prince Albert. At 0.5 (25.5) km past the transition to gravel, a stream flanked by taller vegetation passes under the road. This is an excellent site for **Protea Seed-eater***, particularly in the tall streamside growth and in the adjacent stands of Waboom, a tall, greyish-leaved protea. Protea Seed-eater* is, in fact, common in taller vegetation on both sides of the pass. More conspicuous species to be found in this vicinity are **Cape Sugarbird*, Orange-breasted Sunbird, Neddicky, Cape Bulbul, Cape Grassbird** and **Malachite Sunbird. Victorin's Scrub-Warbler*** is very common in the impenetrable undergrowth, supported by seeps, along the entire ascent of the pass (from here to the summit); look for them at the streams at 3.8 (22.2), 5.0 (21.0) and 7.3 (18.7) km. As the road approaches its highest altitude, the terrain becomes ever-rockier and cooler. The rocky ridges to the east and west of the pass's summit at 9.2 (16.8) km ('Die Top') are well worth a walk in quest of **Ground Woodpecker*, Cape Rock-jumper*, Sentinel** and **Cape Rock-Thrushes** and **Cape Siskin***.

North of the summit, the landscape becomes noticeably drier, revealing spectacular geological contortions. Keep an eye out for classic mountain raptors such as **Verreaux's** and **Booted Eagles, Jackal Buzzard** and **Rock Kestrel**. The road descends through progressively arid country and ultimately joins a river in a dry gorge at 22.2 (3.8) km. The hillside scrub flanking it hosts such typically kloof-loving Karoo species as **Fairy Flycatcher, Layard's Tit-Babbler** and, usually flying overhead, **Pale-winged Starling**. At 25.7 (0.3) km, a picnic site lies on the left-hand side alongside a band of fearsomely thorned acacia trees. This thicket offers **Southern Tchagra*, Pririt Batis, Namaqua Warbler*** and **Red-billed Firefinch**. From the junction at 26.0 (0.0) km, the road runs for 2 km through a broad valley to the sleepy town of Prince Albert and the Great Karoo beyond.

Callan Cohen

The arid slopes of Swartberg Pass

ROUTE 5
BUSHMANLAND & NAMAQUALAND

Bushmanland and Namaqualand form the westernmost districts of the Karoo, a vast and sparsely populated semi-desert of stark beauty. The region's stony plains are scattered with low bushes, punctuated by arid mountain ranges and the occasional dunefield. The freedom of these open spaces will be a welcome respite for those wearied by the stresses of city life, and the dedicated birder will equally appreciate its wealth of highly desirable southern African endemics.

TOP 10 BIRDS

- Ludwig's Bustard
- Burchell's Courser
- Red Lark
- Sclater's Lark
- Black-eared Sparrowlark
- Karoo Eremomela
- Cinnamon-breasted Warbler
- Cape Eagle-Owl
- Barlow's Lark
- Black-headed Canary

Bushmanland hosts one of the world's highest diversity of larks, with an amazing 14 species occurring regularly. Furthermore, Red Lark* is a true endemic to Bushmanland, and Sclater's Lark* and Black-eared Sparrowlark* are most easily seen in this region. It is a poorly defined area, bounded roughly by the Namaqualand highlands in the west, the Orange River in the north, and the towns of Kenhardt, Van Wyksvlei, Calvinia and Loeriesfontein in the east and south. Most of the rain falls in summer. The best times of year for birding are the transitional seasons: bird activity is usually good in spring and autumn, and there is relief from the bitter nights of mid-winter and the scorching heat of summer. Although many species here are nomadic, moving unpredictably in response to rain and seeding grasses, it is quite possible to find the majority during a short visit.

Namaqualand is best known for its spectacular spring floral displays. This winter-rainfall desert, which lies between Bushmanland and the coast, is home to a unique arid-land flora. The region forms the largest portion of the Succulent Karoo biome (see p.16), recognised as the only desert biodiversity hotspot on earth and hosting the world's greatest variety of succulent plants. It is also the most accessible place in the world to see the endemic Barlow's Lark, and offers the best sites in the region for Ludwig's Bustard* and Cape Eagle-Owl*. Namaqualand is best visited during August and September, when the floral displays are at their peak (see box p.86). Overall, birding is best in spring and winter, and poorest in late summer.

Those with limited time can see all the Bushmanland specials in the vicinity of the desolate little town of Brandvlei, easily reached in a relaxed day's drive from Cape Town. However, those with an affinity for huge, near-empty landscapes and desert birds will enjoy a week exploring this vast area. One excellent circular route is along the N7 north from Cape Town to Vanrhynsdorp, and then on to Calvinia to the east, and up to Brandvlei. Bird around Brandvlei for a full day before heading north to Kenhardt, with the option of including a Kgalagadi Transfrontier Park (p.88) loop at this point.

From Kenhardt, travel west to Pofadder and Aggeneys, where you can easily spend a day birding. Leaving Bushmanland, proceed into Namaqualand, spending a day around Springbok, with an excursion to Port Nolloth.

Much of this region is partitioned off as private sheep farms. Good birding can be had at the roadside, but please ask permission before exploring farms. Away from the main arteries of the N7, N14 and R27, there are long, desolate sections of unsurfaced road (see Driving, p.12).

49 Nieuwoudtville ✔

Nieuwoudtville is world famous for its wild flowers, and the incredible density and diversity of bulb species produce a spectacular spring floral display each year. Flower-watching is at its best in the Nieuwoudtville Flower Reserve (3 km east of town on the Calvinia road) and at Glenlyon Wildflower Farm. Look out for **Cape Clapper Lark***, **Southern Black Korhaan** and **Grey-winged Francolin** in these areas.

The scrub in the rocky areas surrounding Nieuwoudtville Falls, which are signposted 10 km along the Loeriesfontein road, holds an interesting selection of birds, including **Layard's Tit-Babbler** and **Cape Eagle-Owl*** (elusive). The agricultural fields stretching for the first two kilometres on either side of the Loeriesfontein road as you leave town are excellent for **Ludwig's Bustard***, also seen along the Calvinia road together with **Booted Eagle**, **Black Harrier*** and **Greater Kestrel**.

50 Calvinia to Brandvlei ✔✔

At Calvinia, check the trees and reeds along the Oorlogskloof River, near the Shell service station, for **Namaqua Warbler*** and **African Reed-Warbler** (summer). Turn into Hospitaal Street near the big silos and make your way to the nearby Akkerendam Nature Reserve. This is your last chance to see **Karoo Lark** (look on the plains shortly after you enter the reserve) as, in Bushmanland proper, only the similar but more localised **Red Lark*** occurs. Park near the dam and walk along the broad path that leads into a huge amphitheatre. The hillside scrub here holds **Layard's Tit-Babbler**, **Karoo Prinia**, **Karoo Scrub-Robin**, **Mountain Wheatear**, **Cape Bunting** and **Black-headed Canary***, while **Fairy Flycatcher**, **Cape Penduline-Tit** and **White-backed Mousebird** prefer the taller vegetation along the river course on the right. This reserve is also excellent for **Cinnamon-breasted Warbler***, which is best searched for on the rocky slopes to the left of the broad path that enters the amphitheatre. Scan the skies for **Verreaux's** and **Booted Eagles** and **Jackal Buzzard**.

From Calvinia, take the R27 north to Brandvlei. As you enter Bushmanland, the landscape becomes more open and the bushes become lower and sparser. From this point on, keep alert for **Black-eared Sparrowlark***, a nomadic species which can be found throughout Bushmanland, and which often moves around in flocks. While driving, you may spot the conspicuous, all-dark males fluttering over the road, although they invariably land frustratingly behind the bushes by the time you have stopped the car!

Nico Myburgh

Black-eared Sparrowlark

About 54 km north of Calvinia (95 km south of Brandvlei), check the pan on the left for **Greater Flamingo**, **Black-necked Grebe**, **Pied Avocet** and **South African Shelduck**. The latter two may be seen on any pool of water in the region. **Blue Crane** can regularly be spotted on the isolated patch of cultivated land 55 km south of Brandvlei, where **Large-billed** and **Red-capped Larks** are common. There are colonies of **South African Cliff-Swallow** (active Sept-Apr) under road culverts at 67 km, 97 km and 107 km south of Brandvlei.

GETTING THERE

The area is best explored along the 2WD gravel roads of varying quality. Accommodation is available at the Brandvlei Hotel.

51 Brandvlei ✔✔✔

Brandvlei is a small town situated on the plains of central Bushmanland. Its unprepossessing appearance is deceptive, as excellent birding may be had close to the town.

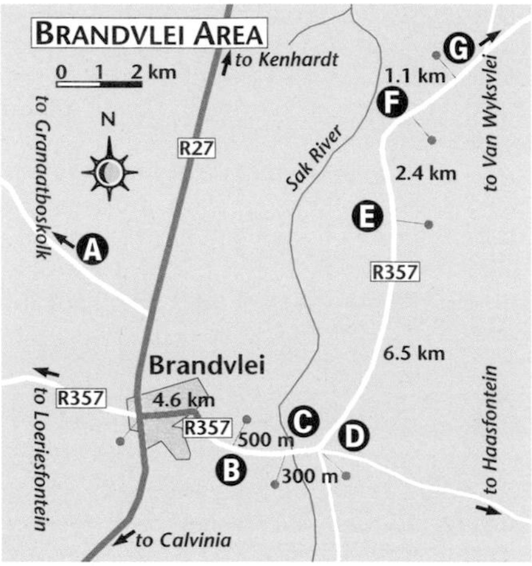

SPECIALS: Ludwig's Bustard*, Karoo Korhaan, Burchell's Courser*, Red* and Sclater's* Larks, Karoo Eremomela*, Black-headed Canary*.
SEASON: All the specials may be present year-round; note that summer is very hot.
HABITATS: Stony, gravel plains with occasional acacia-lined watercourses.
BIRDING: Although **Red Lark*** can be quite localised, it is found widely in the Brandvlei region and may be common where the vegetation is suitable. One such locality is 23.6 km south of Brandvlei (1.1 km south of a roadside picnic site), where a lone windmill stands among a large tract of scrubby vegetation on the east side of the road. For the best chance of success, get here early and listen out for their calls. It is the 'plains form' of the Red Lark* that occurs here, which is much browner than the richly-coloured 'dune form' occurring near Pofadder (p.82). Karoo Lark does not occur here.

In addition, look out for the localised **Karoo Eremomela*** here and in the scrub 10 km south of Brandvlei. This is a relatively scarce species in Bushmanland, unlike the **Yellow-bellied Eremomela**, which is common over much of the region.

Red Lark* also occurs closer to town: follow the R27 for 2 km north of town, and turn left along the unsurfaced road to Granaatboskolk. Continue for about 2 km along here, and check the scrub on either side of the road at Ⓐ.

Tractrac and **Karoo Chats** are the most common chats in the region, although **Familiar**, **Sickle-winged** (uncommon) and **Ant-eating Chats** may also be seen. The stocky **Chat Flycatcher** often perches on telephone wires, while **Karoo Long-billed Lark**, the region's most widespread lark, is often seen perched on fence posts. **Rufous-eared Warbler**, **Black-chested Prinia** and **Bokmakierie** are common on the scrubby plains, whereas **Cape Penduline-Tit** prefers drainage lines. Look out for **Ludwig's Bustard*** and the occasional **Kori Bustard**, which are often seen in flight, especially in the morning and early evening. The most common raptors are **Pale Chanting Goshawk**, **Greater Kestrel** and **Lanner Falcon**, while **Martial Eagle** and **Black-chested Snake-Eagle** are also often seen.

Claire Spottiswoode

Scan the open, stony plains for Sclater's Lark.

The area to the east of Brandvlei offers some excellent Bushmanland birding. From Brandvlei, take the gravel R357 towards Van Wyksvlei. Check the slightly thicker scrub (especially at Ⓑ and Ⓔ on the site map) for **Karoo Eremomela***. Continue to the bridge at Ⓒ, where **European Bee-eater** breeds in summer, and where **Pririt Batis** occurs in the sparse riparian vegetation. Look for **Dusky Sunbird** around the occasional flowering bush (often on rocky koppies) and in riverine trees.

FINDING SCLATER'S LARK

This highly sought-after, nomadic species is by no means guaranteed on a trip to the region.

Sclater's Lark is fairly common, albeit elusive throughout Bushmanland. However, with knowledge of its favoured habitat and inconspicuous yet distinctive flight call, the dedicated birder stands a good chance of finding the lark. These birds occur largely on very stony substrate with little vegetation. When walking through this habitat, be aware of their particular characteristics in order to locate them. The best strategy is often to wait patiently near a water trough or small dam adjacent to suitable habitat, and spend the otherwise unproductive heat of the day watching for birds coming in to drink, usually in pairs or small groups.

Warwick Tarboton

Sclater's Lark

Shortly after the bridge, you will be faced with a staggered, three-point intersection at Ⓓ. Take the northerly road, signposted 'Van Wyksvlei'. The entire route from Brandvlei to Van Wyksvlei is excellent country for **Sclater's Lark*** (see box above). In particular, check the habitat at Ⓖ, and at 3 km beyond this point along the R357. Much of the road towards Van Wyksvlei is also recommended for this species, as well as **Burchell's Courser***, and both can be found by driving along and stopping at their characteristically open habitat, although Burchell's Courser* occurs sparsely here and over the whole of Bushmanland. Watch for them running away from you in the distance when walking through suitable habitat, which is usually the most open, sparsely vegetated area available – from open stony plains to the grassy edges of dry pans. Their unusual flight call often attracts attention. Look out for them while driving, too, as their white wing patches are quite conspicuous in flight.

Check the small farm dams at 10.1, 12.3 and 16.5 km past Ⓓ for **Sclater's Lark***.

Another rewarding route for both these species is the Haasfontein road: start from Ⓓ, and look especially on the plains around the farm Toekoms, 27 km from here. **Red Lark*** may be found 1 km east of Ⓓ.

You may also see **Karoo Korhaan** and **Double-banded Courser** at the roadsides, and **Black-eared Sparrowlark*** is usually present in the area. A very common bird of the stony plains is the enchanting **Spike-heeled Lark**. These birds move about in small, active groups, scuttling along in a stop-start fashion over the pebbles, and digging with their bills into the soft sand accumulated around the bases of bushes. **Lark-like Bunting** is often abundant. **Red Lark*** occurs sparsely in the taller vegetation over this whole area: check at Ⓕ, and also at 17.7 km beyond Ⓖ on the R357. **Namaqua Sandgrouse** is often seen flying to water in the mornings, delivering its characteristic, bubbling 'kelkiewyn' call.

52 Kenhardt to Pofadder ✔✔

The tarred route from Brandvlei to Kenhardt is good for most of the specials mentioned above, although birding is often more productive along gravel side roads. As one heads further north, the countryside becomes more grassy. After good rains, follow the side roads (for instance, 'Afdeling Pad 2984', on the right, 68 km north of Brandvlei) into the newly grassy plains, which often yield **Black-eared Sparrowlark*** and, occasionally, in years of good rainfall, **Pink-billed Lark**. **Sclater's Lark*** is also common in this area: wait for drinking birds at the farm dams 25-40 km south of Kenhardt. In particular, check the two dams (on either side of the road) 36 km south of Kenhardt, near the farm sign 'Knapsak'. Also keep a lookout for **Stark's Lark**, which is most often seen in the northern areas of Bushmanland. Check the patch of trees 100.1 km south of Kenhardt for **Chestnut-vented Tit-Babbler**, **Pririt Batis** and **Fairy Flycatcher**.

The town of Kenhardt is worth visiting for the kokerboom forest, which lies just to its south. The giant nests of **Sociable Weaver** may be seen on the telephone poles here; keep a lookout for the associated and uncommon **African Pygmy Falcon**, which also breeds in the Sociable Weaver nests.

Kori Bustard is regularly seen on the plains north of the town. To complete a Bushmanland loop, take the signposted road, 8 km south of Kenhardt, to Pofadder (marked on some maps as passing through Kraandraai or Bossiekom, although note that these are not towns and no fuel is available). After 35 km along this road, check the stony desert plains near the intersection of powerlines for **Sclater's Lark***. This long and lonely road finally meets the R358 some 27 km south of Pofadder.

53 Pofadder & Onseepkans ✔✔

This stereotypical South African one-horse town bears the name of the Puff Adder (*Bitis ariens*), a sluggish and highly toxic snake found throughout southern Africa. All the Bushmanland specials may be found a short drive from the town.

SPECIALS: Ludwig's Bustard*, Karoo Korhaan, Burchell's Courser*, Stark's and Sclater's* Larks, Black-headed Canary*, and Rosy-faced Lovebird.

SEASON: All the specials are present year-round; note that summer is hot.

HABITATS: Arid mountains, rocky canyons, stony gravel plains, acacia-lined watercourses; dense riverine vegetation, palms (along the Orange River).

BIRDING: Acacia Pied Barbet, **African Red-eyed Bulbul** and **Pale-winged Starling** occur in the town itself. The giant nests of **Sociable Weaver** are common in this part of Bushmanland. A particularly picturesque assemblage of these nests, with a resident pair of **African Pygmy Falcon**, is found in some Camel-thorn trees exactly 11 km east of Pofadder (**A** on map below).

The 50 km unsurfaced road that leads from Pofadder to the Orange River at Onseepkans offers excellent birding across a diversity of habitats, from arid rocky gorges and dusty plains to

> **GETTING THERE**
> The area is best explored along the 2WD gravel roads of varying quality. Accommodation is available at Pofadder.

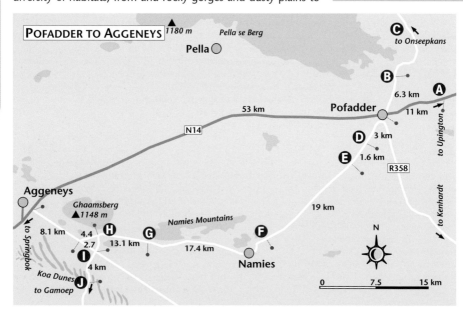

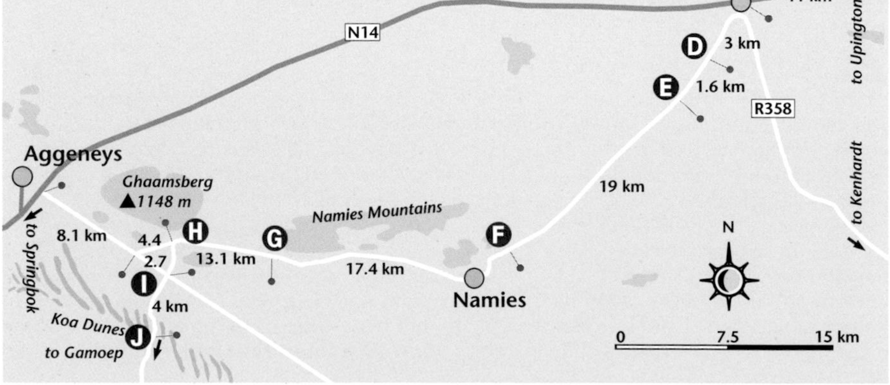

The road from Pofadder to Onseepkans

lush riparian vegetation. The large-billed subspecies of **Sabota Lark** (known as Bradfield's Lark), **Karoo Long-billed Lark** and **Karoo Chat** are common along the first section of this road. The acacia-lined watercourse **B** that crosses the road (6.3 km from Pofadder) contains **Acacia Pied Barbet** and **Pririt Batis**.

Check the open plains that lie 15 km or more from Pofadder (from **C** onwards) for **Burchell's Courser*** and **Stark's Lark**, and after 20 km look for **Sabota** and **Fawn-coloured Larks** in the low thorn trees on the right-hand side. Thirty-three kilometres from Pofadder, a beautiful gorge falls away on the left of the road: look here for **Cinnamon-breasted Warbler***, **Pale-winged Starling**, **Dusky Sunbird** and **Black-headed Canary***.

As you reach the border post hamlet of Onseepkans, check the palms and taller trees for breeding **Rosy-faced Lovebird** (extremely localised in South Africa) and **African Palm Swift**. **African Fish-Eagle** and **African Darter** frequent the river. The riparian vegetation offers **Swallow-tailed Bee-eater**, **Lesser Swamp-Warbler**, **African Reed-Warbler** (summer), **Namaqua Warbler***, **Red-billed Quelea** and **Southern Red Bishop**. The peachy-flanked **Orange River White-eye** is common here, as is **Black-throated Canary**. **Zitting Cisticola** displays over the agricultural fields close to the Orange River.

From Pofadder, take the gravel road to the south-west, towards Namies. This is the P2961 (not the R358), reached by turning into Buitenkant Street (on the western edge of the town) from the N12. At the T-junction with Springbok Street, turn right and follow this road, which becomes gravel after a short while. Continue along the gravel and turn left into the P2961 after 0.3 km. At **D**, search the open plains, and at **E**, check the water trough for **Sclater's Lark***.

At dawn and dusk, listen for the frog-like duet of the **Karoo Korhaan**, one of the characteristic sounds of South Africa's arid plains.

NOCTURNAL MAMMALS OF THE KAROO

If you have a spotlight, it is always worth taking a night-drive along remote gravel roads. Night-drives in the Karoo can be every bit as exciting as those in the renowned game reserves of the savanna regions. There may be no lions, but for many the experience of seeing such unique and bizarre mammals as Aardvark, Caracal, Cape Porcupine and Aardwolf will be even more memorable. More common predators are Bat-eared Fox, African Wild Cat, Cape Fox and Black-backed Jackal.

Rufous-cheeked Nightjar is often common on the plains in summer, and **Cape Eagle-Owl*** may sometimes be seen near rocky areas.

Aardvark are nocturnal.

54 Koa Dunes

IBA ✓✓✓

The Koa 'River Valley' Dunes are arguably the world's best site for **Red Lark***, a little known bird whose nest was discovered as recently as 1986.

SPECIALS: Red Lark*, Karoo Korhaan, Stark's and Sclater's* Larks, Cinnamon-breasted Warbler*, Black-headed Canary*.

SEASON: All the specials are present year-round; summer is hot.

HABITATS: Arid mountains, rocky canyons, stony gravel plains, red dunes (Koa 'River Valley').

BIRDING: The Namies Mountains can be reached by following the Namies road from Pofadder, where **Cinnamon-breasted Warbler*** occurs on the rocky slopes at F and G (see map p.80). Be particularly careful when driving on the unsurfaced road in this area, as there are a number of treacherously sharp corners. **Sabota Lark** (Bradfield's form) and **Karoo Long-billed Lark** are common; look for the former in the taller scrub, where it most often draws attention to itself with its canary-like song. Also look out for overflying **Bradfield's Swifts**. At night, listen for the deep hoot of the **Cape Eagle-Owl***, which is resident on the slopes here, especially in the vicinity of the Ghaamsberg H. This mountain is a treasure chest of biological diversity and threatened plants, which are at risk of destruction in the face of a proposal to initiate an open-cast zinc mine on its summit.

Warwick Tarboton

Red Lark matches the sand colour.

Check the water troughs at I for large numbers of drinking **Namaqua Sandgrouse** and **Lark-like Bunting**. Continue to J, where the road slices through intensely red dunes, and there is a stock enclosure lined with tyres on each side of the road. The dunefield is surrounded by sparsely grassed and mesmerisingly flat expanses, punctuated by the occasional mountain. This is the best-known site for the richly coloured 'dune form' of **Red Lark***, which is in fact one of the most common birds in the vicinity. The larks are most easily found in the morning and late afternoon, when their rattling calls drift across the dune crests. Between bouts of calling from the dune scrub, they feed on the ground, and can usually be seen running about between the bushes.

GETTING THERE

The Koa River Valley can be reached on the gravel road via Namies or on tar via Aggeneys. The area is best explored along the 2WD gravel roads of varying quality. Diepvlei Guest Farm ☎ along the gravel road between Aggeneys and Gamoep is recommended, although accommodation is also available at Pofadder.

Claire Spottiswoode

The Koa Dunes are excellent for Red Lark.

Other common birds here include **Grey-backed Sparrowlark**, **Scaly-feathered Finch**, and **Ant-eating Chat**. **Fawn-coloured Lark** occurs less frequently.

From **J**, either retrace your steps to **I** and turn left towards the tarred N14 near the mining town of Aggeneys (note that there is no accommodation available here) or, if well prepared with fuel and water, continue along the scenic gravel road to Springbok via Gamoep. The first 15 km or so of this road will prove rewarding for **Karoo** and **Northern Black Korhaans**; also check carefully for **Sclater's*** and **Stark's Larks**.

OTHER ANIMALS: Black-footed Cat and Aardvark have been seen on night-drives on the farm Diepvlei on the road to Gamoep. Springhare and Bat-eared Fox are common at night.

55 Aardvark Kloof, Gamoep ✔✔

At Aardvark Kloof, sandy spits from the open Bushmanland plains to the east meet the rocky Namaqualand interior, creating a mosaic of gentle, sandy-bottomed valleys flanked by boulder-covered slopes. This is one of western South Africa's great endemic bird sites, where the diversity of habitats supports a bird community that will leave any desert-bird enthusiast twitching with indecision about where to look first.

SPECIALS: Cinnamon-breasted Warbler*, Karoo Eremomela*, Karoo Lark, Dusky Sunbird, Damara and Black-headed* Canaries.

SEASON: All the specials are present year-round, although spring birding is best.

HABITATS: Rocky slopes and sandy, scrubby valley bottoms with acacia-lined watercourses.

BIRDING: The calls of confiding **Cinnamon-breasted Warbler*** echo through the roadside boulders. **Karoo Lark** is found in the small bushes on the right-hand side of the road. Such open areas (especially back towards Gamoep) support plains birds such as **Large-billed** and **Karoo Long-billed Larks**, and **Karoo Eremomela***.

The rocky jumbles on the left-hand side of the road are home to **Cinnamon-breasted Warbler*** and other endemics, including good numbers of **Grey Tit**, **Mountain Wheatear**, **Layard's Tit-Babbler**, **Fairy Flycatcher**, **Pale-winged Starling**, **Dusky Sunbird** and **White-throated**, **Black-headed*** and **Damara Canaries**.

Small groups of **Ground Woodpecker*** may be found on rocky slopes throughout the area. Scan the skies for **Verreaux's** and **Booted Eagles**, and **Jackal Buzzard**. **Cape Glossy Starling** is common here. **Pririt Batis** and **Acacia Pied Barbet** inhabit the acacia-lined watercourse on the right-hand side of the road.

OTHER ANIMALS: Leopard is rare; Smith's Red Rock Rabbit and Klipspringer are common.

GETTING THERE

Aardvark Kloof lies near Gamoep, south-east of Springbok, and can be reached via the R355 (note that Springbok is your last source of petrol and water). Follow the R355 straight past the final Airport/Goegap Nature Reserve turn-off, at the point where the tarred road turns to gravel. The unsurfaced roads in this region can be rather poor in places and should be negotiated with caution. Continue for 67 km beyond Springbok to Gamoep, a small cluster of houses. Ignore the turn-off here (signposted 'Pofadder', 'Aggeneys', and others) and continue for a further 2.6 km before turning right towards Kamieskroon. Follow this road for 8.4 km and bird the area just beyond the livestock grid in the road.

56 Goegap Nature Reserve ✔✔

This 15 000-hectare reserve is situated in the rugged interior of Namaqualand, 15 km east of Springbok, the region's principal town. It offers spectacular flowers and scenery, and several Karoo specials, among them **Cinnamon-breasted Warbler*** and **Karoo Eremomela***, both found in classic Namaqualand landscapes.

To reach the reserve (which opens at 08h00), follow the signs from Springbok to the airport (via the R355) and turn along another tarred road for a few kilometres past the airport

Callan Cohen
Goegap Nature Reserve

to the reserve gates. There is an attractive succulent garden at the Goegap office – also the starting point of a 17-km tourist loop road that covers a cross-section of the reserve's habitats. Look in the vicinity of the offices for **Acacia Pied Barbet**, **Dusky Sunbird**, **White-backed Mousebird**, **Cape Glossy Starling**, and **White-throated Canary**. **Cinnamon-breasted Warbler*** is a common but inconspicuous inhabitant of rocky slopes throughout the reserve, and may even be seen on the hillsides behind the offices.

Other birds characteristic of the rocky slopes of the reserve, which can be accessed at a number of points along the tourist loop (such as at 5 and 8.5 km from the offices), include **Verreaux's** and **Booted Eagles**, **Ground Woodpecker***, **Grey Tit**, **Mountain Wheatear**, **Layard's Tit-Babbler** and **Dusky Sunbird**. **Cape Eagle-Owl*** is resident on the rocky slopes at Goegap, and can be seen by driving along roads adjacent to the reserve at night. In the more open areas along the loop road (at 4 km and at 8 km from the offices, for example), search for small groups of **Karoo Eremomela*** among the low shrubs. Other birds that may be seen along here include **Common Ostrich**, **Ludwig's Bustard***, and **Karoo** and **Large-billed Larks**.

57 Port Nolloth to Orange River IBA ✔✔

To find **Barlow's Lark**, you will have to descend from the baking and mountainous Namaqualand interior to the breezy scrublands of the coastal plain at Port Nolloth. Port Nolloth is a damp, salty town, often swathed in dense, rolling Atlantic fog. Most of the coastal strip of this region is frustratingly off-limits to birders (it supports rich alluvial diamond deposits), but the region between Port Nolloth and Springbok is, nonetheless, rewarding for birders. The private mining town of Alexander Bay has started to encourage ecotourism in the area and provides access to the mouth of the Orange, South Africa's largest river.

SPECIALS: Barlow's Lark, Cape Long-billed Lark*, Cape Penduline-Tit, and Damara Tern*.

SEASON: All the specials are present year-round, except for **Damara Tern***, which is only present during summer.

HABITATS: Coastal shrublands, rocky shoreline (Port Nolloth), river estuary (Orange River).

BIRDING: Take the N7 from Springbok north to Steinkopf, checking for **Lanner Falcon**, **Jackal Buzzard** and **Cape Crow** perched on the telephone poles. Note that **Jackal Buzzard** in this area shows a high incidence of variable white mottling on the breast, often causing confusion with the closely related Augur Buzzard, which only occurs much further north, in Namibia. From Steinkopf, take the R382 down Anenous Pass, which links the mountains to the coastal plain and eventually brings you to Port Nolloth.

Callan Cohen
Barlow's Lark at Port Nolloth

Because **Barlow's** and **Karoo Larks** (see box opposite) are quite similar, it is worthwhile familiarising yourself with the locally occurring subspecies of the latter. You will have this opportunity 5 km before reaching Port Nolloth, where Karoo Lark (reddish-brown upperparts) occurs commonly in the roadside scrub. For Barlow's Lark, take the road towards Alexander Bay, and about 1.6 km beyond the buildings and the town's last tarred side-road, you will see

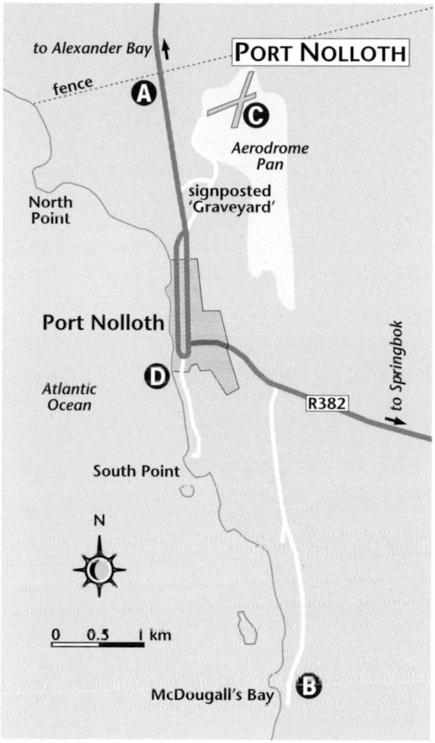

on your left a fence demarcating the beginning of the mining area at **A** (the fence is perpendicular to the road). Search the low coastal dunes on the Port Nolloth side of the fence for the lark, which is common here. However, note that this site is just on the edge of a zone of hybridisation between Barlow's and Karoo Larks; be careful to distinguish 'pure' birds from the much scarcer hybrids (see box below). Karoo Lark occurs again at McDougall's Bay **B**, a few kilometres to the south of Port Nolloth.

Other birds found in the scrubby strandveld vegetation in this area are **Cape Long-billed Lark***, **Grey Tit**, **Cape Penduline-Tit**, as wekk as **Malachite** and **Southern Double-collared Sunbirds**.

Port Nolloth can also be a good place to see **Damara Tern***, which breeds in low numbers from November to February on the large pan on the northern edge of town **C**. Seabirds and waders along the Port Nolloth coast at **D** include **Bank*** and **Crowned Cormorants**, **African Black Oystercatcher***, **White-fronted Plover** and, in summer, **Grey Plover**, **Ruddy Turnstone** and **Sanderling**.

The Orange River Estuary is an internationally recognised RAMSAR wetland, offering good birding. The more notable species here include **Greater Flamingo**, **South African Shelduck**, **Maccoa Duck**, **African Fish-Eagle**, **Pied Avocet**, **African Marsh-Harrier**, **Caspian Tern**, **Damara Tern*** (uncommon), and **Orange River White-eye**.

To find a pure population of **Barlow's Lark** (that is, away from the hybrid zone), continue past the turn-off to town, along the main road, which becomes unsurfaced as it swings inland along the Orange River. Check the area between Beauvallon and Brandkaros (10-20 km beyond Alexander Bay), where Barlow's Lark (sandy-peach upperpart coloration) is present in the sparsely bushed areas on the right-hand side of the road. Retrace your route to return to Springbok.

BARLOW'S/KAROO LARK HYBRID ZONE

Close examination of these confiding birds reveals clear contrasts between **Barlow's** and **Karoo Larks**. Barlow's Lark is relatively easily distinguished by its clear, unstreaked flanks and heavier bill. Upper-part coloration is more complicated, as populations of both species on the white coastal sands show cold brown upper parts, which change in the inland populations (on the redder sands) to a reddish-brown in Karoo Lark, and a sandy-peach colour in Barlow's Lark. There are also subtle differences in call.

Despite the fact that Barlow's and Karoo Larks are each well-differentiated species, they do hybridize over a narrow zone between Port Nolloth and Alexander Bay. The only place where this zone is publicly accessible is in the vicinity of Port Nolloth.

The best way to distinguish hybrids is by flank streaking: 'pure' Barlow's Lark shows none of this (see picture), while 'pure' Karoo Lark shows marked streaking. Hybrids typically show an intermediate streaking pattern, with faint, scattered streaks on the flanks. Barlow's Lark tends to prefer the more arid, open habitat towards Alexander Bay and into Namibia, while Karoo Lark prefers the denser scrub found further inland, and its range extends southwards into much of Namaqualand.

VIEWING THE FLOWERS

Dazzling floral displays are synonymous with Namaqualand: for a short period in spring, the region is carpeted with some of the world's most impressive shows. These usually occur from about mid-August to mid-September, but can be remarkably local and susceptible to rapid wilting. Indeed, Namaqualand holds the world's greatest diversity of succulent species, spanning a mind-boggling array of growth forms, from the giant aloes to the minute 'stone plants'. The Knersvlakte, a lowland expanse at the southern edge of Namaqualand, consists of a mosaic of quartz-strewn plains and is perhaps best known for the diversity of miniature succulent plants which survive on the seemingly barren, rocky plains. It is definitely worth a brief roadside stop to see these bizarre succulents, large numbers of which can be observed adjacent to the N7 – for example, opposite the 'Douse-the-Glim' sign (22.6 km north of Vanrhynsdorp).

Claire Spottiswoode

Springtime flowers in Namaqualand

58 Namaqualand's Mountains

Aardvark Kloof (see p.83) is also the start of an excellent scenic drive that winds its way back to the N7 at Kamieskroon, taking in spectacular landscapes that hold rock-loving hillside birds, including **Cinnamon-breasted Warbler*** and **Black-headed*** and **Damara Canaries.** (Note that the road is unsurfaced and slow-going in places.)

Callan Cohen

Damara Canary

Turn towards Leliefontein to head south through the Kamiesberg and Studer's Pass before arriving at Garies on the N7. Although the mountains of central Namaqualand are a stronghold of **Cape Eagle-Owl***, extensive night-driving along the unsurfaced mountain roads is not recommended. However, you may wish to take a short nocturnal excursion along the gravel route that leads from Kamieskroon towards Leliefontein (follow the signs from Kamieskroon). Scan for the owl on the telephone poles along the first 10 km of this road. Also, listen out for **Freckled Nightjar**, which frequents rocky areas in this region.

ROUTE 6

SOUTHERN KALAHARI

The Kalahari Desert is a vast and almost unpopulated area, stretching from the northern region of South Africa's Northern Cape province into central Botswana. Though the southern Kalahari is not a 'true' desert, its classic dune landscapes and dry riverbeds, lined with gnarled acacia trees, give it a wonderful atmosphere.

Inhabitants of the Kgalagadi Transfrontier Park (previously known as the Kalahari Gemsbok and the Gemsbok national parks, and now a vast conservation area straddling two countries) include big game such as Lion, Cheetah and Gemsbok, a notable diversity of raptors, and also a colourful selection of dry woodland birds.

TOP 10 BIRDS

- Bateleur
- Red-necked Falcon
- African Pygmy Falcon
- Kori Bustard
- Burchell's Sandgrouse
- Verreaux's Eagle-Owl
- Bradfield's Swift
- Monotonous Lark
- Long-tailed Pipit
- Pink-billed Lark

Visitors approaching the Kalahari by road from the south will pass through the regional centre of Upington, sprawling along the Orange River's verdant banks. A little to the west is the Augrabies Falls National Park, where the river plunges into a magnificent gorge carved through glistening granite. The bird life here displays an interesting mix of Karoo and Kalahari elements, and well deserves exploration.

The red sand, yellow grass and sculpted acacias continue on the south-eastward passage to Kimberley. Here, a selection of bird species characteristic rather of South Africa's more wooded eastern regions add a tropical flavour to the birding.

A minimum of two full days should be devoted to the Kgalagadi Transfrontier Park, although those with more time will find a week or more successfully spent. The Upington region and the Witsand Nature Reserve, in addition to being good birding spots in their own right, provide pleasant staging posts to break the otherwise gruelling full-day drives from Cape Town to the entrance of the park, and from here to the Kimberley region. A suggested optimal birding route for those spending three to four nights in the park is to travel from Twee Rivieren northwards to Nossob (day 1) and possibly Union's End (day 2), followed by an arc southwest to the Auob riverbed via the central dune sea, before returning to Twee Rivieren (day 2 or 3). Note that the drive between the Twee Rivieren and Nossob rest camps is long – allow at least half a day without stops.

Good roads (mostly tarred) link all the sites described below, and they can easily be combined with a loop through Bushmanland (p.76). Visitors should note that Kalahari distances are vast, and should take particular care to allow sufficient travel time on unsurfaced roads (see p.12).

Richard du Toit

Gemsbok in the Kgalagadi Transfrontier Park

59 Kgalagadi Transfrontier Park IBA ✔✔

This vast wilderness area, spanning 3.6 million hectares, offers the alluring combination of abundant game, superb landscapes and good birding, all within 2WD access. The park is best known in birding terms for its remarkable diversity and abundance of raptors.

SPECIALS: Bateleur, Red-necked and African Pygmy Falcons, Kori Bustard, Verreaux's Eagle-Owl, Burchell's Sandgrouse* and Pink-billed Lark.

SEASON: Birding is good year-round, and although summer is hot, large numbers of migrants may be present at this time. Winter is best for game-viewing.

HABITATS: Dry riverbeds, acacia stands, grassy dunescapes.

BIRDING: At Twee Rivieren Ⓐ, have a look around the stand of thorn trees to your right as you enter the main park gate for typical thornveld birds such as **Crimson-breasted Shrike**, **Common Scimitarbill**, **Swallow-tailed Bee-eater**, **Kalahari Scrub-Robin**, **Marico Flycatcher**, **White-browed Sparrow-Weaver** and **Ashy Tit**. All three of the Kalahari rest camps, especially Nossob, are excellent for owls, and a night walk to follow up on calls in any of the three is likely to turn up **Southern White-faced Scops-Owl**, **African Scops-Owl**, **Pearl-spotted Owlet**, **Spotted Eagle-Owl** and **Barn Owl**. Ask the staff to point out their daytime whereabouts. **African Pygmy Falcon** regularly hunts inside Twee Rivieren camp, and is, in fact, fairly common throughout the park.

We recommend that you spend the first night at Twee Rivieren, in order to make an early morning start northwards into the park. Shortly after leaving the rest camp, take the first turn-off to Mata Mata, and in the first 3 km of dunes Ⓑ look for **Pink-billed** and **Eastern Clapper Larks** and, if there have been good rains, **Kurrichane Buttonquail**. **Fawn-coloured Lark** is the park's most common lark and is also likely to be seen here, as is **Desert Cisticola**. Return now to the main Nossob road, and continue northwards past the junction of the Nossob and Auob riverbeds, aiming to reach the waterholes of Leeuwdril Ⓒ, Rooiputs Ⓓ and Kij-Kij Ⓔ 2-4 hours after sunrise. This will maximise your chances of seeing the scarce **Burchell's Sandgrouse*** (best in winter and spring), alongside the much more abundant **Namaqua Sandgrouse**. In years when rainfall has been high, listen for the incessant calls of **Monotonous Lark** along the river valleys.

Raptor-watching in the park is superb. **Gabar Goshawk**, **Lanner** and, more scarcely, **Red-necked Falcon** regularly harry the drinking seed-eaters from their vantage points in the thorn trees adjacent to waterholes. Other common birds of prey in the park are **Martial** and **Tawny Eagles**, **Brown** and **Black-chested Snake-Eagles**, **Bateleur**, **Secretarybird**, **Greater Kestrel** and **Pale Chanting Goshawk**. These are augmented in summer by **Steppe Eagle** and

GETTING THERE

The Kalahari Gemsbok National Park has officially been joined to the Gemsbok National Park in adjacent Botswana to form southern Africa's first transfrontier park, the Kgalagadi, a vast conservation area spreading over 3.6 million hectares of the southern Kalahari. If you wish to enter the Botswana section of the park from South Africa, you must be equipped with 4WD vehicles and have checked in at the Gemsbok/Bokspits border post, 60 km south of Twee Rivieren.

The southern (South African) segment of the park forms a vast triangle enclosed by the Namibian border in the west, the Nossob River (also the Botswana border) in the north and east and, approximately, the Auob River in the south. These two rivers remain dry for decades on end, but are punctuated by numerous artificial waterholes that concentrate the game along the otherwise parched riverbeds. The principal roads in the park run along the length of the Nossob and Auob riverbeds; the only other roads are two short-cut routes across the central dune sea between the two rivers. The park roads are all unsurfaced, but are well maintained and fully accessible to sedan cars. The 260-km approach route from Upington is, however, tarred for all but the final 60 km of its length. Allow at least three and a half hours for the drive from Upington north to Twee Rivieren.

There are three rest camps in the park: Twee Rivieren at the entrance (the south-eastern extremity), Mata-Mata on the Namibian border in the far west, and Nossob in the north, halfway up the Nossob River.

Claire Spottiswoode

Suricates, also known as Meerkats

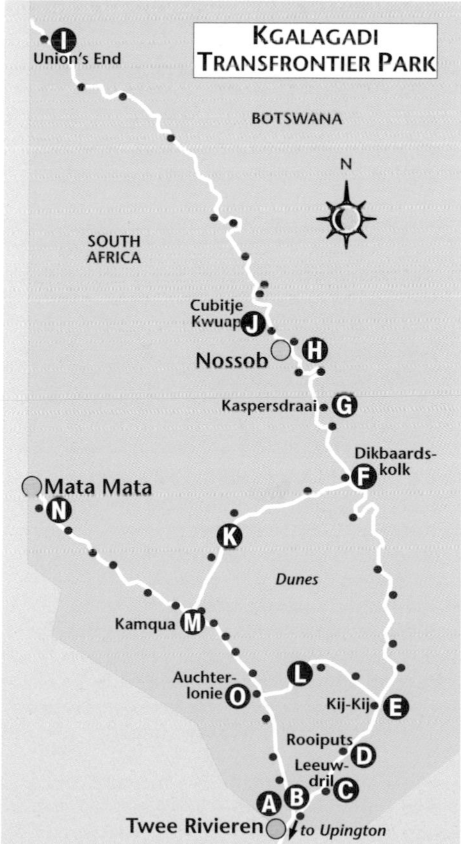

small numbers of **Lesser Spotted Eagle**. In wetter years, harriers may be seen, including **Black** and **Montagu's Harriers**. The most common vulture is **White-backed**, followed by **Lappet-faced**, while **White-headed Vulture** is rare.

All of the Kgalagadi's waterholes are invariably lined with jostling flocks of drinking seed-eaters making nervous forays to the water's edge, especially in winter. The most common among these are **Scaly-feathered** and **Red-headed Finches**, **Sociable Weaver** and **Lark-like Bunting**. During the summer months, huge flocks of **Common Swift** are in evidence overhead, **Lesser Grey Shrike** is commonly seen from the roadside and **Great Spotted Cuckoo** is also present.

Continue towards Nossob rest camp. Dikbaardskolk picnic site **F**, which makes a good lunch spot, is frequented by Ground Squirrels and a selection of skinks and agamas. As you approach the camp, particularly northwards of Kaspersdraai **G**, several additional species start becoming more evident: waterholes attract **Violet-eared Waxbill** and its brood parasite, **Shaft-tailed Whydah**. **Red-necked Falcon** also becomes more common as you head north – look out for hunting birds targeting the flocks of drinking seed-eaters; the falcons also regularly hunt over the Nossob rest camp.

If you are spending two nights at Nossob rest camp **H**, it is possible to make the full day's excursion to the park's northern fingertip at Union's End **I**. As you head north from Nossob and towards

Richard du Toit

Secretarybird is common here.

Richard du Toit
Red-necked Falcon

Union's End (try looking out for **Burchell's Sandgrouse*** at Cubitje Kwap Ⓙ waterhole), bushveld elements such as **Lilac-breasted Roller, Southern Yellow-billed Hornbill, Golden-tailed Woodpecker** and **Temminck's Courser** become more evident. The Union's End waterhole at the lonely junction of three national states – South Africa, Namibia and Botswana – is notable for occasionally hosting drinking flocks of **Rosy-faced Lovebird**. Nossob rest camp itself offers similar birding to Twee Rivieren. Ask the staff to show you the daytime roost of resident **Southern White-faced Scops-Owl**.

Two roads Ⓚ and Ⓛ cut across the central dunefield between the two riverbeds. There is little game along these routes, but either road is well worth the drive not only for the landscape and short-cut to the Auob, but also for **Pink-billed Lark**. This species is difficult to find in much of the Northern Cape and undertakes local movements. Look out for foraging birds around the bases of grass clumps, and do not be put off by their apparently white (not buff) outer tail feathers. Despite this incongruence with the field guides, they are indeed Pink-billed and not Botha's Larks (the latter has a localised distribution in eastern South Africa). **Northern Black Korhaan**, **Ant-eating Chat** and **Grey-backed Sparrowlark** are also particularly common along these roads.

Having reached the broad and shallow Auob riverbed near Kamqua waterhole Ⓜ, you have the option of either making a detour to Mata Mata rest camp Ⓝ on the Namibian border, or completing your loop through the park by returning to Twee Rivieren. The Auob riverbed is superb Cheetah country. It is also an excellent place to see **Verreaux's Eagle-Owl**; check the huge and gnarled Camel-thorn trees that line the riverbed at Auchterlonie Ⓞ.

OTHER ANIMALS: Antelope such as Gemsbok and Springbok are common, and the park is also arguably one of the best places in the world to watch big cats, such as Lion, Leopard and particularly Cheetah, while they hunt. Look out for groupings of Suricate (Meerkat) foraging in the dry riverbeds. Spotted and Brown Hyaenas also occur here. The latter is actually the more common, but is rarely seen due to its crepuscular habits. Enquire about current game-viewing conditions, and about the highly recommended night drives that depart from both the Twee Rivieren and Nossob rest camps about an hour before sunset.

60 Upington to the Kgalagadi ✔

Allow at least three-and-a-half hours for the drive from Upington north to Twee Rivieren. If you have time to spare, the Spitzkop Nature Reserve lies just 13 km north of Upington and consists of open grassy country which is excellent for larks. **Eastern Clapper**, **Fawn-coloured** and **Spike-heeled Larks** are all common here; other birds include **Northern Black Korhaan**, **African Pygmy Falcon**, **Chat Flycatcher** and **Ant-eating Chat**.

Sixty kilometres north of Upington, the landscape changes from open Karoo plains to sand, and the road takes a roller coaster route over parallel dunes. Watch for **Burchell's Courser*** and **Black-eared Sparrowlark*** along the initial Karoo expanses. **Northern Black Korhaan**, **Double-banded Courser** and, in wet years, **Pink-billed Lark**, are all likely to be spotted along the grassy dune sections of the road. Look out for the occasional **African Pygmy Falcon**, which is dependent on the numerous **Sociable Weaver** nests ingeniously attached to the telephone poles.

Near Andriesvale, 60 km south of the Kgalagadi park, the road joins the confluence of the Molopo and Nossob rivers, which are wooded with giant Camel-thorn trees. This woodland, especially near Molopo Lodge, offers good roadside birding, including **Lilac-breasted Roller**, **Golden-tailed Woodpecker** and **Groundscraper Thrush**.

61 Upington Area ✔

Situated on the banks of the Orange River, Upington is the major centre of the north-western Cape. Die Eiland Holiday Resort, situated on the south side of town, offers good birding, representative of this section of the river. To reach it from the town centre, follow the signs to 'Palm Avenue' (the longest palm-lined road in the southern hemisphere), which is the first turn to the left after you cross the river on the N14/N10 to Groblershoop. Birding in the riverine thicket along the river is likely to turn up characteristic Kalahari birds such as **Pearl-spotted Owlet, Swallow-tailed Bee-eater, Ashy Tit, African Red-eyed Bulbul** and **Brubru**, together with the more characteristically southerly **Namaqua Warbler*** and **Karoo Thrush**. Keep a look-out for **Abdim's Stork** in the vicinity (summer).

62 Augrabies Falls National Park IBA ✔✔

Boulder landscape at Augrabies

The park can be reached along a 39 km road that leads north-west from the riverside town of Kakamas, which is 88 km west of Upington on the N8 national road. The focus of the park is the falls, and most visitors venture little further than the river. However, the surrounding plains and rocky outcrops provide good birding, offering such typical Karoo species as **Double-banded Courser, Ludwig's Bustard*, Burchell's Courser*, Spike-heeled** and **Karoo Long-billed Larks** and **Chat Flycatcher**. Both **Stark's Lark** and **Black-eared Sparrowlark*** are erratic, and not always present in dry years. Two sought-after species of the rocky outcrops adjacent to the river are **Short-toed Rock-Thrush** (look on the outcrops around the camp site) and **Cinnamon-breasted Warbler*** (look at the viewsites along the gorge, such as those at Oranjekom, Swartrand and Echo Corner).

The acacia thicket of the camp site at the park headquarters is also rewarding. Here, you can see **Golden-tailed Woodpecker, Acacia Pied Barbet, Ashy Tit, African Red-eyed Bulbul, Namaqua Warbler*** (common), **Black-chested Prinia, Pririt Batis, Pale-winged Starling, Dusky Sunbird**, and the attractively peachy-flanked **Orange River White-eye**. The short walk from the camp to the falls themselves may produce cliff-nesting species such as **Black Stork, Verreaux's Eagle** and **Peregrine Falcon**, as well as huge mixed flocks of aerially feeding swifts and swallows. You are also likely to see the multicoloured Broadley's Flat Lizards that sun themselves conspicuously on the burnished granite.

63 Witsand Nature Reserve ✔

Witsand is so-named because of its strikingly white reef of dunes, which interrupts the red sea of the Kalahari sands. Adjacent to the dunes lies unexpectedly dense woodland and savanna, offering all the typical arid savanna birds of the Kgalagadi Transfrontier Park, as well as species that prefer denser woodland. These include **Green-winged Pytilia, Black-faced** and **Violet-eared Waxbills, Southern Yellow-billed Hornbill, Lappet-faced Vulture** and, in wet years, **Monotonous Lark**. Witsand is unique in hosting the only sandgrouse bird hide in the world: **Burchell's*, Namaqua**, and the scarcer **Double-banded Sandgrouse** may be seen drinking here; numbers vary, but are greatest in winter.

Witsand offers pleasant, immaculately maintained camping and chalet accommodation. See the pull-out map for directions: it can be approached from either the north or the south (look out for conspicuous signposts just west of Olifantshoek, or 10 km east of Groblershoop).

An isolated population of **African Rock Pipit*** is found in the adjacent Langeberg; turn east 13 km north of Witsand and follow the road to the Bergenaars Pass. North-east of Witsand, the small nature reserves adjacent to the towns of Kathu and Kuruman provide a host of woodland species and are worth visiting if you are passing through. Kathu is the most southerly place where **Red-billed Spurfowl** and **Southern Pied Babbler** are regularly observed.

64 Vaalbos National Park ✔

The park, 40 km north-west of Kimberley, incorporates a productive area of grassland and savanna, and is reached by following the signposted left turn 19 km west of Barkly West. It also includes a stretch of Vaal River frontage, rich in alluvial diamond deposits. Indeed, mining and other pressures have reduced the park to the point where it may be facing de-proclamation within the next few years. It remains well stocked with big game, however, including African Buffalo and Black and White Rhinoceroses.

Vaalbos's main attraction for birders lies in a largely isolated population of **Short-clawed Lark***, more typically a bird of overgrazed countryside in south-eastern Botswana. At Vaalbos, it is uncommon: search for it where the open grassy plains are punctuated by small acacia trees, such as those near Block Dam (a map is obtainable at the gate). The open savannas around Block Dam are worth searching for **Buffy** and **Kimberley Pipits** and **Rufous-naped Lark**, while the nearby patch of trees holds such typical arid savanna species as **Brubru**, **Shaft-tailed Whydah**, **Crimson-breasted Shrike**, **Pririt Batis** and **Golden-breasted Bunting**. Wooded habitats throughout the park hold **Red-crested Korhaan** and, scarcely, **Shikra**. Grassland, such as that below the southern powerlines, offers **Northern Black Korhaan**, **Ant-eating Chat**, and **Eastern Clapper** and **Spike-heeled Larks**. The Vaal River banks, accessed from the Riverside picnic site, offer **African Black Duck**, **Giant Kingfisher** and **White-fronted Bee-eater**.

65 Kimberley Area IBA R ✔✔✔

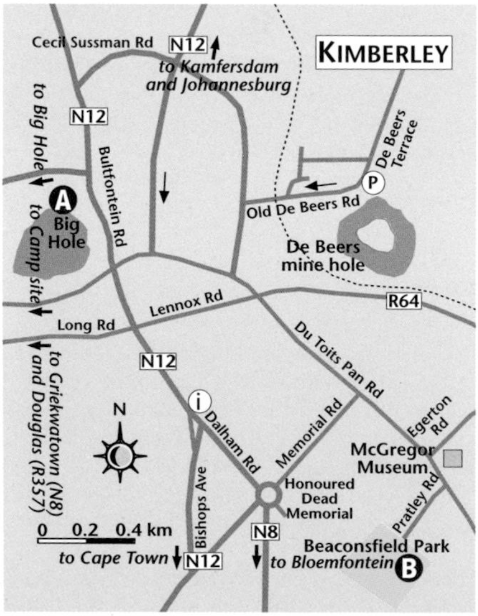

Kimberley is renowned as the site of a 19th-century diamond rush of unprecedented madness. Today, despite its status as the industrial and administrative centre of the Northern Cape, the city is surrounded by natural areas and flanked on virtually all sides by private game farms that offer good dryland savanna birding.

Often underestimated as a birding destination, despite entering the birding limelight with the discovery here of two controversial pipit species new to science, **Long-tailed** and **Kimberley Pipits**, the city also offers access to several other species that are challenging to see in South Africa, such as **Bradfield's Swift**. A number of species that occur here, such as **Red-breasted Swallow, Crested Barbet** and **Golden-breasted Bunting,** are more characteristic of South Africa's eastern regions, and reach their western point of distribution in this area. The city proper offers access to the much sought-after **Bradfield's Swift** as well as

Long-tailed and **Kimberley Pipits**. Look out for the former at the Big Hole Ⓐ (follow the signs from the N12) where they breed, or observe them flying overhead anywhere in the city. **Long-tailed Pipit** is best sought at its type locality, Beaconsfield Park Ⓑ (also known as Keeley Park): follow the signs to the McGregor Museum and, leaving from the gate of the museum, turn right and take the first left into Du Toits Pan Road and then the first right into Pratley Road. Continue to the big gates at the end of the road. Enter the park on foot, and turn left towards the series of playing fields. Although pipit numbers are variable, you will likely see pipits of all descriptions, including **Long-tailed** (winter), **Plain-backed, Buffy, African (Grassveld)** and **Kimberley Pipits**. The thorn trees between the fields and the gate support **African Hoopoe, Lesser Honeyguide, Acacia Pied Barbet, Fiscal Flycatcher, Orange River White-eye** and **Black-throated Canary. White-backed Vultures** can sometimes be seen soaring over the city.

Callan Cohen

De Beers' Mine Hole in Kimberley

De Beers, in conjunction with the Kimberley local bird guides association ☎, has recently allowed birding access to its private farms that surround much of the city. Now visitors can hire a local guide for day trips into these areas in search of specials such as **Pink-billed Lark, Burchell's Courser*** and **Orange River Francolin**. The latter species may be found where tall, scattered acacia trees stand above the grassy flats. This species, which calls in the early morning and is responsive to playback, displays a remarkable capacity to remain concealed, even though it is reasonably common in the Kimberley area.

Another option is Marrick Game Farm, which welcomes day visitors and also provides accommodation. It is conspicuously signposted, 11 km west of Kimberley on the R357 to Douglas ☎. Marrick offers a good combination of both savanna and open grassland species, as well as an ephemeral vlei that occasionally hosts large numbers of water birds. The woodland abounds with typical acacia thornveld species such as **Common Scimitarbill, Ashy Tit, Kalahari Scrub-Robin** and **Crimson-breasted Shrike**. Also present is the more easterly, small billed subspecies of **Sabota Lark**. The open grasslands near the pan supply an entirely different selection of birds, including **Northern Black Korhaan, Double-banded Courser** (common here), **Ant-eating Chat, Eastern Clapper, Spike-heeled** and **Red-capped Larks** and sometimes, with careful checking, **Pink-billed Lark**.

Just north of Kimberley, on the N12 to Johannesburg, lies the vast expanse of Kamfersdam, one of the few perennial water bodies in the Northern Cape and, as such, supporting an exceptional number and diversity of water birds. Access is possible from a turn-off to a culvert next to the adjacent N12 road. Water birds include **Greater** and **Lesser Flamingos, Black-necked Grebe** and small numbers of **Chestnut-banded Plover**. In wet years, reedbeds support **Yellow-crowned Bishop**, here at the edge of its range. **South African Cliff-Swallow** feeds over the adjacent grassland. Spitskop Dam, an hour's drive to the north of Kimberley, regularly hosts national rarities such as **Black-tailed Godwit** and **Lesser Black-backed Gull**. Contact the Kimberley bird guides association for access information.

KIMBERLEY'S NEW PIPITS

In the 1990s, Dr Richard Liversidge, of the McGregor Museum, described two new species of pipit in Kimberley. The distribution and movements of the first species, **Long-tailed Pipit**, are poorly known, although it seems to be a non-breeding winter visitor (May to early Sept) to the Kimberley area. Pipit field identification is notoriously subjective, and separating Long-tailed from the similar **Plain-backed** and **Buffy Pipits** is less than clear. You will need to spend some time familiarising yourself with the selection at Beaconsfield and elsewhere before attempting to sort them out.

ROUTE 7

THE N1 ROUTE (SOUTH AFRICA)

TOP 10 BIRDS

- Melodious Lark
- Blue Korhaan
- Orange River Francolin
- South African Cliff-Swallow
- Lesser Kestrel
- African Rock Pipit
- Ludwig's Bustard
- Long-tailed Widow
- Short-clawed Lark
- Mottled Spinetail

The N1 extends from Cape Town, via Gauteng, to the country's northern border with Zimbabwe. It is South Africa's longest national road and is typically used as a conduit for birders exploring the country. Rather than being viewed as an inevitable slog en route to other birding destinations, the N1 should be appreciated as a fine birding area in its own right, and a few strategic stops along this road can complement a trip along this seemingly barren road rather well.

From African Penguins bobbing in the Atlantic off Cape Town, the N1 stretches across the country to the haunt of the Pel's Fishing-Owl in the riverine forests of the Limpopo. It offers birding opportunities that span the majority of South Africa's habitats, including coasts, wetlands, mountain fynbos, the desolate expanses of the Succulent and Nama Karoo, rivers, highveld grassland, wooded bushveld, Afromontane forest and, in its far northern reaches, lowveld.

Apart from the high diversity of species that is found along its length, certain southern African endemics such as Melodious Lark*, Orange River Francolin and Blue Korhaan are most easily seen along this route. The N1 also passes through the main wintering grounds of the migrant Lesser Kestrel, which gather nightly in their thousands to roost in eucalyptus stands in small towns along this road.

The purpose of this chapter is to draw together disparate sites situated along the road, and to make reference to other sites that are easily reached from the road but covered in the other chapters. In particular, this route draws together sites from the heart of the country, the Free State.

Warwick Tarboton

Blue Korhaan is often seen along the N1.

Callan Cohen

The N1 in winter

Cape Town to Colesberg

Claire Spottiswoode

The Karoo in bloom near Worcester

Starting in the city of Cape Town at the Atlantic Ocean, the N1 heads north-east and the first birding sites adjacent to the road are Table Bay (p.38), the turn-off to Milnerton (p.45), and the Blouvlei wetland (p.38), which lies just off this road. Continuing beyond the city, **White Stork** and **Great White Pelican** are often seen from the road in the vicinity of the Tygerberg Zoo turn-off (exit 39), and the winelands town of Paarl (p.42) offers both fynbos and wetland birding.

While it is possible to drive through the 4 km long Huguenot Tunnel, birders might consider the scenic alternative over Du Toit's Kloof Pass, where **Cape Sugarbird*** and **Protea Seed-eater*** can be seen from the road on the descent. Shortly after passing over the Du Toit's Kloof Mountains, you will reach Worcester and the Karoo National Botanical Garden, signposted on the N1 opposite the town. The garden offers pleasant birding in scenic surrounds (interesting species include **Fairy Flycatcher**, **Booted Eagle** and **Acacia Pied Barbet**).

From Worcester, you can also take the R60 southwards to Robertson, where the nearby Dassieshoek and Vrolijkheid (described below) nature reserves offer a huge contrast between fynbos and Karoo endemics respectively.

Beyond Worcester and the Hex River Valley, the N1 passes the R46 turn-off to the north, which leads to the well-known birding destination of Karoopoort and the Tanqua Karoo (p.55). Shortly before reaching the town of Touws River, the N1 passes through the last of the Cape mountains and reaches the Karoo plains. At Prince Albert Road, the R407 leads southwards to the town of the same name, and the northern end of Swartberg Pass (p.75). An excellent place to spend the night is the Karoo National Park south of Beaufort West, which offers prime rocky-slope birding and exciting night drives (see p.96).

At Three Sisters, birders en route to Gauteng should consider taking the much quieter N12 northwards towards Victoria West, which eventually leads to Jo'burg and only adds an hour onto the travelling time. This road passes through Kimberley (p.92) and then the Sandveld Nature Reserve (p.206), both offering sightings of **Pink-billed Lark** and **Orange River Francolin**.

66 Vrolijkheid Nature Reserve ✔

This attractive reserve, with a number of bird hides and trails, offers the closest Karoo birding to Cape Town. From the N1 at Worcester, take the R60 to Robertson, and from there follow the road towards McGregor for 15 km. The main entrance and parking area is on the left. **Karoo Long-billed Lark** occurs in the old fields adjacent to the car park. The Caracal Trail to the left leads to the open plains, where **Karoo Chat**, **Pale Chanting Goshawk**, **Southern Black Korhaan**, **White-throated Canary**, **Rufous-eared Warbler**, **Cape Penduline-Tit**, **Layard's Tit-Babbler** (rocky slopes), **Namaqua Dove** and **Large-billed Lark** occur. **African Rock Pipit*** and **Ground Woodpecker*** occur on the mountain ridges at the back of the reserve, and are not easily accessed.

The Heron Trail (to the right) leads along the edge of the dam to the bird hides, which are set in dense acacia thicket. **Fairy Flycatcher**, **Chestnut-vented Tit-Babbler**, **African Reed-Warbler** (summer), **White-backed Mousebird**, **Namaqua Warbler*** (especially near the second hide) and **Red-billed Firefinch** (scarce) are present in the thickets, while **African Spoonbill** and **South African Shelduck** are among the water birds that may be present.

67 Dassieshoek Nature Reserve ✔✔

Situated close to Robertson, this small reserve with its dramatic mountain scenery offers a host of fynbos and forest specials. From the N1 at Worcester, follow the R60 to Robertson. Once in town, turn left into Paul Kruger Street, and just before it ends, turn left into Coetzee Street. Turn right at the next T-junction, left at the next stop street, and then follow the gravel road for a further 6 km, past a quarry, until you reach the entrance gate on the right (opposite a lake where **African Black Duck** occurs). Follow the main track into the reserve, bearing left to reach the picnic site. Walk from here, following the trail westwards across the stream and into the fynbos beyond. **Olive Woodpecker**, **Cape Batis**, **Streaky-headed Seed-eater**, **Tambourine Dove**, **Swee Waxbill**, **Southern Tchagra** and **Greater Double-collared** and **Amethyst Sunbirds** may all be found in the trees at the stream crossing. The fynbos along the first 500 m of the main track holds **Victorin's Scrub-Warbler*** (best detected by its call), **Cape Sugarbird***, **Orange-breasted Sunbird**, **Cape Siskin*** and the inconspicuous **Protea Seed-eater***.

68 Karoo National Park IBA ✔✔

The mountainous Karoo National Park, near the regional centre of Beaufort West (five hours' drive on the N1 from Cape Town), provides a representative cross-section of Karoo birding. Apart from being a very worthwhile birding destination, it serves as an excellent staging post en route from Cape Town to Johannesburg.

The park protects an exceptionally fine tract of mountainous Karoo landscape, and is well stocked with game, including Black Rhino, Black Wildebeest, Gemsbok and Cape Mountain Zebra. It also boasts an excellent selection of Karoo specials, providing you with easy access to three tricky rock-loving species, namely **Cinnamon-breasted Warbler***, **African Rock Pipit*** and **Short-toed Rock-Thrush**.

Another of the park's attractions is the opportunity to join guided night-drives, where some exciting Karoo mammals (see box, p.81), as well as **Cape Eagle-Owl***, albeit very occasionally, may be seen.

The entrance to the park is on the N1 national road, 5 km south of Beaufort West. A tarred road leads to the park's headquarters and rest camp **A**, where **Mountain Wheatear**, **African Red-eyed Bulbul** and **Cape Bunting** are tame and conspicuous. **Verreaux's Eagle** regularly passes overhead.

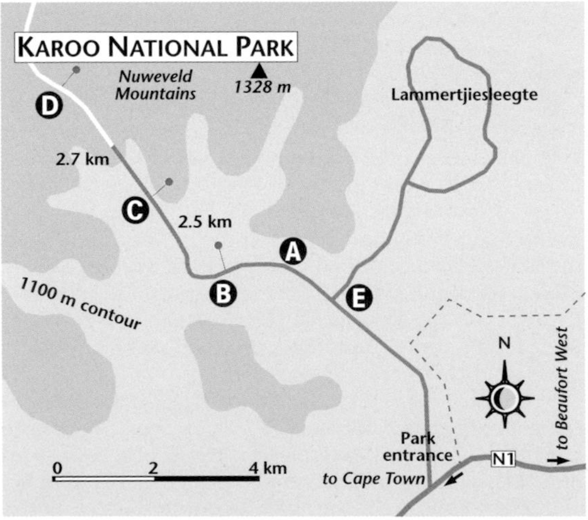

Take an amble around the nearby camp site **B**, set in dense acacia thicket, as it offers some of the best birding in the park. **Namaqua Warbler***, **Southern Tchagra**, **Acacia Pied Barbet**, **Cardinal Woodpecker**, **Dusky Sunbird**, **Pririt Batis**, **Chestnut-vented Tit-Babbler** and **Fairy Flycatcher** are all vocal but inconspicuous thicket dwellers. Rather more obvious are all three of the South African mousebird species – **Red-faced**, **Speckled**, and **White-backed Mousebirds**.

A drive up Klipspringer Pass, which winds up the escarpment of the plateau behind the rest camp, provides access to the three specials of rocky country; check the slopes at the base of the pass (in the vicinity of **C**) for **Layard's Tit-Babbler**, **African Rock Pipit*** and **Short-toed Rock-Thrush**. The latter occurs scarcely but regularly along the length of the meandering road up to the Klipspringer Pass. The vicinity of the fenced lookout point at the summit of the pass at **D** is a good site for both **Cinnamon-breasted Warbler*** and **African Rock Pipit***, neither of which is likely to be seen without staying very alert to their calls, which drift across from the cliff faces. The pipit also occurs on the rocky hillocks of the plateau itself, alongside the similarly rock-loving **Long-billed Pipit**. Other mountain species that are typical of the cliffs along the Klipspringer Pass are **Verreaux's** and **Booted Eagles**, **Ground Woodpecker*** and **Pale-winged Starling**. Also drive the Lammertjiesleegte loop **E** for Karoo plains birds, including **Karoo Korhaan** and **Rufous-eared Warbler**.

Callan Cohen

Rocky slopes in the Karoo National Park

Colesberg to Gauteng

From Colesberg northwards, the Karoo gradually gives way to the grasslands that dominate the high plateaux in the eastern half of the country. One option here is to take the 110 km detour from Colesberg, along the quieter R717 to Philippolis, to rejoin the N1 at Trompsburg. This route is about the same length as the N1 that it avoids, but has less traffic and is better for open-country birding (look out for **Blue Korhaan**).

Oviston Nature Reserve, signposted about 60 km west of Colesberg on the R58 towards Venterstad, provides a convenient stopover (accommodation available). This reserve, in hilly country on the edge of the Gariep Dam, offers birding with a Karoo flavour (specials include **Verreaux's Eagle**, **Ludwig's Bustard***, **Karoo Korhaan**, and **Spike-heeled**, **Eastern Long-billed**, **Large-billed** and **Eastern Clapper Larks**), and a variety of water birds.

Continuing north to Springfontein, either detour along the R701 towards Tussen-die-Riviere Game Reserve, or continue with the N1 northwards to Bloemfontein (this stretch is good for **Blue Korhaan**). A convenient place to bird along this stretch is the 'Stofplaas/Kruger' off-ramp off the N1, 110 km south of Bloemfontein. Turn west at the top of the off-ramp, and bird the grassy fields for the first few kilometres for **Melodious Lark***, **Cloud Cisticola*** and **Eastern Clapper Lark**.

Even better, stay at Vendutiekop Guest Farm near Jagersfontein, which has **Melodious Lark***, **Kimberley Pipit** and **African Rock Pipit***; night drives here have produced Aardwolf, Springhare, South African Porcupine and even Aardvark. Take the Jagersfontein turn-off 90 km south of Bloemfontein; the farm is exactly 30 km along this dirt road (it is necessary to book in advance, ☎).

South African Cliff-Swallow is common in the grasslands in summer and many of the road bridges support active colonies. Passing through Bloemfontein, a detour to the productive Soetdoring Nature Reserve, just 30 km north-west of the town, will lend a distinctly Kalahari element to the birding, and specials include **Orange River Francolin**. Continuing further north still, the well-signposted Willem Pretorius Game Reserve is only 8 km off the N1, 30 km north of Winburg (19 km south of Ventersburg). The reserve surrounds the Allemanskraal Dam and lists over 240 species, and accommodation is available. **Double-banded Courser**,

Colin Paterson-Jones

Highveld grassland along the N1

Melodious* and **Pink-billed Larks**, **Orange River Francolin**, **Black Harrier*** (winter), **Secretarybird** and **Blue Korhaan** are present in the grassland in the southern section of the reserve. **Common Scimitarbill**, **Acacia Pied Barbet**, **Ashy Tit** and **Brown-crowned Tchagra** occur in the surrounding acacia woodlands.

The highveld grasslands, such as those 20 km south of Kroonstad, support large numbers of birds in summer. These include **Amur Falcon**, **Lesser Kestrel**, **Black-winged Pratincole** (an erratic visitor), and **Pallid** and **Montagu's Harriers** (both rare). **Long-tailed Widowbird** is a common sight in many of the grasslands towards Gauteng.

About 60 km north of Kroonstad, Koppies Dam may be worth a stop for some good grassland birding (including **Blue Korhaan**, **Secretarybird**, and a host of larks and cisticolas). Take the turn-off from the N1 to Koppies, and follow the signs to the reserve (about 16 km from the N1).

If you are entering the grasslands just south of Gauteng in the early morning or late evening, look for **Marsh Owl** perched on low fence posts along the road.

69 Tussen-die-Riviere Game Reserve ✔

From the N1 north of Colesberg, take the R701 for 30 km past Bethulie before turning south to Goedemoed; the entrance to the reserve is signposted from this latter road. From Bloemfontein, take the N6 south to Smithfield, and then follow the R701 westwards towards Bethulie before reaching the south turn to Goedemoed described above.

The reserve consists of rocky ridges and ravines, open plains and riverine thickets along watercourses. Birds found in the reserve include **Eastern Clapper**, **Spike-heeled**, **Red-capped** and **Large-billed Larks**, **Double-banded Courser**, **Sickle-winged** and **Karoo Chats**, and **Rufous-eared Warbler**. Look out too for **Grey-winged** and **Orange River Francolins**, **Ludwig's Bustard***, **Karoo Prinia**, and **Buffy** and **Long-billed Pipits**, the latter especially in rocky areas.

Vegetated, rocky hillsides are host to a number of interesting species, including **Karoo Scrub-Robin**, **Layard's Tit-Babbler**, **Grey-backed Cisticola**, **African Rock Pipit***, **Grey Tit**, **Short-toed Rock-Thrush** (often perched on telephone poles along the roads in the reserve), **White-throated Canary** and **Lark-like Bunting**. **Namaqua Warbler*** occurs in the reedbeds along the river.

70 Soetdoring Nature Reserve ✔

Situated some 30 km west of Bloemfontein, Soetdoring provides an excellent range of typical Karoo and Kalahari birds. The reserve incorporates a section of the Modder River, which feeds the Krugersdrift Dam, a large impoundment in the reserve, used mainly for irrigation of farmlands downstream. Access is from the tarred Bloemfontein-Bultfontein road (R700). Limited self-catering accommodation is available.

Over 270 bird species have been recorded in the reserve and up to 140 species can be expected in a single day during summer. Habitats include open water and exposed shoreline, grasslands, karoo scrub, wooded hillsides and acacia-dominated riparian thickets associated with the Modder River. Various kingfishers (**Giant**, **Pied** and **Malachite Kingfishers**) are frequently seen along stretches of the Modder River, as is **White-fronted Bee-eater**, while **Namaqua Warbler*** is common, and skulking species such as **Little Bittern** can also often be found here.

Birds characteristic of the grassland areas include **Northern Black Korhaan**, **Orange River Francolin**, **Ant-eating Chat**, and various larks, including **Eastern Clapper**, **Large-billed** and **Melodious* Larks**.

There are a number of picnic sites in the thicket areas close to the river, and the surrounding area yields **Swainson's** and **Natal Spurfowl**, **Cardinal Woodpecker**, **Crested** and **Acacia Pied Barbet**, **Kalahari** and **Karoo Scrub-Robins**, **Ashy Tit** and **Pririt Batis**. The bridge over the Modder River just outside the entrance to the reserve has breeding **South African Cliff-Swallow**.

Gauteng to Musina (formerly Messina)

North of Gauteng, the N1 descends from highveld grasslands into the vast bushveld woodlands, offering some of South Africa's most characteristic birding. The N1 then snakes through patches of Afromontane forest in the Soutpansberg range, before descending again to the mopane and baobabs of the Limpopo Valley. Unlike the previous sections of the N1 further south, this area falls largely within the routes already covered in this book.

Baobabs near Musina

Lanz von Hörsten/IOA

Birders travelling on the N1 north from Pretoria should consider a detour at the Pienaars River off-ramp to the very productive Zaagkuildrift road (see p.168) for excellent acacia birding. At Kranskop Toll Plaza, take the off-ramp to Modimolle (formerly Nylstroom) if you want to detour to Nylsvley Nature Reserve (p.100). The Mokopane (formerly Potgietersrus) off-ramp offers access to Percy Fyfe (p.182) and Doorndraai nature reserves (p.182). **Short-clawed Lark*** may be seen from the bypass road past Polokwane, but is more reliable in the reserve itself, just a short drive from the N1 (p.183). The N1 passes directly through Machado (formerly Louis Trichardt), the base for Soutpansberg birding, which includes species such as **African Broadbill***. The route comes to an end shortly after Musina, at Beitbridge on the Limpopo. The R572 leading west from Musina joins the Limpopo at the newly proclaimed Mapungubwe National Park (p.190), where riverine forest holds **Pel's Fishing-Owl***.

71 Musina Nature Reserve ✔

This nature reserve, situated on the N1 just 5 km south of Musina town, is an ideal stopover for those travelling to Zimbabwe or to the Pafuri region of the northern Kruger National Park.

Originally established for the purpose of conserving the large concentrations of baobab trees in the area, this birder-friendly reserve offers accommodation in tents or chalets.

Birding in the reserve is good and holds interesting species such as **Verreaux's** and **Martial Eagles** and **African Hawk-Eagle**, **Mottled Spinetail**, **Dickinson's Kestrel**, **Meyer's Parrot**, **Mosque Swallow**, **Broad-billed Roller**, and **African** and **European Golden Orioles** (summer). **White-crowned Shrike**, **Red-billed Buffalo-Weaver**, and **Mocking Cliff-Chat** all commonly occur in the area.

EASTERN SOUTH AFRICA

Eastern South Africa is a magnificent birding area: the tropical influence here results in a stupendously high bird diversity, and colourful bird families (hornbills, rollers and turacos) are common and conspicuous. This combines with excellent game-watching.

The eastern half of South Africa is treated together with the independent countries of **Lesotho** and **Swaziland**, and birding routes link to those in neighbouring South Africa. For the purposes of this book, we've divided eastern South Africa into 10 birding routes. The Eastern Cape Route (R8) is most famous for its excellent coastal birding. The Southern KwaZulu-Natal Route (R9) encompasses excellent forests and rises to the alpine heights of Sani Pass in Lesotho. The birding sites around Durban and Pietermaritzburg (R10) include numerous small urban birding sites. But perhaps the most exciting birding in KwaZulu-Natal is found in the tropical savannas and forests of the coastal plains of Zululand (R11).

Rising to over 3 000 m in this part of South Africa is a prominent mountainous spine. We've combined the very best of the highland sites here – hosting some of the region's most sought-after endemics – into the Highlands Endemics Route (R12), which extends from Swaziland, through South Africa's famous sites at Wakkerstroom in Mpumalanga, Memel in the Free State and the Drakensberg in KwaZulu-Natal southwards to the alpine reaches of Lesotho. The Gauteng & Surrounds Route (R13) is centred on Johannesburg and Pretoria, and routes 14 to 17 are focused on their respective regions. The world-famous birding and game-watching area of the Kruger National Park (R16) has an entire route devoted to it.

NOTE: The N1 Route (R7) originates in western South Africa (and is covered in that section) and follows South Africa's main national road through the centre of the country. It covers many sites in the Free State province that are not covered on other routes.

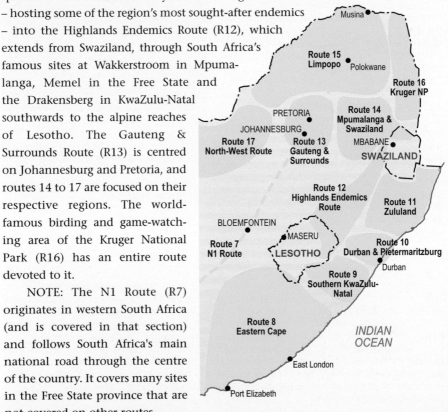

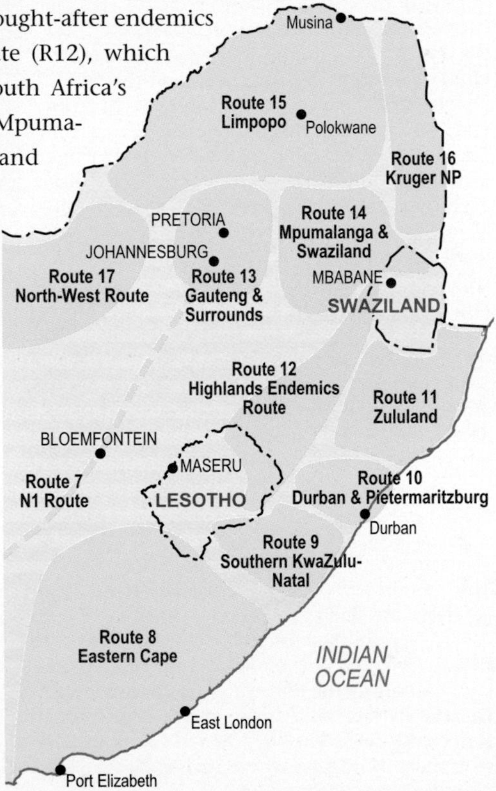

ROUTE **8**

EASTERN CAPE

TOP 10 BIRDS

- Knysna Woodpecker
- Brown Scrub-Robin
- Roseate Tern
- Cape Vulture
- Barrow's Korhaan
- European Oystercatcher
- Mangrove Kingfisher
- Cape Parrot
- Southern Tchagra
- Barred Owlet

Warwick Tarboton

The Eastern Cape is the stronghold of the Knysna Woodpecker.

The Eastern Cape is the main meeting point of the country's biomes, and the birding here is a diverse mixture of western endemics and tropical eastern species. Although no species are unique to this region, and many of its birds can be seen at more traditional sites in surrounding provinces, the Eastern Cape is the best place in southern Africa to see Knysna Woodpecker* and Roseate Tern. Furthermore, the province boasts some excellent sites for Mangrove Kingfisher*, Spotted* and Orange Ground-Thrushes, Bush Blackcap*, Brown Scrub-Robin, Forest Buzzard*, Knysna Warbler, Cape Parrot*, Knysna Turaco, Buff-spotted Flufftail, African Crowned Eagle, Southern Tchagra*, Mountain Pipit, African Rock Pipit*, Ludwig's and Denham's Bustards*, Barrow's* and Karoo Korhaans and Ground Woodpecker*. The series of estuaries along its coast are a magnet for rarities such as Eurasian Oystercatcher and Crab Plover*, which regularly attract dedicated birders from across the country.

The Eastern Cape is best known for the forest patches that occur along the entire length of the coast, ranging from easily accessible reserves close to the main centres of Port Elizabeth and East London to the more remote and poorly known forest patches of the Wild Coast. Inland forests in the mountains at Hogsback offer a different set of species, and heading further inland still, Naudésnek Pass offers montane endemics on this southern edge of the Drakensberg. Most of the western areas comprise expansive Karoo plains, easily accessed from Graaff-Reinet. Wader-watchers and rarity-seekers would do well to concentrate on the many estuaries, the most productive being the Kromme, Gamtoos, Swartkops and Sundays. Egyptian Vulture, previously believed extinct in southern Africa, may even still occur in remote areas of the former Transkei.

72 Gamtoos River Estuary IBA R ✔✔

The Gamtoos River Mouth is well known to South African twitchers for the diversity of migrant waders that occur on the mudflats here in summer, including a long-staying **Eurasian Oystercatcher**. To reach the estuary from Humansdorp, take the Mondplaas off-ramp and turn right under the N2. At the T-junction turn left; proceed to the narrow steel bridge, and cross over. Turn right immediately onto a gravel road that runs parallel to the Gamtoos River. At the T-junction, turn right onto the tarred road that leads into the reserve and park at the parking area, which is some distance from the river mouth.

From Port Elizabeth turn left at the Thornhill off-ramp (about 2 km from the end of the dual carriageway). After about 150 metres turn west (right) towards Jeffrey's Bay. Turn left onto a tarred road, which leads to the reserve a few kilometres further on.

From the parking area, walk onto the sand and cross the little stream, heading towards the sand dunes opposite. Turn left to get to the freshwater reedbeds and right to go to the mudbanks, which are on the way to the river mouth.

The reedbeds and marshes hold **Baillon's Crake**, which may be seen in short vegetation near the reedbeds in the early morning. Also look out for **African Rail** and **Hottentot Teal**. Bush-loving **Southern Tchagra*** occurs in the dense vegetation that lines the river.

The estuary's mudbanks attract hundred of waders, which are best viewed from just outside the reserve's gates, or from the bird trail that starts approximately 100 m before the gates, on the western side. Apart from the usual selection of common migrant waders, **Terek Sandpiper** and **Greater Sand Plover** are regular visitors, and a **Eurasian Oystercatcher** has been present in this area for many years. Recent recorded rarities include **Mongolian Plover** and **Pacific Golden Plover**. Also keep an eye out for **Little Tern** and **Eurasian Hobby** flying overhead. A **Citrine Wagtail** was present here for a month in 1998.

The nearby Kromme River Mouth, close to St Francis Bay, offers similar birding (good waders in summer include **Eurasian Curlew**, **Greater Sand Plover** and **Bar-tailed Godwit**) and the possibility of a vagrant! The estuary at the Seekoei River Nature Reserve, just south of Jeffrey's Bay, is also worth a visit.

Mondplaas Ponds, visible just inland from the Mondplaas N2 off-ramp described above, offer a high diversity of skulking water birds in the reedbeds (**African Rail** and **Little Bittern**) and open water (**African Jacana** and **Hottentot Teal**).

73 Baviaanskloof Wilderness Area IBA ✔

This huge wilderness area that lies between Willowmore and Patensie has an impressive bird list, including a variety of South African endemics, but much of Baviaanskloof is inaccessible to birders on a tight schedule. Forest and fynbos specials that occur in the eastern and central areas include **Cape Siskin***, **Cape Sugarbird***, **Victorin's Scrub-Warbler***, **Denham's**

FINDING BARROW'S KORHAAN AROUND HUMANSDORP

A number of roads here are good for an isolated population of the inconspicuous **Barrow's Korhaan***, which inhabits longish grass, although it may forage in much shorter grass nearby. This bird tends to be very wary when breeding and is far easier to see during the winter months; mornings are best – be sure to listen out for their distinctive frog-like calls. From Humansdorp, drive towards St Francis Bay and after 6-7 km turn down a dirt road on the left, signposted 'Paradise Beach' and 'Lombardi Game farm'. After 4 km along this road (also good for **Blue Crane**), turn left at the intersection. Proceed through a shallow valley, and where the road levels out at the top of the dip, scan the field on the right. Early morning is essential. Barrow's Korhaan* can be found on other routes from Humansdorp: look out for it 17 km from the town on the R330 towards Hankey; also between 22 and 26 km from Humansdorp on the R62 towards Kareedouw.

Bustard*, **Verreaux's Eagle**, **Black Harrier***, **White-backed Night-Heron***, **Half-collared Kingfisher**, **Protea Seed-eater***, **Booted Eagle**, **Yellow-throated Petronia** and **Knysna Woodpecker***, while the arid western Willowmore side is characterised by Karoo species such as **Layard's Tit-Babbler**, **Namaqua Warbler*** and **Rufous-eared Warbler**.

74 Port Elizabeth: Settlers' Park & Island Forest Reserve ✔

Settlers' Park, situated in Walmer in Port Elizabeth, is easily accessed from a number of the city's streets: Howe Avenue off Park Drive, off Chelmsford Avenue, Cudmore Street, or Third Avenue. The park offers several walks along well-maintained paths, and also wheelchair-accessible areas around the main car park at Howe Avenue, as well as at the observation point overlooking the water feature next to this car park. Up to six species of sunbird (**Greater** and **Southern Double-collared**, **Malachite**, **Grey**, **Amethyst** and **Collared Sunbird**) as well as **Fiscal Flycatcher** and **African Firefinch** can be seen near the Information Centre. Thickets around the nursery hold **Southern Tchagra*** and **Terrestrial Brownbul**, and **Peregrine Falcon** is often seen at the cliffs below the Chelmsford Avenue entrance.

The Island Forest Reserve is reached from the Sea View off-ramp from the N2, some 15 km west of Port Elizabeth. Follow the Sea View road for 6 km; the reserve is signposted on your left. The reserve offers several trails and a picnic area.

The reserve's legendary birdbath at the picnic area is its main attraction, particularly when secretive species such as **Lemon** and **Tambourine Doves**, **Knysna Turaco** and **Forest Canary** come to drink. Look in the trees around the picnic area for **Black-bellied Starling**, and follow the 1 km loop path that starts near the gatehouse and descends into the valley for **Chorister Robin-Chat**, **Brown Scrub-Robin** and **White-starred Robin**.

Van Staden's Wildflower Reserve, a mere 40 km west of Port Elizabeth off the N2 (take the Van Staden's Pass turn-off), offers walking trails through fynbos (**Cape Sugarbird***, **Orange-breasted Sunbird**, **Victorin's Scrub-Warbler***) and forest (**Knysna Turaco** and **African Crowned Eagle**).

75 Cape Recife Nature Reserve R ✔✔

An excellent site for shorebirds and terns, and a classic site for **Roseate Tern**, Cape Recife is conveniently located on the south-east edge of Port Elizabeth.

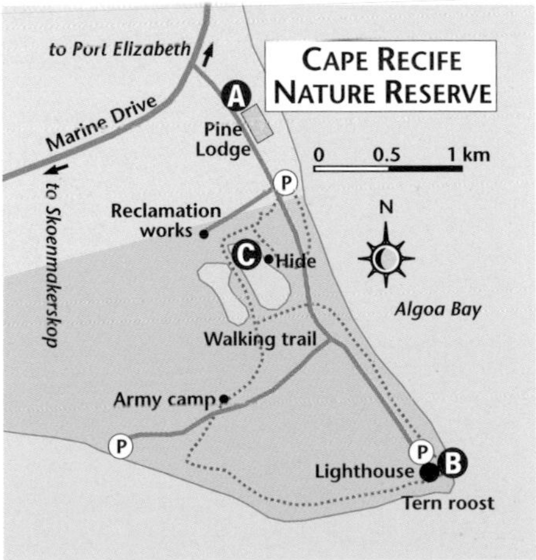

SPECIALS: Roseate, Damara* and Antarctic* Terns, African Black Oystercatcher*.

SEASON: **Roseate Tern** is best seen between Jun-Sept and is virtually absent in summer. **Antarctic Tern*** is present in winter only. **Damara Tern*** is most frequent in spring and autumn.

HABITATS: Seashore, sewage reclamation ponds, coastal bush.

BIRDING: Just outside the reserve, stands of alien trees line the road into Pine Lodge Ⓐ, and these host **Knysna Woodpecker***. Once in the reserve, follow the main road towards the lighthouse Ⓑ, park here and walk to the shore. Terns, gulls and waders are best searched for on the beach and on the rocks in front of the lighthouse (high

tide is best, as the rising waters push the birds closer; check the local newspaper for times). A **Bridled Tern**, a vagrant to South Africa, has been returning to the tern roost here for five years. **African Black Oystercatcher*** is common on the shoreline, while **African Penguin** and **Cape Gannet** can often be seen out at sea here. The first sewage pond, which has a bird hide Ⓒ, is signposted from the main road. Reed-loving species such as **African Purple Swamphen**, **Black Crake** and **African Rail** may be seen. **Southern Tchagra*** may be found in the dune vegetation.
OTHER ANIMALS: African Clawless Otter.
NEARBY SITES: Pelagic trips may be organised from Port Elizabeth (see p.23).

GETTING THERE

The entrance to the Cape Recife Nature Reserve is off Marine Drive, just past the Pine Lodge Resort (obtain an entry permit here) and 2.5 km south of Summerstrand. The reserve is open all hours, and an entrance fee is payable for all vehicles. A good road runs through the reserve to the lighthouse.

76 Swartkops Estuary

IBA R ✔✔

Swartkops provides some of the best estuarine birding to be found on the east coast, and may hold up to 10 000 birds in summer, although access can be tricky. A number of national rarities have been recorded here over the years, including the first southern African record of **Hudsonian Godwit**.
SPECIALS: Eurasian Curlew, Bar-tailed Godwit, Terek Sandpiper, Greater Sand Plover, Black-necked Grebe, Little Tern and Southern Tchagra*.
SEASON: Summer (Oct-Apr) is by far the best, when the highest number of migrant waders are present.
HABITATS: Estuary, intertidal banks, salt marsh, salt pans and thicket vegetation.
BIRDING: A large variety of migrant waders can be seen feeding on the mudbanks at low tide (consult the local newspapers for tide timetable); the best places to look for them are at Ⓐ and Ⓑ. It's not always easy to view the mudflats from the edge of the road, and access is not possible along the entire length of the shore. Specials here include **Eurasian Curlew** (alongside the smaller **Common Whimbrel**), **Terek Sandpiper**, **Greater Sand Plover** and **Bar-tailed Godwit**. **Caspian** and **Little Terns** may be seen, and scan the salt marsh for **Goliath Heron**. The saltpans at Ⓒ and Ⓓ (go past the brick factory)

GETTING THERE

Swartkops village is signposted from the N2 on the north-eastern edge of Port Elizabeth.

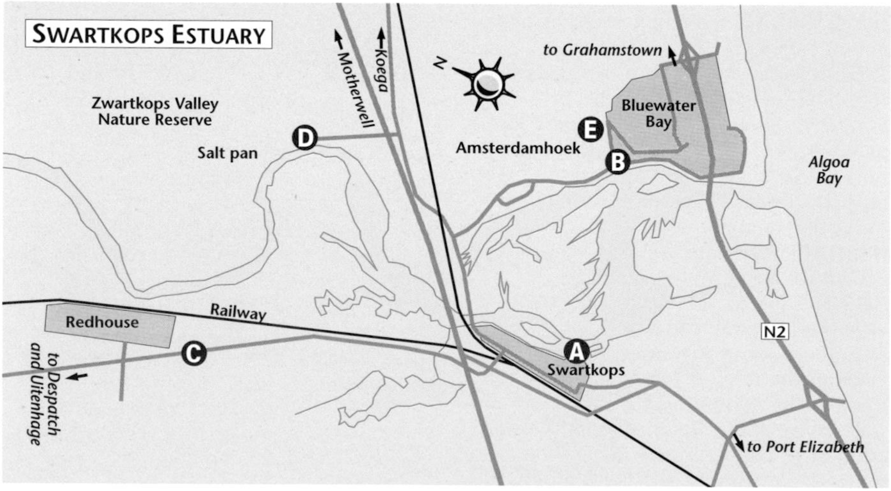

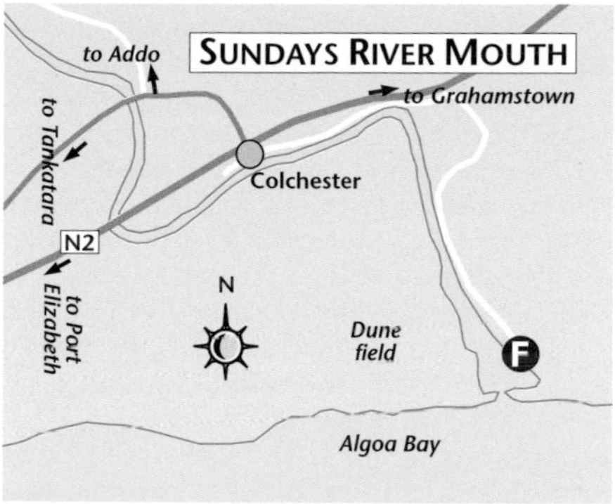

support **Greater Flamingo, South African Shelduck, Cape Teal** and **Black-necked Grebe** (especially at **C**). **Grey-backed Cisticola** is found in low bushes (look near **D**), while **Southern Tchagra*** prefers dense scrub (**E**, the Aloe Reserve, is a good place to look for it).
NEARBY SITES: The Sundays River Mouth (take the Colchester turn-off from the N2 and follow the road through the caravan park and eastwards along the river to the estuary **F**) has hosted a number of rarities, including **Crab Plover*** and **Eurasian Oystercatcher**.

77 East London & Gonubie ✔✔

A network of small reserves around the main centre of East London provides access to a diversity of forest, thicket and wetland species.
SPECIALS: Southern Tchagra*, Brown Scrub-Robin, Knysna Woodpecker*, Buff-spotted Flufftail, Knysna Warbler*, Water Thick-knee, Terek Sandpiper, Little Tern, African Finfoot*, Mountain Wagtail, Narina Trogon*, Red-capped and Chorister Robin-Chats.
SEASON: Birding is good year-round, although migrant waders are present in summer only.
HABITATS: Seashore, dune forest, mudflats, mangrove and coastal forest, thickets.
BIRDING: *Nahoon River Estuary:* Scan the tidal mudflats in the nature reserve at low tide for a selection of migrant waders including **Terek Sandpiper** and **Common Whimbrel. Water Thick-knee** can be found on the river banks. The Dassie Trail, which leads through the adjacent coastal and dune forest, is good for the secretive **Knysna Warbler***, which is best detected by its piercing call. Take care to distinguish it from the closely similar **Barratt's**

GETTING THERE

Nahoon River Estuary: To reach the nature reserve on the east bank, take the M11 or R72 north out of East London en route to Beacon Bay. Cross Batting Bridge, and take the first turn to the right into Beaconhurst Drive. Some 500 m past the sports club, the road veers left up the hill to Beacon Bay; turn right here into Blue Water Road. Park on the verge opposite the block of flats and walk down the gravel road to the stile marking the start of the Dassie Trail. To reach the mouth of the Nahoon River on the eastern side, continue up Beaconhurst Drive and turn right at the Engen garage into Hillcrest Drive. Continue to the Blue Lagoon Hotel car-park, and follow the path and boardwalk through the dune forest to the beach.

Amalinda Nature Reserve: To reach Amalinda, proceed north up Oxford Street and turn left into Connaught Avenue at the traffic lights near the museum. Drive past the hospital and shopping centre, and turn left 4.6 km after the museum (the reserve is signposted), and then right at McClelland Centre.

Umtiza: Proceed north up Oxford Street and turn left into Connaught Avenue at the traffic lights near the museum. Continue past the hospital along Amalinda Main Road. Where the road takes a sharp right (just before Crewe School), turn left into Woolwash Road and immediately left into Buffalo Pass Road. Cross over the bridge to the reserve entrance. Park near the second gate. The reserve is open during daylight hours. There are picnic and braai areas, and walking trails.

Gonubie: To reach Gonubie Nature Reserve, follow the North-East expressway from East London to the N2, and take the Gonubie off-ramp. Turn right onto the M10 to Gonubie, then right into Seventh Street (just before the Municipal Offices). Continue until you reach the T-junction; turn right again to the entrance and parking area, 100 m ahead. The reserve entrance is about 1 km from the Gonubie River Estuary. It is equipped with a good hide, which is open on weekdays (keys can be obtained at the local branch of BirdLife SA ☎). The reserve can also be birded by walking around the perimeter fence.

Warbler, which may visit from higher altitudes during winter months. Forest and thicket birding is productive, with **Brown** and **White-browed Scrub-Robins**, **Red-capped** and **Chorister Robin-Chats**, **Olive Bush-Shrike**, **Southern Tchagra***, **Dark-backed Weaver**, **Knysna Turaco**, **Knysna*** and **Olive Woodpeckers**, **African Dusky Flycatcher** and **Cape Batis**. The krantz opposite the mangrove forest is a favourite area for **Trumpeter** and **Crowned Hornbills**.

Amalinda Nature Reserve: The mix of habitats in this 134 ha reserve produce a diversity of species. Scan the reservoir for water birds (including **Giant** and **Malachite Kingfishers**), and listen in summer for **Marsh-Warbler** in thickets surrounding the dam. **Lesser Swamp** and **Little Rush Warblers**, **Thick-billed**, **Cape** and **Yellow Weavers**, **Southern Red Bishop** and **Fan-tailed Widowbird** all occur in the reedbeds. Forest patches hold **Red-capped Robin-Chat**. Typically bushveld species here include **Orange-breasted Bush-Shrike**, **Chinspot Batis** and **White-browed Scrub-Robin**.

Umtiza Nature Reserve: Umtiza is a large tract of protected forest and the excellent network of trails provides access to the best forest birding in East London. Forest birds are best located by walking slowly and quietly along the paths, listening for mixed-species foraging flocks and stopping frequently. Look out for **Knysna Woodpecker***, **Knysna Turaco**, **Narina Trogon***, **Yellow-throated Woodland-Warbler**, **Brown Scrub-Robin**, **Red-capped** and **Chorister Robin-Chats**, **Blue-mantled Crested Flycatcher**, **Dark-backed Weaver**, **Olive Bush-Shrike** and **Ashy Flycatcher**. Scan the rivers with overhanging vegetation for **African Finfoot***, which is resident here.

Gonubie Nature Reserve: This small reserve provides wetland birding, including breeding **Grey Crowned Crane**.

Skulking reed dwellers are the reserve's speciality, and patience should also reveal **Little Bittern**, **African Rail**, **Black Crake**, **Great Reed-Warbler** (summer), **African Purple Swamphen** and **Baillon's Crake**.

NEARBY SITES: Black-winged Lapwing may be seen on the short grass at Potter's Pass Nature Reserve, along Marine Drive near the Grand Prix track in East London.

Pelagic trips may be organised from East London (see p.23).

D. Bristow/Photo Access

The Eastern Cape coast offers both forest and grassland specials.

78 Morgan Bay ✔

Morgan Bay, and the adjacent Kei Mouth and Double Mouth, offers a good combination of forest, grassland and estuarine birding. The turn-off to Morgan Bay is signposted off the R349 (accessed 50 km east of East London on the N2) shortly before Kei Mouth. The Morgan Bay Hotel offers accommodation and staff here can direct you to the best forest and grassland walks in the area.

The forests and rank grasslands surrounding the dam, 1.3 km beyond Morgan Bay on the road leading to Kei Mouth, provide good birding opportunities. The sheltered valleys support **African Crowned** and **Long-crested Eagles**, **Buff-spotted Flufftail**, **Narina Trogon***, **White-starred Robin**, **Brown Scrub-Robin**, **Chorister Robin-Chat**, **Knysna*** and **Olive Woodpeckers**, **African Emerald Cuckoo** and a variety of other typical coastal forest species. Many of the **Green Woodhoopoes** in this area have leg-rings as part of a long-term study to examine their social behaviour. **Trumpeter** and **Crowned Hornbills** are common in the Morgan Bay village itself. **Red-necked Spurfowl** call in the early morning and late afternoon and are occasionally seen crossing the roads. **Black-rumped Buttonquail**, **Croaking Cisticola** and **Broad-tailed Warbler** occur in moist grasslands on the ridges, while areas with sparser grass (often burnt) are best for **Black-winged Lapwing**. **Grey Crowned Crane** may be seen at the estuary.

79 Naudésnek ✔✔

This mountain pass in the southern Drakensberg offers vehicle-bound birders a good selection of mountain and high-altitude grassland endemics, similar to those of Sani Pass.

SPECIALS: Drakensberg Rock-jumper, Ground Woodpecker*, Sentinel Rock-Thrush, Drakensberg Siskin, Cape Vulture*, Lammergeier*, Mountain and African Rock* Pipits.

SEASON: Spring to autumn (Sept-Apr); peak time Oct-Mar.

HABITATS: High-altitude grassland, mountain slopes, wooded kloofs.

BIRDING: Follow the road that leads beyond Rhodes to the grassy moorlands at the top of Naudésnek, the highest pass in South Africa at 2 740 m. **Mountain Pipit** is very common on open grassy fields at the top of the pass in summer, but beware confusion with the closely similar **African Pipit**. Look out for **Drakensberg Rock-jumper**, **Ground Woodpecker***, **Sentinel Rock-Thrush** and **African Rock Pipit*** on rocky outcrops close to the road towards the top of the pass. **Drakensberg Siskin** and **Wailing Cisticola** should also be seen, and scan above for **Cape Vulture*** and **Lammergeier***. **Grey-winged Francolin** also occurs in these pastures, and **Yellow-breasted Pipit*** is recorded from moister grasslands on the Maclear side of the pass. Lower down, the road traverses thicket-lined streams where **Barratt's Warbler** occurs.

Callan Cohen

The alpine heights of Naudésnek

GETTING THERE

To get to Rhodes from Aliwal North, travel on the R58 to Barkly East and then on the R396 to Rhodes. Rhodes can also be approached from Queenstown via the N6; take the R56 turn-off to Dordrecht. Vehicle access in the area is via gravel roads. Good accommodation is available in the village of Rhodes.

80 Karoo Nature Reserve, Graaff-Reinet

IBA ✔

The reserve, the western section of which is easily reached on the Murraysburg Road (R63) from Graaff-Reinet, offers a range of easy-to-see Karoo specials. A drive into the Valley of Desolation, situated within the reserve, well worth the effort for its scenic splendour alone, is a good area for **Verreaux's Eagle**, **Pale-winged Starling** and **Layard's Tit-Babbler**.

Search the open plains for **Sickle-winged Chat**, **Chat Flycatcher** and **Rufous-eared Warbler**, and the acacia-lined watercourses for **Pririt Batis**, **Southern Tchagra***, and **Namaqua Warbler***.

In the flat country to the south of Graaff-Reinet (travelling along the R75 towards Jansenville), **Kori** and **Ludwig's* Bustards** and **Karoo** and **Northern Black Korhaans** are all commonly seen. Commando Drift Dam Nature Reserve, situated 58 km from Cradock on the Cradock/Tarkastad gravel road, offers good Karoo birding with acacia thickets (**Namaqua Warbler***) and open plains (**Ludwig's Bustard***). The Bosberg Nature Reserve adjacent to Somerset East has patches of Afromontane forest that are good for **Bush Blackcap***.

81 Hogsback

✔✔

Forest patches surrounding this quiet mountain town offer excellent forest birding, and include the most southerly population of **Orange Ground-Thrush**, as well as **Cape Parrot***, which overflies the town.

SPECIALS: Cape Parrot*, Orange Ground-Thrush, Bush Blackcap*, Knysna Woodpecker*, Brown Scrub-Robin, African Emerald Cuckoo, African Crowned, Martial and Long-crested Eagles, African Wood-Owl, Cape Eagle-Owl*, Grey-winged Francolin and Buff-streaked Chat.

SEASON: Early summer months (Sept-Dec) are best, although birding is generally good all year round.

HABITATS: Indigenous forest, exotic plantation, montane grassland, protea stands.

BIRDING: There is good birding in the village, where you can see **Cape Batis**, **Cape** and **Forest Canaries**, **Black** and **African Emerald Cuckoos**, **Southern Black Flycatcher** and a variety of sunbirds. Raptors include **African Harrier Hawk** and **African Crowned**, **Martial** and **Long-crested Eagles**. At dusk, flocks of **Cape Parrot*** may be seen flying overhead to their roosts. In the indigenous forest, such as that along the walk to the Big Tree or the contour path, look for **Orange Ground-Thrush**, **Brown Scrub-Robin**, **Chorister Robin-Chat**, **White-**

GETTING THERE

Hogsback is 270 km from Port Elizabeth. When approaching from Fort Beaufort, take the R63 eastwards for 25 km, then turn north onto the R345. Hogsback is a further 25 km along this road. A permit, obtained from the Forestry Office during working hours or from the Forest Guard on duty at Oak Avenue over weekends, is required. Access in the area is mostly on gravel roads and walking paths. Good accommodation is available.

Hein von Hörsten/IOA

Look out for Cape Parrot above the forests at Hogsback.

starred Robin, **Bush Blackcap***, and **Olive** and **Knysna* Woodpeckers**. In the exotic plantations, look for **Yellow-fronted Canary, Streaky-headed Seed-eater, Grey Cuckooshrike, Barratt's Warbler** (scrub along the edges), **Yellow-throated Woodland-Warbler, Green-backed Camaroptera**, and **Red-necked Spurfowl**; at night, listen for **African Wood-Owl**. In the mountain fynbos and grassland, such as on Gaika's Kop on the road to Cathcart, **Southern Red** and **Yellow-crowned Bishops, Denham's Bustard*, Blue** and **Grey Crowned Cranes, Common Quail, Secretarybird**, and **Cape Longclaw** all occur. Also look out for **Sentinel Rock-Thrush, Mountain Wheatear, Sickle-winged Chat, Cape Eagle-Owl*, Ground Woodpecker*** and **Drakensberg Rock-jumper** (scarce) in high, rocky areas.
OTHER ANIMALS: Hogsback supports the most southerly population of Samango Monkey.
NEARBY SITES: The Kologha Forest near Stutterheim offers another extensive patch of Afromontane forest, and offers similar specials to Hogsback, including the endangered **Cape Parrot***. Continue out of Stutterheim on the gravel road to Keiskammahoek until the turn-off (to the right after 7 km) to the Kologha picnic site and forest trails. A series of trails is laid out from here that offer good birding; look out for **Cape Parrot*, Knysna Turaco, Orange Ground-Thrush, White-starred Robin, Brown Scrub-Robin, Chorister Robin-Chat, Bush Blackcap*, Narina Trogon*** and others. Along the forest margins look for raptors such as **African Crowned** and **Long-crested Eagles**, and **Forest Buzzard***. The marshy areas are home to **Red-chested Flufftail** and **Dark-capped Yellow Warbler**. The montane grassland above the forest is worthwhile for grassland species such as **Buff-streaked Chat, Ground Woodpecker***, both **Cape** and **Gurney's Sugarbirds***, and **Wing-snapping, Wailing** and **Levaillant's Cisticolas**.

82 Greater Addo National Park IBA ✔

The park, originally set aside for a small herd of Elephant, has been expanded to include six different biomes, including Afromontane forest patches in the northern Zuurberg section. In the main Elephant Park, the pachyderms tend to overshadow the birding, although the park does offer a variety of western endemics, as well as more common and widespread eastern species. The best drive for birding is the Nzipondo loop: look out for **Southern Black Korhaan, Secretarybird, Blue Crane, Southern Tchagra*, Green-spotted Wood-Dove** and **Pearl-breasted Swallow**, among others.

Denham's Bustard* may be encountered on the Gorah loop. Reintroduced **Red-billed Oxpecker** (scarce) occurs on game animals. Raptors include **Jackal Buzzard, Southern Pale Chanting Goshawk**, and **Martial** and **Booted Eagles**. Birding is good around the camp, and **Black Crake** can be seen from the bird hide at the pond. **Cape** and **Dark-capped Bulbuls** occur side by side in the camp, and these two species and **African Red-eyed Bulbul** have all been recorded hybridising in the Eastern Cape.

The main gate is 15 km north of Addo village (approximately 85 km north of Port Elizabeth on the R335). There are chalets and a camping area in the park, as well as privately run camps. A tarred road leads to the park, and good gravel roads traverse it.

The Alexandria Forest Reserve, signposted from Alexandria town, is now part of the Greater Addo National Park. Look out for **Brown Scrub-Robin, Crowned** and **Trumpeter Hornbills, Knysna Turaco, Red-fronted Tinkerbird** and a host of forest species along the well-maintained trail.

83 Mountain Zebra National Park ✔✔

Located south-west of Cradock, this reserve offers good Karoo birding with an excellent list of South African endemics.
SPECIALS: Layard's Tit-Babbler, Namaqua Warbler*, Karoo Prinia, White-throated Canary, Cape Eagle-Owl*, Ground Woodpecker*, Large-billed, Spike-heeled and Eastern Clapper Larks, African Rock Pipit*, and Lesser Kestrel.

> **GETTING THERE**
> The park is situated just off the R61 that runs between Cradock and Graaff-Reinet. Take the Middelburg road out of Cradock and turn onto the Graaff-Reinet road after 4.2 km. The turn-off to the park is 6 km further on. The park has good gravel roads, a restaurant, chalets and a camping ground.

SEASON: Birding is good year-round.
HABITATS: Acacia thornveld, karroid scrub, rocky mountain slopes, grassy plateaux.
BIRDING: Birding is good from the main circular drive, as well as from walks starting from the camp. As with many other parks, birding is excellent in and around the camp itself, and **African Rock Pipit*** may be seen on the rocky hillsides above the hutted camp (listen for its distinctive call). Also scan the steep, rocky slopes for **Cinnamon-breasted** and **Cape Buntings, Ground Woodpecker*, Cape** and **Sentinel Rock-Thrushes, Mountain Wheatear**, and **Pale-winged Starling**. Scrubby hillsides should be searched for **Layard's Tit-Babbler, Dusky Sunbird, Black-headed Canary*** and **White-throated Seed-eater**, while **Sickle-winged Chat** and **Rufous-eared Warbler** prefer flatter areas. Thicker areas of acacia thornveld hold **Southern Boubou, Southern Tchagra*** and **Red-fronted Tinkerbird**.

Flat areas with grass hold **Large-billed, Spike-heeled** and **Eastern Clapper Larks**, while **Namaqua Warbler*** is to be found in reedbeds and thickets along watercourses. Raptors include **Verreaux's** and **Booted Eagles, Jackal Buzzard, African Goshawk, Rock Kestrel, African Harrier Hawk** and **Cape Eagle-Owl***. **Buff-streaked Chat** occurs on the Kranskop Loop.
OTHER ANIMALS: The park was formed to protect the endangered Cape Mountain Zebra, especially since its numbers were reduced to less than 50 individuals last century.

84 Wild Coast

IBA ✔✔

The area north of the Kei River offers several remote sites with fantastic birding potential. Access is quite feasible, but most areas take longer to get to than other comparable birding spots in KwaZulu-Natal and further south.

Superb coastal forests are found at Wavecrest (Nxaxo), Dwesa and Cwebe Nature Reserves, Silaka Nature Reserve (between Port St Johns and Umgazi Mouth), Hluleka Nature Reserve and Mkambati Nature Reserve (contact local tourism authorities for access information and road conditions). **Mangrove Kingfisher*** and **Spotted Ground-Thrush***, both best located by their calls in summer, may be fairly common in these forests, along with a host of more widespread specials such as **Knysna Woodpecker*** and **Brown Scrub-Robin**. At night, listen for **Barred Owlet** (rare – see box below) and the haunting calls of Southern Tree Hyrax, which emanate from the forest.

Short grasslands along the Wild Coast should be scanned for **Black-winged Lapwing**. Wavecrest is well known for the **Grey Crowned Crane** that roost here. Mkambati, accessed via Flagstaff, is the largest reserve and includes spectacular scenery (with two **Cape Vulture*** colonies). In addition to forest patches, it has extensive rolling grasslands (look for **Southern Ground-Hornbill*, Swamp Nightjar** and **Broad-tailed Warbler**). A lone pair of **Egyptian Vulture** is believed to be resident in the northern part of this region in the vicinity of the Tsitsa and Tina river gorges, and is seen from time to time from the N2 in this area.

> **BARRED OWLET REDISCOVERED**
> A curiously isolated and little-known *capense* subspecies of this secretive owl, described in 1834 from Kenton-on-Sea, was rediscovered in the area as recently as 1980. There are no reliable sites for this species, but there have been a handful of recent records at Bathurst and Hluleka Nature Reserve on the Wild Coast (with unconfirmed records of the bird calling from the camp site at Cremorne Estate ☎ near **Port St Johns**). Searching dense riverine woodlands and forests of the Wild Coast might reveal other sites in which this owl may be found. Please contact the authors ☎ if you do have any updated records.

ROUTE 9

SOUTHERN KWAZULU-NATAL

The lush, subtropical coast south of Durban is one of South Africa's premier domestic tourist destinations. Though greatly fragmented by holiday homes, golf courses and retirement villages, much of the coastal forest remains intact, providing excellent forest birding. At Port Shepstone, the N2 swings inland to avoid the rugged coastal topography, climbing through a cool mist-belt region, which eventually rises to the ramparts of the Drakensberg range that form the international boundary with Lesotho. Sani Pass is by far the most famous and frequently visited site in the southern highlands and provides easy access to the full range of high-altitude Drakensberg endemics, although visits to some of the lesser-known sites may reward the discerning birder with a selection of highly sought-after species that are difficult to find elsewhere in the southern African subregion.

For the visitor with little time, the key sites in southern KwaZulu-Natal are the Southport area (Magpie Mannikin*), Oribi Gorge Nature Reserve (Knysna Woodpecker*), Mount Currie Nature Reserve (Striped Flufftail*), Sani Pass (high-altitude specials, Bush Blackcap*) and the Creighton area (Black-rumped Buttonquail, Cape Parrot* and Blue Swallow*), all of which could be covered on a brisk four-day loop. Vernon Crookes Nature Reserve and Umdoni Park offer diverse birding close to Durban.

TOP 10 BIRDS

- Lammergeier
- Drakensberg Rock-Jumper
- Drakensberg Siskin
- Mountain Pipit
- Cape Parrot
- Blue Swallow
- Southern Bald Ibis
- Black-rumped Buttonquail
- Magpie Mannikin
- Knysna Woodpecker

Nigel Dennis/OA

Sani Pass is a top site for montane specials such as Lammergeier.

85 Umdoni Park ✔

Situated a mere 50 km south of Durban's international airport along the N2, Umdoni Park makes an excellent first stop on a loop through southern KwaZulu-Natal, but can also easily be covered as a day trip from Durban. The mosaic of forest, grassland and golf course incorporated into this private residential estate provides an excellent opportunity to track down a variety of tricky forest birds.

Specials to watch and listen for are **Scaly-throated Honeyguide**, **Narina Trogon***, **Green Malkoha** and **Brown Scrub-Robin**, all of which are common here. **Spotted Ground-Thrush*** is regular in small numbers in winter, and is best seen in the early morning near the cottage on the left en route to the trails' parking area. The scrubby forest edges are especially suited to seed-eaters, making Umdoni Park one of the best sites in the country for **Grey Waxbill**. **Red-backed Mannikin** is plentiful, but study flocks carefully, as the rare **Magpie Mannikin*** is also possible. Other noteworthy forest birds fairly common here include both **Knysna** and **Purple-crested Turacos**, **Lemon** and **Tambourine Doves**, **Grey Cuckooshrike**, **Square-tailed Drongo**, **Black-bellied Starling**, and **Grey Sunbird**.

To reach the site from the north, turn off the N2 at the Umzinto North/Park Rynie/Pennington sign and head east towards the coast (or continue straight across the N2 if coming from Vernon Crookes Nature Reserve), bearing right at the traffic lights on the R102 towards Pennington. Turn left into Pennington after 8.5 km and follow the indistinct signs to the Umdoni Park Golf Course. The boom gate to the estate is reached after a further 1.6 km. Continue past the 'Wildlife Society Trails and Parking' sign on the right (100 m past the boom) to the clubhouse, where you can park and obtain permission to bird in the park.

Take the 2 km long track, which passes through forest patches and along the edge of the golf course, to the trails' parking area. There is good birding along the way. The final 500 m (before you reach a permanently chained gate) winds through superb coastal forest, where the full range of coastal forest birds may be found.

86 Vernon Crookes Nature Reserve ✔✔

Vernon Crookes is a popular venue among Durban's birding fraternity, providing high quality grassland and forest birding close to Durban, and boasting a bird list that exceeds 300 species. Although its forest birds are more easily found elsewhere, the reserve remains one of the best sites in the country for such elusive grassland species as **Pale-crowned Cisticola** and **Broad-tailed Warbler**.

SPECIALS: Knysna Turaco, Narina Trogon*, African Crowned Eagle, Grey Crowned Crane, Pale-crowned Cisticola, Broad-tailed Warbler, Short-tailed Pipit* and Green Twinspot*.

SEASON: Summer is the best time for the grassland specials, although the forest is productive year-round.

HABITATS: Coastal forest and grassland, acacia woodland, man-made dams.

BIRDING: An indistinct walking trail starts 25 m uphill of the first picnic site (2.2 km beyond the entrance gate Ⓐ); this productive grassland area holds both **Broad-tailed Warbler** and **Short-tailed Pipit***. However, the latter is tricky and only in short grass.

Listen for the distinctive '*twink!*' display call of the warbler emanating from unburnt grassy slopes along the trail, or scan for them perched on grass stems in the early morning. **Short-tailed Pipit*** is even more secretive (Oct-Nov is best), and is usually only seen when flushed underfoot. The pipits may also be found on burnt grasslands in winter, but even then they remain inconspicuous. Another highly sought-after grassland denizen which is occasionally found here is the **Black-rumped Buttonquail**, but

GETTING THERE

The reserve is located 80 km south of Durban, off the N2 at Park Rynie/Umzinto. Head inland along the R612 for 12 km; turn right at the signpost, and continue a further 4 km to the reserve entrance. An entrance fee is payable at the gate, which is open from dawn to dusk. Facilities include a 12 km road network, several excellent hiking trails, a picnic site and chalet accommodation.

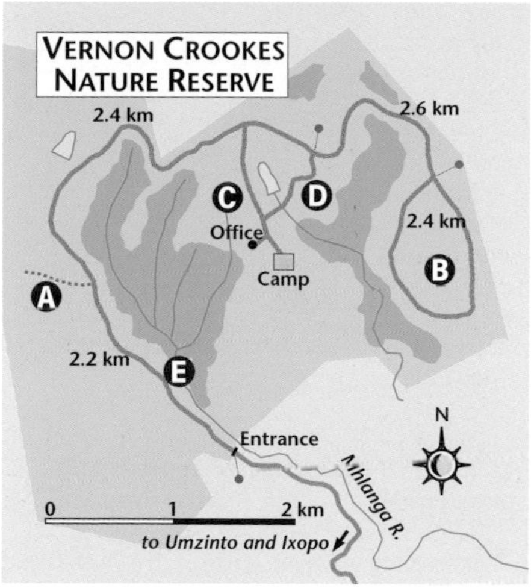

beware of confusion with the more common **Kurrichane Buttonquail**.

Further exploration on foot is likely to be rewarded, as the above specials may also be found in suitable habitat elsewhere in the reserve. The shorter grassland of the high plateau Ⓑ is best for **Croaking, Pale-crowned** and **Zitting Cisticolas**, all of which are easily found along the loop road beyond the office.

Grey Crowned Crane has nested on the dam near the office Ⓒ. A variety of forest birds, notably **Green Malkoha, Brown Scrub-Robin, Knysna Turaco**, and **Green Twinspot***, may be seen from the excellent loop trails that start at the main picnic site Ⓓ. Listen for **African Broadbill** at Ⓔ.

OTHER ANIMALS: Larger mammals in the park include Plains Zebra, Blue Wildebeest, Blesbok, Impala, Oribi, Southern Reedbuck, Bushbuck, Blue and Common Duikers, and Vervet Monkey; African Clawless Otter, Cape Porcupine, and Large Grey Mongoose are less frequently encountered inhabitants.

MAGPIE MANNIKIN

The small village of Southport, situated on the R102 south of Hibberdene, has become famous as the only reliable site in South Africa for the localised and highly erratic **Magpie Mannikin***. Originally discovered in the area by a local resident, who contacted her birding son in Durban with concerns that she was 'overfeeding the Bronze Mannikins', this rare bird is most easily seen at feeder tables in private gardens. A local birder may be contacted to arrange a sighting ☎. Alternatively, spending time in the area may reveal small flocks flying overhead.

Turn inland (west) off the R102 in Southport, 16 km south of its northern junction with the N2, and immediately left into Kloof Rd. The birds inhabit well-wooded gardens along this road.

87 Oribi Gorge Nature Reserve ✔✔

Situated less than 2 hours' drive from Durban, the spectacularly scenic Oribi Gorge is famous among birders as a convenient KwaZulu-Natal site for the endemic **Knysna Woodpecker***, but also boasts a fine supporting cast of forest birds, notably **African Crowned Eagle, Spotted Ground-Thrush*** and **Brown Scrub-Robin**.

SPECIALS: Knysna Woodpecker*, Narina Trogon*, Trumpeter Hornbill, African Crowned Eagle, Spotted Ground-Thrush*, Brown Scrub-Robin, and Green Twinspot*.

SEASON: The specials are present year-round; winter is often extremely productive.

HABITATS: Scarp forest, small patches of coastal grassland.

BIRDING: Knysna Woodpecker* is fairly common but inconspicuous in the gorge and may be found at any point along the road. Listen for its

GETTING THERE

The reserve is signposted from the N2, 20 km inland of Port Shepstone. Watch for the KwaZulu-Natal Wildlife Reserve sign (i.e. do not take the first sign-posted turn-off to Oribi). Birding is easiest from the tarred road that traverses the gorge, although a number of hiking trails allow fuller exploration. An excellent visitors' guide, sold at the office, contains a park map and lists of birds, mammals and trees. Self-catered hutted accommodation and camping is available at the rest camp.

'squeaky gate' call, or follow mixed flocks of forest birds with which it frequently associates. Search especially at the first picnic site Ⓐ, or along the final stretch of road before the Umzimkulwane River Ⓑ.

A pair of **African Crowned Eagle** has nested in a large, roadside tree uphill from the first picnic site, which is also frequented by a wide variety of forest birds, notably **Knysna Turaco**, **Grey Cuckooshrike**, **Olive Bush-Shrike** and **Yellow-throated Woodland-Warbler**. The open grassland area 500 m downhill from the picnic area Ⓒ is an excellent site for **Green Twinspot***, **Grey** and **Swee Waxbills**, and **Red-backed Mannikin**, while **African Broadbill*** (of the scarce *capensis* subspecies) is often heard along the forest edges here.

Oribi Gorge

The Hoopoe Falls Walk Ⓓ follows the Umzimkulwane River upstream along its northern bank, passing through superb forest, where **Narina Trogon***, **Lemon Dove**, **Spotted Ground-Thrush*** (winter), **Brown Scrub-Robin** and **Barratt's Warbler** all occur. **Knysna Warbler*** has also been recorded in the area.

Scan the river and river banks for **African Black Duck**, **African Finfoot**, **Half-collared Kingfisher** (scarce) and **Mountain Wagtail**, as well as African Clawless Otter. Back at the rest camp Ⓔ, a walk along the short Baboon View Walk, which loops down to the edge of Oribi Gorge, should turn up **Lanner Falcon**, **Cape Rock-Thrush**, **Mocking Cliff-Chat** and **Striped Pipit** along the cliffs. Listen for **Freckled Nightjar** at night.

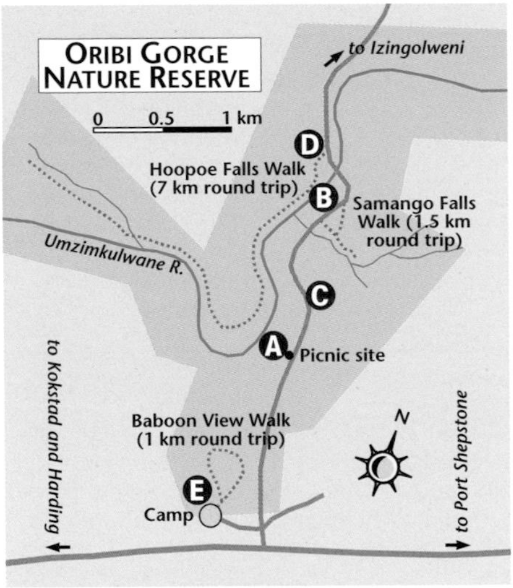

OTHER ANIMALS: Bushbuck, Blue Duiker, Vervet and Samango Monkeys, and African Clawless Otter inhabit the forest, while the antelope for which the reserve is named is restricted to grasslands on the northern side of the gorge, often occurring alongside Common Reedbuck.

NEARBY SITES: Similar species, including **Knysna Woodpecker***, may be found at the Umtamvuna Nature Reserve, which lies inland of Port Edward. The reserve also boasts a colony of the endemic **Cape Vulture***, and **Gurney's Sugarbird*** is present at the ranger's house in winter. From Oribi, the N2 climbs inland through plantations of introduced pine and blue gum, where **Jackal** and **Forest Buzzards** (winter), and **Long-crested Eagle** are often seen on roadside telephone poles.

88 Weza-Ngele Forest

IBA ✔

Weza-Ngele Forest, a relict patch of Afromontane forest, straddles the N2 between Kokstad and Harding, and can be birded either from the roadside or from one of the hiking trails that commence at the well-signposted Ingeli Forest Lodge, 114 km west of Port Shepstone. This is one of the most accessible and reliable sites in southern KwaZulu-Natal for **Forest Buzzard*** (winter), small numbers of which may be seen in flight over the forest, especially at mid-morning. Purchase a permit and trail map from the lodge.

Other Afromontane forest specials encountered along the trails include **Orange Ground-Thrush** (common) and **Bush Blackcap***. The once numerous **Cape Parrot*** is now rare.

89 Mount Currie Nature Reserve ✔

This small, quiet reserve is a good site for the highly elusive **Striped Flufftail***, which is resident in moist grassland near the camp site at the foot of Mount Currie. Park in the day visitors' parking area, and cross the shallow marsh to the north-eastern side of the reservoir, where two or three pairs of **Striped Flufftail*** inhabit the steep, well-grassed slopes. Their laughing '*ki! kiddy! kiddy!*' alarm calls are often heard, especially in the morning and late afternoon, but this extreme skulker is only likely to be seen after dark during the summer breeding season, when territorial males may be located by careful spotlighting. Pinpointing the birds' exact location is not easy, as the sound seems ventriloquial and the birds stop calling when they detect disturbance, but with luck and patience this beautiful rallid may finally be seen. The best technique is by means of 'triangulation', with at least three people in different positions pointing at the apparent source of the sound. The birds usually freeze momentarily in the torchlight, when they can be studied at leisure, only to resume calling again within minutes.

African Rail and **Red-chested Flufftail** will almost certainly be heard in the nearby marsh. A walk up to the ridge east of the dam should reward the energetic birder with **Ground Woodpecker***, **Buff-streaked Chat** and **Gurney's Sugarbird***.

The reserve lies 5 km north of Kokstad, and is signposted off the R617 to Franklin.

The vast Franklin Marsh holds exciting species such as **White-winged Flufftail** and **Eurasian Bittern**, but is privately owned and difficult to access.

90 Matatiele Mountain IBA ✔✔

One of the best sites in southern Africa for the endemic **Yellow-breasted Pipit***, this mountain south of the remote East Griqualand village of Matatiele (4 hrs from Durban) is also home to **Drakensberg Rock-jumper**, the globally threatened **Rudd's Lark*, Gurney's Sugarbird*** and **Mountain Pipit**. If it wasn't such an out-of-the-way birding location, Matatiele Mountain would rival Sani Pass and Wakkerstroom in excellence.

SPECIALS: Ground Woodpecker*, Cape Eagle-Owl*, Drakensberg Rock-jumper, Buff-streaked Chat, Rudd's Lark*, Gurney's Sugarbird*, and Yellow-breasted*, Striped, African Rock*, African and Mountain Pipits.

SEASON: Best during the summer (Oct-Mar) breeding season.

HABITATS: High-altitude grasslands, protea woodland, rocky gorges; a trout lake and surrounding moist grassland (Mountain Lake Nature Reserve).

BIRDING: Scan the rocky escarpment left of the main track on the initial ascent for **Ground Woodpecker*, Buff-streaked Chat, Mountain Wheatear**, and **African Rock Pipit***. Listen for the pipit's distinctive call at dawn. Roadside protea stands here hold **Gurney's Sugarbird*** and **Malachite Sunbird**, while the first level grassland left of the road a few hundred metres beyond should be carefully combed for the elusive **Short-tailed Pipit***.

After reaching the plateau, turn right into 'High Street' (the last gate on the right before reaching the entrance to Mountain Lake Nature Reserve). This track leads through heavily grazed grasslands that support numerous **Yellow-breasted*** and **Mountain Pipits**, as well as a few pairs of **Rudd's Lark***. **Mountain Pipit** is present only from Oct-Feb, but beware of confusion with the very similar **African Pipit**. **Grey-winged Francolin, Denham's Bustard*, Black-winged Lapwing** and **Black Harrier*** (winter) are other notable

GETTING THERE

The R56 from Kokstad becomes Main Road in Matatiele village. Turn left into Jagger Street and right a further 500 m on, onto a gravel road that continues past a rocky escarpment and protea stands to the radio mast at the top of the mountain plateau. All birding may be done from this mountain road, which becomes tricky during bad weather but is usually accessible with 2WD vehicles. There are no access restrictions. There is a single chalet at Mountain Lake Nature Reserve ☎, atop the mountain, and accommodation is available in Matatiele.

birds in this area. After 3 km, the track reaches a rocky gorge to the left that is home to **Drakensberg Rock-jumper** and a pair of **Cape Eagle-Owl***. **Rufous-chested Sparrowhawk*** may be seen in the eucalyptus stands.
OTHER ANIMALS: Oribi, Grey Rhebok and the scarce Natal Red Rock Rabbit may be seen on the mountain.

91 Sani Pass 4X4 ✔✔✔

The spectacular Sani Pass is justly famous as the most accessible site (a mere 3 hrs from Durban) in southern Africa for the high-altitude specials of the Drakensberg massif, and is an essential stop on any endemic-hunter's birding route. Sightings of such highly sought-after species as **Drakensberg Rock-jumper**, **Gurney's Sugarbird*** and **Drakenberg Siskin** are almost guaranteed on a day trip up the pass in summer.
SPECIALS: Grey-winged Francolin, Ground Woodpecker*, Cape Eagle-Owl*, Lammergeier*, Cape Vulture*, Southern Bald Ibis*, Drakensberg Rock-jumper, Sentinel Rock-Thrush, Buff-streaked Chat, Barratt's Warbler, Bush Blackcap*, Gurney's Sugarbird*, Mountain Pipit, Fairy Flycatcher and Drakensberg Siskin.
SEASON: The best time to visit Sani Pass is in summer (Oct-Feb), when **Mountain Pipit** is present and wild flowers are at their peak.
HABITATS: Protea-studded grasslands, 'Ouhout' (*Leucosidea*) thicket, ericaceous scrub, tussock grass, cliffs and scree slopes, Afro-alpine grassland, seasonal bogs.
BIRDING: Search the 'Ouhout' (*Leucosidea*) thickets near the river, especially near the Mkomazana bridge, 4.2 km past the entrance to Sani Pass Hotel Ⓐ, for **Brown-backed Honeybird, Bush Blackcap*** and **Swee Waxbill**, and the protea stands 3.5 km beyond Ⓑ for **Malachite Sunbird** and **Gurney's Sugarbird***. **Ground Woodpecker*, Cape Rock-Thrush** and **Buff-streaked Chat** are conspicuous on rocky slopes from here to the South African border post Ⓒ, while both **Red-winged Francolin** and **Cape Grassbird** are plentiful but more commonly heard than seen. **Greater Double-**

GETTING THERE

Turn north at Underberg, pass through Himeville, and turn left onto a signposted gravel road 2 km north of Himeville. Although the lower pass is officially open to 2WD vehicles, the condition of the road deteriorates after heavy summer rains, when access may be restricted to 4WD only. The South African border post is open strictly 8am to 4pm, and passports are essential. A range of accommodation is available in Himeville and Underberg, and at the fairly basic but highly recommended Sani Top Chalet, at the head of the pass in Lesotho. The chalet boasts the highest pub in southern Africa (2 874 m), and sells local Maluti Lager – no better place to toast those highland lifers!

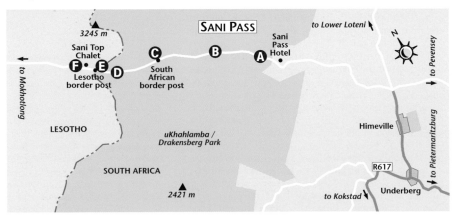

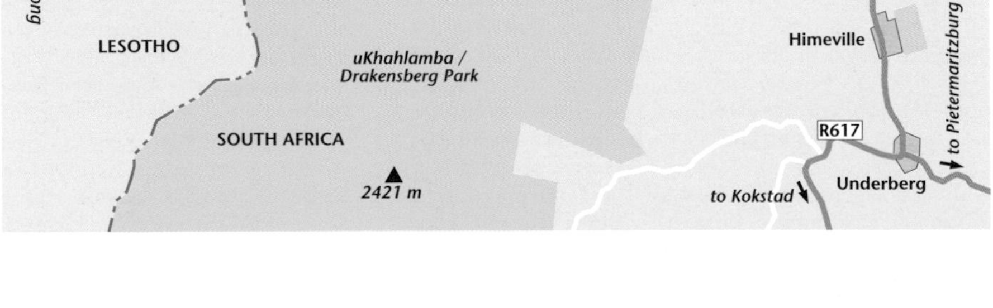

Callan Cohen

Look out for Drakensberg Rock-jumper and Drakensberg Siskin near the top of the pass.

collared Sunbird is regularly seen on the 'red-hot pokers' at the South African border post, while **Barratt's Warbler** and **Drakensberg Prinia** are common in the riverside thicket just beyond. Compare this saffron-breasted prinia with its greyer cousin, **Karoo Prinia**, which occurs in the roadside scrub 5.5 km higher up the pass.

Fairy Flycatcher, **Grey Tit**, **Wailing Cisticola** and **Layard's Tit-Babbler** are also regular in the scrub towards the head of the pass, and in similar habitat in Lesotho. **Drakensberg Rock-jumper** and **Drakensberg Siskin** are frequent on the final switchbacks near the top (D).

Check in at the Lesotho border post (E), then walk across the boggy plains west of the Sani Top Chalet (F), looking for **Southern Bald Ibis***, **Sickle-winged Chat**, **Large-billed Lark** and **Mountain Pipit** (summer only). **Grey-winged Francolin** prefers grassier slopes to the north. **Drakensberg Rock-jumper**, **Sentinel Rock-Thrush** and **Drakensberg Siskin** are frequent around the chalet itself, while **Lammergeier***, **Cape Vulture***, **Verreaux's Eagle** and **Jackal Buzzard** may be seen overhead. The sheer cliffs at the head of the pass are home to **Cape Eagle-Owl***, which is occasionally seen near the chalet at dusk.

A drive further into Lesotho is a worthwhile cultural experience, which may also reward you with **Black Stork** along the river, or **Sickle-winged Chat** and **Yellow Canary** in the karroid scrub.

OTHER ANIMALS: Chacma Baboon, Rock Hyrax, Eland, Mountain Reedbuck and Grey Rhebok are frequently seen on the pass.

NEARBY SITES: Stop frequently along the first 20 km as you drive east of Underberg, as fallow fields here regularly hold **Denham's Bustard***, **Grey Crowned Crane**, **Secretarybird** and **Southern Bald Ibis***.

92 Creighton & Xumeni ✔✔

The secluded village of Creighton makes a good base to explore the surrounding mist-belt forests and grasslands, home to some rare and highly sought-after birds. Foremost among these is the critically endangered **Cape Parrot***.

SPECIALS: Cape Parrot*, Black-rumped Buttonquail, Southern Bald Ibis, Knysna Turaco, Denham's Bustard*, Southern Bald Ibis*, Orange Ground-Thrush, Chorister Robin-Chat, Buff-streaked Chat, Barratt's and Broad-tailed Warblers, Bush Blackcap*, Gurney's Sugarbird*, Swee Waxbill, and Forest Canary.

SEASON: Although most of the specials are resident, summer is a more rewarding time to visit.

GETTING THERE

Follow the R612 through Donnybrook and bear right – 20 km south of the town – to Creighton. There is dedicated birders' accommodation in the area, where one can hire a guide to arrange access to private land ☎.

Blue Swallow is threatened by commercial forestry.

HABITATS: Scattered patches of mist-belt forest and grassland, upland marshes, agricultural fields.
BIRDING: Various patches of relict Afromontane forest remain in the area, the most accessible of which is Xumeni, near Donnybrook. A dirt road runs through the tiny forest from behind the Donnybrook railway station; to reach it, turn off the R612 just north of the railway bridge that lies 1 km north of town.

Xumeni's most famous residents are its **Cape Parrots***, at least a few pairs of which still survive here. If you stand any chance of seeing this mega-rarity, you will have to wait at the forest edge in the very early morning (before the mist lifts) or late afternoon, and listen for their high-pitched flight calls as they circle over the forest.

Other forest species may be found by walking slowly along the forestry track through the trees (a distance of 1 km), and exploring the few trails that lead off from the track. **Bush Blackcap*** is resident along the forest edge at the start of the track, where **Barratt's Warbler** and **Swee Waxbill** are also relatively common. Look out for **African Goshawk** and the less numerous **Forest Buzzard*** overhead. Further into the forest, listen for the calls of mixed-species foraging flocks, which may contain **Olive Woodpecker**, **Grey Cuckooshrike**, **Blue-mantled Crested Flycatcher**, **Cape Batis**, **Bar-throated Apalis** and **Yellow-throated Woodland-Warbler**. The far-carrying calls of **African Emerald Cuckoo** and **Knysna Turaco** dominate the forest in summer, while the softer, more melodious songs of **Orange Ground-Thrush**, **White-starred Robin** and **Chorister Robin-Chat** are the best means of locating these skulkers.

Larger, less accessible forest patches elsewhere in the Creighton area share a similar avifauna, although many boast larger populations of **Cape Parrot***. Ask a local for advice.

The farmlands and remaining grassland areas (mostly privately owned land) around the village of Creighton support such difficult species as **Black-rumped Buttonquail** (more reliable here than at any other site in South Africa), **Blue Swallow***, **Short-tailed Pipit*** and **Broad-tailed Warbler**, although numbers vary from year to year according to rainfall and grassland conditions.

93 Impendle Nature Reserve

IBA ✔

This site is easily accessed on a day trip from Pietermaritzburg, or as a side trip en route to Sani Pass. The bulk of the reserve, which lies north of the Mkomazi River some 50 km west of Pietermaritzburg, consists of mid-altitude grassland favoured by **Blue Swallow***; at least three pairs of these handsome birds breed here annually. A walk through the reserve between Oct and Mar should almost guarantee a sighting, as well as offering **Broad-tailed Warbler**.

Contact the Officer in Charge ☎ to arrange a visit. There are currently no amenities in the reserve.

Take the R617 between Underberg and Howick and just west of the village of Boston, take the gravel road to Impendle (approximately 45 km before Howick). The reserve is signposted 9.6 km along this road.

ROUTE 10
DURBAN & PIETERMARITZBURG

Durban's subtropical climate and warm ocean have made it a popular destination for holiday-makers seeking sun and surf, while for the itinerant birder it serves as a gateway to the country's most bird-rich province. The Greater Durban Metropolitan area alone boasts over 350 species of bird, although almost all of these may be found more easily on the birding loops to the north or south of the city. For those with limited time, a few hours' birding the Bayhead mudflats and mangroves before heading north is time well spent, as this is the most accessible site in South Africa for Terek Sandpiper, Greater Sand Plover, Lesser Black-backed Gull (summer), and also Mangrove Kingfisher* (winter). For those with more time, or those mixing business with pleasure, there is much of interest in and around the city. Consider an early morning visit to one of the coastal forest reserves or the Umgeni River Mouth, or, using Durban as a base, take a day trip to the excellent Shongweni Resources Reserve and Umvoti River Mouth.

TOP 10 BIRDS

- Red-headed Quelea
- Mangrove Kingfisher
- Spotted Ground-Thrush
- African Crowned Eagle
- Lesser Black-backed Gull
- Black-winged Lapwing
- Pale-crowned Cisticola
- Terek Sandpiper
- Brown-backed Honeybird
- Baillon's Crake

The so-called Natal Midlands is centred on the provincial capital of Pietermaritzburg, which lies approximately 80 km inland of Durban at an altitude of 900 m. A diverse array of habitats, including montane grasslands, mist-belt forest and thornveld, is protected in reserves a short drive from the city centre, providing a host of superb birding opportunities. Afromontane forest endemics and a breeding population of localised Red-headed Quelea* are likely to be the main attractions for birders, but the Midlands is also an excellent area in which to search for more widely distributed but scarce species that often 'slip through the net' on a birding tour of South Africa, such as Coqui Francolin, Baillon's Crake and Dark-capped Yellow Warbler.

Peter Steyn

This route is one of the best areas on the continent for seeing African Crowned Eagle.

SITES IN AND AROUND DURBAN

94 Durban Bayhead

R ✔✔

The most accessible and productive birding area in the harbour is at Durban Bayhead, where the remnant patch of mangroves and some mudflats have been afforded protection in the Bayhead Heritage Site. The area is an important wintering site for Palearctic waders, with **Common Whimbrel**, **Common Greenshank**, **Curlew Sandpiper**, **Grey** and **Common Ringed Plovers**, and smaller numbers of **Terek Sandpiper**, **White-fronted Plover** (uncommon) and **Greater Sand Plover** (rare). The best time for waders is two hours before high tide (consult the local newspapers for exact times), when the feeding shorebirds are pushed towards the bird hide by the advancing water. At peak high tide, the waders may move up to the artificial dune 100 m to the north of the hide. A telescope is very useful here.

Scan **Common Tern** roosts for the occasional **Lesser Crested Tern** (mid- to late summer), and check the gulls carefully as **Hartlaub's Gull** (a rarity on the east coast) and **Lesser Black-backed Gull** (summer migrants) are sometimes seen. **Common Black-headed**, **Franklin's** and **Slender-billed Gulls** have been recorded as vagrants. **Osprey** is frequent in the bay, while **African Fish-Eagle** is commonly seen overhead. **Little Bee-eater**, **Rattling Cisticola** and **Brimstone Canary** are all numerous in the vicinity of the hide.

At least four **Mangrove Kingfishers** frequent the mangroves in winter (end Mar to end Sept) and these are best sought out from the path along the eastern side of the mangroves. Listen for their far-carrying calls, or scan the forest edge in the early morning, when they often perch out in the open. They usually retreat into the mangroves later in the day, and may be seen along the mangrove boardwalk, where **Black-throated Wattle-eye** (uncommon) and **Purple-banded Sunbird** also occur.

To reach Bayhead from the Durban city centre, follow the signs to Maydon Wharf from the south-western end of Victoria Embankment, bearing left into Maydon Road. After passing

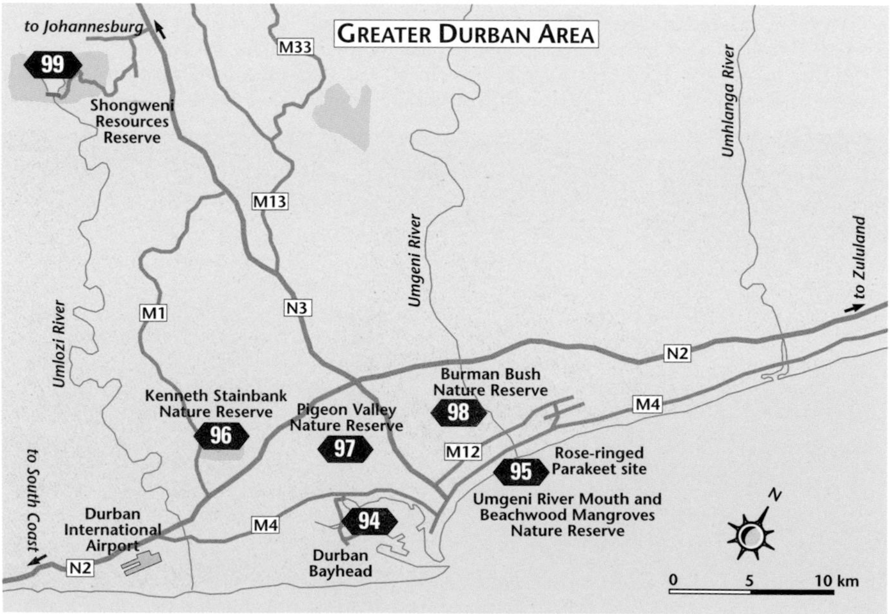

the dry dock, turn left into Bayhead Road, and left again (signposted) into the harbour area shortly after crossing the Mhlatuzana River canal. Just after the railway bridge at the northern end of the mangroves, turn left again to the parking area.

95 Umgeni River Mouth R ✔✔

The estuarine habitats near the mouth of the Umgeni River support a wide range of water birds, and at the same time provide the vagrant-hunter with one of the best sites in KwaZulu-Natal for unexpected avian visitors.

SPECIALS: Lesser Black-backed Gull and Terek Sandpiper.

SEASON: Oct-Mar.

HABITATS: Estuarine mudflats and river, with adjacent mangroves.

BIRDING: The number of water birds varies greatly with the season, tides and river water levels, but the highest totals recorded have been at low tide in late summer. Under these conditions, Palearctic waders are present, with small numbers of **Terek Sandpiper**, **Grey Plover** and **Greater Sand Plover** (rare) among the more numerous **Curlew Sandpiper**, **Sanderling**, **Little Stint** and **Common Ringed Plover**.

Red-necked Stint, **Broad-billed Sandpiper**, **African Black Oystercatcher***, **Pacific Golden Plover**, **Mongolian Plover** and **Crab Plover*** have all occurred as vagrants.

Large tern roosts, consisting primarily of **Common Tern**, with lesser numbers of **Caspian**, **Lesser Crested** (uncommon in recent years), **Swift**, **Sandwich**, **Little** and **White-winged Terns**, often form at low tide. **Lesser Black-backed Gull** is a rare summer visitor, and this remains the best place in southern Africa to find this scarce migrant.

Vagrants in these mixed roosts have included **Common Noddy**, **Common Black-headed** and **Franklin's Gulls**, and **Roseate**, **Black-naped**, **Bridled**, **Sooty** and **Black Terns**.

Great White and **Pink-backed Pelicans** are erratic visitors, while **Grey**, **Goliath** and **Purple Herons**, **Sacred Ibis**, **African Spoonbill** and **Woolly-necked Stork** are more regular. A few **Water Thick-knee** (conspicuous by their vocalisations, especially in the evening) reside on the north bank just upstream of the lowest bridge. **Osprey** may fly overhead in summer.

Waterfowl are most plentiful in winter, with **White-faced** and **Yellow-billed Ducks**, and **Egyptian** and **Spur-winged Geese** being the dominant species. A pair of **South African Shelduck**, escapees from the Umgeni Bird Park, 2 km upriver on the north bank, is also occasionally present. The reedbeds upstream of the second (M12) bridge support **Red-faced** and **Rufous-winged Cisticolas** and this is also the best area in which to find **Malachite**, **Pied** and **Giant Kingfishers**, as well as a selection of widowbirds and weavers.

The car-park on the south bank of the river, at the inaccurately named 'Blue Lagoon', provides a vantage point from which to view the sand spit at the mouth of the river, where a tern roost sometimes forms at dusk on a high tide. A telescope is usually necessary to obtain satisfactory views of these birds and of the **Subantarctic Skuas** that are regularly offshore here. Scan the sea carefully, as tropicbirds and **Greater Frigatebird** have also been recorded, mainly after cyclonic conditions in the Mozambique Channel in late summer. Late summer is also the season to watch overhead at dusk for **Sooty Falcon**, which roosts occasionally in the mangroves. A less salubrious resident of the car-park is the introduced **House Crow.**

NEARBY SITES: The Northern Wastewater Treatment Works, in Johanna Road, hosts a good selection of waterfowl, and migrant warblers such as **Great Reed-Warbler**.

GETTING THERE

The north bank is the best side from which to view the main mudflats, and it is reached via the first turn-off north of the Umgeni River bridge on the Leo Boyd highway (M4), signposted 'Prospect Hall Rd/Riverside Rd'; bear left at the T-junction into Riverside Road. Park at any of the numerous parking areas along the road and walk along the bank. To reach the south bank and 'Blue Lagoon', take the turn-off south of the M4 Umgeni River bridge, signposted 'Athlone Drive/Blue Lagoon'.

96 Kenneth Stainbank Nature Reserve ✔

This reserve, adjacent to Yellowwood Park in southern Durban, protects a rich mosaic of coastal forest and grassland, and is one of the city's most popular birding venues. It remains the best place in the greater Durban area to find **White-eared Barbet**, **Green Malkoha**, and the elusive **Lemon Dove** (uncommon), although it holds much more besides. Knowledge of the strange 'ticking' call of the malkoha is essential, as this species is highly vocal yet notably secretive; the best way to find the dove is to listen for fairly noisy scratching sounds emanating from the undergrowth, especially in sloping areas with deep leaf litter.

The nature reserve can be reached by taking the Edwin Swales Drive/Queensburgh exit from the N2 South ('Outer Ring Road'). Continue east for 1 km; turn right at the Bellair Road intersection, and bear left into Cliffview and then Sarnia roads. Turn right into Coedmore Road at the second set of traffic lights, and continue over the Mhlatuzana River to the reserve entrance. All the forest trails hold similar birds, and each is worth exploring. The reserve is open from 06h00-17h00 and a small entrance fee is payable.

97 Pigeon Valley Nature Reserve ✔

This tiny reserve (10 ha), which lies a few minutes' drive from the city centre, comprises a remnant of the coastal forest that once blanketed Durban's Berea Hills. Named after the rare **Eastern Bronze-naped** (or **Delegorgue's**) **Pigeon***, which was first discovered here by French explorer Adulphe Delegorgue in 1847, Pigeon Valley is now an island of forest in a sea of suburbia. Despite this, the reserve offers a good selection of coastal forest birds, most notably the elusive **Buff-spotted Flufftail**, the rare and localised **Spotted Ground-Thrush*** (Mar-Oct), and **Green Twinspot***, conveniently close to Durban. Unfortunately, the Eastern Bronze-naped Pigeon* is no longer present in the reserve.

Park outside the gate, and walk up the main path, which follows the small valley. The **Spotted Ground-Thrush*** is often ridiculously easy to find, hopping about on the lawns near the office at the entrance, or at the edges of the forest along the main track. If it proves elusive here, take one of the loop trails off into the forest (the northern loop at the upper edge of the reserve is best), and listen for the scratching sounds of the thrushes working through the leaf litter. **Red-capped Robin-Chat** and **Terrestrial Brownbul**, both common residents, may raise a false alarm. Areas with dense undergrowth, particularly around the tiny dam above the entrance gate, support a small population of **Buff-spotted Flufftail** and this is as good a site as any to see this frustratingly skulking yet spectacular bird. Listen for the haunting 'hoot' of the male, usually heard at dawn and dusk, and position yourself in an area with as wide a view of the understorey as possible. Use playback sparingly, with the volume on low. Sit absolutely motionless and with luck and patience this phantom of the forest may materialise as a beautifully spotted creature stalking stealthily across the leaf litter. An alternative tactic is to wait at the dam at dawn or dusk (take mosquito repellent), when the flufftails may emerge from cover to feed. A pair of **Black Sparrowhawk** has nested in the reserve for a number of years and are seen frequently, while other notable species include **Grey**

Nico Myburgh

Buff-spotted Flufftail

Sunbird, **Purple-crested Turaco** and **Green Twinspot*** (listen for their flight calls, which are even higher-pitched than those of the numerous **Collared Sunbirds**).

Take the Tollgate/Ridge Road exit from the N3 west of the city centre, and turn south into South Ridge Road at the traffic lights. Continue for 2 km, and then turn left into King George V Road in response to the sign to Pigeon Valley Nature Reserve, when you will see the forest on your right. Bear right after 500 m into Princess Alice Avenue, and park in the road outside the entrance gate, which is open from 07h00-16h30 daily.

Alan Wilson/Photo Access

Pigeon Valley is good for Spotted Ground-Thrush in winter.

98 Burman Bush Nature Reserve ✔

Administered by the Thekwini Municipality, Burman Bush Nature Reserve holds many coastal forest species in common with Pigeon Valley Nature Reserve. **Spotted Ground-Thrush*** is less likely here, but **Southern Tchagra***, **Green Twinspot*** and **Grey Waxbill** may all be seen, although they are all uncommon. The forest edges along the upper part of the reserve are particularly productive. Among the mammals frequently seen here are Blue Duiker and Vervet Monkey. Burman Bush overlooks the Umgeni River from the northern end of the Berea Hills. It can be reached by following Umgeni Road from the Durban city centre, and turning left into St Mathias' Road, just before the Connaught Bridge over the Umgeni River.

DAY TRIPS FROM DURBAN

99 Shongweni Resources Reserve ✔✔

Shongweni Resources Reserve is centred on Shongweni Dam. In addition to an interesting mix of forest and bushveld birds, the area boasts a handful of sought-after specials that can be easily overlooked at other birding sites in KwaZulu-Natal.

SPECIALS: African Black Duck, Red-throated Wryneck, Narina Trogon*, African Pygmy-Kingfisher, African Crowned Eagle, Black Stork, Southern Tchagra*, Mocking Cliff-Chat, Mountain Wagtail, Striped Pipit, and Green Twinspot*.

SEASON: Birding is good year-round.

HABITATS: Valley bushveld, cliffs, dams.

BIRDING: Of particular interest here are the cliff-associated species, **Cape Rock-Thrush**, **Mocking Cliff-Chat** and **Striped Pipit**, all of which may be found on the rock faces along the road down to the dam wall. Stop at the only look-out point, pull your

GETTING THERE

Follow signs from the Shongweni/Assagay exit, 5 km inland of the tollgate on the N3 Toll Freeway between Durban and Pietermaritzburg. Tarred roads wind down to picnic sites at the base of the dam wall and the south-eastern edge of the dam, with a more extensive gravel road network that may be explored on arranged game drives only. A small fee is payable at the entrance gate, where reserve maps are available.

car off the road (300 m uphill from the dam wall), and scan the cliffs above and below (disturbance by rock-climbers has made these species more difficult to see in recent years). The rare **White-backed Night-Heron*** has bred below here, near the edge of the dam. **African Black Duck** is regular on the dam itself, and **Mountain Wagtail** occurs along the river below the wall. Continue to the picnic site below the wall (access possible on weekends only), and park alongside the abandoned settling ponds. Impressive sandstone cliffs opposite sometimes support a pair of nesting **Black Stork**, although it may require intensive scanning to find them; **Lanner Falcon** and **African Black Swift** are considerably more conspicuous. Also scan for **Verreaux's Eagle**.

From the northern picnic area, a trail loops up the hill and follows a well-wooded watercourse. Here, **African Broadbill*** can sometimes be seen. This area holds an excellent selection of woodland birds, including **Crowned** and **Trumpeter Hornbills**, **Narina Trogon***, **African Pygmy-Kingfisher** (summer), **Black Cuckooshrike**, **Southern Tchagra***, **Black-bellied Starling**, **Gorgeous Bush-Shrike**, **Grey** (scarce) and **Swee Waxbills**, and **Green Twinspot***. **African Crowned Eagle** breeds here, and is frequently seen in display flight.

The Ntini Trail from the main picnic site traverses some excellent valley bushveld and grassland. On the way out, watch for **Red-throated Wryneck** in eucalyptus trees near the entrance gate.

100 Umvoti River Mouth R ✔✔

Sandbars and mudflats at the mouth of the Umvoti River are protected on the private Jex Estate. Just as interesting for the vagrant hunter are the Palearctic waders, vast flocks of terns, and scarce passerines that turn up here in summer. This is one of the most productive estuaries for rarities on southern Africa's east coast.

SPECIALS: Collared Pratincole, Black-throated Wattle-eye, Rufous-winged Cisticola, Yellow Wagtail, Southern Brown-throated Weaver, Red-headed Quelea*, and Cuckoo Finch*.

SEASON: Summer is undoubtedly the best time to visit.

HABITATS: Estuary, adjacent reedbeds, flood plain and fallow fields; limited coastal forest.

BIRDING: Collared Pratincole is usually present from Jul-Mar and is easily seen as it roosts on sandbars or hawks insects overhead, although numbers have declined in recent years and it no longer breeds at the site. The number of terns present is directly dependent on whether or not the sandbars are exposed, so be sure to check conditions with Mrs Jex prior to your visit.

Peak conditions prevail in late summer, and roosts comprising more than 3 000 birds are not unusual at this time, with large numbers of **Sandwich, Little** and **Common Terns**, and smaller numbers of **Caspian**, **Lesser Crested**, **Swift** and **White-winged Terns** present. Vagrants recorded include **Roseate**, **Black-naped**, **White-cheeked**, **Sooty** and **Black Terns**. Palearctic waders usually occur in small numbers; **Terek Sandpiper** is regularly seen.

A track running along the western edge of the estuary traverses fallow fields that hold **Collared Pratincole**, and attract **Spotted Thick-knee** and **Yellow Wagtail** (uncommon; summer). **African Rail**, **Red-chested Flufftail** and **Red-faced Cisticola** are heard frequently from adjacent reedbeds, which also host breeding **Southern Brown-throated** and **Yellow Weavers**.

Cuckoo Finch* (rare) and **Red-headed Quelea*** are erratic summer visitors to rank vegetation. **Black-throated Wattle-eye** is resident in the stand of Swamp Barringtonia on the south-western corner of the estuary, while the dune forest east of the homestead holds a variety of coastal forest birds, most notably **Green Malkoha** and **Ashy Flycatcher**.

GETTING THERE

Take the Groutville turn-off from the N2 just north of the Umvoti Toll Plaza, approximately 60 km north of Durban. Head east on a gravel road through sugarcane fields to the checkpoint, then turn right towards the coast and continue to the Jex homestead. The estuary is below the house, and can be reached via a track that skirts the south-western bank. An entrance fee is payable, and access is by prior arrangement only ☎. B&B accommodation is available.

101 Sappi Stanger (Mbozambo Wetland) ✔

The hide at Mbozambo Wetland has proven excellent for obtaining views of skulking wetland species and is best visited in summer. **Baillon's Crake** and **African Rail** have been seen regularly, while scarcer visitors include **Spotted Crake, Allen's Gallinule** and **Lesser Moorhen**. **Southern Brown-throated Weaver** and **Yellow Wagtail** (summer) are common.

Take the Stanger turn-off from the N2 north of Durban, and head towards the town. About 1 km from the N2, take the dirt road to the left, marked 'Paper Mill'. Follow this for about 5 km until you reach the Sappi Paper Mill. Go to the security gate and sign the book to get the key and directions to the hide.

SITES IN AND AROUND PIETERMARITZBURG

102 Darvill Resources Park

This wastewater treatment plant is perhaps Pietermaritzburg's most frequently visited birding venue, as it plays host to a wide variety of water-associated species, of which **Red-headed Quelea*** is the most famous. Water-bird numbers on the larger upper ponds, a short walk from the car-park, vary according to water levels, with healthy numbers of Palearctic shorebirds present in summer, and waterfowl more numerous in winter. Good viewing may be had from the bird hides, although most species are as easily seen from the paths along the banks.

Extensive reedbeds surrounding the top two ponds are home to **Little Rush Warbler** and **Lesser Swamp-Warbler**, with **Sedge-Warbler**, and **African** and **Great Reed-Warblers** (uncommon) swelling their ranks in summer. The localised **Dark-capped Yellow Warbler**, another Darvill speciality, prefers taller, rank vegetation around the ponds. **African Rail** is heard frequently, but seen less commonly, feeding on exposed mud alongside **Black** and **Baillon's** (uncommon) **Crakes** and **African Snipe**.

Marshy edges of the lower, cement-lined strip ponds are the best areas to search for **Orange-breasted Waxbill** and the elusive **Red-headed Quelea***, small flocks of which

Nigel J. Dennis/IOA

Black Crake is a common reedbed rallid.

Nico Myburgh

Orange-breasted Waxbill

may be seen in summer. These edges are also excellent for migrant warblers, and **Green Sandpiper** has been recorded regularly in the vicinity. Scan dead trees here for **Brown-backed Honeybird**, **Red-throated Wryneck** and **Black Sparrowhawk**.

To reach Darvill, take the Scottsville/New England Road turn-off from the N3, and head east on New England Road. Bear left at the service station; drive past Pietermaritzburg Golf Club, and continue for 2 km to the park entrance gate. Proceed to the parking area, where an entrance fee is payable.

103 Ferncliffe (Town Bush) ✔

The mist-belt forest of Ferncliffe, a remnant of the once extensive Town Bush forest, overlooks Pietermaritzburg's western suburbs. A good selection of forest species may be found along the road, or on the trail network radiating from the picnic site.

From the Royal Showgrounds, travel westwards on the Town Bush Road, which narrows and climbs through exotic plantations to the reserve. A gravel track winds through the forest to a picnic site.

Other areas of mist-belt forest worth birding in the Pietermaritzburg area include Queen Elizabeth Park and Doreen Clarke Nature Reserve, near Hilton.

104 Bisley Valley Nature Reserve ✔

The 250 ha Bisley Valley reserve offers thornveld birding close to Pietermaritzburg's city centre. A short walk along the loop trails should yield a wide variety of common bushveld species, such as **Crested Barbet**, **Common Scimitarbill**, **Black Cuckooshrike**, **Brubru**, **Red-backed Shrike**, **Orange-breasted Bush-Shrike**, **Chinspot Batis**, **White-browed Scrub-Robin**, **Violet-backed Starling**, **White-winged Widowbird** and **Golden-breasted Bunting**. **Brown-backed Honeybird** and **Southern Tchagra*** are less common residents. **African Pygmy-Kingfisher** is found in thickets along the small river in summer. The area is best in summer, when migrants are present and the widowbirds, weavers and whydahs are in their breeding finery.

The reserve lies south-west of Oribi Airport, and is best reached via the Alexander Road Extension. The dirt road continues beyond the end of the Alexander Road Extension, leading through agricultural land that supports a surprisingly diverse avifauna. Stop 7 km beyond the tar and scan the grassland for **Blue Crane**, **Secretarybird** and **White Stork**. **Orange-breasted Waxbill** and **African Quailfinch** may be flushed from the roadside, and a plethora of cisticolas – **Croaking**, **Zitting**, **Pale-crowned** and **Wing-snapping** – is present.

105 Albert Falls Resources Reserve ✔

Flanking the Albert Falls Dam, some 20 km north of Pietermaritzburg, this fine reserve incorporates a rich mosaic of woodland, grassland and wetland habitats. Good birding may be had along the road that hugs the dam's southern shore, and visitors are also allowed to explore part of the reserve on foot. Open thornveld along the initial few kilometres supports a wide variety of bushveld birds, notably **Jacobin Cuckoo**, **Spotted Thick-knee** and **Coqui Francolin**, the speciality of the area. The francolin, which is common throughout the reserve, usually draws attention to itself with its crowing call in the early morning. Moist grassland towards the end of the road holds **Common Quail**, **Harlequin Quail** (in wet summers), **African Wattled Lapwing**, **Croaking Cisticola**, **African Quailfinch** and **Orange-breasted Waxbill**, and **Denham's Bustard*** is an occasional visitor. **Black-winged Lapwing** is regularly seen on the lawns near the entrance gate, while **Red-throated Wryneck** is also resident in this area.

The reserve is signposted 23 km along the R33 from Pietermaritzburg to Greytown. Chalet and camp site accommodation can be booked through the reserve office.

106 Midmar Game Reserve ✔

This 1 000 ha reserve on the south bank of Midmar Dam is worth a visit for its grassland specials, many of which are difficult to find elsewhere. A short loop road starts at the Thurlow Gate, traversing moist grassland, where **Black-rumped Buttonquail** (uncommon in summer), **African Grass-Owl*** (rare), **Marsh Owl**, **Denham's Bustard***, **African Wattled** and **Black-winged Lapwings**, **Pale-crowned** and **Wing-snapping Cisticolas**, **Yellow-crowned Bishop**, **Orange-breasted Waxbill** and **African Quailfinch** may be found. **Cuckoo Finch*** is a scarce visitor in wet years.

A regular roosting area for **Grey Crowned** and **Blue Cranes** can be seen to the west of the row of eucalyptus trees at the end of the loop, with **Ground Woodpecker*** and **Eastern Long-billed Lark** often present on the rocky ridge to the south.

Entrance should be arranged in advance with the KwaZulu-Natal Wildlife Midmar office ☎. Thurlow Gate, which is not the main entrance, can be reached from the R617 (from Howick to Bulwer); look out for the conspicuous name on the gate as the reserve is not signposted.

DAY TRIPS FROM PIETERMARITZBURG

107 Howick & the Karkloof IBA ✔✔

A huge variety of habitats are traversed on this fairly short route, and most of the target species may be found with relative ease, making this loop immensely appealing. Because of the range of vegetation, the area provides some of the best birding in the KwaZulu-Natal Midlands – whether you're seeking **Wattled Crane*** or **Bush Blackcap***.

SPECIALS: Maccoa Duck, Brown-backed Honeybird, Olive Woodpecker, Narina Trogon*, Cape Parrot*, Knysna Turaco, Denham's Bustard*, all three species of southern African crane, Buff-spotted Flufftail, Black-winged Lapwing, Forest Buzzard*, Olive Bush-Shrike, Orange Ground-Thrush, Chorister Robin-Chat, Buff-streaked Chat, Bush Blackcap* and Eastern Long-billed Lark.

SEASON: Karkloof is excellent year-round, with the forest and grassland specials most vocal during the spring-summer breeding season; waterfowl, cranes, **Denham's Bustard*** and raptors are more conspicuous in winter.

HABITATS: Mist belt forest and grassland, wetlands, cliffs and gorges, open agricultural lands, thornveld.

BIRDING: *Howick Falls and Umgeni Valley Nature Reserve:* The spectacular 100 m high waterfall is Howick's major tourist attraction, but the adjacent Umgeni Valley Nature Reserve offers birders far more than just scenic beauty. **Cape Rock-Thrush**, **Familiar Chat** and **Mocking Cliff-Chat** are often

Peter Pickford/IOA

Cape Eagle-Owl

GETTING THERE

This loop commences in the Midlands town of Howick, well signposted from the N3, about 30 km north-west of Pietermaritzburg. Immediately after crossing the Umgeni River bridge in Howick, turn right in response to signs to Howick Falls; continue for 300 m to the viewpoint.

present around the Howick Falls viewpoint in town, while a pair of **Lanner Falcon** nest on the cliffs opposite, and they are frequently seen sunning themselves with their young in the early morning.

The woodland along the edge of the bush-filled gorge just to the north of the viewpoint is home to **Red-throated Wryneck**, **Olive Woodpecker**, **African Crowned Eagle**, **Southern Tchagra***, **Olive Bush-Shrike**, **Cape Batis** and **Streaky-headed Seed-eater**. Look and listen for the inconspicuous **Brown-backed Honeybird**. Continuing back to the main road, turn right at the traffic lights and right again towards Karkloof, in response to the sign 'Karkloof/Rietvlei'. The entrance gate to Umgeni Valley Nature Reserve lies 0.8 km along this road. Various hiking trails start at the reserve office and lead into the gorge.

A walk down Indulo Hill may reveal **Lazy Cisticola** and **Striped Pipit** in the rocky grassland, while tall fig trees along the river at the bottom of the gorge attract **Greater Honeyguide**, **Crowned** and **Trumpeter Hornbills**, **Narina Trogon***, **Knysna Turaco** and, occasionally, **African Green Pigeon**.

Shelter Falls Gorge is well known for its resident **Cape Eagle-Owl***, which may be seen (but is more likely to be heard) here at dusk.

The Karkloof: Just 5 km beyond the entrance to Umgeni Valley Nature Reserve, the road passes through alien pine plantations, where **Forest Buzzard*** is seen occasionally, before emerging into open agricultural country. Scan any recently ploughed lands between 15.2 km and 17.2 km from Howick for all three species of southern African crane, which are regular here (in the ratio of about 10 **Grey Crowned**: 3 **Blue**: 1 **Wattled* Crane**). Also look out for **Red-necked** and **Swainson's Spurfowls**, **Long-crested Eagle** and **Black Sparrowhawk**.

At 20.6 km the road becomes gravel, winding through relatively undisturbed grassland that is home to **Red-winged Francolin** (uncommon) and **Yellow Bishop**, before passing the entrance to the private resort of Mbona. The road begins to climb shortly after passing the gate, with a damp, bracken-filled valley on the right, which hosts **Broad-tailed Warbler** and **Dark-capped Yellow Warbler**.

At 32.8 km a junction is reached, with 'York/New Hanover' to the right, and 'Rietvlei' to the left. A pair of **Forest Buzzard*** are frequently seen soaring overhead in the mid-morning. Keep left towards Rietvlei; after 36.4 km, the road passes the turn-off to the D584 on the right, before paralleling a watercourse punctuated with artificial water impoundments. Scan the fallow fields on either side of the road for **Denham's Bustard***, **Secretarybird** and all three species of crane.

After 41.7 km, the road skirts a large dam at the bottom of the valley. The dam regularly holds **White-backed** and **Maccoa Ducks**, **South African Shelduck**, **Cape Shoveler** and **Southern Bald Ibis*** (the latter may often be seen in the surrounding fields). Return to the

Albert Froneman

Southern Bald Ibis is endemic to the highland grasslands of southern Africa.

D584 and follow it for 4.2 km to another small dam on the right, watching the roadside for **Wattled Crane***. Low, rocky outcrops here support **Eastern Long-billed Lark**, and the handsome **Buff-streaked Chat**, while **Southern Ground-Hornbill*** (uncommon), **Blue Crane**, **Black-winged Lapwing**, **Wailing**, **Pale-crowned** and **Wing-snapping Cisticolas**, and **African Quailfinch** frequent the surrounding grasslands.

Return to the junction (at 32.8 km) and, this time, bear left towards York/New Hanover. Between 0.8 and 1.2 km from the T-junction, the road bisects a highly productive patch of mist-belt forest that is home to **Olive Woodpecker**, **African Emerald Cuckoo**, **Grey Cuckooshrike**, **Blue-mantled Crested Flycatcher**, **Olive Bush-Shrike**, **Cape Batis**, **Chorister Robin-Chat**, **Yellow-throated Woodland-Warbler**, **Bush Blackcap***, **Swee Waxbill** and **Forest Canary**.

A further 1.2 km beyond the forest, the road passes the entrance to Benvie Farm. Here, accommodation, which allows access to the magnificent landscaped gardens surrounding the farmhouse, is offered (enquire in advance about day visits ☎). A walk through the quiet gardens in the early morning or late evening is likely to reveal a phenomenal selection of Afromontane forest birds, not least such skulking specials as **Lemon Dove**, **Orange Ground-Thrush**, **White-starred Robin** and, with luck, **Buff-spotted Flufftail**.

In the morning, **Chorister Robin-Chat** and **Red-backed Mannikin** visit Benvie's feeders, **African Olive-Pigeon** and **Forest Canary** often sun themselves atop surrounding trees, and the endangered **Cape Parrot*** may be glimpsed high overhead. To return to Pietermaritzburg, retrace your route to the N3 at Howick, or continue along the York/New Hanover road to the R33, with a stop at Albert Falls Nature Reserve if time permits.

108 Hella-Hella Pass ✔✔

The spectacular Mkomazi Gorge in the vicinity of Hella-Hella Pass boasts a strong breeding population of the globally threatened **Blue Swallow***, as well as an impressive variety of typical Valley Bushveld and mist-belt forest birds. Just an hour's drive from Pietermaritzburg, this is the most accessible site in KwaZulu-Natal for Blue Swallow*.

SPECIALS: Black-rumped Buttonquail, Brown-backed Honeybird, Knysna Turaco, Forest Buzzard*, Blue Swallow*, Lazy Cisticola, Broad-tailed Warbler and Striped Pipit.

SEASON: Hella-Hella is best visited from late Sept to early Mar, when **Blue Swallow*** is present.

HABITATS: Pristine upland grassland, valley bushveld, patches of mist-belt forest, numerous cliffs, rocky slopes, Mkomazi River.

BIRDING: Four pairs of **Blue Swallow*** nest in the grassland and are sometimes seen from the road just before the top of the pass. It is preferable, however, to park off the road (obtain the gate key) and walk east into the grasslands, as **Black-winged Lapwing**, **Black-rumped Buttonquail** (scarce; summer), **Broad-tailed Warbler** (fairly common in the seepages but conspicuous only by call in summer) and **Pale-crowned Cisticola** may also be found here. If the swallows are not immediately apparent, be patient, as they roam widely across the plateau. **Rufous-chested Sparrowhawk*** as well as **African Goshawk** are occasionally observed in flight over the adjacent forest.

Bird the pass back towards the Mkomazi River, keeping an eye out for **Forest*** and **Jackal Buzzards**, **Verreaux's Eagle**, **African Crowned Eagle** and **Black Stork** along the cliffs, **Brown-backed Honeybird**, **Lazy Cisticola** (especially numerous) and **Striped Pipit** on the dry, rocky slopes, and **Crowned Hornbill**, **Knysna Turaco**, **Grey-headed** and **Olive Bush-Shrikes**, **Garden Warbler**, and **Swee Waxbill** in the thicker bushveld along the river. You may be able to spot **African Black Duck** and **Mountain Wagtail** from the Mkomazi River bridge.

GETTING THERE

Highover Nature Reserve is a private reserve and natural heritage site encompassing a variety of habitats in an area of 1 504 ha, and is situated 25 km south-west of Richmond. Turn right into Shepstone Street off the R56, and left at the intersection to enter Richmond. Drive through the village for approximately 2 km, and take the signposted left turn towards Hella-Hella. After 11 km, the road becomes gravel; continue for a further 11 km to the Highover Nature Reserve. The entrance is on the left about 2 km beyond the Mkomazi River bridge. Day visits must be arranged in advance; accommodation is available in chalets ☎.

ROUTE 11

ZULULAND

TOP 10 BIRDS

- Pel's Fishing-Owl
- Green Barbet
- Neergard's Sunbird
- Lemon-breasted Canary
- Pink-throated Twinspot
- Woodwards' Batis
- Eastern Bronze-naped Pigeon
- Swamp Nightjar
- African Broadbill
- Southern Banded Snake-Eagle

Once the bush-covered domain of the great Zulu warrior kings, the land north of the Tugela River boasts some of the greatest natural diversity in South Africa. With the dune forest and coastal wetlands surrounding Lake St Lucia, the world-famous Hluhluwe-Imfolozi Game Park, the forests around Eshowe in the south and the Fever Tree-lined pans of Ndumo Game Reserve on the Mozambique border, Zululand offers the birder unparalleled avian wealth in settings of exceptional natural beauty.

Some of Zululand's premier birding sites, such as Mkhuze and Ndumo game reserves, have achieved legendary status in birding circles through the sheer numbers of birds on their bird lists. Others, such as Ongoye Forest and the Greater St Lucia Wetland Park, are home to restricted species difficult to find elsewhere. It is this richness that makes birding Zululand so exciting and fulfilling.

International visitors will require a minimum of five days in the area, divided between the essential sites of the Eshowe forests, Greater St Lucia Wetland Park, and Mkhuze Game Reserve. Local birders could easily spend the same amount of time exploring any one of these reserves, or the numerous lesser known birding areas in between. The Zululand Birding Route, based in Richards Bay, should be consulted to arrange guides, often from adjacent communities, at many of the localities described below ☎.

Hugh Chittenden

Listen out for the call of Southern Banded Snake-Eagle in Zululand's coastal forests.

Hugh Chittenden

In South Africa, Green Barbet is restricted to Ongoye Forest.

109 Amatikulu Nature Reserve ✔

Most of Zululand's major birding sites lie within an hour's drive of the national N2 highway that runs north along the coast from Durban to the Swaziland border and Mpumalanga. About 15 km after crossing the Tugela Bridge into Zululand (watch for **Goliath Heron** and **Woolly-necked Stork** on the sandbars below), the toll highway (N2) passes the turn-off to Inyoni/Amatikulu Nature Reserve.

This small reserve holds an excellent selection of coastal forest and grassland birds. **Swamp Nightjar***, which has been recorded breeding here, is the reserve's greatest attraction. Employ the services of a local guide, and explore the grassy plains with Lala Palms about 1 km before the pan on the 4WD trail. **Black Coucal** may be seen in summer. Other species in the reserve are **Grey Waxbill**, **Green Twinspot***, **Shelley's Francolin** (very scarce), **Spotted Ground-Thrush*** (winter), **White-fronted Bee-eater** and **Black-throated Wattle-eye** (common).

Little more than 100 km from Durban, and with a well-situated camp overlooking the Amatikulu River, this makes an ideal overnight stop on the Zululand birding loop, or a weekend birding excursion from Durban.

110 Eshowe: Dlinza & Entumeni IBA ✔✔✔

Eshowe, 150 km north-east of Durban, boasts excellent forest birding within the town limits, and the only forest canopy walkway in South Africa. The Dlinza and Entumeni forests provide easy access to a host of difficult forest specials, notably **Eastern Bronze-naped Pigeon***, and **Spotted Ground-Thrush***.

SPECIALS: Eastern Bronze-naped Pigeon*, Spotted Ground-Thrush*, Green Twinspot*, Olive Woodpecker, Scaly-throated Honeyguide, Narina Trogon*, Crowned and Trumpeter Hornbills, Lemon Dove, Buff-spotted Flufftail, African Crowned Eagle, Green Malkoha, Yellow-streaked Greenbul and Chorister Robin-Chat.

SEASON: The optimal time to visit is during the Sept-Dec breeding season, when birdsong is at its peak and **Spotted Ground-Thrush*** has returned from its coastal wintering quarters. Winter is still productive, however, as most of the forest birds are resident and many Spotted Ground-Thrush* overwinter on the breeding grounds.

HABITATS: Evergreen forest (scarp forest), grassland (flanking Entumeni).

BIRDING: *Dlinza:* Bird the forest along the canopy walkway Ⓐ and tower, preferably with a local bird guide, where most of the specials may be found. You should hear the distinctive call of the **Eastern Bronze-naped Pigeon*** from the canopy walkway, although seeing the birds can be tricky. Arrive in the early morning, and watch canopy gaps and fruiting trees. Large fig trees attract good numbers of **White-eared Barbet** and **Trumpeter Hornbill**, while **African Emerald Cuckoo**, **Green Malkoha**, **Scaly-throated Honeyguide** and **Grey Cuckooshrike** may be seen.

Green Twinspot* is also regularly recorded in open patches in the forest, such as around Bishop's Seat Ⓑ, feeding on seeding grasses. **Spotted Ground-Thrush***, **Chorister Robin-Chat**, **Grey Cuckooshrike**, **Cape Batis** and **Olive Sunbird** are all present along the first few hundred metres of the trail.

GETTING THERE

Dlinza Forest lies on the south-western edge of Eshowe, while Entumeni Forest is situated 15 km to the west of the town. Take the N2 north from Durban and turn west onto the R66 at the 'Gingindlovu, Eshowe and Ulundi' off-ramp. About 24 km beyond the toll gate, turn left into the second turning into Eshowe at the only set of traffic lights on the R66, which is Kangella Street. The Dlinza Forest sign is clearly visible after about 2 km (just past Eshowe High School). Dlinza is best birded from the 125 m long canopy walkway, which leads to an observation tower, and the surrounding trails. Entumeni has two longer, fairly rigorous trails, although most of the birds may be seen along the forest edge near the reserve entrance. Ask for directions at Dlinza. The Eshowe B&B ☎ offers birding advice and self-catering accommodation.

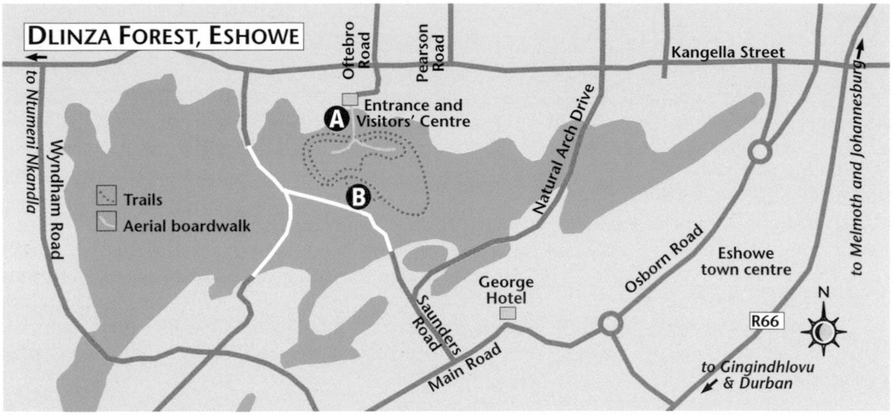

Bishop's Seat picnic site is an excellent spot, as **Olive Woodpecker**, **Narina Trogon*** and **Eastern Bronze-naped Pigeon*** are frequent.

Entumeni Forest: Entumeni shares most of its forest birds with Dlinza, although **Yellow-streaked Greenbul** is only found here. Scan the forested valley from the grassy knoll, 1 km (walking distance) to the north-east of the entrance gate, as **Eastern Bronze-naped Pigeon*** is sometimes seen in flight here, or, if you are lucky, perched on exposed snags in the early morning. **African Goshawk** and **African Crowned Eagle** display overhead in winter. The rank grass supports **Croaking** and **Lazy Cisticolas**, as well as **Drakensberg Prinia** and **Southern Tchagra***.

Hugh Chittenden

Eastern Bronze-naped Pigeon

A trail starting in the car-park runs along the ridge before forking, with both paths dropping steeply down into the valley. **Spotted Ground-Thrush***, **Brown Scrub-Robin** (more common here than Dlinza) and **Yellow-throated Woodland-Warbler** are both fairly common in the drier ridge-top forest.

OTHER ANIMALS*:* Vervet Monkey and the dainty Blue Duiker may be frequently encountered, with Bushbuck and Bushpig more commonly heard than seen.

111 Lake Phobane ✔

Lake Phobane (previously known as Goedetrou Dam), 15 km north of Eshowe, has a few quiet backwaters with plenty of overhanging vegetation. Five breeding pairs of **White-backed Night-Heron*** are resident on the dam and **African Finfoot*** is best seen feeding in these areas along the edges in the early morning. Six species of kingfisher can be seen here, including the elusive **Half-collared Kingfisher**, which is best found in the rocky areas where streams flow into the dam.

The cliff faces that drop into the dam are home to **Southern Bald Ibis***, which breeds here in the late winter months, as well as **Lanner** and **Peregrine Falcons**, **Mocking Cliff-Chat** and **Striped Pipit**.

From Eshowe, head towards Melmoth/Ulundi on the R66. About 10 km out of Eshowe, take the dirt road to your left (signposted 'Lake Phobane and Shakaland'). Follow this road for 7 km, cross the dam wall and park in the parking area on the northern shore (don't leave any valuables in your car). You can organise a boat trip via the Zululand Birding Route, or bird the surrounding woodlands on foot.

112 Mtunzini & Umlalazi

IBA ✔✔

The sleepy, coastal town of Mtunzini is famous among birders for its small population of **Palm-nut Vultures***, here at the southern limit of their breeding range. Although the vultures may be seen relatively easily on a quick visit to the Raphia Palm Monument, further exploration of the adjacent Umlalazi Nature Reserve will reward the birder with an additional selection of coastal specials.

SPECIALS: Palm-nut Vulture*, Mangrove Kingfisher*, Spotted Ground-Thrush*, African Finfoot*, Narina Trogon*, Trumpeter Hornbill, Yellow Weaver*, Black-throated Wattle-eye, Grey Waxbill and Green Twinspot*.

SEASON: **Palm-nut Vulture*** and the majority of specials are resident, while **Mangrove Kingfisher*** and **Spotted Ground-Thrush*** are present only from Apr–Sept.

HABITATS: Dune and swamp forest, grassland, marshes, and mangroves (Umlalazi Lagoon).

BIRDING. **Palm-nut Vulture*** is usually found easily in the forest strips lying north and south of the road into the village, where the birds perch atop the Raphia Palms in the early morning. They may be seen here throughout the day, although they tend to be less conspicuous around midday. The Raphia Palm Monument is home to further pairs of the vultures, as well as to **Black-throated Wattle-eye**. Open grasslands south of the monument support **Red-breasted Swallow** and **Yellow-throated Longclaw**, and **Gorgeous Bush-Shrike** is commonly heard calling from thickets in this area.

Mangrove Kingfisher* winters around the Umlalazi Lagoon. Look and listen for it on the Mangrove Trail, or scan mangrove edges from the road along the north bank. **Woolly-necked Stork** is common on the exposed mudflats and **African Finfoot*** is possible along the quieter stretches upstream.

Forest birds are most easily seen by strolling either around the Indaba camp site, or along the roads through the dune forest. **White-eared Barbet, Yellow-rumped Tinkerbird, Trumpeter Hornbill, Purple-crested Turaco, Red-capped Robin-Chat, Black-bellied Starling, Yellow-bellied Greenbul, Terrestrial Brownbul**, and **Grey, Olive** and **Purple-banded Sunbirds** are common throughout, while **Spotted Ground-Thrush*** (winter) is more readily found in the camp itself. Reedbeds near the entrance gate support **Rufous-winged Cisticola, Dark-capped Yellow Warbler** (winter), and also **Yellow Weaver**.

OTHER ANIMALS: Vervet Monkey, Blue and Red Duikers, Bushbuck, and Bushpig.

GETTING THERE

Mtunzini lies 130 km north-east of Durban, just off the Mtunzini Toll Plaza. The 'Palm-nut Vulture Forest Strips' may be viewed from a parking area 300 m along the road into Mtunzini village (Hely Hutchison Street), or take the first right off Hely Hutchison into Mimosa Drive, and turn right again into Wilderness Drive, a cul-de-sac that provides excellent viewing of the southern forest patch.

To reach Umlalazi Nature Reserve and the Raphia Palm Monument, continue east on Hely Hutchison Street and follow signs in the village. A small road network makes for easy birding, with various trails providing further access. The reserve offers well-situated camp sites and chalets with excellent birding on your doorstep.

Hugh Chittenden

Mangrove Kingfisher is a winter visitor.

113 Ongoye Forest

4X4 IBA ✔✔

Ongoye Forest is the only site in South Africa for the *woodwardi* subspecies of **Green Barbet*** (often considered a separate species), which is found only here and on the Rondo Plateau in south-eastern Tanzania. Ongoye is home to an excellent selection of forest birds, but may be tricky to reach without a high-clearance vehicle.

SPECIALS: Black-rumped Buttonquail, Olive Woodpecker, Green Barbet*, Eastern Bronze-naped Pigeon*, Lemon Dove, Spotted Ground-Thrush*, Chorister Robin-Chat, Brown Scrub-Robin, Yellow-streaked Greenbul and African Crowned Eagle.

SEASON: Bird activity in this subtropical forest remains high year-round.

HABITATS: Coastal scarp forest, grasslands, granite outcrops.

BIRDING: **Green Barbet*** may be seen at any forest patch within Ongoye, but it is common and most easily found in the western part of the forest. Listen for its distinctive '*chop! chop! chop*!' call, or wait at a fruiting fig tree. The remainder of the forest specials are best sought along the first kilometre of track into the forest. The best way to actually see, as opposed to hear, the localised **Eastern Bronze-naped Pigeon***, is to climb atop one of the granite outcrops in the early morning and watch for the birds flying over the forest. Other forest species include **Yellow-streaked Greenbul**, **Green Malkoha** and **Spotted Ground-Thrush*** (uncommon). Surrounding grassland areas may reveal **Southern Ground-Hornbill*** (scarce), **Broad-tailed Warbler** (uncommon; marshy areas), and **Striped** and **Plain-backed Pipits**.

OTHER ANIMALS: Samango Monkey, Blue Duiker and Bushbuck form the staple diet of the forest's resident **African Crowned Eagle**. Other notable denizens are the endemic Ongoye subspecies of Red Bush Squirrel, and the highly localised Zululand Dwarf Chameleon, both of which are regularly seen here.

GETTING THERE

Ongoye is situated inland of Mtunzini, between Eshowe and Empangeni, and is easily accessed from the western side in a 2WD during the dry season.

Fourteen kilometres south of Eshowe on the R66, turn left onto the D884. After 3 kms on a gravel road, turn left again. Drive for a further 7 kms; turn sharp left, proceed for another 7 kms and turn left again, passing a store and school before climbing up to the western edge of the forest. This road passes through about 1 km of forest which is occupied by a number of pairs of Green Barbets, as well as all the other local forest specials.

The forest warden's house (on the right) is situated in the forest along this road and the north-west corner of the fenced area is the easiest site for finding barbets.

About 500 m past the forest is a track on the right, at the top of the ridge, that takes you through 4 kms of grassland and into the forest centre.

114 Richards Bay

✔✔

Richards Bay is one of South Africa's largest estuaries, home to vast numbers of resident water birds, and a magnet to migrants down the east coast. Despite increasing industrialisation, the area offers excellent birding in a variety of wetland and forest habitats. The top wader-watching site on the east coast, Richards Bay is a reliable spot for **Terek Sandpiper**, **Greater Sand Plover**, **Lesser Jacana** and **Lesser Crested Tern**.

SPECIALS: African Pygmy Goose* (winter), Green Malkoha* (winter), Lesser Jacana, Greater Sand Plover, Lesser Crested Tern, Blue-cheeked Bee-eater, Black-throated Wattle-eye, Rudd's Apalis, Southern Brown-throated Weaver and Green Twinspot*.

SEASON: Although birding is excellent here throughout the year, summer is when the migrants are present, and the chance of finding something unusual is at its highest.

HABITATS: Tidal mudflats, mangrove swamps, adjacent freshwater lakes and pans, reeds, papyrus, swamp forest, dune forest, natural coastal grassland.

BIRDING: The extensive mudflats of the *Sanctuary* area Ⓐ and Ⓑ hold the bulk of the migrant waders and are best birded on an incoming tide, when birds are concentrated in a smaller area (see tide tables in the local newspaper). **Common Whimbrel, Common Greenshank, Little Stint, Curlew Sandpiper**, and **Grey** and **Common Ringed Plovers** are the dominant species, although the attractive **Terek Sandpiper** and **Greater Sand Plover** are also pleasantly common. Regular and recent rarities include **Broad-billed Sandpiper, Mongolian Plover, Common Redshank, Pacific Golden Plover**, and **Crab Plover***. The sanctuary supports healthy populations of **African Fish-Eagle, Goliath Heron, Pink-backed Pelican** and **Woolly-necked Stork**, as well as smaller numbers of **Osprey**.

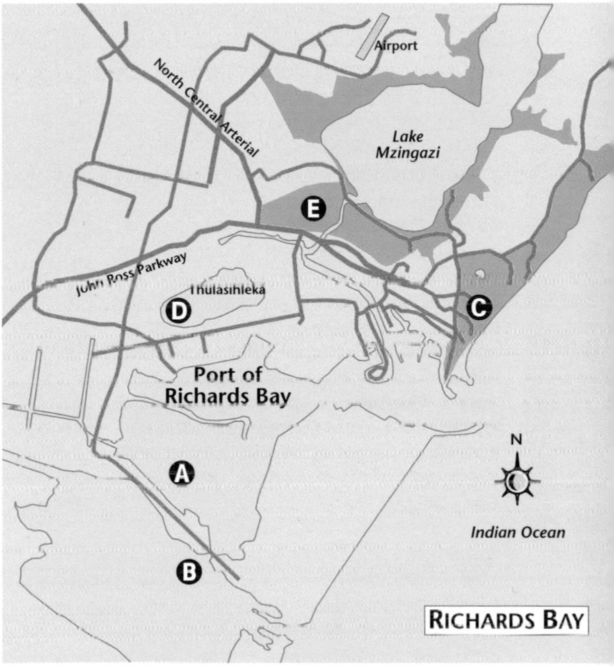

Vast tern roosts regularly form here, especially in summer, when vagrant **Gull-billed** and **White-cheeked Terns** have been discovered among the mixed hordes of **Caspian, Lesser Crested, Swift, Sandwich, Common, Little** and **White-winged Terns. Mangrove Kingfisher*** is present, but its habitat is difficult to access.

The '*Casuarinas*' **C** area offers a selection of waders and roosting terns, including **Greater Sand Plover** and **Lesser Crested Tern,** and, although it is not as productive as the Sanctuary, you do not need a permit to get in. **Mangrove Kingfisher*** may be found here in winter.

'*Thula Pan*' **D** is the most accessible of the freshwater pans, and its reed-fringed borders shelter a wide variety of water-associated species. Scan the open water carefully for **African Pygmy Goose*** and **White-backed Duck**, and the edges of the reedbeds for **Little Bittern, Baillon's Crake** and **Lesser Jacana. Blue-cheeked Bee-eater** may be seen hawking insects overhead in summer. The reedbeds are also excellent for migrants such as **Great** and **African Reed-Warblers**, and **Sedge-Warbler**, and are worth watching for **Southern Brown-throated Weaver** and **Red-headed Quelea*** (scarce).

GETTING THERE

Richards Bay is 170 km north-east of Durban. Contact the Zululand Birding Route office, for updated directions ☎.

Access to the *Sanctuary* harbour area **A** and **B** is currently only possible with a permit from the Zululand Birding Route (to be arranged two days in advance). It is recommended that you employ the services of a local guide, who will have up-to-date information on the presence of rarities, and will also be able to guide you to the more obscure sites in the vast harbour area. A telescope is recommended.

To access the 'Casuarinas' area **C**, take the R34 from the N2, and turn right at the 'Medway/ Harbour Coast' sign and, after 900 m, turn left towards Tuzi Gazi Waterfront. After 1.4 km, turn right onto a small dirt road, cross the railway, and continue for about 4 km to an area of Casuarina trees and sandflats.

To reach *Thula Pan* **D**, head east towards Richards Bay on the R34 from the N2 or Empangeni, and turn right/south into Medway Road at the 7th set of traffic lights, signposted ZBR 12.1.5. A dirt track on the right just before the harbour entrance boom leads off to the pan. There are three hides at the pan, which appears on the right-hand side about 1 km down this road. A map sign along this road gives positions of the hides and trails.

Coastal forest in and around the town, such as at the Sharks Board Office Ⓔ, supports a wide range of forest birds, notably **Scaly-throated Honeyguide**, **Narina Trogon***, **Green Malkoha**, **Rudd's Apalis** and **Black-bellied Starling**, while patches of swamp forest hold **Black-throated Wattle-eye**.

115 Enseleni Nature Reserve ✔

Another gem of a birding site in the area, Enseleni straddles the N2 some 10 km north-east of Empangeni, inland of Richards Bay. The reserve is signposted off the N2, and access to the riparian forest is via the 7 km Nkonkoni and 5 km Mvubu trails. A boat trip with a local guide along the river can be organised through the Zululand Birding Route.

This reserve is primarily known as an excellent spot for the elusive **African Finfoot***, a number of pairs of which live along the Enseleni River. The mature riparian forest in the reserve also boasts **White-backed Night-Heron***, **White-eared Barbet**, and **Scaly-throated Honeyguide**, as well as **Green Malkoha** and **Black-throated Wattle-eye**. Watch overhead for **Sooty Falcon** at dusk in late summer.

Richard du Toit

African Finfoot may be seen at Enseleni.

116 Greater St Lucia Wetland Park IBA R ✔✔

Lake St Lucia is one of the most important breeding areas for water birds in South Africa, and is the most accessible place to see the East Coast littoral endemics and many coastal forest and grassland specials. The recently amalgamated Greater St Lucia Park protects this vital wetland and coastal region, and the surrounding rich mosaic of forests, woodlands and grasslands, spanning a vast region from Mapelane in the south to Kosi Bay in the north. It is a highly recommended part of any Zululand birding itinerary.

SPECIALS: Great White and Pink-backed Pelicans, Southern Banded Snake-Eagle, Crested Guineafowl, Buff-spotted Flufftail, Livingstone's Turaco, Green Malkoha, Swamp Nightjar, Mangrove Kingfisher*, African Broadbill*, Eastern Nicator, Brown and Bearded Scrub-Robins, Rudd's Apalis, Woodwards' Batis, Rosy-breasted Longclaw*, Green* and Pink-throated* Twinspots, and Grey Waxbill.

SEASON: The endemics are reasonably easy year-round, although late summer is best for vagrant shorebirds and seabirds at the mouth of the St Lucia Estuary.

HABITATS: Dune and Sand Forest, mangrove swamp, grassland, marshes, lakes.

BIRDING: Just before the bridge over the St Lucia Estuary, the road crosses an area dense with *Phragmites* reeds: excellent habitat for **Rufous-winged Cisticola** and **Southern Brown-throated Weaver**. Stop at the bridge and scan through the mixed hirundine flocks, which often hold **Wire-tailed Swallow**. **Mangrove Kingfisher*** may be heard, and occasionally seen, in the mangroves downstream of the bridge during the winter months. **Blue-cheeked Bee-eater** is frequent here in summer.

St Lucia village: The best way to see water birds in the 'Narrow Section' of the lake is on a boat cruise. Although water-bird numbers vary greatly according to the salinity of the lake's waters, **Great White** and **Pink-backed Pelicans**, **Saddle-billed** (uncommon), **Yellow-billed** and **Woolly-necked Storks, Caspian Tern, Ruff, Ruddy Turnstone, Grey Plover** and **Pied Avocet** are usually encountered.

Check the mouth of the estuary, reached by turning right at the first T-junction in the village and following the road south past the KwaZulu-Natal Wildlife office, for **Goliath Heron** and roosting terns, including **Caspian, Lesser Crested** and **Little Terns**. The sandspit here has hosted numerous rarities, especially after cyclonic conditions in the Mozambique Channel, including **Eurasian Oystercatcher, Sooty Tern, Brown Noddy**, and **Greater Frigatebird**.

Dune Forest: For the endemic-hunter, however, it is the dune forest that is St Lucia's greatest attraction, with the most accessible patch being along the short Gwalagwala trail that runs from the KwaZulu-Natal Wildlife office and the Iphiva camp site. Both **Livingstone's** and **Purple-crested Turacos** are fairly common and easily seen: listen for their raucous calls, or wait at a fruiting fig tree. **Brown Scrub-Robin** and **Woodwards' Batis** are equally numerous, although perhaps less conspicuous than at Cape Vidal's camp site. Other noteworthy species to watch for include **Green Malkoha, Buff-spotted Flufftail, Square-tailed Drongo, Blue-mantled Crested Flycatcher, Black-bellied Starling** and **Grey Waxbill.**

Coastal Grassland: The coastal grassland en route to Cape Vidal in the north is flooded seasonally, and a scan from the road in likely-looking habitat may produce **African Pygmy-Goose*, White-backed** and **Fulvous Ducks, Lesser Jacana, Grey-rumped Swallow, Pale-crowned Cisticola** and the beautiful **Rosy-breasted Longclaw*** (uncommon; only found nearer Cape Vidal). Check roadside forest patches for **Southern Banded Snake-Eagle**, which is uncommon but seen more easily here than anywhere else in southern Africa. **Swamp Nightjar** roosts under palms at the edge of moist depressions and may be located after dark by its slow *chook-chook* call.

Cape Vidal: The dune forest at Cape Vidal is arguably the best locality in South Africa for **Brown Scrub-Robin** and **Woodwards' Batis.** Both species are readily found along the roads or within the camp site, especially at dawn when their distinctive calls seem to ring from all around. Other species that are common and conspicuous by their vocalisations are **Green Malkoha, Livingstone's Turaco, Narina Trogon*, Blue-mantled Crested Flycatcher, Eastern Nicator, Yellow-breasted** and **Rudd's Apalis** (the latter restricted to acacia thickets within the coastal forest), and **Grey Sunbird. African Wood-Owl** is heard commonly in the camp site at night. Check patches of seeding grass at the roadside for mixed groups of **Green Twinspot*, Grey Waxbill** and **Red-backed Mannikin.** Trails behind the Iphiva camp site (at the Eastern Shores gate) hold grassland and thicket species, including **Rudd's Apalis.**

Western Shores: The three reserves on the western shores of the lake, namely False Bay Park, Fanie's Island and Charter's Creek, share similar habitats, including dry woodland, Sand Forest and grassy lake margins. The best of the three is False Bay Park. **Pale Flycatcher** is found regularly near the entrance gate; **African Broadbill*** and both **Green*** and **Pink-throated* Twinspots** are located in thickets along the entrance road, and **Bearded Scrub-Robin**, and **Rudd's Apalis** in the camp site.

The Nibela Peninsula, an exciting new birding area with extensive flood plain areas, is located on the north-western side of Lake St Lucia and can be accessed on the new tarred road from Hluhluwe to Sodwana (turn south opposite the Phinda sign, about 30 km north of Hluhluwe). The area holds most of the Maputaland (northern Zululand) specials, as well as **Rosy-breasted Longclaw*, Short-tailed Pipit*** (winter) and **Swamp Nightjar***. When

GETTING THERE

St Lucia village makes an excellent base from which to explore this vast wetland reserve, having numerous B&Bs, restaurants and shops, while Cape Vidal offers a KZN Wildlife-administered camp with chalets, and a camp site. St Lucia Tourism Association offers launch cruises of the lake. Mapelane (signposted from the N2 south of Imfolozi village), Sodwana Bay (signposted from the N2 10 km north of Hluhluwe village), and the reserves on the Western Shores (Charter's Creek, False Bay Park and Fanie's Island: all signposted from the N2) have rest camps with cabins, a camp site and trails. Contact KZN Wildlife for bookings and information.

conditions are right, tens of thousands of waterfowl and waders may be seen here. Raptors include **Sooty Falcon** (summer) and **Southern Banded Snake-Eagle**. A 4WD vehicle is necessary to explore this area, and a local guide, organised through the Zululand Birding Route, is strongly recommended to inform on water levels and to navigate the maze of tracks in the area.

117 Hluhluwe-Imfolozi Park

IBA ✔✔

Hluhluwe-Imfolozi is more famous for its megafauna than for its avifauna, although the diligent birder should be rewarded with well over 100 species in a single day's visit in summer. The park's healthy population of mammalian predators and huge extent (almost 100 000 ha) mean that Hluhluwe-Imfolozi supports 'indicator species' largely extirpated from other parts of the province, notably **Southern Ground-Hornbill***, **Bateleur** and **Lappet-faced Vulture**. This Big Five reserve is situated only three hours' drive from Durban.

SPECIALS: Southern Ground-Hornbill*, Narina Trogon*, African Finfoot*, Bronze-winged Courser, White-backed Night-Heron*, Southern Bald Ibis*, Gorgeous Bush-Shrike, and Bushveld Pipit.

SEASON: Birding is good year-round, although **Southern Bald Ibis*** is present only in winter.

HABITATS: Hilly terrain, open thorn savanna to dense valley bushveld, riverine forest, coastal scarp forest, grassland, rivers, cliffs.

BIRDING: Many of the park's birds are widespread and common species typical of the acacia savanna of south-eastern Africa. A good variety of these can be found on game drives and by exploring the numerous picnic sites and game-hide parking areas on foot. The Gontshi Loop starts at Memorial Gate Ⓐ, traversing a marshy area where **Black Coucal** and **Red-headed Quelea*** are uncommon, but should be watched for in summer. Wait quietly at the Gontshi stream crossing Ⓑ, as the elusive **African Finfoot*** is often seen here. At least two pairs of these secretive water birds are also resident along the Hluhluwe River upstream of Maphumulo picnic site Ⓒ, and may be seen from the various river viewpoints and the guided boat cruise. If possible, arrange a private cruise or join a like-minded group, as the **White-backed Night-Heron*** (scarce) may also be found through careful scrutiny of waterside vegetation. Riverine fig trees here and at other viewpoints, such as Sitezi Ⓓ, attract a plethora of frugivorous and insectivorous birds, such as **White-eared** and **Black-collared Barbets**, **Yellow-rumped Tinkerbird**, **Crowned** and **Trumpeter Hornbills**, **Narina Trogon***, **Purple-crested Turaco**, **African Green Pigeon**, **Ashy Flycatcher**, **Grey Tit-Flycatcher**, and **Black-bellied Starling**. A similar host of birds, including African Finfoot*, may be found at the picturesque Siwasamakhosikazi picnic site Ⓔ. This site overlooks a cliff, where small numbers of **Southern Bald Ibis*** nest from May-Oct. **Lanner Falcon, Mocking**

GETTING THERE

The park is approximately 220 km north of Durban, and is signposted from the N2. The southern Nyalazi gate lies 30 km from Mtubatuba along the R618 (west), and this is the best access point for the Imfolozi section of the park, while Hluhluwe is best reached via the northern Memorial Gate, 13 km off the N2 near Hluhluwe village. A good road network spans the reserve, which boasts a variety of accommodation ranging from hutted rest camps to bush camps and luxury lodges. Shops at the main camps of Hilltop and Mpila sell basic foodstuffs and detailed park maps. Numerous game-viewing hides, guided game and night drives, boat cruises on the Hluhluwe River and the ever-popular Wilderness Trails complete the list of amenities.

V. Burger/Photo Access

Birding in Hluhluwe-Imfolozi

Cliff-Chat and **Striped Pipit** are other residents of the rocky slope.

Hilltop Camp **F** commands an impressive position overlooking the well-watered valleys of northern Hluhluwe, and adjoins a patch of coastal scarp forest known as Mbhombe. A short, self-guided trail starts near the swimming pool and winds through forest before emerging near Chalet 2. **Narina Trogon***, **Green Malkoha**, **Lemon Dove**, **Buff-spotted Flufftail**, **Blue-mantled Crested Flycatcher**, **Olive Bush-Shrike**, **Cape Batis**, **Chorister Robin-Chat** (winter) and **Green Twinspot*** are all regular here, although patience may be required to see them, while coveys of **Crested Guineafowl** are frequent on the camp lawns.

The more open savanna in the southern Imfolozi sector of the park, and the so-called Corridor that links it to Hluhluwe, is the best area for game-viewing. Watch overhead for **White-backed**, **White-headed** (uncommon) and **Lappet-faced Vultures**, **Bateleur**, or **Tawny Eagle**, all of which are attracted to predator kills. **Southern Ground-Hornbill*** and **Secretarybird** favour open ground, especially in the Nqabatheki and Msasaneni areas, while a pair of **Verreaux's Eagle-Owl** are resident near Thiyeni hide **G** and are frequently heard booming in the early morning.

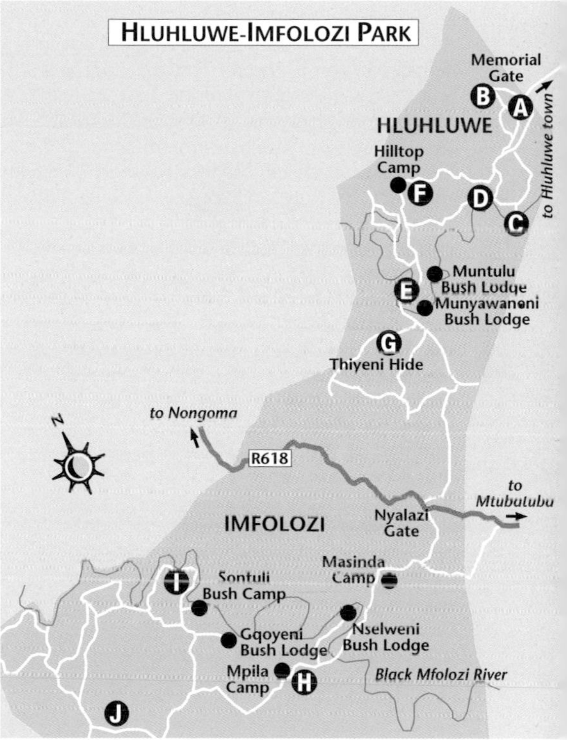

Mpila Camp **H** attracts a variety of birds from the surrounding bushveld, notably **Mocking Cliff-Chat** and **Green-winged Pytilia**, and serves as the starting point for drives in Imfolozi. The Sontuli loop **I** along the Black Mfolozi River may produce **White-fronted Bee-eater**, **Water Thick-knee** and **Black Stork**, while the open thorn savanna in the Msaneni area **J** should be searched for **Bearded Woodpecker**, **Black-bellied Bustard**, **Red-backed Shrike**, **Brown-crowned Tchagra**, **White Helmet-Shrike**, **Fiscal Flycatcher** (winter), **Flappet** and **Sabota Larks**, and **Bushveld Pipit**.

Guided night drives depart from both Hilltop and Mpila camps each evening and may produce **Bronze-winged Courser**, **Water** and **Spotted Thick-knees**, **African Scops-Owl** and **Southern White-faced Scops-Owl** (uncommon), **Spotted Eagle-Owl**, **Fiery-necked Nightjar** and a selection of nocturnal mammals. **African Wood-Owl** is resident at Hilltop and can be seen easily on a spotlighting walk around the camp.

OTHER ANIMALS: Hluhluwe-Imfolozi is famous as the reserve that brought the endangered White Rhinoceros back from the brink of extinction and nowhere are these leviathans easier to see than here. The remainder of the 'Big Five' are all well represented, with Black Rhinoceros, Hippopotamus, Cheetah and African Wild Dog present too.

118 Bonamanzi Game Reserve ✔✔

This superb private reserve borders the Greater St Lucia Wetland Park and boasts an impressive selection of east coast littoral specials. Bonamanzi's appeal lies in the fact that visitors are allowed to search for these specials on foot and unescorted in certain parts of the reserve. **African Broadbill***, **Rudd's Apalis** and **Pink-throated Twinspot*** are all common, and it is arguably the best site anywhere for the scarce endemic, **Lemon-breasted Canary***. The reserve is situated a mere three hours' drive from Durban, and day visitors are allowed.

SPECIALS: African Pygmy Goose*, Green Malkoha, Swamp Nightjar, Senegal Lapwing, African Cuckoo Hawk, Southern Banded Snake-Eagle, African Broadbill*, Gorgeous Bush-Shrike, Bearded Scrub-Robin, Eastern Nicator, Rudd's Apalis, Neergaard's Sunbird*, Pink-throated Twinspot*, Grey Waxbill, and Lemon-breasted Canary*.

SEASON: Spring, when birdsong is at its peak, is the best time. A visit in summer may be hot, although this is when **Lemon-breasted Canary*** is more reliable, while **Southern Banded Snake-Eagle** is more conspicuous in winter.

HABITATS: Tongaland Sand Forest (the southernmost in the country), Lala Palm (*Hyphaene*) savanna.

BIRDING: Sand Forest covers most of Bonamanzi, and many of the reserve's specials, such as **Green Malkoha, Narina Trogon***, **Square-tailed Drongo, Bearded Scrub-Robin, Sombre** and **Yellow-bellied Greenbuls, Eastern Nicator, Rudd's Apalis**, and **Purple-banded Sunbird** are common throughout. **African Broadbill*** prefers particularly dense Sand Forest, especially the areas around Tree-house 5 and along the road to Lalapanzi Camp from the office. Look and listen for small parties of **Pink-throated Twinspot*** and **Grey Waxbill** in more open areas along this road. The flowering trees around the office attract a plethora of birds year-round, and time spent here in summer may be rewarded with very scarce **Neergaard's Sunbird***. This endemic is at the extreme southern end of its range at Bonamanzi, and may be found more readily further north in Zululand. The open Lala Palm savanna in the west of the reserve, easily reached by walking north from the entrance gate, holds **Senegal Lapwing** (especially after burning), and **Lemon-breasted Canary***. The canaries may be found nesting in the palms in summer, but they are nomadic, moving here in response to grass seeding, and may be absent in winter. They are also seen frequently at the roadside between the entrance gate and Hluhluwe village. Beware confusion with washed-out immature **Yellow-fronted Canary**, especially between late summer and early winter.

OTHER ANIMALS: A spotlighting excursion may reward you with the Four-toed Elephant-Shrew, Greater Bushbaby, White-tailed Mongoose, Large-spotted Genet, or even a Leopard.

GETTING THERE

Bonamanzi lies approximately 250 km north of Durban, and is signposted from the N2 either from the south via the Bushlands turn-off (right off the N2 onto a gravel road, left at the T-junction and 4 km north to the signposted reserve entrance) or from the north via Hluhluwe village (east through the village, right at the T-junction, and 6 km south to the entrance gate). Entry is restricted to residents. A small road network allows access to the 600 ha of the reserve that is open to the public. The flood plain of the Hluhluwe River may be visited from Bonamanzi. Accommodation includes self-catered tree-houses, and fully catered lodges ☎.

Hugh Chittenden

African Broadbill displays at dawn and dusk.

119 Hluhluwe River Flood Plain ✔

The Hluhluwe River flood plain is the most reliable site in South Africa for the exquisite **Rosy-breasted Longclaw***. Access is easy through the well-situated Bonamanzi Lodge (or via Hluhluwe River Lodge ☎). Contact the lodge for permission to enter, although access to the flood plain is free.

After arranging access at the Bonamanzi office, the local guide will take you to the flood plain. Scan for **Rosy-breasted Longclaw*** in moist grassland along the edge of the Hluhluwe River. They are often in the company of **Yellow-throated** and **Cape Longclaws**. **Collared Pratincole** and **Blue-cheeked Bee-eater** are common overhead in summer, while **Grey-rumped Swallow** is more plentiful in winter. **Kurrichane** and **Black-rumped** (rare) **Buttonquails** may be flushed from the grassland, and **African Crake** and **Greater Painted Snipe** from marshy edges. **Southern Brown-throated** and **Golden** (uncommon) **Weavers** breed in the reedbeds, while **Red-headed Quelea*** (summer) and **Lemon-breasted Canary*** are irregular visitors. Numbers of water birds in the small ponds at the southern edge of the flood plain (distantly visible from the lodge) vary according to water levels, but may include **African Pygmy Goose***, large numbers of ducks, storks, **Great White Pelican**, and **Goliath Heron**.

120 Mkhuze Game Reserve IBA ✔✔✔

Mecca of southern African birders, Mkhuze offers the heady mix of avian wealth, endemicity and unpredictability that makes birding the Zululand coastal plain so exciting. Not only are most of its specials relatively easily seen on a short visit, but its impressive bird list numbers over 450 species, a tally in South Africa second only to that of the vast Kruger National Park. Mkhuze's magnetism lies in its incredible diversity of habitat.

SPECIALS: Broad-billed Roller, Pel's Fishing-Owl*, Senegal Lapwing, African Cuckoo Hawk, Southern Banded Snake-Eagle, African Broadbill*, Gorgeous Bush-Shrike, Bearded Scrub-Robin, Eastern Nicator, Rudd's Apalis, Olive-tree Warbler*, Neergaard's Sunbird*, Bushveld Pipit, Green and Pink-throated Twinspots*, Grey Waxbill, and Crested Guineafowl.

SEASON: Sept-Nov sees most of the specials at the peak of their breeding activity (helpful for locating such elusive birds as **Green Malkoha, Buff-spotted Flufftail, African Broadbill*** and **Eastern Nicator**), and the exposed muddy margins of Nsumo Pan ideal for a variety of both resident water birds and Palearctic migrants. Breeding activity continues into Dec and Jan, when summer rainfall may eliminate muddy margins in Nsumo Pan but attract a variety of exciting 'rain migrants'. The Sand Forest hides are at their best towards the end of the winter dry season (roughly Jul-Oct), and the raptors and the **Yellow-billed Stork** breeding colonies are also at their peak at this time.

HABITATS: Sand Forest, Fig Forest, acacia and Lala Palm (*Hyphaene*) savanna, grassland, rocky ridges and gorges, as well as wetlands in the form of subtropical pans and rivers.

BIRDING: Nsumo Pan and the Sand Forest hides are undoubtedly the birding focal points of Mkhuze, and are excellent places from which to commence your exploration of the reserve.

Sand Forest, easily accessed from the parking areas and walkways to the Kubube Ⓐ and Kumasinga Ⓑ hides, is home to **Narina Trogon***, **Square-tailed Drongo**, **Bearded Scrub-Robin**, **Sombre** and **Yellow-bellied Greenbuls**, and **Rudd's Apalis**, as well as comical coveys of **Crested Guineafowl**. Listen for the distinctive *koing-koit!* of a skulking **Gorgeous Bush-Shrike**, or the quiet tinkling of the beautiful **Pink-throated Twinspot***, both common here.

Dense bush surrounding Kubube parking area is the best place to hear the mechanical purring of the elusive **African Broadbill***, while the more open woodland around Kumasinga supports a few pairs of **Barred Owlet** and the localised endemic, **Neergaard's Sunbird***. Listen for the distinctive call of the latter, which distinguishes it from the similar and more common **Purple-banded Sunbird**. Kumasinga is also the better of the two hides for water birds, with **Woolly-necked Stork** regular and **Dwarf Bittern**, **Lesser Moorhen** and **Allen's Gallinule**

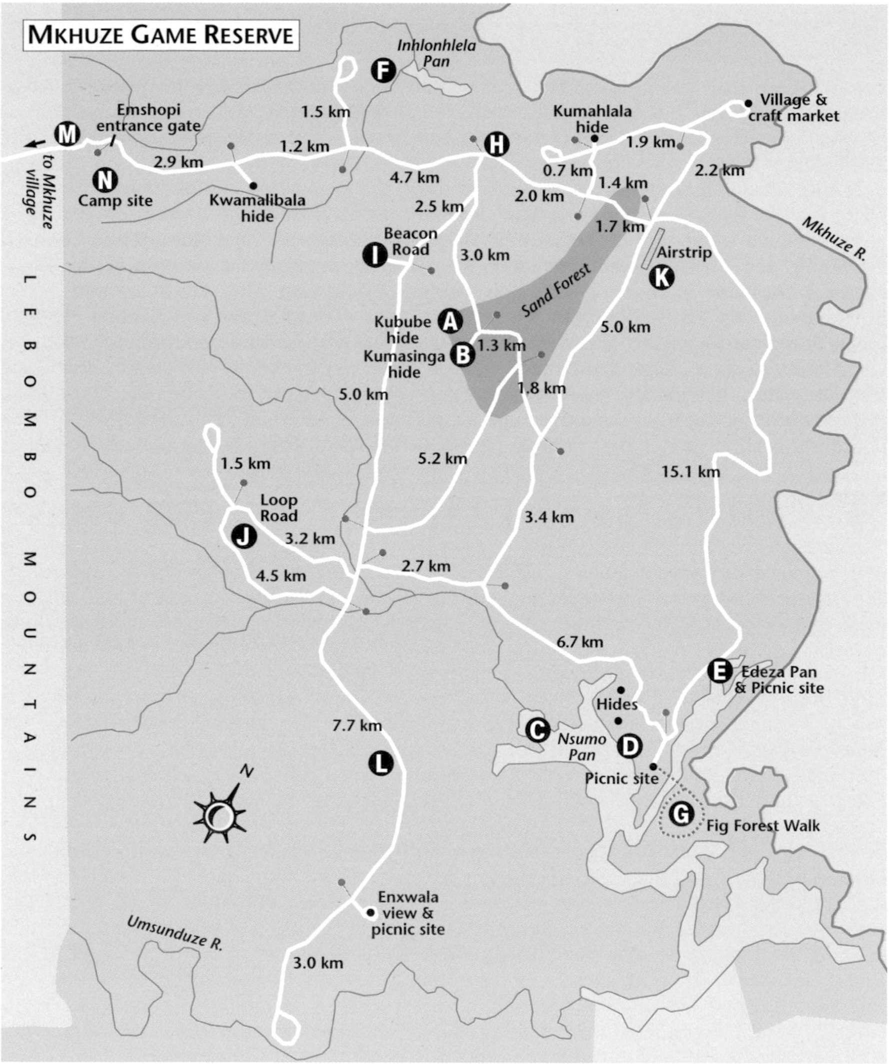

occasional in wet summers. The reedbeds support breeding **Lesser Masked-Weaver** and **Thick-billed Weaver**, and provide cover for drinking seed-eaters, notably the elusive **Green Twinspot*** and **Grey Waxbill**. The throngs of birds and mammals that utilise Kumasinga at the end of a dry winter are truly spectacular, providing superb photographic opportunities. Enquire about the guided walk in the Sand Forest, which is excellent for **African Broadbill***.

Formerly an oxbow lake flooded only in peak rainfall years, the vast Nsumo Pan **C** is now connected directly to the Mkhuze River, and water levels are erratic. However, when the water is low enough to expose muddy margins in spring, the pan attracts a wide variety of water birds, including large numbers of waterfowl and Palearctic waders. **African Purple Swamphen**, **African Jacana**, **African Wattled Lapwing**, **Water Thick-knee**, **Whiskered** and **White-winged Terns**, **African Fish-Eagle**, **Great White** and **Pink-backed Pelicans**, **Yellow-billed** and **Woolly-necked Storks**, **African Openbill** and **Goliath Heron** all occur here. Watch overhead for

Collared Pratincole, small numbers of which breed on the pan, and flocks of **Blue-cheeked Bee-eater**. Scrutinise the Fever Trees around the pan, especially in the vicinity of the picnic site, as **Pel's Fishing-Owl***, **Southern Banded Snake-Eagle** and **Sooty Falcon** have all been recorded in the area. The picnic site **D** is also an excellent place to search for the endemic **White-throated Robin-Chat**, and **Pink-throated Twinspot***.

A number of other wetland areas in Mkhuze are well worth birding, especially when water conditions in Nsumo Pan are less than ideal.

Edeza Pan **E**, another oxbow of the Mkhuze River, is worth a scan and is best viewed from the Edeza picnic site.

The best place in Mkhuze to find **African Pygmy Goose*** and **Southern Banded Snake-Eagle** is the exquisite, lily-covered Inhlonhlela Pan **F**, accessible either from the well-appointed Inhlonhlela Bush Lodge, or on a guided walk from Mantuma Camp. Small numbers of **Allen's Gallinule** have also bred here in recent years.

Hugh Chittenden

Neergaard's Sunbird

Another jewel in Mkhuze's crown is the Fig Forest Walk **G**, which is now accessible only on guided walks. It is essential to book in advance to ensure an early start and a like-minded group of co-walkers. After initially traversing open acacia savanna frequented by **Eastern Nicator** and **Rudd's Apalis**, the trail crosses the Mkhuze River by means of a long suspension bridge, and loops through a beautiful riverine forest of Sycamore Figs and Fever Trees.

Conspicuous in their vocalisations are **White-eared Barbet** and its brood parasite, **Scaly-throated Honeyguide**, as well as the frugivorous **Crowned** and **Trumpeter Hornbills**, **Narina Trogon***, **Brown-headed Parrot** (uncommon), **Purple-crested Turaco**, **African Green Pigeon** and **Black-bellied Starling**. Mixed-species foraging flocks of insectivores may contain **Square-tailed Drongo**, **Blue-mantled Crested Flycatcher**, **Black-throated Wattle-eye** (uncommon), **Grey Tit-Flycatcher**, **Yellow-breasted Apalis**, **African Yellow White-eye**

Claire Spottiswoode

A suspension bridge leads into the Fig Forest.

GETTING THERE

Mkhuze lies approximately 275 km north of Durban. From the south it is reached off the N2 via the well-signposted Bayala road (20 km of gravel road) or, from the north, via Mkhuze village (17 km of gravel road). The reserve's birder-friendly facilities include an 80 km road network covering all the main habitats, a range of self-guided and guided walking trails, guided night drives, and a number of hides (excellent for photography), viewing platforms and picnic sites. Accommodation options include a camping ground near the entrance gate (petrol is available in the reserve), bush lodges at Inhlonhlela and Umkhumbe, and a variety of accommodation at the main Mantuma Camp. There is also a restaurant near the swimming pool at Mantuma, while the office sells basic foodstuffs. Enquire about the new entrance on the D820.

and **Collared Sunbird**. Scan dense canopy foliage for **Pel's Fishing-Owl*** and exposed snags for **Broad-billed Roller, African Cuckoo Hawk** and the scarce **Southern Banded Snake-Eagle** and search for the elusive **Green Malkoha**. Another worthwhile walk (self-guided) is the short River Trail that overlooks the Mkhuze River below Mantuma Camp Ⓗ, where **White-fronted Bee-eater, Broad-billed Roller, White-throated Robin-Chat** and **Pink-throated Twinspot*** may be found.

The bulk of Mkhuze is covered in the more open acacia savanna ('bushveld') typical of much of eastern Africa, supporting many widespread and well-known woodland birds. The Beacon Ⓘ and Loop Ⓙ roads are especially productive for raptors, notably **White-headed** and **Lappet-faced Vultures, Bateleur, Lizard Buzzard**, and **Martial Eagle**, as well as **Crested Francolin, Bearded Woodpecker, Black-bellied Bustard, Grey-headed Bush-Shrike, Flappet** and **Sabota Larks**, and **Bushveld Pipit**.

Areas of denser thicket flanking the road south of the airstrip Ⓚ support **Senegal Lapwing, Grey Penduline-Tit, Olive-tree Warbler*** (uncommon summer migrant), and **Burnt-necked Eremomela**, while the moist Lala Palm savanna along the Enxwala Road Ⓛ is home to the localised **Lemon-breasted Canary*** (scarce). **Mocking Cliff-Chat, Striped Pipit** and **Jameson's Firefinch** are best sought along the rocky slopes near the park's entrance gate Ⓜ.

A guided night drive increases the birder's chance of encountering **African Scops-Owl** and **Spotted Eagle-Owl, Pearl-spotted** and **Barred** (scarce) **Owlets, Bronze-winged Courser, Fiery-necked Nightjar** and a variety of nocturnal mammals. The camp site Ⓝ has resident **African Wood-Owl**.

OTHER ANIMALS: Mkhuze is one of the country's top game reserves, providing excellent mammal-viewing. Notable species include Leopard, White and Black Rhinoceroses, Elephant, Hippopotamus, White-tailed Mongoose, Four-toed Elephant-Shrew, and the localised antelopes, Nyala and Suni. Nsumo Pan boasts enormous Nile Crocodile.

NEARBY SITES: The adjacent Phinda Reserve also offers fantastic birding with luxury accommodation and guided excursions.

121 Lower Mkhuze & Muzi Pans IBA ✔✔

This exciting new birding area, with riverine gallery forest, coastal grassland and reed-fringed freshwater pan systems, has proven reliable for **Pel's Fishing-Owl*** throughout the year. East Coast littoral specials such as **Lemon-breasted Canary*** and **Rudd's Apalis** may also be seen here.

Lower Mkhuze/Muzi is reached on the main Sodwana road from Hluhluwe. About 50 km beyond Hluhluwe you will reach the Mkhuze River bridge. For Muzi pans, drive another 1 km beyond the Mkhuze River bridge, and take the D820 turn-off to the left. You will see the pans and wetlands, one of the best areas for birding, on both sides of the road after 2 km. A short distance beyond the pans is the KwaJobe community centre, where guides can be met by arrangement with the Zululand Birding Route ☎.

Likely birds in the area include **Pink-backed Pelican, Goliath** and **Black Herons, African Openbill, Comb** and **White-backed Ducks, African Pygmy Goose*, African Marsh-Harrier, Lesser Moorhen, Allen's Gallinule, Lesser Jacana, Senegal Lapwing, Long-toed Lapwing** (rare), **Greater Painted Snipe, Collared Pratincole, Black Coucal, Rufous-winged Cisticola, Blue-cheeked Bee-eater** and **Lemon-breasted Canary***.

The main special of the Lower Mkhuze area is undoubtedly **Pel's Fishing-Owl***. Ask your guide to obtain permission from KZN Wildlife and lead you to the best spot in the riparian fig forest along the river south of the road for this elusive species. The fig forest and adjacent vegetation allows access to **White-eared Barbet, Green Malkoha, Scaly-throated Honeyguide, African Emerald Cuckoo, Rudd's Apalis, Grey-rumped Swallow, Eastern Nicator, White-browed Robin-Chat, Gorgeous Bush-Shrike, Bearded Scrub-Robin, Red-faced Cisticola, African Yellow White-eye, Grey Sunbird, Lemon-breasted Canary*** and **Brown-headed Parrot**. Future developments include a bird hide and camp site, and arranged canoe trips on the pan.

122 Ndumo Game Reserve

IBA ✔✔

This remote Maputaland reserve has achieved legendary status in southern African birding circles, boasting a bird list that is high in both quantity and quality.

SPECIALS: Scaly-throated Honeyguide, Narina Trogon*, Broad-billed Roller, Pel's Fishing-Owl*, Senegal Lapwing, Southern Banded Snake-Eagle, Sooty Falcon, African Broadbill*, Gorgeous Bush-Shrike, Retz's Helmet-Shrike, Black-throated Wattle-eye, Bearded Scrub-Robin, Eastern Nicator, Rudd's Apalis, Green-capped Eremomela, Neergaard's Sunbird*, Bushveld Pipit, Pink-throated Twinspot*, and Grey Waxbill.

SEASON: Ndumo is at its best in early summer, when most of the specials are breeding and before summer rainfall covers the margins of the pans.

HABITATS: Wetlands, riverine forests, flood plain, Sand Forest; acacia woodland (south-west).

BIRDING: Start birding at the observation tower on Ndumo Hill Ⓐ, which affords spectacular views across the flood plain of the Pongola River. The taller woodland here is good for cuckoos in summer, and is one of the best areas in the reserve to search for **Retz's Helmet-Shrike** and **Green-capped Eremomela**, both scarce in KwaZulu-Natal.

A slow drive on the one-way loop through Mahemane Bush Ⓑ should reward the birder with a selection of species typical of Sand Forest thicket, such as **Crested Guineafowl, Narina Trogon*, Square-tailed Drongo, Gorgeous Bush-Shrike, Bearded Scrub-Robin, Terrestrial Brownbul, Yellow-bellied Greenbul, Eastern Nicator** and **Rudd's Apalis**. The highly sought-after East Coast littoral endemics, **Neergaard's Sunbird*** and **Pink-throated Twinspot***, are common here, but it requires patience and a knowledge of their calls to track them down. The area around Skhove bird hide Ⓒ holds most of the aforementioned species, as well as a colony of **White-fronted Bee-eater**. Spend time in the vicinity of the picnic site at Red Cliffs Ⓓ, as **Broad-billed Roller** and **African Green Pigeon** are seen frequently in riverside trees, and **African Broadbill*** is resident here.

Guided walks in the company of an armed guard (many of the guards have excellent local bird knowledge) is the only way of reaching the pristine riverine forest. The 5 km North Pongola Walk Ⓔ is highly recommended, traversing riparian forest that is home to **Scaly-throated Honeyguide, White-eared Barbet, Narina Trogon*, Woodland Kingfisher**, and **Purple-crested Turaco**. With luck, you may see **African Finfoot*** along the river, or find a **Pel's Fishing-Owl*** at its day roost.

Another superb walk is through the Sycamore Fig Forest along the edge of Shokwe Pan Ⓕ,

Shaen Adey/IOA

Fever trees at the edge of a pan in Ndumo

GETTING THERE

Ndumo lies on the Mozambique border in far northern Zululand, approximately 380 km from Durban. Take the Jozini turn-off, signposted 'Ndumo and Sodwana', from the N2 north of Mkhuze village, and follow signs to the reserve. All but the final 15 km of road is tarred, but it is potholed in places and wandering livestock present a hazard. The KwaZulu-Natal Wildlife rest camp has chalet accommodation, a camping site, a small shop and a swimming pool, while the upmarket lodge on Banzi Pan is run by Wilderness Safaris. Roads traverse the Sand Forest and western bushveld areas, although the more interesting riverine forest and the pans are accessible only on guided walks and drives. These can be reserved in advance or on arrival at the camp. Other facilities include picnic sites, a bird-viewing hide and an observation tower.

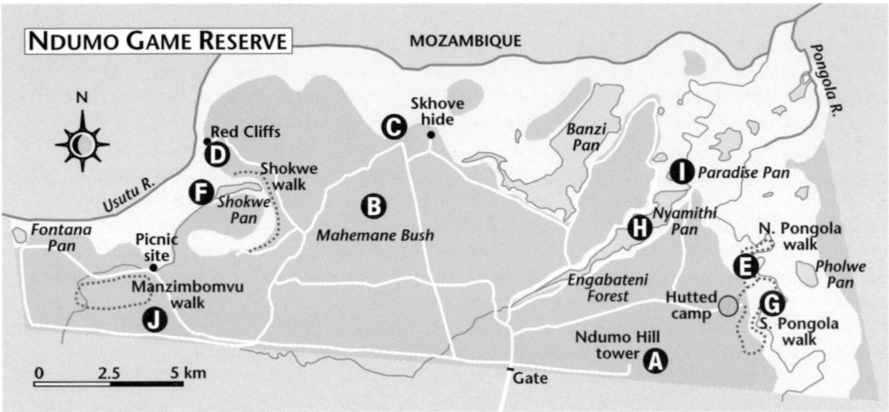

an oxbow lake of the Usutu River. **Southern Banded Snake-Eagle** and **African Cuckoo Hawk** are seen regularly, and both **Verreaux's Eagle-Owl** and **African Barred Owlet** are resident and heard frequently in the late afternoon; **African Broadbill*** is common in thickets along the forest edge. Also watch for **Green Malkoha** and **Black-throated Wattle-eye**.

The South Pongola Walk G is also excellent, and although it is not quite as productive as its northern counterpart, **Pel's Fishing-Owl*** is seen here more regularly.

The Fever Tree-lined Nyamithi Pan H is the largest and most picturesque pan on the Pongola flood plain. A guided drive here in early summer is rewarding, as the lower water levels attract large concentrations of waterfowl, such as **Fulvous Whistling-Duck** and **Comb Duck**, Palearctic waders, **African Jacana**, **Water Thick-knee**, **Whiskered** and **White-winged Terns**, **Glossy Ibis**, and **Yellow-billed**, **Woolly-necked** and **Saddle-billed** (scarce) **Storks**, as well as **African Openbill**, and **Goliath Heron**. **Sooty Falcons** are seen regularly in the Fever Trees from Dec-Apr, and this is one of the best sites in the subregion for this scarce migrant. **Eastern Saw-wing** has also been recorded here recently. Scrutinise any **Black Heron** carefully, as a vagrant **Slaty Egret*** has made its home here for the past few years. The bird hide overlooking Nyamithi Pan is excellent for water birds.

The marshy Paradise Pan I, actually a northern extension of Nyamithi Pan, should be scanned for **African Pygmy Goose***, **Black Coucal** (uncommon), **Lesser Moorhen**, **Greater Painted Snipe**, **Lesser Jacana**, **Rufous-bellied Heron**, **Southern Brown-throated Weaver** and, with luck, **Red-headed Quelea***.

The southern edge of Banzi Pan may also be visited on a guided drive and holds similar species to Nyamithi, but it is more difficult to access.

More open woodland west of the hutted camp and along the southern boundary fence, on the Manzimbomvu Loop J, holds typical bushveld species such as **Bearded Woodpecker**, **Bateleur**, **Gabar Goshawk**, **Grey-headed Bush-Shrike**, **Grey Penduline-Tit**, **Burnt-necked Eremomela**, **Flappet** and **Sabota Larks**, and **Marico Sunbird**. **Senegal Lapwing**, **Stierling's Wren-Warbler**, **Bushveld Pipit** and **Long-tailed Paradise-Whydah** are less commonly encountered. **Bennett's Woodpecker**, a rarity in KwaZulu-Natal, is resident in the tall Knobthorn woodland, 7 km west of the entrance gate.

OTHER ANIMALS: Ndumo is more famous for its birds than its large mammals, although White and Black Rhinoceroses, Hippopotamus and Giraffe may be seen. The secretive Suni and Red Duiker are common but skulking in the dense Sand Forest.

123 Tembe Elephant Park

4X4 ✔✔

Situated just to the east of Ndumo, Tembe Elephant Park protects the last wild Elephant herds in KwaZulu-Natal. Although it holds many of the same birds as its more famous cousin, Tembe also offers the birder the only reasonable chance in South Africa of finding **Plain-backed Sunbird**, a species otherwise restricted to the Mozambique coastal plain.

SPECIALS: Similar to Ndumo, although Woodwards' Batis and Plain-backed Sunbird are seen regularly, while birds of the drier bushveld are largely absent.

SEASON: Plain-backed Sunbird is present all year-round.

HABITATS: Sand Forest, coastal grassland, marshes.

BIRDING: Plain-backed Sunbird has been found at various places in the park, although it is seen most regularly in the tall woodland a few hundred metres west of the observation tower (also search the northern end of the Gowanini Loop, near the picnic site). Park here and listen for its distinctive call, or wait for mixed flocks of insectivorous birds. **Woodwards' Batis** is plentiful both here and in dense woodland throughout the park. Birding (no more self-guided trail here after Lion introduced) near the reserve entrance may reveal **African Broadbill***, **Woodwards' Batis**, **Retz's Helmet-Shrike**, **Neergaard's Sunbird*** and **Pink-throated Twinspot***. Lion have been introduced into the reserve.

GETTING THERE

The entrance to Tembe lies 20 km to the east of the final turn-off to Ndumo Game Reserve. A network of sandy tracks traverse the reserve, which also has two observation hides. The only accommodation is a private tented camp run by Tembe Elephant Lodge ☎. The pristine sand forests and coastal grasslands of this remote reserve can only be explored in a 4WD vehicle.

Some 20 km east of the Tembe gate, the tar road crosses the palm-studded kwa-Ngwanase grasslands. These grasslands provide excellent birding, especially when flooded in summer. **African Pygmy Goose***, **White-backed Duck**, **Lesser Jacana**, **Whiskered Tern**, and **Squacco Heron** are frequent at roadside ponds, 8-16 km west of Manguzi village, while adjacent areas should be scanned for **African Wattled Lapwing**, **Collared Pratincole**, **Grey-rumped Swallow** and **Montagu's Harrier**.

The far-carrying calls of **Coqui** and **Shelley's Francolins** may help you locate coveys of these elusive birds in the grassland, although the main prize here is undoubtedly the beautiful **Rosy-breasted Longclaw***. A few pairs are resident south of the road, 16 km west of Manguzi. Both **Swamp*** and **Square-tailed Nightjars** are commonly encountered here after dark. In peak rainfall years, **Black-rumped Buttonquail**, **Allen's Gallinule**, **Lesser Moorhen**, **Rufous-bellied Heron** and even **Eurasian Bittern** may be flushed from the edges of flooded grassland. **Senegal Lapwing** moves onto the burnt grasslands in winter and this is one of very few places where it may be directly compared to its larger cousin, the **Black-winged Lapwing**.

Richard du Toit

Pink-throated Twinspot

124 Kosi Bay Nature Reserve

IBA ✔

Kosi Bay Nature Reserve protects a unique estuarine system, and its surrounding coastal grassland and forest, in a remote wilderness setting. The thick coastal forest around the KwaZulu-Natal Wildlife camp is home to a selection of East Coast littoral specials, including **Woodwards' Batis** and **Brown Scrub-Robin**.

Leatherback and Loggerhead Turtles lay their eggs on the beaches here in summer, and may be seen on nocturnal excursions from the KwaZulu-Natal Wildlife camp.

Kosi, situated in the far north-eastern corner of KwaZulu-Natal, lies 150 km from the N2 via Jozini and Manguzi villages.

Kosi Forest Lodge and, further north, Rocktail Bay Lodge offer excellent coastal forest birding and luxury accommodation.

125 Pongola Nature Reserve

IBA ✔

This small KZN Wildlife-administered reserve, which surrounds Jozini (Pongolapoort) Dam, is of interest primarily to birders seeking to enlarge their KwaZulu-Natal bird lists. **Olivetree Warbler** may be found in thorn thickets in summer. **Magpie Shrike** and **Burchell's Starling**, rare or absent further south in the province, are common in the camping ground, which is accessed through the reserve entrance gate in the Swaziland border town of Golela. Northern bushveld species to watch out for include **Bennett's Woodpecker**.

126 Ithala Game Reserve

IBA ✔✔

Situated in north-western KwaZulu-Natal, Ithala is a good site for birds typical of mid-altitude grassland and thornveld, most notably the elusive **Barrow's Korhaan***.

SPECIALS: Barrow's Korhaan*, Shelley's Francolin, Brown-backed Honeybird, Southern Ground-Hornbill*, Half-collared Kingfisher, Freckled Nightjar, African Hawk-Eagle, Southern Bald Ibis*, Buff-streaked Chat, and Mocking Cliff-Chat.

SEASON: The specials are present year-round, although **Southern Bald Ibis*** and **Barrow's Korhaan*** are easier to locate during the winter dry season, when they move onto burnt areas.

HABITATS: Mid-altitude grassland, rocky ridges and gorges, streams.

BIRDING: Ntshondwe Camp is an excellent place to start birding Ithala, with frugivores such as **Red-fronted Tinkerbird**, **Trumpeter Hornbill**, **Purple-crested Turaco** and **African Green Pigeon** attracted to fruiting fig trees, and **Mocking Cliff-Chat** and **Striped Pipit** common in the surrounding rocky terrain. **Freckled Nightjar** may be heard here after dark.

The park's grassland specials are most easily seen along the Onverwacht Loop, just north of the entrance gate. **Barrow's Korhaan*** is a fairly common, but elusive resident, and is most easily seen in winter, when it feeds in heavily grazed or burnt grasslands. These areas are also favoured by **Southern Ground-Hornbill***, **Southern**

GETTING THERE

Ithala lies 60 km north-east of Vryheid in northern KwaZulu-Natal, between the town of Louwsberg and the Pongola River. The reserve is signposted from the R69, about 400 km from Durban. A wide range of camping and hutted accommodation is available. Good roads permit access to all the major birding areas, while a number of self-guided trails radiate from the main camp at Ntshondwe. An entrance fee is payable.

Richard du Toit

Plains Zebra in Ithala Game Reserve

Bald Ibis*, **Denham's Bustard***, **Black-winged Lapwing**, and **Plain-backed Pipit**. Other grassland specials to watch for are **Croaking, Zitting, Cloud*** and **Wing-snapping Cisticolas** and, with luck, their brood parasite, the scarce **Cuckoo Finch***.

A wide variety of common bushveld species may be encountered along the Ngubhu and Dakaneni Loops, most notably **Shelley's Francolin**, **Brown-backed Honeybird**, **White-throated Robin-Chat**, and a host of large 'indicator' species, such as **Lappet-faced Vulture**, **Bateleur**, **Martial Eagle** and **Secretarybird**, largely absent from adjacent parts of KwaZulu-Natal. The uncommon **Half-collared Kingfisher** inhabits the fast-flowing streams in the reserve, and is seen frequently around the Mbizo Bush Camp and picnic site.

OTHER ANIMALS: Ithala boasts a full complement of plains' game, with the notable exception of Lion. Interesting smaller mammals include Serval, Aardwolf, and African Striped Weasel.

127 Chelmsford Nature Reserve IBA ✔

Chelmsford Nature Reserve is a reliable site for the localised **Barrow's Korhaan***, a bird rarely recorded on traditional birding routes. Listen for the strange croaking calls of family groups from the various loop drives through the game park. They are particularly vocal at dawn and dusk, but may be difficult to see in the grasslands. Other noteworthy species include **African Grass-Owl*** (uncommon), **Marsh Owl**, **Denham's Bustard***, **Blue Crane**, **Southern Bald Ibis***, which breeds at the edge of the reserve and is encountered regularly on burnt ground in winter, and **Pink-billed Lark** (a relative rarity in KwaZulu-Natal). **Montagu's Harrier** is seen occasionally over the grasslands in summer, while **Corncrake** is a scarce visitor.

The reserve, which is also home to healthy populations of Black Wildebeest and Oribi, lies some 25 km south of Newcastle, and is signposted off the N11. Camping and picnic sites are available.

128 Vryheid Area ✔

Forest patches in Vryheid Hill Nature Reserve, situated in the town itself, hold **African Crowned Eagle** and **Bush Blackcap***, while the grassy areas hold **Broad-tailed Warbler**. The Klipfontein Bird Sanctuary, on the R34 south of Vryheid, east of the Dundee turn-off, hosts a variety of water birds, including **South African Shelduck** and **Baillon's Crake**, as well as **Red-chested Flufftail** and **Grey Crowned Crane**.

129 Ladysmith Area ✔✔

In summer, the reedbeds and flooded grasslands of the Ladysmith Sewage Works (Malandeni) are excellent for skulking species such as **Baillon's Crake**, **African Rail** and **Little Bittern**, while **Eurasian Bittern** and **Striped Crake*** are rare visitors. To get to the sewage works from either Murchison or Lyell streets, turn east into Princess Street, cross the river on the new bridge, turn left into Kandahar Avenue, and take the first right, which is Madras Road. Turn left into Circle Road after crossing the railway lines, and the entrance to the works is 150 m beyond the double railway line.

The grasslands, mainly on the western side of Ladysmith, particularly the Bluebank, air-port and Elandslaagte areas, are very productive for **Wing-snapping**, **Cloud***, **Zitting**, **Desert** and **Croaking Cisticolas**, **Melodious Lark*** and **Barrow's Korhaan***.

Spioenkop Nature Reserve, accessed from the R74 between Bergville and Winterton, offers a mix of rocky country and bushveld species, and grasslands here hold **Melodious Lark***, **Shelley's Francolin** and **Barrow's Korhaan***. Weenen Nature Reserve, on the R74 west of Weenen town, offers excellent bushveld birding. Grassy areas hold Barrow's Korhaan* and in summer **Icterine Warbler** should be searched for in areas of acacias.

ROUTE **12**

HIGHLANDS ENDEMICS ROUTE

Sites on this Highlands Endemics Route, which meanders along the well-watered eastern edge of the Great Escarpment, offer the avid endemic-hunter a host of rare and range-restricted birds in an area of outstanding natural beauty. Spanning a distance of some 500 km as the Lammergeier* flies, from Swaziland's flagship montane national park of Malalotja in the north-east to the bleak Afro-alpine heights of Lesotho's Maluti Mountains in the south-west, this route encompasses South Africa's famous birding site of Wakkerstroom and the recently recognised adjacent Memel area, as well as the Drakensberg peaks to the south. Each site merits extensive exploration, particularly taking into account the considerable scenic attractions, and birders may choose weekend visits (or longer) to fully appreciate these areas. For the international visitor with limited time, the individual sites can easily be included in standard birding loops through eastern South Africa. Taken together, however, the Highlands Endemics Route offers a chance of finding all southern African highland specials!

TOP 10 BIRDS

- Blue Korhaan
- Southern Bald Ibis
- Bush Blackcap
- Rudd's Lark
- Botha's Lark
- Lammergeier
- Drakensberg Rock-jumper
- Yellow-breasted Pipit
- Mountain Pipit
- Drakensberg Siskin

The Great Escarpment, which separates South Africa's coastal plain from its inland plateau, is steepest and highest in the east, especially between the Eastern Cape and Mpumalanga, where it forms the dramatic Drakensberg range. Summer – when the migrants have returned, the avian endemics are more conspicuous due to their territorial displays, and the landscapes are verdant and studded with wild flowers – is undoubtedly the best time to visit this region. Winters are clear and cold, especially at night, with regular snowfalls on higher ground, and some of the birds vacate the dry, golden grasslands for warmer climes.

Walter Knirr/IOA

South Africa's highlands are rich in endemics.

Numerous avian endemics are restricted largely to this area; among these are some of the most enigmatic and sought-after birds in southern Africa. They can be divided into birds that occur in medium to high altitude grasslands, and those that are restricted to the highest alpine grasslands (2 800 m and above). The former group includes Blue Korhaan, all three southern African crane species – Blue, Wattled and Grey Crowned, White-winged Flufftail, Southern Bald Ibis*, Blue Swallow*, Rudd's and Botha's Larks*, Gurney's Sugarbird*, the striking Yellow-breasted Pipit*, with Bush Black-cap* and Barratt's Warbler in adjacent scrub. The true alpine specials are Drakensberg Rock-jumper, Drakensberg Siskin, Lammergeier* and Mountain Pipit. See also Sani Pass (p. 116) for another alpine site.

130 Malalotja NR (Swaziland)

IBA ✔✔

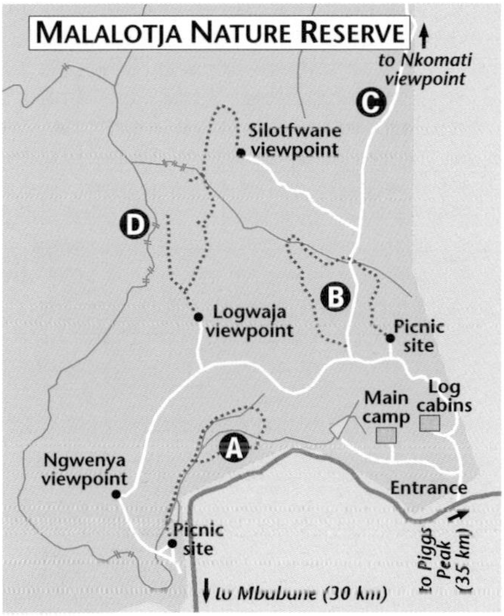

An easy four-hour drive from Gauteng, the 1 800 ha Malalotja Nature Reserve is home to one of southern Africa's rarest birds, the magnificent **Blue Swallow***. It is arguably Swaziland's most attractive reserve, lying at the edge of the Drakensberg escarpment and protecting a wide variety of habitats that range in altitude from below 800 m to above 1 800 m. The bird list of more than 280 species is correspondingly diverse and it is possible to see more than 100 species in a day here during the summer months.

SPECIALS: Denham's Bustard*, Ground Woodpecker*, Striped Flufftail*, Black-winged Lapwing, Southern Bald Ibis*, Sentinel Rock-Thrush, Buff-streaked Chat, Blue Swallow*, Broad-tailed Warbler, Short-tailed Pipit*, and Gurney's Sugarbird*.

SEASON: The **Blue Swallow*** is present only in summer. This is the best time also for most of the grassland specials, although **Southern Bald Ibis*** colonies are active only from June-Oct.

HABITATS: Montane grassland, gorges and rocky slopes, wetlands (montane vleis, dams and rivers), patches of mist-belt and riverine forest.

BIRDING: **Blue Swallow*** is undoubtedly the star attraction here, and a few pairs of this endangered species breed in disused Aardvark burrows in the pristine montane grassland. These elegant birds are best viewed by walking in the area between the entrance gate and Malalotja Vlei Ⓐ, and along the main track beyond the picnic site near Ⓑ. Malalotja Vlei is worth checking for **Broad-tailed Warbler** and a variety of more common water birds.

The gravel roads in the park are easily traversed in 2WD vehicles, and provide access to good grassland and rocky slope habitat such as at Ⓒ. Driving slowly and scanning the surroundings should turn up coveys of **Red-winged Francolin** (especially in the early morning), **Ground Woodpecker***, **Denham's Bustard***, **Black-winged Lapwing**, **Cape** and **Sentinel** (rare) **Rock-Thrushes**, **Buff-streaked Chat**, **Mocking Cliff-Chat** and **Short-tailed Pipit***. Cisticolas are particularly well represented, and are best identified by their breeding displays in summer. Listen for **Zitting**, **Croaking** (widespread), **Wing-snapping** (gentle, short-grass slopes), **Wailing** (tall-grass slopes), **Lazy** (rocky slopes) and **Levaillant's** (wetlands) **Cisticolas**, and **Neddicky** (scrubs and trees), as well as for the jumbled melody of **Cape Grassbird** (rank vegetation).

Two colonies of **Southern Bald Ibis*** are present during winter; look out for them in the vicinity of Malolotja Falls Ⓓ. Also keep an eye out here for **Black Stork** (a year-round resident of the park), **Jackal Buzzard**, **African Crowned Eagle** and **African Cuckoo Hawk**, which can be seen in the forest patches in the upper Malalotja Valley.

OTHER ANIMALS: Malalotja is an excellent area for viewing a variety of grassland mammals, the most interesting of which include Black Wildebeest, Blesbok, Oribi, Mountain and Common Reedbuck, Grey Rhebok, and Klipspringer. Serval, Caracal, Leopard and Cape Porcupine are also present.

GETTING THERE

The reserve lies approximately 30 km north of Mbabane on the road to Piggs Peak, and is well signposted. Log cabins and camping facilities are available near the reserve entrance. Bird and mammal lists, and excellent leaflets covering recommended walks, are available from the informative museum at the entrance gate.

131 Wakkerstroom

IBA ✓✓✓

Warwick Tarboton

Rudd's Lark

Once a sleepy hamlet in a forgotten part of the country, the presence of rare highland birds in its vicinity has propelled Wakkerstroom into the international birding limelight. Its grassland specials, such as the localised **Rudd's** and **Botha's Larks*** and the beautiful **Yellow-breasted Pipit***, are its major drawcards for international twitchers. Wakkerstroom also boasts an excellent wetland at the edge of town, and a birder-friendly infrastructure, complete with local bird guides, bird-viewing hides, and comfortable accommodation. Although one clement summer day here may be enough to find most of the target species, the unpredictability of the weather and the superb birding conditions mean that a stay of two to three days is a far more reliable and enjoyable option.

SPECIALS: Red-winged Francolin, Ground Woodpecker*, Denham's Bustard*, Blue and Barrow's* Korhaans, Grey Crowned and Blue Cranes, Black-winged Lapwing, Southern Bald Ibis*, Sentinel Rock-Thrush, Buff-streaked Chat, Bush Blackcap*, Drakensberg Prinia, Rudd's*, Eastern Long-billed, Pink-billed (rare) and Botha's* Larks, Yellow-breasted Pipit*, African Rail and Pale-crowned Cisticola.

SEASON: Good birding may be enjoyed at Wakkerstroom at any time of the year, although most of the specials are easiest to locate in early summer (Oct-early Dec).

HABITATS: Open grassland, forest patches, gorges, cliffs, extensive wetland habitat (vleis, pans and dams).

BIRDING: Using Wakkerstroom as a base, a number of easy morning or day trips may be taken. If you are not accompanied by a guide, please obtain permission before walking across any fields in the Wakkerstroom area.

Botha's and Rudd's Larks Loop: This drive covers approximately 60 km of road, and traverses a range of excellent grassland habitats, providing the opportunity to find most of Wakkerstroom's grassland specials, including the elusive **Botha's Lark***. If you have time for only one drive from Wakkerstroom, this is it!

Take the gravel road towards Amersfoort for 9 km, and turn left towards Volksrust shortly after crossing the railway line for the second time. The birding is excellent from this point on Ⓐ, and **Blue Korhaan** (common, and easily located by its croaking call), **Blue Crane**, **Southern Bald Ibis***, **Spike-heeled** and **Red-capped Larks** and **Cape Longclaw** are all reasonably conspicuous. Common summer migrants to the area include **Amur Falcon** and **Banded Martin**, with **Denham's Bustard*** and **Lesser Kestrel** occurring in smaller numbers. The dominant sound at this time comes from ubiquitous **Wing-snapping Cisticola** and **African Pipit**, which display high overhead, while bumble-bee-like **Yellow-crowned Bishop** frequently perches on roadside fences. Check the rocky hillside on the right after 6 km Ⓑ for **Ground**

GETTING THERE

Wakkerstroom lies in eastern Mpumalanga, some 300 km from Gauteng, and can be visited easily as a weekend excursion from Johannesburg, or connected with Zululand via Piet Retief. Accommodation in town includes some of the best-known birding establishments in the country, such as Weaver's Nest, Toad Hall and Beautiful Just Birding, although it is by no means restricted to these guest houses. BirdLife South Africa has a project office at Wakkerstroom and can arrange the services of a local guide. It is situated a few kilometres west of town on the road to Volksrust, has three bird hides situated on the property, and camping is possible near the office. A camping and caravan site, known as De Oude Stasie, is situated on the opposite side of the Wakkerstroom vlei from the town, near the old railway station. Warwick and Michele Tarboton's superb *Wakkerstroom Bird and Nature Guide*, complete with comprehensive maps and bird, mammal and wildflower finding information, is highly recommended.

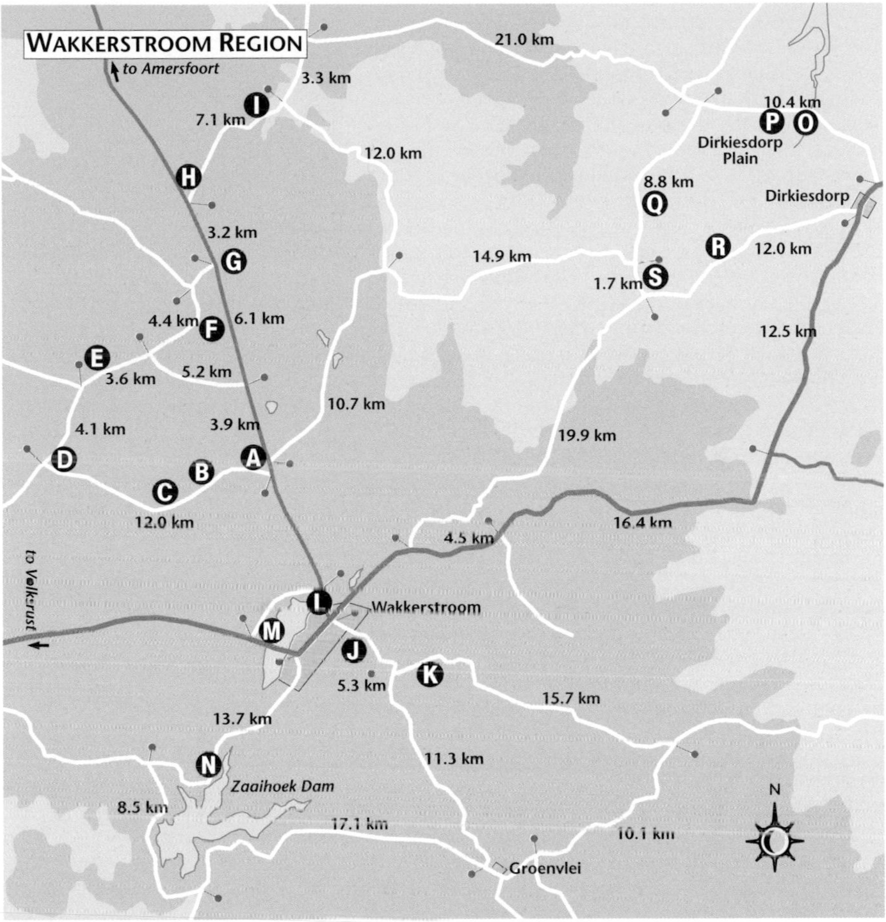

Woodpecker*, **Sentinel Rock-Thrush**, **Buff-streaked Chat** (uncommon), **Mountain Wheatear** and **Eastern Long-billed Lark**. Scan the road verges carefully from this point, as this is one of the best stretches for the nomadic **Botha's Lark***, and **Rudd's Lark*** is often present here too **C**. Their breeding sites vary from year to year according to the timing of the veld burning, so it is important to locate suitable areas of short grass. Note that it is ill-advised to trespass in these fields and the services of a local guide are recommended to locate the most current areas and walk in the fields.

Turn right at the T-junction **D** (signposted 'Wydgelegen'), 12 km from the Wakkerstroom-Amersfoort road, and continue the loop, with regular stops to scan and listen for resident species. The next 5 km is good for **Rudd's Lark***: listen for the distinctive song, given in high aerial display, but don't despair if they are silent, as more reliable sites exist along the Wakkerstroom-Amersfoort road. Immediately west of the railway line (opposite the 20 km marker), a small farm track leads off left for 2 km to Fickland Pan **E**, a seasonal wetland that often holds all three southern African grebe species (**Great Crested, Black-necked** and **Little Grebes**), **Maccoa Duck**, **Southern Pochard**, and **Whiskered Tern**. An entry fee needs to be paid at the kraal. Return to the road and continue the loop, passing a signposted road back to Wakkerstroom. The grassland along this road holds many of the same species as the remainder of the loop (but not Rudd's and Botha's Larks).

Scanning for Yellow-breasted Pipit near Wakkerstroom

Rather than return directly to Wakkerstroom, continue north-eastwards, climbing a ridge Ⓕ that is good for **Red-winged Francolin**, **Ground Woodpecker***, **Buff-streaked Chat** and **Sentinel Rock-Thrush**. To reach the best site for **Rudd's Lark***, turn left at the T-junction with the Wakkerstroom-Amersfoort Ⓖ road and continue towards Amersfoort. After 3.2 km Ⓗ, turn right. Listen in this area for the larks, a few pairs of which usually breed in the field to the left (north) of this road. A short detour to a patch of Ouhout woodland at Ⓘ may yield **Bush Blackcap***. To complete the loop, drive the 20 km or so back to Wakkerstroom along the Wakkerstroom-Amersfoort road, watching in rocky areas for **Eastern Long-billed Lark**, which is especially common here.

Yellow-breasted Pipit Drive:* This route heads southwards out of Wakkerstroom, climbing to the high-altitude grassland favoured by this handsome endemic. Take the road signposted 'Utrecht', and scan the rocky hillsides and the quarry on the right Ⓙ for **Ground Woodpecker***, **Sentinel Rock-Thrush**, **Buff-streaked Chat** and **Mountain Wheatear**. Turn left after 5.3 km, along the road towards Paulpietersburg. Stop after approximately 1 km, and enter the large field on the right Ⓚ at the wire entrance gate. (This is public land and permission is not required to walk here.) Walk to the right towards the crest of the hill, watching for **Eastern Long-billed Lark**, **Sentinel Rock-Thrush** and, especially, **Yellow-breasted Pipit***. The best way to locate the birds is to listen for their calls, frequent during early summer. **Rudd's Lark*** also frequents this area, but is not as easy to find here as it is on the 'Botha's and Rudd's Larks Loop'. **Black Harrier** is regular in late summer/early autumn.

The Wetland Loop: As the name suggests, this route circles the large Wakkerstroom vlei, allowing good views of the wetlands at the edge of town. Take the Amersfoort road and, just before the Utaga River bridge, stop and park on the left. Here, a boardwalk trail Ⓛ leads along the river to a bird hide. **South African Cliff**, **White-throated** and **Greater Striped Swallows**, and **Little** and **White-rumped Swifts** all nest under the Utaga River bridge, where they are often joined by **Barn Swallow**, and **House** and **Brown-throated Martins**. Watch for **African Rail**, **Malachite Kingfisher** (and African Clawless Otter) along the boardwalk, and **African Grass-Owl*** (scarce) in the thick cover near the hide in the evening.

The hide affords good views of the wetland in the morning, although it rarely proves more productive than scanning from the raised section of the Amersfoort road (north of the Utaga River bridge, where the road traverses an arm of the vlei). **Grey Crowned Crane**, **African Purple Swamphen**, **Purple Heron**, **Yellow-billed Egret**, a variety of waterfowl (including **South African Shelduck**), **Levaillant's Cisticola** and **Little Rush Warbler** are usually conspicuous from the high road. Careful scanning should also reveal **African Snipe**, and this is one of the best sites in southern Africa to see the skulking **African Rail**. **Little Bittern** is fairly regular, and both **Red-chested Flufftail** and **Baillon's Crake** have been seen.

The mega-rare **White-winged Flufftail*** is found in the vlei and the only way to see it is on the occasional outings organised by BirdLife South Africa Ⓜ ☎. The gorge below the Zaaihoek Dam wall Ⓝ is productive for birds common in rocky highland areas, as well as for **African Rock Pipit*** (erratic) and **Ground Woodpecker***. Another bird hide worth visiting is located near the BirdLife South Africa project office.

The Dirkiesdorp plain is at a lower altitude than the other Wakkerstroom sites, and is particularly good for bustards and korhaans, especially **Barrow's Korhaan*** (although **Blue Korhaan** is rare here). From Wakkerstroom, take the main Piet Retief road for 33 km. After passing the small Dirkiesdorp settlement on your left, continue for about 1 km and turn left (signposted 'Amersfoort'). After about 2 km, you will reach the bridge Ⓞ over the Assegaai River, where **South African Cliff Swallow** nests in summer (also look for **Red-headed Finch**). Beyond the bridge Ⓟ, open pastures are good for **Black-winged Lapwing** outside of the summer seasons. Barrow's Korhaan* is common in this whole area, and is best looked for on the left where there is natural grassland at Ⓠ and Ⓡ. This area is also good for **Black-**

bellied and **Denham's* Bustards** (especially in the winter months). You can return to Wakkerstroom via the Jantjieshoek road (turn right at the T-junction at Ⓢ), where patches of Ouhout thickets hold **Bush Blackcap***, **Cape Batis**, **Drakensberg Prinia** and **Greater Double-collared Sunbird**. Rocky areas along this road are particularly good for **Buff-streaked Chat**. The roads may be in a poor state – enquire about their condition before getting there.

OTHER ANIMALS: Wakkerstroom's mammals provide an often unexpected bonus to visitors, and include Yellow Mongoose, Suricate and African Clawless Otter. Grey Rhebok and reintroduced Black Wildebeest and Blesbok occur on many private farms around town.

132 Memel Area

IBA ✔✔✔

The avian riches of the village of Memel, which lies 70 km south of Wakkerstroom in the Free State, have only recently gained recognition, and this exciting birding 'hub' is now considered one of the top highland birding sites. Not only do Memel's wetland and grassland areas match those of its better-known Mpumalanga neighbour, but it boasts populations of two sought-after species rarely recorded around Wakkerstroom, namely **Wattled Crane***, and the near-mythical **White-winged Flufftail***.

SPECIALS: Red-winged Francolin, Ground Woodpecker*, Denham's Bustard*, Blue Korhaan, Grey Crowned, Blue and Wattled* Cranes, White-winged Flufftail*, African Rail, Black-winged Lapwing, Southern Bald Ibis*, Sentinel Rock-Thrush, Buff-streaked Chat, Bush Blackcap*, Drakensberg Prinia, Rudd's*, Eastern Long-billed, Pink-billed and Botha's* Larks and Yellow-breasted Pipit*.

SEASON: Summer is the best season to locate the numerous specials.

HABITATS: Extensive high-altitude grassland, wetlands, cliffs, patches of mist-belt forest.

BIRDING: The Grasslands Specials Loop runs south from Memel, traversing high-altitude plateau grasslands – where almost all of the special birds associated with this habitat may be found – before returning to Memel via the Klip River valley. A short deviation to the top of the spectacular Normandien Pass is a must.

From Memel, travel south-west along the gravel road (S56) to Verkykerskop, and turn left after 9.8 km onto the S471 (signposted 'Normandienpas/Mont Pelaan'). The road immediately begins to climb out of the valley, passing an extensive rocky area on the left Ⓐ, where **Ground Woodpecker***, **Mountain Wheatear** and **Wailing Cisticola** are commonly seen. **African Rock Pipit***

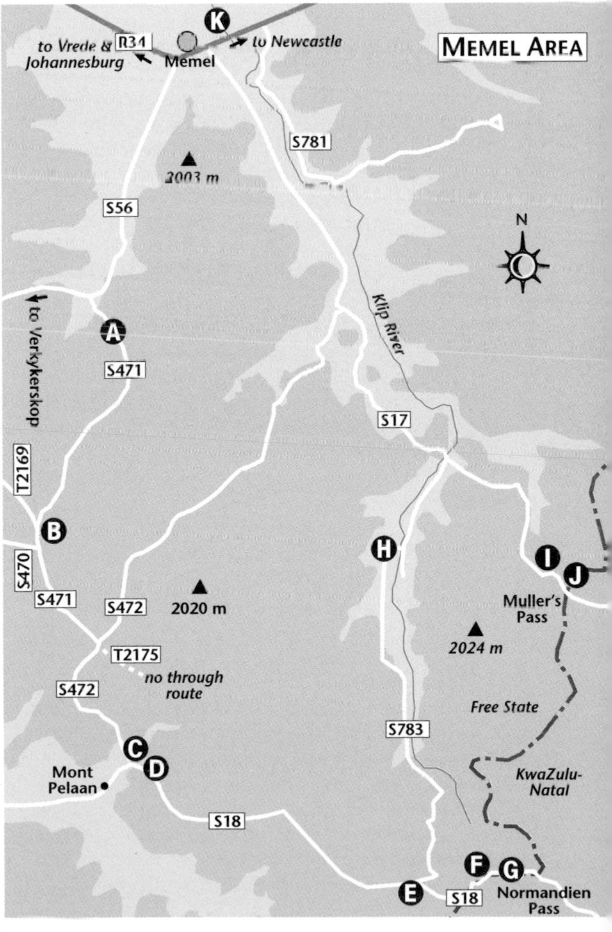

and **Grey-winged Francolin** are resident, best located by call in the early morning. The road levels out and runs south across a plateau at about 2 050 m, where high-altitude grassland on both sides of the road holds small numbers of **Rudd's***, **Botha's*** and **Pink-billed Larks**, as well as **Yellow-breasted Pipit***.

Warwick Tarboton

Yellow-breasted Pipit

At 11.1 km from the S56, just after some obvious silver cattle pens on the right Ⓑ, a tertiary road (T2169) angles back to the right. Stop here to scan and listen, as this is an especially productive area for larks. Good habitat is found on either side of the T2169 for at least 2 km. Keep an eye out for **Blue Korhaan**, **Blue Crane**, **Black Harrier*** (winter), **Burchell's Courser*** (scarce) and **Yellow-breasted Pipit***.

Return to the cattle pens and continue on the S471 to the 4-way junction with the S472, and turn right to Mont Pelaan. When you are 20 km from the S56, the road drops steeply into a small valley, where the rocky hillsides Ⓒ provide good habitat for **Cape Eagle-Owl***, **Ground Woodpecker***, **Buff-streaked Chat**, **Eastern Long-billed Lark** and **Cape Bunting**. Keep left Ⓓ (22 km from the S56), and then right Ⓔ (34 km from the S56) in response to the signs 'S18/Normandienpas', with the road climbing to a rocky ridge (37 km from the S56) where **Buff-streaked Chat**, **Eastern Long-billed Lark**, **Yellow-breasted** and **African Rock Pipits*** may be seen Ⓕ.

A further 1 km on Ⓖ, the road reaches the crest of the escarpment at a dramatic viewpoint that overlooks KwaZulu-Natal. The small patch of Afromontane forest below the viewpoint holds **Red-chested Cuckoo**, **Southern Boubou**, **Bush Blackcap***, **Barratt's Warbler**, **Cape Batis** and **Southern Double-collared Sunbird**. These species may all be found in another forest patch situated in the narrow valley left of the road, a further 2 km down the pass.

To continue the loop back to Memel, return along the S18 for 5 km from the top of the pass and turn right at Ⓔ, signposted 'S783/Roodepoort'. The road crosses the Klip River after about 14.7 km, and follows its course northwards down the valley. Keep an eye out for **Blue** and **Grey Crowned Cranes** in the cultivated fields Ⓗ, and scan any visible water in the oxbows of the Klip River, as **African Black Duck**, **African Snipe** and even **African Rail** may be seen here. Turn left at the T-junction with the S17, which leads back to town.

The best wetland birding in the Memel area is to be found on the northern outskirts of town at the large Seekoeivlei wetland Ⓚ, a RAMSAR site that constitutes a third of the 5 000 ha Seekoeivlei Nature Reserve. The reserve can be accessed either on its western side, via a gate 3 km north of town on the S782, or from its eastern side at the main entrance 17 km from town along the S465. Keys to the gates may be obtained from the Mahem Country House or from the Memel Getaways office in the village ☎.

Scan the marsh for assorted waterfowl, herons, **Glossy Ibis**, and **Grey Crowned** and **Wattled* Cranes**. Pairs of handsome **Whiskered Tern** dance over the wetland in summer, and **Southern Bald Ibis*** often roosts in the conspicuous dead trees here. **Blue Korhaan**, and both **Red-winged** and **Grey-winged Francolins**, are frequently heard calling in the surrounding grasslands, while **African Rail** and **Red-chested Flufftail** inhabit the reedbeds. Listen also for the insect-like song of **Pale-crowned Cisticola** high over the wetland edges in summer. The western entrance provides access to the farm Waterval, where a small knoll provides a superb view of the flood plain and the oxbows below.

To reach Vanger Vlei, one of only a few sites where **White-winged**

GETTING THERE

Memel lies in the eastern Free State and is easily reached on good tarred roads from Gauteng (240 km, or about 3 hours) or KwaZulu-Natal. A network of well-maintained gravel roads, all suitable for 2WD vehicles, allows access to the main birding areas. The newly created Memel-Zamane Wetlands Trust offers a number of birding hides on the eastern side of Seekoeivlei. Birder-friendly accommodation is also available in town at the Mahem Country House ☎, where access to private land around Memel can be arranged.

Warwick Tarboton
Botha's Lark

Flufftail* has been reported, take the S17 turn-off, just out of town on the R34 to Newcastle. Once 19 km from Memel, take the left fork to Muller's Pass. Vanger Vlei **I** is reached after a further 7 km (look out for the National Heritage board). It is a Natural Heritage Site in excellent condition, and one may obtain permission to go onto the farm from Mahem Country House. Other good water-bird species recorded here include **African Marsh-Harrier, Whiskered Tern, Little Bittern** and **African Rail**.

If you continue towards Muller's Pass, you can visit the extensive Ncandu Forest, which contains a selection of Afromontane birds such as **Bush Blackcap*** and **Barratt's Warbler**. Either turn off to Moorefield at 3.1 km beyond the Vanger Vlei Natural Heritage board (an entrance fee is payable here), or stop at the hairpin bend **J** 4.5 km beyond the board to reach an excellent viewsite at a good patch of forest.

OTHER ANIMALS: Hippopotamus, for which Seekoeivlei is named, have been reintroduced into the reserve. African Clawless Otter occurs here, and Mountain Reedbuck, Grey Rhebok and Suricate (Meerkat) may be seen on birding loops through the surrounding grasslands. A variety of other large mammals, such as Black Wildebeest, Blesbok (including a number of 'white' individuals), Red Hartebeest and even Buffalo, have been introduced or reintroduced onto farms in the area.

133 Golden Gate National Park IBA ✓✓

This exceptionally scenic national park is most famous for its spectacular geology, although it also offers excellent highland birding. Most of the avian specials may be found a short distance from the roads, although the birder with the time and energy to explore the area on foot will be handsomely rewarded.

SPECIALS: Red-winged Francolin, Black-rumped Buttonquail, Ground Woodpecker*, Cape Eagle-Owl*, Blue Korhaan, Blue Crane, Lammergeier*, Cape Vulture*, Verreaux's Eagle, Black Stork, Southern Bald Ibis*, Drakensberg Rock-jumper, Sentinel Rock-Thrush, Buff-streaked Chat, Gurney's Sugarbird*, Greater Double-collared Sunbird, Yellow-breasted and African Rock Pipits[W], and Drakensberg Siskin.

SEASON: Many grassland species descend to lower altitudes during winter.

HABITATS: Highland grasslands, protea woodland, rugged cliffs, small patches of sparse Afromontane forest.

BIRDING: The road spanning the park drops more than 1 000 m from west to east, providing easy access to a variety of high-altitude habitats. Magnificent sandstone cliffs provide breeding habitat for **Verreaux's Eagle**, **Jackal Buzzard**, **Lanner** and **Peregrine Falcons**, **Rock Kestrel** and **White-necked Raven**. Watch the road cuttings in the higher western parts of the park for **Drakensberg Rock-jumper** and **Drakensberg Siskin**, the latter especially in the vicinity of streams. **Grey-winged Francolin** and **Mountain Pipit** also favour higher altitudes, although Mountain Pipit is only present during their summer breeding season.

The camp is set at the base of one of the most dramatic sandstone outcrops and is the starting point for a number of hiking trails into the surrounding mountains (enquire at the parks office for a trail map). Avian residents here tend to be widespread, common species, but watch for **African Black Duck** along the river, **Alpine** and **African Black Swifts** overhead, and **Cape Eagle-Owl*** after dark. Birds are most plentiful in the lower-altitude sector of the park, east of the camp, where rocky slopes hold **Ground Woodpecker***, **Sentinel Rock-Thrush**, **Buff-streaked**

GETTING THERE

Golden Gate lies immediately to the east of Clarens in the eastern Free State. A luxury hotel, bungalows and an attractive camp site are located in a pleasant riverside setting in the park. Good roads allow access to the lower parts of the park and an excellent system of hiking trails provides ample opportunity for exploration of the surrounding areas.

Gerald Cubitt

Golden Gate National Park

Chat, Mountain Wheatear, Lazy Cisticola and also **Cape Bunting**.

Areas of short or burnt grass are favoured by **Southern Bald Ibis***, **Blue Crane**, **Barrow's*** and **Blue Korhaans** and **Secretarybird**. A vulture restaurant is frequented by **Cape Vulture*** and, occasionally, **Lammergeier*** (although both are more frequently seen at the Sterkfontein Dam Vulture Restaurant on the R74, to the east of Golden Gate).

Walking through taller, moist grassland in the valley bottoms should reveal **Wailing Cisticola**, **Cape Grassbird**, **Yellow-crowned Bishop** and, with luck, **Black-rumped Buttonquail** (uncommon). Areas of scattered proteas support the sought-after **Gurney's Sugarbird*** and **Malachite Sunbird** in summer, while any of the small patches of forest growing in rocky, sheltered areas may turn up **Mocking Cliff-Chat**, **Fairy Flycatcher**, **Bush Blackcap*** (scarce), **Greater Double-collared** and **Southern Double-collared Sunbirds**, **Cape Canary** and **Cinnamon-breasted Bunting**.

OTHER ANIMALS: Black Wildebeest and Blesbok are conspicuous in the park, and Southern African Hedgehog (uncommon) may, with luck, be found around the camp at night.

134 Witsieshoek ✔✔

Situated high in the Drakensberg range above Phuthaditjhaba, Witsieshoek Mountain Resort is well situated to find high-altitude Drakensberg specials without having to have a 4WD vehicle.

GETTING THERE

From Johannesburg, follow the N3 towards Harrismith. At Harrismith, take the N5 west and then the R712 to Phuthaditjhaba. Continue straight through town and follow the Fika Patso Dam signs. Once beyond the first Fika Patso Dam road, the way to Witsieshoek is marked. Just before the resort, the road forks; the right-hand road becomes dirt and winds up to the Sentinel lookout. There is basic accommodation and a restaurant.

SPECIALS: Lammergeier*, Cape Vulture*, Verreaux's Eagle, Drakensberg Rock-jumper, Mountain Pipit, Drakensberg Siskin.

SEASON: Best from Oct-Mar.

HABITATS: Alpine grassland, rocky slopes, riverine forest.

BIRDING: Star of the show here is the **Lammergeier***, and sightings of this magnificent raptor are a regular occurrence. A vulture restaurant near the resort is worth a visit, although always keep an eye skywards as the vultures regularly fly overhead. Other birds to look out for include **Southern Bald Ibis***, **Black Stork**, **Verreaux's Eagle** and **Cape Vulture***. Examine all flocks of canaries for **Drakensberg Siskin**. The road up to the Sentinel lookout is good for **Drakensberg Rock-jumper** and **Sentinel Rock-Thrush** – check all scree slopes for these species. All pipits should be carefully examined, as **Mountain Pipit** does occur in summer.

135 uKhahlamba-Drakensberg Park IBA ✔✔

A perennial favourite of hikers and other outdoor enthusiasts, the rugged mountain landscapes of KwaZulu-Natal's Great Escarpment have been formally protected in the 243 000 ha uKhahlamba-Drakensberg Park. Although the focal points of this site are Royal Natal National Park and Giant's Castle Nature Reserve, many other excellent birding camps (including Monk's Cowl, Injasuti and Garden Castle) and a host of lesser known reserves in the area all offer birders the full complement of Drakensberg specials in a setting of spectacular natural beauty.

Although most of the specials mentioned below may be found on short walks from any of the rest camps at the foot of the escarpment, a number of the high-altitude endemics, such as **Drakensberg Rock-jumper** and **Drakensberg Siskin**, require a longer hike and birders with limited time or hiking ability are advised to visit Sani Pass (p.116), Katse Dam (p.160), Matatiele (p.115) or Witsieshoek instead.

SPECIALS: Half-collared Kingfisher, Grey-winged Francolin, Ground Woodpecker*, Cape Eagle-Owl*, Lammergeier*, Cape Vulture*, Forest Buzzard*, Denham's Bustard*, Striped Flufftail*, Southern Bald Ibis*, Black Stork, Drakensberg Rock-jumper, Sentinel Rock-Thrush, Buff-streaked Chat, Barratt's Warbler, Broad-tailed Warbler, Bush Blackcap*, Gurney's Sugarbird*, Yellow-breasted*, Mountain and Short-tailed* Pipits, and Drakensberg Siskin.

SEASON: Birding is good year-round, although altitudinal migrants are present only in summer and the Giant's Castle vulture hide is only open from May-Sept.

HABITATS: Three broad altitudinal zones, i.e. Montane zone (1 280-1 830 m): moist grassland, protea stands, patches of Afromontane forest, scrub. Sub-alpine zone (1 830-2 865 m): sparse high-altitude grassland. Alpine zone (2 865-3 500 m): alpine grassland and heath.

BIRDING: The stretch of road between the entrance gate to *Royal Natal National Park* and the main rest camp passes through indigenous bush, including Ouhout thickets, where **Red-necked Spurfowl, Olive Woodpecker, Drakensberg Prinia, Bush Blackcap*, Greater Double-collared Sunbird** and **Swee Waxbill** are seen regularly. Watch for **Half-collared Kingfisher** and **Mountain Wagtail** along the river on the short walk up Queen's Way, and scan the protea-studded hillside beyond for **Ground Woodpecker*, Cape Rock-Thrush, Wailing Cisticola, Malachite Sunbird** and **Gurney's Sugarbird*. Verreaux's Eagle, Lammergeier*, Cape Vulture*** as well as **Jackal Buzzard** frequently soar above the spectacular cliffs.

The *Giant's Castle* area provides the vehicle-bound birder with some of the most accessible birding in the Drakensberg. Rocky slopes between the entrance gate and the camp are excellent for **Red-winged Francolin, Ground Woodpecker*, Cape Rock-Thrush, Buff-streaked Chat, Lazy** and **Wailing Cisticolas, Malachite Sunbird** and **Gurney's Sugarbird*** (protea stands), although the real prize is the scarce and elusive **Short-tailed Pipit***, a few pairs of which probably breed here in summer. Scan, or preferably walk along, the grassy slopes 1-2 km before the camp entrance, from where you may flush this small dark bird with a jizz somewhere between a large cisticola and an eclipse-plumaged bishop. Thick bush around the camp and along the river walk to the Main Caves holds **Barratt's Warbler** and **Bush Blackcap*** in summer, and **Fairy Flycatcher** in winter. **Red-necked Spurfowl** is commonly seen on the camp's lawns, while flowering aloes attract **Gurney's Sugarbird*, Greater Double-collared Sunbird** and **Malachite Sunbird.**

A three-hour hike up the Langalibalele Ridge to the moist grasslands along the contour track should reward the energetic birder with a sighting of the beautiful **Yellow-breasted Pipit***, but you will need to climb even higher, preferably up Bannerman's Pass, to reach suitable habitat for **Drakensberg Rock-jumper** and **Drakensberg Siskin.**

Lammergeier*, Verreaux's Eagle, Cape Vulture*, Jackal Buzzard, Lanner Falcon and **White-necked Raven** are all commonly seen overhead at Giant's Castle, as well as at the excellent Bearded Vulture Hide. A similar range of species may be found throughout the uKhahlamba-Drakensberg Park, with other excellent camps for birding being Monk's Cowl, Injasuti and Garden Castle.

OTHER ANIMALS: Chacma Baboon, Rock Hyrax, Eland, Klipspringer, Mountain Reedbuck and Grey Rhebok are all present in the park.

GETTING THERE

The various camps are all well signposted from the N3 (approximately 3 hrs from Durban), and all are accessible to 2WD vehicles. A range of hutted and camping facilities is provided in most rest camps, with mountain huts and caves available for use by hikers. Trail maps are sold in the respective reserves. Giant's Castle boasts the famous Bearded Vulture Hide; open on weekends from May-Sept, it is extremely popular with photographers, so advance booking is essential ☎.
Visitors are driven up to the hide by reserve staff in the morning and allowed to remain there for the day, returning to the camp on foot in the evening (a 1 hr hike).

136 Mafika-Lisiu Pass & Katse Dam IBA ✔✔

This once remote corner of Lesotho's Maluti Mountains, centuries ago the sole domain of the Basutu herders, is today easily reached by means of the spectacular Mafika-Lisiu Pass. The excellent tarred road, used during the construction of the Lesotho Highlands Water Project, provides vehicle-bound birders with access to an almost 'full house' of high-altitude Drakensberg specials.

SPECIALS: Grey-winged Francolin, Ground Woodpecker*, Cape Eagle-Owl*, Lammergeier*, Cape Vulture*, Black Stork, Southern Bald Ibis*, Drakensberg Rock-jumper, Sentinel Rock-Thrush, African Rock* and Mountain Pipits, and Drakensberg Siskin.

SEASON: Midsummer (Nov-Feb) is definitely the best time to visit, as Mafika-Lisiu Pass is often bitterly cold and closed by snowfalls during winter, when many of the special birds vacate the area for warmer altitudes or latitudes.

Lesotho Highlands in winter

HABITATS: Afro-alpine grasslands, cliffs and gorges, scrubby farmlands, riverine Ouhout thickets, and open water (in the form of a dam).

BIRDING: Great high-altitude birding can be had immediately upon reaching the top of Mafika-Lisiu Pass, although roadside rock-jumpers or **Lammergeier*** cruising overhead may induce a premature birding stop on the ascent. Spend a few minutes appreciating the view back towards Hlotse, as **Black Stork** and **White-necked Raven** are often seen soaring around their breeding sites on adjacent cliffs, and this is also one of the most reliable spots to see **Lammergeier***.

Most of the area's passerine specialities are fairly common and easily found on the plateau immediately beyond the crest of the escarpment, with the shrill piping of **Drakensberg Rock-jumper** regularly heard from rocky outcrops, and flocks of **Drakensberg Siskin** frequent at the roadside. The new information centre at the top of the pass is worth a visit, especially as **Sentinel Rock-Thrush** often perches on its roof.

Short walks into the surrounding area should turn up **Ground Woodpecker***, **Sickle-winged Chat**, **Large-billed Lark**, **Cape Bunting**, and both **African Rock*** and **Mountain Pipits**, although the former is more numerous lower down. Coveys of **Grey-winged Francolin** are often flushed from underfoot, although they are most easily located by their shrill calls in the early morning. Good numbers of raptors are another attraction. **Jackal Buzzard** is most conspicuous, preying on the plentiful Sloggett's Vlei Rat, although **Cape Vulture***, **Lammergeier***, **Lanner Falcon**, and **Rock Kestrel** are regular overhead.

After about 5 km, the road begins its steep descent towards Ha Lejone and Katse, passing between low cliffs, where **Cape Eagle-Owl*** has been found roosting during the day if you are very lucky.

Because it is a deep, highland dam, Katse holds few water birds, the notable exception being a large population of **African Black Duck**. Scrubby thickets along the Katse River and around the dam may yield **Fairy Flycatcher** and **Layard's Tit-Babbler**.

GETTING THERE

Enter Lesotho from South Africa at the Ficksburg/Maputsoe border and at the first T-junction (5 km beyond the border post), turn left towards Hlotse/Leribe. On the outskirts of Hlotse/Leribe town (15 km from the first T-junction), turn to the right at the road to Pitseng/Katse. This road heads eastwards across the highveld, and crests the Mafika-Lisiu Pass after about 50 km, before descending to Ha Lejone village and continuing on to Katse town and the dam wall. While it is possible to find all the specialities easily on a day's excursion from a base in South Africa, a stay of at least one night is recommended. Good accommodation is available at Katse Lodge in the town, and very basic lodging may be found in Ha Lejone. Fill your petrol tank in Ficksburg, as fuel supplies in this area are erratic.

ROUTE 13

GAUTENG & SURROUNDS

The bustling province of Gauteng incorporates South Africa's political and commercial capital cities, Pretoria and Johannesburg respectively. Despite the region being the gateway for many visitors to the country, few realise that the fringes of its largest urban areas provide easy access to a remarkable bird diversity.

TOP 10 BIRDS

- Melodious Lark
- Orange River Francolin
- African Grass-Owl
- Short-toed Rock-Thrush
- Ovambo Sparrowhawk
- Tinkling Cisticola
- Cuckoo Finch
- Black-winged Pratincole
- Orange-breasted Waxbill
- Marsh Owl

Approximately 400 species, including about 60 southern African endemics and near-endemics, are regularly found in a variety of habitats less than an hour's drive from Johannesburg and Pretoria. The wider Gauteng birding region is situated at an altitude of between 1 000 and 1 800 m.

Remnant patches of the province's once extensive 'highveld' grassland biome are best explored at Suikerbosrand to the south, or on the Bronkhorstspruit Loop to the east.

Acacia thornveld (arid woodlands) in northern Gauteng and the adjacent Limpopo and North-West Provinces offer the highest diversity of bird species, and a trip to sites such as Zaagkuildrift, Borakalalo and Vaalkop Dam can produce over 150 species on a day in summer.

For the dedicated birder with limited time, a trip to Suikerbosrand can be combined with a visit to the wetlands at Marievale – an expedition that will result in an extremely productive day's birding. Add bushveld birding in the Seringveld, Buffelsdrift or Zaagkuildrift areas for a day's tally of close to an impressive 200 species!

Gauteng's key specials include the local subspecies of Short-toed Rock-Thrush (*pretoriae*), Melodious Lark*, and African Grass-Owl*.

Numerous wetlands offer a diverse range of water birds, and Greater Painted Snipe, Baillon's Crake, Red-chested Flufftail, and Greater Flamingo are regularly encountered. Due to the number of birders in the province, monitoring of rarities is relatively intensive and species such as Slaty Egret*, Spotted Crake, Western Marsh-Harrier, Baird's Sandpiper, Pectoral Sandpiper and Black-tailed Godwit are regularly reported.

Albert Froneman

Long-tailed Widowbird

137 Marievale Bird Sanctuary R ✓✓

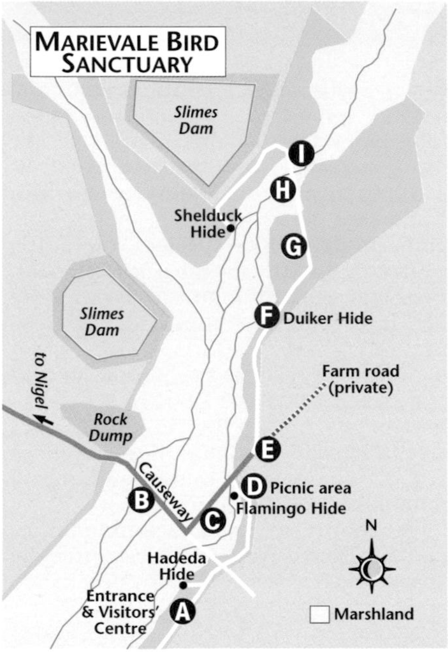

This sanctuary falls within Blesbokspruit, a modified high-altitude wetland that possibly offers the best waterbirding on the highveld, with regular rarities – in particular, **Spotted Crake** and **Slaty Egret*** – and a number of tricky specials.

SPECIALS: Great Crested Grebe, Little Bittern, Yellow Canary, Fan-tailed Widowbird, African Marsh-Harrier, Goliath Heron, African Rail, African Crake, Black Heron, Red-chested Flufftail, Greater Painted Snipe, Black-winged Pratincole, Yellow Wagtail, and Cuckoo Finch. Marievale regularly produces rarities such as Slaty Egret*, Spotted Crake, Western Marsh-Harrier, Baird's Sandpiper, Black-tailed Godwit, Pectoral and Buff-breasted Sandpipers, Pacific Golden Plover, Red Phalarope and Black Coucal.

HABITATS: Extensive reedbeds, seasonally flooded sedges and grasses, open water, mudflats, grasslands, agricultural land.

SEASON: Summer months (Sept-Mar) are best. Early summer (Oct-Dec) is best for elusive rallids as vegetation is low. Species that favour saline conditions, such as **Cape Teal** and **Pied Avocet**, tend to be more numerous in the dry season (May-Sept).

BIRDING: A very early start is usually productive. You may spot **African Rail** on the muddy verges of the tarmac entrance road at **C**, where **African** and **Baillon's Crakes** have also been recorded. Look out for **Little Bittern** in the reedbeds along the causeway, especially at **B** (near the hide), and scan the open water on both sides of the entrance road for **Great Crested Grebe**, **Cape Shoveler**, **Southern Pochard** and **Hottentot Teal**.

Waders are found on suitable mudflats, and any extensively muddy area will yield **African Snipe**, **Ruff**, **Curlew Sandpiper** and **Little Stint**.

Drive past the picnic area **D** on the right, and through the main gate **E** on the left; follow the track past the Duiker Hide **F** to the left. Continue across the grassland at **G**, keeping a look-out for migrant **Western Marsh-Harrier** and **Montagu's Harrier** or resident **African Marsh-Harrier**, **Marsh Owl** (on winter mornings and in the evenings) and, a little further on, **Fan-tailed Widowbird**. Listen also for **Cloud** and **Zitting Cisticolas** and **Common Quail**. On the causeway, watch carefully for **Yellow Wagtail** and **Orange-breasted Waxbill**. Keep an eye skywards for **Horus Swift**, which breeds on the nearby mine dumps.

Park in the small parking area (just before an oddly shaped hide on the left **H**), which marks the most productive birding area in the reserve. **African Rail**, **Greater Painted Snipe** and **Baillon's Crake** may be spotted on the verges of the reedbeds early in the morning. Scan the areas on both sides of the

GETTING THERE

Follow the N3 from Johannesburg towards Heidelberg. Take the R550 Glenroy/Kliprivier off-ramp and turn left. Continue for 20 km until you reach a T-junction. Turn right towards Nigel, and continue through the town. A slip-road to the left is signposted, after which you keep right as you pass a rather derelict defence force base. Gate times are from 05:30 to 19:30 (Oct-Mar) and 06:30 to 18:00 (Apr-Sept); however, a significant part of the wetland can be viewed from the access road at any time. Marievale has a new visitors' centre **A**, several hides, a picnic site with ablution facilities, and a short walking trail.

road. The surrounds have produced many rarities, and the hide is also a good place from which to watch for the secretive **Slaty Egret*** and the more commonly seen **Black Heron**. In summer, this area is alive with warblers, including **African Reed**, **Lesser Swamp** and **Sedge Warblers**. In summer, open verges in the area should be patiently searched for **Spotted Crake**. The bridge at **I** is a good vantage point.
OTHER ANIMALS: Blesbok, African Clawless Otter and Yellow Mongoose occur in the reserve.

138 Suikerbosrand Nature Reserve ✔✔

Suikerbosrand is a diverse and rewarding site, comprising unspoilt, high-altitude grassland highveld), rugged hilly terrain, well-wooded valleys, and in the south-western reaches of the reserve, dry acacia thornveld.
SPECIALS: Grey-winged, Red-winged and Orange River Francolins, Jackal Buzzard, Cape Rock-Thrush and Sentinel Rock-Thrush (winter), Eastern Long-billed, Eastern Clapper and Melodious* Larks, Yellow Bishop, and African Rock Pipit*.
HABITATS: High altitude grassland, rocky outcrops, wooded valleys, Ouhout thickets, protea woodland, grass plains, dry acacia thornveld, artificial dams and wetlands.
SEASON: Summer is best.

Johan Kramer/Photo Access

Rocky koppies and grassland at Suikerbosrand

BIRDING: Begin birding at **A**, 3 km along the R550, where you can look for **South African Cliff-Swallow**, **Red-capped Lark** and **Melodious Lark*** (Oct-Jan, when grass cover is adequate). The grassland on the left often yields a variety of widowbirds and bishops, including **Long-tailed Widowbird** and **Southern Red Bishop**, as well as **Marsh Owl**, which quarters the area, particularly on winter mornings or afternoons, and **Amur Falcon** (summer). About 200 m

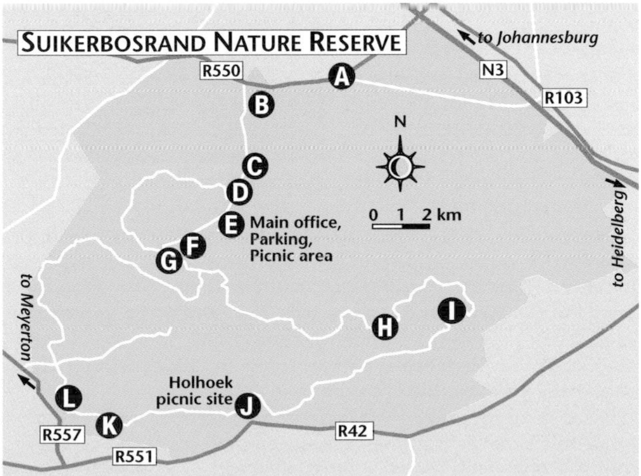

GETTING THERE

The reserve can be reached from the N3 South from Johannesburg. Take the R550 Glenroy/Kliprivier off-ramp and turn right. The entrance gate lies to the left, 6 km along the R550. The gate opens at 07:00 (weekends), and 07:30 (weekdays). Latest permissible entry is 15:30. Bird lists, maps and information guides can be purchased at the office. There is a 60 km circular game drive, and picnic sites with ablution facilities in the reserve, and accommodation (caravans only) is available at Kareekloof resort.

after turning left, at Ⓑ listen for **Melodious Lark*** and **Orange River Francolin**, which are best searched for here before the gate at Ⓓ opens. The dams at Ⓒ to the east of the entrance road are good for **White-backed Duck** and **Sand Martin** (summer).

The parking and picnic area around the main office Ⓔ are good for **Cape Weaver**, **Cape Grassbird**, **Acacia Pied Barbet** and **African Red-eyed Bulbul**.

The 60 km circular drive requires at least four hours, and traverses a number of habitats. Lower valleys hold **Red-throated Wryneck**, **Cape Grassbird**, **Malachite Sunbird** and, in winter, **Fairy Flycatcher**. **Brown-backed Honeybird** often occurs in Ouhout thickets. The steep, rocky area on the left before you reach the top of the ridge Ⓕ and the ridge top itself near the junction Ⓖ is a good spot for **African Rock Pipit*** (erratic in summer). At the top of the ridge, listen for **Eastern Long-billed Lark**, which usually calls from an exposed rocky outcrop (anywhere from Ⓖ to Ⓗ). **Mountain Wheatear** is common, and **Sentinel Rock-Thrush** is conspicuous in winter. **Wing-snapping Cisticola** is common here, and most easily detected in summer when displaying. Areas of shortish grass offer the best chance to see francolins, **Grey-winged Francolin** being most likely on the high ground. **Red-winged Francolin** occurs both on the higher ground and on slopes, while **Orange River Francolin** occurs in the scrubby grassland once you have descended the mountain (at Ⓘ). **Yellow-breasted Pipit*** has been recorded in the grasslands in winter (in non-breeding plumage).

The Holhoek picnic site, at Ⓙ, is a good place to stop and bird for **Chestnut-vented Titbabbler**, **Ashy Tit**, **Cape Rock-Thrush**, **Mocking Cliff-Chat**, **Bokmakierie**, **Fairy Flycatcher** (winter), **African Red-eyed Bulbul** and **Acacia Pied Barbet**.

The thornveld 5 km beyond the picnic spot, particularly at Ⓚ, is also good for **Ashy Tit**, as well as a variety of other acacia species such as **Common Scimitarbill**, **Kalahari Scrub-Robin**, **Green-winged Pytilia**, **Yellow Canary** and **Black-faced Waxbill**. The slopes beyond the powerlines at Ⓛ are particularly productive for **Acacia Pied Barbet**, **Ashy Tit**, Black-faced Waxbill and **Long-tailed Paradise Whydah**.

139 Elandsvlei (Dickin's Pan) R ✔✔

A natural pan, Elandsvlei offers a wide variety of ducks and waders, and it regularly produces rarities such as **Pectoral Sandpiper**, **Slaty Egret*** and **Chestnut-banded Plover**. **African Grass-Owl*** breeds here.

Peter Steyn
African Grass-Owl

SPECIALS: African Grass-Owl*, Black-winged Pratincole (summer), Black-necked Grebe, South African Shelduck, Western Marsh-Harrier and Montagu's Harrier (summer).

SEASON: Nov-Mar. Good for flamingos, **Pied Avocet** and **Cape Teal** in winter. Summer brings visiting harriers, and a large variety of ducks, as well as migrant pratincoles and shorebirds. Note that the water level is variable and the pan may dry up.

HABITATS: Open water, mudflats, reedbeds, lakeside grasses, sedges; alien plantations, agricultural lands.

BIRDING: As you enter the pan area, you will see the first, smaller 'secondary pan' on your right. This pan should be scanned intensively for waders and waterfowl. **Pectoral Sandpiper** has been recorded here. In summer, **Whiskered Tern** in breeding garb flutters at the lake edge, and **African Purple Swamphen** struts over low, emergent vegetation. Keep an eye out, too, for **African Jacana**, **Cape Shoveler**, **White-backed Duck**, **Purple Heron**, **African Snipe** and **Black-winged Stilt**. **Orange-breasted Waxbill** is common in rank vegetation.

There is a hide at the main pan on the left, a short distance beyond this smaller pan, and here birding can be excellent, depending on water levels. Alternatively, drive around the track

GETTING THERE
The pan is situated on private land near Bapsfontein, and access must be arranged ☎.

that circles the pan, stopping regularly to scan the shoreline for the many waders that are present here, particularly in summer. **African Grass-Owl*** and **Marsh Owl** are both present and roost in the rank grass and sedges that flank the water's edge. Wait until dusk, when you have a good chance of seeing these species, especially if equipped with a spotlight.

During the day, scan the skies for raptors, as the large number of water birds and doves seems to attract a variety of birds of prey. In summer, **Pallid*** and **Montagu's Harriers**, and **Western Marsh-Harrier** have been recorded, as have **Black** and **Ovambo Sparrowhawks**, and **Lanner Falcon**. **Amur Falcon** is often seen in the area in large numbers at this time of year; check flocks for the occasional **Red-footed Falcon**.

140 Zonderwater & Cullinan ✔

Situated on the grounds of Zonderwater Prison, this good wetland area supports specials such as **Dark-capped Yellow Warbler**, **African Grass-Owl***, **Red-chested Flufftail** and **African Rail**.

From the N4 (travelling in an easterly direction), take the R515 off-ramp to Cullinan/Rayton. After 10 km, you will cross a railway line; continue to the prison entrance, which is to your right. Request permission from the guard at the gate to enter and bird.

Proceed straight along the main tar road. Look for a track that runs off to the right across the wetland, and is flanked by a line of tall trees. The vlei below this track is a good site for **Red-chested Flufftail**.

After exploring this area, continue along the main tar road with the stream bed on your right. Turn right onto the dirt track that leads towards the recreational/birding area and past a small sewage works. Follow the track until you reach the grassy verge of a dam close to an ablution block. You can either walk over the small spillway and onto the dam wall, or walk down to the track that runs below the wall, and crosses the stream bed further on.

The reedbeds between these two tracks support **Dark-capped Yellow Warbler** (best seen, and heard, in the tall reeds or bushes along the lower path), **Lesser Swamp-Warbler**, **African Reed-Warbler**, **Little Rush Warbler**, **African Rail**, **Red-chested Flufftail**, **Cape** and **Southern Masked Weavers**, **Common** and **Orange-breasted Waxbills** and **Southern Red Bishop**. **Marsh Owl** and (less common) **African Grass-Owl*** roost in dense grassland on the rim of the wetland, on the far side from where you will have parked. The best way to see them is to spend some time slowly patrolling the grassland at dawn and dusk.

NEARBY SITES: Only 10 minutes from Zonderwater, the Premier Mine Quarry in Cullinan is a good spot for swifts and raptors. **Horus**, **African** and, occasionally, **Alpine Swifts** are present here in summer, and **Peregrine Falcon** is resident. **White-fronted Bee-eater** breeds in large numbers on the edge of the vast quarry, while **Striped Pipit** can be found along the rim of the quarry, where **Ayres' Hawk-Eagle*** has also been recorded. The quarry is best viewed from the lookout at the west end of the main street in Cullinan.

141 Ezemvelo ✔

To reach Ezemvelo, take the N4 east from Pretoria. Turn left onto the R25, towards Groblersdal. After a further 4 km, turn right to Vlakfontein. Follow the Ezemvelo signs for about 20 km. There are hiking trails, picnic spots, chalets and caravan/camp sites in the reserve. Guided game drives and night drives are available. An entrance fee is payable.

This reserve offers good highveld grassland birding. **Barrow's Korhaan*** (scarce) occurs here, and may be seen on the game drives near the north-western boundary fence. **Eastern Longbilled** (rocky ridges), **Eastern Clapper**, **Fawn-coloured**, **Spike-heeled** and **Melodious* Larks** are present, and can all be heard calling in summer. **Denham's Bustard***, **Blue Crane** and **Grey Crowned Crane** occur irregularly.

A host of francolins occur throughout the reserve, including **Coqui**, **Red-winged**, **Orange River** and **Shelley's Francolins**; a dawn vigil is the best way to locate them. **Mocking Cliff-Chat** is resident at the visitors' centre.

The Wilge River bridge is a good spot for **African Finfoot***, **Half-collared** and **Giant Kingfishers**, and **African Black Duck**. Poplar thickets along drainage lines are best for **Dark-capped Yellow Warbler**.

In winter and early summer (Sept-Oct), an area of rolling hills to the north provides the best opportunity to see **Barrow's Korhaan***. Leave Ezemvelo and, after 11 km on the gravel road, turn right at the T-junction. After 8.5 km, turn right at the T-junction (R25) towards Groblersdal. Continue on this road for 20 km to Verena, and then for a further 8.5 km, where you will see a road to the left, which follows a game fence. The rolling hills in this area are excellent for the korhaan, which favours areas of longer grass.

The next 6 km are not only good for this species, but **Denham's Bustard***, **Secretarybird**, **Melodious Lark***, and **Shelley's Francolin** also occur along here. If you continue on this road for 12 km, you will come to another T-junction; turn left here to return to Verena.

NEARBY SITES: Rietvlei Dam Nature Reserve is closer to Pretoria, and can also be reached from Bapsfontein on the R50 (it is well signposted). This large grassland reserve offers a good bird hide and an extensive dam with associated water birds such as **Goliath Heron** (rare), **African Darter** and **Red-chested Flufftail**.

Specials here include **Long-crested Eagle**, **Secretarybird**, **Dark-capped Yellow Warbler**, **Spike-heeled Lark**, **Buffy Pipit** and **Cape Longclaw**. **Barrow's Korhaan*** and **Melodious Lark*** also occur here, but are difficult to find in this big reserve.

Bronkhorstspruit Dam is Gauteng's best site for **Caspian Tern** (winter); however, the reserve also holds good grassland birds, including **Spike-heeled** and **Pink-billed Larks**.

To reach the dam, take the N4 towards Bronkhorstspruit. Turn right onto the R25 towards Delmas/Bapsfontein. Turn left after 3.8 km, onto the R42 to Delmas. The road to the dam is 13.7 km further on, to the right (70 km from Pretoria).

142 Rooiwal Sewage Works ✔

Just north of Pretoria, this sewage works offers excellent water birds and a few other specials not easily found in the region. **Long-crested Eagle** is resident in the area, and **Yellow Wagtail** is regular in summer.

To reach Rooiwal, follow the R101 from Pretoria until you reach the power station. Alternatively, take the N1 north to the off-ramp signposted 'Pyramid'. Turn left and drive for 6.5 km to the T-junction on the old Pretoria-Warmbaths road (R101). Turn right, and after 1.5 km, turn right again, onto the Rooiwal/Mabopane road. The entrance to Rooiwal is on your left, just beyond the bridge. To reach the sewage works keep left. Permission must be obtained in advance ☎.

Birding is best around the settling ponds, and around the irrigated lands opposite the main entrance, where waders are present in numbers (summer). **Southern Pochard**, **White-backed Duck**, **Comb Duck** and several other duck species are usually present.

In summer, check flocks of **Amur Falcon** for the occasional **Red-footed Falcon**, and check flocks of **Barn Swallows** for **Sand Martin**. The lawns that lie between the upper settling ponds hold **Yellow Wagtail**.

143 Seringveld Conservancy ✔✔

The Seringveld Conservancy offers accessible birding in excellent broad-leaved woodland habitats. It's the most accessible area for **Tinkling Cisticola*** and other tricky woodland birds.

SPECIALS: Tinkling Cisticola*, Green-capped Eremomela, Fawn-coloured Lark, Pale Flycatcher, African Cuckoo Hawk, Flappet Lark, Short-toed Rock-Thrush (*pretoriae*), Striped Kingfisher, and Bushveld Pipit.

SEASON: The majority of the specials are resident, but are most conspicuous in early to mid-summer (Oct-Dec).

HABITATS: Deciduous to semi-deciduous broad-leaved woodland, on sandy soils, rocky ridges, cliffs, wooded gorges, man-made dams and associated wetlands; alien eucalyptus plantations.

BIRDING: Follow the Bynespoort road (Cobra-weg) eastwards for about 1 km. **White-throated Robin-Chat** is found in the thick bush at the base of the hill to the left, and **Short-toed Rock-Thrush**, both **Lesser** and **Greater Honeyguides**, and **Black Cuckooshrike** also inhabit the bush. Turn left at the brick-paved road marked 'Rinkhalsweg'. The road levels out near the brow of the hill, and **Flappet Lark** can often be heard displaying in the sky above. **Striped Pipit** is present on the hill to the left, and may be heard calling in summer. This is also a good area for **Yellow-fronted Tinkerbird** and **Striped Kingfisher**, and **Pale Flycatcher** and **Coqui Francolin** may be encountered here too.

Continue down the slope to where the road turns sharply to the right. Stop about 100 m beyond the right turn, and scan the woodland on both sides of the road for **Tinkling Cisticola***, **Pale Flycatcher** and **Green-capped Eremomela**. **African Cuckoo Hawk** is resident in the area. Look out for **Bushveld Pipit**, **Southern Black Flycatcher**, **Brown-backed Honeybird** and **Pearl-breasted Swallow**.

Once you have birded this area, retrace your steps to the tar road where you joined the Bynespoort road and turn right, to continue northwards on the main tar road. Drive for 200 m and then turn right into Mamba Road, and follow the bumpy track, keeping an eye out for the resident population of **Pearl-breasted Swallow**, which breeds in Aardvark burrows in this vicinity.

After 3.5 km, the road enters an area of substantial broad-leaved woodland, with a wide road verge on the right. This is a good spot for **Tinkling Cisticola***, **Green-capped Eremomela** and **Flappet Lark**. **Fawn-coloured Lark** favours more open areas with sandy substrates, and may often be seen on the roadside here and further along this road.

OTHER ANIMALS: Vervet Monkey, Black-backed Jackal, Steenbok, and Yellow Mongoose occur here.

NEARBY SITES: The Buffelsdrift Conservancy is close to Pretoria, and offers good thornveld birding. An isolated population of **Yellow Canary** occurs in the area, and **White-backed Mousebird** is regular. This is also a good site for **African Firefinch** and **Black-faced Waxbill**. On night-birding excursions, **Southern White-faced Scops-Owl**, a range of nightjars and, occasionally, **Bronze-winged Courser** may be seen here. (To arrange night birding or get directions, see ☎.)

Callan Cohen

The Seringveld is one of the most accessible areas for Tinkling Cisticola: listen out for its distinctive call.

GETTING THERE

Seringveld is situated only 1 hour from Johannesburg, or 20 minutes from Pretoria. Follow the N1 north past Pretoria. Take the Zambezi Drive off-ramp, and turn east (right) towards Cullinan (R513). Proceed straight across the large intersection with traffic lights, and continue through two four-way stops. Four kilometres beyond the second stop, turn left onto the road signposted 'Kameelfontein'. Turn right after 11 km, onto the gravel Bynespoort road. This is the south-western corner of the conservancy, and the land here is privately owned. Permission must be obtained to bird off the public roads described here ☎.

144 Rust de Winter Nature Reserve ✔

Good bushveld birding in both acacia thornveld and broad-leaved woodland habitats, as well as a diversity of water birds, make Rust de Winter a good destination for a day visit.

The gravel approach road to Rust de Winter passes through good acacia thornveld where **Ashy Tit**, **Great Sparrow**, **Crimson-breasted Shrike**, **Marico Sunbird**, and **Kalahari Scrub-Robin** may be found. Water birds at Rust de Winter dam include **Goliath** and **Black Herons**, **Comb** and **White-backed Ducks**, and, occasionally, **African Pygmy Goose***. The broad-leaved woodlands hold **Coqui** and **Shelley's Francolins**, **Red-crested Korhaan**, **Flappet Lark** and **Yellow-throated Petronia**. Acacia woodland that lines the road some 3.5 km into the reserve holds **Cape Penduline-Tit**, **Southern Pied Babbler**, **Barred Wren-Warbler**, **Black-faced Waxbill** and **Fairy Flycatcher** (winter).

The reserve is 80 km north of Pretoria, and can be reached by following the N1 (Polokwane Highway) north, and taking the Hammanskraal/ Boekenhoutkloof off-ramp 45 km north of Pretoria. Turn left shortly afterwards towards Rust de Winter. After 27 km, turn right at the T-junction, and the reserve is signposted on the right. Sign in at the gate. Camping is allowed (bush toilets only). Luxury lodge accommodation is available at Genius Loci Game Lodge, some 5 km from the reserve. The lodge offers good bush birding.

145 Zaagkuildrift & Kgomo-Kgomo ✔✔

The Zaagkuildrift gravel road runs from east to west along the Pienaars River. The roadsides offer superb acacia thornveld birding, and Wolfhuiskraal – a local birder-friendly stock farm – offers further secure and undisturbed birding in prime thornveld. Kgomo-Kgomo village is situated at the western end of this road, and is adjacent to a large seasonal flood plain, with very interesting birding at all times. In fact, the whole area offers excellent diversity in summer, with experienced local birders recording up to 160 species – including an array of arid woodland endemics and tropical wetland birds – before breakfast!

SPECIALS: Southern Pied Babbler, Barred Wren-Warbler, Olive-tree* and River Warblers, Common Whitethroat, Great Sparrow, Southern Carmine and Blue-cheeked Bee-eaters, Shaft-tailed Whydah, African Crake, Cape Penduline-Tit, Greater Painted Snipe, Allen's Gallinule, and Lesser Moorhen (in wet years).

SEASON: Oct-Mar is best.

HABITATS: Arid thornveld savanna, thornveld bush with thick tangles, and taller riverine woodland. Old agricultural lands have created areas of open grassland. Heavily grazed flood-plain verges with seasonal swampland and lily-covered pools.

BIRDING: From the start of the gravel road, search the grasslands on the left for **Northern Black Korhaan**, **Rufous-naped Lark**, and **Desert Cisticola**. In late summer, **Southern Carmine** and **Blue-cheeked Bee-eaters** often perch on the telephone lines, and **Secretarybird** is frequently seen on the plains to the left. Stop at the farm gate on the left of the road after 1 km and scan the dam, which is good for aerial feeders, especially in summer, with **Blue-cheeked Bee-eater** virtually guaranteed. The area just beyond the gate, on the right-hand side of the road, is a reliable site for **Olive-tree*** and **Icterine Warblers** (late Nov-Feb).

From this point on for the next 5 km, there is excellent roadside birding, and some of the specials that you are likely to encounter here include **Southern Pied Babbler**, **Crimson-breasted Shrike**, **Southern Yellow-billed Hornbill**, **Ashy Tit**, **Common Scimitarbill** and **Barred Wren-Warbler**. Some 4.3 km from the farm gate, open acacia gives way to dense thickets, and here **White-throated Robin-Chat**, **Grey-backed Camaroptera**, and **African Firefinch** may be encountered.

The sandy turn-off to the right is also a good place to stop and look around. **Gabar Goshawk** is resident, and, in summer, **Black**, **Levaillant's** and **Jacobin Cuckoos** are present.

A further 2 km along, you will reach an old quarry on the right, which often holds some water. This is a good spot for **Kalahari Scrub-Robin** and, in high summer, **Dwarf Bittern** has often been seen here, along with **African Black Duck** and a variety of waxbills that come to drink, including **Black-faced** and **Violet-eared Waxbills** and also **African Quailfinch**.

A short distance further on you will see a green signboard at the gate of Wolfhuiskraal farm.

From here to Kgomo-Kgomo, the road passes through drier country, where **Scaly-feathered Finch** and **Shaft-tailed Whydah** (late summer) are common, and **Barred Wren-Warbler** is also present. Look for **Great Sparrow** anywhere along this road and, in late summer, migrant warblers such as **Icterine** and **Olive-tree* Warblers**, as well as **Common Whitethroat**, may be present in stands of larger acacias.

At Kgomo-Kgomo, you will see the first patch of seasonal flood plain, and then traverse a section of dry thornveld before a road reaches a junction. Veer left and proceed past the village. The field just before the village on your left is a site for **Temminck's Courser**, while the very dry plains opposite the village are usually good for **Chestnut-backed Sparrowlark, Red-headed** and **Cut-throat Finches, Red-capped Lark, Kittlitz's Plover**, and **Capped Wheatear. Caspian Plover** has been recorded on the plains on the left. Turn left into the first road and proceed to the bridge (where the road becomes tar), a good vantage point from which to scan for birds. In wet years, the flood plain is inundated and water birds are common. Careful scrutiny may be rewarded with sights of **Lesser Moorhen, African Crake, Greater Painted Snipe, Yellow-billed Stork**, and **Allen's Gallinule**. In most years you are likely to see **Great Egret, Squacco Heron, African Jacana** and **Blue-cheeked Bee-eater** from the bridge, which is also an excellent spot for harriers (**Montagu's** and **Western Marsh-Harrier** are present in wet years).

NEARBY SITES: Mkhombo Dam site is well suited to the adventurous birder, and can be excellent in wet summers, when extensive wetland habitats attract water birds such as **Allen's Gallinule, Lesser Moorhen**, and even **Eurasian Bittern**. The dam surrounds offer excellent thornveld birding, and regular migrant warblers include **Common White-throat** and **Olive-tree Warbler***. Birders should contact BirdLife Northern Gauteng ☎ for access details.

GETTING THERE

To reach the Zaagkuildrift road, take the N1 highway northwards from Gauteng. Continue past Pretoria for 65 km, then take the Rust de Winter/Pienaarsrivier off-ramp. Turn left at the top of the off-ramp and then right onto the R101 north. After 800 m, take the first left turn over the railway line to 'Zaagkuildrift'. Ignore the left turn back towards the town, and follow the bend to the right. The distance from here to Kgomo-Kgomo is about 24 km, and the road is generally quiet. Some13 km from the start of this road, a sign on the left indicates Wolfhuiskraal farm. Visits to the farm can be made, and a rustic old farm-house serves as basic accommodation ☎.

146 Walter Sisulu Botanical Gardens ✔✔

The botanical gardens provide the classic peri-urban site for **Verreaux's Eagle** (a pair of which have a conspicuous nest near the waterfall in the gardens, and are best seen from May-Sept when they are in attendance at the eyrie) and the best Gauteng site for **Greater Double-collared Sunbird**. Other birds include **Striped Pipit, Black Sparrowhawk, Cape Rock-Thrush, Bokmakierie**, and **Malachite Sunbird**, as well as **Fairy Flycatcher** in winter months.

To reach the gardens, take the R28 Krugersdorp highway to the four-way stop at Muldersdrift, approximately 41 km from the N1-R28 interchange. Turn left onto the M47 at the four-way stop. After about 3.5 km, turn right into Handicap Street. After about 1.5 km, turn right into Malcolm Street, which will take you directly to the entrance to the gardens. There are picnic sites and trails in the gardens. An entrance fee is payable.

147 Magaliesberg ✔

This prominent mountain range runs from east to west, roughly from Pretoria to Rustenburg. It is notable as one of the global strongholds of **Cape Vulture*** and offers fairly good mountain birding. Access to the mountains is best via Breedtsnek Pass, which is reached from Maanhaarrand in the south via the Marikana road, or at the Kgaswane Mountain Reserve (p.202).

ROUTE 14

MPUMALANGA & SWAZILAND

For many visiting birders and others interested in wildlife, the Mpumalanga escarpment area serves as a convenient stopover en route to the Kruger National Park from the Gauteng region. However, the diversity of altitudes and habitats makes it a superb birding area in its own right, and a few days spent here will complement a Kruger itinerary rather well.

TOP 10 BIRDS

- Taita Falcon
- White-winged Flufftail
- Gurney's Sugarbird
- Orange Ground-Thrush
- Black-winged Lapwing
- Blue Swallow
- Bush Blackcap
- Short-tailed Pipit
- Yellow-breasted Pipit
- Wattled Crane

This route, centred largely on South Africa's Mpumalanga province, includes not only the high-lying areas in the west, but also the lowveld to the east, extending southwards into Swaziland.

The northern Drakensberg range, which forms the backbone of the escarpment here, is somewhat more spread out and less dramatic than the southern Drakensberg. It separates the cooler, temperate highveld from the hot, sub-tropical lowveld.

This region experiences summer rainfall, and parts of the lowveld are fairly arid, while parts of the escarpment receive over 1 600 mm of rain annually, supporting lush Afromontane forests with a host of specials, including Orange Ground-Thrush and Bush Blackcap*. Best accessed at sites such as Mount Sheba and Peddlar's Bush, these forest specials complement the more widespread woodland species of lower altitudes.

To the west of the escarpment proper, there is a disjunct belt of montane grassland, which is best represented in the high regions near Dullstroom, at a height of about 2 000 m. Even though they are strictly in Mpumalanga, the famous southern highlands in the area of Wakkerstroom are covered in the Highlands route on p.152. Areas of montane grassland covered in this route, such as at Dullstroom and Kaapsehoop, do offer the best sites for a number of endemics and uncommon species, including Wattled Crane*, Short-tailed and Yellow-breasted Pipits*, Blue Swallow*, Striped Flufftail* and Africa's rarest rallid, the White-winged Flufftail*. Apart from these, many grassland endemics are well represented here, including Southern Bald Ibis*, Ground Woodpecker*, Sentinel Rock-Thrush, Buff-streaked Chat and Blue Crane.

Rugged parts of the escarpment have large areas where cliffs, gorges and rocky peaks dominate. These areas are particularly good for raptors and, in the vicinity of the Blyde River Canyon, provide refuge for one of Africa's most endangered raptors, the Taita Falcon*. A nest site here, situated close to a public road and monitored by a local guide, has become the best site globally to see this elegant and sought-after species.

Peter Ginn

The rare and localised Taita Falcon

148 Dullstroom Area

IBA ✔✔

This area of highland grassland, vleis and ridges is a prime spot for grassland endemics. Although it lacks a few highland specials, this is more than made up for by the presence of others, including **Gurney's Sugarbird***, and by the ease with which grassland endemics such as **Buff-streaked Chat** and **Yellow-breasted Pipit*** are located.

SPECIALS: Ground Woodpecker*, Sentinel Rock-Thrush, Rufous-chested Sparrowhawk*, Southern Bald Ibis*, Gurney's Sugarbird*, Wattled* and Blue Cranes, Denham's Bustard*, Pale-crowned Cisticola, Black-winged Lapwing, Cape Eagle-Owl*, Yellow-breasted Pipit* and Buff-streaked Chat.

HABITATS: Montane grassland, protea copses, extensive wetlands and sponges, trout dams with fringing vegetation, stands of alien trees, cultivated land, rocky outcrops.

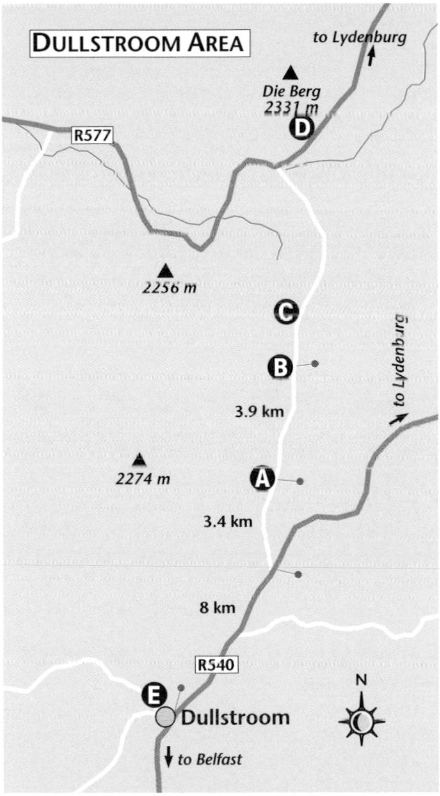

SEASON: Best from Sept–Jan.

BIRDING: Travel northwards on the R540 from Dullstroom for 8 km, then turn left onto the road signposted 'Die Berg'. Check stands of alien trees for **Rufous-chested Sparrowhawk***. Search the protea-covered slopes on the left **A** (after 3.4 km) for **Gurney's Sugarbird***, **Malachite Sunbird**, and **Long-billed Pipit**. After 7.3 km **B** you will pass some rocky outcrops on the left, where **Ground Woodpecker*** and **Buff-streaked Chat** are present. The marsh on the right holds **Yellow Bishop**.

A little further on, a left turn leads to Verlorenvalei Nature Reserve, which can be visited by arrangement only. Bypass this turn-off and continue straight until you enter an area of pristine grassland, at **C**, that extends for the next 8 km. Note that birding is only permitted from the road itself. Rocky outcrops hold **Sentinel Rock-Thrush**, **Eastern Long-billed Lark** and **Mountain Wheatear**. Check grassy slopes for **Red-winged Francolin**; **Wing-snapping** and **Pale-crowned Cisticolas** are both present on the flats, the latter around marshy areas, where you should also look for **Wattled Crane***. On the slopes of the wide, open valley, and along the road further on, look for **Yellow-breasted Pipit*** (common), **Black-winged Lapwing** (often detected by call), Wattled Crane* and, if you are lucky,

WHITE-WINGED FLUFFTAIL

White-winged Flufftail*, one of Africa's rarest birds, occurs in a tightly controlled vlei in the area, to which visits are arranged from time to time by the Middelpunt Wetlands Trust ☎. Believed to be extinct until rediscovered in the 1980s, this small rallid is only regularly recorded in South Africa (where it is present in summer) and in Ethiopia. Joining one of these outings is the only realistic way of seeing the bird.

GETTING THERE

From Johannesburg take the N12 east, which then joins the N4 towards Nelspruit. Take the R500 through Belfast to Dullstroom (35 km beyond the N4).

the shy **Denham's Bustard***, as well as **Blue Crane** and **Secretarybird**.

Once you get to the tar road, turn right and proceed a short distance until protea trees are visible on both sides of the road **D**. **Gurney's Sugarbird*** can be seen here when the proteas are in flower.

Rather than returning to Dullstroom the way you came, continue instead along the tar road until you reach a signposted turn to 'Vermont' on the right. Once on the dirt road, keep right, until you reach the main Lydenburg-Dullstroom road again. This extension of the birding loop is very productive.

Callan Cohen

Scan the marshy plains for Wattled Crane.

An alternative circular route starts 7 km out of Dullstroom on the Belfast road. Turn left to Machadodorp and, after 5 km, take a left turn to Valleyspruit. After a further 7 km, turn right towards Kruisfontein and, another 14 km on, take a sharp left towards Morgenson. This road will bring you back to the R540 just north of Dullstroom. This route can be good for **Grey Crowned** and **Blue Cranes** as well as **Wing-snapping** and **Pale-crowned Cisticolas**, which may be found in moister areas at vlei edges.

The rocky outcrop above the municipal dam in Dullstroom **E** itself is the site of a **Cape Eagle-Owl*** roost, which can often be seen from the municipal camp site at dusk. The vlei just before the camp site usually holds **Dark-capped Yellow Warbler**, **African Rail** and **Red-chested Flufftail**. **Striped Flufftail*** is also recorded from moist slopes with extensive stands of bracken and ferns.

149 Gustav Klingbiel Nature Reserve ✔

Situated just east of Lydenburg on the R37 to Sabie, this reserve offers a diverse combination of upland grassland and savanna (**Barrow's Korhaan***, **Shelley's Francolin**, **Lazy Cisticola**), rocky slope (**Buff-streaked Chat**, **Sentinel** and **Cape Rock-Thrushes**) and even acacia thornveld (**Chestnut-vented Tit-Babbler**) specials. The stand of eucalyptus near the entrance gate holds **Ovambo Sparrowhawk**, and protea-studded slopes in the reserve, visible from the R37 as one ascends Long Tom Pass, are good for **Gurney's Sugarbird***.

150 Mount Sheba Nature Reserve ✔✔✔

One of the better escarpment forest and grassland sites, Mount Sheba offers easy access to excellent Afromontane forest birding and is arguably the best southern African site for **Orange Ground-Thrush**. It also has some interesting grassland and forest verge birding.

SPECIALS: Orange Ground-Thrush, Wing-snapping Cisticola, Buff-streaked Chat, Gurney's Sugarbird*, White-starred Robin, Southern Tchagra*, Yellow-streaked Greenbul, Barratt's Warbler, Red-necked Spurfowl, Narina Trogon*, and Buff-spotted Flufftail.

SEASON: The specials are present year-round; early summer is best.

HABITATS: Afromontane forest, montane grasslands, rocky outcrops.

GETTING THERE

Mount Sheba is a private nature reserve and hotel, but day trips can be arranged ☎. A good network of trails exists in the reserve. Mount Sheba can be reached via Robber's Pass from Pilgrim's Rest; 14 km outside of Pilgrim's Rest, take the signposted turn to the left. From Lydenburg, take the Pilgrim's Rest road and before Robber's Pass turn right onto the signposted Mount Sheba Road.

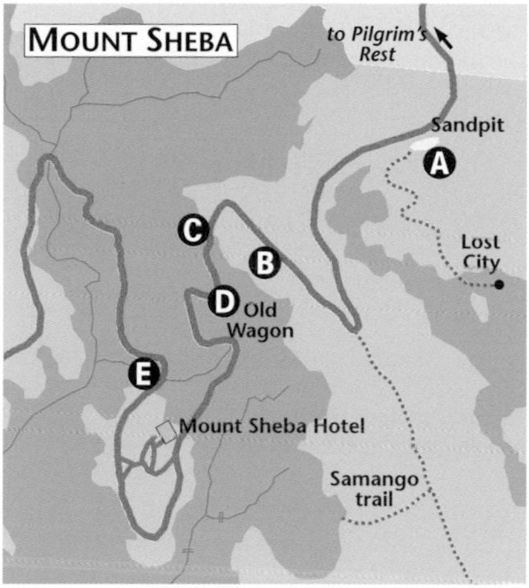

BIRDING: The grassland on either side of the road leading into the reserve is good for **Wing-snapping Cisticola** in summer; listen for the high-pitched *'see-see-see'* calls of displaying birds. **Black-winged Lapwing** occur from time to time, especially after the grasslands have been burnt. Scan the grass for **Denham's Bustard*** and **Secretarybird**, and keep a careful look out for **Levaillant's Cisticola** and **Yellow Bishop**.

The road enters a long avenue of oak and eucalyptus trees – a good area for raptors such as **Rufous-chested*** and **Black Sparrowhawks** and, occasionally, **African Cuckoo Hawk**.

Follow the road until you reach a sandpit at **A** on your left. Here a small sign indicates the trail to the 'Lost City'. Park and lock your car, and follow the path on foot into an impressive rocky outcrop, which holds **Buff-streaked Chat**, **Cape Rock-Thrush**, and **Cape** and **Cinnamon-breasted Buntings**. **Cape Eagle-Owl*** has been found here too. Scrub and protea bushes in this area offer **Wailing Cisticola**, **Drakensberg Prinia**, **Cape Grassbird**, **Gurney's Sugarbird*** and **Malachite Sunbird**.

Return to your car, and follow the road as it winds down towards the forest; the last stretch just above the forest is where the shy **Southern Tchagra*** has been recorded; try locating it by call at **B**.

Birding at the top of the forest road **C** is good, especially for specials that prefer forest fringes, such as **Bush Blackcap***, although this species is scarce and not always present. The first sharp turn to the right **D** – at an old wagon – is a good spot to look for the stunning **Orange Ground-Thrush**. The road down to the hotel is excellent for birding. Maps and information on the trails at Mount Sheba are available at hotel reception.

The Samango Trail (steep in places) runs along the upper verge of the forest, and birds that prefer the scrubby forest-grassland ecotone may be seen here. Listen for the low, churring call of **Barratt's Warbler** in summer. This bird occasionally responds to spishing, and you may be fortunate enough to catch a quick glimpse of it under these circumstances. Other birds to look out for at the forest edge include **Red-necked Spurfowl**, **Black Saw-wing**, **Cape Robin-Chat**, **Bush Blackcap***, **African Dusky Flycatcher**, **Swee Waxbill** and **Forest Canary**. If you spend the night at Mount Sheba, listen for **African Wood-Owl** and **Buff-spotted Flufftail** in the evenings, or on misty mornings.

Forest-birding can be hard work, and the best approach is to walk quietly and stop often, all the while listening for mixed-species foraging flocks. Typical parties may include **Yellow-throated Woodland-Warbler**, **Terrestrial Brownbul**, **Yellow-streaked Greenbul**, **Cape Batis**, **Olive Woodpecker**, **White-starred Robin**, **Chorister Robin-Chat**, **Green-backed Camaroptera**, **Bar-throated Apalis**, **Olive Bush-Shrike**, **Blue-mantled Crested** and **African Paradise Flycatchers**, and **Sombre Greenbul**. Listen, too, for the **Orange Ground-Thrush** and **Lemon Dove**, as they scratch through the leaf litter on the forest floor. **Olive Thrush**, commonly confused with Orange Ground-Thrush, is also found in the area. Forest canopy birds include **Grey Cuckooshrike**, **Knysna Turaco**, **Emerald Cuckoo**, **African Olive-Pigeon** and **Scaly-throated Honeyguide**.

Hugh Chittenden

Barratt's Warbler

For those who prefer a shorter outing, walk the road that leads down from the hotel (past Chalet 1). The road beyond the first small stream at **E** is a good spot for

Narina Trogon*, **White-starred Robin** and **Blue-mantled Crested Flycatcher**. The hotel grounds are good for **Swee Waxbill, Greater Double-collared Sunbird, Drakensberg Prinia,** and **African Dusky Flycatcher**; scan the surrounding valley for raptors such as **African Goshawk, African Crowned Eagle** and **Jackal Buzzard**.
OTHER ANIMALS: Bushbuck and Samango Monkey inhabit the forest, and Mountain Reedbuck may be seen on the grassy slopes.
NEARBY SITES: The nearby Crystal Springs Mountain Lodge, a 5 000 ha private reserve, offers a wider range of bushveld and grassland habitats.

151 Saddleback Pass & Peddlar's Bush ✔✔

Peddlar's Bush is a fine patch of indigenous forest located above Barberton, and easily accessible from Nelspruit. Saddleback Pass offers fine montane grassland birding, which can be done en route to the forest.
SPECIALS: Orange Ground-Thrush, Brown Scrub-Robin, Narina Trogon*, Knysna Turaco, Yellow-streaked Greenbul, Bush Blackcap*, Chorister Robin-Chat, White-starred Robin, Grey Cuckooshrike, Barratt's Warbler, Square-tailed Drongo, Scaly-throated Honeyguide, Emerald Cuckoo, Buff-spotted Flufftail, Olive Sunbird, Olive Woodpecker, Green Twinspot*, Forest Canary, Gurney's Sugarbird*, Broad-tailed Warbler, Drakensberg Prinia, Buff-streaked Chat.
SEASON: Forest birding is rewarding throughout the year, although spring and early summer (Sept-Dec) are best.
BIRDING: *Saddleback Pass:* Use the parking spots provided to stop and explore the slopes. Search protea stands for **Gurney's Sugarbird***, and **Greater Double-collared** and **Malachite Sunbirds**. Look for areas of rank grass on the left in the valley – a good spot for **Broad-tailed Warbler**. Rocky areas harbour **Buff-streaked Chat**, and the skies should be scanned for soaring raptors, including **African Crowned Eagle**, **Jackal Buzzard** and **African Goshawk**.

Peddlar's Bush: A dawn start along the forest track offers good possibilities of **Orange Ground-Thrush**, **Chorister Robin-Chat**, and even **White-starred Robin**.

Buff-spotted Flufftail and **Barratt's Warbler** call from within the forest, but are difficult to see. Move slowly through the forest, stopping regularly; listen out for mixed-species foraging flocks. Species you are likely to see include **Narina Trogon***, **Knysna Turaco**, **Yellow-streaked Greenbul**, **Grey Cuckooshrike**, **Olive Woodpecker**, **Green Twinspot***, **African Emerald Cuckoo**, **Square-tailed Drongo**, **Olive Sunbird**, and **Brown Scrub-Robin**, which all have localised distributions in Mpumalanga. Stop and listen for motion on the forest floor – **Lemon Dove** and **Orange Ground-Thrush** may be seen foraging among the leaves. **Bush Blackcap*** is best searched for at forest edges, and is most easily located in spring. **Forest Buzzard*** also occurs here – particularly near the pine plantations.

GETTING THERE

From Barberton, take the Bulembu road towards the Swaziland border. The first few steep kilometres of this road make up the Saddleback Pass. Once at the top, take the first left turn, signposted 'Shayalongubo Dam'. After 9 km, you will reach the indigenous forest of Peddlar's Bush; for road safety reasons, don't stop at the start of the forest, but rather continue to where it ends, some 10.5 km from the tar road, and turn sharply to the right. Follow this narrow road, keeping to the right until you reach an area of forest where you can stop and walk. No facilities are available.

Claire Spottiswoode

The hills above Barberton offer excellent forest birding.

152 Kaapsehoop

IBA ✔✔

A picturesque village with a number of walks and trails, Kaapsehoop is best known as one of the few accessible and reliable sites for **Blue Swallow***. The area hosts other montane grassland species, and also offers the opportunity for some good forest birding. Most of the local specials are best found with the assistance of a local guide ☎.

SPECIALS: Blue Swallow*, Drakensberg Prinia, Red-winged Francolin, Black-rumped Buttonquail, Striped Flufftail*, Gurney's Sugarbird*, Buff-streaked Chat, Bush Blackcap*, Knysna Turaco, Olive Bush-Shrike and Yellow-streaked Greenbul.

HABITATS: Montane grassland, rocky outcrops, Afromontane scarp forest patches.

SEASON: The swallows are present from Oct-Apr.

Warwick Tarboton

Commercial forestry is encroaching on ever-dwindling patches of Blue Swallow habitat.

BIRDING: **Blue Swallow*** breeds in the nearby Blue Swallow Natural Heritage Site which, in summer, provides a very reliable chance of finding this species. In addition to the **Blue Swallow***, the Natural Heritage Site holds **Black-rumped Buttonquail** and **Striped Flufftail*** (locally common but difficult to see), as well as **Cape Longclaw, Yellow Bishop, Drakensberg Prinia** and **Wailing** and **Wing-snapping Cisticolas**. **Black-winged Lapwing** is present in winter, and **Red-winged Francolin** occurs in small numbers.

The rocky outcrops just outside of the town on the path to the viewpoint provide good opportunities for **Mocking Cliff-Chat, Buff-streaked Chat, Long-billed Pipit** and **Cape Rock-Thrush**. In the village itself, flowering aloes host **Gurney's Sugarbird*** and **Greater Double-collared** and **Malachite Sunbirds**, and one or two pairs of **Red-throated Wryneck** are resident; **Bokmakierie** also occurs scarcely here. **Cape Weaver, Amethyst Sunbird**, and **Bar-throated Apalis** are common in the village.

The small forest patches at the escarpment edge (best visited with a local guide) provide an important habitat for key birds such as **Bush Blackcap*, Knysna Turaco, Olive Bush-Shrike, Yellow-streaked Greenbul, Olive Woodpecker, Blue-mantled Crested Flycatcher, Yellow-throated Woodland-Warbler** and **Narina Trogon***, while the forest edges hold **Swee Waxbill, Forest Canary** (scarce), **Barratt's Warbler**, and **Southern Double-collared Sunbird**. The scarce **Red-necked Spurfowl** occurs in small numbers.

Broad-tailed Warbler has been recorded in the tall grass near the forest, but it is easily overlooked.

Follow the road that leads out of town (past the rocky outcrops and the small forest patches) to the viewpoint. The cliff habitat of **Speckled Pigeon**, and **Alpine** and **African Swifts** can be observed from the viewpoint. When birding in the area always keep an eye skyward for passing **Jackal Buzzard, Long-crested Eagle**, and the occasional **Black Sparrowhawk**.

OTHER ANIMALS: The Natural Heritage Site is home to Oribi and Mountain Reedbuck.

GETTING THERE

Kaapsehoop can be reached either from Nelspruit via the airport road, or from the N4 at Ngodwana. There are a number of other trails in and around the town. Access to the Blue Swallow Natural Heritage Site is by arrangement only ☎.

153 Nelspruit Birding ✔

Nelspruit offers accessible, quality lowveld birding and complements a trip to the Kruger National Park, or the escarpment areas already covered.

The *Lowveld Botanical Gardens* are reached by taking the main road towards White River. After crossing the Crocodile River from Nelspruit, turn right at the second traffic light, and left at the small traffic circle to reach the new gate. Gates open at 08h00.

Follow the path to the suspension bridge over the Crocodile River; search the fig trees for **African Green Pigeon** and **Purple-crested Turaco**, then look for riverine species such as **Mountain Wagtail** and **African Black Duck**. Well-wooded areas inside the gardens offer **White-browed** and **Red-capped Robin-Chats**, **Yellow-rumped Tinkerbird**, **Collared Sunbird**, **Spectacled Weaver**, and **Yellow-breasted Apalis**. More open areas away from the river offer species such as **Grey-headed** and **Orange-breasted Bush-Shrikes**, **Klaas's Cuckoo** and **Yellow-fronted Tinkerbird**.

The *Nelspruit Nature Reserve* offers woodland and reedbed habitats in a more natural setting. From Nelspruit centre, take the main Barberton Road, turning left at Piet Retief Street and the suburb of Sonpark. Turn right into Celliers Street, and left into Andries Pretorius Street; this leads to the Trim Park entrance. This is where you should park your vehicle. There are a number of footpaths in the area and the vlei can be reached by crossing Trim Park in a northerly direction, going under the culvert and turning right to follow the dirt path along the vlei edge. A host of weavers are present here, including **Golden** and **Thick-billed Weavers**, as well as **Red-collared Widowbird**.

Warwick Tarboton

Grey-headed Bush-Shrike

Continue along this path to the Impala Street entrance. Thorn thickets near here hold **Gorgeous Bush-Shrike**. Other woodland species present include **Southern Boubou**, and **White-browed**, **Red-capped** and **White-throated Robin-Chats**, **Purple-crested Turaco**, **Little Bee-eater**, **African Goshawk**, **African Wood-Owl**, **Red-faced Cisticola**, **Green Twinspot***, **Tambourine Dove**, and **Bronze** and **Red-backed Mannikins**. **Olive Bush-Shrike** and **Brimstone Canary** are resident in the reserve. Altitudinal migrants (present in winter) include **Narina Trogon***, **Cape Batis**, and **Grey Cuckooshrike**.

154 Blyde River Canyon IBA ✔

GETTING THERE
The canyon can be accessed from the south via the R532 through Sabie and Graskop, or from the north via the R36 Lydenburg/Ohrigstad road.

This very scenic area, with a wide variety of birds, is a popular tourist attraction and the largest canyon in South Africa. **Southern Bald Ibis*** may be seen at the Three Rondavels, and Aventura Blydepoort is a good base for birding the area. The God's Window area is excellent for raptors and montane grassland, where **Blue Swallow*** has been recorded. The lower areas are best accessed at Aventura Swadini.

156 Misty Mountains ✔✔

Misty Mountains Natural Heritage Site holds **Blue Swallow*** and other grassland birds. Permission to enter must be obtained from Misty Mountains Resort ☎, 25 km south-west of Sabie on the Long Tom Pass between Sabie and Lydenburg. The resort is signposted; ask here for directions to the adjacent Natural Heritage Site. **Striped Flufftail*** is found here, and may be heard calling from the grassland.

155 The Taita Falcon Eyrie

The cliff face above the JG Strijdom Tunnel is the only accessible South African site, and arguably the best site globally, for the extremely rare **Taita Falcon***. This diminutive falcon is one of Africa's most poorly known and scarce raptors and has a very localised distribution.

This site is situated just off the R36 between Lydenburg and Tzaneen/Kruger Park, and is close to a curio stall Ⓐ, 1.3 km above (south of) the tunnel. From the stall, cross the road and walk 25 m downhill to a big rock, where a makeshift viewing position is evident.

The local guide, who can usually be found at the cluster of curio stalls, will know the habitual movements of the birds. However, they are possible to spot without assistance. Scan the white-stained areas that lie about two-thirds up the cliff face directly in front of you Ⓑ, or watch overhead for the distinctive flight of the Taita, which is 'parrot-like' in fashion. Also listen for its piercing call.

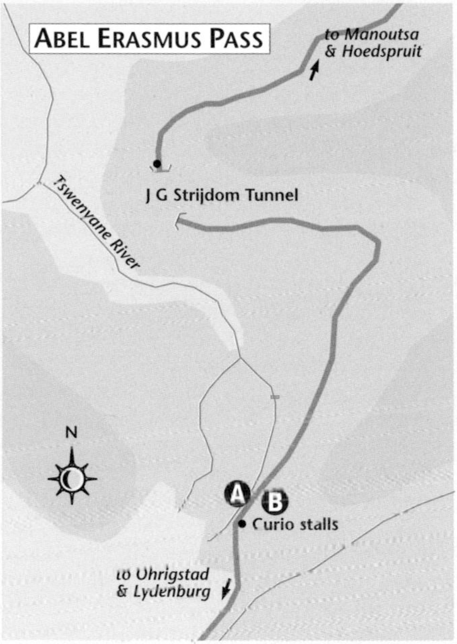

157 Chrissiesmeer

IBA ✔

This small village serves as the gateway to Lake Chrissie and a vast number of pans and wetlands (270 pans within a radius of 20 km). Apart from a wealth of variable wetland birding, the surrounding area offers interesting grassland birding.

Specials include **Blue** and **Barrow's* Korhaans**, **White-backed Duck**, **Chestnut-banded Plover**, **Grey-winged Francolin**, **Southern Bald Ibis***, **Wattled*** and **Blue Cranes**, **Black Stork** and a range of ducks and waders. However, since most of the pans fluctuate from year to year, and are on private land, it is best to contact local birder-friendly lodges for maps, current advice and permission to bird ☎.

158 Doornkop Fish & Wildlife Reserve

✔

This is one of the few known sites where **Short-tailed Pipit*** breeds (early summer). Fortunately, the reserve management is attempting to manage the reserve in such a way that suitable habitat is maintained. Doornkop is half-way between Machadodorp and Carolina on the R36. Other species that occur here include **Southern Bald Ibis***, **Red-throated Wryneck**, **Half-collared Kingfisher**, **Denham's Bustard***, **Broad-tailed Warbler** and **Cuckoo Finch**. **Black-rumped Buttonquail**, **Striped Flufftail*** and **Corncrake** have also been recorded here, and there are also patches of escarpment forest to explore.

The reserve is signposted on the left (if you are coming from Machadodorp), and is then 9 km from the main road. Day visitors are welcome, although visitors usually have to be escorted to the pipit sites. It is advisable to contact the reserve before you arrive; guide fees are payable ☎.

159 Swaziland: Mlawula

IBA ✔✔

This scenic 16 500 ha reserve lies in the foothills of the Lebombo Mountains along Swaziland's north-eastern border with Mozambique, and incorporates a variety of habitats that support over 350 species of bird.

SPECIALS: Scaly-throated Honeyguide, Thick-billed Cuckoo*, Black Coucal, Barred Owlet, African Finfoot*, White-backed Night-Heron*, Retz's Helmet-Shrike, Bearded Scrub-Robin, Eastern Nicator*, African Broadbill*, Grey Sunbird (Lebombo Mountains) and Pink-throated Twinspot* (the latter two largely restricted to the east coast littoral).

SEASON: Birding is good throughout the year.

HABITATS: Lowveld thicket, acacia savanna, moist woodland, riverine forest, grassland, rocky slopes.

BIRDING: The road from the main entrance to Siphiso camp site runs up the broad Siphiso Valley, passing through excellent moist savanna, where a variety of typical lowveld birds may be found. Watch out for **African Finfoot*, Black Stork** and **Wire-tailed Swallow** at the crossing over the Mlawula River, and **Crested Guineafowl, Gorgeous Bush-Shrike, Bearded Scrub-Robin** and **Eastern Nicator** in dense thickets along the Siphiso River.

The area around the camp site is productive and easily explored by means of self-guided hiking trails. Watch especially for parties of the characterful **Retz's Helmet-Shrike** and its brood parasite, **Thick-billed Cuckoo***. The cuckoos are scarce and highly elusive, but may occasionally be seen (or more likely, heard) in display flight above the woodland in early summer.

More open savanna areas along the road to Siphiso camping site may produce **Black-bellied Bustard, Bronze-winged Courser** and, when burnt, the savanna may hold **Senegal Lapwing** (especially outside the reserve). **Black Coucal, Harlequin Quail** and **African Crake** are occasionally seen in the Mbuluzi area after good summer rains.

Access to the northern and eastern parts of the reserve is via a road opposite the main entrance. It passes the Environmental Centre, and follows first the Mlawula and then the large Mbuluzi River towards the Mozambique border. Most of the riparian woodland has been decimated by cyclone-created floods, but the few remaining patches still support **Scaly-throated Honeyguide, Crowned** and **Trumpeter Hornbills**, and the thickets are home to **African Broadbill*, Eastern Nicator** and **Pink-throated Twinspot***. A night drive (request permission at the office) may produce **White-backed Night-Heron*, Barred Owlet**, and even **Pel's Fishing-Owl***. **Bennett's Woodpecker, Green-capped Eremomela** and **Brown-headed Parrot** are best seen near Simunye Village, from the golf course.

GETTING THERE

The entrance to the reserve lies off the Manzini-Lomahasha road, 10 km north of Simunye in Swaziland. Just south of this village, the road traverses the Hlane National Park, which offers self-contained cottage accommodation, although the birding is better within the combined Mlawula/Mbuluzi nature reserves and camping in one of the two camp sites is recommended. The road network is variable, but adequate for normal saloon cars. There are self-guided trails, a camping site and accommodation in the form of pre-erected tents in the reserve.

160 Mahushe Shongwe Nature Reserve

✔

This reserve is an excellent lowveld site for a range of eastern birds that are not easily found in the nearby southern Kruger Park. It may well harbour a wider range of lowland specials than has been recorded. To date these include **Gorgeous Bush-Shrike, Eastern Nicator, African Wood-Owl, Retz's Helmet-Shrike, Bearded Scrub-Robin, Purple-crested Turaco** and **Red-headed Weaver**. Mahushe Shongwe covers 700 ha along the Mzinti River.

From Nelspruit, take the N4 eastwards towards Komatipoort. Outside Malelane, take the Jeppe Reef turn-off; continue for 12 km to the Tonga road. Turn left and continue for 15 km. Turn right to Mzinti; the reserve entrance is within 3 km on the right. Accommodation is available in a tented camp ☎.

ROUTE 15

LIMPOPO

Limpopo Province bustles with tropical diversity of a truly African flavour, and is one of the frontiers of birding in South Africa. Many species from east and central Africa reach their southern limit here, and for those restricting their birding to South Africa, this region offers a whole suite of exciting and range-restricted birds. Vast wooded bushveld areas, descending into lowveld along the region's riverine borders, are punctuated in the north and east by the Soutpansberg and northern Drakensberg escarpment respectively. These ranges support isolated patches of Afromontane forests, adding to a tremendous diversity of habitats and associated birds. Although there are a number of famous sites here, many of the northern areas are poorly explored and birders travelling off the beaten track will be sure to make exciting birding discoveries.

TOP 10 BIRDS

- Pel's Fishing-Owl
- Short-clawed Lark
- African Finfoot
- African Broadbill
- Blue-spotted Wood-Dove
- Black-fronted Bush-Shrike
- Thick-billed Cuckoo
- Mottled Spinetail
- Bat Hawk
- Pennant-winged Nightjar

The region is peppered with prime birding sites. Accessible in a day trip from Gauteng, Nylsvley offers excellent bushveld and wetland birding in late summer. Further north along the N1, the Polokwane area offers the most accessible area for Short-clawed Lark*, while Magoebaskloof – in the mountains to the east – offers some of the best forest birding in the country, and is a reliable site for the ever-elusive Bat Hawk*. The Soutpansberg offers a diversity of sites that are among the best areas for African Broadbill* and African Finfoot*. Perhaps most exciting is the newly discovered patch of miombo woodland in a remote area of the range, which supports birds not usually recorded in South Africa, such as Southern Hyliota. Heading into the lowveld, the riverine forests (Pel's Fishing-Owl* and Thick-billed Cuckoo*) of the Limpopo Valley itself can be accessed either in the Kruger National Park (p. 191), Pafuri River Camp, the newly proclaimed Mapungubwe National Park, or the Tuli Block, which spans the border with Botswana. To the south is the Blouberg, made famous by the single Rüppell's Vulture that frequents the Cape Vulture* colony here.

This route is also the best place in the country to see scarce or localised species such as Grey-headed Parrot, Arnot's Chat, Mottled and Böhm's* Spinetails, Slaty Egret*, Striped Crake*, Dickinson's Kestrel, Tinkling Cisticola*, White-breasted Cuckooshrike, Three-banded Courser* and Meves's Starling. Wetland species such as Dwarf Bittern, Allen's Gallinule and Lesser Moorhen are regular in wet years, and are joined by uncommon migrants such as Montagu's and Pallid* Harriers, African Golden Oriole, Dusky Lark*, and Steppe and Lesser Spotted Eagles.

Warwick Tarboton

The Nyl River flood plain is famous for water birds in season.

161 Waterberg & Marakele

IBA ✔

The Waterberg, which runs from north-east of Thabazimbi in the south-west, to near Potgietersrus, is about 150 km in length. A wide variety of public and private nature reserves are dotted throughout the mountains; the following reserves are worth visiting from a birding perspective: Entabeni Game Reserve, Mokolo Dam Nature Reserve, Lapalala Wilderness and Masebe Nature Reserve. For more information, contact the Waterberg Birding and Raptor Group ☎.

Marakele National Park, in the south-west corner of the Waterberg range, provides excellent bushveld birding, as well as access to interesting high-altitude habitats at the top of Kransberg Mountain, and is easily accessible from Thabazimbi on a tarred road. **Short-toed Rock-Thrush** is recorded from rocky outcrops, or in woodland on rocky hillsides. The road up to Kransberg provides a complete contrast, and the protea-covered hillsides near the top have **Gurney's Sugarbird*** in the winter months. Look for **Buff-streaked Chat** on grassy slopes with boulders. Kransberg is the site of the second largest **Cape Vulture*** colony in the world. The western areas of the reserve consist of dry Kalahari thornveld. A safari-tent camp and camp site are available for visitors and bookings can be made through South African Parks ☎.

162 Nylsvley Nature Reserve

IBA ✔✔

A unique ephemeral flood plain, this area offers superb wetland birding that in good seasons is comparable with the best in the region. Timing and conditions are, however, vital, as the wetland is dry much of the time.

SPECIALS: Slaty Egret*, Dwarf Bittern, Rufous-bellied Heron, African Pygmy Goose*, Lesser Moorhen, Allen's Gallinule, African Crake, Barred Wren-Warbler, Tinkling Cisticola*, Southern Pied Babbler, African Rail, Ashy Tit, Kalahari Scrub-Robin, Black-faced Waxbill.

SEASON: In wet years, the best period for wetland birding is typically later summer (Jan-Mar). Woodland birding is good year-round, but best in summer (Oct-Feb). It is very important to check local conditions before planning a visit.

HABITATS: Open water, sedge and reed areas, flooded grassland in season, dry grassland, acacia thornveld, broad-leaved woodland.

BIRDING: Vogelfontein Ⓐ is best early in the morning (you'll need to get a key at the reserve entrance). In good years, almost all the herons, egrets and ducks can be found from the hides and raised dykes here. Patient observation of flooded areas from the hides in late summer is usually rewarded with sightings of **Lesser Moorhen** and **Allen's Gallinule**; look for areas where taller vegetation gives way to shorter inundated vegetation, and watch for movement. **Dwarf Bittern** roosts in thickets and trees on the flood plain verges, and is common in wet years – look for it on the eastern edge of the flood plain (continue on the road past Vogelfontein for 300 m and scan trees on both sides of the road). Pools of open water hold a number of duck species such as **White-faced** and **White-backed Ducks**, and occasionally **African Pygmy Goose***. The edges of the flood plain (as you approach Vogelfontein on the right) are often good for a range of herons and storks, including **Black Heron**.

Every few years, when the flood plain is fully inundated, a range of rare and difficult species occurs. However, given the amount of habitat present (15 000 ha), a good deal of time and effort needs to be dedicated to seeing these birds. The best time is from late Jan-Apr, depending on conditions. As the flood plain dries up, birds congregate along the

GETTING THERE

The reserve is reached from the old road (R101) between Mookgopong and Modimolle (you'll have to leave the toll road). Travelling north, take a right turn to Boekenhout Station. After the railway crossing, turn left for Vogelfontein, or continue straight on to the reserve. To reach Vogelfontein, continue parallel to the railway line, taking a sharp right turn towards the flood plain. Camping is available in the reserve, and a range of other accommodation is available nearby, including the self-catering birders' base at Sericea ☎.

channels, and one should look for exposed marshy areas that are close to denser vegetation. Very patient watching, preferably in the early morning, may be rewarded with sightings of **African**, **Baillon's**, and maybe even **Spotted** and **Striped* Crakes**. **Baillon's** and **Spotted Crakes** require fairly dense and substantial vegetation, whereas Striped Crake* is found in more open areas, with muddy pools and sparser grasses – and may breed in wet years. **Corncrake** inhabits fairly tall vegetation – often some way away from the water, and a large amount of habitat must be traversed to give one a chance of flushing this elusive species.

Watch the birds commuting up and down the wetland in the early morning and evening. **Slaty Egret*** has often been seen this way, and can be picked out by its narrow wings and all-yellow legs. Listen too for the *chop-chop* of the **Black Coucal**, or the booming of the **Eurasian Bittern**. Although both species appear on the flood plain in good years, it requires a big dose of luck to see the latter. **Streaky-breasted Flufftail** is also heard every few years – it inhabits sparser, more temporary flooded grassland, and is recorded on smaller, 'tributary' wetlands, which surround Nylsvley proper.

African Marsh-Harrier is regularly present and the section of trees on the 'island' to the south of the road should also be scanned for **Dwarf Bittern** and **Rufous-bellied Heron**.

Kurrichane Buttonquail is common in well-grassed areas in the reserve. The most accessible acacia birding is along the approach road to Vogelfontein, especially at **B**, where the road turns away from the railway track. Look here for **Ashy Tit**, **Southern Pied Babbler**, **Yellow-bellied Eremomela**, **Cape Penduline-Tit** and **Scaly-feathered Finch**. Just north of the flood plain is an area of large acacia trees and thickets, where **Barred Wren-Warbler**, **Crimson-breasted Shrike** and **Black-faced Waxbill** are present. Areas of trees and thickets on the flood plain and flood plain edges are excellent for warblers (especially the large patch south of the road at Vogelfontein), and a search in late summer is likely to turn up **Common Whitethroat**, **Marsh-Warbler** and **Great Reed-Warbler**.

The Jacana Hide **C** inside the Nylsvley Nature Reserve is reached along a walkway from a parking area. This hide offers some of the same water birds as Vogelfontein, as well as being a good area for **Great Reed-Warbler** and **African Rail** (summer). Parts of the path are frequently flooded in wet seasons. This area also offers good acacia woodland birding, with species such as **Chestnut-vented Tit Babbler**, **Burnt-necked Eremomela** and **Crimson-breasted Shrike** being common.

Good broad-leaved woodland requires more effort, and the easiest to reach is that along the south-eastern border fence **D**. From Vogelfontein, continue south-east for about 5 km. At a set of power lines, turn right on a sandy track (suitable for sedan vehicles). This track follows the south-eastern boundary of the Nylsvley Nature Reserve, and takes you through some prime broad-leaved woodland. Look out here for **Tinkling Cisticola***, **Pale Flycatcher**, and **Green-capped Eremomela**, as well as raptors such as **Wahlberg's**

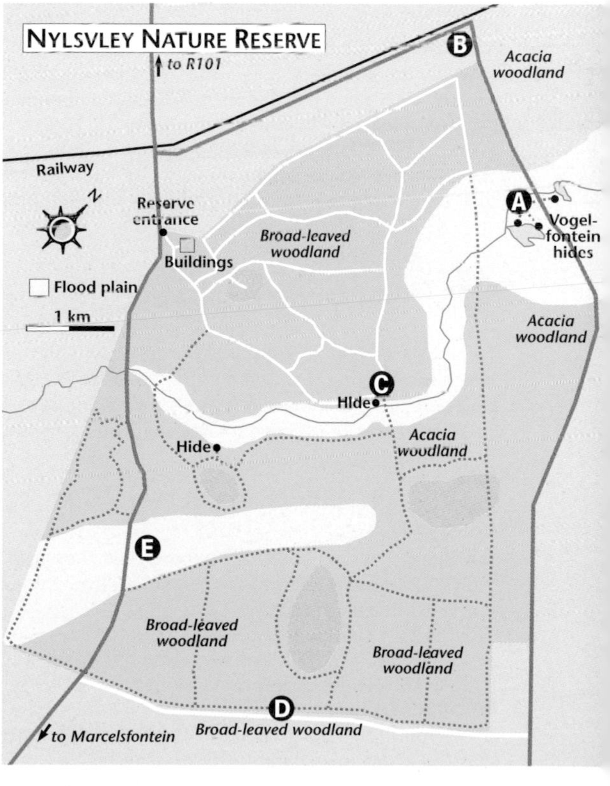

Eagle (summer), **African Hawk-Eagle** and **Brown Snake-Eagle. Tinkling Cisticola*** is best located by call in transitional areas where the woodland is verging on more open areas. In summer this area also holds a variety of cuckoos, as well as **European Golden Oriole**. This road eventually joins a bigger road and you turn right to get back to Nylsvley, crossing a secondary grassland/flood plain **E** (which can also be good when flooded).

Pearl-spotted Owlet and **Southern White-faced Scops-Owl** can be heard at night, and followed up with a torch. **African Scops-Owl** occurs in broad-leaved woodland, and **Fiery-necked** and **Rufous-cheeked Nightjars** are common. When water levels permit, a winter evening walk along the road across the flood plain near the Jacana Hide may produce **African Grass-Owl***, which breeds in the area.

OTHER ANIMALS: Nylsvley has a substantial herd of the rare Roan Antelope, as well as more common game such as Giraffe and Plains Zebra. Black-backed Jackal are common in the area.

Lesser Moorhen arrives with good rains.

NEARBY SITES: Doorndraai Dam Nature Reserve: the reserve includes the large Doorndraai dam and is set amid hilly country south-west of Mokopane (Potgietersrus). The main camp site is good for **Striped Pipit** (winter), and the broad-leaved woodland holds **Grey Tit-Flycatcher**, **Little Sparrowhawk**, **Green-capped Eremomela**, **Pale Flycatcher**, **Brubru**, **Yellow-throated Petronia** and **Flappet Lark**. Doorndraai is reached via the 'old' R101, north of Mookgopong (Naboomspruit). Take the left turn-off to Sterkrivier and after about 16 km a well-signposted left turn leads to the reserve after a further 6 km.

163 Percy Fyfe Nature Reserve ✔

This small reserve, 35 km north of Mokopane (Potgietersrus), is a site for **Short-clawed Lark***, which may be found near the entrance gate. The areas of open grassland, broad-leaved woodland and rocky granite outcrops also hold **Shelley's Francolin** and **Bushveld Pipit**. Follow the R101 north out of Mokopane, and you will soon reach the turn-off to the reserve.

164 Blouberg Nature Reserve IBA ✔✔

The Blouberg is an isolated inselberg that rises some 1 200 m from the surrounding plain in the north-west of Limpopo Province. A lone **Rüppell's Vulture** has bred here with a **Cape Vulture***, in a large colony of the latter.

SPECIALS: Cape* and Rüppell's Vultures.

SEASON: Best time is May-Oct, when the Rüppell's Vulture is most often present on the cliff.

HABITATS: Cliff faces and rocky slopes, broad-leaved and acacia woodlands.

BIRDING: Enquire at the Environmental Education Centre about access to the **Cape Vulture*** colony and for help in locating the **Rüppell's Vulture**. Other raptors include **Lappet-faced Vulture**, **Verreaux's Eagle**, **African Hawk-Eagle**, and **Pale Chanting** and **Gabar Goshawks**.

GETTING THERE

From Polokwane (formerly Pietersburg), take the R521 Dendron/Vivo/Alldays road. At Vivo (37 km from Dendron) turn left onto the Bochum road. Travel for about 10 km, to a small shopping complex on the right-hand side called Kgobokanang (kiosk, petrol station, bottle store, tyre repairs & building supplies). Turn right toward Kromhoek. The reserve is 8.4 km down this road on the left-hand side. Drive through the entrance and go to the office.

There are drives in the reserve, but it is very sandy and rocky and a 4WD vehicle is recommended. A vulture restaurant with a hide has been established.

Rustic accommodation is available at Tamboti Bush Camp by arrangement. An entrance fee is payable for day and overnight visitors. Because of the remoteness of this reserve, it is advisable to contact the reserve management if you intend to visit and to enquire about the availability of accommodation ☎.

165 Langjan Nature Reserve ✔

Langjan is a small provincial nature reserve situated 21 km north of Vivo on the R521 from Polokwane. It is an ideal spot to stay over for those travelling to or from Botswana (79 km from the Pontdrif border post) or as a base to visit Blouberg or the northern Soutpansberg area. One of the main reasons for the proclamation of this reserve was the protection of a very isolated natural population of Gemsbok. These animals thrive in this Kalahari-type thornveld, which also hosts typical dry west birds such as **Crimson-breasted Shrike** and **Southern Pied Babbler**. Other interesting species that occur here include **Kori Bustard**, **Martial**, **Tawny** and **Steppe Eagles** (late summer), **Bronze-winged Courser** (summer) and **Dusky Lark*** (summer). Langjan is one of the few spots in the country where **Egyptian Vulture** has been recorded on more than one occasion. Accommodation consists of safari tents and thatched huts ☎.

166 Polokwane Game Reserve IBA ✔✔

This classic site for **Short-clawed Lark*** and a range of other thornveld and plains birds lies conveniently close to the N1.

SPECIALS: Short-clawed Lark*, Northern Black Korhaan, Double-banded Courser, Barred Wren-Warbler, Black-faced Waxbill, Bushveld Pipit and Tinkling Cisticola*.

SEASON: The lark may be found throughout the year but is most conspicuous from Sept-Jan.

HABITATS: Arid thornveld, open grassland, acacia thickets, granite outcrops.

BIRDING: The general game-drive roads offer plenty of good **Short-clawed Lark*** habitat, and you can ask at the gate for advice on where to go to look for this species. Alternatively, look for open grassland with scattered trees and shrubs at Ⓐ, Ⓑ and Ⓒ, especially the evergreen, broad-leaved *Gymnosporia*, which is favoured by the bird as a calling post. The males are most conspicuous from Sept-Jan, when they perform an aerial display. Beware of confusion with the similarly plumaged **Sabota** and **Rufous-naped Larks**, which can be distinguished by call.

Northern Black Korhaan and **Ant-eating Chat** are common in the open grassland areas, which also sometimes hold **Double-banded Courser**. In late summer, moist grasslands and ephemeral pans may hold **Dwarf Bittern**, **Harlequin Quail** and **African Crake**. Check the acacia woodlands for **Kalahari Scrub-Robin**, **Crimson-breasted Shrike**, **Burnt-necked** and **Yellow-bellied Eremomelas**, **Black-faced Waxbill**, **Barred Wren-Warbler**, **Ashy Tit**, **Brown-backed Honeybird** and **Marico Flycatcher**.

A large variety of raptors occurs here, including **African Hawk-Eagle**, **Black-chested**

GETTING THERE

To reach the reserve (formerly known as Pietersburg Nature Reserve) from the Tzaneen bypass road (R81) (east of Polokwane), take the right turn to Silicon. From Polokwane itself, take Dorp Street (southerly direction), which then becomes Silicon Road. Drive into the caravan park and to the reserve entrance. The reserve is open from 07h00 and an entrance fee is payable. A good network of roads and several hiking trails cover most of the habitats.

Snake-Eagle, **Secretarybird**, **Booted Eagle**, **Greater Kestrel**, and **Montagu's Harrier** (the latter is a summer visitor). The **Gabar Goshawk** population in the reserve is largely made up of the melanistic form of this species. Look for **Bushveld Pipit** at **D**.

A vulture restaurant attracts **Cape*** and sometimes **White-backed** and **Lappet-faced Vultures**, and nocturnal birds are well represented, with six owl species and four nightjars. **Bronze-winged Courser** is found in the late summer.

OTHER ANIMALS: A variety of large ungulates, including Sable Antelope, Eland, Gemsbok, Giraffe, Plains Zebra, Red Hartebeest, Tsessebe, and also White Rhinoceros, inhabit the reserve.

NEARBY SITES: Most of the length of the Polokwane bypass road intercepts areas frequented by **Short-clawed Lark***. From south of Polokwane, follow the R81 to the R71. The area near the junction of this road and the R36 is particularly productive.

Search acacia thickets in the small Polokwane Bird Sanctuary for migrant **Olive-tree Warbler*** (on the tracks between the dams) and **Common White-throat**. The sanctuary, which also has a diversity of wetland and riverine woodland birds, including breeding **Ovambo Sparrowhawk**, is 3 km out of town on the R521 to Dendron (the turn-off is opposite a SASOL filling station).

Southern Bald Ibis* breed at Turfloop Dam Nature Reserve, beyond the University of Limpopo, 24 km along the R71.

Warwick Tarboton

Black-faced Waxbill

Robby Sandrock

Short-clawed Lark

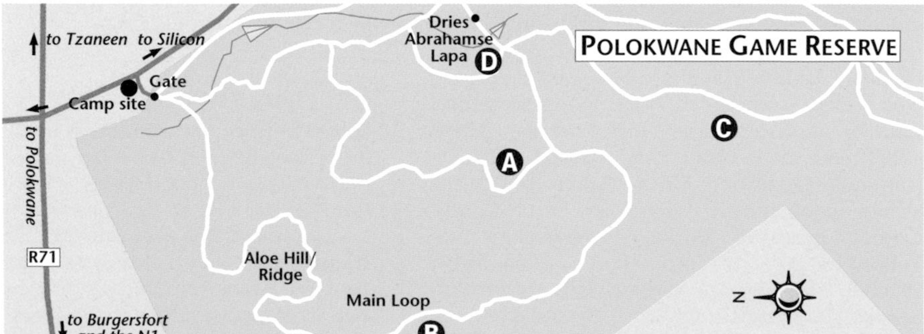

167 Magoebaskloof

IBA ✔✔✔

The Magoebaskloof area on the far northern escarpment offers arguably the best forest birding in South Africa, and is certainly the best place for **Black-fronted Bush-Shrike*** and **Bat Hawk***.
SPECIALS: Black-fronted Bush-Shrike*, Cape Parrot*, Bat Hawk*, Chorister Robin-Chat, Brown Scrub-Robin, White-starred Robin, Knysna Turaco, Orange Ground-Thrush, Narina Trogon*, Buff-spotted Flufftail, African Crowned Eagle, African Emerald Cuckoo, Grey Cuckooshrike, Yellow-streaked Greenbul, Green Twinspot*, Mountain Wagtail, Blue Swallow*, and Barratt's Warbler.
SEASON: Birding is good year-round, but is best in spring and summer, when the birds are more vocal.
HABITATS: Afromontane forest, pine plantations, mountain streams.
BIRDING: It is often worthwhile visiting the lookout point Ⓓ at dawn, where the endangered **Cape Parrot*** may be seen flying in the valley or heard calling.

Woodbush Forest Drive itself offers excellent birding; stop regularly to listen for calls and scan at breaks in the forest – which provide a spectacular view across the valley – for soaring raptors such as **African Crowned Eagle** and **African Goshawk**. In winter and spring, the calls of **Yellow-streaked Greenbul** and **Square-tailed Drongo** draw attention to a jackpot of forest birds: mixed-species foraging flocks.

Knysna Turaco, Grey Cuckooshrike, Scaly-throated Honeyguide, African Emerald Cuckoo and **Olive Bush-Shrike** feed in the upper reaches of the trees. **Black-fronted Bush-Shrike***, however, is the undisputed canopy special in this area, and is best located by its haunting call (look especially between sites Ⓔ and Ⓕ). **Narina Trogon*** lurks in the mid-storey, as do **Cape Batis** and **Blue-mantled Crested Flycatcher**.

Barratt's Warbler, which skulks in undergrowth on the forest edge, can be difficult to find if you are not familiar with its call. To see some of the shyer species, such as **White-starred Robin, Brown Scrub-Robin, Orange Ground-Thrush** and **Olive Thrush**, leave your car and walk a short distance into the forest, and

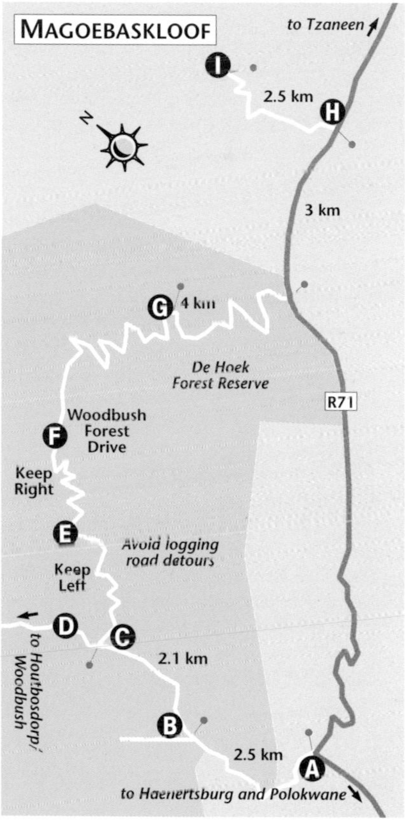

GETTING THERE

Access is primarily via Woodbush Forest Drive, and may be limited by poor road conditions during periods of heavy rain. To reach Woodbush Forest Drive, take the R71 from Polokwane past the small town of Haenertsburg. About 2 km past the Magoebaskloof Hotel, turn to the left onto the gravel road to Houtbosdorp/Woodbush Ⓐ. After 2.5 km, at Ⓑ, take the right fork to the Woodbush Forest Reserve, which passes through stone gateposts. After passing the hikers' huts (2.1 km past the previous junction), take the sharp right fork Ⓒ, which is Woodbush Forest Drive; this road can be birded for about 13 km. The left fork leads to a lookout point (identifiable by the benches on the right) after 500 m Ⓓ. A local bird guide can assist with up-to-date information ☎.

stop where you see a trail or a small opening. Listen for calls, and the sounds of thrushes and robins scratching through leaf litter on the forest floor.

By car, the entire drive down to the Debengeni Falls turn-off **G** should take from three to four hours if you cover it thoroughly, and most of the Magoebaskloof specials can be recorded on this drive. The entire Woodbush Forest Drive is about 16 km long, and rejoins the R71 some 4 km after Debengeni.

Forest edges and tangles offer **Green Twinspot*** and **Buff-spotted Flufftail**, and are good sites for raptor watching. The Debengeni Falls area is good for **Mountain Wagtail** and **Red-backed Mannikin**, and **Grey Wagtail** (a national rarity) has even been recorded a few times here. **Blue Swallow*** may be found in a small patch of montane grassland in the area, but it is necessary to be accompanied by a local bird guide to visit the site.

OTHER ANIMALS: Bushpig, Samango Monkey, Bushbuck and Leopard all inhabit the forest depths.

NEARBY SITES: Kurisa Moya is a birder-friendly guesthouse positioned in the heart of an indigenous forest near Magoebaskloof. The area has the full range of Afromontane forest species of the Magoebaskloof region, including **Black-fronted Bush-Shrike*** and **Orange-Ground Thrush**. Day visitors are permitted by prior arrangement ☎.

168 Finding Bat Hawk

To reach the **Bat Hawk*** site from Woodbush Forest Drive, continue past Debengeni to the R71, and turn left towards Tzaneen. After 3 km, you reach the 'Commonwealth Plantation' sign (at the first fields of tea); take the gravel road to the left here **H** (if coming directly from Polokwane, this turn is exactly 13.5 km from the Magoesbaskloof Hotel). Immediately after you cross over the stream, veer to the left and take the right fork. Follow this road for 2.5 km until you get to a T-junction (opposite a massive eucalyptus tree) **I**. Bat Hawk* has bred in this immediate vicinity for some years and, although the nest site varies from time to time, the birds can often be seen roosting in one of the three large bluegums that are visible from the junction. You will need to scan carefully to pick up a roosting bird in these large trees, although they are active at dusk.

This area is also good for other raptors such as **Eurasian Hobby** (summer) and **Long-crested Eagle**.

Peter Ginn

Bat Hawk

169 Hans Merensky Nature Reserve ✔

This reserve, which includes the 'Eiland' Holiday Resort, holds fine tracts of mopane woodland, and offers good birding along the Letaba River. The special here is **Arnot's Chat**, which is best located by taking a drive in the main portion of the reserve and searching the areas of mature mopane woodland.

The Eiland Resort attracts the usual collection of bushveld species such as **Greater Blue-eared Starling**, **Red** and **Southern Yellow-billed Hornbills**, and **Bennett's Woodpecker**. **White Helmet-Shrike** is common and **Stierling's Wren-Warbler** occurs in the surrounding woodland. The River Walk (good for **Red-headed Weaver**) starts from the reserve office and passes through riverine woodland; **Thick-billed Cuckoo*** occurs here in the summer months.

Take the R71 east of Polokwane towards Gravelotte, and turn north along the R529 just before Letsitele. Hans Merensky is found 37 km along this road.

170 The Soutpansberg Range

IBA ✔✔

The Soutpansberg forms the northernmost range of mountains in South Africa, with the closest major town being Makhado (formerly Louis Trichardt). A rich diversity of habitats provides an impressive range of birds.

SPECIALS: African Broadbill*, White-backed Night-Heron*, African Finfoot*, Gorgeous Bush-Shrike, Orange Ground-Thrush, Eastern Nicator, Bat Hawk* and Blue-spotted Wood-Dove.

SEASON: A visit will prove most productive in early summer (Oct-Nov) but most specials are resident year-round. Mid- to late summer (Dec-Feb) can be wet, especially up in the mountains. Winter birding can be very rewarding as the climate is mild.

HABITATS: Afromontane forest, riverine thickets, acacia woodland, farmlands (mainly orchards), wetland and alien plantations.

BIRDING: *Entabeni Forest Reserve:* Tracts of Afromontane forest remain at Entabeni **A**, which hosts good populations of **Orange Ground-Thrush** (look especially along the 2.2 km-long trail to Matiwe Kop) and **Yellow-streaked Greenbul**. The highly localised **Black-fronted Bush-Shrike*** occurs here but is not common. Other species include **Scaly-throated Honeyguide**, **Knysna** and **Purple-crested Turacos**, **Southern Double-collared Sunbird**, **Chorister** and **Red-capped Robin-Chats**, **Swee Waxbill**, **Blue-mantled Crested Flycatcher**, **Grey Cuckooshrike**, **African Olive-Pigeon**, **Lemon Dove**, and **Yellow-throated Woodland-Warbler**. **African Goshawk** display over the canopy in the early morning, and **Jackal** and **Forest* Buzzards** and **Long-crested Eagle** can all be found in the vicinity. **Blue-spotted Wood-Dove** occurs, but prefers the lower, more disturbed slopes of the mountain away from true forest. It is also locally common nearby, especially along the edges of disturbed agricultural land, such as near macadamia plantations. Look for it along the R524 road to Levubu, especially at Muirhead Dams, 21 km east of Makhado. Turn off the R524 at Royal Macadamia, keep right and proceed to the dams, where a hide and series of trails have been laid out.

Roodewal Forest **B**: From the gate, proceed on foot, pass to the left of the stand of pine trees and bird the dense scrub forest on the left of the track. This is the best site for **African Broadbill***, which may be located from the track that continues straight on. You can also follow the overgrown trail to the left and explore the dense vegetation along the stream gulley that runs parallel to the track. **Eastern Nicator**, **Gorgeous Bush-Shrike** and **Narina Trogon*** are more easily heard than seen here. Also keep a look out for **Green Twinspot***.

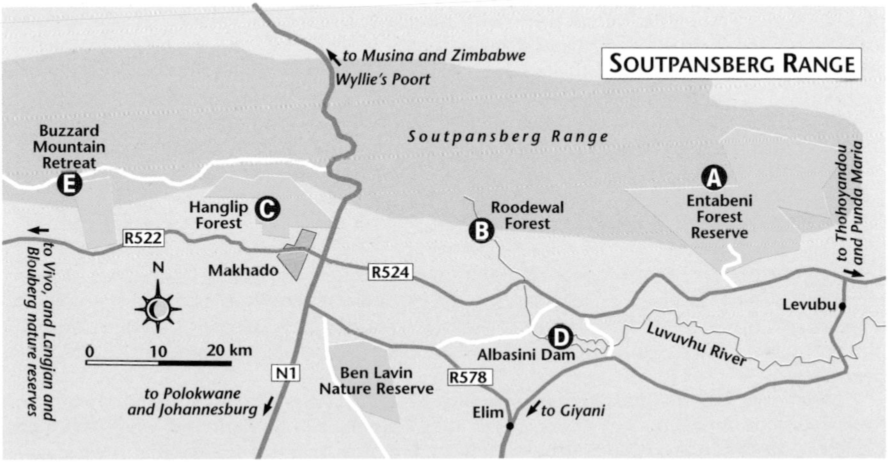

GETTING THERE

All these areas are easily accessible from Makhado, and the Soutpansberg-Limpopo Birding Route ☎ can provide up-to-date information and recommended accommodation.

Entabeni Forest Reserve: Travel on the R524 towards Thohoyandou from Makhado for 36 km, and turn left towards 'Entabeni/Timbadola'. Go through the boom gate and follow the signs to the Kliphuis, and you will reach the indigenous forest after 8 km.

Roodewal Forest: Take the Thohoyandou/Punda Maria road from Makhado for 15.8 km, and turn left at a sign marked 'Welgevonden' (in red letters) and 'Textures'. Follow the gravel road for 4.1 km, keeping left at any forks you encounter. At the end of a macadamia nut orchard, a small, concealed track runs steeply down to the left into a thick patch of forest.

Hanglip Forest: Easily accessible from Makhado and therefore a good stop if travelling northwards to Musina or Zimbabwe. From Makhado, take Krogh/Forestry Street due north, following the road through the Hanglip gate and for a further 8 km to the picnic site, where forest trails are indicated by signboards.

Albasini Dam: This area is best accessed from Shiluvan Lakeside Lodge ☎, a birder-friendly establishment which also offers boat rides on the dam. From Pretoria/Johannesburg, take the N1 north towards Makhado. Just before Makhado, take the R576 (signposted 'Giyani'). Follow this road for about 19 km to a 4-way stop in the town of Elim. Turn left to Levubu and follow the road for 4.5 km to the dam.

Hanglip Forest: Listen out for the resident **Scaly-throated Honeyguide** in the picnic site **C** and take one of the short trails where **Knysna Turaco, Crested Guineafowl, Narina Trogon*, Olive Woodpecker, Chorister Robin-Chat** and other typical forest species occur.

Albasini Dam: A boat ride on Albasini Dam **D** provides excellent viewing of many wetland species, and is one of the best areas in the country to see the elusive **African Finfoot***. Other species include **White-backed Night-Heron***, several kingfisher species, notably **Giant** and **Half-collared Kingfishers, Osprey, African Fish-Eagle, Woolly-necked Stork**, as well as a host of ducks and herons. The elusive **Bat Hawk*** has been seen in the vicinity of the dam wall on a number of occasions.

The dam is fringed by broad-leaved woodland and riverine thickets, which at times can become dense. **African Broadbill*** has been recorded in these thickets and **Gorgeous** and **Olive Bush-Shrikes** sometimes occur together in the riverine woodland. **Cape** and **Chinspot Batis** occur side by side, as do **Bar-throated** and **Yellow-breasted Apalis. Yellow-bellied** and **Sombre Greenbuls, White-browed Scrub-Robin** and **White-throated Robin-Chat** are best located by call.

The bush and grassland in the area surrounding the dam and the lower-lying area harbour **Shelley's Francolin, Yellow-throated Longclaw, Croaking Cisticola, Scarlet-chested Sunbird, Lizard Buzzard** and **Marico Flycatcher**.

OTHER ANIMALS: Forest and thicket mammals found here include Red Duiker, Bushbuck, Bushpig and Samango Monkey.

NEARBY SITES: Buzzard Mountain Retreat **E**, signposted 20 km north-west of Makhado on the Vivo road, offers excellent Soutpansberg birding and self-catering accommodation.

171 Venda Miombo Woodland 4X4 ✔✔

The recent discovery of a relict patch of miombo woodland in the remote mountains of Venda represents one of the most exciting birding opportunities in South Africa. This characteristic habitat type, previously only known from Zimbabwe northwards (see box on typical miombo birding, p.267), still has to be fully explored and may yet reveal bird species unrecorded in South Africa.

Initial exploration of the Gundani area has revealed species typical of miombo woodland further north in Africa, but which also occur in low numbers in similar moist woodland types. The most exciting is arguably **Southern Hyliota**, a typical miombo species that is very scarce outside of its favoured habitat. Gundani is the only reliable place in South Africa to see this species, and it should be searched as it gleans the outer branches of the *Brachystegia* trees. **White-breasted Cuckooshrike** is also characteristic of bird parties in miombo. Other species currently recorded favour dense thickets and include **Pink-throated*** and **Red-throated Twinspots, Bearded Scrub-Robin, Gorgeous Bush-Shrike, Eastern Nicator, Terrestrial Brownbul and Narina Trogon*. Blue-spotted Wood-Dove** has also been recorded in the area. Further exploration of these parts is sure to be rewarded with birding surprises.

Callan Cohen

An isolated patch of miombo woodland exists in Venda.

The miombo patch is accessed from the village of Gundani, which lies approximately 60 km north of Thohoyandou on the road to Muswodi, and is difficult to access without a 4WD and detailed directions to navigate the maze of mountain tracks. Birders are advised to contact the Soutpansberg-Limpopo Birding Route ☎ for guidance and to obtain permission from the local chief, as well as to use the new camp site.

172 Pafuri River Camp ✓✓

Offering easy access to riparian and woodland habitats in the north-eastern corner of Limpopo Province, Pafuri River Camp is close to the Kruger National Park.

SPECIALS: Eastern Nicator, Black-throated Wattle-eye, Yellow White-eye, Lemon-breasted Canary*, Grey-headed Parrot, Mottled Spinetail, Dickinson's Kestrel, African Finfoot*, Thick-billed Cuckoo*, Narina Trogon* and African Golden Oriole.

SEASON: Summer is best for bird numbers as many migrants are present; however, conditions can be very hot and humid.

HABITATS: Riverine forest and thicket, rocky outcrops, mopane woodland.

BIRDING: The camp provides access to a number of different and diverse habitats – making this one of the most rewarding areas in the region. Riverine forest along the Mutale and Pafuri rivers holds very similar birds to Pafuri in the Kruger National Park, including **Narina Trogon*, Eastern Nicator, Black-throated Wattle-eye, Broad-billed Roller, Tropical Boubou** and **Thick-billed Cuckoo*** in summer months. Common species here include **Ashy Flycatcher, Yellow-bellied Greenbul, African Green Pigeon, Woodland Kingfisher** (summer) and a host of bee-eater species including **White-fronted** and **Little Bee-eaters**.

Mopane woodland, which is the dominant habitat type away from the river near the camp, is good for **Arnot's Chat** and **White-breasted Cuckooshrike**, and is where the scarce **Racket-tailed Roller*** is occasionally recorded. Other species of mature mopane woodland include **African Golden Oriole, Red-headed Weaver** and **Retz's Helmet-Shrike**.

Callan Cohen

Mottled Spinetails roost in the Segole Big Tree.

GETTING THERE

Also known as Waller's Camp, this destination, which offers accommodation in tree houses alongside the Mutale River ☎, is close to the Pafuri Gate of the Kruger National Park.

Ask at the camp, or in advance from the Soutpansberg-Limpopo Birding Route, to be directed to the nearby Segole Big Tree, where a large number of **Mottled Spinetail** roost in this gargantuan Baobab. **Pennant-winged Nightjar*** occurs across this area in summer, and **Freckled Nightjar** is common on rocky outcrops.

NEARBY SITES: Pafuri River Camp is an ideal base from which to explore the area, and also to visit the Pafuri area within Kruger, as it is only 6 km from the Pafuri gate. Makuya Park is a beautiful and remote reserve bordering the far northern reaches of Kruger National Park that will appeal to adventurous birders keen on a wilderness experience. Birding is similar to Pafuri, and specials include **Mottled Spinetail** and **Lemon-breasted Canary***. Four-wheel-drive vehicles are advisable. Several rustic camps are open to the public; bookings and enquiries about day visits and directions can be made through the offices of Limpopo Parks and Tourism and the Soutpansberg-Limpopo Birding Route ☎.

173 Mapungubwe National Park ✔✔

This new park, protecting some of South Africa's most famous archaeological sites, is situated on the Limpopo/Shashe confluence in the north-western corner of Limpopo Province. It is one of the most exciting new birding venues in the country and provides access to a remarkable variety of habitats, including excellent riverine forest and mixed and mopane woodland, with scenic sandstone ridges, granite outcrops and arid plains.

Access to the riverine forest is enhanced by the construction of a canopy walkway and offers similar birding to that at Pafuri (p.189), with **Pel's Fishing-Owl***, **Thick-billed Cuckoo***, **Meyer's Parrot**, and **Senegal Coucal** among the specials on offer. Rocky wooded areas hold **Pennant-winged Nightjar***, and open plains offer species such as **Caspian Plover** (summer), **Monotonous Lark** and **Kori Bustard**. **Three-banded Courser*** occurs in the park. African Wild Dog features on an impressive mammal list.

There are plans to include an adjacent area known as the Den Staat farms into the park. Extensive wetlands here offer the spectacle of great numbers of water birds, including **Saddle-billed** and **Yellowbilled Storks**, **African Openbill**, **Rufous-bellied Heron**, **African Pygmy-Goose***, **Western Marsh-Harrier** (summer), **Lesser Moorhen**, **Allen's Gallinule**, **White-backed Duck**, **Lesser** and **Greater Flamingos**, **Grey Crowned Crane**, **Pel's Fishing-Owl***, **Osprey** and **White-backed Night-Heron***. Currently, access to Den Staat is via the Mopane Bush Lodge ☎.

174 The Tuli Block ✔✔

The Tuli Block lies in the eastern corner of Botswana, adjoining South Africa and Zimbabwe. This is a vast area of big game reserves – all privately owned and offering the classic African safari experience. The area has an excellent diversity of woodland birding, and the Limpopo River provides some superb riparian birding with exceptional diversity of birds and specials like **Pel's Fishing-Owl***, but access is difficult for the independent birder. Other specials include **White-crowned Lapwing** (Limpopo River), **Meves's Starling**, **Bronze-winged** and **Three-banded* Coursers** (latter in mopane woodlands), **White-backed Night-Heron*** (riverine thickets), **Tropical Boubou** and **Thrush Nightingale*** (summer).

Access – now easier than in the past – must be arranged through private lodges and game farms. The area is usually reached from the South African side via the Pontdrift, Platjan or Zanzibar border posts, which may be impassable to vehicles when the water level of the Limpopo is high. Most of the lodges have their own airstrips, and charters can be arranged. Accommodation arrangements should be made in advance; game reserves and lodges will be able to assist with directions and advice on local conditions. A variety of accommodation is available, although the area caters primarily for upmarket safaris. Access can be arranged through the following reserves: Tumelo Game Lodge, Mashatu Game Reserve, Tuli Safari Lodge and Stevensford Game Reserve. Ratho Bush Camp in South Africa has **Pel's Fishing-Owl*** in gallery forest, and offers accommodation and camping ☎.

ROUTE 16

KRUGER NATIONAL PARK

This vast reserve is one of Africa's best known safari areas and, apart from its impressive mammal diversity, boasts a bird list in excess of 500 species. The Kruger National Park is set apart from many similar big-game areas elsewhere in Africa because of the ease with which it can be visited on an independent basis, making this vast reserve a mecca for self-drive birders and nature enthusiasts. Apart from the high diversity of woodland birds, at 20 000 km² Kruger is a safe haven for a number of the region's larger birds, including Saddle-billed Stork, Hooded, White-backed, Lappet-faced and White-headed Vultures, Tawny and Martial Eagles, Bateleur, Kori Bustard, Pel's Fishing-Owl* and Southern Ground-Hornbill*. Other species with limited distribution in southern Africa that occur here include Yellow-billed Oxpecker, Greater Blue-eared Starling, Meves's Starling, Retz's Helmet-Shrike, Stierling's Wren-Warbler, Thrush Nightingale*, Bearded Scrub-Robin, Thick-billed Cuckoo*, Senegal Lapwing, African Finfoot*, and Brown-headed Parrot.

TOP 10 BIRDS

- Saddle-billed Stork
- Mottled Spinetail
- Thick-billed Cuckoo
- Senegal Lapwing
- White-headed Vulture
- Brown-headed Parrot
- Yellow-billed Oxpecker
- Southern Ground-Hornbill
- Monotonous Lark
- White-crowned Lapwing

Visits to Kruger are generally done as part of a wider birding trip, and despite its enormous wealth of birds, visitors wanting a more representative southern African list are advised to combine Kruger with other habitats nearby. These include escarpment forests at Magoebaskloof (Limpopo) and Mount Sheba, and high-altitude grassland birding around Dullstroom or Kaapschoop.

The sheer size of the Park can be overwhelming, and to this end we offer below several recommended itineraries.

Callan Cohen

Southern Ground-Hornbill

Visiting birders who are not familiar with the area are advised to be very conservative when planning an itinerary. Given the speed limits and the number of birds on offer, distances on the map may be deceptive, and even a short drive of 10 km can take three or four hours to complete! Be sure to return to camp before the designated closing times.

Because birding on foot is only allowed in the rest camps and at certain designated spots, most of Kruger can only be birded from the confines of one's vehicle. Although this has its limitations, it can also be very rewarding, as birds are much more approachable from a vehicle. We recommend that you don't spend less than three nights in the Park. If you are a focused birder with experience of the common species and don't mind driving long distances, you might consider Punda

Maria (2-3 nights), Mopani (1 night), Satara (1 night), Lower Sabie (1 night), Skukuza (1 night) and Pretoriuskop (1 night). However, relaxed birders could happily spend a week just between Skukuza, Pretoriuskop and Lower Sabie. Generally, the southern region offers an excellent diversity of birds, especially bushveld species. It is also the most popular game-viewing area in the Park. The northern area, near Punda Maria and Pafuri, offers a taste of more tropical birds, and hosts a number of local species.

Because this entire route is located within the confines of a single national park, we have summarised the access, seasons and habitat information to all areas of the Park in this introduction, and have confined the site accounts to birding information. Birding is highly rewarding year-round, although birds are most vocal during the wet summer months (Nov-Mar), when the migrants are also present. Winter months have the advantage of having superb weather, better game-viewing opportunities, and lower malaria risk.

> **GETTING THERE**
> Nine points of entry along Kruger's western and southern borders provide access to an exceptional tourist infrastructure, with an excellent road network, numerous bird hides, night drives, day walks, walking safaris, shops and restaurants, and a number of camps offering a range of accommodation ☎. An excellent map is available from each of the rest camps, as well as each entry point.

The Kruger Park can be characterised as a mosaic of lowland savannas and woodlands, bisected by wooded, seasonally flowing rivers, with dams and seasonal pans dotted throughout. Soil type plays a major role in determining habitat structure, dividing Kruger's savanna habitats into open, grass-dominated savannas in the east (basalt soils) and well-wooded bushveld in the west (granitic soils). The bushveld can further be divided into mixed bushveld, with both acacia and broad-leaved woodland south of the Olifants River, and mopane-dominated bushveld to the north. Punda Maria and Pretoriuskop are at slightly higher elevation than the rest of Kruger, with cooler, moister conditions prevailing in the mesic broad-leaved woodlands. A number of major rivers run west to east, providing a mixture of riverine forest, riverine thicket and alluvial acacia bushveld, particularly at Pafuri and along the Sabie and Crocodile rivers.

Game-viewing is diverse and as the park has the highest mammal diversity of any protected area in Africa, we haven't mentioned these species individually.

SOUTHERN KRUGER

175 Skukuza to Lower Sabie

IBA ✔✔

The largest camp and administrative hub of the park is Skukuza Ⓐ, within which there is some successful birding to be had. Walk from the reception towards the camping area (visitors are issued with a map upon arrival at reception), set among dense thickets where **Terrestrial Brownbul**, **Bearded Scrub-Robin** and **Green-backed Camaroptera** can be found.

The camping ground, which contains a number of large, dense Umbrella Thorns, plays host to **Grey Tit-Flycatcher** and **Burnt-necked Eremomela**. Then visit the corner of the camp towards the Selati Restaurant, where areas of thick vegetation harbour species such as **White-throated Robin-Chat**. **Kurrichane Thrush**, **White-browed** and **Red-capped Robin-Chats**, **White-browed** and **Bearded Scrub-Robins**, **Eastern Black-headed Oriole**, **Brubru**, **Marico**, **Collared**, **Scarlet-chested** and **White-bellied Sunbirds**, **Orange-breasted** and **Grey-headed Bush-Shrikes**, **Southern Black Flycatcher**, **Yellow-breasted Apalis**, **Southern Black Tit**, and **Violet-backed Starling** are all found here, as are **Cape Glossy** and **Greater Blue-eared Starlings**, providing a great opportunity to get to grips with these two very similar species.

Along the Sabie River, the main attraction is the opportunity to see the uncommon **African Finfoot***. Patiently watch the river margins, particularly sections with dense, overhanging reedbeds. Other water birds found along the river include **Goliath** and **Green-backed Herons**, **Pied** and **Giant Kingfishers**, **African Pied Wagtail** and **Wire-tailed Swallow**. Reedbeds and rank vegetation adjacent to the river often hold a host of seed-eaters, including **Red-backed** and **Bronze Mannikins**, **Red-billed** and **African Firefinches** and **Thick-billed Weaver**, as well as **Tawny-flanked Prinia** and **Red-faced Cisticola**. Large figs along the river are a hive of activity when fruiting, and **African Green Pigeon** and **Black-collared Barbet** are conspicuous, while **Trumpeter Hornbill** sometimes make an appearance.

Nigel Dennis/IOA

Lilac-breasted Roller is common in southern Kruger National Park.

DRIVES AROUND SKUKUZA

There are many excellent drives around Skukuza **A**. For general bushveld birding the area south of Skukuza, towards Pretoriuskop, holds a rich diversity of species.

Take the H1-1 south towards Pretoriuskop, keeping an eye out for more widespread species such as **Golden-breasted Bunting**, **Southern White-crowned Shrike**, **White Helmet-Shrike**, **Orange-breasted Bush-Shrike**, **White-browed Scrub-Robin**, **Woodland Kingfisher** (summer), **Cardinal** and **Bearded Woodpeckers** and **Southern Yellow-billed Hornbill**. After five kilometres, turn left onto the gravel road (S114). At **B**, scan the sparsely grassed areas for **Senegal Lapwing**, which may join the more common **Crowned Lapwing**. **Red-billed Hornbill**, **Magpie Shrike**, **Sabota Lark** and **Burchell's Starling** are also usually present, and **Burnt-necked Eremomela** may be heard calling from the thickets. After another 3 km, turn right onto the S22, making the detour to the Stevenson Hamilton Memorial Tablet, situated on top of a small koppie **C**. Here you may alight from your vehicle. Scanning the rocks should reveal **Mocking Cliff-Chat**, and **Striped Pipit** (which may respond to playback). **White-throated Robin-Chat** also occurs around the parking area. Back in the car, carry on to the S112, turning right, and right again onto the H3. Turn left onto the H1-1 towards Pretoriuskop at **D** and right at **E** onto the Waterhole road (S65). This road is good for a variety of less common bushveld species. The first few kilometres may well yield **Grey Penduline-Tit**, **Yellow-bellied Eremomela**, **Coqui Francolin**, **Levaillant's**, **Jacobin** and **African Cuckoos**, **Black Cuckooshrike**, **Bushveld Pipit**, **Jameson's Firefinch**, **Yellow-throated Petronia**, **Pallid Flycatcher** and **Stierling's Wren-Warbler**. After 14 km, the Waterhole road ends. Turn left onto the Doispane road (S1) and stop at the narrow watercourse **F** to listen out for bird parties. At **G**, look for **Bennett's Woodpecker** before turning right. On reaching the S4, turn right and follow the course of the Sabie River back to Kruger Gate. The first 2 km often yield **Retz's Helmet-Shrike** and, if you are very lucky, the scarce **Thick-billed Cuckoo*** that parasitises it. Its piercing call may be heard anywhere in the Skukuza area, particularly in November.

The road also provides good riverine forest, especially at **H**, and holds all the species that are found in Skukuza rest camp. From Kruger Gate, return to Skukuza rest camp along the main road, stopping in at the Lake Panic Bird Hide. **Grey Tit-Flycatcher** is regularly seen in the car park here. Spend the last 30 minutes before sunset on the low-level bridge over the Sabie River, which is one of the better sites for **African Finfoot***.

LOWER SABIE

The smaller Lower Sabie camp is also set alongside the Sabie River, 46 km downstream from Skukuza. A popular spot here is the viewing deck in front of the restaurant, which offers the opportunity to watch water birds while sipping cocktails! Depending on water levels, viewing from the deck may produce an assortment of herons and waders, **African Finfoot***, **White-crowned Lapwing**, **African Fish-Eagle** and other raptors, while **Water Thick-knee** and **Red-faced Cisticola** are usually close by. The shady camp is good for **Grey-headed Bush-Shrike**, **Ashy Flycatcher**, **Grey Tit-Flycatcher**, **Golden-tailed Woodpecker**, **Brown-headed Parrot** and a variety of weaver species.

Sunset Dam is close to Lower Sabie on the main Skukuza road, and is good for water birds, including storks and herons. The road follows the southern bank of the Sabie River, and **River Warbler** has been recorded calling from thickets along the banks during late summer. **White-crowned Lapwing** occurs on the exposed sandbanks, such as those below Nkuhlu picnic site. **African Finfoot*** prefers quieter backwaters, and one such site is the high-level bridge 12 km from Skukuza. From this bridge, return to Lower Sabie along the Salitjie road, north of the Sabie River, for good bushveld and open savanna birding.

The more open country to the north and south of Lower Sabie supports a different variety of birds. A drive to Mlondozi Dam picnic spot (returning via Mlondozi road) is good for **Black-bellied Bustard**, **Senegal Lapwing**, **Temminck's Courser** and **Kori Bustard**. Mlondozi Dam lookout and the road northwards (H10) can be excellent for **Yellow-throated Longclaw** and **Croaking Cisticola**, while the picnic spot is good for **Mocking Cliff-Chat**, **Cinnamon-breasted Rock Bunting**, and water birds. **Black Coucal** has been seen in the grasslands on the H10, 10 km north of Lower Sabie, after good rains. Another rewarding drive from Lower Sabie is the southward loop via Nhlanganzwane Dam, and Duke waterhole (S137).

176 Pretoriuskop to Berg-en-dal IBA ✔✔

Pretoriuskop camp (I) is situated in mesic broad-leaved woodland, with a number of large, densely vegetated outcrops nearby. Sunbirds abound in the camp's gardens, while **Green-capped** and **Yellow-bellied Eremomela**, **Grey Penduline-Tit** and a host of other woodland species occur in the woodlands surrounding it. **Brown-headed Parrot** often flock in the camp's trees in large numbers during the winter months. **Purple-crested Turaco**, **Yellow-fronted Tinkerbird**, and **Groundscraper Thrush** all also occur. **Red-headed Weaver** nests colonially here – look out for its distinctive, long-tunnelled nests, for example, outside the restaurant.

Shabeni and Pretoriuskop loops: The numerous loops in the Pretoriuskop area provide for some excellent birding. In addition to the species that can be found in the rest camp ((I) on map), **Gorgeous Bush-Shrike** is fairly common in dense thickets on koppie fringes – try Shabeni Koppie (J) or Marungu Kop (K) (near the camp). The rocky Shabeni Loop is also good

J Rossouw

Red-headed Weaver breeds in Pretoriuskop camp.

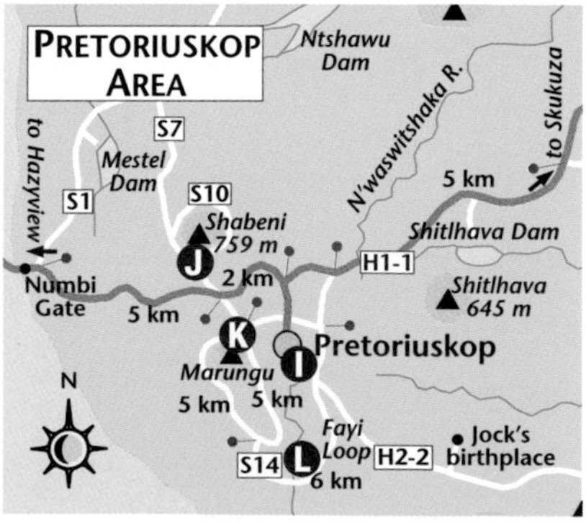

for **Mocking Cliff-Chat**, **Striped Pipit** (occasional), and **Croaking** and **Lazy Cisticolas**. **Southern Boubou** and **White-throated Robin-Chat** are common in the thicker vegetation. The area is also particularly good for **Lizard Buzzard**. The S8 and S14 Ⓛ, as well as parts of the H2-2 closer to Pretoriuskop, provide good opportunities to find **Bushveld Pipit** and **Flappet Lark**, as well as **Yellow-throated Longclaw** (in the taller, moister grass). Look out, too, for **Yellow-throated Petronia**, **Pallid Flycatcher** and **Striped Kingfisher**. A night drive from Pretoriuskop offers an excellent chance of **Freckled Nightjar**.

Berg-en-dal, a rest camp to the south of Pretoriuskop, is good for general bushveld birding, and the small dam in the camp is an excellent spot for **White-backed Night-Heron***, which can be seen at dusk. **African Finfoot*** is also sometimes seen here. **Orange-winged Pytilia** has been recorded several times drinking at the camp waterhole.

177 Satara IBA ✔

The Satara rest camp is surrounded by open savanna, and offers a range of plains birds, particularly after good rains. **Common Ostrich**, **Kori Bustard**, **Southern Ground-Hornbill*** and **Secretarybird** can be found, and **Sabota Lark** and **Chestnut-backed Sparrowlark** are common. The S90 is an excellent road for Palearctic visitors such as **Montagu's** and **Pallid* Harriers**, as well as **Lesser Grey Shrike**. After good rains, **Harlequin Quail** and **Kurrichane Buttonquail** can be common. In mid- to late summer, **Red-billed Quelea** colonies and termite alate irruptions attract a host of raptors, often with impressive numbers of **Steppe** and **Lesser Spotted Eagles**.

At the camp itself, it is worth spending a few hours birding around midday. **Bennett's Woodpecker**, **Red-billed Buffalo-Weaver**, **Burchell's Starling**, **African Mourning Dove**, **Brown-headed Parrot** and **Groundscraper Thrush** are almost always present. **African Scops-Owl** roosts in the camp by day (ask the cleaning staff for the birds' current roost site). **Pearl-spotted Owlet** is common in the area, and often ventures onto the verge of the rest camp. Other camp specials include **Grey-backed Camaroptera** and **Red-capped Robin-Chat**, which favour thickets near the staff quarters.

An excellent drive for woodland birds is the circular route to Timbavati picnic spot, via the H7, S40 and S127. Carry on along the main road for a few kilometres west past Nsemani Dam, as the thornveld here is excellent for the smaller bushveld birds.

NORTHERN KRUGER

178 Pafuri IBA ✔✔✔

Pafuri produces arguably the most exciting birding in Kruger. The picnic site can be reached by making an early start from Punda Maria, or staying at the Pafuri River Camp (p.189) near

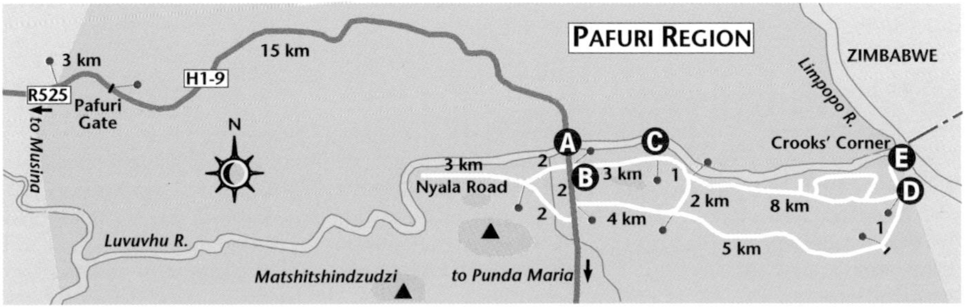

Nigel Dennis/IOA

Well-developed woodland along the Luvuvhu River

Pafuri Gate. Upon entering Pafuri Gate, head for the Luvuvhu River bridge, keeping an eye out for **Arnot's Chat** (uncommon) in the well-developed mopane woodlands. The bridge Ⓐ provides a good vantage point for scanning the river; look out for **African Finfoot***, **Green-backed Heron** and, among the large trees just south of the river, **Tropical Boubou**, **Eastern Nicator** and other woodland species. This area is also the best site for spotting spinetails; **Mottled Spinetail** nests in a nearby Baobab and is often seen in this area, as is **Böhm's Spinetail***. Also keep a lookout for **Horus Swift**, which nests in the river banks. Just 200 m south of the bridge, a dirt road follows the river in an easterly direction Ⓑ, passing through acacia thicket and riverine forest to the picnic site Ⓒ. En route, watch out for **Crested Guineafowl**, **Common Scimitarbill**, **Yellow-bellied Greenbul**, **Meves's Starling**, **Grey Tit-Flycatcher**, **Ashy Flycatcher**, **Bearded Scrub-Robin**, **White-browed Scrub-Robin**, **White-throated Robin-Chat**, **Retz's Helmet-Shrike**, and **Broad-billed Roller**. **Purple Indigobird** and its host, **Jameson's Firefinch**, may also be seen here, although beware of confusion with the more common **Village Indigobird** and their **Red-billed Firefinch** hosts. This section of road has also proved excellent for a range of uncommon warblers, with **Common Whitethroat** and **Olive-tree Warbler***, as well as **Thrush Nightingale***, being recorded during most summers, especially in years of good rain. Follow the signs to the picnic site and bird the perimeter. Many of the above-mentioned species can be seen here, where the thick riparian forest attracts **Green-capped Eremomela**, **Purple-crested Turaco**, **Tropical Boubou** and **Black-throated Wattle-eye**. **Pel's Fishing-Owl*** sometimes roosts in the dense riverine trees – ask the caretaker or local bird guide if it is around. The river in front of the picnic spot is also good for **White-crowned Lapwing**, **Water Thick-knee** and other water birds, including the occasional **African Finfoot***.

From the picnic site, continue eastwards, checking the large baobabs about 200 m beyond the picnic site turn-off for both **Böhm's*** and **Mottled Spinetails**, which appear to have taken up residence here for the first time recently. After 9 km, you reach a T-junction with an area of open palm savanna straight ahead Ⓓ. This is the best site in Kruger for **Lemon-breasted Canary***, although also check the palms just south of the bridge at Ⓑ. Listen for the typical canary-like call coming from the palms. Continuing left towards the river, you will pass through a dense patch of forest, where **African Crowned Eagle**, **Narina Trogon***, **Gorgeous Bush-Shrike**, **Eastern Nicator**, **Black-throated Wattle-eye** and **Tambourine Dove** occur, before meeting up with the confluence of the Limpopo and Luvuvhu rivers, known as Crooks' Corner Ⓔ; here **Senegal Coucal** and **Blue-cheeked Bee-eater** may be found.

From Crooks' Corner, retrace your steps to the tarred road and continue upstream along the river for more excellent riverine birding.

179 Punda Maria

IBA ✔✔

Punda Maria camp Ⓕ offers superb woodland birding. It is situated on a hillside (good for soaring raptors), in dense woodland. **Yellow-bellied Greenbul**, **White-throated Robin-Chat** and **Bearded Scrub-Robin** occur around the camp, particularly behind the shop, and in the thickets between the camp ground and the bungalows. The Flycatcher Trail within the camp area is also excellent for birding, and **African Scops-Owl** is present in tall trees in the camp ground. The prime birding area here is, however, the Mahonie Loop. Moist wood-

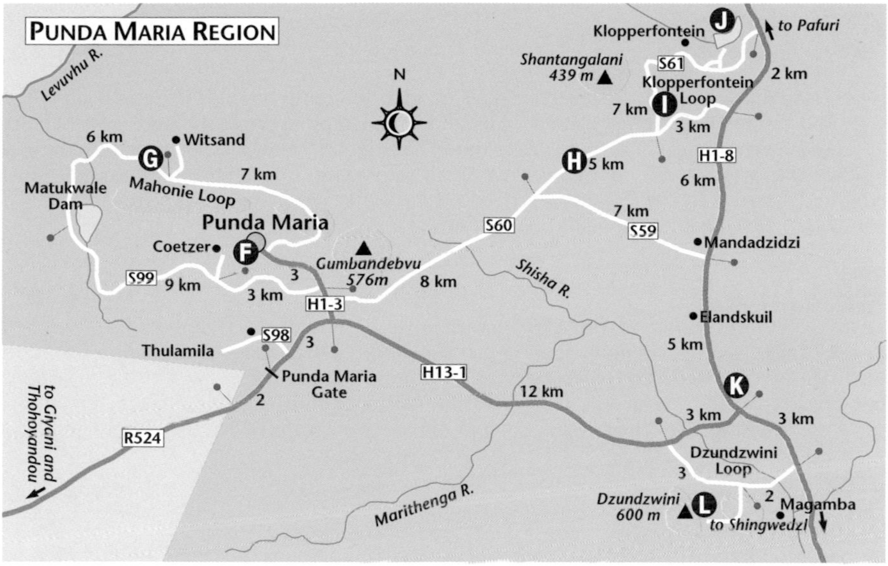

lands along this route are among the best for **Eastern Nicator, Narina Trogon*, Eurasian Golden Oriole, Mosque Swallow, Broad-billed Roller, White-breasted Cuckooshrike** and **Grey-headed Parrot**. The parrot is best looked for in the early morning and late afternoon, when noisy flocks commute to and from roost sites; the best area to search is 7-10 km along the loop in an anti-clockwise direction (G). Night drives in early summer may produce **Pennant-winged Nightjar*** (see p.198), which can also be seen at dawn and dusk. Although rare, **Sooty Falcon, River Warbler, Thrush Nightingale*, Racket-tailed Roller*** and **Southern Hyliota** have all been recorded here.

East of Punda Maria, the S60 passes through mature stands of mopane woodland and is good for **Arnot's Chat**; try 3 km east of the S59-S60 junction (H), where **White-breasted Cuckooshrike** may also be seen. Search the plains (I) in the Klopperfontein area (S61) for **Dickinson's Kestrel** and **Harlequin Quail**.

In wet seasons, **Lesser Moorhen** is present on small wetlands (such as that at Klopperfontein, (J) on map), and **Black Coucal** in wetlands with tall grasses (such as near the junction of the H13-1 and H1-8, (K)). **Monotonous Lark** may irrupt into the area in large numbers. In summer, open grasslands in this northern area often hold flocks of **Amur Falcon, Red-footed Kestrel, Pallid*** and **Montagu's Harriers, Harlequin Quail** and, during wet summers, **Corncrake**. Check all Buffalo herds for **Yellow-billed Oxpecker**. Dzundzwini Hill (L) offers broad-leaved woodland birding, including **White Helmet-Shrike**.

180 Shingwedzi Area

IBA ✔✔

Shingwedzi rest camp holds a number of interesting species. **Red-headed Weaver, Bennett's Woodpecker** and **African Mourning Dove** are resident, and **Collared Palm-Thrush** has been recorded around tall Lala Palms – check the palms in the camp (such as near Hut 25) and those between the camp and the high-level bridge. Also keep a lookout for **Cut-throat Finch**.

Nearby, Kanniedood Dam provides some excellent waterbirding, and usually has a number of waders (including **White-fronted Plover** occasionally) and storks (including **African Openbill** and **Saddle-billed Stork**). Some of the best grassland birding can be had to the south of Shingwedzi, between the Nyawutsi bird hide and Nshawu no. 1 (see Mopani/the Tropic of Capricorn Loop, overleaf).

181 Letaba

IBA ✔

Letaba Camp is well spread out and birding is good in the camp grounds, especially along the river. **Red-capped Robin-Chat**, **Barred Owlet** and **Green-capped Eremomela** are resident here.

Letaba provides easy access to several good river loops, where **Grey-rumped Swallow** is resident (keep an eye out for the swallows along the river in front of the camp too). **White-crowned Plover** (on the Olifants River) and a variety of water birds occur in the vicinity, particularly at Mingerhout and Engelhardt dams.

182 Olifants

IBA ✔

As with most camps, birding is good in camp, where **Orange-breasted** and **Grey-headed Bush-Shrikes** and **Red-headed Weaver** are common. The lookout in front of the restaurant not only provides a panoramic view over the savannas, but is a good place for raptor-spotting. **Mocking Cliff-Chat** may be seen in the rocky outcrops within the camp.

183 Mopani

IBA ✔

Mopani is situated within relatively unproductive mopane savanna, but there are several good birding opportunities in the vicinity of this camp. The camp overlooks Pioneer Dam, which often hosts breeding **Collared Pratincole** and a range of other water birds.

Nshawu Dam is one of the more interesting dams in the Park, and often yields a range of water birds, including **Kittlitz's Plover**. **Collared Pratincole** has bred here. **Rufous-winged Cisticola** can be found in the reedbeds along the Nshawu River, such as at Nshawu No. 2.

The Tropic of Capricorn Loop leads across the open plains, where **Kori Bustard** and **Secretarybird** are present. This area also supports **Red-crested Korhaan**, **Black-bellied Bustard** and **Chestnut-backed Sparrowlark**. After good rains, **Harlequin Quail** may be seen here, as well as migratory **Pallid*** and **Montagu's Harriers**.

NIGHT DRIVES IN THE KRUGER

Sunset and night drives run every night from the larger camps in the Park. Pre-booking is essential. Each camp offers drives starting at different times and of different duration, so it is important to enquire beforehand.

Nightjar spotlighted on the road

Fiery-necked, **Square-tailed** and **European Nightjars** (latter in summer only) occur throughout the Park, although Square-tailed Nightjar is usually localised at the margins of larger rivers. **Freckled Nightjar** is found on rocky outcrops, such as Mathekenyane near Skukuza and Shabeni near Pretoriuskop, or on the Mahonie Loop at Punda Maria. **Pennant-winged Nightjar*** is also best seen along this loop, particularly during early summer (Nov-Dec).

Verreaux's (particularly at Mathekenyane near Skukuza) and **Spotted Eagle-Owls**, **Pearl-spotted Owlet**, **African Scops-Owl** and **Barn Owl** are common in the Park, while **Marsh Owl** occurs in areas with seasonal wetlands, and **African Barred Owlet** occurs along the larger watercourses and in the moist woodland on the Mahonie Loop.

Spotted and **Water Thick-knees** and **Bronze-winged Courser** (uncommon) are widespread. **White-backed Night-Heron*** is scarce along well-wooded rivers, but may be seen at the Olifants River bridge on the H1-4, and the Sabie River crossing just east of Lower Sabie.

ROUTE 17

NORTH-WEST ROUTE

The North-West Route – basically, the north-western reaches of the Limpopo Province, Gauteng, and the North-West Province – is mostly covered by arid woodland and grassland. On its north-south axis, the North-West Province is characterised by a remarkably consistent divide at 26° S that separates the higher altitude grasslands to the south from the lower altitude woodlands to the north. This divide essentially follows the watershed, with north-flowing rivers going into the Limpopo Basin to the north, and south-flowing rivers into the Vaal/Orange basin.

TOP 10 BIRDS

- Yellow-throated Sandgrouse
- Short-clawed Lark
- Southern Pied Babbler
- Crimson-breasted Shrike
- Barred Wren-Warbler
- Short-toed Rock-Thrush
- Kalahari Scrub-Robin
- Orange River Francolin
- Pink-billed Lark
- Olive-tree Warbler

Much of the Great North-West is remote, and well away from the better-known birding routes. The focus of this route is thus on the more accessible and better known game areas and nature reserves, which offer a great variety of species, and are particularly rich in southern African near-endemics. Notably, the area offers easy access to a number of range-restricted or tricky birds, including Short-clawed Lark*, Yellow-throated Sandgrouse, Melodious Lark*, Orange River Francolin, Cape Vulture^ and Barrow's Korhaan*. Other interesting birds that are to be found in this region include White-backed Night Heron*, African Finfoot*, Burchell's Sandgrouse* and Short-toed Rock-Thrush (subspecies *pretoriae*).

Common near-endemics that occur on the North-West Route include Pale Chanting Goshawk, Northern Black Korhaan, White-backed Mousebird, Acacia Pied Barbet, Southern Yellow-billed Hornbill, Crimson-breasted Shrike, Kalahari Scrub-Robin, Eastern Clapper, Fawn-coloured and Spike-heeled Larks, Grey-backed Sparrowlark, Ashy Tit, Cape Penduline-Tit, Southern Pied Babbler, Red-eyed Bulbul, Karoo Thrush, African White-throated Robin Chat, Burchell's Starling, Barred Wren-Warbler, Black-chested Prinia, Orange River White-eye, Marico Flycatcher, Black-faced Waxbill, Red-headed Finch and Shaft-tailed Whydah.

The ranges of several species, namely African Pygmy Falcon, Sociable Weaver, Burchell's Courser*, Swallow-tailed Bee-eater, Pririt Batis (extreme south and west), Rufous-eared Warbler, Dusky Sunbird (extreme west), Chat Flycatcher and Namaqua Sandgrouse, extend into this region from the west.

Richard du Toit

Yellow-throated Sandgrouse come to drink.

184 Vaalkop Dam & Bird Sanctuary ✔✔

This site, relatively close to Gauteng, offers excellent bushveld birding, complemented by a good number of endemics and an array of water birds. Vaalkop also offers regular rarities and some good raptors.

SPECIALS: Blue-cheeked Bee-eater, Short-toed Rock-Thrush, Pale Chanting Goshawk, Olive-tree Warbler*, Common Whitethroat, Southern Pied Babbler, Barred Wren-Warbler, Shaft-tailed Whydah, Ashy Tit. Barrow's Korhaan* is seen in the North-West Parks section.

HABITATS: Acacia thornveld, broad-leaved woodland, rocky hillsides with thick bush, riverine woodland, open savanna, open grassland (dry years), open water, well-vegetated backwaters and reedbeds.

Pale Chanting Goshawk

BIRDING: As you go in at the entrance gate, follow the sharp left turn. Keep left, and cross the canal. A few hundred yards further on, acacia trees become dominant. This area is excellent for acacia thornveld species such as **Kalahari** and **White-browed Scrub-Robins**, **Barred Wren-Warbler**, **Cape Penduline-Tit**, **Violet-eared** and **Black-faced Waxbills**, and **Green-winged Pytilia**. Watch overhead for raptors, and in summer for **European** and **Blue-cheeked Bee-eaters**, as well as displaying **Shaft-tailed Whydah** and **Long-tailed Paradise-Whydah. Pale Chanting Goshawk** is present in the area. Follow the fence until you reach a spot where an old quarry was dug quite near the fence, and is surrounded by large low thorn trees. In late summer, this is a good locality for **Olive-tree Warbler***, **Common Whitethroat**, and other warblers. The shoreline is easily accessible and yields **Goliath Heron**, **Kittlitz's Plover**, and **White-winged Tern**; keep a lookout for **Osprey**.

To bird the north side, go back past the gate, cross the river (worth a stop) and go up the hill. The woodland against the koppie on the right is a regular spot for **Short-toed Rock-Thrush**, as well as **Bar-throated Apalis**, **Yellow-fronted Tinkerbird**, **Striped Pipit** and **Grey-backed Camaroptera**. Watch above for **African Hawk-Eagle**. Along the dam wall you may see **Water Thick-knee**, **Green-backed Heron** and **Blue-cheeked Bee-eater.** Examine flocks of swifts and swallows for **Horus Swift**, which is regular at the dam wall.

Irrigated and fallow lands on the Beestekraal road always offer something interesting; check for **Chestnut-backed Sparrowlark**, **Red-capped Lark**, **Long-tailed Paradise** and **Shaft-tailed Whydahs** and **Temminck's Courser**.

The Bird Sanctuary, managed by North-West Parks, provides access to the northern end of the dam, and more open country. The area around Bushwillow is also excellent for **Great Sparrow**, **Southern Black Flycatcher**, **Magpie Shrike** and **Red-billed Buffalo-Weaver. Double-banded Sandgrouse** is regular along roads, and the manager knows where **Barrow's Korhaan*** can be seen. **Pale Chanting Goshawk** is common in open savanna areas.

GETTING THERE

From Gauteng, take the N4 toll road to Brits, and then proceed northwards (R511) towards Thabazimbi. After about 35 km (just after a railway bridge) follow the sign to the left towards Vaalkop Dam. Cross the Crocodile River, and at the T-junction, turn right. After 12 km (of prime birding road) turn left at the Vaalkop Dam sign. The entrance is about 1 km further on the right-hand side, and just before this is the road to 'Bushwillow', which takes one through to the Bird Sanctuary, managed by North-West Parks. Access to the latter needs to be arranged in advance ☎.

185 Borakalalo Game Reserve ✔✔

This is a large game reserve north-west of Pretoria with a good diversity of bushveld and water-bird habitats and a nice variety of big game, including White Rhinoceros. It features the large Klipvoor Dam, the Moretele River and the scenic Mogoshane hills.

SPECIALS: Short-toed Rock-Thrush, White-backed Night-Heron*, African Finfoot*, Purple Roller, Grey-headed Kingfisher, Grey Tit-Flycatcher, Meyer's Parrot, Southern Pied Babbler, Barred Wren-Warbler, Shaft-tailed Whydah, Ashy Tit.

HABITATS: Woodland habitats, including acacia thorn-veld, riverine woodland and broad-leaved savanna, including an area of tall *Burkea* woodland; rocky hill-sides, and extensive open water with fringing reedbeds and shoreline.

GETTING THERE

Borakalalo is just over 100 km from Pretoria and Johannesburg via Brits. Entering Brits via the R511, take the turn-off in the middle of town, which is signposted to Borakalalo Game Reserve. After 17 km, turn right to Legonyane. From here on keep to the left on the tarred roads for 50 km, until you reach the reserve gates. Gates open at 06h00. Accommodation is available in two furnished tented safari camps, and bookings should be made in advance, particularly on weekends ☎. A park checklist and map are available at the gate.

BIRDING: The main picnic site Ⓐ is worth a stop for waxbills, pipits and woodpeckers. Look for **Familiar Chat** and **Groundscraper Thrush**. Beyond the picnic site, the hillside to the left Ⓑ should be scanned for **Short-toed Rock-Thrush**, which is resident in this area, and is often seen opposite the dam wall. This species can also be seen around the quarry, which can be reached by keeping left past the dam wall.

Below the dam wall, the road forks. The right-hand fork leads to the river Ⓒ, and is a likely spot for **African Finfoot***, which is sometimes seen just below the low bridge. Park beyond the bridge and take a small footpath along the right-hand bank of the river, which goes downstream. The river takes a wide bend to the right, and then turns left. **White-backed Night-Heron*** has bred in this area, and is fairly regular in summer, but is usually well concealed in a dense tangle overhanging the water. Look out for **Giant Kingfisher, Green-backed Heron, African Fish-Eagle** and **Half-collared Kingfisher**.

The River Walk, starting at Moretele Camp Ⓓ, passes through tall acacia woodland, which is good for **Grey Tit-Flycatcher** and **Lesser Honeyguide**. Also look for **Red-headed Weaver, Meyer's Parrot** and **Levaillant's** and **African Cuckoos** (summer). The thickets along the river's edge are home to **White-throated Robin-Chat** and **Grey-backed Camaroptera**;

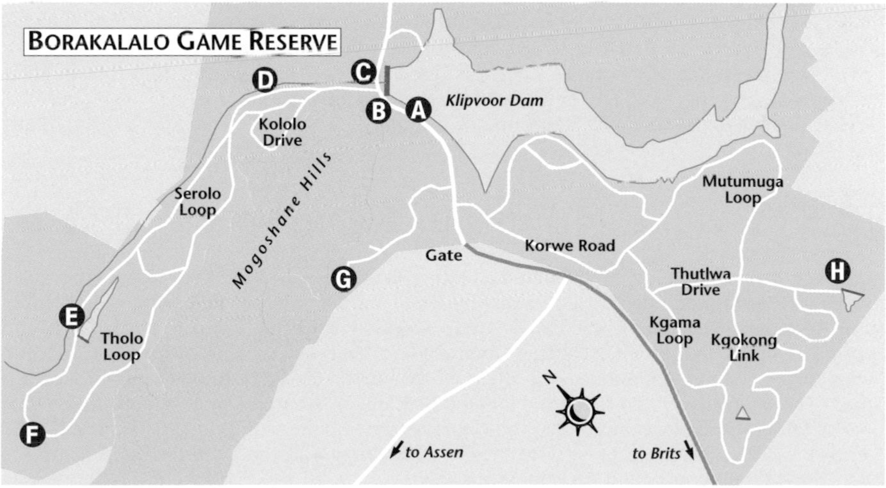

Warwick Tarboton

Crimson-breasted Shrike

Little Sparrowhawk and **Shikra** are also common. **African Finfoot*** and **Half-collared Kingfisher** are present everywhere along the river, but it requires considerable patience to see them.

Moretele Camp **D** lies alongside the river. This is as good an area as any for **African Finfoot***, which is most easily seen by patient watching from a chair on the river bank.

Below Moretele Camp, follow the drive in a westerly direction. In summer, **European Golden Oriole** is common in trees along the river, as is **Grey-headed Kingfisher**, although the latter is less conspicuous than **Woodland Kingfisher**.

After 5 km you reach Ga Dinonyane hide **E** on the left. This is set amid dry acacia thornveld, and **Crimson-breasted Shrike** and **Ashy Tit** are often present. Further down, below Ga Dinonyane, a drier stretch is a good spot for **Southern Pied Babbler**. Common birds here include **White-browed Sparrow-Weaver**, **Burchell's Starling**, **Blue Waxbill** and **Red-billed Firefinch**. In summer, a range of waders visit the area, and **Greater Painted Snipe** and **Dwarf Bittern** may be seen from the hides. In the early evening, **Double-banded Sandgrouse** arrives.

Continue on the road past the hide. At the extreme western end of the drive, the road enters a fine stand of tall woodland **F**. Look here for **Purple Roller**, **Bennett's Woodpecker**, **Woodland Kingfisher** (summer) and **Red-billed Buffalo-Weaver**. Stop at the picnic spot here and look out for **Grey-headed Kingfisher** (summer). **Yellow-throated Petronia**, **Southern Black Tit**, **White Helmet-Shrike** and **Southern Black Flycatcher** are also common in this area.

If staying at Phuduphudu Camp **G**, you can explore the excellent broad-leaved woodland around the camp for **Pallid Flycatcher** and **Bennett's Woodpecker** and, in open areas, **Coqui Francolin** and **Bushveld Pipit** can be found. Other woodland species common in the area include **Yellow-fronted Tinkerbird**, **Red-billed Hornbill** and **Black Cuckooshrike**.

Pitjane camp site (Fisherman's Camp) is good for thornveld species. Sefudi Dam **H** is worth a visit, and may hold **Lesser Moorhen** in wet seasons.

OTHER ANIMALS: Borakalalo has a range of big game, including White Rhinoceros, Giraffe and Leopard.

186 Kgaswane Mountain Reserve IBA ✔

Kgaswane Mountain Reserve (Rustenburg Nature Reserve) is an accessible Magaliesberg site in a pristine setting. Specials include **Sentinel Rock-Thrush** (winter), **Red-winged Francolin**, **Wing-snapping Cisticola**, **Cape Eagle-Owl***, **Freckled Nightjar**, **African Black Swift** and **Striped Pipit**, as well as a host of raptors including **Verreaux's Eagle**, **Cape Vulture*** and **Jackal Buzzard**. From Rustenburg (travelling westwards on the R27), turn left into Wolmarans Street. Follow this road and the signs for about 6 km to the main gate. The entrance gate opens at 08h00 and closes at 16h00, and one must leave before 18h00 (summer) and 17h30 (winter). Facilities include a game drive, hiking trails, short walks and a bird hide. A camp site offers good birding, including **African Scops-Owl**.

187 Pilanesberg National Park IBA ✔✔

This popular big game reserve is a scenically spectacular crater with a range of good birding habitats and excellent game-viewing opportunities. Birds include **Short-toed Rock-Thrush** (subsp. *pretoriae*), various raptors and thornveld species, including **Southern Pied Babbler, Ashy Tit, Great Sparrow** and **Barred Wren-Warbler.**

Callen Cohen

Southern Pied Babbler

SPECIALS: Short-toed Rock-Thrush, Southern Pied Babbler, Flappet Lark, Barred Wren-Warbler, Kalahari Scrub-Robin, Black-faced and Violet-eared Waxbills, Shaft-tailed Whydah, Pale Chanting Goshawk and Secretarybird.

SEASON: Summer months are best (late Oct-Feb).

HABITATS: Hillsides, rocky ridges, grassy plains, mixed and acacia woodland, dams and seasonal vleis.

BIRDING: The park's camps, lodges, picnic spots and hides are all good. Drive from the Kwa-Maritane camp towards the exit gate, and then turn left towards Mankwe Dam via the tar road. This drive leads through some good thornveld, and the bird hide at Mankwe Dam can be very productive, with **African Fish-Eagle**, waders and herons – sometimes **White-backed Night-Heron***. The picnic spot overlooking the dam is good for **Short-toed Rock Thrush.**

Manyane Camp is particularly good for acacia thornveld birds such as **Crimson-breasted Shrike, Southern Pied Babbler, Chestnut-vented Tit-Babbler, Barred Wren Warbler, Great Sparrow** and **Kalahari Scrub-Robin.** Visit the excellent walk-in aviary, and follow the short walking trail through good birding habitat.

In the Sun City complex, visitors can walk around freely. Typically, areas around the golf courses, crocodile farm and Lost City all offer good bushveld birding. Much excellent birding can be done from a car – drive slowly and stop and examine bird parties (especially in winter).

Look in wooded areas for **Southern Yellow-billed Hornbill, Emerald-spotted Wood-Dove, Marico Flycatcher, White-browed Scrub-Robin** and **Long-billed Crombec.**

Close to hillsides you may encounter **Short-toed Rock-Thrush, Cinnamon-breasted Bunting, Flappet Lark** and **White Helmet-Shrike.**

In more open areas, **Rufous-naped Lark, Desert Cisticola, Lilac-breasted Roller, Secretarybird, Pale Chanting Goshawk** and **Magpie Shrike** all abound. Watch for **Northern Black Korhaan** in these areas. **Red-crested Korhaan** is common in areas with scattered trees and bushes.

The vulture restaurant near Manyane Gate (on the eastern side of the reserve) may at times be good for vultures, including **Cape*, White-backed** and occasionally **Lappet-faced Vultures.**

OTHER ANIMALS: The full spectrum of big game occurs, including Elephant, Black and White Rhinoceroses, Lion, Cheetah, Burchell's Zebra, Giraffe, Kudu, Impala, Blue Wildebeest, Common Duiker and Chacma Baboon, as well as a range of smaller mammals.

NEARBY SITES: A Big Five reserve, Madikwe Game Reserve is situated close to the Botswana border in the North-West Province, and covers over 750 km^2. It is a reasonably reliable site for **Yellow-throated Sandgrouse,** as well as a host of large raptors and larks. Casual visits are discouraged, and visitors need to book through one of the lodges in the reserve.

GETTING THERE

From Gauteng, take the N4 past Hartbeespoort Dam, or connect to the Rustenburg road via the R512. The shortest route is via the R556 towards Sun City; keep straight on for Sun City or turn right onto the R510 to reach the Manyane Gate. Gates open at 06h00 (Apr-Aug) and 05h30 (Sept-Mar). Maps, checklists and park guide booklets can be obtained at the gate.

188 Yellow-throated Sandgrouse

The Northam-Thabazimbi area is a classic site for **Yellow-throated Sandgrouse**, and is centred on Northam. From Rustenburg, take the R510 northwards for 97 km. From Gauteng, take the R511 towards Thabazimbi and via Brits for 76 km. Turn left at the Northam-Dwaalboom sign, and travel 30 km to the Northam crossroads. From here there are two accessible sites.

Bierspruit Dam is reached by taking the western road at the four-way crossing (turn left if coming along the R510 from Rustenburg/Pilanesburg; straight if approaching from Brits). After 13 km turn left towards Swartklip Mine (if you reach a dirt road, you have gone too far). After 4 km the road passes through a village on the right. The gates to the dam are about 2 km further on. Sign in at the gate, and immediately look for a track to the left, which takes you to the eastern side of the dam. **Yellow-throated Sandgrouse** usually drinks here after sunrise, up until about 09h00, and sometimes again before sunset. Reliability depends on local movements, but there are usually some birds drinking here daily.

If a morning visit to Bierspruit Dam fails to produce the sandgrouse, take the R510 northwards from the crossroads (turn right if coming from Brits) and head north on the R510 for 4 km. Turn right to Middledrift/Koedoeskop; the best areas are after 9 km. Yellow-throated Sandgrouse has adopted cultivated lands as its habitat, and can be found if you stop and scan year-old fallow or stubble lands of maize or sunflowers (their preferred crop is soya, now seldom planted). The north to south road running through the farming community of Koedoeskop is also good for these birds. The sandgrouse sometimes sits underneath irrigation sprinklers in the early morning, and also drinks from the pools created by the sprinklers. Other interesting species in the same habitat include **Temminck's Courser**, **Chestnut-backed Sparrowlark** and, in summer, **Caspian Plover** (rare).

189 Faan Meintjies Nature Reserve ✔

This small reserve provides access to a number of tricky grassland endemics typical of South Africa's interior. These include **Melodious Lark***, **Eastern Clapper Lark** and **Orange River Francolin**. The latter is best seen at dawn and is relatively common.

Other plains birds include **Ant-eating Chat**, **Spike-heeled Lark**, **Double-banded Courser** and **African Quailfinch**; the latter is more easily seen here than at many other localities. Woodland areas hold typical thornveld species such as **Kalahari Scrub-Robin** and **Violet-eared Waxbill**. The reserve is situated 12 km from Klerksdorp and is best birded on a circular route following the good gravel roads. This reserve is well worth a stop en route to the Kalahari or Bushmanland regions. The road to the reserve is well signposted at all entrances to Klerksdorp. Entry is from 07h00.

190 Botsalano Game Reserve ✔

Situated 38 km north-east of Mafikeng on the Ramatlabama road towards Botswana, this 5 800 ha reserve lies at the edge of the arid Kalahari, and is a reliable site for the range-restricted **Short-clawed Lark***, which occurs in open areas with scattered trees. The reserve is covered with acacia woodland with some open grassy plains, and also has some patches of thicker bush. Other common species in the reserve include **Northern Black Korhaan**, **Yellow Canary**, **Burnt-necked Eremomela**, **Red-headed Finch**, **Crimson-breasted Shrike** and **Barred Wren-Warbler**. **Burchell's Sandgrouse*** and **Double-banded Courser** also occur here. This reserve provides a good stopover for those visiting southern Botswana, or en route to the Kalahari. There is a tented camp and camp site at Botsalano.

To reach Botsalano from Mmabatho, take the R52 towards Lobatse, and at the border post turn right towards Jagersfontein. After 8 km, turn right onto the Klippan/Botsalano road. The reserve entrance is 10 km further on.

191 Barberspan Nature Reserve IBA R ✓✓

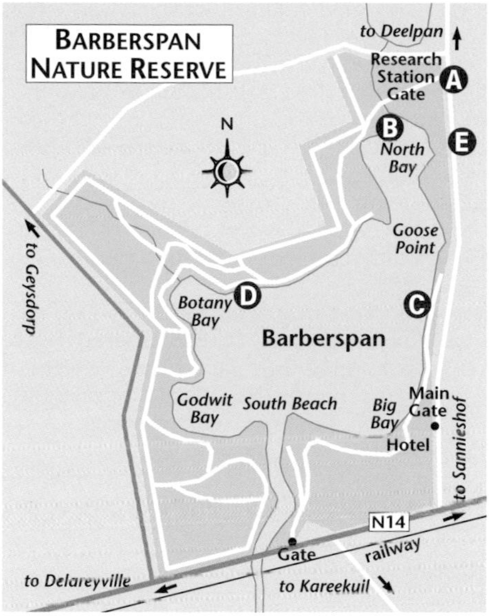

An internationally recognised Ramsar Wetland, Barberspan is known for its vast quantities of water birds which, in spring, may number more than 40 000. Nearby Leeupan is more saline, and offers a different suite of water birds.

SPECIALS: Osprey, African Grass-Owl*, Rufous-eared Warbler, Swallow-tailed Bee-eater, Pink-backed Pelican, Pink-billed Lark and South African Shelduck. Irregular migrants include Chestnut-banded Plover, Lesser Black-backed Gull, Caspian Tern, Ruddy Turnstone and Grey Plover. Vagrant waders have included Black-tailed and Bar-tailed Godwit, Black-necked Grebe, Buff-breasted Sandpiper and Green Sandpiper.

SEASON: For water birds, Sept and Oct; alternatively, Mar-Apr.

HABITATS: Semi-saline lake, mudflats, lake verges and marshland, grassland with scattered trees and alien copses.

BIRDING: Twenty kilometres outside of Sannieshof on the way to Delareyville/Barberspan, there is a signposted right turn to Deelpan. To reach the office and nature reserve, travel for 5 km along this road (the pan is very close to the road here, and you will see numerous birds from the car) until the Research Station entrance is on your left **A**. Turn in and cross the causeway, where you can enjoy some good birding from the car. There is a parking area just before the crossing. The offices are a bit further on, located under some giant Bluegums. Report here for more information, and keys to the hides. If you continue past the Deelpan road, you will see the main gate to the public recreational area on the south shores.

The reserve has a diverse list and almost all of South Africa's inland water-bird species have been recorded here. The best areas for water birds are the northern **B** (near the office) and eastern **C** (close to the Deelpan road) shores in the nature reserve and at Botany Bay **D** on the north-west shore. There is also a dedicated birding site and hide at the inlet, which is at the main public entrance. There are hides available at other spots, but keys must be obtained from the offices. The hides are moved from time to time depending on water levels.

Good birding is to be had around the research station. Look out for raptors on utility poles, and for **White-backed Vulture** in the trees. Scrubby areas with small bushes near the entrance gate **E** to the Research Station usually yield **Rufous-eared Warbler**.

It is a good idea to work the eastern shore during the morning, and the northern section later, to keep the sun behind you.

NEARBY SITES: Lichtenburg Game Breeding Centre, situated close to the town of Lichtenburg on the R52 towards Koster, has a productive vulture restaurant and makes a good stop for open country species.

GETTING THERE

From Gauteng, take the N14 westwards towards Vryburg. Barberspan is close to the N14 between Delareyville and Sannieshof.

Nigel J. Dennis

Swallow-tailed Bee-eater

192 Sandveld & Bloemhof Dam NRs IBA ✔✔

These two reserves, which straddle the Vaal and Vet rivers and the Bloemhof Dam, have a host of specials and represent the eastern distribution limit for several species.

SPECIALS: Double-banded Courser, Orange River Francolin, Pink-billed and Fawn-coloured Larks, Tinkling Cisticola*, Rufous-eared Warbler, Pririt Batis, Sociable Weaver, Orange River White-eye, Violet-eared and Black-faced Waxbills.

HABITATS: Large dam and shoreline, marshy areas, grassland, Karoo scrub, Kalahari thornveld savanna and woodland.

BIRDING: Large numbers of waterfowl, including **Comb Duck**, may be seen at times. A heronry comprising up to 12 different species of heron, egret, ibis and cormorant is usually occupied during seasons of good rainfall. Interesting water birds include **Goliath Heron** (common) and **Caspian Tern**, especially at Ⓐ.

The main camp Ⓑ offers a good selection of thornveld specials including **Crimson-breasted Shrike**, **Kalahari Scrub-Robin**, **Marico Flycatcher**, and **Scaly-feathered Finch**. Grassland areas such as Ⓒ will produce **Eastern Clapper** and **Rufous-naped Larks**, **Northern Black Korhaan** and **Ant-eating Chat**. **Orange River Francolin** is best located by call in the morning. **Marsh Owl** is common, and usually seen on winter mornings and evenings.

Common Scimitarbill is fairly common in woodland areas such as Ⓓ, as are **Red-crested Korhaan** and **Barred Wren-Warbler** (both easier to hear than to see!). **Tinkling Cisticola*** is fairly common but hard to find, and is best located in the transitional zone on the edge of the woodland areas – listen for its distinctive calls. **Sociable Weaver** colonies are con-

Nigel Dennis/IOA

Sociable Weaver

GETTING THERE

The reserves are situated on the R34 between Hoopstad (Free State) and Bloemhof (North-West Province), about 35 km from Hoopstad and 10 km from Bloemhof. A good network of roads traverses a variety of habitats on the Sandveld (Free State) side. Chalet accommodation and camping facilities are available at the reserve. A map is available from the reserve office, and night drives can be arranged.

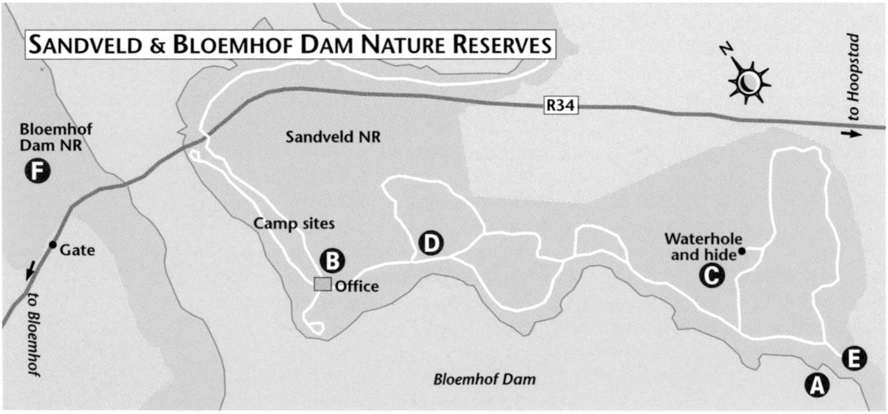

Nigel Dennis/IOA

Sociable Weaver nest in a Camel-thorn tree in the southern Kalahari

spicuous; search the vicinity of the weaver nests for **African Pygmy Falcon** (rare). **Double-banded Courser** may be seen in an area of Karoo scrub bordering the easternmost loop road (E), closest to the dam (in the bare patches between the grass and bushes), while **Rufous-eared Warbler** may be found in the low scrub/bush clumps here. **Pink-billed Lark** (rare) also occurs. **Double-banded Courser** is more easily seen in the sparse, short grassland areas of the adjacent Bloemhof Dam Nature Reserve (F), across the Vaal River in neighbouring North-West Province.
OTHER ANIMALS: Black and White Rhinoceroses, Buffalo, Giraffe, Eland, Roan and Sable Antelope, Gemsbok, Kudu, Red Hartebeest, Tsessebe, Plains Zebra, Springbok and Steenbok are all present in the reserve. Aardwolf may also be seen.
NEARBY SITES: The Aventura resort near the village of Christiana offers alternative accommodation, as well as good river frontage. Birds that may be encountered here include **Ashy Tit, Yellow Canary, Orange River White-eye** and **Pririt Batis.**

The small Wolwespruit Nature Reserve is situated on the banks of the Vaal River, upstream from Bloemhof. This tract of sandveld bush yields excellent lark sightings. **Grey-backed Sparrowlark, Eastern Clapper Lark**, and **Pink-billed** and **Spike-heeled Larks** are just some of the species that may be seen here. **Pririt Batis** is common, while **Swallow-tailed Bee-eater** and **Double-banded Courser** also occur in the reserve. To reach Wolwespruit, travel west from Orkney on the R502, go through Leeudoringstad, and then turn left to Kommandodrif. Follow the signs to Klipspruit and then to Rustkraal, which takes you to the reserve entrance.

193 Molopo Game Reserve 4X4 ✔

This remote 2 500 km² tract of Kalahari grassland and thornveld, situated in the far western corner of the North-West Province, is good for raptors and typical Kalahari endemics. Specials here include **Southern Pied Babbler, Burchell's Sandgrouse*** (more conspicuous in winter) and **Monotonous Lark** (vocal in wet years). The reserve is located on the Botswana border approximately 250 km north of Vryburg and 7 km west of the village of Vorstershoop. A 4WD vehicle is strongly recommended. Self-catering accommodation and camping facilities are available ☎.

NAMIBIA

From the ochre dunes of the Namib Desert to the expansive plains of Etosha National Park, and from the flamingo-thronged coastal lagoons of the cold Atlantic Ocean to the land-locked papyrus swamps of the Okavango River, Namibia offers excellent birding in an amazing variety of bird-rich habitats. With one endemic, almost 20 near-endemics and a host of specials that are difficult to see elsewhere, a visit to Namibia is an essential part of the southern African birding experience.

The cold Benguela Current that washes Namibia's 1 470 km-long Atlantic coastline supports one of the world's richest marine environments and is the best place globally to see the endangered Damara Tern. The Namib Desert's spectacular dune sea stretches for nearly 400 km north of Lüderitz and some 120 km inland. It is here that the only bird entirely endemic to Namibia, the handsome Dune Lark, finds its home.

Near Walvis Bay, the dunes give way to the vast gravel plains of the Skeleton Coast. This stony desert supports a host of highly specialised birds such as Gray's Lark, Burchell's Courser and Rüppell's Korhaan. The Namib escarpment, a discontinuous belt of broken mountains and inselbergs that forms the country's backbone, incorporates such massifs as the Naukluft, Brandberg, Spitzkoppe and Erongo Mountains. This region boasts the majority of the country's near-endemic birds, notably Hartlaub's Spurfowl, Monteiro's Hornbill, Rüppell's Parrot, Rosy-faced Lovebird, Violet Wood-Hoopoe, Damara Red-billed Hornbill, White-tailed Shrike, Carp's Tit, Herero Chat, Rockrunner, Bare-cheeked Babbler and Benguela Long-billed Lark.

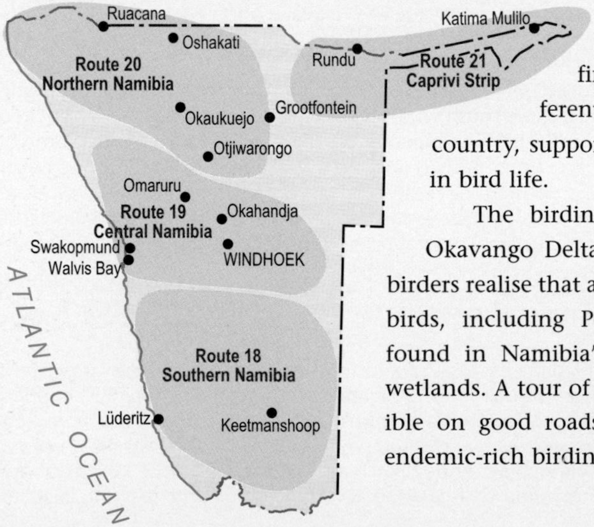

The Caprivi Strip, a finger of land distinctly different from the remainder of the country, supports tropical woodlands rich in bird life.

The birding wonders of Botswana's Okavango Delta are well known, but few birders realise that all of the Okavango's special birds, including Pel's Fishing-Owl, are also found in Namibia's Okavango and Zambezi wetlands. A tour of the wetlands, easily accessible on good roads, can be linked with the endemic-rich birding loops of the dry west.

ROUTE 18

SOUTHERN NAMIBIA

TOP 10 BIRDS

- Dune Lark
- Gray's Lark
- Barlow's Lark
- Burchell's Courser
- Rüppell's Korhaan
- Ludwig's Bustard
- Karoo Korhaan
- Rosy-faced Lovebird
- Damara Canary
- Herero Chat

The driest part of a dry land, southern Namibia lies between Windhoek and the Orange River, bounded in the west by the dune sea of the Namib Desert and in the east by the fiery red sands of the Kalahari. While traversing the southern Namibian region's seemingly never-ending gravel plains, the birder could be forgiven for thinking them lifeless. Although avian diversity is low, a number of desert-adapted birds thrive in these waterless conditions and southern Namibia is an excellent area to get to grips with such specials as Ludwig's Bustard*, Rüppell's Korhaan, and Dune, Barlow's and Gray's* Larks. The main tourist attractions of the region, the shifting dunes at Sossusvlei and the dramatic Fish River Canyon, are both worth visiting in their own rights. The approach road to Sossusvlei is one of the best places in southern Africa to see the endemic Burchell's Courser*.

International visitors birding Namibia alone will access the area via the excellent B1 south of Windhoek, while road entry from South Africa is restricted to the border posts of Arlamsvlei on the B3/N10 in the east (from Gauteng), and Noordoewer on the Orange River further west (from Cape Town).

Claire Spottiswoode

The Namib Desert consists of open gravel plains in addition to the famous sea of red dunes.

194 Rosh Pinah to Aus

IBA ✔✔

Shortly after crossing into Namibia at Noordoewer, a good gravel road follows the Orange River westwards to Rosh Pinah and the C13. This remote and starkly beautiful area supports a host of birds typical of dry, rocky environments, notably **Cape Eagle-Owl***, **Freckled Nightjar**, **Verreaux's Eagle**, **Mountain Wheatear**, **Karoo Long-billed Lark** and **Damara Canary**. **Namaqua Warbler*** is common in the reedbeds along the Orange River, and riparian acacia woodland is home to **White-backed Mousebird**, **Fairy Flycatcher**, **Pririt Batis** and **Cape Penduline-Tit**. Informal camp sites dot the banks of the Orange River between Noordoewer and Rosh Pinah.

The recently described **Barlow's Lark**, a localised species found only between Port Nolloth (see p.84) and Lüderitz, is easily found along the C13 between Rosh Pinah and Aus. Search suitable bushy habitat, especially at the roadside 30 km north of Rosh Pinah and in the vicinity of the junction with the D727. If you fail to find the bird along the C13, drive west from Aus on the B4 to Lüderitz for about 75 km, to an area of low euphorbia scrub north of the road, about 3.5 km west of the road sign that reads 'Lüderitz 50 km'. The larks are best located in the early morning, when they sing from the tops of bushes. **Tractrac Chat** and **Lark-like Bunting** are other inhabitants of this barren environment.

Callan Cohen

Low scrub east of Lüderitz

195 Fish River Canyon

✔

The Fish River Canyon, the world's second largest canyon, is one of Namibia's most famous natural spectacles, and is signposted from the B1 near Grunau.

Birders visiting the main camp at Ai-Ais (keep an eye out for **Freckled Nightjar** near the lights at night) will be rewarded with a similar suite of species to those found along the Orange River gorge, but should also watch for **Karoo Korhaan** and **Karoo Eremomela*** along the road from Ai-Ais to the main canyon viewpoint. Chalets and camping facilities are available.

196 The B1 & Hardap Dam

✔

To connect with the birding route of central Namibia, either follow the tarred B1 north from Keetmanshoop to Windhoek, which is much quicker, or traverse the Namib-Naukluft Park to Walvis Bay via Sesriem and Sossusvlei.

Be alert while crossing the desolate, gravel plains on the B1 north of Keetmanshoop, as **Ludwig's Bustard***, **Karoo Korhaan**, and **Burchell's Courser*** are frequently seen. **Grey-backed Sparrowlark** and **Stark's Lark** are often common at the roadside, but watch carefully for **Black-eared Sparrowlark***, **Pink-billed Lark** and the nomadic **Sclater's Lark***. Scan the conspicuous **Sociable Weaver** colonies for **African Pygmy Falcon**.

Twenty kilometres north of Mariental, the B1 passes Hardap Dam, the country's largest body of fresh water. Most of the birds found at the resort here are widespread and readily seen elsewhere, although **Rufous-eared Warbler** and **Karoo Eremomela*** may merit an overnight stop. Both occur on open, bush-studded plains in the game park south of the dam. Keep a look out for **Rosy-faced Lovebird** and **Short-toed Rock-Thrush** near the dam wall. Between Mariental and Windhoek, scan the roadside Camel-thorn trees for **Lappet-faced Vulture** nests, which occasionally also host colonies of **Chestnut Weaver** in mid- to late summer.

197 Spreetshoogte Pass ✔✔

If you choose this scenic and adventurous route across the Namib Desert to Walvis Bay or Sossusvlei, be sure to carry adequate water (and preferably two spare tyres, as the road is stony and traffic sparse). Look out for **Monteiro's Hornbill** after leaving Windhoek and, as the vegetation becomes sparser, scan for **African Pygmy Falcon** near the conspicuous nests of **Sociable Weaver**. The scenic Spreetshoogte Pass plunges off the Namib escarpment to the desert plains below. Look for **Mountain Wheatear** at the top viewpoint and look and listen for **Herero Chat***, a tricky near-endemic, on the lower half of the pass. It may be found perching in scattered, low trees, or along the low fence, although is perhaps easier seen at Spitzkoppe (see p.219). To search for the elusive **Cinnamon-breasted Warbler***, here at the northern limit of its range, scan the rocky slopes and listen for its far-carrying call. It also occurs in suitable habitat along the C14 between Solitaire and Maltahöhe. Cinnamon-breasted Warbler* is scarce here, however, and perhaps better searched for further south in the Karoo.

198 Sossusvlei IBA ✔✔

The picturesque red sands of the Namib dune sea at Sossusvlei are another of Namibia's premier tourist attractions, although the surrounding gravel plains and rocky escarpments of the

Callan Cohen

A lone Gemsbok in classic Dune Lark habitat at Elim Dune

Namib-Naukluft Park are of equal interest to the birder. This is an excellent area for desert birds, notably **Rüppell's Korhaan**, the scarce **Burchell's Courser***, and the Namibian endemic, **Dune Lark**.

SPECIALS: Common Ostrich, Ludwig's Bustard*, Rüppell's Korhaan, Burchell's Courser*, Dune Lark.

SEASON: All the specials are present year-round; note that summer is extremely hot.

HABITATS: The primary birding habitats in the Sossusvlei area are the gravel plains and grassy dunes along the access road from Sesriem. North of the Kuiseb River, along the C14 and C28, the Namib-Naukluft Park lacks sand

GETTING THERE

Sesriem, the access point to Sossusvlei, lies approximately 300 km south-west of Windhoek, and is signposted off the C36 between Solitaire and Maltahöhe. The 65 km road south-west from Sesriem Ⓐ to Sossusvlei Ⓕ within the park is tarred except for the last few kilometres to the vlei itself. A variety of accommodation is available in the area, ranging from up-market lodges and guest farms to camp sites. Two good gravel roads traverse the northern part of the Namib-Naukluft Park: the C14 from Solitaire to Walvis Bay via the Kuiseb Pass, and the C28 from Windhoek to Swakopmund via the spectacular Gamsberg Pass.

dunes, although additional birding habitats are present in the form of Camel-thorn-lined watercourses and rocky canyons.

BIRDING: The tarred road to Sossusvlei traverses gravel plains where **Namaqua Sandgrouse, Ludwig's Bustard*** and both **Burchell's*** and **Double-banded Coursers** are regularly seen. The **Common Ostriches** found here and in Etosha National Park are among the only genetically pure, truly wild ostriches in southern Africa. Stop at various points along the roadside in the early morning and scan the gravel plains for any sign of movement that may reveal the presence of **Stark's Lark**.

Ludwig's Bustard moves in after rain.

The special lark of this area is the handsome **Dune Lark**, which favours well-vegetated sand dunes. Small numbers may be found at the grassy bases of the dunes to the north of the road. The base of Elim Dune **B**, reached by taking the first road to the right shortly after entering the Park at Sesriem **A**, is best searched for this species in the early morning. Alternatively, look at the Sossuspoort lookout **D** or scan the dune on the right **C**. The plains at **C** and **E** are good for **Burchell's Courser***. **Swallow-tailed Bee-eater, Pririt Batis, Black-chested Prinia, Dusky Sunbird, Scaly-feathered Finch** and **Great Sparrow** are among the few passerines to be seen in the picturesque Camel-thorn trees in this area, such as at **D**.

Rüppell's Korhaan is best seen between Solitaire and Sesriem (look for them sheltering under shady bushes in the heat of the day), while **Gray's Lark*** is most easily found on the barren plains of the Namib-Naukluft along the C14 between the Kuiseb Pass and Walvis Bay. **Common Ostrich, Stark's Lark** and the pale, almost white desert form of **Tractrac Chat** also occur along this stretch.

OTHER ANIMALS: Gemsbok (Southern Oryx) crossing the dunes are classic favourites of wildlife photographers. A host of smaller creatures, such as fog-basking toktokkie (Tenebrionid) beetles and Wedge-snouted Lizards, may be seen on the dunes. Common Barking Gecko is responsible for the 'tapping' call that dominates at dusk.

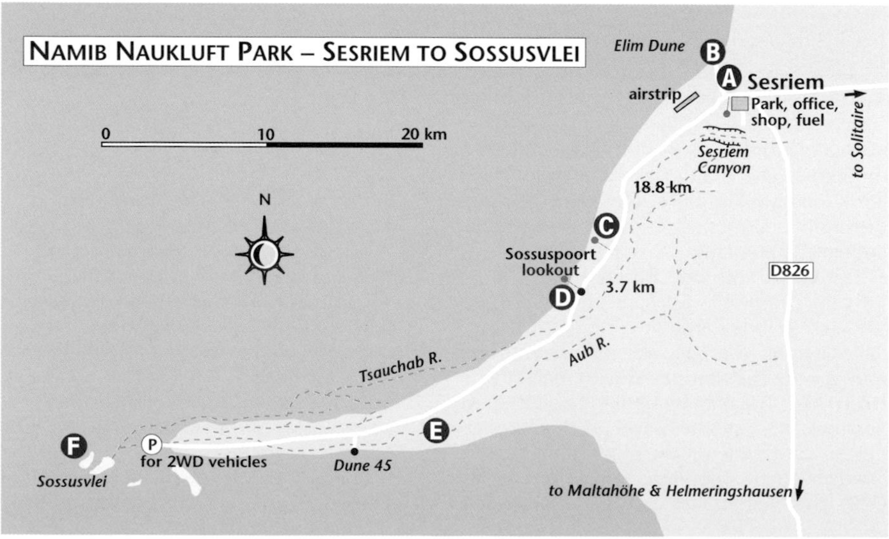

ROUTE 19

CENTRAL NAMIBIA

Lagoons pink with flamingos, sculpted granite inselbergs standing sentinel over barren desert plains, and German beer gardens harking back to colonial days all add to the flavour of central Namibia, the cultural and economic heart of this arid land. A road journey between the capital, Windhoek, and the main port of Walvis Bay takes the visitor from the highest part of the Namibian escarpment, across the stony wasteland of the Namib Desert, to the inky, nutrient-rich waters of the Atlantic Coast. For the birder, this classic transect of the country provides an opportunity to find the full suite of Namibian escarpment endemics, including such gems as Rockrunner*, the elusive Herero Chat*, charismatic White-tailed Shrike and the rock-dwelling Hartlaub's Spurfowl*, along with the Namib Desert endemics, comprising Rüppell's Korhaan, and Gray's* and Dune Larks. Add to this the thrill of working through the immense wader flocks that winter annually in one of Africa's finest coastal wetlands, and it isn't hard to understand why Central Namibia is such an alluring birding destination.

TOP 10 BIRDS

- White-tailed Shrike
- Rockrunner
- Hartlaub's Spurfowl
- Herero Chat
- Monteiro's Hornbill
- Gray's Lark
- Dune Lark
- Rüppell's Korhaan
- Benguela Long-billed Lark
- Damara Tern

Most visitors fly into Windhoek or approach the town along the main B1 highway from the south; either way, an overnight stop in the capital city is worthwhile, not only for a taste of the culture but also for a superb introduction to birding in the area. The tiny Daan Viljoen Game Park, on the western outskirts of town, forms the birding focal point, and can usually be adequately covered in a day. Most travellers head westwards by means of the excellent tarred B2 to the coast, though adventurous birders are advised to take one of the less travelled passes off the escarpment, as much for the scenery as for the bird life.

Although the old German colonial town of Swakopmund has more charm, Walvis Bay is undoubtedly a better base for birders, situated as it is at the edge of the superb Walvis Bay lagoon. A minimum of two nights is recommended here, though waderphiles could happily incorporate twice that time. Continuing northwards towards Etosha National Park, the only two essential stops are the Spitzkoppe, famous for Herero Chat*, and the Erongo Mountains for Hartlaub's Spurfowl*. The memory of this rugged central Namibian route is likely to remain in birders' minds long after the Namib dust has worked its way out of their binoculars.

Callan Cohen

Hartlaub's Spurfowl is best seen at dawn.

199 Windhoek & Surrounds ✔✔

Namibia's capital city, Windhoek, is surrounded by the mountains of the Khomas Hochland range, at an altitude of 1 650 m asl. Many of the Namibian near-endemics are easily seen on the outskirts of the city, and birders flying into the country should consider spending at least one night in the area, preferably at Daan Viljoen Game Park. **Bradfield's Swift** is a regular feature above the city, especially in the eastern parts.

From Windhoek airport, head for Avis Dam, visible on the right of the B6 a few kilometres before the city (just west of the railway bridge). Follow the sign to the parking area on the eastern edge of the dam and scan the water for **White-throated Swallow, South African Shelduck** and **Red-billed Teal**. Surrounding acacia woodland supports **White-backed Mousebird, Monteiro's Hornbill, Cape Penduline-Tit, Ashy Tit, Black-faced Waxbill, Shaft-tailed Whydah** and **Black-throated Canary**, while the dry, grassy slopes are home to the scarce **Orange River Francolin** (best located by their calls at dawn) and **Rockrunner***. The local subspecies of **Grey-backed Cisticola**, a very different-looking bird to the southern race and which may be a different species, can be found among rank wetland vegetation. Weekdays are best for visiting, as the area is very popular with dog walkers.

At Windhoek's sewage works, the reed-fringed pans and surrounding acacia thickets offer an excellent diversity of birds, including local specials such as **Maccoa Duck, Purple Heron, Baillon's Crake, Black-necked Grebe** and a variety of warblers. Follow the C28 out of Windhoek towards Daan Viljoen, and 1.8 km after passing under the B1, take the road marked 'Otjomuise' to the right. After 3.9 km, a short road on the left leads to the Gammams Water Care Works. Sign in at the gate and bear right immediately after. Follow the paved road until it ends at a big blue building, from where you can follow the gravel road to the settling ponds.

Warwick Tarboton

Look out for Violet-eared Waxbill near acacia bushes.

200 Daan Viljoen Game Park ✔✔

Superb dry-country birding can be found just a short drive from downtown Windhoek. Situated in the rugged Khomas Hochland Mountains that overlook the city, this park makes a convenient base for further exploration of the city surrounds, and provides an excellent introduction to the birds of the dry west, including **Monteiro's Hornbill** and **Rockrunner***.

SPECIALS: Monteiro's Hornbill, Short-toed Rock-Thrush, Carp's Tit, Barred Wren-Warbler, Rockrunner*, Long-billed Pipit and Black-faced Waxbill, Orange River Francolin.

SEASON: The specials may be found year-round, although they are most conspicuous in early summer.

HABITATS: The bulk of the park consists of hilly terrain covered in arid acacia savanna, with tall Camel-thorn trees and dense thorn thicket along the watercourses. The well-watered gardens of the rest camp provide additional birding habitat, and also allow access to some nearby cliffs.

BIRDING: One of the advantages of birding in Daan Viljoen is the relative ease with which

GETTING THERE

The park is approximately 20 km west of Windhoek along the **C28**, and is easily reached by following signs along Sam Nujoma Drive from the city centre. A short loop ('detour') road provides access to excellent birding habitat. There is a good restaurant and bar in the park's resort area, which offers chalet accommodation and a well-appointed camping site. Reservations should be made in advance, especially over weekends, when Daan Viljoen is flooded with day visitors from Windhoek.

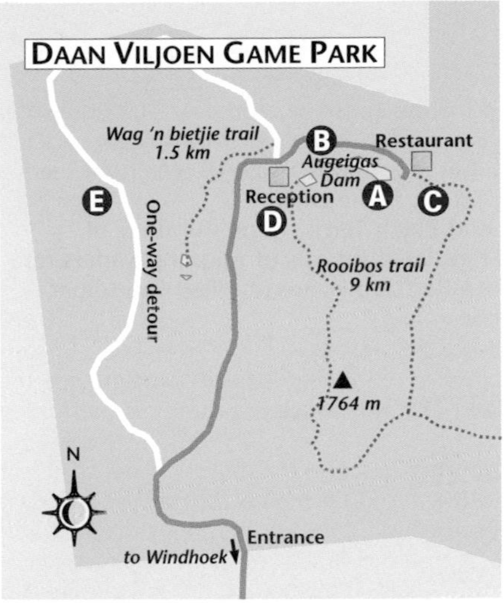

many of the specials may be seen. The small Augeigas Dam at A forms the focal point of the resort, and attracts a selection of water birds, most interesting of which are the occasional **Maccoa Duck** and **South African Shelduck. Mountain Wheatear, Short-toed Rock-Thrush** and **Pale-winged Starling** frequently perch on the chalet roofs, while **Red-billed Spurfowl, Crimson-breasted Shrike, Great Sparrow, Long-billed Pipit** and **White-browed Sparrow-Weaver** often feed on the lawns in the camp site at B. Search the rocky area just below the dam wall at C for **Rockrunner*, Cape** and **Cinnamon-breasted Buntings**, and the sparsely wooded slopes across the dam from the restaurant for **Swallow-tailed Bee-eater, Cape Penduline-** and **Ashy Tits, Burnt-necked Eremomela, Scaly-feathered Finch**, and the exquisite **Violet-eared Waxbill** and its brood parasite, **Shaft-tailed Whydah.**

Bearded Woodpecker, Pririt Batis, Carp's Tit (uncommon), **Barred Wren-Warbler** and **Black-faced Waxbill** prefer thicker vegetation along the watercourse at D, and are easily attracted by a whistled imitation of the call of **Pearl-spotted Owlet**, which is plentiful here. Summer rains bring an influx of migrants, which may include **Great Spotted Cuckoo** and **Icterine Warbler**; the repetitive song of **Monotonous Lark** may also be heard at this time (especially around the entrance to the park).

The elusive **Orange River Francolin** is best sought along the grassy ridges to the north-west of the resort, easily accessed along the loop road shortly after entering the reserve. Coveys may be seen sunning themselves in the early morning, although the birds are more commonly located by their piercing calls. **Monteiro's Hornbill, Purple Roller, Sabota Lark, Rockrunner*** and **Short-toed Rock-Thrush** are also regularly encountered along this loop road at E, while **White-tailed Shrike** is present but uncommon.

OTHER ANIMALS: The game park is home to a healthy ungulate population, notably Gemsbok, Eland, Blue Wildbeest and Greater Kudu, as well as the handsome Hartmann's Mountain Zebra. Giraffe, Warthog and Chacma Baboon also occur. In rocky areas, look for Rock Hyrax and the endearing but shy Dassie Rat.

Callan Cohen

Arid acacia savanna covers Daan Viljoen Game Park.

201 Walvis Bay

IBA R ✔✔✔

With its extensive mudflats, artificial salt pans and marine coastline, and over 100 000 water birds present every summer, the Walvis Bay area is southern Africa's premier coastal wetland for birds. A mecca for shorebird enthusiasts, it is also a convenient site to search for marine cormorants, **Damara Tern*** and the Namibian endemic, **Dune Lark**.

SPECIALS: Chestnut-banded Plover, Damara* and Black Terns, huge numbers of Greater and Lesser Flamingos, Dune Lark, and regular sightings of migrant waders rare in southern Africa: Black-tailed Godwit, Common Redshank, Broad-billed Sandpiper, Red-necked Phalarope and Eurasian Oystercatcher.

SEASON: Summer is best for **Damara Tern*** and vagrant waders.

HABITATS: Vast tidal mudflats in the lagoon and extensive surrounding salt pans provide the birding focal point, with a small freshwater wetland and the vegetated dunes of the Kuiseb delta providing additional interest.

BIRDING: The strikingly abundant water-bird-thronged lagoons at Walvis Bay are in direct contrast to the apparently desolate desert plains a few hundred metres inland. The mudflats in Walvis Bay lagoon are easily viewed from the Promenade between the Yacht Club **A** and the first salt pans south of town **B**, a distance of about 1.5 km. Thousands of flamingos of both species are usually present, forming one of Walvis Bay's major tourist attractions. Smaller numbers of **Great White Pelican** frequent the area around the Yacht Club, feeding on scraps tossed out by fishermen.

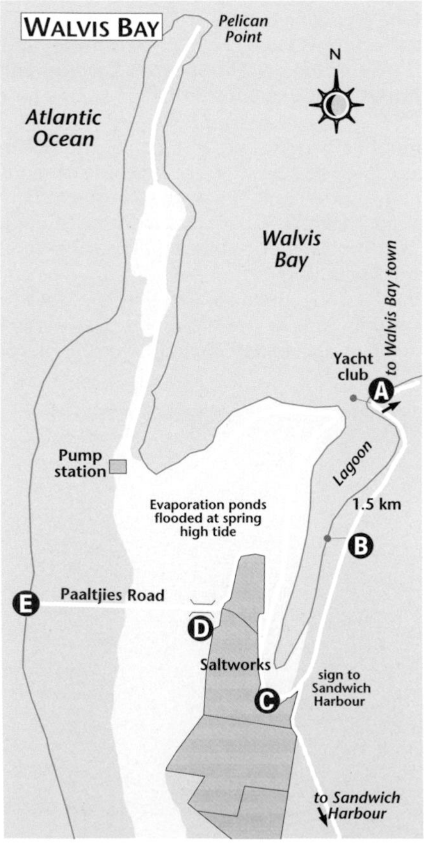

In summer, the mudflats are covered with Palearctic shorebirds, notably large numbers of **Sanderling, Bar-tailed Godwit**, **Curlew Sandpiper** and **Red Knot**. **Terek** and **Broad-billed Sandpipers**, **Common Redshank, Black-tailed Godwit**, and **Greater Sand Plover** are almost annual rarities along this stretch. **Chestnut-banded**, **White-fronted** and **Common Ringed Plovers** may also be seen here. Large roosts of terns (including **Caspian Tern**) also form, and both **Parasitic** and **Pomarine Jaegers** may be seen harassing them over the bay. The highly localised **Damara Tern*** is the key species to watch for, though it is often more easily seen in the vicinity of the salt pans.

To reach the salt pans, continue south from the Promenade and turn right towards Paaltjies just before the salt factory **C**. The public road runs along a series of pans that frequently hold high concentrations of flamingos,

GETTING THERE

Namibia's largest port lies an easy 4 hr drive from Windhoek along the B2. A variety of accommodation is available, including hotels and self-catering holiday cottages. The excellent oyster farm on the west side of Walvis Bay can be accessed by collecting a key at the main gate of the saltworks by prior arrangement; visitors might want to contact local birders for updates on access and rarities ☎.

before crossing a sluice bridge **D**, where shallow ponds north and south of the road attract the full range of Palearctic waders, including the rarities mentioned above. Rafts of **Black-necked Grebe** are frequent, **Black Tern** may be seen dancing over the water, and this is the best place in Walvis Bay to search for **Red-necked Phalarope**, small numbers of which occur here annually. **Chestnut-banded Plover** occurs along the road.

The privately owned oyster farm on the northern side of these pans has achieved fame among southern African birders as the most reliable site in the subregion for **Eurasian Oystercatcher**, a rare but annual visitor. **African Black Oystercatcher*** and **Eurasian Curlew** are easily seen here.

Callan Cohen
Flamingos in Walvis Bay lagoon

Continue on to the beach at Paaltjies **E**, where scanning the cold ocean in the early morning may turn up **Cape Gannet**, **White-chinned Petrel**, **Sooty Shearwater** and, rarely, **African Penguin**. The guano platform visible 10 km along the road to Swakopmund is good for large numbers of **Cape Cormorant**, which breeds alongside smaller numbers of **Crowned Cormorant**.

Check the coastline between the guano platform and the mouth of the Swakop River, 30 km further north, for **Crowned** and **Bank* Cormorants**, **African Black Oystercatcher*** and especially **Damara Tern***, which occurs here at higher densities than anywhere else in southern Africa (listen out for their distinctive, high-pitched call). Bank* and Crowned Cormorants can be elusive, and both are more easily found near Cape Town (see p. 17).

The freshwater wetland of Walvis Bay Bird Sanctuary (access may not always be possible), formed by the town's waste-water outflow, lies south of the main traffic circle at the junction of the B2 and C14 and is easily reached by turning west off the C14, just south of the circle. A small observation tower offers a good vantage point over the ponds, where **Maccoa Duck**, **Cape Shoveler** and **Great Crested Grebe** may be seen. **African Purple Swamphen**, **Purple Heron** and **Lesser Swamp Warbler** are inconspicuous residents of the reedbeds. Many rarities have been recorded here over the years, including **Franklin's** and **Black-headed Gulls**.

The 'Nursery' in the Kuiseb delta, 5 km south-east of the saltworks, is the nearest place to Walvis Bay to find the endemic **Dune Lark**. The birds are easily located in the early morning, when they perch conspicuously atop the grassy dunes. Look out too for **Bokmakierie** and **Orange River White-eye** around the nursery, although the latter is also common in suburban gardens in Walvis Bay. Follow signs towards Sandwich Harbour from just north of the saltworks, bear left at the 'Rooibank' sign, and continue for 2 km to the nursery. The road traverses some sandy patches, and a 4WD is essential.

An accessible 2WD site for **Dune Lark** lies further south in the Kuiseb River, near Rooibank. Drive out towards Walvis Bay Airport for 6 km on the C14, turn right at the sign to Rooibank and continue south on a gravel road for 24 km to the settlement on the north bank of the dry Kuiseb River.

From Rooibank, walk west through the well-vegetated dunes on the south side of the Kuiseb riverbed, but be sure to visit early or late as the larks rest up in vegetation during the heat of the day.

OTHER ANIMALS: Cape Fur Seal, Common Bottlenose Dolphin, the strange-looking Sunfish, and the Benguela endemic, Heaviside's Dolphin, are regularly encountered on the highly recommended dolphin-watching launch cruises in the bay.

NEARBY SITES: A natural lagoon flanked by the giant sand dunes of the Namib dune sea, Sandwich Harbour holds even greater numbers of birds (although the species are similar) than Walvis Bay. It is far more difficult to access, lying some 50 km south of Walvis Bay, and accessible only by 4WD, with requisite permit: birders should contact Turnstone Tours ☎.

202 North of Swakopmund

IBA ✔

The famous Welwitschia Drive in the Namib-Nauklauft Park lies close to Swakopmund, and a map and permit can be obtained in the town. Aside from the numerous specimens of this ancient and remarkable plant, **Gray's Lark*** and **Tractrac Chat** can also be seen here.

Callan Cohen

The pale desert form of Tractrac Chat

One can also follow the C34 up the coast from Swakopmund, turning towards the coast at the Mile 4 Saltworks some 7 km north of town. These salt pans support a similar suite of water birds to those found around Walvis Bay, although concentrations of flamingos (of both species), **African Black Oystercatcher*** and **Cape Cormorant** here are even more impressive at times. **Great Crested Grebe** is resident, and small groups of **Red-necked Phalarope** are regularly present in summer. **Gray's Lark*** may be encountered on the gravel plains between the saltworks and the main road.

The C34 continues northwards along the Skeleton Coast, and mammal enthusiasts might consider a detour to the massive Cape Fur Seal colony at Cape Cross, where it is worth checking for **Damara Tern***, **Chestnut-banded Plover** and vagrant waders at the lagoon.

203 Brandberg

IBA ✔✔

Namibia's highest mountain, towering over the desolate plains of the Namib Desert at 2 573 m, is known primarily for its spectacular rock art. Although the birding can be difficult owing to high temperatures during the summer, the area offers a large variety of the country's near-endemics. From Uis continue north on the C35 (to Khorixas) for 14.5 km (search for **Herero Chat*** along this stretch), and turn west onto the D2359 that leads to the car park at the base of the Tsisab Ravine 26 km on.

Birding is good along an easy trail winding up the ravine to the rock overhang containing the world-famous *White Lady* petroglyph; here **Mountain Wheatear** is particularly common. The desert plains along the D2359 are home to **Ludwig's Bustard***, **Rüppell's Korhaan**, **Double-banded Courser**, **Namaqua Sandgrouse**, **Tractrac Chat**, and both **Stark's** and **Gray's* Larks**. However, it is not necessary to climb the mountain to see one of the area's most strategic specials. The Brandberg forms the southern limit of the range of **Benguela Long-billed Lark***, recently elevated to full species status, and easily found on the plains at the base of the inselberg. Listen for its descending 'fee-ooh!' display call, and search for birds hiding under bushes during the heat of the day. Look for it around the D2359 turn-off, or continue along the C35 and search for it at 18.2 km and 35.2 km north of Uis respectively. Also look out for the **Herero Chat*** and the white-rumped nominate subspecies of **Karoo Chat** in this area.

Geoff McIlleron: Firefly Images

Rüppell's Korhaan

204 Spitzkoppe ✔✔✔

One of the country's premier sites for the localised **Herero Chat***, the Spitzkoppe also offers a superb supporting cast of dry-west specials, and some of Namibia's most spectacular scenery.

SPECIALS: Herero Chat*, Monteiro's Hornbill, Rosy-faced Lovebird, Bradfield's Swift, Rüppell's Korhaan, Augur Buzzard, Booted Eagle, White-tailed Shrike and Dusky Sunbird.

SEASON: The specials are resident and may be found throughout the year, although temperatures soar during summer.

HABITATS: Camel-thorn-lined watercourses and shrubby vegetation at the base of granite inselbergs, which are surrounded by semi-desert.

BIRDING: Spitzkoppe's special bird, the **Herero Chat***, favours scrubby vegetation at the base of the inselbergs and may be found throughout the area. One place to see them is on the south side of the main dirt track heading through the middle valley of the Spitzkoppe and eventually joining the road to Henties Bay. Stop just before the narrow pass (B) that exits the Spitzkoppe, and walk south along the base of the large granite dome. The rocky slopes (C) 500 m west of camp sites 10 and 11 have also proved particularly reliable. The chats are relatively inconspicuous, however, and it may require considerable effort to track them down. Listen for their warbling song at dawn.

GETTING THERE

From the B2, take the D1918 towards Henties Bay and turn right after 18 km onto the D3716 towards Spitzkoppe. After 11 km, cross the dry riverbed and bear left (signposted) to the community-run office (A) and camp site, which has basic ablution facilities. An entrance fee is payable. Follow the tracks around to camp sites 10 and 11 on the south-western side of the Gross Spitzkoppe, an excellent birding area and recommended camping site.

Other denizens of the jumbled boulders here are **Mountain Wheatear, Ashy Tit, Black-chested Prinia, Layard's Tit-Babbler** (here near the northern limit of its distribution) and **Dusky Sunbird**.

Monteiro's Hornbill, Rosy-faced Lovebird and **Pale-winged Starling** breed in the abundant rock crevices, while **Bradfield's Swift** is frequently seen overhead. The lovebirds are best seen early in the morning, before they head out onto the surrounding plains to forage. Scan the skies

Callan Cohen

Herero Chat occurs at the base of the Spitzkoppe.

carefully for **Augur Buzzard**, a few pairs of which breed here, and for **Peregrine Falcon**.

Swallow-tailed Bee-eater and the dapper **White-tailed Shrike** favour taller Camel-thorn trees away from the base of the rocks; in wet summers, colonies of the nomadic **Chestnut Weaver** also utilise these trees. **Sabota Lark** (large-billed Bradfield's form) is common.

Watch for **Ludwig's Bustard*** (uncommon), **Rüppell's Korhaan**, **Burchell's Courser***, **Namaqua Sandgrouse** and **Stark's Lark** along the entrance road to Spitzkoppe, particularly near the junction of the D1918 and D3716 and further west towards Henties Bay. Birding the barren desert 10-15 km west of this junction should produce **Tractrac Chat** and **Gray's Lark***.

OTHER ANIMALS: Western Rock Elephant-Shrew, Dassie Rat, Rock Hyrax, Klipspringer and the brilliantly coloured Namibian Rock Agama add interest during the day, while a nocturnal spotlighting excursion may reveal Common Barking Gecko, or the night-hunting Giant Ground Gecko.

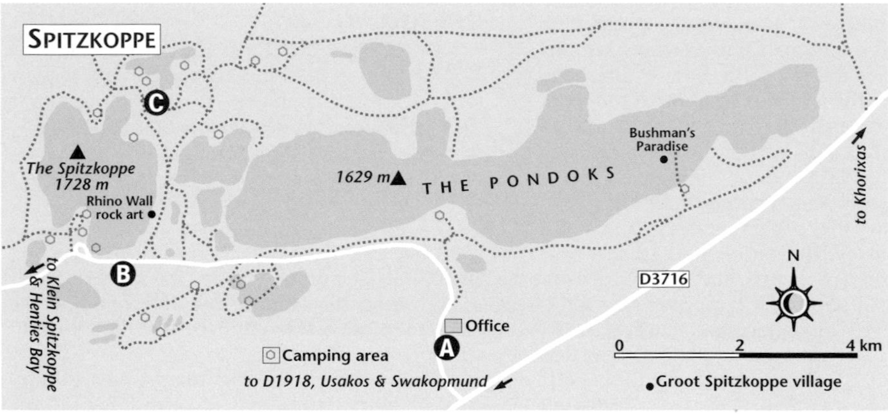

205 Erongo Mountains ✔✔✔

The magnificent granite domes of the Erongo Mountains lie 60 km to the east of the Spitzkoppe and offer quality endemics in one of Namibia's most atmospheric settings. This is the most accessible site in the country for **Hartlaub's Spurfowl***.

SPECIALS: Hartlaub's Spurfowl*, Monteiro's and Damara Red-billed Hornbills, Rüppell's Parrot*, Southern White-faced Scops-Owl, Freckled Nightjar, White-tailed Shrike, Short-toed Rock-Thrush and Rockrunner*.

SEASON: All the specials are present year-round.

HABITATS: Acacia-lined watercourses and rocky slopes at the base of granite inselbergs.

BIRDING: The key species here is the localised **Hartlaub's Spurfowl***, which is best seen in the rocky jumbles at the base of the huge granite domes that dominate this area. Coveys vocalise from the tops of the boulders at dawn. To increase the chances of an encounter, find a vantage point and scan surrounding areas in the direction of the spurfowls' raucous calls. You should be in position at dawn. Even then the spurfowl may prove elusive, in which case the only chance of seeing them is by

GETTING THERE

Take the C33 from Omaruru towards Karibib, and turn right 2 km after the Omaruru River bridge onto the D2315, signposted 'Etemba'. Follow the gravel road for 10 km, when you will pass through the gate of the Erongo Conservancy. The Erongo Wilderness Lodge is situated among the inselbergs near Paula's Cave, immediately on your left. Although, strictly speaking, all Erongo's key birds can be found from this public road (birding beyond the road is not permitted unless you are resident at the lodge), a stay at this elegantly designed (although moderately expensive) lodge is highly recommended and will ensure your best chance of success ☎. A range of accommodation is also available in Omaruru.

scrambling around the rocky landscape in the hope that one may dart in or out of the boulders. By far the best area for the spurfowl is at the edge of the Erongo Wilderness Lodge grounds, although they can be seen from the road early in the morning at almost any point where large granite outcrops occur.

Rosy-faced Lovebird, White-tailed Shrike (there is a colour-ringed population in the vicinity of the lodge), **Pale-winged Starling, Short-toed Rock-Thrush, Carp's Tit** and **Rockrunner*** are all relatively easily seen here. The lodge's dining area overlooks numerous waterholes that attract a continual stream of birds, including four species of bunting and, occasionally, **Chestnut Weaver**. Keep an eye on the cliffs for **Verreaux's Eagle** and **Peregrine Falcon. Freckled Nightjar** may also be seen at night.

Thornveld in this area is home to **Monteiro's** and **Damara Red-billed Hornbills, Swallow-tailed Bee-eater, Great Spotted Cuckoo** (summer), **Pririt Batis, Barred Wren-Warbler, Black-faced** and **Violet-eared Waxbills**, and **Shaft-tailed Whydah.**

Rüppell's Parrot* may be found in the wooded riverbed that is intersected by the D2315 road, 21 km west of Omaruru.

Verreaux's Eagle-Owl roosts in gallery woodland along the Omaruru River; access is gained by walking westwards along the sandy riverbed from the bridge in Omaruru town. The scarce **Bat Hawk*** is occasionally seen here at dusk. **Violet Wood-Hoopoe** breeds in the Omaruru camp site, and may be seen in early evening moving along the river fringes towards their roost. The camp site is also good for **African Scops-Owl, Pearl-spotted Owlet, African Cuckoo, Crimson-breasted Shrike** and **Lesser Honeyguide.**

OTHER ANIMALS: The agile Klipspringer and the curious Dassie Rat are regularly seen, the latter being easy to spot in the vicinity of the Erongo Wilderness Lodge. The lodge is one of the best places to see Black Mongoose, a scarce and little-known Namibian near-endemic.

NEARBY SITES: Just 21 km north of Usakos the C33 crosses the dry bed of the Khan River, where the tall gallery woodland is home to **Violet Wood-Hoopoe, Rüppell's Parrot*, Southern Pied Babbler, Damara Red-billed Hornbill, Ovambo Sparrowhawk, Pearl-spotted Owlet** and **African Scops-Owl.**

Claire Spottiswoode

The granitic domes and woodlands of the Erongo Mountains are home to a host of Namibian near-endemics.

ROUTE 20

NORTHERN NAMIBIA

For most first-time visitors to the country, northern Namibia means Etosha National Park. Boasting prolific mammals and birds, plentiful waterholes (three of which are floodlit after dark), and an excellent road network, this unique game reserve is understandably one of the highlights of a visit to southern Africa. While Etosha is undoubtedly the area's main attraction, it is by no means its only one. To the south-east lies the attractive Waterberg Plateau National Park, enticing birders with a good chance of the scarce Rüppell's Parrot*, while the private concession of Hobatere, west of Etosha, offers a plethora of Namibian endemics. For adventurous spirits, however, it is Ruacana in the far north that quickens the pulse, beckoning with a mix of wild landscapes, traditional Himba villages, and some of the most exciting birding in southern Africa.

Birders should allow a minimum of three full days in Etosha National Park, although five would certainly not be wasted, especially if one's interests extend to photography and general wildlife. Two nights is adequate in the smaller reserves to the south, while a trip to the Kunene River merits at least three nights to savour the area's multiple attractions.

TOP 10 BIRDS

- Cinderella Waxbill
- Hartlaub's Spurfowl
- Bare-cheeked Babbler
- Violet Wood-Hoopoe
- Madagascar Bee-eater
- Grey Kestrel
- Rufous-tailed Palm-Thrush
- Rüppell's Parrot
- Kori Bustard
- Carp's Tit

Cinderella Waxbill occurs along the Kunene River, Namibia's northern border with Angola.

206 Waterberg Plateau NP

IBA ✔✔

The Bernabé de la Bat rest camp is set in tall woodland at the foot of the rugged Waterberg Plateau, supporting a handful of elusive dry-west specials. This is a reliable site for the near-endemic **Rüppell's Parrot***.

SPECIALS: Hartlaub's Spurfowl*, Bradfield's and Monteiro's Hornbills, Violet Wood-Hoopoe, Rüppell's Parrot*, Rosy-faced Lovebird, Bradfield's Swift, Freckled Nightjar, Short-toed Rock-Thrush, Carp's Tit and Rockrunner*.

SEASON: The specials are present year-round.

HABITATS: Cliffs, boulder-strewn slopes, tall acacia woodland along the base of the sandstone plateau, and adjacent thorn thickets are the major habitats of interest to the birder.

BIRDING: Most of the Waterberg's special birds are conspicuous and easily located around the rest camp. Raucous cackling may reveal the location of a family group of loudly chattering **Violet Wood-Hoopoes** (watch out for **Green Wood-Hoopoes**, which may also be in the area), while fruiting fig trees in the vicinity of the swimming pool attract **Damara, Bradfield's** and **Monteiro's Hornbills**, as well as **Rüppell's Parrot***. Bradfield's Hornbill may be found more easily on the plateau, or by following the D2512 for about 20 km beyond the entrance gate. The parrot is also frequently seen in the camp site, and has even bred in the trees in front of the main park office. The liquid call of the handsome **Rockrunner*** is frequently heard along the short trails ascending the plateau, while **Rosy-faced Lovebird, Bradfield's Swift, Augur Buzzard, Peregrine Falcon, African Hawk-Eagle, Verreaux's** and **Booted Eagles** and **Short-toed Rock-Thrush** are commonly seen along the cliffs. **Hartlaub's Spurfowl*** is also resident on the boulder-strewn slopes to the west of the camp, but is not easy to see.

Dense thorn thicket between the reception and the entrance gate supports a host of birds typical of dry thorn savanna, such as **Red-billed Spurfowl, Crimson-breasted Shrike, Marico Flycatcher, Barred Wren-Warbler, Southern Pied Babbler, Violet-eared Waxbill, Shaft-tailed Whydah** and, in summer, **Great Spotted** and **Jacobin Cuckoos** and **Icterine Warbler**. A spotlighting excursion may reward the diligent birder with sightings of **Freckled Nightjar** and **Southern White-faced Scops-Owl**. The plateau game drives are not only a worthwhile mammal-viewing experience, but also visit a vulture restaurant, where **Cape*, White-backed** and **Lappet-faced Vultures** may be observed at close quarters.

OTHER ANIMALS: The diminutive Damara Dik-dik is plentiful in the camp. Larger game on the plateau include Black and White Rhinoceroses and the scarce Roan and Sable Antelopes. In the early evening, South African Galago is active around the camp.

Callan Cohen

Spectacular cliffs of the Waterberg Plateau

GETTING THERE

Waterberg Plateau National Park lies 60 km east of Otjiwarongo, and is signposted from the B1 north of Windhoek. The Bernabé de la Bat rest camp offers chalet accommodation and a camp site. Guided game drives are conducted to the plateau, which can also be explored on overnight hiking trails. The network of short trails above the rest camp is excellent for birding.

207 Hobatere

IBA ✔✔

This 35 000 ha reserve immediately to the west of Etosha National Park straddles the endemic-rich Namibian escarpment, and is one of the premier sites for such localised birds as **Rüppell's Parrot***, **Bare-cheeked Babbler*** and **Violet Wood-Hoopoe**. A wide variety of Namibian endemics are present in the immediate vicinity of the Hobatere Tourist Lodge.

SPECIALS: Monteiro's and Damara Hornbills, Violet Wood-Hoopoe, Rüppell's Parrot*, White-tailed Shrike, Short-toed Rock-Thrush, Carp's Tit, Rockrunner*, Bare-cheeked Babbler*, Madagascar Bee-eater (summer) and Hartlaub's Spurfowl*.

SEASON: The specials are present year-round, but are particularly easy to find in winter, when they congregate along the watercourses.

HABITATS: Arid mopane woodland covers much of the area, which has an undulating topography broken by granite outcrops. Taller gallery woodland along the usually dry water-courses supports most of the specials.

BIRDING: **Rüppell's Parrot***, **Damara Hornbill**, **White-tailed Shrike**, **Meves's Starling**, **Carp's Tit** and **Bare-cheeked Babbler*** are usually easily located in well-developed mopane woodland around the lodge, while finding the scarce **Violet Wood-Hoopoe** may require more extensive exploration of surrounding woodland. The lodge's birdbaths also attract **Rosy-faced Lovebird**, and a plethora of seed-eaters that may include **Black-faced Waxbill**, **Red-headed Finch**, **Black-throated Canary**, and **Lark-like** and **Cinnamon-breasted Buntings**. Many thousands of **Chestnut Weavers** and **Red-billed Queleas** may gather here seasonally. **Gabar Goshawk**, **Shikra** and, less commonly, **Little** and **Ovambo Sparrowhawks** prey on small passerines in the lodge grounds. A few coveys of the elusive **Hartlaub's Spurfowl*** are resident in the granite outcrops south of the lodge, and are best located by their raucous dawn chorus. **Monteiro's Hornbill**, **Short-toed Rock-Thrush** and **Rockrunner*** are also fairly common in this area. Listen out for **Orange River Francolin**.

Summer sees the arrival of a number of migrants from the Afrotropics, notably **Madagascar Bee-eater**, which is often conspicuous near the lodge. Night drives are especially worthwhile, with **African Scops-Owl**, **Southern White-faced Scops-Owl**, **Verreaux's Eagle-Owl**, **Pearl-spotted Owlet**, **Rufous-cheeked Nightjar** and even **Bronze-winged Courser** all possible.

OTHER ANIMALS: Lion and Elephant are found in the immediate vicinity of the unfenced lodge. Gemsbok, Eland, Hartmann's Mountain Zebra, Kudu, African Wild Cat and Small-spotted Genet are all common in the area.

NEARBY SITES: From Hobatere, the good gravel C35 skirts the western boundary of Etosha National Park and heads, straight as an arrow, towards Ruacana.

GETTING THERE

From Kamanjab at the western end of the C40, take the C35 towards Opuwo and Ruacana for 65 km, to the turn-off marked 'Hobatere Tourist Lodge', where accommodation is available. Access to the private concession is restricted to residents. Contact Hobatere Tourist Lodge for reservations ☎. There is also a camp site.

Callan Cohen

Hartmann's Mountain Zebra at Hobatere

208 Ruacana & Kunene River IBA ✔✔✔

Wild, remote and exotic, Ruacana's legendary status among birders is well deserved. One of the only sites on earth for the localised and evocatively named **Cinderella Waxbill***, and one of the few sites for **Rufous-tailed Palm-Thrush***, the area was entirely closed to visitors during the long Angolan war. With the onset of peace, birders can again experience the avian treasures of this unique wilderness area. Ruacana's birds and scenery more than compensate for its remote location, soaring summer temperatures and basic facilities.

Callan Cohen

White-tailed Shrike

SPECIALS: Cinderella Waxbill*, Rufous-tailed Palm-Thrush*, Hartlaub's Spurfowl*, Monteiro's Hornbill, Madagascar Bee-eater, Rüppell's Parrot*, Grey Kestrel, White-tailed Shrike, Bare-cheeked Babbler* and Chestnut Weaver.

SEASON: The best time to visit Ruacana is in the summer, when **Madagascar Bee-eater** and **Chestnut Weaver** are present, although it is very hot at this time. Most specials may be found year-round.

HABITATS: The thin riparian strip of *Hyphaene* palm woodland and riverine thicket along the Kunene River forms an oasis that is bordered by arid mopane and acacia woodland extending up the rocky slopes of the river valley.

BIRDING: Most of Ruacana's special birds occur in the riparian fringe along the Kunene River just downstream of the falls, such as at the camp site at Hippo Pools (A), which is located 15 km north-west of Ruacana town. **Madagascar Bee-eater** and **Chestnut Weaver** are usually common and conspicuous in midsummer, while a walk downstream from the camp site should reveal **Rosy-faced Lovebird** and **Rufous-tailed Palm-Thrush***, both of which breed in the *Hyphaene* palms at (B). The poorly marked path along the river can be reached on the western edge of the camp site, or by following a track to the river 500 m after the end of the tar road. **Verreaux's Eagle-Owl**, **Freckled Nightjar** and **Barred Owlet** are commonly heard after dark and, with luck, **Bat Hawk** may be seen feeding over the river at dusk. Other notable denizens of the riparian strip are **Red-necked Spurfowl** (of the distinct *cunensis* race; try at (C)), **Grey-headed Kingfisher**, **White-browed Coucal**, **African Golden Oriole**, **African Mourning Dove**, **Bare-cheeked Babbler***, **Swamp Boubou**, **Meves's Starling** and **Golden Weaver**, most of which represent disjunct populations far west of their usual ranges. The local race of **Bennett's Woodpecker** is fairly common: this subspecies has totally plain underparts and may warrant specific status.

An early morning walk up one of the small watercourses that run down from the rocky escarpment south of the camp site may turn up **Hartlaub's Spurfowl*** (also try on the rocky, wooded slopes on the edge of the road 10 km west of Ruacana town at (G)), as well as **Monteiro's Hornbill**, **Rüppell's Parrot***, **White-tailed Shrike**, **Short-toed Rock-Thrush**, **Carp's Tit** and **Bare-cheeked Babbler***.

Another of Ruacana's special birds, **Grey Kestrel**, occurs only in small numbers; check the electricity pylons along the roadside around Ruacana town, or scan from vantage points (H) over the valley in the evening. The pylons and powerlines around the power station (I) at the falls are probably the most reliable spot for this species. Alternatively, continue with the untarred road over the hill from Hippo Pools camp site for 7 km and take a turn (at a small settlement) to the river on your right (J). **Grey Kestrel** is often seen here, and **Rufous-tailed Palm-Thrush*** is resident. **Augur Buzzard** and **African Hawk-Eagle** are other noteworthy raptors regularly encountered in the dry woodland. **Herero Chat*** may be found on the escarpment, further inland from the river. **Benguela Long-billed Lark***, which favours sparsely vegetated, rocky areas,

GETTING THERE

Ruacana is reached either along the C35 or from Tsumeb via the much longer (450 km) but tarred B1 and C46. The Ruacana Lodge in Ruacana town is the only accommodation in the area ☎. A clearing overlooking the Kunene River at Hippo Pools (Otjihampuriro) is the traditional camp site (A), although it is not always well maintained.

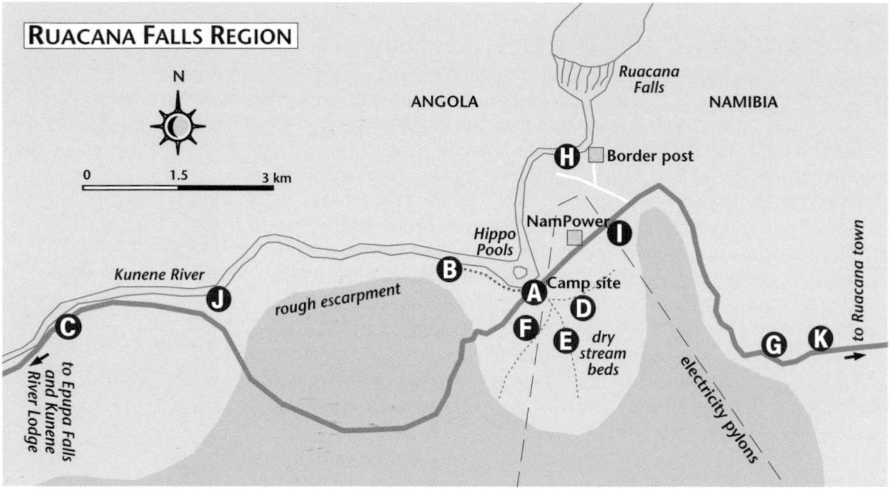

should be searched for on the level ground behind Ruacana town.

Most of the Kunene specials, including **Grey Kestrel**, **Rufous-tailed Palm-Thrush*** and **Cinderella Waxbill***, are also known from riparian vegetation in the vicinity of the Kunene River Lodge ☎ approximately 66 km west of Ruacana along a gravel road. Intrepid birders following the 4WD road westwards to Epupa Falls will be rewarded with spectacular scenery (that may be relegated to the annals of history if the government's plans for a hydro-electric scheme at Epupa proceed) and good birding opportunities. Check livestock in the area for **Yellow-billed Oxpecker**.

OTHER ANIMALS: Hippopotamus (rare), African Clawless Otter and Nile Crocodile still occur in the Kunene River. The attractive Striped Tree Squirrel is common in the riparian fringe.

NEARBY SITES: On the south side of the road between Ruacana and Ombalantu is the Olusati Dam. This is worth a stop. Here **Grey-rumped Swallow** is regular, and **Pink-billed Lark** often frequents the heavily grazed areas around the dam. **Squacco Heron** and other herons are fairly common, and there are often large flocks of swallows and martins to sift through in search of the elusive **Angola Swallow**.

FINDING CINDERELLA WAXBILL

Cinderella Waxbill*, Ruacana's most sought-after bird, is erratic and may require considerable effort and exploration to track down. The waxbills are more reliably seen further away from the river, and the best time to see them is in the heat of the day, when they come to drink at small pools in otherwise dry tributaries of the main river that line the escarpment to the south, such as at **D**, **E** and **F**.

Jameson's and **Red-billed Firefinches** and the white-billed form of **Steel-blue Indigobird** can also be seen here.

Walk up the dry riverbed that ends at Hippo Pools (near the end of the tarred road), and, where the tributary forks, take the left fork and continue walking upriver until you find a small pool with plenty of nearby or overhanging vegetation, often including tough sedges. The *crrk* contact call is often the first sign that waxbills are present.

The pipeline that runs alongside the northern side of the road between Ruacana town and the Kunene River is good for **Cinderella Waxbill*** and **Hartlaub's Spurfowl***. Search for drinking Cinderella Waxbill* during the heat of the day at the leaking pipe that lies just below a partially hidden pump station (**K** just beyond a blue wrecked car) 13 km from Ruacana town en route to Hippo Pools. A rough track follows the pipe down the valley at the point where the pipe leaves the roadside, and Hartlaub's Spurfowl* may be found 300 m along this track.

209 Etosha National Park

IBA ✔✔✔

Namibia's most famous game reserve, and the subject of many a wildlife documentary, Etosha is also a superb birding destination. The arid woodlands and grassy plains surrounding the vast pan are home to a wide variety of northern Namibian specials, and provide excellent, easy birding in one of Africa's top game parks.

SPECIALS: Common Ostrich, Violet Wood-Hoopoe, Rüppell's Parrot*, Kori Bustard, Blue Crane, Caspian Plover (rare), African Pygmy and Red-necked Falcons, Black-faced*, Southern Pied and Bare-cheeked* Babblers, and Pink-billed Lark.

SEASON: The dry and cooler winter season, when both avian and mammalian activity at the waterholes is at its peak, is also the peak tourist season. Summer rain, which falls mainly in the form of thunderstorms that commence any time from October to January, disperses the animals from the waterholes and, in exceptionally wet years, may even flood Etosha Pan. Summer temperatures are high but the intra-African and Palearctic migrants are present and bird breeding is in full swing. For birders, this is undoubtedly the most exciting time to visit.

HABITATS: The 'Great White Place' of Etosha Pan covers almost a quarter of the approximately 20 000 km^2 park, and remains bone-dry except in years of exceptional rainfall. Arid grassland and open woodland in the western part of the park, around Okaukuejo, give way to denser, broad-leaved woodland around Halali, and finally to taller woodland around Namutoni in the east.

BIRDING: As with many African parks, the rest camps, which visitors may explore freely on foot, are excellent places for birding. A **Sociable Weaver** colony (look on game drives in the vicinity of the camp for **African Pygmy Falcon**) is present in the Okaukuejo camp site Ⓐ, and a variety of the more common acacia woodland species may be found in the tall trees near the swimming pool, including **Pearl-spotted Owlet**, **Crimson-breasted Shrike**, **Pririt Batis**, **Barred Wren-Warbler** and, in summer, **Jacobin** and **Great Spotted Cuckoos**, and **Icterine Warbler**. **Violet-eared Waxbill**, **Shaft-tailed Whydah**, **Black-throated Canary** and flocks of **Red-billed Quelea** gather to drink at the waterhole in the heat of the day, where they often fall prey to resident **Gabar Goshawk**.

Liquid calls herald the arrival of **Double-banded Sandgrouse** at the floodlit waterhole in the evening, when **Rufous-cheeked Nightjars** may be seen hawking moths over the water,

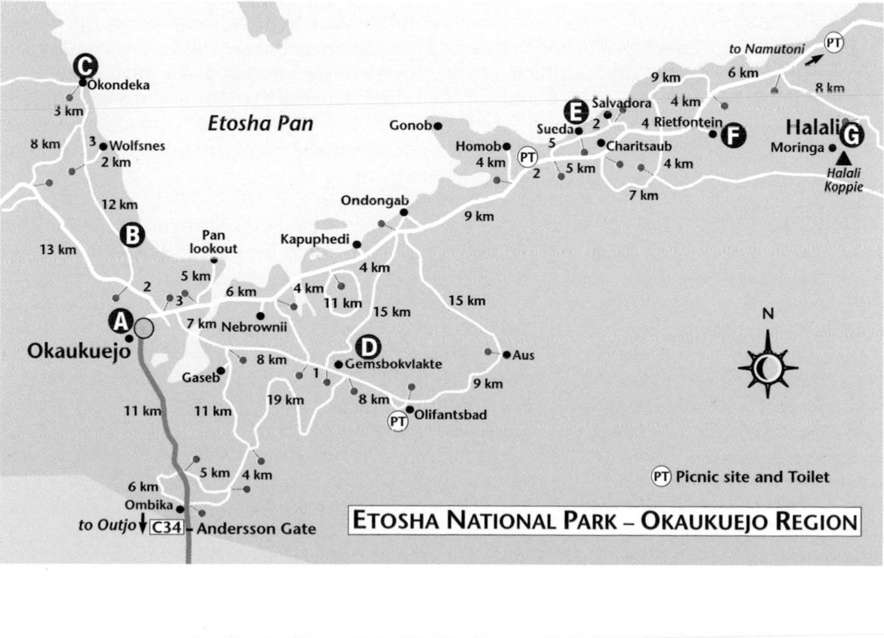

Search Halali for Bare-cheeked Babbler.

with **Barn Owl**, **Spotted Eagle-Owl** and **Verreaux's Eagle-Owl** patrolling the peripheries. A pair of the last roost regularly in the large tree on the left edge of the waterhole.

North of Okaukuejo, **Common Ostrich**, **Kori Bustard**, **Northern Black Korhaan**, **Southern Pale Chanting Goshawk** and **Ant-eating Chat** are all conspicuous on the grassy plains, while careful scanning may also reveal **Ludwig's Bustard*** (rare; pre-rains), **Caspian Plover** (rare; summer), **Double-banded** and **Burchell's*** (rare) **Coursers**, **Black-chested Snake-Eagle**, **Greater Kestrel**, **Desert Cisticola**, as well as **Spike-heeled** and **Red-capped Larks**. Another key species of the open plains is **Pink-billed Lark**, which can be found alongside **Grey-backed** and **Chestnut-backed** (erratic) **Sparrowlarks**, especially on the road to Okondeka waterhole. Look especially in the vicinity of the airstrip, about 4 km north of Okaukuejo **B**. **Eastern Clapper Lark** breeds in this area and is best located by its calls in the early morning near Okondeka **C**, when you will also be treated to the spectacle of thousands of **Namaqua Sandgrouse** flying in to drink on the western edge of Etosha Pan.

Low scrub east of Okaukuejo, 14 km along the road towards Halali, supports an isolated population of **Rufous-eared Warbler**, while the plains around Gemsbokvlakte **D** to the south hold a few pairs of **Red-necked Falcon**, as well as good numbers of vultures, which are attracted to the regular lion kills in the area. Salvadora and Sueda **E** waterholes are also worth visiting (these areas are good for Cheetah), as is Rietfontein **F**.

Halali Camp **G** is famous among birders for **Violet Wood-Hoopoe** and **Bare-cheeked Babbler***. Both are resident and often conspicuous, moving about in noisy parties, although frequently feeding in the woodland beyond the borders of the camp. Listen for their distinctive cackling calls, but beware of confusion with the very similar **Green Wood-hoopoe**, which may also occur here.

The camp acts as an oasis, with **Groundscraper Thrush, Damara Red-billed Hornbill**, **Southern White-crowned Shrike** and **Greater Blue-eared Starling** feeding on the lawns, while **African** and **Eurasian Cuckoos**, **Shikra**, **Little Sparrowhawk**, **White Helmet-Shrike**, **Purple Roller** and **Carp's Tit** are attracted to the surrounding woodland. Ask one of the camp attendants if they know the whereabouts of the resident pairs of **African Scops-Owl**, **Pearl-spotted Owlet** and **Southern White-faced Scops-Owl**, which frequently provide excellent photographic opportunities. The small granite outcrop in the camp makes a good vantage point from which to scan for raptors such as **African Hawk-Eagle** and the spectacular **Bateleur**, with the adjacent floodlit waterhole attracting **Cinnamon-breasted Bunting** during the day, and **Double-banded Sandgrouse** and **Rufous-cheeked Nightjar** after dark.

The scrub mopane north of the camp is home to **Monotonous Lark** in late summer, while the open plains along the pan support many of the species to be found north of Okaukuejo, although **Secretarybird** is more common here. Look for **Dusky Lark*** in summer, sometimes in loose flocks numbering 100 or more. Be sure to visit Kalkheuwel **H** (**Meyer's Parrot**) and Rietfontein (good for water birds).

The acacia thicket in Namutoni Camp **I**, which is centred on an old German fort in the eastern part of the park, is home to **Barred Wren-Warbler**, **Burnt-necked**

GETTING THERE

Etosha lies about 430 km north of Windhoek along excellent tar roads, and is clearly marked on all tourist maps. The park can be accessed via the Andersson Gate near Okaukuejo in the west, or the Von Lindequist Gate near Namutoni in the east. Three well-equipped rest camps at Okaukuejo, Halali and Namutoni, each with hutted accommodation, a camp site, restaurant, shop (where a map of the park can be obtained), swimming pool and floodlit waterhole, are located along the southern edge of Etosha Pan.

Eremomela, Southern Pied Babbler and **Violet-eared Waxbill**, while **African Palm-Swift** and **Red-billed Buffalo-Weaver** are resident in the palms near the swimming pool. **Lesser Masked Weaver** breeds in the tree in front of the shop. The fort's tower is an excellent place to catch the breeze during the heat of the day, and a good place to scrutinise the thermals for **White-backed, Lappet-faced** and **White-headed Vultures, Tawny Eagle** and **Bateleur**. Keep a careful watch for **Egyptian Vulture**, as Etosha is the only park in southern Africa where this species is recorded with any regularity. Groot and Klein Okevi **J** waterholes, just north of the camp, are excellent for acacia bird species.

The shallow Fischer's Pan **K**, to the north of the camp, is an eastern extension of the main Etosha Pan, and water levels vary enormously from year to year, with the pan often lying completely dry. After good summer rains, however, it comes to life, supporting large numbers of **Red-billed Teal, Cape Shoveler, South African Shelduck, Black-necked Grebe** and **Greater** and **Lesser Flamingos**, as well as **Yellow-billed Stork**. In peak seasons, the grassy *omuramba* (drainage line) that enters the pan's north-eastern corner hosts breeding **Lesser Moorhen, Greater Painted Snipe** and even **Spotted Crake**. The best areas lie along the road to Aroe waterhole, which occasionally holds **Chestnut-banded Plover**. Even when dry, the loop

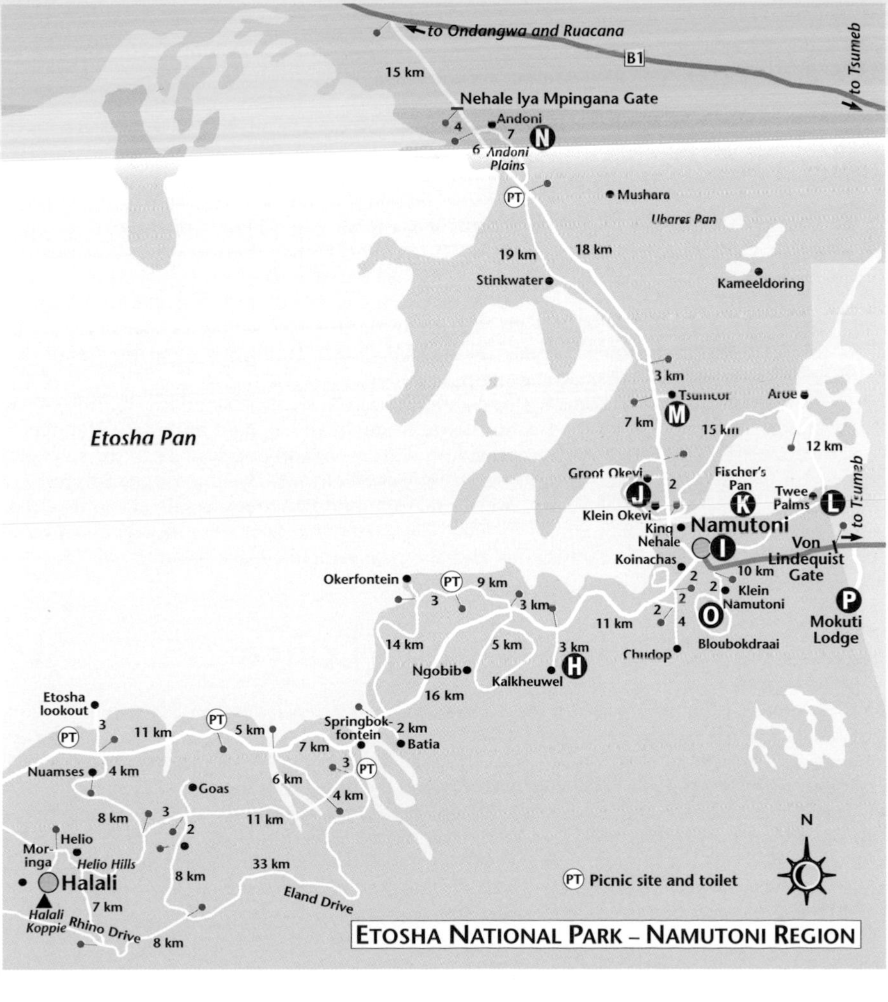

ETOSHA NATIONAL PARK – NAMUTONI REGION

Richard du Toit

Etosha's waterholes attract large numbers of animals.

around Fischer's Pan is worth driving, as sandy areas north of the pan are home to the scarce **Burchell's Sandgrouse*** (sometimes spotted mid-morning at Tsumcor Waterhole Ⓜ). **Red-necked Falcon** is frequently encountered between the camp and Twee Palms waterhole (check the palm trees at Twee Palms Ⓛ for resting birds). At Andoni Plains Ⓝ, the extensive grasslands are home to **Kori Bustard**, **Blue Crane** and **Secretarybird**, as well as large herds of Gemsbok, Blue Wildebeest and Springbok. Passerines are not plentiful, but listen out for the display calls of **Eastern Clapper Lark** and **Desert Cisticola**.

The localised **Black-faced Babbler*** may be found around Bloubokdraai (Dikdik) Drive Ⓞ, south of Namutoni. This species can be elusive, and the best strategy is to drive Bloubokdraai loop at dawn, listening and watching for family groups at the roadside. Failing this, they can be found in the gardens of the Mokuti Lodge Ⓟ, just outside the park's eastern gate. **Red-billed Spurfowl, Red-crested Korhaan**, **Carp's Tit**, **Red-billed Hornbill, Kurrichane Thrush**, **Barred Wren-Warbler** and **Chinspot Batis** are other birds to watch for in the tall woodland.

OTHER ANIMALS: Etosha is justly famous as one of the greatest game reserves in Africa, and the concentration of animals around the waterholes at the end of the dry season has to be seen to be believed. Burchell's Zebra, Blue Wildebeest, Springbok and the handsome Gemsbok (Southern Oryx) all occur in large numbers, forming the main prey base of the park's large predators, Lion, Leopard, Cheetah and Spotted Hyaena. Floodlit waterholes in all three camps are often excellent, attracting large numbers of Elephant and Black Rhinoceros (up to 10 animals together), as well as providing visitors with an opportunity to see such elusive nocturnal mammals as Leopard, African Wild Cat and Brown Hyaena. Honey Badgers are a particular speciality of Halali Camp, and frequently raid the rubbish bins at night. Other mammals recorded on game drives include Cape Fox, Aardwolf, South African Ground Squirrel, Red Hartebeest, Damara Dik-dik and the near-endemic Black-faced Impala. Banded Mongoose is often seen at Namutoni.

210 Tandala Ridge Wildlife Lodge ✔

Tandala Ridge is a lightly wooded private game farm, which includes a small research station, situated 79 km from Etosha's Andersson Gate (near Okaukuejo) on the D2695. The cottages are situated on a prominent rocky ridge, where the main attraction must be the confiding covey of **Hartlaub's Spurfowl*** that regularly wanders among the houses. **Orange River Francolin** is resident and may also be found in the vicinity, and the surrounding bush supports **White-tailed Shrike, Rüppell's Parrot*** (subject to local movements), **Bare-cheeked Babbler***, **Carp's Tit** and **Monteiro's Hornbill**. An array of raptors regularly harry small passerines (including **Chestnut Weaver**) at the waterhole below the ridge. **Red-crested Korhaan** and **Southern Pied Babbler** are common on the D2695 along the approach to the farm. Visits and bird-ringing demonstrations are by prior arrangement only; contact Tim and Laurel Osborne ☎.

ROUTE 21

CAPRIVI STRIP

A strange quirk of history attached this geographically, biologically and ethnically distinct finger of land to the arid body of Namibia, and the Caprivi Strip has far more in common with the well-watered areas to the north than it does with the remainder of the country. Much of the region is flat, essentially featureless and blanketed in broad-leaved woodland, but it has been blessed with a number of tropical rivers, most famous of which are the Okavango and the Zambezi. Where their productive alluvial flood plains traverse the bird-rich tropical woodlands, such as in Mahango Game Reserve or along the Kwando River, they support an especially diverse avifauna, and these sites form the obvious focal points in the region. While the Caprivi Strip falls within the territory of Namibia, we have included the northern Botswanan birding sites of Shakawe and Kasane in this route, as they are most accessible from the Caprivi and are most sensibly combined in itineraries.

The Caprivi Strip offers truly exhilarating birding, with the top daily tallies in summer almost reaching 300 species, although it is more the prospect of exciting tropical species that attracts birders to this remote region. Foremost are the so-called 'Okavango specials', such as Slaty Egret*, Coppery-tailed Coucal and Chirping and Luapula Cisticolas, as well as other more widespread but uncommon water-associated species, such as African Skimmer*, Rock Pratincole*, White-backed Night-Heron*, and the charismatic Pel's Fishing-Owl*. Others come in search of certain scarce endemics of south-central African woodlands, such as the ever-elusive Sharp-tailed Starling*, here at the southern extreme of its range, while vagrant-hunters dream of Green Sandpiper, Souza's Shrike*, Angola Swallow, Ross's Turaco*, or even a new species for the southern African region. Whatever your reason to visit, the Caprivi Strip offers superlative birding in a wild corner of Africa.

TOP 10 BIRDS

- Pel's Fishing-Owl
- Slaty Egret
- White-backed Night-Heron
- African Skimmer
- Rock Pratincole
- Western Banded Snake-Eagle
- Brown Firefinch
- Hartlaub's Babbler
- Coppery-tailed Coucal
- Sharp-tailed Starling

Richard du Toit

The elegant Slaty Egret is endemic to the swamps of south-central Africa.

211 Roy's Camp ✔✔

Black-faced Babbler* is the undeniable special of this small camp, situated on the B8 just 55 km north of Grootfontein. A large family group of the babblers, most reliably encountered in the morning, is regularly found around the waterhole overlooked by the restaurant. A wide variety of seed-eaters drink at the birdbath, offering excellent photographic opportunities. The surrounding woodland holds a good selection of widespread species. Accommodation options include rustic cottages and camping ☎.

212 Bushmanland 4X4 IBA ✔✔

A spirit of adventure and a fleet of 4WD vehicles are necessary to explore Bushmanland properly, and those who get the logistics and the timing right will be rewarded with some of the most exciting birding in southern Africa. In bizarre contrast to its surrounds, ephemeral pans around the remote town of Tsumkwe are transformed into a wetland paradise after heavy summer rains, attracting huge numbers of migratory water birds, notably crakes and rare Palearctic waders. The town is also the access point for Kaudom National Park, which offers a suite of woodland birds, including **Sharp-tailed Starling***, similar to those found in the more accessible areas further east. Bushmanland should not be confused with the Karoo birding region of the same name (see p.76).

SPECIALS: Bradfield's Hornbill, Wattled Crane*, Lesser Moorhen, Great Snipe, Caspian Plover, Black-winged Pratincole, Pallid Harrier*, Dickinson's Kestrel, African Hobby*, Slaty Egret*, White-breasted Cuckooshrike, Sharp-tailed Starling*, Rufous-bellied Tit, Tinkling Cisticola*, Stierling's Wren-Warbler, Green-capped Eremomela, Wood Pipit, and Black-faced Babbler*.

SEASON: Some of the pans may retain water throughout the dry season, although the area is at its best when recently flooded by summer rains. This may make access to the pans and Kaudom National Park even more difficult, however. April and May are a good compromise, as many of the tracks have dried out by then.

HABITATS: The Bushmanland Pan System comprises an extensive arc of shallow pans of varying character, surrounded by grassland and mixed woodland. Smaller pans may be found just to the north in Kaudom National Park, most of which is covered in broad-leaved woodland.

BIRDING: After good rains, the Nyae-Nyae area provides one of southern Africa's great birding spectacles, with vast numbers of waterfowl, herons, rails, crakes and waders present.

Small groups of **Wattled Crane*** stand along shallow, flooded wetlands thronging with **Red-billed Teal**, **Southern Pochard**, egrets (including good numbers of both **Slaty*** and **Yellow-billed Egrets**), herons, ibises and storks. **Black-tailed Godwit**, **Common Redshank** and **Great Snipe** are regular among the flocks of **Curlew**, **Marsh** and **Wood Sandpipers**, **Common Greenshank** and **Ruff**. Both **Greater** and **Lesser Flamingos** are attracted to more alkaline pans, although they are nomadic and their presence unpredictable. **Lesser Moorhen** often move into the area in large numbers to breed alongside smaller numbers of **African** and **Baillon's Crakes**, **Allen's Gallinule** and **Greater Painted Snipe** after the rains. Watch for **Black-winged Pratincole** and both **Pallid*** and **Montagu's Harriers** over the surrounding grassland in summer, and scan bare ground for flocks

GETTING THERE

Tsumkwe lies about 250 km east of Grootfontein along the C44. The main pan systems of Nyae-Nyae and Pannetjies Veld lie about 20 km to the south and east of Tsumkwe respectively, and are accessible along sandy 4WD tracks running from town. Kaudom National Park is reached from Tsumkwe via Klein Dobe and Dorslandboom, or from the north via the B8; the reserve is signposted about 120 km east of Rundu. Access to this wilderness area is controlled by the Ministry of Environment and Tourism (MET) and is restricted to convoys of a minimum of two fully self-sufficient 4WD vehicles. There are basic huts and camping sites at the northern Kaudom and southern Sikereti camps, which require advance booking through MET Central Reservations.

of **Caspian Plover**, and **Temminck's** and **Double-banded Coursers**. The mixed woodland along the roads may turn up a host of interesting species that favour Kalahari sands, notably **Burchell's*** and the scarce **Yellow-throated Sandgrouse**, **Magpie Shrike**, **Kalahari Scrub-Robin**, **Southern Pied** and **Black-faced* Babblers**, **Violet-eared Waxbill** and **Shaft-tailed Whydah**.

Kaudom's pristine teak woodlands are of greatest interest to the birder, providing an opportunity to find such scarce birds as **White-breasted Cuckooshrike**, **African Hobby***, **Sharp-tailed Starling***, **Rufous-bellied Tit**, **Tinkling Cisticola***, **Green-capped Eremomela**, **Wood Pipit** and, with luck, **Green-backed Honeybird**.

OTHER ANIMALS: Kaudom's remoteness still protects such rare mammals as Roan Antelope and African Wild Dog.

Callan Cohen

Woodlands south of Rundu

213 Rundu Area ✔✔

The woodlands and wetlands around Rundu, a small town on the Okavango River, are home to a number of northern specials, and are the most accessible and reliable area in the subregion for **Rufous-bellied Tit**.

SPECIALS: African Pygmy Goose*, Bradfield's Hornbill, Coppery-tailed Coucal, Grey-headed Parrot, Allen's Gallinule, Lesser Moorhen, Lesser Jacana, Dickinson's Kestrel, African Hobby*, Rufous-bellied Heron, Dwarf Bittern, Swamp Boubou, Arnot's Chat, Sharp-tailed Starling*, Rufous-bellied Tit, Tinkling Cisticola*, Green-capped Eremomela, Hartlaub's Babbler, Wood Pipit and Brown Firefinch.

SEASON: Good year-round, but particularly productive in summer when termite emergences attract large concentrations of migrant raptors. The nomadic and migratory water birds are most abundant in mid- to late summer.

HABITATS: Broad-leaved woodland and natural and man-made wetlands along the Okavango River.

BIRDING: *Sewage Works:* The upper settling ponds of the sewage works attract a variety of ducks and waders, with numbers varying according to water levels, and are worth checking for the scarce migrant **Green Sandpiper**, and the attractive inland subspecies of **White-fronted Plover** (rare). It is, however, the larger, lower ponds and reedbeds to the west that are of greatest interest to the birder. **African Pygmy Goose*** and **Lesser Jacana** are regular on the ponds, and **Red-chested Flufftail**, **African Rail**, **African** and **Spotted Crakes**, **Allen's Gallinule**, **Lesser Moorhen**, **Greater Painted Snipe**, **Slaty Egret***, **Rufous-bellied Heron** and **Little Bittern** are often present on the flood plain, particularly when it floods in summer.

Three coucal species, the giant **Coppery-tailed** and the smaller **Senegal** and **White-browed Coucals**, are all common inhabitants of the

GETTING THERE

To reach the Rundu sewage works turn left off the B8 at the sign for Rundu, and right at the T-junction in Rundu town. After 4 km the settling ponds become visible on the left. Access is unrestricted. Woodland areas worth birding may be found in the vicinity of the radio mast, 20 km south-west of Rundu on the B8, and at various points along the B8 between Rundu and Divundu. Further south, subsistence agriculture and burning for charcoal has had an impact in some areas, including around the legendary Katere mast, but pristine woodland can still be found between 26 km and 100 km east of Rundu. A variety of private accommodation is available along the Okavango River near Rundu. Birding is especially productive at Sarasunga River Lodge at the edge of Rundu, and at Shamvura ☎.

reedbeds and surrounding thickets, which also host **Swamp Boubou**, and, in summer, a plethora of *Acrocephalus* warblers. **Eurasian Reed-Warbler** is probably an annual visitor in small numbers, but is almost impossible to separate in the field from the much more common **African Reed-Warbler**. Adjacent thorn thickets should be searched for **Dwarf Bittern**, **Hartlaub's Babbler** and **Brown Firefinch**. Bee-eaters are often plentiful in the vicinity of the sewage ponds, with large flocks of **Blue-cheeked**, **European** and **Southern Carmine Bee-eaters**, and smaller numbers of **White-fronted** and **Little Bee-eaters** present. A similar selection of rails and herons may be found along the B8 about 5 km south-west of town, where the B8 crosses a broad drainage line (*omuramba*). If overnighting in Rundu, it is worth watching overhead in the evening in the vicinity of the sewage ponds for **African Hobby*** and, more rarely, **Bat Hawk***.

Ayres' Hawk-Eagle inhabits moist woodlands.

Woodland birding: Twenty kilometres before Rundu, on the left of the B8, stands what is obviously a radio mast, the first essential woodland birding site in the Rundu area. Dry, broad-leaved woodland along the 1.5 km track leading to the radio mast south of Rundu is one of the best sites in southern Africa for the inconspicuous **Rufous-bellied Tit**. The woodland is also home to scarcer birds, here on the western edge of their range, such as **African Cuckoo Hawk**, **African Golden Oriole**, **White-breasted Cuckooshrike**, the striking **Arnot's Chat**, **Tinkling Cisticola***, and **Stierling's Wren-Warbler**. The area sometimes seems almost devoid of birds, but perseverance here should be rewarded with sightings of **Green-capped Eremomela**, **Neddicky**, **Wood Pipit** and, with luck, **Green-backed Honeybird**.

Most of these species may also be found in mature woodland along the B8 east of Rundu, where **Bradfield's Hornbill** and the scarce **Sharp-tailed Starling*** are more likely to be seen. The rare and elusive **Souza's Shrike***, an inconspicuous bird that is usually found perching quietly in the upper levels of broad-leaved woodland, has been recorded here. During summer, **Racket-tailed Roller*** (scarce) can be seen almost anywhere along the road from Rundu to Mahango.

Keep an eye on the sky while driving, as **European Honey-Buzzard*** and **Ayres' Hawk-Eagle*** are other regularly recorded rarities. By visiting the area after good summer rains between October and January, you stand a chance of witnessing the emergence of termite alates, with vast numbers of birds attracted to the flying insects. Flocks of aerial-feeding **Yellow-billed Kite**, **Dickinson's Kestrel**, **Red-footed** and **Amur Falcons**, and **Eurasian** and **African* Hobbies** may be joined at this time by **Bateleur**, **Dark Chanting Goshawk**, and **Lesser Spotted**, **Tawny**, **Steppe** and **Wahlberg's Eagles**, all of which waddle about on the ground bingeing on the insect smorgasbord. A motley assortment of hornbills, rollers, kingfishers, storks, orioles, drongos, shrikes and starlings often join the fray, creating an enjoyable birding spectacle.

A spotlighting excursion along the same road may turn up **African** and **Southern White-faced Scops-Owls**, **Bronze-winged Courser** and a host of nightjars, such as **European** (uncommon), **Rufous-cheeked**, **Fiery-necked**, **Square-tailed** and **Pennant-winged*** (uncommon) **Nightjars**.

214 Popa Falls

IBA ✔✔

This beautiful rest camp, set in lush surroundings at the foot of Popa Falls, makes an excellent base from which to explore Mahango Game Reserve and the western Caprivi Strip. It is also a wonderful birding site in its own right, being one of the best places in the subregion to find **Rock Pratincole*** and **Brown Firefinch**.

SPECIALS: White-browed Coucal, Rock Pratincole*, White-backed Night-Heron*, Hartlaub's Babbler and Brown Firefinch.

SEASON: Good year-round, although **Rock Pratincole*** and **African Skimmer*** may be absent between March and July.

HABITATS: Dense riparian woodlands flank the rapids, with mid-stream rocks being the favoured breeding habitat of **Rock Pratincole***.

BIRDING: **Rock Pratincole***, easily seen roosting on rocks in the rapids, or hawking insects overhead, is particularly conspicuous in the early morning and late afternoon. Scan for them from the viewpoint at the north end of the camp site, or clamber over the top of the rapids from the loop trail. The patch of riverine woodland traversed by the loop trail is home to **Yellow-fronted Tinkerbird, White-browed Coucal, African Mourning Dove, African Green Pigeon, African Goshawk, Swamp Boubou, Grey Tit-Flycatcher, White-browed Robin-Chat, Yellow-bellied Greenbul, Terrestrial Brownbul** and **Hartlaub's Babbler**.

Clumps of papyrus along the river channels are home to **Greater** and **Lesser Swamp-Warblers**, and **Golden Weaver** has also been recorded along the trail. **African Emerald Cuckoo**, **African Cuckoo Hawk** and **White-backed Night-Heron*** are more rarely seen. Search the thorn thickets around the camp site for **Brown, Red-billed** and **Jameson's Firefinches**. Both **African Wood-Owl** and **Barred Owlet** are frequently heard in the camp site at night.

OTHER ANIMALS: Nile Crocodile is common in the Okavango River, and Hippopotamus feed on the island at night, so exercise caution on spotlighting excursions! Spotted-necked Otters are regularly seen in the river.

NEARBY SITES: The camp site (N//goabaca) on the opposite side of the river to Popa Falls also offers good birding; cross the bridge at Divundu and turn to the south (signposted) onto a sandy track just before the prison.

GETTING THERE

Popa Falls lies 5 km south of Divundu Bridge on the D3403 to Botswana. The camp (administered by MET) has chalets and camping facilities. A short loop trail provides access to the small patch of riverine forest.

J. Rossouw

Rock Pratincole

Geoff McIlleron: Firefly Images

White-backed Night-Heron

215 Mahango Game Reserve IBA ✓✓✓

This magnificent game reserve, stretching along the Okavango River flood plain in the western Caprivi Strip, is one of southern Africa's top birding spots. Although it covers only 25 000 ha, it boasts a bird list of over 400 species, including an impressive selection of Okavango specials. The fact that one is allowed to explore the reserve on foot, despite the presence of Lion, Elephant and Buffalo, only adds to the excitement of birding (see p.10 on dangerous wild animals). Mahango is expected to become part of the new Bwabata Reserve.

SPECIALS: Coppery-tailed Coucal, Wattled Crane*, Burchell's Sandgrouse*, Greater Painted Snipe, Long-toed Lapwing, African Skimmer*, Western Banded Snake-Eagle, Dickinson's Kestrel, African Hobby*, Slaty Egret*, Dwarf Bittern, Swamp Boubou, Rufous-bellied Tit, Tinkling* and Chirping Cisticolas, Greater Swamp-Warbler, Green-capped Eremomela, Hartlaub's Babbler, Rosy-breasted Longclaw*, Wood Pipit, Southern Brown-throated and Golden Weavers, and Brown Firefinch.

SEASON: Although **African Skimmer*** may be absent between October and May, depending on water levels in the Okavango River, summer is the most exciting time to visit Mahango.

HABITATS: The flood plain of the Okavango River, and its adjoining riverine woodland and savanna, are the most productive birding habitats in the reserve. Two shallow drainage lines may flood during peak summer rains, providing habitat for migrant crakes. Dry, broad-leaved woodland occurs in the west, but is largely inaccessible without 4WD.

BIRDING: This birding paradise is easily covered from the 2WD loop road, which initially runs down the Mahango *omuramba* at (A) before following the flood plain. Bare areas in the drainage line in early summer attract **Temminck's Courser** and a variety of larks, including **Rufous-naped, Flappet, Fawn-coloured, Red-capped** and, with luck, **Dusky* Larks**, as well as **African** and **Plain-backed Pipits**.

Raptors are plentiful in this area, so scan the dead trees in the adjacent woodland for **Brown Snake-Eagle, Dark Chanting Goshawk, Martial Eagle, Dickinson's Kestrel** and **African Hobby*** (rare). When the drainage line floods after heavy summer rains, stroll through the rank grassland for **African, Baillon's, Spotted** and **Striped*** (rare) **Crakes, Great** (rare) and **African Snipes, Greater Painted Snipe** and **Dwarf Bittern**, all of which may also be found at seasonal pools further south along the road (4.5 km from the D3403 junction). Acacia thickets around the seasonal pools host **Black-faced Babbler*** (scarce), **Green-winged Pytilia**, and **Violet-eared** and **Black-cheeked Waxbills**, while taller woodland immediately to the south supports **Southern White-crowned Shrike, Burchell's** and **Meves's Starlings** and **Stierling's Wren-Warbler**.

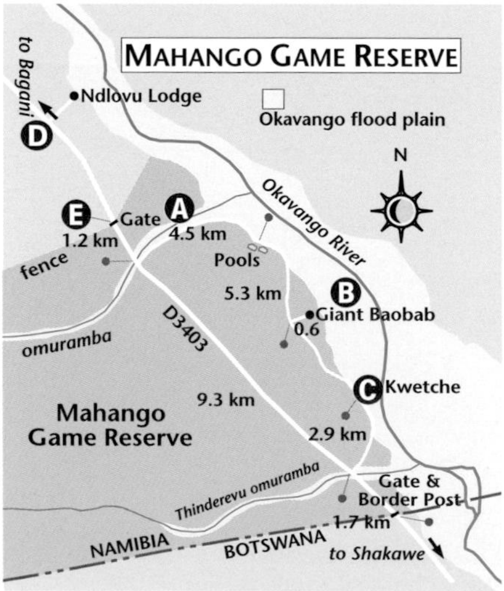

The road then returns to the flood plain, allowing unobstructed views of lily-clad ponds favoured by **African Pygmy Goose*, White-backed Duck, Hottentot Teal, Allen's Gallinule, African** and **Lesser** (uncommon) **Jacanas, Water Thick-knee** and **Squacco Heron**. The shy Sitatunga may also be seen along the edge of the papyrus here in the late afternoon, while **White-backed Night-Heron*** feeds here after dark. The best place from which to access the flood plain, however, is at the Giant Baobab (B). Scan from the viewpoint or, if Buffalo, Lion and Elephant are not present, consider walking out onto the flood plain (at your own risk), where **Blue-cheeked** and **Southern Carmine Bee-eaters, Black** (rare) and **Coppery-tailed Coucals, Wattled Crane*, Long-toed** and **African**

Wattled Lapwings, Collared Pratincole, African Marsh-Harrier, Slaty Egret* (erratic), **Black** and **Goliath Herons, African Openbill, Saddle-billed Stork** (rare), **Banded Martin, Grey-rumped** and **Wire-tailed Swallows, Luapula Cisticola, Rosy-breasted Longclaw*** (scarce) and **Cuckoo Finch*** (rare) may all be found. **Collared Palm-Thrush** has been seen here.

Continue on to the Kwetche picnic site **C**, which overlooks a scenic backwater of the Okavango River. **Swamp Boubou, Hartlaub's Babbler** and **Brown Firefinch** inhabit the waterside thickets, and adjacent papyrus beds are home to **Southern Brown-throated** and **Golden Weavers**. Another two Okavango specials, **Chirping Cisticola** and **Greater Swamp-Warbler**, are equally common in the papyrus, but it may require tape recordings to lure them out of cover. A walk through the beautiful riparian woodland south of the picnic site is highly recommended, although both Elephant and Buffalo are common here, so beware. **African Skimmer*** is often seen patrolling the main river (but is usually absent when flood waters cover the sandbars from Oct/Nov to May), while **Barred Owlet, Western Banded Snake-Eagle, Little Sparrowhawk, White-backed Night-Heron*** and **Retz's Helmet-Shrike** are less frequently recorded. A pair of the highly sought-after **Pel's Fishing-Owl*** once resided in this riparian strip, which is now badly damaged by Elephant.

GETTING THERE

Mahango Game Reserve straddles the D3403 to Botswana, about 20 km south of Bagani Bridge. A 2WD track loops east off the D3403 and follows the edge of the flood plain to a picnic site overlooking the river, while a longer 4WD track loops west along the Mahango and Thinderevu drainage lines. There are no overnight facilities in Mahango, although the highly recommended MET camp at Popa Falls (see entry p.235), 15 km to the north, offers both chalets and a camp site. Private accommodation is also available along the river between Popa Falls and Mahango.

OTHER ANIMALS: Although Mahango boasts Lion, Elephant and Buffalo, its ungulates are of greatest interest to the mammal connoisseur: two Okavango specials, the elegant Red Lechwe and the swamp-dwelling Sitatunga, and the rarely seen woodland antelopes, Roan, Sable and 'Chobe' Bushbuck (with distinctly brighter colouring and clearer markings typical of the northern populations), all occur.

NEARBY SITES: The D3403 from Popa Falls south to Mahango initially passes through settled areas which hold few birds (although **Black-faced Babbler*** occurs and **Burchell's Sandgrouse*** may be seen flying over prior to the rainy season, especially 1.8 km south of the Popa turn-off). Good quality woodland **D** 5 km before the gate holds a reasonable selection of broad-leaved woodland birds. Bird the roadside, or walk west along the fence from the entrance gate **E**.

Both **Tinkling Cisticola*** and **Green-capped Eremomela** are fairly common here, while **Rufous-bellied Tit, Stierling's Wren-Warbler, White-breasted Cuckooshrike** and **Wood Pipit** are less frequently seen.

The seldom-seen **Sharp-tailed Starling*** should also be looked out for. Lodges along the Okavango River offer launch trips that almost guarantee sightings of **African Skimmer*** in season, and often a wide variety of other water birds, notably **Allen's Gallinule, Long-toed Lapwing** and, at dusk, **White-backed Night-Heron***.

Callan Cohen

Elephant in Mahango Game Reserve

216 Okavango Panhandle: Shakawe (Botswana)

IBA ✔✔✔

Shortly after traversing the Caprivi Strip, the Okavango River meanders into Botswana through the Okavango Delta's upper reaches, commonly known as the Okavango Panhandle. Although it lacks much of the charismatic megafauna of the eastern delta's game parks, the panhandle is every bit as good for birds, and considerably more accessible to birders. A number of well-established birder-friendly lodges and camps make much sought-after birds such as **White-backed Night-Heron*** and **Pel's Fishing-Owl*** a definite possibility.

SPECIALS: African Pygmy Goose*, Slaty Egret*, White-backed Night-Heron*, Western Banded Snake-Eagle, Greater Painted Snipe, Long-toed Lapwing, African Skimmer*, Coppery-tailed Coucal, Southern Carmine Bee-eater, Hartlaub's Babbler, Chirping and Luapula Cisticolas, Greater Swamp-Warbler, Swamp Boubou, Southern Brown-throated and Golden Weavers, and Brown Firefinch.

SEASON: Sep-Nov is probably the best time to visit, as Afrotropical and Palearctic migrants begin to arrive, **Southern Carmine Bee-eaters** are at their colonies, and rising water levels have not yet covered the **African Skimmer*** roosts. However, late summer, when a host of exciting water birds turn up along the flood plain, is equally interesting.

HABITATS: Well-developed riparian woodland and the Okavango flood plain, with its extensive papyrus beds, quiet backwaters and flooded grasslands.

BIRDING: The attractions at Shakawe Lodge are many, not least the resident **Pel's Fishing-Owls***, which sometime feed from the lily-covered pond adjacent to the dining room. The fishing-owls roost behind the cabins in superb riverine woodland, which also supports **African Wood-Owl**, **Barred Owlet**, **Western Banded Snake-Eagle** and **Retz's Helmet-Shrike**. All the Okavango specials, including **Hartlaub's Babbler**, **Greater Swamp-Warbler**, **Chirping Cisticola** and **Brown Firefinch**, inhabit the reedbeds and thickets in the immediate vicinity of the camp. Drotsky's Camp is set in an even larger patch of impressive riparian woodland overlooking the river, and boasts a similar suite of Okavango specials, as does Xaro Lodge, where a pair of **Pel's Fishing-Owl*** regularly roost in the riparian woodland adjacent to the tented camp.

Pel's Fishing-Owl

Boat cruises offered by all camps along the papyrus-fringed channels and into the lily-covered backwaters provide the opportunity of seeing **Slaty Egret***, **Rufous-bellied Heron**, **African Pygmy Goose*** and **Lesser Jacana** (scarce). **African Skimmer***, **Collared Pratincole** and **Long-toed Lapwing** roost on the regular sandbars. And, while on a cruise, there is an excellent chance of sighting **Pel's Fishing-Owl*** and **White-backed Night-Heron*** on their day roosts. Shakawe Lodge offers a unique spotlighting launch cruise, allowing one to experience the sounds of the Okavango night, and offering one of the best chances of White-backed Night-Heron* and Pel's Fishing-Owl*. The Shakawe area is renowned for its breeding colonies of **Southern Carmine Bee-eaters** in spring and early summer.

GETTING THERE

Drotsky's Camp ☎ and Shakawe Lodge, both offering catered accommodation, camping sites and boat excursions, are signposted from the excellent tarred road, 30 km south-east of the Namibian border. Xaro Lodge visitors are taken by boat from Drotsky's Camp. Nxamaseri Camp lies a further 30 km downstream and visitors are met and escorted along the 4WD track to the camp.

217 Divundu & Beyond ✔✔

Returning to northern Caprivi, the B8 stretches eastwards from Divundu Bridge across flat country, where formerly pristine woodland has suffered heavily at the hands of charcoal-makers. Nevertheless, stop in any semi-intact patches between the Okavango and Kwando rivers, as the birding is excellent and many widespread species of Africa's wooded savannas are represented. Watch especially for **Coqui Francolin**, **Bennett's Woodpecker**, **Racket-tailed Roller***, **Ayres' Hawk-Eagle***, **Dickinson's Kestrel**, **White-breasted Cuckooshrike**, **Arnot's Chat** and **Sharp-tailed Starling*** (such as 33 km west of Kongola). At points 146 km, 178 km and 191 km east of Bagani Bridge, the B8 traverses narrow, grassy clearings, which could be explored for **African Crake**, **Greater Painted Snipe** and **Dwarf Bittern**, especially after summer rains. The Kwando River, which forms the western limit of the Eastern Caprivi wetlands, is reached 194 km from Divundu Bridge.

218 Kwando River Area IBA ✔✔

Most of the Okavango's special birds may be found along the Kwando River, with the MET camp site at Susuwe providing easy access to excellent riparian woodland, and the remote national parks of Mudumu and Mamili offering viable wilderness alternatives to Botswana's Okavango Delta.

SPECIALS: Bradfield's Hornbill, Narina Trogon*, Racket-tailed Roller*, Black and Coppery-tailed Coucals, Pel's Fishing-Owl*, Pennant-winged Nightjar*, African Cuckoo Hawk, Western Banded Snake-Eagle, African Hobby*, Slaty Egret*, Rufous-bellied Heron, White-backed Night-Heron*, Swamp Boubou, Arnot's Chat, Tinkling Cisticola*, Stierling's Wren-Warbler, Hartlaub's Babbler, Copper Sunbird and Red-headed Quelea*.

SEASON: Summer, when the migrants have returned, is generally the best time.

HABITATS: Dense riparian woodland and a narrow, fairly dry flood plain along the Kwando River in the Susuwe area, with broad-leaved woodland and more extensive riverine wetlands, including papyrus swamps and forested islands, in Mudumu and Mamili national parks.

BIRDING: The tall woodland in the immediate vicinity of Susuwe supports a number of birds that are scarce or absent elsewhere in Namibia, notably **Grey-headed Parrot** (scarce), **Narina Trogon*** and **Racket-tailed Roller***. Look for **Western Banded Snake-Eagle**, **Copper Sunbird** and **Brown Firefinch** along the edges of the riparian forest, and in the drier, broad-leaved woodland nearby, for **Bradfield's Hornbill**, **Arnot's Chat**, **Hartlaub's Babbler**, **Tinkling Cisticola*** and **Stierling's Wren-Warbler**. The Kwando River is fairly narrow at this point, with more productive wetland habitat to be found downstream in Mamili National Park, although **Rufous-bellied Heron**, **Black Heron**, a variety of storks and **Chirping Cisticola** may be found along the river near the B8.

Peter Ginn

Racket-tailed Roller

GETTING THERE

Susuwe Camp is a MET-operated camping area set in riparian woodland on the west bank of the Kwando River, 4 km north of the B8 on a reasonable 2WD track. The fantastic Susuwe Island Lodge is also situated on the Kwando River in this vicinity. Mudumu, accessible via reasonable 2WD roads, has accommodation ranging from the Nakatwa camp site to the upmarket Lianshulu Lodge, while Mamili, set up to protect the vast Linyanti Swamp, is accessible to 4WD only and camping is the sole accommodation option.

219 Katima Mulilo ✔✔

The remote outpost of Katima Mulilo lies on the banks of the Zambezi River at the eastern edge of the Caprivi Strip and, like its border counterparts of Kasane in Botswana and Victoria Falls in Zimbabwe, boasts a staggeringly diverse avifauna.

SPECIALS: Coppery-tailed Coucal, Grey-headed Parrot, Schalow's Turaco, Pel's Fishing-Owl*, Pennant-winged Nightjar*, African Finfoot*, African, Baillon's and Striped* Crakes, Allen's Gallinule, Lesser Moorhen, Greater Painted Snipe, Lesser Jacana, White-crowned Lapwing, Rock Pratincole*, African Skimmer*, Bat Hawk*, Western Banded Snake-Eagle, Dickinson's Kestrel, Slaty Egret*, Rufous-bellied Heron, White-backed Night-Heron*, Dwarf Bittern, Swamp Boubou, Hartlaub's Babbler, Shelley's Sunbird*, Copper Sunbird.

SEASON: November, before the water levels rise in the Zambezi, and when the migrants are back in town, is the best time to visit. From December to April, **Rock Pratincole*** and **African Skimmer*** may be absent, although migrant water birds are likely to be at their peak.

HABITATS: Broad-leaved woodland, and both natural and man-made wetlands along the Zambezi River.

BIRDING: An impressive variety of birding habitats are to be found in and around town, resulting in Katima Mulilo's bird list now exceeding 400 species. The sewage works on the southern edge of town, although it has become rather overgrown in recent years, is famous for its rails and crakes, and a dawn visit in summer may still produce **African Rail, African** and **Baillon's Crakes, Allen's Gallinule, Lesser Moorhen**, and possibly **Spotted Crake. Striped Crake*** has been recorded, but is not easily seen. Walk around the large, reed-fringed ponds to the south of the cement-lined settling pans, watching for the secretive **Black Coucal, African Snipe, Greater Painted Snipe, Rufous-bellied Heron** and **Dwarf Bittern**. Although viewing the cement-lined ponds may be tricky due to high reed growth, it is worth scanning the open water for **Fulvous** and **White-backed Ducks**, and **Hottentot Teal. Copper Sunbird** and **Thrush Nightingale*** may also be found in thickets here.

The mixed broad-leaved and acacia woodland in the immediate vicinity of the sewage works is also highly productive, especially in summer, when **Eurasian Hobby, Jacobin** and **Great Spotted Cuckoos**, and *Sylvia* warblers join the resident **Southern White-crowned Shrike, Retz's Helmet-Shrike, Burchell's Starling** and **Tinkling Cisticola***.

The dense woodland along the Zambezi River, particularly along the golf course near Zambezi Lodge and in the vicinity of Hippo Lodge, supports a number of birds that are tricky to find elsewhere in Namibia, notably **African Emerald Cuckoo, Narina Trogon***, the spectacular **Schalow's Turaco**, and **Grey-headed Bush-Shrike**, all of which are best located by their distinctive calls. Both **Yellow-bellied Greenbul** and **Terrestrial Brownbul**

GETTING THERE

Katima Mulilo, the administrative capital of the Caprivi Strip, lies 310 km east of Bagani Bridge along the tarred B8. To reach Katima Mulilo sewage works, drive north from the BP service station on the B8 south of town, and turn left after 600 m, opposite the huge radio mast, onto an indistinct track signposted 'Buche Buche', which leads to the edge of the ponds. A variety of accommodation is available along the Zambezi River, of which Zambezi Lodge, Hippo Lodge and Kalizo Lodge are highly recommended as birding spots in their own right.

Callan Cohen

The Golden Highway traverses the moist woodlands of the Caprivi Strip.

are common in the thickets, which are also home to both **Tropical** and **Swamp Boubous, White-browed** and **Red-capped Robin-Chats, Bearded Scrub-Robin,** and **Hartlaub's Babbler**, and, in summer, **Thrush Nightingale*** is also present. **Retz's Helmet-Shrike** is fairly common in taller woodland, and there have been a number of recent records of its brood parasite, the elusive **Thick-billed Cuckoo***.

Warwick Tarboton
African Pygmy-Kingfisher

Small flocks of **Grey-headed Parrot** may be seen in noisy flight over the golf course, but they are scarce, while flowering trees in town should be checked for **Purple-banded Sunbird** and **Copper Sunbird** (erratic). Other noteworthy woodland birds to watch for along the golf course are **African Pygmy-Kingfisher, Grey-headed Kingfisher, African Cuckoo Hawk, Little Sparrowhawk, Ashy Flycatcher,** and **Grey Tit-Flycatcher**.

Sundowners enjoyed while overlooking the river are recommended for a variety of reasons, not the least of which is the opportunity to watch a **Bat Hawk*** swallowing its first victim of the evening. The crepuscular hawk has also been seen around the lights on the golf course after dark, where **African Scops-Owl, African Wood Owl** and **Barred Owlet** are commonly present. The most reliable way of finding **Pel's Fishing-Owl***, however, is to hire a boat from one of the lodges in town, and explore the quiet backwaters of the Maningi Manzi and Hippo Island areas, where the secretive **African Finfoot*** and **White-backed Night-Heron*** may also be found. The boat drivers often know the whereabouts of roosting birds. No boat is necessary to see **White-crowned Lapwing, African Skimmer*, Collared Pratincole** and **African Openbill**, all of which are conspicuous on exposed sandbars during periods of low water in the Zambezi River. **Rock Pratincole*** prefers the rocky areas around the rapids west of town, which can be viewed from near the pump station. To the south-east of town, along the road towards Kasane, this mixed woodland is replaced by extensive mopane woodland. Although relatively depauperate in terms of birds, both **Arnot's Chat** and **Wood Pipit** are fairly common residents. Mopane is also the favoured habitat of the globally threatened **Black-cheeked Lovebird***, which has been reported from this area (see p.335). **Shelley's Sunbird*** is regularly recorded at Kalizo Lodge ☎.

OTHER ANIMALS: Although few large animals survive in the vicinity of Katima Mulilo, Nile Crocodile are plentiful in the river and grazing Hippopotamus remain a danger while spotlighting along the river banks at night.

220 Kasane & Chobe NP (Botswana)

IBA ✔✔✔

Over 450 species have been recorded from this area of flood plains and mixed woodlands in far northern Botswana, famous for its game-viewing. The main road from Caprivi en route to Victoria Falls in Zimbabwe, passes directly through the town of Kasane and the Chobe National Park, where almost 300 bird species have been recorded in a single day!

SPECIALS: Slaty Egret*, Rock Pratincole*, African Skimmer*, African Finfoot*, Rufous-bellied Heron, African Hobby*, Bat Hawk*, Coppery-tailed Coucal, Chirping Cisticola, Luapula Cisticola, Greater Swamp-Warbler, River Warbler*, Thrush Nightingale*, Western Banded Snake-Eagle, Allen's Gallinule, African Pygmy Goose*, Broad-tailed Paradise-Whydah, Three-banded Courser*, Collared Palm-Thrush, Swamp Boubou, Brown Firefinch, Copper Sunbird, Racket-tailed Roller*, Arnot's Chat.

HABITATS: Open flood plains with grass, reeds and papyrus beds, riparian thicket vegetation, open river habitats with patches of water lilies, temporary pools, teak, acacia and mopane woodland.

SEASON: Summer, when most of the migrants are present, is the most exciting time. **African Skimmer*** and **Rock Pratincole*** may be absent from mid to late summer, as the rising river levels cover their sand and rock perches.

BIRDING: A good first stop in Kasane is Mowana Lodge Ⓐ, where the grounds offer confiding **Collared Palm-Thrush**, a local special. **Southern Brown-throated Weaver**, **African Mourning Dove**, **Brown Firefinch** and **Copper Sunbird** may also be seen in the gardens, and **Thrush Nightingale*** may be heard in summer.

The riverside trail is excellent for thicket species including **Bearded Scrub-Robin**, **White-browed Robin-Chat**, **Terrestrial Brownbul**, **Yellow-bellied Greenbul**, **Swamp Boubou** and **Hartlaub's Babbler**, while **Red-faced Cisticola** may be found in the waterside vegetation. The bird hide here offers sightings of **Rock Pratincole*** perched on the rocks in the river in spring and early summer, **White-backed Night-Heron*** hiding in the dense riverside vegetation, and the occasional **Half-collared Kingfisher**.

African Skimmer* may sometimes fly past, although these elegant birds are best seen on sandbars in the river while taking a boat cruise. Kubu Lodge Ⓑ has some good riverine vegetation, and one should scan carefully for **African Finfoot*** along the river's edge here.

The Chobe Safari Lodge Ⓒ provides good views over the river and flood plain. Sundowners on the deck may reward the patient birder with a foraging **African Hobby***, and, at twilight, a **Bat Hawk***.

A boat trip along the Chobe River, which heads westwards into the park (although good birding can also be had in the Kasaai channel to the north) is highly recommended. Although some of these species here can be seen by scanning with a telescope from Kasane itself, or by scanning from the road that leads westwards out of town towards the Chobe entrance gate Ⓓ, a boat trip is far more productive. Scan the river edges for **Slaty Egret***, **Rufous-bellied Heron**, and **White-crowned** and **Long-toed Lapwings**, while **African Fish-Eagle** and **Collared Pratincole** fly overhead. Search patches of water lilies for **African Pygmy Goose*** and **Lesser Jacana**, the thick vegetation on the water's edge for skulking **Allen's Gallinule** and **Lesser Moorhen**.

Coppery-tailed and **White-browed Coucals** and **Luapula Cisticola** call from the herbage along the river edge, and may be seen perched on top of the vegetation, while **Chirping Cisticola** and **Greater Swamp-Warbler** prefer the papyrus beds. **Red-headed Quelea*** may be seen in reedbeds, such as those in the vicinity of Sedudu Island Ⓔ, in late summer (Feb-Apr).

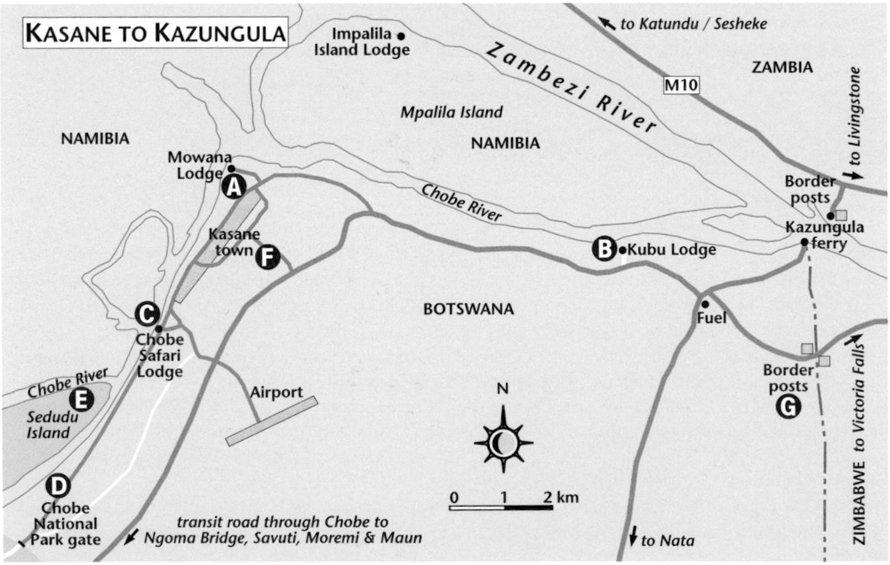

Southern Carmine Bee-eaters are very common and breed in sandy banks along the river's edge in spring and early summer. Moist grasslands along the river edge host **Rosy-breasted Longclaw*** and sometimes **Black Coucal**. Look and listen for **Western Banded Snake-Eagle**, **Meyer's Parrot**, **Broad-billed Roller** and **Trumpeter Hornbill** in large waterside trees.

Teak woodlands, in the forest reserve behind Kasane town Ⓕ (beware of Elephants and deep sandy tracks) and along the road southwards from the Natanga/Ngoma Road junction, hold **Racket-tailed Roller*** and **Stierling's Wren-Warbler**. There is also excellent teak woodland on the main road from Ngoma to Kasane.

Other species to look out for here include **African Cuckoo Hawk**, **Ayres' Hawk-Eagle***, **Coqui Francolin**, Wood Pipit, **Southern Ground-Hornbill*** and **Retz's Helmet-Shrike**. **Broad-tailed Paradise Whydah** may be seen in later summer (Feb-Apr), while scarcer teak woodland residents include **Golden-backed Pytilia**, **Miombo Rock-Thrush** and **Green-backed Honeybird**.

Richard du Toit

Trumpeter Hornbill

The woodlands around Kasane town are really good for migrant warblers, with **Olive-tree Warbler*** and **Common White-throat** preferring acacia, while the grassy understorey of the teak woodlands (such as in the Kasane Forest Reserve) support high numbers of the secretive **River Warbler** when conditions are right. Listen for them, especially when they are most vocal prior to departing in Feb and Mar.

Turn south along the sandy road to Lesoma just before the border post at Kazungula to reach the 10 km Lesoma track, along which the acacia woodland Ⓖ holds **Crimson-breasted Shrike**, **Violet-eared Waxbill** and a host of migrant warblers.

Three-banded* and **Bronze-winged Coursers**, **Verreaux's Eagle-Owl** and **Pennant-winged Nightjar*** (the last may be found widely in the Kasane area in early summer) are regularly recorded on night drives.

Seasonal pans in the Chobe National Park, such as those that begin 40 km south of the Natanga/Ngoma road junction, hold impressive numbers of wading birds and waterfowl, including **Dwarf Bittern** (check especially Kwikamba pan). The nearby Seleko plains (near Nogotsaa) are a good area for **Yellow-throated Sandgrouse**, which favours black-cotton soils (but beware, these soils are notoriously treacherous when wet). The network of seasonal pans extends towards the Mababe Depression (excellent for game-viewing) and Savuti, where **Slaty Egret*** and **Wattled Crane*** may be seen on the fringes.

The Savuti area is famous for its game-viewing and birding, but is quite remote and often subject to flooding in summer. Scan the dry edges of the Savuti marsh for **Kori Bustard**, and check the trees in the camp site at Savuti for **Bradfield's Hornbill**. Mopane woodland across the park holds **Arnot's Chat**. For birding in the south of the Chobe National Park, see p.261.

OTHER ANIMALS: This area offers a wide diversity of game, including Lion, Buffalo, Elephant, African Wild Dog, Leopard, Hippo, 'Chobe' Bushbuck and Red Lechwe.

NEARBY SITES: The upmarket Impalila Island Lodge, situated on an island in Namibia, but accessible by boat from Kasane, offers similar waterside and woodland birding in a magnificent setting. It offers access to a nearby island, which is the only place south of the Zambezi River where the highly distinctive *ruwenzori* subspecies of **Olive Woodpecker** is to be found.

GETTING THERE

A variety of accommodation and camping is available in Kasane town and there are camp sites in the Chobe National Park. A number of Kasane tour operators will arrange boat cruises, including Chobe Safari Lodge, which also has a good camp site. Because almost all the areas off the main roads here are very sandy and are only suitable for 4WD vehicles, we have concentrated our birding information on the most accessible areas.

BOTSWANA

Dominated by the dry woodlands of the Kalahari Desert, Botswana boasts a popular combination of wonderful wilderness landscapes, abundant wildlife, and good infrastructure. For many visitors, the enormity and solitude of Botswana's arid interior leave as great an impression as the bird-filled, game-studded swamps of the Okavango Delta. Vast areas of the country are extraordinarily thinly populated, and 17 per cent of Botswana's land area is formally protected by parks and reserves, many of which are acknowledged to be among the continent's finest for mammal-viewing. Bird diversity is famously high in the north, and about 580 species have been recorded in the country as a whole. Although Botswana has no true endemics, it is one of the best places in the world to see many key Kalahari, grassland, swamp and flood-plain specials, and is also a particularly important region for Palearctic migrants.

The country offers a wide range of facilities for visitors, from luxurious fly-in safaris to rustic camp sites for independent overland travellers. Although a good network of well-maintained tar roads allows for efficient travel between far-flung sites, birders aiming to travel within any of the country's major parks and reserves are strongly advised to take at least one 4WD vehicle. Deep sand all year round and heavy mud during the wet season necessitate the use of a 4WD. However, during the dry season, it is often possible to get by in a 2WD with high clearance and deflated tyres. Please see p.12 for further comments on driving in remote parts of southern Africa. Note that it is especially ill-advised to drive at night in Botswana, as both game and livestock present very real and serious hazards. Fuel and supplies are widely available in larger towns.

Albert Froneman

Burchell's Sandgrouse favours red Kalahari sands.

ROUTE 22
EASTERN BOTSWANA

TOP 10 BIRDS

- Short-clawed Lark
- Boulder Chat
- Olive-tree Warbler
- Cape Vulture
- Maccoa Duck
- Eurasian Reed-Warbler
- White-throated Robin
- South African Cliff-Swallow
- Sociable Weaver
- Montagu's Harrier

Fringing the eastern border of Botswana's sand-filled Kalahari basin is a stretch of harder soils, interrupted by several ranges of low, rocky hills and granite koppies and predominantly covered in mixed woodlands. Known as the Hardeveld, this is the more densely populated part of Botswana, and both of the country's principal cities are situated in this wetter area.

Birding here is concentrated in the vicinity of the capital, Gaborone, and could be considered to have two components. On the one hand, the wetlands, thornveld and hills in the immediate vicinity of the city provide an excellent diversity of species, and always produce a good day's birding. It is relatively easy to see in excess of 150 species in a dedicated day within 25 km of Gaborone, but these are predominantly species that have fairly widespread distributions in southern Africa. On the other hand, the grasslands and scrub of the south-eastern corner of Botswana, particularly between the villages of Pitsane, Good Hope and Ramatlabama, produce lower overall diversity, but host a number of sought-after species. Most notable among these is the localised Short clawed Lark*, which, but for a curiously disjunct small population in the Limpopo Province, South Africa, is almost restricted to Botswana. Gaborone and south-eastern Botswana thus supply both diversity and endemism, and perhaps deserve greater attention.

Most birders travelling further north in Botswana will pass the eastern towns of Palapye and, near the Zimbabwean border, Francistown. This area is best known for its accessible Boulder Chat* sites.

Roger de la Harpe/IOA

Eastern Botswana has significant Cape Vulture colonies.

221 Ramatlabama Grasslands

IBA ✔✔

Ramatlabama is a small settlement on the South Africa/Botswana border. The grasslands just to the north provide excellent birding, particularly after good rainfall. At all times, there is a near certainty of finding the highly localised **Short-clawed Lark***, which is common here.

Callan Cohen

Habitat of Short-clawed Lark

SEASON: Birding in the grasslands is much more productive in summer, especially during wet years, when several additional species move into the area. However, **Short-clawed Lark*** is vocal and easy to find all year round.

SPECIALS: Montagu's and Pallid* Harriers, Short-clawed* and Pink-billed Larks, South African Cliff-Swallow and Sociable Weaver.

HABITATS: Dry Kalahari grassland, grazed grassland with sparse thornveld.

BIRDING: The best areas of natural grassland to bird are present immediately north of the border post at Ramatlabama, whereas **Short-clawed Lark*** prefers the grazed land closer to Lobatse. Leaving the border village of Ramatlabama, and heading north towards Lobatse, look out for Botswana's only breeding colony of **South African Cliff-Swallow**, recently established on the small building just beyond the BP garage. A second, larger colony is present under the Moselebe River bridge, 25 km further on. Also scan the savanna on the opposite side of the road from the BP garage, where a large **Sociable Weaver** nest (among one of the only accessible nests in south-eastern Botswana) is visible in a Camel-thorn tree about 80 m from the road, and can be reached along a track over the railway line.

Excellent grassland extends for 4 km on the road towards Lobatse. Stop anywhere along here and walk into the grassland west of the road. It is for larks that this area is most famous, and up to eight species may be seen in a single day after good rain. **Rufous-naped** and **Eastern Clapper Larks** are easily located by their songs, whereas **Chestnut-backed Sparrowlark** is often seen feeding at the roadsides. **Pink-billed Lark** is usually flushed while walking, but also scan for it at pan edges. **Monotonous** and **Melodious* Larks** probably only move into the areas in wetter years and, if present, may be located by their songs. Common and typical grassland species include **Northern Black Korhaan, Cape Crow, Ant-eating Chat, Desert Cisticola, African Quailfinch** and, in wetter years, **Long-tailed Widowbird** – here at the edge of its range. You might even flush a **Kurrichane Buttonquail**. Summer also brings large numbers of aerial feeders, including **Red-breasted Swallow, Banded** and **Sand Martins, Common Swift** and **Lesser Kestrel**. Also scan carefully for the scarce migrants, **Montagu's** and **Pallid* Harriers**, which also quarter this area. More common raptors of the area include **Cape Vulture*** (feeding birds from the Mannyelanong colony), **White-backed** and **Lappet-faced Vultures, Tawny Eagle, Greater Kestrel** and **Lanner Falcon**. The wooded drainage lines running through the grassland at intervals supply typical acacia species.

Moving further north towards Pitsane, the grassland becomes more wooded, and, despite the fact that it is largely overgrazed, bird numbers increase. The sparse, short-grass acacia shrublands are the habitat of **Short-clawed Lark***. It is a common bird here, vocal year-round, and often perches conspicuously on fences or bushes. A short walk in appropriate habitat will usually turn up several individuals. In particular, try 14 to 16 km north of Ramatlabama. Do take note that the similar **Rufous-naped Lark** also occurs here – usually, but not exclusively, in areas of taller grass.

Other species occurring in the acacia scrub are **Sabota** and **Fawn-coloured Larks, Barred Wren-Warbler, Bokmakierie** and **Scaly-feathered Finch**. In summer, listen carefully for the characteristic, harsh song of **Olive-tree Warbler***, which sometimes occurs in denser thickets throughout this area.

GETTING THERE

Access is along public, tarred roads. Fuel and basic supplies are available in Ramatlabama; the nearest accommodation is in Lobatse, 50 km to the north.

222 Mannyelanong Hill (Otse) IBA ✔

Mannyelanong Hill is one of just two of Botswana's breeding sites of the globally threatened **Cape Vulture***, and is protected by the Mannyelanong Game Reserve, close to the village of Otse. About 50 pairs now breed on the southern sandstone cliffs of the hill, which is distantly visible from the main A1 road from Gaborone to Lobatse. However, it can be approached more closely: turn off at the Otse sign, 21 km north of Lobatse (or 50 km south of Gaborone). Drive towards the village, taking the leftmost branch of the staggered three-way intersection, 1.2 km past the railway line. At the T-junction 500 m further on, turn right and continue for 300 m until you reach the Department of Wildlife and National Parks building, where you are asked to sign in. From here, it is a further 2.1 km along a track to the gate of Mannyelanong Game Reserve. To avoid disturbing the vultures, you should leave your car here and walk the last hundred metres into the reserve, towards an inner fence at the base of the cliff. The vultures will be very obvious on the cliffs above all year round. Cape Vulture* is a highly sensitive species, so please take great care not to disturb it, and on no account try to approach closer than the inner fence.

Other breeding species here are **Black Stork**, **Verreaux's Eagle**, **Rock Kestrel** and **Lanner Falcon**. There is also pleasant birding, similar to that at Kgale Hill, in the tall, moist woodland around the gate.

223 Kgale & Modipe Hills ✔

Kgale and Modipe are wooded hills close to Gaborone, and they provide easy access to a high diversity of species localised in the Gaborone area, but relatively widespread in the broader southern African context. These include thicket and moist woodland species such as **White-throated Robin-Chat**, **Grey Tit-Flycatcher**, **Bar-throated Apalis**, **Violet-backed Starling** and, in summer, **Garden Warbler**.

To reach Kgale Hill Ⓐ from central Gaborone, follow the A1 south towards Lobatse, until you reach the stile and small parking area on the right-hand side of the road, 2 km south of the Lobatse roundabout. Two paths lead to the hill summit from this point; both provide good birding. Car break-ins have been recorded at this spot, so park your car as conspicuously as possible and do not leave valuables inside. Modipe Hill Ⓑ is perhaps a safer place to walk, but further from town. To reach it, drive through Modipane and look out for a track leading to the base of the hill, on the right-hand side of the road 2.5 km from the water tower on the outskirts of the village.

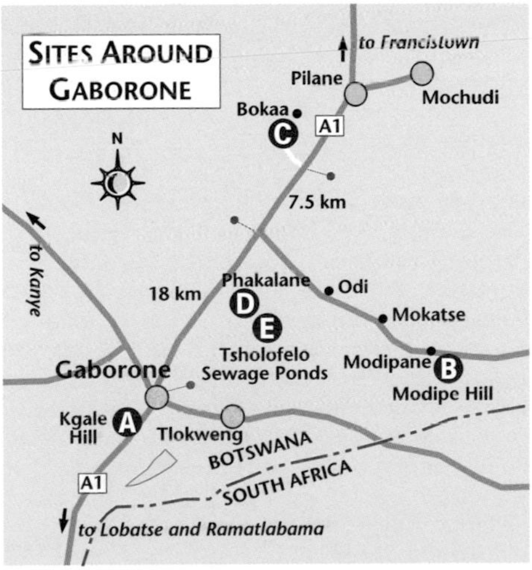

Typical species of the rocky slopes are **Natal Spurfowl**, **Mocking Cliff-Chat**, **Short-toed Rock-Thrush**, **Striped Pipit**, **Lazy Cisticola** and **Cinnamon-breasted Bunting**. Overhead raptors often include **Verreaux's Eagle** (which breeds here), as well as **African Hawk-Eagle**, **Booted Eagle** and **Lanner Falcon**.

Nigel J. Dennis/IOA

Natal Spurfowl

224 Bokaa Dam

IBA ✔

Bokaa Dam Ⓒ (map on previous page) can be a good spot for water birds, although this depends to a large extent on the local rainfall and dam water levels. The surrounding acacia thicket is an excellent site for the scarce migrant **Olive-tree Warbler***, with **Short-clawed Lark*** in the scrubby fields nearby. To reach the dam from central Gaborone, take the A1 towards Francistown, and turn left at the 'Bokaa Dam' signpost, 7.5 km past the Odi turn-off (the latter is 18 km from Gaborone). Follow this gravel road for 3.5 km, carefully scanning the fallow fields with low acacia bushes for Short-clawed Lark*, until you reach a gate and some buildings. Before the gate, bear left and follow the fence for 1 km, until you reach a gap in the fence with a 'Private Property' (although birders are permitted here) sign alongside. Drive through the gap and follow the meandering track to the water's edge (taking either branch where it forks). Care should be taken along the last stretch, as heavy rains sometimes damage the road.

Concentrate your efforts along the southern shore of the dam, as a village on the northern shore impacts on birdlife here; however, when water levels are high, the area around the inflow is better, as the water is shallower here and a heronry is also present. Small numbers of **Pink-backed Pelican** and **Greater Flamingo** sometimes occur, and **Black-winged Pratincole** and **Yellow Wagtail** may be found on the drying lake shores in summer. **Great Crested Grebe** and **Southern Pochard** are sometimes numerous. **Western Marsh-Harrier** has been recorded above the moist grasslands and reedbeds at the upper reaches of the dam.

The acacia thicket along the southern shoreline is very good for migrant warblers in summer. Listen for the rich warble of the **Olive-tree Warbler*** from deep within the acacia thickets, and the telephone-like trill of the **Barred Wren-Warbler** in the more open woodland.

225 Phakalane Sewage Ponds

IBA R ✔

There are a number of artificial wetlands close to Gaborone, all of which hold important waterbird populations. Of these, Phakalane Ⓓ (map on previous page), just 12 km north of Gaborone, is the best known and most easily accessed by birders. It consists of a series of four large sewage ponds, fringed by rock, mud and reeds and surrounded by acacia thornveld. The Tsholofelo Sewage Ponds Ⓔ, 3 km away, provide similar species and are also worth a look.

To reach Phakalane from central Gaborone, take the A1 to Francistown, turning off to the right (signposted 'Phakalane'), 7 km north of the airport roundabout. Continue beyond the railway crossing, and turn right at the roundabout. The road passes a Spar supermarket and turns to gravel. After 200 m of gravel, turn right into the bush along a track that leads to the entrance gates. Park here and explore the pans on foot. Watch out for thieves – do not explore alone and leave no valuables in your vehicle. In summer, you will be plagued by aggressive ants, so take insect repellant or wear boots and socks. Tsholofelo is reached via the 'crematorium' road from Broadhurst suburb.

These spots are best known for the localised **Maccoa Duck**; other waterfowl regularly seen include **Black-necked Grebe**, **Fulvous Duck**, **Cape**, **Red-billed and Hottentot Teal**, **Southern Pochard**, **Black Crake**, **African Purple Swamphen**, occasionally **Greater** and **Lesser Flamingo** and, where there is surface vegetation, **White-backed Duck**. Check the tree-studded lagoon for **African Black Duck**. The pan edges are good for Palearctic migrant waders, most commonly **Wood**, **Common**, and **Marsh Sandpipers**, **Ruff**, **Common Greenshank** and **Little Stint**. Rarities here include **Spotted Crake**, **Black-tailed Godwit**, **Lesser Moorhen** and **Basra Reed-Warbler**. Warblers are plentiful in the stands of *Typha* reeds, and include **Lesser Swamp-Warbler**, the Palearctic migrant **Sedge Warbler**, **African**, **Great**, and surprisingly large numbers of **Eurasian Reed-Warblers**, and **Little Rush Warbler**. The thornveld around the ponds holds typical woodland species such as **Jacobin** and **Black Cuckoo**, **Striped** and **Woodland Kingfishers**, **Marico Flycatcher**, **Swallow-tailed** and **Little Bee-eaters**, **Sabota Lark** and **Southern White-crowned Shrike**.

226 Khama Rhino Sanctuary ✔

This community-run reserve is just north of Serowe on the Orapa road and an easy 65 km drive from the main Gaborone-Francistown highway at Palapye. Offering excellent camp-site and chalet accommodation, it makes an ideal stop-over en route north, and is also the best place in Botswana to obtain good sightings of **Burchell's Sandgrouse*** – look especially at the hide at one of the 'Small Pans' south-west of the camp, where the birds drink in the early mornings. There is a good mix of other Kalahari birds on the grass-covered Serowe Pan and surrounding woodlands, and a healthy population of reintroduced White Rhinoceros.

227 Francistown Region ✔✔

Francistown, surrounded by mixed woodlands, is the second largest town in Botswana, and is best known to birders because it provides easy access to the intriguing and localised **Boulder Chat***. This bird of rocky hillsides under cover of broad-leaved woodland is found only at a scattering of sites in Botswana, Zimbabwe and Malawi.

The Nata and Plumtree (towards the Zimbabwe border) roads, respectively north-west and north-east of Francistown, are lined with low, wooded koppies, most of which support this species. On the Nata road, the pair of koppies situated on either side of the road, 62 km from Francistown, are good for this chat. Along the A1 to Zimbabwe, try the koppie 31.5 km from Francistown, opposite the intersection of the A1 and the minor road to Mabudzane. The birds are easily located by their unusual 'squeaky-bicycle' call, and are usually seen running and ducking about the boulders in pairs. **Mocking Cliff-Chat** also occurs here.

If in Francistown, you might also consider taking a short walk around the gardens and camp site of the Marang Hotel, where a strip of riparian trees provides good birding, including singing **Thrush Nightingale*** and **Garden Warbler** in the thickets in summer; **River Warbler*** has also been recorded here. Other species include **Little Sparrowhawk**, **Woodland Kingfisher**, **Grey-headed Bush Shrike** and **Tropical Boubou**. Shashe Dam, just south-west of Francistown, provides a good variety of water birds, including both **White** and **Pink-backed Pelicans**, and breeding **White-fronted Plover** and **Collared Pratincole**. Take the signposted turn-off to the west about 24 km south-west of Francistown on the A1; just before the fenced works area, turn right onto a small track towards the yacht club, and follow it along the indented shoreline to the dam's inflow at its northern end, where birding is best.

Callan Cohen

Boulder Chat is found at this koppie, 62 km north of Francistown.

ROUTE 23

CENTRAL KALAHARI

TOP 10 BIRDS

- Pallid Harrier
- Kalahari Scrub-Robin
- Barred Wren-Warbler
- Caspian Plover
- Crimson-breasted Shrike
- Chestnut-backed Sparrowlark
- Burchell's Sandgrouse
- Pink-billed Lark
- Great Sparrow
- Yellow-throated Sandgrouse

The Kalahari is the largest unbroken stretch of sand in the world, filling a vast basin extending from the Orange River to the Congolese rainforests with a layer of sand up to 200 m in depth. The central Kalahari Desert is not a true desert, but rather an arid savanna punctuated by fossil valleys and lakes. Most spectacular among the latter are the vast Makgadikgadi Pans, which, together with the Okavango Delta, formed part of the greatest lake in Africa twenty thousand years ago. Today, the Makgadikgadi is periodically flooded by outflow from the Okavango Delta from the west, via the Thamalakane and Boteti rivers, and by the Nata River from the north. The Kalahari and Makgadikgadi form a tremendously beautiful and thinly populated region, heavily exploited for diamonds and soda ash in certain areas and by widespread cattle grazing in others; however, vast tracts remain largely pristine and still host abundant populations of big game.

This region forms the centre of a number of southern African endemic and near-endemic species' distribution, and most are fairly common where they occur. Some are reasonably common, such as Eastern Clapper Lark, Kalahari Scrub-Robin, Barred Wren-Warbler, Marico Flycatcher and Crimson-breasted Shrike, whereas others, such as Orange River Francolin, Burchell's Sandgrouse* and Pink-billed Lark, usually require a little dedicated effort. The Kalahari is also an important wintering area for Palearctic migrants, and some of the more sought-after species include Pallid Harrier*, Red-footed Falcon, Caspian Plover and Olive-tree Warbler*, although the latter is more common in acacia thickets of eastern Botswana.

A number of other, lesser-known sites in wonderful wilderness areas also provide excellent birding, including an extraordinary diversity and abundance of raptors.

The area is most easily tackled from the north, using the Francistown-Nata-Maun tar road as an axis. It is now also possible to cross the entire basin on the Trans-Kalahari highway, which crosses central Botswana to link Johannesburg, Gaborone and Windhoek. Birders heading north to the Chobe area from South Africa have easy access to great Kalahari birding en route to the Nata area, with access to the Makgadikgadi Pans through the Nata Sanctuary. Nxai Pan National Park and the Central Kalahari Game Reserve are more suited to self-sufficient visitors with capable vehicles (4WD is strongly advised) and some experience of driving on sand and mud (great care should be taken when crossing pan areas during the rains).

Callan Cohen

Northern Black Korhaan

228 Central Kalahari GR

4X4 IBA ✔✔

The Central Kalahari Game Reserve (CKGR) is one the great wilderness areas of southern Africa, protecting a tract of Kalahari sandveld substantially larger than Switzerland. Although established primarily for the benefit of permitting the Bushman (San) people, who live mostly in the southern half of the park, to pursue their traditional lifestyle, it is now steeped in a controversy relating to government plans to resettle them. Only opened to the public fairly recently, the reserve has received little attention from birders. Although it boasts no exclusive specials, general birding is excellent and the experience of spending a few days alone among the abundant game of its pan country and great fossil valleys is highly recommended. Deception Valley lies in the most scenic and easily accessible north-eastern section of the park. The valley, its surrounds, and other similar habitats within the park, including the adjacent Khutse Game Reserve, all offer similar birding opportunities.

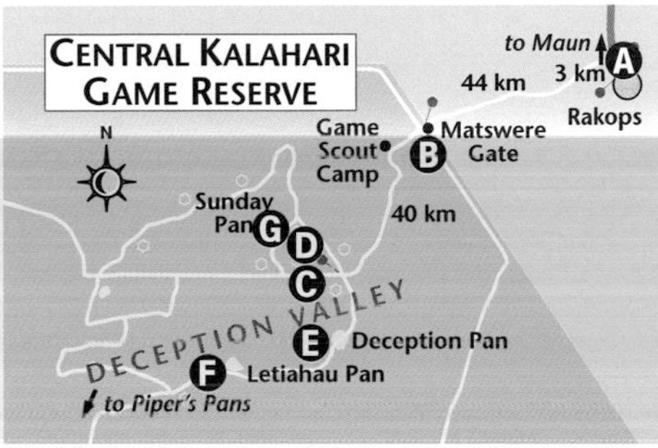

SEASON: It is well worth visiting at any time of year, although game is more plentiful in summer when numerous migrant birds are also present. However, road conditions are undeniably easier in the dry season.

SPECIALS: Pallid Harrier*, Caspian Plover, Pink-billed Lark, and Rufous-eared Warbler.

HABITATS: Kalahari savanna, scrub, grassy pans and fossil valleys, and acacia thicket and woodland. There are some artificial waterholes, which are periodically dry.

BIRDING: The turn-off to the park is approximately 3 km north of Rakops Ⓐ. As you take the turn-off, the road almost immediately crosses an open pan (grassy after rain), where **Pink-billed Lark** can be abundant. Shortly thereafter, the road crosses the Gidikwe Sand Ridge, where you will soon discover whether your vehicle is capable of making it through to the park. The park gate at Matswere Ⓑ, on the infamous Veterinary Cordon Fence, is 44 km from the Rakops turn-off, and the latter part of the drive is through wooded grassland. These more wooded areas support species that are not typical of the Deception Valley area, such as **African Grey Hornbill, Common Scimitarbill, Southern White-crowned Shrike** and **Shaft-tailed Whydah**. You also may flush **Harlequin Quail** in wet years.

From the park gate, it is another 40 km to Deception Valley Ⓒ. Deception is a broad, flat, fossil valley, grassy after rain and usually teeming with game. The valley and the park as a whole can be excellent for raptors, and a few days in summer can produce in excess of 20 species. The most common are **White-backed Vulture, Tawny Eagle, Pale Chanting Goshawk, Gabar**

Callan Cohen

Springbok in the Central Kalahari Game Reserve

GETTING THERE

Access by 4WD only is recommended. However, with careful driving and selective deflation of tyres, it is possible to reach the vicinity of Deception Valley with a high-clearance 2WD. Visitors need to be completely self-sufficient and should ensure that their vehicles – preferable more than one – are in good running order. The closest access to fuel, water and supplies is in Rakops. Rakops is 135 km south of the tar road between Nata and Maun, and the turn-off is 226 km west of Nata.

Double-banded Courser

Goshawk and **Shikra** (the latter two near acacia stands), **Black-shouldered Kite**, **Lanner Falcon** and **Greater Kestrel**, with smaller numbers of **Lappet-faced** and **White-headed Vultures**, **Martial Eagle** and **Bateleur**. In summer, these are supplemented by **Pallid*** and especially **Montagu's Harriers** (these can be remarkably common in wet years), **Lesser Kestrel**, **Red-footed Falcon** and **Eurasian Hobby**.

A series of camp sites (no facilities) called Kori Camp **D** is set among acacia trees along the western flank of Deception Valley, and these are good places for **Red-necked Falcon** and thornveld species such as **Striped Kingfisher**, **Acacia Pied Barbet**, **Southern Pied Babbler**, **Kalahari Scrub-Robin**, **Chestnut-vented Tit-Babbler**, **Barred Wren-Warbler**, **Marico Flycatcher**, **Pririt Batis**, **Ashy Tit**, **Crimson-breasted Shrike**, **Brubru**, **Violet-eared** and **Black-faced Waxbills** and **Red-headed Finch**, together with numerous Palearctic migrant shrikes, warblers and flycatchers. Similar species occur in acacia stands elsewhere in the park (such as around Letiahau). While camping here, night sounds will probably include **Southern White-faced** and **African Scops-Owls**, and **Pearl-spotted Owlet**, as well as Lion, Black-backed Jackal and the evocative Common Barking Gecko. **Marsh Owl** can be common in the fossil valleys. Note that Kori Camp is unfenced, and Lion are a concern; take appropriate precautions, such as sleeping inside tents or vehicles, and do not wander around after dark (see p.10).

From Deception, head south-west towards Piper's Pans, through Deception **E** and Letiahau Pans **F**. In summer, the pans may attract large numbers of **Caspian Plover**, usually distributed in loose groups of up to 30 birds. These are remarkably cryptic when immobile, so scan carefully and look out for flying birds. **Temminck's** and **Double-banded Coursers** are usually the easiest to spot. Areas of bare ground or short grass on the pan surface usually provide **Spike-heeled**, **Pink-billed** and **Red-capped Larks**, **Grey-backed** and **Chestnut-backed Sparrowlarks**, and **Capped Wheatear**, and the scrubby areas on the calcrete at the pan edges hold **Rufous-eared Warbler**. Longer grass provides **Kori Bustard**, **Eastern Clapper Lark** and **Desert Cisticola**. Sunday Pan **G** once even produced a lone and short-lived male **Buff-spotted Flufftail**!

The landscape becomes more wooded south of Letiahau Pan, and again north and north-west of Deception, towards Leopard Pan and the Passarge Valley. Species in slightly denser areas include **Fawn-coloured Lark**, **Burchell's Starling** and (scarce) **Bronze-winged Courser**.

OTHER ANIMALS: After rain, this can be one of the prime game-viewing areas in southern Africa. Large numbers of Gemsbok, Springbok and Blue Wildebeest move into the area, followed by Lion, Cheetah, Black-backed Jackal and Brown Hyaena. Springhare are abundant at night.

NEARBY SITES: The Khutse Game Reserve, along the CKGR's southern border, is just 3 hours' drive from Gaborone on a good tar road to Letlakeng via Molepolole, and then on a reasonable dirt road from Letlakeng to the reserve gate. Khutse's mixed Kalahari woodland and series of excellent pans hold much the same species as the CKGR's Deception region. Nxai Pan National Park and Makgadikgadi Pans National Park also offer excellent Kalahari birding, scenery and game-viewing, but are less accessible without a 4WD.

229 Nata Sanctuary

IBA ✔✔

The Nata Sanctuary, at the northern edge of Sowa (Sua) Pan, provides easy access to the edge of the Makgadikgadi Pans, which are otherwise accessible only to 4WD expeditions. Furthermore, this community-run sanctuary protects the Nata Delta, which, when holding water, can host huge concentrations of water birds. Birding in the surrounding grasslands is also always worthwhile for a good selection of Kalahari species.

SEASON: The Nata Delta is at its best in midsummer (about Oct-Feb) in a wet year; however, during some years it remains wholly dry, and in others it can remain flooded until early in the dry season. Summer is also preferable for grassland birding, although many of the specials are resident and may be seen year-round.

SPECIALS: Red-necked Falcon, Chestnut-banded Plover, Yellow-throated Sandgrouse, Grey Crowned Crane, Southern Pied Babbler, and water-bird and raptor diversity.

HABITATS: Grasslands, salt pans, seasonal marshes, mixed woodland.

BIRDING: Although birding at Nata Sanctuary is focused mostly on the delta area, there are a number of interesting species in the grasslands to look out for along the 20 km drive from the gate (B) to the delta (C). **Northern Black Korhaan**, **Eastern Clapper Lark** and **Desert Cisticola** display above the grass, **Double-banded Courser**, and **Kori Bustard** and **Secretarybird** occur in short and longer grass areas respectively. **Montagu's** and, more scarcely, **Pallid* Harriers** quarter here in summer. Other summer raptors are **Wahlberg's** and **Steppe Eagles**, and **Lesser Spotted Eagle** (in decreasing order of abundance), and **Red-footed Falcon** and **Lesser Kestrel**, whereas residents include **Bateleur**, **Martial Eagle**, **White-backed**, **Lappet-faced** and **White-headed Vultures** and **Red-necked Falcon**. **Black-winged Pratincole** also occasionally feeds overhead. In wetter years, you may flush a **Harlequin Quail** while driving.

Also keep an eye out for small groups of **Yellow-throated Sandgrouse** – usually flushed – which is one of the sanctuary's specials, but is not seen by many visitors. This scarce species favours the dense black-cotton soil that fringes the pan. **Burchell's Sandgrouse***, a Kalahari sand specialist, also occurs irregularly, but in some years may descend in large numbers to drink at freshwater pans, such as those en route the hide. **Orange River Francolin** can sometimes be heard calling in the grasslands at dawn, but usually takes some effort to see. Mopane species such as **Meves's Starling** occur in the woodland around the camp site and entrance gate.

To reach the Nata Delta (C), turn right just beyond the entrance gate. (The roads are largely signposted and there is a map at the entrance.) This road joins the Nata River 14 km further on, and more or less follows

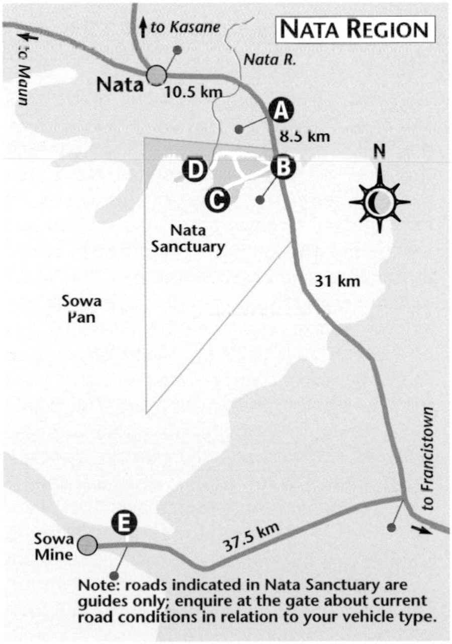

Note: roads indicated in Nata Sanctuary are guides only; enquire at the gate about current road conditions in relation to your vehicle type.

GETTING THERE

The entrance to the sanctuary is 19 km south of Nata, on the Francistown road. Although most of the sanctuary is accessible to 2WD vehicles, please take great care when driving on the roads closer to the pan edge, such as in the vicinity of the delta. The mud can be treacherous, even while the surface may look deceptively firm. If unsure, rather get out and walk. There is a camp site near the gate, and it is also possible to camp or hire a bungalow at Nata Lodge (A), 8.5 km up the road towards Nata.

the river bank as far as the delta. The river does not flow every year, and birding conditions at the delta are hence extremely variable. When the river does come down, it usually holds water around Oct-Feb; however, this is not reliable, as water and good numbers of birds can sometimes persist until May, and in some years it remains bone-dry throughout the wet season.

Scattered waders and other water birds occur along the river banks **D**, and in summer there are also good numbers of **Blue-cheeked** and **Southern Carmine** (late summer) **Bee-eaters** and sometimes **Olive-tree Warbler*** in the thickets. Also scan the larger riverside trees for **Verreaux's Eagle-Owl**. Spectacular numbers of **Red-billed Quelea** can occur in this area. The best birding is at the delta proper; when conditions are right, water birds here number in their thousands, and **Greater** and **Lesser Flamingos** even in their tens of thousands at times. Other seasonally abundant species include **Great White Pelican** (there is a breeding colony at the mouth of the Nata River when there is water in the pan), **Red-billed** and **Hottentot Teal**, **White-winged Tern** and **Chestnut-banded Plover**. Other salt-pan specialists include **Cape Teal** and **Black-necked Grebe**.

Waders such as **Pied Avocet** and **Black-winged Stilt** may be supplemented in summer by huge numbers of Palearctic migrants, predominantly **Little Stint**, **Curlew Sandpiper**, **Ruff** and **Common Greenshank**, but also, sometimes, Botswana rarities such as **Grey Plover**, **Sanderling**, **Eurasian Curlew**, **Black-tailed Godwit** and **Lesser Black-backed Gull**. Other notable water birds are **African Openbill**, and **Saddle-billed**, **Yellow-billed** and **Marabou Storks**, **Goliath** and **Black Herons**, **Cape Shoveler** and, on occasion, **Grey Crowned Crane**, which has bred here. **Caspian** and **Whiskered Terns** and **Grey-headed Gull** sometimes occur in large numbers, and **Western Marsh-Harrier** also occasionally visits in wet years. When the pan is completely dry, **Kittlitz's**, **White-fronted** and **Chestnut-banded Plovers** usually still occur around the edges.

Consider visiting the observation platform at the pan edge (reached along a straight road heading directly south from the gate) to view the pan and, if there is water, scan for the vast flocks of flamingos that often visit the area.

Birding in the grounds of and mixed woodland adjacent to Nata Lodge **A** can also be productive for thornveld and mopane species. Groups of sometimes tame **Red-billed Spurfowl**, **Meyer's Parrot** and **Southern Pied Babbler** are usually present in the lodge grounds. In summer, the thickets around the lodge are good for Palearctic migrants such as **Garden** and **Icterine Warblers** and, occasionally, **Thrush Nightingale***. Carefully scan the palm trees for quietly perching **Red-necked Falcon**, which is resident here.

NEARBY SITES: Sowa Pan **E** is usually reached by birders from Nata Sanctuary. However, if there has been rain and the pan holds water, it is well worth taking the short drive towards the soda-ash mining factory at Sowa (see map), where the view of hundreds of thousands of **Greater** and **Lesser Flamingos** can be breathtaking. Although not as scenic as the untouched parts of the pan, this site is at least very easily and rapidly accessed in any kind of vehicle. The turn-off to Sowa (sometimes spelt Sua) is 39 km south of Nata on the Francistown road. Follow this tarred road for 37.5 km, then turn right (north), opposite a waterhole, to 'Point Tango' and an artificial saltworks. This gravel road reaches a locked boom after 3.9 km, from where you should have a good view northwards over Sowa Pan. Better still, continue on the tar road through the town, until a veterinary fence is reached, just before the airfield. Do not pass through the fence, but turn left and drive along it until you reach the pan.

Callan Cohen

The observation platform in Nata Sanctuary

230 Kalahari Roadside Birding ✔

An inevitable component of independent travel in Botswana is *a lot of road.* Distances are substantial and towns few and far between. However, this results in good roadside birding, notably an often remarkably high density of raptors. This is particularly true for the Nata-Maun drive, and, to a slightly lesser extent, Francistown-Nata and the Trans-Kalahari Highway between Gaborone, Ghanzi and Maun. Typical resident species such as **Tawny** and **Martial Eagles**, and **Black-chested Snake-Eagle** are supplemented in summer by **Steppe, Lesser Spotted** and **Wahlberg's Eagles, Red-footed Falcon, Eurasian Hobby**, and **Lesser Kestrel**. Also look out for **Dickinson's Kestrel** and **Red-necked Falcon** between Nata and Maun, especially in the vicinity of palm trees, and in the more heavily wooded sections of the Trans-Kalahari.

The most common vulture is always **White-backed**, but **Lappet-faced** and **White-headed Vultures** can, fortunately, still be widely seen in Botswana, even outside the large reserves. At Tholo Park, a mine-owned reserve near Jwaneng, a camp site is maintained around a large **White-backed Vulture** colony. Donkeys, when not posing a serious road hazard, provide platforms for **Red-billed Oxpeckers**.

Nigel J. Dennis

Lappet-faced Vulture

Conspicuous roadside species are **Kori Bustard, Northern Black** and **Red-crested Korhaans, Secretarybird**, and sometimes remarkable numbers of **European** and **Lilac-breasted Rollers**.

231 Mabuasehube GR

IBA ✔

This reserve, which now forms the eastern section of the vast Kgalagadi Transfrontier Park, is relatively little-known among birders, yet provides good Kalahari birding in a beautiful wilderness setting. It is reached via the town of Tshabong, situated near the South African border, and the section of the park that is situated in Botswana is also directly accessible from here. A 4WD vehicle is essential, as there are areas of deep sand. The park consists primarily of Kalahari woodland and scrub, together with an abundance of very attractive pans. In wet years, these fill and rapidly attract surprisingly good numbers of water birds and waders. The woodland provides classic Kalahari species, including **Monotonous Lark** after rain, and relatively numerous **Red-necked Falcon**. In addition to the typical antelope, there are also good numbers of Lion in the park, as well as Cheetah and Brown Hyaena.

ROUTE **24**

OKAVANGO DELTA

The improbable green fan of the Okavango Delta results from a series of geological faults in a vast expanse of exceptionally flat country. This perturbation diverted the course of the Zambezi and Okavango rivers about two million years ago, creating a permanent and verdant swamp buried in the middle of dry Kalahari sandveld. The Delta is one of southern Africa's most famous wildlife-viewing and ecotourism regions, particularly for the more exclusive fly-in safari market. However, overland travellers can also experience the swamps via the Moremi Game Reserve or the Delta's north-western Panhandle region; it is even possible to access the latter without a 4WD vehicle (see p.238).

TOP 10 BIRDS

- Pel's Fishing-Owl
- Slaty Egret
- Chirping Cisticola
- Coppery-tailed Coucal
- White-backed Night-Heron
- Hartlaub's Babbler
- Western Banded Snake Eagle
- Long-toed Lapwing
- Brown Firefinch
- Lesser Jacana

The Delta and associated areas form the southernmost extreme of the range of more typically south-central African swamp species, which have become known as 'Okavango specials' in the southern African context, and many further exciting tropical flood-plain and woodland birds are easily seen here, such as Pel's Fishing-Owl*, Slaty Egret*, Coppery-tailed Coucal and Chirping Cisticola. Many of these species occur seasonally in the immediate vicinity of Maun, situated at the Delta's southern extremity. Although Maun is a convenient venue in that you can see many Okavango specials in this area without venturing further north, it would be a pity to miss the memorable wilderness experience of Moremi and the Delta's interior.

Callan Cohen

View from a boat in the backwaters of the Okavango Delta

232 Maun

IBA ✔✔

Maun is a sprawling, bustling town situated on the Thamalakane River at the southern extremity of the Okavango Delta. It is the springboard for most trips north into the Delta and into associated areas. In addition to good thornveld and riparian woodland birding, there are several good sites around the town that are accessible in any vehicle and which, when wet, provide a very good sample of the Okavango waterbird specials.

SEASON: Birding in the vicinity of Maun is highly seasonal. Although riparian woodland species can be seen at any time of year, waterbirding is excellent only when the Thamalakane comes down in flood (not every year, and usually between mid Jul and about Mar) – at other times it can be a dustbowl, although after good floods water remains in pools throughout the year.

GETTING THERE

There are many roads to Maun; it can be reached from the east on an excellent tar road that links it with Kasane and Nata or from the Trans-Kalahari highway (and hence Windhoek and Kanye) on a short-cut road skirting Lake Ngami (see overleaf). From the western Caprivi Strip, Maun can also be approached via the good tar road that runs through Sepupa and Gumare. Although it is possible to reach the Delta directly from the north-east via Chobe National Park, be sure that you have the time and equipment to negotiate the many hundreds of kilometres of sand roads that lie in between, especially during the wet season, and particularly when traversing the Mababe Depression.

Maun is a town of substantial size, with modern banking, transport, medical and shopping facilities. There are innumerable camps and accommodation possibilities around it, and all are accessible by 2WD vehicle. The Boteti River lies south of town, and can be reached via the Samedupi Bridge on the Nata road or via the Waste Disposal Site, near Xobe, south-west of town.

SPECIALS: Slaty Egret*, Rufous-bellied Heron, African Pygmy Goose*, Red-necked Falcon, Dickinson's Kestrel, Long-toed Lapwing, Bradfield's Hornbill, and Olive-tree Warbler*.

HABITATS: Riparian woodland, dry acacia savanna, wetlands with emergent vegetation.

BIRDING: While driving through Maun, keep an eye out for **Red-necked Falcon** around the numerous *Hyphaene* palm trees in town; other raptors, including **Dickinson's Kestrel**, **Bateleur**, **African Fish-Eagle**, the occasional **Ayres' Hawk-Eagle** and large numbers of assorted vultures constantly pass overhead. At dusk, watch for **Bat Hawk** along the Thamalakane River. **Southern Carmine Bee-eater** is common in town from Sept–Mar. Most visitors to Maun stay at one of the several safari camps along the Thamalakane, which all offer camping and hutted accommodation of a high standard. At the eastern end of the town, near the Boro River junction, lie Audi Camp Ⓐ, Crocodile Camp Ⓑ and Island Safari Lodge Ⓒ. Birding around the camps is much the same, and common and usually tame species around the camp sites include **Red-billed Spurfowl**, **African Mourning Dove**, **Terrestrial Brownbul**, **White-browed Robin-Chat**, **Hartlaub's** and **Arrow-marked Babblers**, **Grey-backed Camaroptera**, **Swamp Boubou** and **Spectacled** and **Golden Weavers**. **African Green Pigeon**, **Meyer's Parrot** and **African Golden Oriole** also occur in the larger trees.

Bradfield's Hornbill sometimes enters the camps (mainly in winter), although its movements are poorly known. **Senegal Coucal** is fairly common. At night, several owl species, including **African Scops-Owl**, **Barred** and **Pearl-spotted Owlets** and **Barn Owl**, are often heard simultaneously.

Wendy Dennis/IOA

African Pygmy Goose

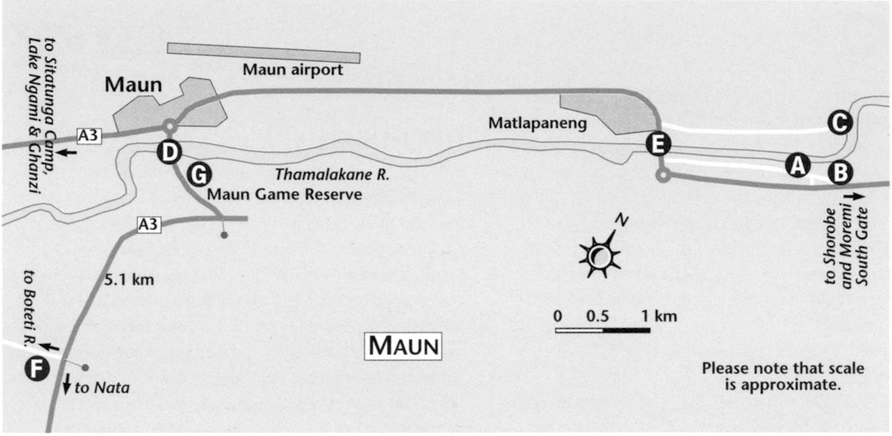

Red-billed Hornbill and **Meves's** and **Burchell's Starlings** are plentiful in the mopane woodland along the access road to Island Safari Lodge.

When the Thamalakane holds water, superb waterbirding is possible here too, and many Okavango specials are easily seen. Good places to access the river are from all of the camps mentioned above (especially Sitatunga Camp – see below), from the main bridge **D** on the Nata road or from the old Matlapaneng Bridge **E** beyond the Sedia Hotel.

West of Maun, on the Thamalakane River, lies Sitatunga Camp, set in attractive riparian woodland. Sitatunga also offers the advantage of year-round waterbirding and a water-bird roost at an adjacent crocodile farm (the pens are good for **Allen's Gallinule**, but beware of the crocodiles). **Retz's Helmetshrike** and **Yellow-breasted Apalis** occur at the camp itself.

The Waste Disposal site **F** en route the Boteti River, holds vast numbers of **Marabou Stork** and **White-backed Vulture**, and thornveld birding along the road is very productive. Flooded grassland at the Boteti River edges, such as here and at Sitatunga, is particularly rewarding, often supplying good numbers of **Rufous-bellied Heron**, **African** and **Black Crakes**, **Allen's Gallinule**, **Long-toed Lapwing**, **Coppery-tailed Coucal** and even the occasional **Slaty Egret***, **Striped Crake*** (quite common in wet years in flooded grasslands) or **Greater Painted Snipe**. Stretches of water with emergent vegetation are dotted with **White-backed Duck**, **African Pygmy Goose***, **Lesser Moorhen**, and **African** and (more scarcely) **Lesser Jacanas**. Aggregations of waterfowl may include **Southern Pochard**, **Hottentot** and **Red-billed Teals** and **Knob-billed Duck**.

Some good acacia thickets are situated adjacent to Island Safari Lodge (walk out the northern end of the camp), and in the Maun Game Reserve **G**. Typical species include **Swallow-tailed Bee-eater**, **Southern Pied Babbler**, **Kalahari Scrub-Robin**, **Chestnut-vented Tit-Babbler**, **Burnt-necked Eremomela**, **Marico Flycatcher**, **Marico Sunbird**, **Red-billed Firefinch** and **Black-faced Waxbill**. **Olive-tree Warbler*** can be locally common from Dec-Mar. Look particularly in the thornveld on the northern outskirts of the Island Safari Lodge, and along the road past the dump at **F** (especially 2-3 km along once you've left the tar road). The warbler usually sings concealed from the densest thickets, but is fairly easily located and seen once its call is heard. Up to 10 birds have been heard singing in an area of about 100 m diameter on the dump road. **Burchell's Sandgrouse*** may drink at the Thamalakane drifts here in the early morning.

OTHER ANIMALS: Red Lechwe venture very close to town, and can sometimes be seen grazing on the Thamalakane flood plain.

NEARBY SITES: Lake Ngami usually remains dry and often grass-covered, but when it periodically floods (as last happened in 1992 and 2005), thousands of water birds descend to breed. Lake Ngami is crossed by the sandy short-cut road from Sehitwa (101 km west of Maun on the Shakawe road) south to the Ghanzi road.

233 Okavango Delta & Moremi GR IBA ✔✔

As one of the most famous wildlife and wilderness areas in Africa, the Okavango Delta needs little introduction. In addition to a selection of key south-central African swamp birds, the Delta provides a superb diversity of raptors, water birds and riparian woodland species. However, these species are also accessible in the Delta's Panhandle and at many sites in Zambia and elsewhere.

SEASON: Traditionally, the best time to visit is May-Oct, when game-viewing is optimal, roads are in a good state, and daytime temperatures are pleasant. Most of the Okavango specials are resident, but birding is more diverse during the wet season and there are fewer tourists with whom to share the landscape.

SPECIALS: White-backed Night-Heron*, Slaty Egret*, Rufous-bellied Heron, Bat Hawk*, Western Banded Snake-Eagle, Wattled Crane*, Lesser Jacana, African Skimmer*, Coppery-tailed Coucal, Pel's Fishing-Owl*, Arnot's Chat, Chirping and Luapula Cisticolas, Greater Swamp-Warbler, and Brown Firefinch.

Callan Cohen

African Skimmers are among the superb range of birds to be found at the Delta.

HABITATS: Flood plain, permanent rivers and swamps, papyrus and *Typha* reedbeds, tall riparian woodland, open palm savanna, mopane woodland.

BIRDING: For most, the overriding memory of a visit to the Okavango Delta is that of being poled silently through clear, lily- and reed-lined waterways, watching big game and exciting tropical water birds as one glides by. Lily-covered pools and channels usually hold **African Pygmy Goose*, White-backed Duck** and the occasional **Lesser Jacana** among the abundant **African Jacana**, while **Blue-cheeked** and **Southern Carmine Bee-eaters** feed overhead. Reedbed edges are invariably adorned with **Malachite Kingfisher**, while **Pied** and **Giant Kingfishers** hunt over the open water, and **Chirping** (common) and **Luapula Cisticolas** call explosively from the reedbed interiors. **Greater Swamp-Warbler** especially favours papyrus beds and, though skulking, is easily lured with a playback of its loud and distinctive song. **Coppery-tailed Coucal** is common and most conspicuous at dawn, when it hauls itself above the reeds to bask, and at dusk, when it is often seen flying heavily to roost.

GETTING THERE

The Okavango Delta is peppered with camps of varying cost and degrees of accessibility. The largely luxurious camps of the central Delta are accessible only by boat or air (the latter usually by Cessna transfer from Maun). The best options for overland travellers are any of the camps situated in the Delta's north-western Panhandle region (see p.238), the lovely Makwena Camp in the Etsha 6 district, or camps in the Moremi Game Reserve (note that 4WD is essential within Moremi at all times of year).

Enter Moremi at South Gate, drive to Xakanaxa and take a boat or *mokoro* trip into the Delta from here. To reach Moremi's South Gate, take the 47 km tar road from Maun to Shorobe and continue for 20 km along a gravel road to the buffalo fence. Shortly after the latter, a sand road runs off to the north until you reach the gate. Moremi is also accessible from the north-west, and can be entered directly from Chobe National Park via North Gate on the Khwai River. The Khwai region has a particularly good diversity of habitats.

Note that park fees are applicable for camps that lie within the Moremi reserve.

Boats can be hired from Xakanaxa camp site. Most of the Delta's camps have 'resident' *mokoro* polers, who will take you into the Delta.

Conspicuous species of flooded grassland include **Woolly-necked, Marabou, Yellow-billed** and **Saddle-billed** (uncommon) **Storks, African Openbill, Squacco** and **Rufous-bellied Herons, Black Heron, Slaty Egret*, Fulvous** and **Knob-billed Ducks, Long-toed** and **Blacksmith Lapwings**, and the occasional pair of **Wattled Crane***. If lucky, you may encounter a seasonal aggregration of the latter, in which they may number in their hundreds. **African Skimmer*** may turn up anywhere in the Delta, but is most reliably seen in the Shakawe region of the Panhandle (see p.238).

To see the more elusive flood-plain specials, it is necessary to take a walk and carefully scan the wet grass at flood-plain edges in the early morning and evening, when many species emerge uninhibitedly into shorter grass areas to feed. These may include **African Crake, African Rail, Red-chested Flufftail, Lesser Moorhen, Allen's Gallinule, Ethiopian** and, less commonly, **Greater Painted Snipe** and **Rosy-breasted Longclaw***.

In summer, scan short-grass areas for **Collared Pratincole** and **Yellow Wagtail**, and long-grass areas for **Black Coucal**.

African Fish-Eagle is predictably numerous, but tall trees at the wetland edges should also be scanned for **Western Banded Snake-Eagle** (not uncommon, and also helpfully vocal), **Pel's Fishing-Owl***, and **White-backed Night-Heron*** roosting in the densest tangles. If taking a *mokoro* (dugout) safari, ask your polers about the latter two, as they may well know of daytime roosts; better still, find out whether they will take you on a night boat trip, which regularly result in sightings of these stunning species.

Most of the Delta's islands are rimmed with magnificent riparian Jackal-berry and Sycamore Fig trees, and birds characteristic of this habitat are usually tame and conspicuous around the camps, often remaining active throughout the day. Typical species include **African Green Pigeon, African Mourning Dove, Arrow-marked** and **Hartlaub's Babblers, Terrestrial Brownbul, Yellow-bellied Greenbul, White-browed Robin-Chat, Ashy Flycatcher, Swamp Boubou, Golden** and, occasionally, **Southern Brown-throated Weavers**, and flocks of other seed-eaters, including **Jameson's** and **Red-billed Firefinches** and the odd group of **Brown Firefinch**. Carefully scan larger trees for roosting **Verreaux's Eagle-Owl** and **Pel's Fishing-Owl***. In the evening, just as the mosquitos descend, a vigil across a swamp edge with tall trees may well reveal the rapid, silent passage of a **Bat Hawk*** emerging to hunt.

Walks through the beautiful ilala palm savanna of many of the Delta islands' interiors are likely to turn up **Red-necked Falcon, Dickinson's Kestrel** (scan the palm crowns), **African Palm Swift, Meyer's Parrot** and perhaps **Black-bellied Bustard** and **Grey-rumped Swallow** and occasionally **Banded Martin** feeding over barer areas. **Brown Firefinch** favours tangles of grass and bush at the woodland edges. Any trees are likely to turn up a diversity of woodland birds, including numerous species of cuckoo, kingfisher, woodpecker and barbet.

Large raptors are common throughout the Delta and adjacent woodlands and include, in addition to those already mentioned, **Hooded, White-headed** and **Lappet-faced Vultures, Bateleur, Martial** and **Tawny Eagles, African Hawk-Eagle, Brown Snake-Eagle** and **Dark Chanting Goshawk**; these are joined in summer by **Wahlberg's, Steppe** and **Lesser Spotted Eagles** (the latter relatively scarce, though occasionally abundant) and **Yellow-billed Kite**. At night, the frequently deafening chorus of frogs, crickets, Hippopotamus and, occasionally, Lion and Hyaena is accompanied by the calls of **Barred Owlet**, and even the impossibly deep call of **Pel's Fishing-Owl***.

At Moremi, particularly good flood-plain areas are accessible in the Khwai River, Xakanaxa and Mboma loop areas (signposted from Third Bridge); the latter two are especially good for **Swamp Nightjar***. There are particularly good water-bird roosts and heronries at the Xakanaxa and nearby Gadikwe lagoons, easily accessible by boat (these can be hired from Xakanaxa camp site).

If entering Moremi overland through South Gate, you will pass through extensive tracts of woodland in the 'mopane tongue' that extends into the eastern Delta from here to Xakanaxa and Third Bridge. **Arnot's Chat** is one of the most common birds of this habitat; other characteristic species include **Dark Chanting Goshawk, White Helmet-Shrike, Meves's Starling** and **Red-headed Weaver** and, in summer, the occasional **Dusky Lark*** in areas with bare ground. Listen for the resounding boom of **Southern Ground-Hornbill*** just before dawn.

There are good pan areas in the last 10 km from South Gate to Third Bridge, as well as along the Xakanaxa to North Gate road. Another good area to bird is at the Dombo Hippo pools, about mid-way along the latter road, where there is a hide at the adjacent swampy pools.

In the North Gate area, check the pan beyond Magwexhlana Pool (near Fourth Bridge) for **African Skimmer***; flocks regularly occur here after breeding. Exceptionally good raptor-watching is possible on the various loops along the Khwai River; this is also an ideal place to search for **Wattled Crane*** without taking to a boat.

OTHER ANIMALS: Moremi can be one of the best game-viewing areas on the continent, particularly during the dry season, although game-viewing is excellent year-round throughout the Delta. Elephant and Red Lechwe are abundant; other common species are Lion, African Buffalo, Impala and Giraffe and, less commonly, Cheetah and African Wild Dog. Sitatunga, Hippo and Crocodile lurk in the swamps, and you may be lucky enough to encounter one of these shy, marsh-dwelling antelopes on a night boat ride.

234 Chobe NP: Savuti Marsh IBA ✔✔

The southern part of the Chobe National Park has a landscape quite distinct from the verdant rivers of the Linyanti and Kasane regions. The Savuti Marsh is now a dry, sand-filled basin within the Mababe Depression, with a classic landscape of (drowned) dead trees scattered among game-filled grassy plains. There are numerous pans, some of which are maintained by pumps and can be excellent for **Collared** and **Black-winged Pratincoles**, and waders such as **White-fronted Plover**. Also look for drinking **Burchell's Sandgrouse***.

Savuti provides great game-viewing and many grassland species, including **Temminck's Courser, Kurrichane Buttonquail, Caspian Plover** (summer), **Chestnut-backed** and **Grey-backed Sparrowlarks** and **Grey-rumped Swallow**, and remarkably numerous **Kori Bustard**, often with **Southern Carmine Bee-eater** perched on their backs, poised to catch insects flushed by the striding bustard. In summer, **Montagu's** and **Pallid* Harriers** visit in moderately good numbers, as do **Amur** and **Red-footed Falcons**, and around bare ground, **Dusky Lark*** sometimes occurs.

Army worm eruptions occur in wet years and attract staggering numbers of various storks, including **White** and **Abdim's Storks. Olive-tree Warbler*** occurs in summer in acacia thickets around the margins of the Savuti Marsh. The whole area is superb for raptors, and together with Moremi, can rate among the best raptor sites in Africa. With luck you may encounter a summer termite emergence, when multi-species feeding aggregations of storks, bush birds and hundreds of assorted raptors descend.

Savuti Camp is one of the most pleasant in this region; **Bradfield's Hornbill** may occur in the camp, as well as around the Mababe Depression. Be sure to secure your possessions at night, as Spotted Hyaena are particularly common and persistent here. Beware too of the infamously treacherous black-cotton soil of the Mababe Depression when driving from Maun to Savuti after rain; compensation for any mishap may be had in the form of **Yellow-throated Sandgrouse**, a specialist of this soil type that may be flushed by your vehicle. For birding in the northern part of Chobe, see p.241.

Callan Cohen

White-fronted Bee-eater

ZIMBABWE

Zimbabwe lies at a crossroads of birding in southern Africa, with an interesting mix of northern tropical and southern temperate elements. It supports a diverse bird community, with over 650 species recorded, and offers the birder one of the best opportunities to see one of the continent's most sought-after species – African Pitta.

While the country has no true endemics, Roberts' Warbler, Chirinda Apalis and Swynnerton's Robin of the Eastern Highlands forests are all unlikely to be seen elsewhere. For many, Zimbabwe is epitomised by the spectacular granite landscapes cloaked in miombo woodland and occupied by the scarce and near-endemic Boulder Chat. This species, of mysterious taxonomic affinities, is endemic to the granite koppie country of south-central Africa. Miombo woodland, often dominated by *Brachystegia* trees (see box on p.267), and which also occurs in Zambia, Malawi, Angola and Mozambique, is home to many endemic bird species such as Miombo Rock-Thrush and Southern Hyliota. Furthermore, the flooded grasslands of the central plateau are the most reliable place in southern Africa to see migratory rallids and flood plain species, including Streaky-breasted Flufftail, Striped Crake and Rosy-breasted Longclaw.

African Pitta

Zimbabwe is endowed with a wealth of wild scenic landscapes that range from the world-famous Victoria Falls, to Mana Pools National Park in the Middle Zambezi Valley and the Eastern Highlands.

Ongoing political change in Zimbabwe is not without its logistical considerations for the visiting birder. Note that fuel may be in short supply, and many of the access details could change.

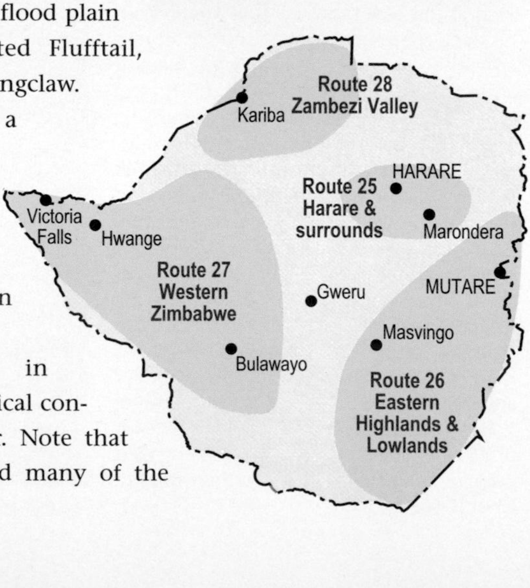

ROUTE 25

HARARE & SURROUNDS

Zimbabwe's capital city is well known among the international birding fraternity as a hotspot for wet grassland specials, such as the summer migrant Streaky-breasted Flufftail and Striped Crake*. In addition, birders have easy access to a number of miombo specialists (see box p.267) including Spotted Creeper*, Whyte's Barbet, Cinnamon-breasted Tit and Miombo Rock-Thrush, and to several species that are confined to granite inselberg country, such as Boulder Chat*.

TOP 10 BIRDS

- Striped Crake
- Streaky-breasted Flufftail
- Whyte's Barbet
- Cinnamon-breasted Tit
- Spotted Creeper
- Miombo Rock-Thrush
- Boulder Chat
- Black Coucal
- Cuckoo Finch
- Locustfinch

Situated in the north-eastern Mashonaland Province and on the central watershed at approximately 1 500 m above sea level, Harare is surrounded by natural drainage lines, along which extensive grasslands and miombo woodlands are found.

Harare provides a convenient base for vlei birding, which is best a few weeks after the first rains have reached the Mashonaland Plateau (usually late Dec-Feb).

Most of the miombo specials are resident and can be seen year-round. Suburban greenbelts, the National Botanic Gardens, Haka Park and Cleveland Dam, Mukuvisi Wood-lands and Marlborough and Monavale vleis all provide excellent birding within the city limits.

All of the surrounding sites are easily reached from the city, although a commute to Gosho Park in Marondera for an early morning birding session will require an early start. Dedicated birders with little time can combine morning and afternoon woodland walks in the Mukuvisi Woodlands, Haka Park, along the shores of Lake Chivero, or in Mazowe or Ewanrigg botanical gardens, with midday vlei birding at Marlborough or Monavale.

Claire Spottiswoode

Situated within the city limits, Marlborough (above) and Monavale vleis are excellent for migrating rallids, such as Striped Crake and Streaky-breasted Flufftail.

235 Harare's Vleis & Dambos

R ✔✔✔

The mystery surrounding Harare's vlei birds and the excitement associated with birding them are internationally renowned. In particular, the enigmatic **Streaky-breasted Flufftail** and **Striped Crake*** breed here and there is a plethora of other unusual species making for an unforgettable birding experience.

SPECIALS: Western Marsh-Harrier, Corncrake, Striped Crake*, Streaky-breasted Flufftail, Lesser Moorhen, Black Coucal, Grey-rumped Swallow, Rosy-breasted Longclaw*, Cuckoo Finch*, Yellow-mantled Widowbird, Pale-crowned Cisticola.

SEASON: Dec-Feb is the best for rallids.

HABITATS: The eastern section of Marlborough Vlei is kept permanently wet through the discharge of effluent from the adjacent sewage works. This maintains marshy conditions here and associated plant growth in addition to the seasonal dambo habitats.

BIRDING: Marlborough and Monavale vleis share many of their birds and habitats and because the former is the more extensive of the two areas with greater numbers of birds, we treat it as the basis of this account. The squelch zone of the south and south-western reaches of Marlborough Vlei Ⓐ holds nesting **Streaky-breasted Flufftail**. Other ground-dwellers that prefer wet conditions here include **Blue Quail*** and **Black-rumped Buttonquail**. **African Crake** and the migrant **Corncrake** are tolerant of drier conditions, but like most crakes, they

GETTING THERE

To reach Marlborough Vlei, turn into Elizabeth Windsor Road from Harare Drive. At the end of the housing development on the right, turn right into Princes Margaret Road. Turn left into a small road jutting into the vlei, where a car guard can be found and hired for a small fee. Monavale Vlei can be accessed from Fenella Drive (just before the golf course), via Lyndhurst Road, which can be reached from Quendon Road. Crake Cottage Ⓓ, a B&B that caters for birders, is located at Monavale Vlei and the owners can be contacted for updated conditions and access information on both vleis ☎.

DAMBOS AND DAMBO BIRDING

The word 'vlei' is a South African colloquialism for a wetland, and in Zimbabwe it is used to describe any open grassy area in a relatively well-wooded landscape. Thus the word 'dambo' has been adopted by many scientists to describe specifically the streamless, seasonally inundated open depressions among areas of miombo woodland.

Dambo birding is a great challenge because so many of the dambo birds are under cover of grass. Thus, knowledge of dambo birds' calls is essential. However, because so many species are secretive ground-dwellers that will flush at any time of day, an ethical approach to vlei birding is required so as not to disturb them.

Many of the species characteristic of the dambo avifauna are nomadic, moving into an area when the conditions are suitable. For example, **Streaky-breasted Flufftail** arrives on the Mashonaland Plateau a few weeks after the rains have set in (late Dec), breeds, and then departs for equatorial areas when the vleis begin to dry out (Mar-Apr).

The dambo microhabitat of particular interest is what is termed the 'squelch zone' – an area of short, knee- to waist-high grassland, usually on the lower slopes of vleis, where seepage from adjacent higher ground keeps the grassland wet to a depth of a few centimetres (even if there are dry days in between periods of direct rainfall). **Streaky-breasted Flufftail** nests here and **Striped Crake*** breeds in the grassy parts of deeper pools in the squelch zone. **Blue Quail*** and **Black-rumped Buttonquail** also favour short, wet grassland and **Lesser Moorhen** breeds in the larger pools.

Other wet grassland species include **Black Coucal**, **Broad-tailed Warbler**, **Rosy-breasted Longclaw***, **Yellow-mantled Widowbird**, **Locust Finch** and **Cuckoo Finch***. The **African Crake** is tolerant of drier conditions and is the most frequently flushed large rail. **Corncrake** is commonly encountered in the drier, taller grassland at the vlei margin, as well as in a range of drier habitats. **Red-chested Flufftail** and **African Rail** can be found in the permanently wet and marshy areas, which are more thickly vegetated.

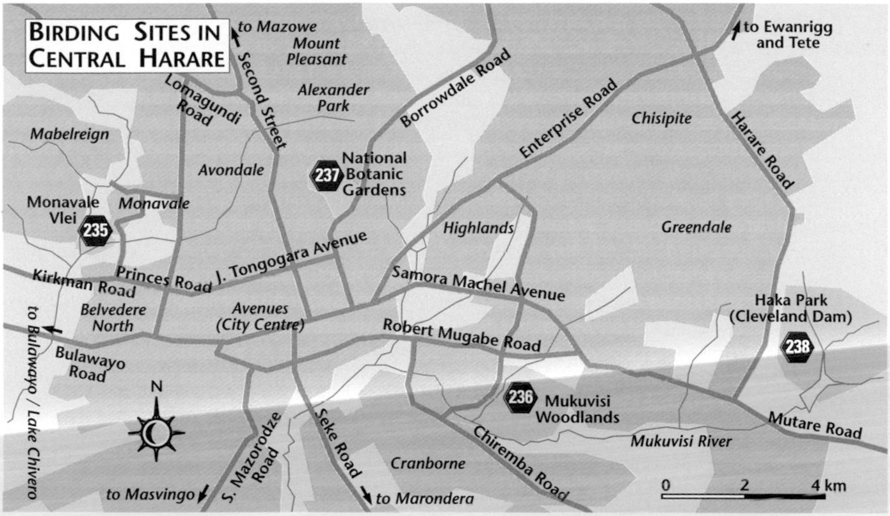

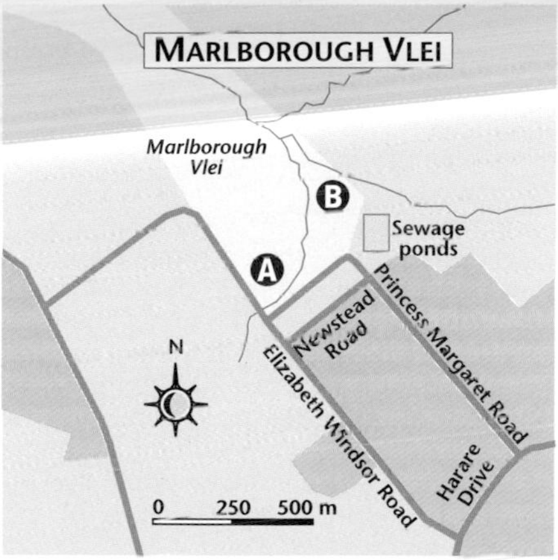

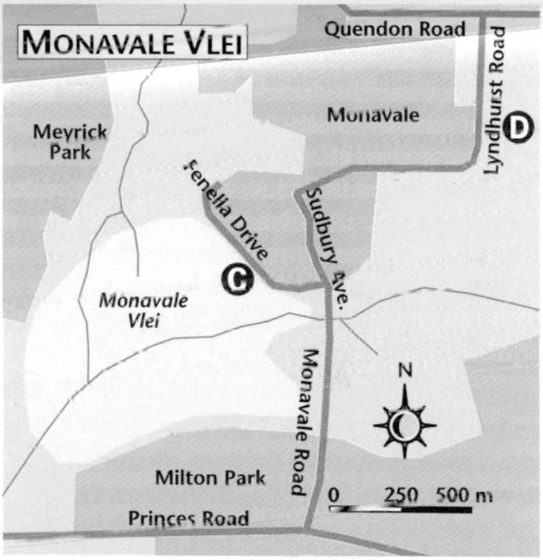

prefer shorter grass that is not too dense to walk through. **Striped Crake*** nests in deeper grassy pools. **Lesser Moorhen** nests in deeper grassy pools too, often in fairly thick vegetation. **African Rail** and **Red-chested Flufftail** can be heard calling from the marshy area near the sewage works **B**. **Rosy-breasted***, **Cape** and **Yellow-throated Longclaws** co-occur in Marlborough Vlei, the striking Rosy-breasted Longclaw* being the most common, preferring short, wet grassland. **Yellow-mantled Widowbird** breeds here too.

Zitting and **Croaking Cisticolas** are common, while **Pale-crowned** and **Wing-snapping Cisticolas** are less so; the cisticolas' brood parasite, the **Cuckoo Finch***, is also

Striped Crake is best seen at Monavale.

found here. The impressive **Broad-tailed Warbler** may be seen during the rains. **Streaky-breasted Flufftail** seeks refuge in the thicker vegetation growing on the drier, more aerated soils on termitaria. These are dotted through the area, and **Black Coucal** can be seen sunning itself here in the early morning and after a storm.

Overhead, **Grey-rumped** and **Greater Striped Swallows** may be seen. Once a rarity in Zimbabwe, **Western Marsh-Harrier** is now regularly recorded. This species and **Pallid*** and **Montagu's Harriers** quarter the extensive open landscape over Marlborough Vlei.

With luck, a walk though taller, thicker grass may result in a flushed **African Grass-Owl***. During the dry season, Marlborough Vlei is used as a daytime dormitory by **Marsh Owl,** and it is a remarkable experience to watch tens of these owls quartering the vlei in the golden glow of early evening.

Monavale Vlei Ⓒ offers similar habitats and birds, and, although it is smaller, the deeper grassy pools near Fenella Drive offer the birder the best chance of **Striped Crake*** in Harare; one has even been seen in the small pond in the front garden of Crake Cottage Ⓓ! After six years of lobbying, Monavale Vlei is now protected and a conservation scout is permanently employed.

236 Mukuvisi Woodlands ✔✔

The Mukuvisi Woodlands are a classic place to look for **Spotted Creeper***. The distribution of this miombo bird is centred on the Mashonaland Plateau and, interestingly, it is absent from miombo over most of the eastern districts.

SPECIALS: Spotted Creeper*, Pennant-winged Nightjar*, Whyte's Barbet, White-breasted Cuckooshrike, Miombo Tit, Green-capped Eremomela, Stierling's Wren-Warbler, Wood Pipit, Miombo Blue-eared Starling, Miombo Rock-Thrush.

SEASON: Birding is good throughout the year.

HABITATS: Miombo woodland, with a river and seep area.

BIRDING: The Mukuvisi Woodlands support a number of pairs of the charismatic **Spotted Creeper***. It is a frequent member of bird parties and is usually located by its distinctive high-pitched whistle. Individuals forage by working their way upwards along the trunks and main branches of larger trees and are usually spotted as they move between the top of one tree and the base of the next. The tall woodlands Ⓐ–Ⓓ usually yield these birds.

Mukuvisi also provides a breeding ground for the magnificent **Pennant-winged Nightjar***, which arrives mid-Sept to breed, and displays until Dec.

Green-capped Eremomela, **Cardinal Woodpecker** and **African Yellow White-eye** are commonly found in bird parties, while **Yellow-fronted Tinkerbird**, **Grey Penduline-Tit** and **Red-headed Weaver** are less frequent.

Miombo Rock-Thrush, Miombo Tit and **White-breasted Cuckooshrike** may be encountered at Ⓑ or Ⓒ; listen carefully for the cuckooshrike's thin, wispy call.

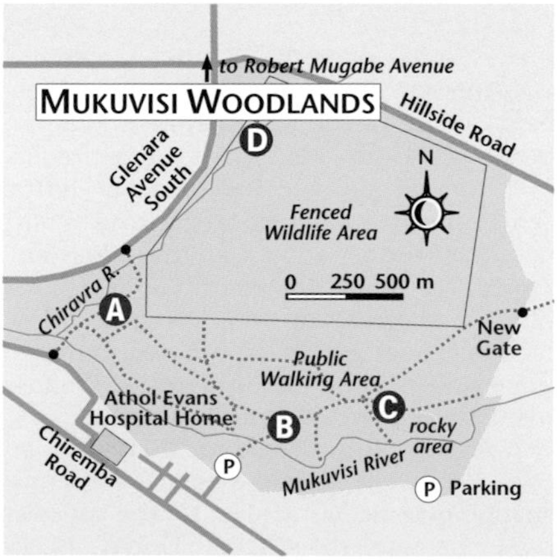

GETTING THERE

At this stage, access to the public walking area is gained by obtaining a key from the Mukuvisi Woodlands Association offices, which are situated east of the city centre at the junction of Glenara Ave South and Hillside Road at. Ⓓ The best access point is at gate Ⓑ; exact directions may be obtained from the office, or from BirdLife Zimbabwe ☎. The resident guide employed by the association usually knows the location of several creeper nests. Enquire at the offices Ⓓ.

The ringing call of **Stierling's Wren-Warbler** is commonly heard. **Whyte's Barbet** is fairly common, and perches conspicuously in the canopy. **Miombo Blue-eared Starling** breeds in the woodlands. **Miombo Double-collared Sunbird** is common, particularly at nectar sources provided by parasitic mistletoes.

Little Rush Warbler may be enticed from the reedbeds along the edge of the Mukuvisi River, where **Red-collared Widowbird** and **Thick-billed Weaver** nest. During the summer months, the migrant **Diderick Cuckoo, African Golden Oriole** and **African Paradise-Flycatcher** are common. The repetitive call of **African Cuckoo** may be heard in the summer; beware the very similar call of the **African Hoopoe**.

237 Harare National Botanic Gardens ✔

Although a typical miombo species, **Whyte's Barbet** is more likely to be encountered in areas where fig trees, on which it feeds, grow, such as gardens in the more wooded areas of Harare and the fig section at the centre of the National Botanic Gardens.

Miombo Double-collared and **Variable Sunbirds** are common in the botanic gardens, while **Copper Sunbird** feeds in indigenous trees in vleis during the wet season, and is frequently seen in gardens in suburbs adjacent to large vlei areas. **Black-throated Wattle-eye** occurs, and watch for **Magpie Mannikin** when the bamboo is in flower.

In the rainy season, large flocks of **Amur Falcon** fly low over the suburbs, feeding on termite alate emergences.

MIOMBO AND MIOMBO BIRDING

Miombo is a general term applied to the moist woodland in which trees of the genera *Brachystegia, Julbernardia* or *Isoberlinia* are dominant. This classic African vegetation type is almost endemic to the area covered by this book, and covers much of the plateau areas of south-central Africa from Angola to southern Tanzania, and south to Zimbabwe and Mozambique. Miombo endemics include such species as **Miombo Rock-Thrush, Red-capped Crombec, Cinnamon-breasted Tit, Olive-headed Weaver*, Black-necked Eremomela, Southern Hyliota, White-winged Babbling Starling*** and **Anchieta's Sunbird**. In southern Africa **Green-backed Honeybird, Yellow-bellied Hyliota** and **Spotted Creeper*** are confined to miombo.

A walk through miombo will include periods in which the woodland is quiet, followed by short bursts during which the forest canopy seems alive with birds. In fact, miombo is best birded by listening for the first signs of a party – for example, the jumbled whistles of **Chinspot Batis**, or the grating calls of a group of **Green-capped Eremomelas** – and then heading in that direction. Up to 24 different species have been recorded in a single bird party. In the breeding season (mainly Sept-Nov), birds are less vocal around the nest. Late Aug to early Sept is potentially the easiest for miombo birding, although the specials may be seen all year round.

In springtime (Aug-Sept), red and orange miombo literally blanket the landscape, transforming it into a mosaic of colour and creating one of the most spectacular natural scenic sights in southern Africa.

A. Lizek

Miombo woodland

238 Haka Park & Cleveland Dam ✔✔

The park offers excellent miombo and vlei birding, together with the opportunity to view game on foot, right in Harare.

SPECIALS: Miombo Rock-Thrush, White-breasted Cuckooshrike, Green-backed Honeybird, Cuckoo Hawk, Locustfinch*, Miombo Tit, Southern Hyliota, Pennant-winged Nightjar*, Spotted Creeper*, African Pygmy Goose*, Coqui Francolin, Whyte's Barbet.

SEASON: The miombo birding is good throughout the year, while the vleis are most active from Dec-Feb.

HABITATS: Miombo woodland, vlei.

BIRDING: The best miombo is in the south-west and south-east. **African Pygmy Goose*** and **White-backed Duck** are resident on the upper reaches of the dam **B**, and **Allen's Gallinule** skulks in the sedges at the water's edge from Dec-May.

The unobtrusive **Miombo Rock-Thrush** can remain motionless on a branch within the canopy for some time, and some patience is required to track down this species. Familiarity with its call will lead you to the general vicinity of this bird, but then you will have to watch carefully for the slightest movement; a sighting of the mottling on the mantle of the male is certainly worth the effort. There are a number of pairs resident in the smaller patches of miombo woodland in the south-east. In particular, try taller woodland with fairly sparse undergrowth around **C** and **D**.

The excitement of the activity associated with a bird party is heightened by the good probability of **Green-backed Honeybird** sightings. It can be inconspicuous as it moves in the canopy, and the flash of white in the outer tail feathers is usually the first indication of its presence. **Brown-backed Honeybird** has also been recorded in the park.

The busy **Southern Hyliota** is a common party member and there is a good probability of **Miombo** and **Southern Black Tits**, as well as **White-breasted Cuckooshrike.** A good sighting of the cuckooshrike often entails some quick legwork through the woodland, as individuals fly some distance between perches. However, once the bird alights, it often spends some time there searching for food, with its characteristically pensive head movements. There is a good chance of encountering a **Wood Pipit** along the roads – listen for its call. **Spotted Creeper*** is fairly common here. A pair of **Cuckoo Hawk** has bred in this patch of woodland; watch for them flying overhead; they may also be flushed from a perch in the area (try around **E**).

Listen for the distinctive call of **Coqui Francolin** in the morning and evening, and keep an eye out for **Pennant-winged Nightjar***. The latter seems to prefer the open woodland on the eastern side of the vlei. The spectacular males can be seen in display flight in the

GETTING THERE

Haka Park is open every day of the year from 07h00. The main entrance gate **A** to the Cleveland Dam public area is locked at 18h00, so visitors should be out of the park by 17h50. Follow the Mutare Road out of Harare through the traffic circle at the junction with Harare Drive and continue past the large wholesaler (Jaggers) on the right, immediately turning left into the Cleveland Dam road **A**. The roads within the park are gravel and in wet years Hacha Drive and the road along the northern fence are sometimes closed. Check with the gate attendant on the conditions of the roads. Much can be seen by parking at the main gate and walking along one of the many paths through the miombo in the south-east.

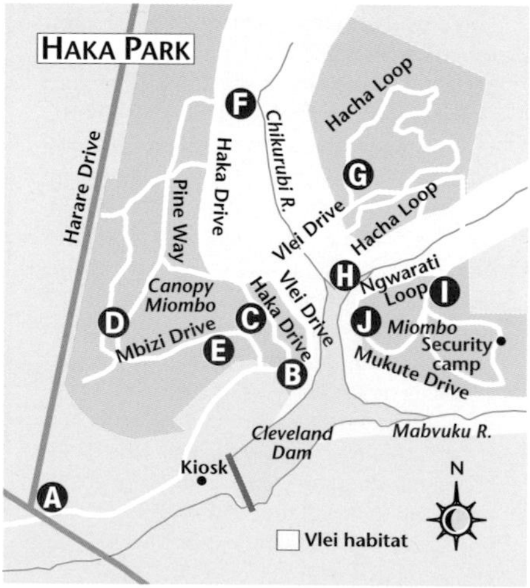

open area enclosed by Musasa Loop and Mhofu and Hacha drives between Sept and Nov. Several interesting species have been recorded in the vlei, among these **Locustfinch***. This species is believed to wander extensively in the dry season in search of suitable wet habitat. At this time, it is worth trying the wet, bare, trampled ground close to the spring near the head of the Chikurubi River **F**. During the wet summer months this habitat becomes flooded downstream. **Harlequin Quail** has been recorded from the more open grassland at **G**. Interestingly, **Great Snipe**, now rarely recorded in southern Africa, has been flushed from the thicker growth here.

The rocky outcrops **H** and **I** support a different type of vegetation. **Whyte's Barbet** favours the wild figs that grow here, and the erythrinas are a good source of food for sunbirds – including **Miombo Double-collared Sunbird** – when they flower in winter.

Spotted Creeper on its lichen-encrusted nest

The sight of the large number of **Amur Falcon** which roost in the trees at **J** during the wet season is impressive.

OTHER ANIMALS: A wide selection of game animals, including Sable Antelope and Giraffe, is kept. Although the park is named from the chiShona for Ground Pangolin, this rare mammal is unlikely to be found here!

239 Mazowe Botanical Reserve ✔

The boulder-strewn slopes of the granite koppies, blanketed with the beautiful miombo woodland, provide habitat for the specialist **Boulder Chat***. You may be fortunate enough to pick up its repetitive whistle at the koppie closest to the car park. This is also a good place to look for the uncommon **Green-backed Honeybird**. In particular, try the woodland on the higher ground adjacent to the car park, where bird parties may also include **Red-faced Crombec** and **Southern Hyliota**. The raucous **Broad-billed Roller** breeds in the dead trees in the area. With a bit of luck, you may find a **Half-collared Kingfisher** in the forest and thicket along the Mazowe River. Listen for the soft call of the **Red-throated Twinspot** here.

Take the Golden Stairs Road north out of Harare, towards Mazowe. Turn right at the 22.5 km peg into Christon Bank Road. Continue to the end of this road; the parking area for the reserve is on the right.

240 Lake Chivero ✔

The Robert McIlwaine Recreational Park, including 2 630 ha of dam, is 5 550 ha in size and under the control of the Department of National Parks. Situated just 30 km outside Harare, the lake was built to supply water to the capital. A game park of some 1 600 ha is situated on the southern bank of the lake and most large mammal species, including White Rhinoceros, have been reintroduced here.

The park is well known for its water birds (**Slaty Egret*** makes the odd appearance on the exposed shoreline, best when the lake level drops from May-Dec) and miombo specials. **Spotted Creeper*** and **Southern Hyliota** are among the most frequently recorded species in the bird parties, but also keep a lookout for **Black-eared Seed-eater**, **Wood Pipit**, **Brown-backed** and **Green-backed Honeybirds** and **Miombo Blue-eared Starling**.

Pennant-winged Nightjar* is a common visitor in the summer. **Thrush Nightingale*** can be heard calling from thickets in the area. Follow the Bulawayo road for 32 km from Harare. Turn left immediately after crossing the Manyame River. The road is clearly signposted and leads towards the dam wall, but turn right at the fork to the game park.

The garden of the Hunyani Hills Hotel holds **Western Violet-backed Sunbird** (always inconspicuous), while the nearby camp site is excellent for **Spotted Creeper*** and **Orange-winged Pytilia**. **Barred Owlet** may be seen here at night. The camp site also offers access to the flood plain.

To reach the Hunyani Hills Hotel, turn left 27 km from Harare at the Turnpike Service Station, and then turn right when you reach the lake, and continue until you see the camp site on the left and the hotel on the right.

Peter Ginn

Barred Owlet

241 Domboshawa ✔

The spectacularly scenic Chinamora, Masembura and Masana communal lands that lie north of Harare, which have several sites of historical and cultural interest (rock art and ruins dating from the time of Great Zimbabwe), also offer great miombo birding. **Mottled Swift**, **Miombo Rock-Thrush**, **Cinnamon-breasted Tit**, **Cabanis's Bunting**, **Western Violet-backed Sunbird** and **Cape Eagle-Owl*** (subspecies *mackinderi*) have all been recorded breeding in the vicinity of Chikupo inselberg. This site lies about one and a half hours' drive north of Harare and directions can be obtained from Birdlife Zimbabwe ☎.

242 Ewanrigg Botanical Garden ✔

The main attraction is the famous aloe collection, which flowers during the winter months and attracts a large number of sunbirds – **Miombo Double-collared**, **White-bellied** and **Scarlet-chested** are the most common, but watch for **Copper**, **Amethyst**, **Western Violet-backed** and **Purple-banded Sunbirds** too.

The enigmatic **Magpie Mannikin*** is regularly recorded from the area; look carefully at flocks of **Bronze** and **Red-backed Mannikins**. Try the rank, grassy area behind the far picnic site. Take Enterprise Road out of Harare and, at the city limit, take the left fork to Shamva. The turn-off to Ewanrigg is to the right after about 15 km. The garden is about 3 km from here, down a good gravel road. Ewanrigg opens at 08h00.

243 Gosho Park, Marondera ✔✔✔

Established to protect 340 ha of generally undisturbed miombo woodland, Gosho Park offers some of the best miombo birding in Zimbabwe, and includes one of the best sites for **Boulder Chat*** and the uncommon and highly localised **Cinnamon-breasted Tit**. The area is also well known for its regular sightings of **Collared Flycatcher**.

SPECIALS: Boulder Chat*, Cinnamon-breasted Tit, Collared Flycatcher, Miombo Rock-Thrush, Western Violet-backed Sunbird, Cabanis's Bunting, Black-eared Seed-eater, Wood Pipit.
SEASON: Birding is good throughout the year. Dec-Jan is best for the migrant **Collared Flycatcher**.
HABITATS: Miombo, granite koppies, streams.
BIRDING: The park offers a good range of miombo specials which can be found by walking between the bush camp (B), and (E). **White-breasted Cuckooshrike**, **Miombo Rock-Thrush**, **Southern Hyliota**, **Green-capped Eremomela**, **Wood Pipit**, **Miombo Double-collared Sunbird** and **Black-eared Seed-eater** are all reasonably common in mixed-species foraging flocks. However, first prize is the uncommon and highly localised **Cinnamon-breasted Tit**, which is usually found in well-developed woodland, searching for food among the epiphytic orchids and lichens, and often in the company of a group of **Miombo Tits**. Listen for the characteristic grating calls of the tits.

GETTING THERE

From Harare take the Mutare Road (take Samora Machel Avenue all the way out of town), through Marondera and on for about 9 km to the entrance to Peterhouse College on the right. Continue for a short distance past the shops on the left, and then take the Springvale turn-off to the left. The entrance to the park is gained through the boom on the left just before you get to the Springvale entrance (A). Gosho Park is open between 07h00 and 18h00 every day of the year. Camping facilities are available in the rustic bush camp.

This area consistently produces records of the non-breeding migrant **Collared Flycatcher** during the summer months (look especially at (D)).

The granite koppies at (E) and (F) are a good place to look for **Boulder Chat*** (listen for its distinctive squeaky-wheel calls). **Miombo Rock-Thrush** and **Lazy Cisticola** are also found near these koppies, and **Shelley's Francolin** may be heard calling from the grassy areas. **Pennant-winged Nightjar*** displays here on summer nights.

During the winter months, **Western Violet-backed Sunbird** may be found at nectar sources within the woodland, otherwise it feeds in the canopy of well-developed miombo. **Wood Pipit** is commonly encountered along roads, from where it flushes into the adjacent canopy. **Cabanis's Bunting** is also often flushed from the ground when feeding. During the summer months, listen for it singing from the top of an exposed tree.

As you drive into the park, look for **Whyte's Barbet** in the tops of the trees in this open area. **Green Sandpiper** has also been recorded along the small stream at (C).
OTHER ANIMALS: A variety of game animals, including Sable Antelope and Giraffe, have been reintroduced.

Peter Ginn

Boulder Chat

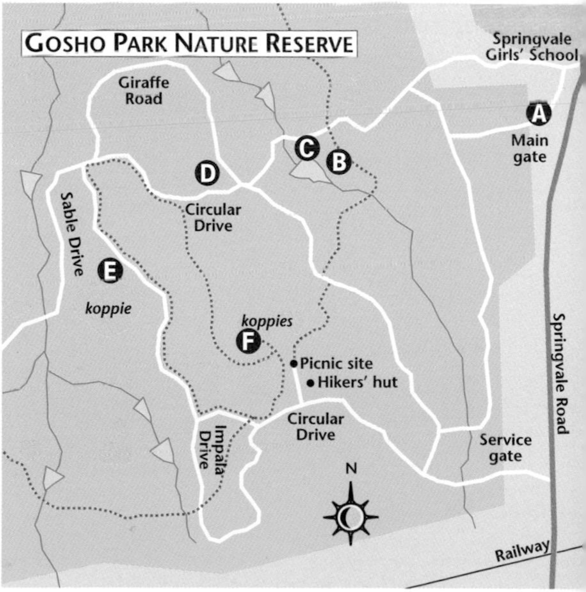

ROUTE 26

EASTERN HIGHLANDS & LOWLANDS

Zimbabwe's mountainous eastern border with Mozambique offers some of the highest species diversity of any route in southern Africa. Rugged mountain ranges loom more than 2 500 m asl over tropical rainforest in the lowlands. Heathlands akin to the southern Cape's fynbos blanket the mountain tops, rolling grasslands are studded with patches of Afromontane forest, and fascinating dwarf miombo woodland covers spectacular granite landscapes.

TOP 10 BIRDS

- Swynnerton's Robin
- Chirinda Apalis
- Roberts' Warbler
- Blue Swallow
- Red-faced Crimsonwing
- Cinnamon-breasted Tit
- Eastern Bronze-naped Pigeon
- Lesser Seedcracker
- Black-and-white Flycatcher
- Anchieta's Tchagra

The region is a centre of endemism for many groups of organisms and this includes birds: Roberts' Warbler, Chirinda Apalis* and a fair number of subspecies are endemic to the highlands here. Furthermore, most of the known sites for the highly localised forest denizen, Swynnerton's Robin*, are found in the Zimbabwean highlands. The marshes in the lowlands hold little-known species such as Lesser Seedcracker* and Anchieta's Tchagra*. Inland lie the moist woodlands and extensive grasslands of the central plateau and to the south, the south-east lowveld's arid woodlands and bushveld stretch as far as the eye can see.

The region's evergreen forest avifauna can be roughly separated into those that inhabit moist evergreen forest at low and medium altitudes (usually less than 1 500 m asl), and those of the moist broad-leaved montane forests at higher altitudes. However, certain species are shared and individuals of several species that inhabit high-altitude forests move downwards during the cold winter months (May-Aug). During the wet season (Dec-Feb), heavy rainfall, particularly on the eastern slopes of the highlands, can last for days and make forest birding difficult, even though most of the roads are tarred.

Peter Ginn

Swynnerton's Robin

Visitors pushed for time can pick up many of the specials in the Bvumba Highlands, an easy half-day's drive from Harare, in 2-3 days, but at least 10 days should be given to explore the region fully. The Eastern Districts are conveniently explored en route to Mozambique or via the south-east lowveld to the border with South Africa at Beitbridge.

244 Nyanga Highlands

IBA ✔✔

The scenic Nyanga Highlands form a spectacular wilderness area that includes widespread grasslands and supports the most extensive forest catena in Zimbabwe's eastern highlands. Centred on the Nyanga Massif, the area ranges in altitude from 2 593 m at the summit of Mount Nyangani (the highest point in Zimbabwe), to 700 m in the Pungwe Valley.

SPECIALS: Chirinda Apalis*, Blue Swallow*, Scarce Swift, Mottled Swift, Striped-cheeked Greenbul, Barratt's Warbler, Roberts' Warbler*, Bronzy Sunbird, Gurney's Sugarbird*, Red-faced Crimsonwing*.

SEASON: Most of the specials are present year-round.

HABITATS: Afromontane grassland, Afromontane forest, miombo, pine and wattle plantations.

BIRDING: The high cliffs over which the Mtarazi River plunges into the Honde Valley to form the spectacular Mtarazi Falls – one of Africa's highest waterfalls – are among the most accessible places to see **Scarce Swift**, a summer breeding migrant (Aug-Feb). The montane forest patches here hold an excellent selection of montane species, including **Chirinda Apalis***, **Striped-cheeked Greenbul**, **Red-faced Crimsonwing***, **African Crowned Eagle** and **Roberts' Warbler*** (although lacking **Swynnerton's Robin***). There is a good chance of seeing the distinctive white-faced race *swynnertoni* of the **Red-necked Spurfowl** along the road close to the picnic site in the early morning or at dusk.

GETTING THERE

The area is one of Zimbabwe's prime tourist attractions, and the wide selection of accommodation facilities range from four-star hotels and quaint country inns to conveniently situated camping sites.

The extensive montane grasslands of the Nyanga Massif support one of the largest breeding populations of the globally threatened **Blue Swallow*** (summer migrant, Aug-Apr), which is best searched for in the grasslands along the Mtarazi River above the falls, at Udu Dam and a few kilometres along the Troutbeck road after turning off from Nyanga village.

Although much of the popular tourist resort of Troutbeck has been overrun with invasive alien pines and wattle, the generally unobtrusive **Red-faced Crimsonwing*** and vocal **Barratt's Warbler** occur in dense, tangled vegetation at the edge of forest, and **Rufous-chested Sparrowhawk*** may be seen flying overhead (try the golf course for the latter). **Augur Buzzards** are commonly seen at nearby World's View, where you can watch the impressive aerial antics of **White-necked Raven**. **Yellow-bellied Waxbill**, **Cape Grassbird** and **Striped Flufftail*** are found in even the smallest patches of indigenous grassland (such as at Rhodes Nyanga Hotel).

The grasslands of the beautiful Nyazengu Nature Reserve on the south-western slopes of Mount Nyangani provide excellent birding opportunities (including **Gurney's Sugarbird*** as well as **Broad-tailed Warbler**).

The extensive miombo woodland that covers the Forestry Commission's York Estate behind Punch Rock Chalets, and in the vicinity of the Inn on the Ruparara or Hidden Rocks, is a good place to look for **Miombo Rock-Thrush**, **Shelley's Francolin**, **Green-backed Honeybird** and **Whyte's Barbet**. **Mottled Swift** breeds in crevices on Susurumba, the granite whaleback that looms over Pine Tree Inn.

Callan Cohen

World's View at Nyanga

245 Honde Valley

IBA ✔✔✔

The Honde Valley has become the classic site at which to find highly localised species such as **Anchieta's Tchagra***, **Moustached Grass Warbler** and **Lesser Seedcracker***.

SPECIALS: Eastern Bronze-naped Pigeon*, Pallid Honeyguide, Scarce Swift, Green-backed Woodpecker, Ayres' Hawk-Eagle*, Palm-nut Vulture*, Silvery-cheeked Hornbill, Moustached Grass Warbler, Red-winged Warbler, Singing and Short-winged Cisticolas, Pale Batis, Anchieta's Tchagra*, and Lesser Seedcracker*.

SEASON: Birding is good throughout the year.

HABITATS: Low-altitude forest, tea plantations, wetlands.

BIRDING: The low-altitude forest near the Aberfoyle Lodge holds forest specials such as **Eastern Bronze-naped Pigeon** (check for these roosting in dead trees near the lodge early in the morning), **Green-backed Woodpecker** and **Black-fronted Bush Shrike**. Also look out for **Silvery-cheeked Hornbill**, **White-eared Barbet**, **Pallid Honeyguide** and **Square-tailed Drongo**. **Scarce Swift** may be seen overhead. This is a particularly good spot for the shy **Green Twinspot***, which can be seen early in the morning behind the cabins; other seed-eaters include **Red-throated Twinspot** and **Grey** and **Yellow-bellied Waxbills**. **Singing Cisticola** calls from the rank growth, **Blue-spotted Wood-Dove** explodes from the sides of the dirt roads and **Eastern Saw-wing** hawks insects over the picturesque tea estates. There is excellent birding too at Eastern Highlands Tea Estate (F).

Anchieta's Tchagra

Watch carefully for **Ayres' Hawk-Eagle*** flying overhead. **Palm-nut Vulture*** breeds in the oil palms close to (A) and may be seen from the nearby golf course. Also enquire about the nearby Gleneagles Reserve (4WD only), which offers similar species.

Wamba Marsh (E) is famous for **Anchieta's Tchagra*** (ask for the 'Wamba Bird'), **Moustached Grass Warbler** and **Lesser Seedcracker***. **Pale Batis** and **Red-winged Warbler** may also be seen around the marsh. Spend some time scanning the marsh from the road alongside, especially in the late afternoon when the warbler perches conspicuously. **Black-winged Bishop** is encountered in reedbeds throughout the Honde Valley.

The area in the vicinity of the airstrip on the Katiyo Tea Estate (B) is well known for **Short-winged Cisticola**, which calls from a prominent perch during the rains. **Collared Palm-Thrush** may be seen here too.

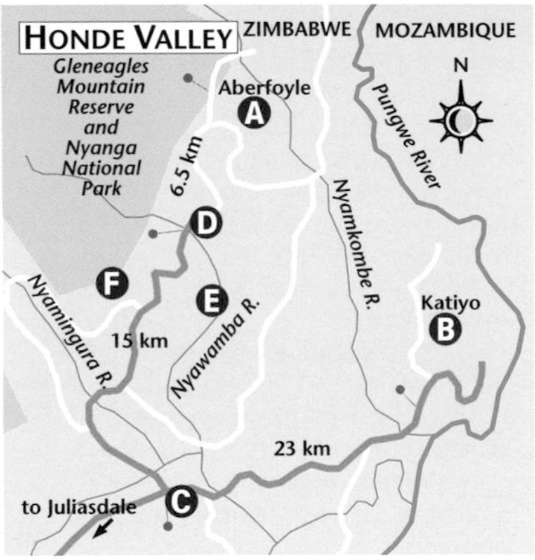

GETTING THERE

The best birding is near Aberfoyle (A) and Katiyo (B) Tea Estates. Take the turn-off to the east off the Mutare/Juliasdale road at the 22 km peg, and follow this winding road into the Honde valley. The turn-off to Katiyo Tea Estate is on the right after about 46 km (C), just before you cross the Pungwe River. (To get to the Katiyo Tea Estate airstrip, enter the estate and take the left fork to the main office at the factory, continuing past the main office for a short distance ☎.) To reach Aberfoyle Tea Estate (A), continue 64 km along the main road down the Honde Valley (enquire here about birding guides). The road to Aberfoyle Lodge ☎ is signposted from here. To get to Wamba Marsh, turn right just before the Wamba Factory (D), about 62 km from the turn-off from the Juliasdale-Mutare Road. Travel for about 2.5 km, taking the hairpin bend to the left. The small marsh (E) is to the right at the headwaters of the dam.

246 Chirinda Forest

IBA ✔✔

Chirinda Forest, the southernmost tropical evergreen forest in Zimbabwe, supports one of the most important populations of **Swynnerton's Robin***, which is common here. The bird community is interesting because it is not typical of either high altitude forests or of those from lower altitudes, and is rather a mix of both that includes canopy specials such as **Chirinda Apalis***, **Livingstone's Turaco**, **Black-fronted Bush-Shrike***, **Silvery-cheeked Hornbill** (check the giant fig trees at the camp site), together with mid-storey birds such as **Black-throated Wattle-eye** and **African Broadbill***.

The *swynnertoni* subspecies of the beautiful Red Squirrel is endemic to Chirinda, and Tree Civet (nocturnal), Sun Squirrel, Samango Monkey and Blue Duiker are among the larger mammals found here.

The forest is about 30 km (on a tarred road) from the small town of Chipinge; turn left at Mount Selinda and, after driving through the middle of the forest, left into the track to the camp site. The nearby Kiledo Lodge ☎ offers good birding (**Green Malkoha**) and logistical advice for birding the Haroni Valley.

247 Bvumba Highlands

IBA ✔✔✔

These rambling, often mist-swathed highlands about 30 km south-east of Mutare are legendary for providing easy and scenic access to three species restricted to eastern Zimbabwe and the Mozambican highlands, and a host of further montane species reach the southern limit of their ranges here. The wild interior of the Bvumba's lush montane forests contrasts with the gentle and almost European landscape of the farms and plantations that lie in between.

SPECIALS: Swynnerton's Robin*, Roberts' Warbler*, Chirinda Apalis*, White-tailed Crested Flycatcher, Stripe-cheeked Greenbul, Red-faced Crimsonwing, Yellow-bellied Waxbill, Blue-spotted Wood-Dove, Bronzy Sunbird, Silvery-cheeked Hornbill, Singing Cisticola, Cinnamon-breasted Tit, Eastern Saw-wing, Buff-spotted Flufftail.

SEASON: All the specials may be found year-round.

HABITATS: Montane forest and grassland, plantations, botanical gardens.

BIRDING: It is well worth stopping along the first ascent into Bvumba, especially the lay-by at a steep bend (Ⓐ on map overleaf) about 25 km from Mutare, to bird in the beautiful miombo woodland here. This is a reliable site for **Cinnamon-breasted Tit**, which may be found in bird parties. Other possibilities here include **Spotted Creeper***, **Miombo Tit** and **Cabanis's Bunting**. As the road rises into montane grassland and patches of forest, look out for **Augur Buzzard** and **Long-crested Eagle** perched on utility poles, and scan the skies for scarce **Ayres' Hawk-Eagle***. Roadside patches of rank grassland and bracken may yield **Singing Cisticola**, **Cape Grassbird** and **Dark-capped Yellow Warbler**.

All the Bvumba specials may be found in one of several easily accessible forest sites around 1 500 m altitude, notably Bunga Forest Reserve Ⓑ, Seldomseen Ⓒ, and the Vumba Botanical Gardens Ⓓ. Of the specials, **Chirinda Apalis*** and **White-tailed Crested Flycatcher** are easily found in the forest, particularly with knowledge of their calls. **Roberts' Warbler*** prefers thicket at forest edges – such as around the gardens at Seldomseen – and is

GETTING THERE

To reach Bvumba, follow the signs from Park Road in Mutare. This is also initially the road to the Mozambique border post at Forbes Road. Bvumba Road leads up a beautiful miombo-wooded pass directly into the mountains. All the key sites are well signposted from this road. Bunga Forest Reserve (Ⓑ on map) can be entered along footpaths leading directly off the tar road that runs through it. The Bvumba caters extensively to tourists, and there are many accommodation possibilities: in addition to a clutch of up-market and well-reputed hotels, recommended and reasonably priced accommodation is available at Seldomseen ☎ and Ndundu Lodge ☎, and there is a well-positioned camp site at the Vumba Botanical Gardens. Seldomseen, a private property with its own forest, offers birding walks with excellent guides.

Peter Ginn

Roberts' Warbler

also noisy and readily found. **Swynnerton's Robin*** typically requires more effort, but is not uncommon, and with some searching is usually found skulking in the forest understorey (listen for its distinctive call).

Stripe-cheeked Greenbul, a localised bird south of the Zambezi, is easily located in any kind of forest. More widespread forest species occurring at all of these sites include **African Goshawk**, **Lemon Dove**, **Livingstone's Turaco**, **Silvery-cheeked Hornbill**, **Yellow-rumped Tinkerbird**, **Yellow-streaked Greenbul**, **Barratt's Warbler**, **Yellow-throated Woodland-Warbler**, **Bar-throated Apalis**, **Orange Ground-** and **Olive Thrushes**, **Black-fronted Bush-Shrike*** and **Dark-backed Weaver**.

The Botanical Gardens **D** present a magnificent view eastwards into Mozambique. Flowering plants here and in the gardens around Ndundu Lodge and Seldomseen invariably attract an impressive array of sunbirds, including **Bronzy**, **Malachite**, **Variable**, **Collared**, **Amethyst**, **Miombo Double-collared** and **Olive Sunbirds**. Also look out for **Gurney's Sugarbird*** on the flowering protea bushes. **Eastern Saw-wing** is widespread, but particularly conspicuous in the Botanical Gardens, which is also one of the few reliable sites in southern Africa for wintering **Tree Pipits**; look in open areas with lawns and scattered trees for the latter. The unmistakeable call of **Gorgeous Bush-shrike** can usually be heard from thickets, and **Red-throated Twinspot** and **Yellow-bellied Waxbill** feed at the lawn edges.

A slow walk along the broad tracks running through the forest below the gardens is highly recommended for easy access to all the Vumba specials; look out too for **Blue-spotted Wood-Dove** and even **Red-faced Crimsonwing** feeding at the roadside. The small bushes lining the main entrance road are particularly good for **Barratt's Warbler**. **Buff-spotted Flufftail** may also be heard here, although this is a species that is frequently encountered on guided walks at Seldomseen.

OTHER ANIMALS: A number of mammals and reptiles are endemic to the Bvumba, including a subspecies of Samango Monkey, conspicuous at the Botanical Gardens, and the elegant little Marshall's Leaf Chameleon – ask at Ndundu Lodge!

NEARBY SITES: Tom Hulley Road **E**, forming a short-cut down to the Burma Valley, provides good miombo birding, including **Whyte's Barbet**, **Green-backed Woodpecker**, **Spotted Creeper***, **Miombo Tit** and **Cabanis's Bunting**. The heavily settled Burma Valley itself, lying 900 m below the Bvumba, provides good lowland birding and is best known for **Zambezi Indigobird***, the little-known brood parasite of **Red-throated Twinspot**.

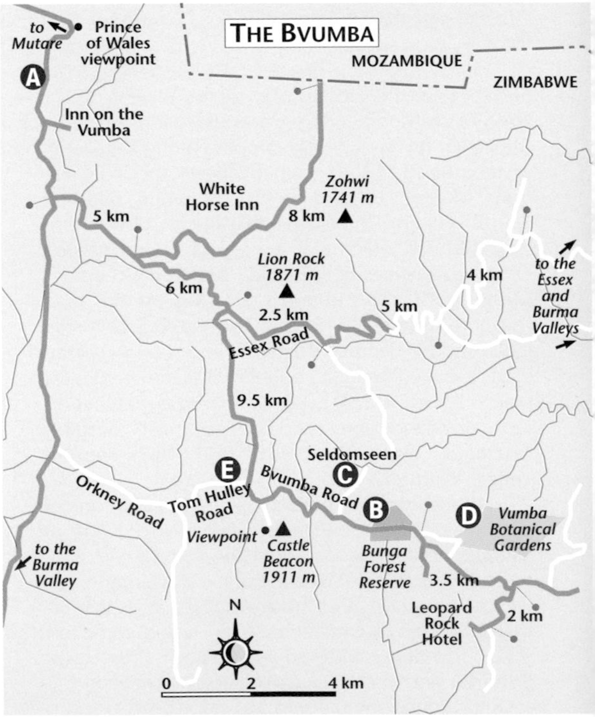

248 Haroni-Rusitu Confluence IBA ✔✔

The well-known but dwindling patches of lowland forest at the junction of the Haroni and Rusitu rivers are almost legendary among southern African birders, even though new sites have been found in Mozambique for many of the lowland forest specials they support.

SPECIALS: Southern Banded Snake-Eagle, Eastern Bronze-naped Pigeon*, Pel's Fishing-Owl*, Blue-spotted Wood-Dove, Pallid Honeyguide, Green-backed Woodpecker, African Broadbill*, Tiny Greenbul, Black-headed Apalis, Singing Cisticola, Red-winged Warbler, Black-and-white Flycatcher*, Black-fronted Bush-Shrike*, Chestnut-fronted Helmet-Shrike*, Black-winged Bishop, Grey Waxbill, Zambezi Indigobird*.

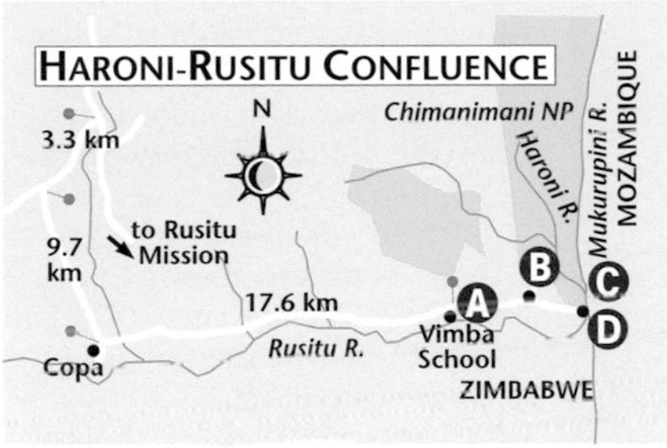

SEASON: The specials may be found year-round, although **Black-and-white Flycatcher*** is best seen in summer.

HABITATS: Lowland forest, farmlands.

BIRDING: Although the Vimba (Nyakwawa) Forest (A) is relatively small, it allows for easier canopy birding than the Haroni-Mukurupini Forest. The bizarre and especially sought-after **Black-and-white Flycatcher*** may be found in the canopy, where knowledge of its call is essential to finding it. Look for **Green-backed Woodpecker, Black-fronted Bush-Shrike*, Black-throated Wattle-eye, Square-tailed Drongo, Dark-backed Weaver, Black-headed, Yellow-breasted** and (in winter) **Chirinda* Apalises** and **Yellow-streaked Greenbul** in bird parties here. **Tiny Greenbul** too is a common member of bird parties.

In the mid-stratum, the otherwise inconspicuous **African Broadbill*** has been seen displaying year-round. This is also a good spot to look for **Green Malkoha**, which creeps through tangles at the forest edge.

Look for **Eastern Bronze-naped Pigeon*** in Vimba Forest, perching on exposed branches. The male's white hind collar stands out on this otherwise dark bird. Watch for pairs of the impressive **Silvery-cheeked Hornbill** flying between trees. **Barred Long-tailed Cuckoo*** is rare and is more often heard, particularly at dusk, than seen. **African Pitta***, another very rare bird here in recent years, feeds on the forest floor and may be detected by its call during summer.

GETTING THERE

The gravel road from Chimanimani town to the confluence is passable in a 2WD with high clearance, although it deteriorates during the wetter summer months (Nov-May) and may become inaccessible. Although the confluence is only about 60 km from Chimanimani town, allow at least 2-3 hours for the drive. Turn left at the Chimanimani turn-off, 13 km before Chipinge town on the Birchenough-Chipinge road. Four kilometres down this tar road, turn right onto the Roscommon Estate-Rusitu Valley Road. After 3 km, this becomes a dirt road; follow it for another 4 km to where the road forks, and take the right-hand fork. After a further 9 km, take the left-hand fork into Roscommon Estate. Continue for 7 km until you get to a T-junction. Turn left and immediately right as you pass through the small business centre. This will take you over a metal suspension bridge. Turn right and follow the road for 15 km to Vimba School. Vimba Forest (A) is a short distance past the school. Note that these directions change occasionally, so at each junction, ask for 'Vimba Forest', 'CAMPFIRE' and 'birdwatching'. The Vimba (Nyakwawa) Forest is sacred to the Vimba people, who kindly allow birders access; as a reciprocal courtesy, please seek permission for entry to the forest at the VEP/CAMPFIRE camp (B). The Vimba Environmental Project (VEP) and CAMPFIRE Association have built an attractive camp site/lodging area close to the Haroni River ☎. Continue for 3 km further along the main road to the Haroni-Mukurupini Forest at the river confluence (C), which is just north of the well-known 'store' at the confluence of the Haroni and Rusitu rivers at (D).

Note: There are old and unsubstantiated rumours that there are landmines on the Mozambique side of the Haroni-Mukurupini Forest; bear this in mind should you decide to cross the river into Mozambique (there are no border signs).

Callan Cohen

The main road passes through Vimba Forest.

Birding the canopy of the much higher and more extensive Haroni-Mukurupini Forest Ⓒ (which can also be accessed from the camp site at Ⓑ) is more difficult, and it is probably best to find a gap and wait for bird parties to move through the area. As in any forest, knowledge of calls is essential to get the most out of birding. Among the canopy-dwellers are **Grey Cuckooshrike** (winter) and **African Crowned Eagle** and **Black-and-white Flycatcher***. The equally prized and even more fantastic **Chestnut-fronted Helmet-Shrike*** is only rarely recorded. And if that is not enough, there is the possibility of **Southern Banded Snake-Eagle** and the rare **Lesser Cuckoo** too (both may be seen on the road between Ⓐ and Ⓓ). **Eastern Saw-wing**, and **Mottled** and **Böhm's* Spinetails**, which, together with **Collared Palm-Thrush**, are associated with *Borassus* palms in the area, may be seen overhead.

The Chizire Forest (near Ⓑ) on the western banks of the Haroni River pays testament to the regenerative powers of the natural vegetation. Originally used by locals as farmland, the forest now houses **Woodwards' Batis**, **Tiny Greenbul** and, in bird parties in the winter months, **White-tailed Crested Flycatcher** and **Striped-cheeked Greenbul**. **Narina Trogon*** lurks in the mid-stratum, while **Livingstone's Turaco** is more conspicuous. **Olive Sunbird** is the most common of the forest 'proper' sunbirds, while **Collared Sunbird** may be found at forest edges and in thickets.

Look for the little-known **Pallid Honeyguide** at forest edges, particularly along the Haroni River, below the camp site Ⓑ. It is similar in appearance to **Lesser Honeyguide** and has probably been generally overlooked in the past. **Half-collared Kingfisher** and **Pel's Fishing-Owl*** also occur along the Haroni River. The short thicket growth on the promontory close to the camp site supports **Eastern Nicator**, **Red-throated Twinspot** and **Red-capped Robin-Chat**.

Rank growth in the cultivated fields below the camp site supports a number of interesting species, including **Singing Cisticola**, **Black-winged Bishop** and (scarce) **Red-winged Warbler**, **Short-winged Cisticola** and much sought-after **Lesser Seedcracker***. **Grey Waxbill** may be found in rank growth at the forest edge.

Blue-spotted Wood-Dove is regularly flushed from rank growth at the roadside on the journey to the confluence. **Taita Falcon*** is sometimes seen overhead.
OTHER ANIMALS: Blue Duiker and Samango Monkey are found in the forest.

HPH Photography/Photo Access

Green Twinspot

249 Chimanimani Mountains

IBA ✔

Albert Froneman

Gurney's Sugarbird

The Chimanimani Mountains are a naturalist's heaven. A possible 60 endemic plant species, including at least three proteas, and several endemic and range-restricted amphibians occur here. It is possible too that the isolated populations and distinctive forms of the **Bokmakierie** and **Cape Bunting** found in the Chimanimani range might warrant specific status, and further investigation is required.

The **Bokmakierie** population of the subspecies *restrictus* is confined to the remotest mountain areas and, therefore, one has to work hard to find it. It is possible that most of the relict population, an estimated 400 individuals, occurs on the eastern side of the range, in Mozambique. On the Zimbabwean side, individuals can be found on the path leading up to Mount Binga (Point 71 on local maps of the area), the highest point of the range at 2 438 m. After locating the bird by its call, you will probably have to scramble over quartzite boulders to find it.

The very dark subspecies *smithersii* of the **Cape Bunting** is far easier to find, as it has become habituated around hikers who spend the night in caves in the mountains.

Blue Swallow* hawks over the magnificent grasslands of the Bundi River plain, and **Gurney's Sugarbird*** feeds on the aloes and proteas in the area. Watch overhead for **Augur Buzzard** and **Scarce Swift** and, with luck, you may even see **Taita Falcon***.

Ask for directions to Bridal Veil Falls in Chimanimani (easily accessed by road). The area hosts a number of forest specials, including **Stripe-cheeked Greenbul**, and **Scarce Swift**. A **Grey Wagtail** has been seen near the base of the falls for a number of years.

Chimanimani Mountains lie at the southern end of the Eastern Highlands massif. Travel through Mutare and access the Birchenough Bridge/Masvingo road. About 70 km along this road, take the major road to the left, which is signposted. This 85 km road is well signposted to Chimanimani town. Just as you enter the town, take the main road to the right, which leads to Chimanimani National Park. Ask for logistical information at Heaven Lodge in town.

250 Lake Mutirikwe & Great Zimbabwe

✔

Excellent miombo birding may be had in the vicinity of Lake Mutirikwe (Lake Kyle Recreational Park) and the adjacent Great Zimbabwe Ruins. The famous Zimbabwe bird statues, originally found within the ruins, are thought to be stylised versions of an African Fish-Eagle or perhaps a Bateleur.

Green-backed Honeybird, **White-breasted Cuckooshrike**, **Miombo Rock-Thrush**, **Red-faced Crombec**, **Southern Hyliota**, **Black-eared Seed-eater** and **Cabanis's Bunting** can all be seen in well-developed miombo canopy in this area. One of the area's more special birds is the elusive **Thick-billed Cuckoo*** (most conspicuous Sept-Dec), which parasitises resident **Retz's Helmet-Shrikes**. Of local interest are the small populations of **Black Saw-wing** and **Swee Waxbill**. The calls of **Mocking Cliff-Chat** resound off the walls of the ruins.

The area can be conveniently visited en route to Harare or the Eastern Highlands. The signposted turn-off to the east is near the Shell Service Station just south of Masvingo. There is an excellent patch of miombo woodland in the Sikato Bay area; take the turn-off directly opposite Great Zimbabwe. Follow this road to Lake Mutirikwe, where **Pallid*** and **Montagu's Harriers** have been recorded in the grasslands at the edge of the lake, and **Collared Flycatcher** in the adjacent miombo.

251 SE Lowveld & Gonarezhou 4X4 IBA ✔✔

The south-east lowveld not only offers some varied savanna birding and access to a number of tricky specials, but also hosts the Big Five game species. Birding on foot is not allowed without a guide.

SPECIALS: Lemon-breasted Canary*, Arnot's Chat, Three-banded Courser*, Thick-billed Cuckoo*, African Finfoot*, Bat Hawk*, White-backed Night-Heron*, Thrush Nightingale, Yellow-billed Oxpecker, Senegal Lapwing, Racket-tailed Roller*, Böhm's* and Mottled Spinetails, Meves's Starling, Collared Palm-Thrush, Dickinson's Kestrel.

SEASON: Most of the specials are resident, and can be seen year-round. **Thick-billed Cuckoo*** and **Thrush Nightingale*** are wet season migrants.

HABITATS: Woodlands, flood plain, pans and riverine vegetation.

BIRDING: Both Tambahata and Muchaniwa pans can be reached from Mahenye Lodge, and both support large numbers of waterfowl in the wet season. **Rufous-winged Cisticola** is found in the emergent vegetation and **Lesser Jacana, Allen's Gallinule** and **Lesser Moorhen** skulk in the dense cover and water lilies at the pan edges. **Senegal Lapwing** is frequently found in the shorter grass in this area.

The dense stands of Ilala palms that lead from Tambahata pan to the Save/Runde junction along the Runde River hold the elusive **Collared Palm-Thrush**; listen for its warbling call, and look in the taller palms. **Dickinson's Kestrel, Red-necked Spurfowl, African Mourning Dove, Mosque Swallow** and **Mottled** and **Böhm's* Spinetails** can be found here too. Large flocks of **Chestnut-backed Sparrowlark** can be found in the overgrazed communal lands near the Save and Runde rivers.

Thick-billed Cuckoo* (rare) calls and displays over thicker riverine growth, such as along the Save River near Mahenye and down towards the Save/Runde junction, a 5 km drive through riparian vegetation. Listen for **Thrush Nightingale*** along the Save River drives.

The dry forest behind Mahenye School at the Save-Runde junction is accessed by driving from Mahenye along the dirt road. The Mahenye School is about 10 km distant, and **Square-tailed Drongo, Tambourine Dove, Woodwards' Batis** (wet season), **Gorgeous Bush-Shrike, Eastern Nicator, Narina Trogon*, African Broadbill*** and **Green Twinspot*** can be found in the area. **Green Malkoha** and **Southern Banded Snake-Eagle** have been seen here, but the grand prize is the rare but regularly recorded **Plain-backed Sunbird**.

Sightings of **Bat Hawk*** and **Pel's Fishing-Owl*** are not uncommon from Mahenye Lodge. Look carefully for small flocks of **Lemon-breasted Canary*** (the similar **Yellow-eyed Canary** is common), particularly in the dry Save riverbed where wild poppies grow.

Large raptors are common throughout the region, which supports one of the highest raptor densities in southern Africa. In Ghonarezhou, there is a large breeding population of **Lappet-faced Vultures**, and **Hooded, White-backed** and **White-faced Vultures** are common here. Guides attached to lodges throughout the area know where to locate secretive species such as **White-backed Night-Heron*** and **Pel's Fishing-Owl***.

Yellow-billed and **Red-billed Oxpeckers** can be found in this big game country, as can **Brown-headed, Meyer's** and **Grey-headed Parrots. Racket-tailed Roller*, Arnot's Chat** and **Retz's Helmetshrike** occur in well-developed mopane, mainly in Malilangwe Trust and Save Valley Conservancies. At Senuko Lodge in the Save Valley Conservancy, look for **Boulder Chat*** among the boulders into which the lodge is built.

GETTING THERE

Exploration of the remote Gonarezhou National Park is by 4WD only in the wet season. Check with National Parks or the neighbouring Malilangwe Trust before embarking on your trip. Malilangwe Trust has two lodges which fully cater for eco-tourists. Much of the area comprises private land, and access is confined to those staying in the accommodation. Camping facilities are available in the park at Chipinda Pools, Chinguli and at Mabalauta. This is big game country and birding on foot is only permitted if birders are accompanied by a guide. The Save-Runde junction is on communal land and the Mahenye CAMPFIRE project is operated from here. Chilo Gorge and Mahenye Lodge are situated at the Save-Runde junction.

ROUTE **27**

WESTERN ZIMBABWE

TOP 10 BIRDS

- White-backed Night-Heron
- Dickinson's Kestrel
- African Finfoot
- Racket-tailed Roller
- Bradfield's Hornbill
- Boulder Chat
- Collared Palm-Thrush
- African Hobby
- Broad-tailed Paradise-Whydah
- Schalow's Turaco

The vast western reaches of Zimbabwe include some of southern Africa's most famous natural landmarks and wilderness areas: Victoria Falls, Hwange National Park and the Matobo Hills. On the Zambezi, birders have access to species found only on the largest African rivers – Rock Pratincole*, African Skimmer* and White-crowned Lapwing. The north-western region supports several species endemic to the savannas of south-central Africa – Dickinson's Kestrel, Racket-tailed Roller*, Bradfield's Hornbill and Brown Firefinch.

The large game herds in Hwange National Park host the localised Yellow-billed Oxpecker. Further south, Boulder Chat* and the magnificent *mackinderi* subspecies of Cape Eagle-Owl* are found in the hauntingly beautiful Matobo Hills, a haven for raptorphiles.

A. Lizek

The granite dome landscape of the Matopos National Park

252 Victoria Falls & Zambezi NP IBA ✔✔

Approximately 2 km wide and cascading 100 m into the gorge below, the Victoria Falls are one of the biggest curtains of falling water in the world. The mighty Zambezi River above the Falls supports special birds such as **Collared Palm-Thrush**, **Rock Pratincole***, **Schalow's Turaco**, **African Skimmer*** and **African Finfoot***. Victoria Falls can also be birded from the Zambian side (see p.334).

SPECIALS: Rufous-bellied Heron, White-backed Night-Heron*, Western Banded Snake-Eagle, Dickinson's Kestrel, Allen's Gallinule, African Finfoot*, White-crowned Lapwing, Rock Pratincole*, African Skimmer*, Schalow's Turaco, Half-collared Kingfisher, Collared Palm-Thrush, Northern Grey-headed Sparrow, Orange-winged Pytilia, Brown Firefinch, Broad-tailed Paradise-Whydah.

SEASON: Oct-Apr is best for most of the specials, with migrants such as **Allen's Gallinule** present in the area in Dec-May, **Rock Pratincole*** in Aug-Jan, and **African Skimmer*** in Jun-Dec. **River Warbler*** is best found in Feb.

HABITATS: Riverine habitat, teak forest on Kalahari sands, grassy vleis, and basaltic gorges with mopane and acacia scrub.

BIRDING: Perhaps the best birding in the area can be had by hiring the services of a guide and booking a private boat trip up the river above the Falls (such as from the A'Zambezi Hotel) Ⓔ on map (p. 334). Head upstream, and ask the guide to take you to Kandahar Island, where **White-backed Night-Heron*** is resident. **African Finfoot*** can be seen by searching under overhanging vegetation along the wooded banks of the small islands. Check the palm trees in the old minefield on the south bank for perched **Dickinson's Kestrel**, and sandbars for **White-crowned Lapwing**. **African Skimmer*** can be found on exposed sandbanks in the Zambezi when the river level is low.

Schalow's Turaco is uncommon and is best viewed in the rainforest Ⓕ area or in the garden of the Victoria Falls Hotel Ⓖ. **Collared Palm-Thrush** may be found in the palm trees along Zambezi Drive between the 'Big Tree' (signposted) Ⓗ and the river, in the camp site situated on the river Ⓘ, or on the golf course. Check the same areas for **Brown Firefinch**, often in the company of **Blue Waxbill** and **Red-billed Firefinch**. **Western Banded Snake-Eagle** may be found anywhere along the river, while **Rock Pratincole*** can be seen upstream from the Falls' edge. **Northern Grey-headed Sparrow** is best found around the industrial sites, the railway marshalling yards and rubbish dumps. **Taita Falcon***, once regular at Third

GETTING THERE

Victoria Falls is a popular tourist destination and offers numerous accommodation options. The National Park has three entrances – one near the Zambian border that allows access by foot to the Victoria Falls, the second 5 km west of the town for vehicular access to the Zambezi Riverside Park, and the third 5 km south of the town on a good dirt road for vehicular access to Chamabonda Vlei. Twitchers Lodge ☎ offers birding advice and budget accommodation in Victoria Falls. Access to the wild areas around the town is easy, but such areas are the haunt of Elephant, Buffalo and Lion, and extreme care should be taken when walking around the forest or along the Zambezi River.

Claire Spottiswoode

Victoria Falls

Gorge, has unfortunately all but disappeared from the area. Lovebirds seen in the area are neither Black-cheeked nor Lilian's; they are, in fact blue-rumped hybridised cage birds that have escaped captivity.

Chamabonda Vlei is the best area in the national park for dry-land migrants, larks and pipits, as well as **Cuckoo Finch*** and **Tinkling Cisticola***.

The main road towards the border at Kazungula passes through wonderful woodland, and even the first 10 km outside the town are worthy of an early morning birding trip. **Broad-tailed Paradise-Whydah** is quite common here in late summer, and **Grey-headed Parrot** flies over early in the morning. The extremely elusive **River Warbler*** may be quite common here, when conditions are right and there is a grassy understorey to the teak woodland. Listen for its predawn, insect-like call in Feb along the length of this road, and sometimes in the town itself. Also keep an eye out for **Orange-winged Pytilia**.

OTHER ANIMALS: Large herds of Sable Antelope occur in the Zambezi National Park and Elephant wander around the edges of the town.

NEARBY SITES: Kazungula Swamps, 70 km west of Victoria Falls, are an excellent place to see many of the Okavango specials more commonly associated with Botswana. The best birding can be had at the private lodge on the Botswana border during the low-water season in Aug-Jan. The lodge, leased by Wild Horizons, lies 75 km west of Victoria Falls via a main tarred road. **Slaty Egret***, **Coppery-tailed Coucal**, **Swamp Nightjar***, **Hartlaub's Babbler**, **Luapula** and **Chirping Cisticolas** may all be found here.

253 Hwange National Park

IBA ✔✔

Hwange is Zimbabwe's largest national park, spanning a huge 14 650 km^2. The park offers a rich variety of bird species, including an excellent diversity of raptors.

SPECIALS: Dickinson's Kestrel, Three-banded Courser*, Racket-tailed Roller*, Bradfield's Hornbill, Mosque Swallow, Southern Pied Babbler, Kalahari Scrub-Robin, Tinkling Cisticola*, Yellow-billed Oxpecker, Arnot's Chat and Dusky Lark*.

SEASON: Birding is good year-round, with migrants present from about Sept-Apr.

HABITATS: Kalahari sandveld supporting teak, or mixed woodlands, mopane, grasslands, and open vleis, plains and pans.

BIRDING: A guided walk around Main Camp **A** may yield **Red-billed Spurfowl**, **Bradfield's Hornbill** and **Crimson-breasted Shrike**; try the birdbath in front of the main office, but be aware of feral **Rosy-faced Lovebirds**! **African Hobby*** may be seen hunting over the camp grounds in the evening.

Martin Harvey

Yellow-billed Oxpeckers on an African Buffalo

GETTING THERE

Turn off the Bulawayo-Victoria Falls road just before the 265 km peg (signposted) and proceed for 23 km to Main Camp. Accommodation should be booked through National Parks Harare. Numerous safari camps also service the area; alternatively Hwange Safari Lodge (hotel) lies about 9 km off the Bulawayo road. Entrance to the park is via the Main Camp gate (a fee is payable). The road to Shumba pans is tarred, with dirt road loops off to the north and south. The road from Shumba to Sinamatella and out through the north gate to Hwange town is dirt (80 km). Ask at Main Camp for route maps, the condition of the roads and opening/closing times.

Three-banded Courser

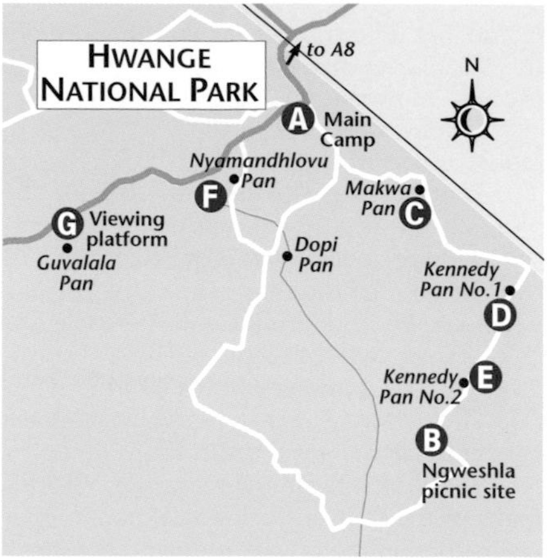

The early morning guided walk from Main Camp is recommended, and sometimes the guides know the location of roosting **Three-banded*** and **Bronze-winged Coursers**. Drive to Ngweshla **B** via Makwa **C**, where **Striped Crake*** breeds in the ponds and ditches during good rains. Stop at all pans, especially in the dry season, when birds and mammals alike come down to the water in their droves.

Continue to Kennedy-1 **D** and Kennedy-2 **E**, where **Kalahari Scrub-Robin** frequents grass/scrub along the eastern verges and **Tinkling Cisticola*** abounds in the scrub. Check the grasslands on the right for **Kori Bustard**.

When passing through woodlands, keep an eye out for **Pale Chanting Goshawk** and **Dickinson's Kestrel**. Stop at Nyamandhlovu **F**, Guvalala **G** and Shumba Platforms, situated off the Sinamatella road. Mandavu Dam, which makes an excellent stop for a diversity of water and bush birds, is 27 km further on. The mopane woodland at the Robin's Camp turn-off holds **Arnot's Chat**. Check game for **Yellow-billed Oxpeckers**.

OTHER ANIMALS: As one of Zimbabwe's premier reserves, all the Big Five species are found here, as well as Bat-eared Fox, Cheetah and a diversity of antelope species.

254 Chizarira National Park 4X4 IBA ✔

It is possible to see two very special species – **Taita Falcon*** and **African Pitta*** – in this remote and very scenic national park that lies on the escarpment south of Lake Kariba. **African Broadbill***, **Eastern Nicator**, **Red-throated Twinspot**, **Ayres' Hawk-Eagle***, **Livingstone's Flycatcher***, **Pennant-winged Nightjar*** and **Three-banded Courser*** are all regular here.

Contact National Parks Harare for reservations and directions. This park is ideal for the bush enthusiast and a 4WD is recommended.

255 Tshabalala Game Sanctuary ✔

Situated on the outskirts of Bulawayo, along the Matopos National Park road, this is the only reserve in Zimbabwe in which acacia thornveld is the dominant vegetation. It is a convenient place to find a number of acacia specialists that are endemic to southern Africa's 'thornbelt'. These include **Burnt-necked Eremomela**, **Ashy Tit**, **Cape Penduline-Tit** and **Kalahari Scrub-Robin**. Also look out for **Bronze-winged Courser** and **Dusky Lark*** in summer. Park at the entrance gate and walk into the reserve. Follow the path from the gate to the staff quarters through fairly dense stands of acacia, where the specials may be seen.

256 Aisleby Municipal Farm

Aisleby Municipal Farm supports a broad range of habitats and offers some of the best bird-watching in the vicinity of Bulawayo, with over 400 species recorded. **Western Marsh-Harrier** is regular near the dams in summer. Dry season visits are particularly productive for water birds, and highlights include sightings of appreciable numbers of **Maccoa Duck**. Small numbers of **Black-necked Grebe** can be seen on the Upper Umgusa Dam.

Wet season visits produce good numbers of migrant warblers, shrikes and waders. **Lesser Jacana** and **Allen's Gallinule** (summer) can be seen in fringing vegetation on the main Umgusa Dam. **Thrush Nightingale*** is often recorded within the rank vegetation fringing the watercourse, while **African Rail** usually responds to playback at Ibis Dam. Bird Dam and its prolific bulrushes is a good place to look for crakes – **Baillon's**, **Striped*** and **Spotted Crakes** have all been recorded here. **Yellow Wagtail** may be seen on the access road.

Take the Victoria Falls road north of Bulawayo for 10 km. Just beyond the Umgusa Yacht Club sign, turn right into Stirling Rd. Travel for 1.5 km, and turn left at the Umgusa Yacht Club and Aisleby signpost.

257 Matobo Hills

Situated 30 km to the south of Bulawayo, the Matobo Hills area stretches over 300 000 ha and includes the Matopos National Park, which is home to a fair number of both Black and White Rhinoceros.

The spectacular granite koppie landscapes are a raptorphile's heaven, and a potential World Heritage Site. The hills are the site of the longest-running raptor research project in the world, and 50 species of raptor have been recorded here. **Verreaux's Eagle** has probably been studied more intensively than any other, as the more than 50 pairs of this species that occupy territories within the area have been monitored for the past 40 years.

Other species that inhabit the rocky landscape include **Boulder Chat*** (such as on the hills near Maleme Dam), **Cape Eagle-Owl*** (subspecies *mackinderi*), **Freckled Nightjar** and **Mottled Swift**.

An isolated population of **Cape Batis** is found in moister woodlands but in close proximity to the similar **Chinspot Batis**.

Roger de la Harpe/IOA

Wooded koppies are favoured by Boulder Chat.

ROUTE 28

ZAMBEZI VALLEY

Zimbabwe's middle Zambezi River Valley teems with wildlife, both within and outside of the reserves, and, for birders, offers an opportunity to see one of the continent's most sought-after species – African Pitta*. In addition, birders can see Lilian's Lovebird and Livingstone's Flycatcher*, as well as Dickinson's Kestrel, Racket-tailed Roller*, Arnot's Chat and Shelley's Sunbird*, which are endemic to the broad-leaved woodlands of south-central Africa.

TOP 10 BIRDS

- African Pitta
- Dickinson's Kestrel
- African Skimmer
- Lilian's Lovebird
- Thick-billed Cuckoo
- Böhm's Spinetail
- Mottled Spinetail
- Racket-tailed Roller
- Livingstone's Flycatcher
- Shelley's Sunbird

Downstream of Lake Kariba, the valley comprises a hot, low-lying expanse, more than one hundred kilometres wide in places and several hundred kilometres long. Mopane woodland is the predominant vegetation type here (with miombo on the plateau areas only), and some of the most exciting birding is to be had in the patches of forest and thicket that fringe the rivers draining the plateaux.

Almost all of the land on the Zimbabwean side of the middle Zambezi is devoted to wildlife and its conservation.

The valley's flagship is Mana Pools National Park, which, during the dry months, plays host to huge congregations of Elephant, Buffalo, Eland, Impala and a diversity of other game species, creating what has been described as an unrivalled wildlife spectacle. However, these large densities have led to the thinning of riverine forest patches, so the most productive areas for African Pitta* are to be found where the riverine fringe is under less pressure. Here, birding is best during the summer months of Nov-Jan, when intra-African migrants such as the pitta have arrived.

Kariba and Mana Pools are both a morning's drive from Harare. The road to Masoka Village is more difficult, and the trip takes longer, making a stopover at the Mavuradonha Wilderness Area well worth the effort.

Those with more time, a spirit of adventure and a healthy respect for wild animals (and a 4WD, especially in the rainy season) who wish to see the best of what the Zambezi River Valley has to offer should plan a round trip from Harare to the Mavuradonha Area and Masoka Village, through the Chewore and Sapi safari areas to Mana Pools National Park, returning via Kariba. Also enquire about Hippo Pools camp in Umfurudzi Safari Area, with rich woodland birding.

Keith Begg/IOA

Mana Pools National Park in the Zambezi Valley

258 Mavuradonha Wilderness Area IBA ✔

The Mavuradonha Wilderness Area lies north-east of Harare on the edge of the Zambezi escarpment, and provides a good stopover point en route to Masoka Village and other sites in the middle Zambezi River Valley.

The reserve offers comfortable camping facilities, as well as varied birding in spectacular surrounds. It is generally vegetated with miombo woodland and is a good place to look for **Miombo Rock-Thrush**, which calls in the evenings some distance behind the camping area along the path to Banirembizi.

A walk to Eagle's Crag should produce **Broad-tailed Paradise-Whydah** (in late summer when breeding) and **Cabanis's Bunting**, which is flushed from the ground where it feeds. **Spotted Creeper*** and **Miombo Tit** also occur in the miombo. Watch for raptors such as **Ayres' Hawk-Eagle*** and **Taita Falcon*** from Eagle's Crag.

In the camping area, look out for **Red-faced Crombec** in the trees, and **Red-throated Twinspot** in the surrounding undergrowth.

259 Mana Pools National Park 4X4 IBA ✔✔

This World Heritage Site is one of the very few reserves with dangerous game in southern Africa where visitors are free to bird on foot. The area offers unforgettable big game experiences, such as the sight of an Elephant herd wading in the Zambezi River, backed by picturesque blue-purple valley escarpment, and a host of bird specials. Areas of dense flood plain *Vetivaria* grassland, colloquially termed 'adrenaline grass' because of the big game that hides here, are best avoided!

SPECIALS: African Skimmer*, Lilian's Lovebird, Livingstone's Flycatcher*, Shelley's Sunbird*, Western Banded Snake-Eagle, Red-necked Falcon, Dickinson's Kestrel, Long-toed Lapwing, Grey-headed Parrot, Thick-billed Cuckoo*, Black and White-browed Coucals, Pel's Fishing Owl*, Mottled and Böhm's* Spinetails, Racket-tailed Roller*, Collared Palm-Thrush and Black-throated Wattle-eye, Meves's Starling.

SEASON: Year-round; migrants from about Sept-Apr. Cool nights during winter; peak season from Aug until the rains start in about Nov.

HABITATS: Flood plain woodland, mopane, thicket and dry woodlands.

BIRDING: It is easier to spot dangerous game in the open flood plain woodland at Mana Pools, so visitors are free to walk about at their own risk; however, as mentioned above, be very careful when entering patches of *Vetivaria* grass and, in fact, any densely vegetated areas where Lion, Buffalo, Elephant and other animals may be concealed (see p.10, *Dangerous animals*).

Most birdwatching is done on the flood plain from the road, with birders hopping out of the vehicle at interesting spots. Look out for flocks of **Lilian's Lovebird** in mopane woodland near the river, especially in the morning.

Thick-billed Cuckoo* (uncommon) and also **Shelley's Sunbird*** (Dec-Feb) occur in the stands of *Faidherbia albida* trees around Nyamepi. Look for the sunbird in the woodland where there is mistletoe; be careful not to confuse it with the abundant **Purple-banded Sunbird. Rufous-bellied Heron** is resident in flood plain pools and weed-covered areas of the river. Check tall trees and riverine patches for **Western Banded Snake-Eagle.**

GETTING THERE

Take the Harare-Chirundu road north, and stop at Marongora National Parks office (306 km) to have your pre-booked permit processed. Continue down the Zambezi escarpment towards Hell's Gate; at 313 km, turn east onto the dirt road. It's about 70 km to Nyamepi Camp from here, with a stop at Nyakasanga Gate (30 km), where you turn north. A high-clearance or 4WD vehicle is recommended, and is essential during the rains. The camp sites at Nyamepi Camp are basic and, unless you have booked lodge accommodation (very hard to get), you will need to be totally self-sufficient! There is no shop or fuel available, so make sure that you have all the necessary provisions, including enough fuel for the 100 km return trip to Makuti.

It is worth driving to Long Pool and Mana airstrip to find **Dusky Lark*** (late summer) on open ground, as well as **Livingstone's Flycatcher*** (year-round) in the Chiruwe riverine vegetation at the top of the airstrip.

Alternatively, drive west towards Vundu and look in the thick woodland just past the sign-posted parking area, where **Collared Palm-Thrush, Bearded Scrub-Robin** and **Black-Throated Wattle-eye** are also found.

Tropical backwaters are rich birding areas.

For **Collared Palm-Thrush,** continue past Vundu (12 km); en route, look for **Arnot's Chat** in the mopane that skirts the Rukomechi concession to the Mana boundary at the Rukomechi River. This extensive area of palms also houses resident **Red-necked Falcon** and a good selection of riverine/thicket birds.

Search for **Mottled Spinetail** around the baobabs on all roads, **Broad-billed** (Sept-Mar) and **Racket-tailed* Rollers** in the tall woodlands, and **Grey-headed Parrot** (mainly active in the mornings and evenings) crossing the river.

The river itself offers a wide range of species, including **Collared Pratincole** (Apr-Jan, mainly dry season), the ubiquitous **White-crowned Lapwing** and, in the weeds, **Long-toed Lapwing**. Clouds of **Southern Carmine Bee-eaters** frequent the banks in the dry season, and **African Skimmer*** forages in flocks over the river (Jun-Dec), while **Böhm's Spinetail*** may be spotted over the channels.

OTHER ANIMALS: Lion, Leopard, Elephant and Buffalo abound in the park, as do Nyala and numerous other antelope species. This is a good place to see African Wild Dog.

260 Masoka Village

4X4 IBA ✔✔✔

Sightings of **African Pitta***, an intra-African migrant, are almost guaranteed in this birding hotspot, especially when it is displaying in Nov-Dec.

SPECIALS: African Pitta*, Southern Ground-Hornbill*, Lilian's Lovebird, Thick-billed* and African Emerald Cuckoos, Pennant-winged Nightjar*, Bohm's* and Mottled Spinetails, Racket-tailed Roller*, Arnot's Chat, Livingstone's Flycatcher* and Meves's Starling.

SEASON: Late Nov-Dec and into Jan is best for **African Pitta***.

HABITATS: Riverine forest/thicket, acacia woodland.

BIRDING: African Pitta* is best located by its frog-like call. It displays from fallen branches or lianas in patches of riverine forest/thicket. This species probably favours older patches with a greater accumulation of leaf litter. Although brightly coloured, it can be remarkably difficult to locate in the forest gloom. It is best searched for by sitting patiently and watching the leaf litter carefully in the dense strip of riverine vegetation below the camp.

The beautiful **Livingstone's Flycatcher*** inhabits the canopy of riparian forest and thicket. Other inhabitants of the thin strips of forest and thicket in the middle Zambezi River Valley include **Eastern Nicator, Black-throated Wattle-eye** and **African**

GETTING THERE

Masoka Village lies in a CAMPFIRE district so please ask for the CAMPFIRE office on arrival. A small admission fee is payable. The rustic but comfortable camp has recently been renovated and a second camp is currently in the process of completion. See ☎ for detailed instructions on how to get to this very remote area, accessed via Mushumbi Pools. A 4WD is essential during the rainy season.

Broadbill*. The characteristic call of **African Emerald Cuckoo** can be heard in summer, and the uncommon **Thick-billed Cuckoo*** is present Oct-May, and is also best located by its call. Also recorded from riparian forest in the district is the rare **Barred Long-tailed Cuckoo***.

Mottled and **Böhm's* Spinetails** can be seen flying around the baobabs located in the school grounds in Masoka Village. **Arnot's Chat**, **Racket-tailed Roller***, **Lilian's Lovebird** and **Meves's Starling** can be seen in the taller 'cathedral' mopane in the area. In the early morning, the deep boom of groups of **Southern Ground-Hornbill*** can be heard from the dry riverbed, and flocks of **Double-banded Sandgrouse** fly in at dusk to drink. The spectacular **Pennant-winged Nightjar*** can sometimes be seen hawking insects over the river at dusk during the summer months.

OTHER ANIMALS: Be aware that this is Big Five country. Tourists are well advised to secure from the CAMPFIRE office the services of a game guide who can watch for Lion, Buffalo and other animals lurking behind bushes while birders peer into the canopy.

CAMPFIRE

Zimbabwe's Communal Areas Management Programme for Indigenous Resources (CAMPFIRE) was one of the world's most successful examples of a Community Based Natural Resource Management (CBNRM) system. The general idea of a CBNRM is that communally owned resources, such as wildlife and indigenous forests, are managed by the very communities who live there.

Masoka Village in the middle Zambezi River Valley was one of the first of CAMPFIRE's projects. By paying the local community to see **African Pitta***, and a host of other specials found in the area, birders are contributing to the preservation of the riverine forest and thicket habitats which the pitta needs in order to breed successfully.

261 Lake Kariba ✔

There are few holiday experiences in Zimbabwe that can compare with a trip on a houseboat on Lake Kariba. While activities other than birding – e.g. cruising within tens of metres of a wading Elephant, or fishing for the legendary tigerfish – most often take precedence, there is also much of interest for the birder.

Long-toed Lapwing makes use of the invasive water hyacinth, such as occurs at Gache Gache. **Goliath Heron** feeds in more exposed areas, where the impressive 'umbrella' feeding of the **Black Heron** is a common sight. Elegant **Collared Pratincole** is common along the exposed shoreline, while large flocks of **African Openbill** may often be found roosting in the dead trunks of submerged trees.

Southern Ground-Hornbill*, **White-fronted** and (in summer) **Southern Carmine Bee-eaters** can be seen along the shoreline.

Red-billed Oxpecker and, to a lesser extent, expanding populations of **Yellow-billed Oxpecker** attend to the herds of Impala; **White-browed Coucal** lurks in thick rank undergrowth. In Kariba village, **Böhms Spinetail*** may be seen overhead, while **Orange-winged Pytilia** occurs in the denser vegetation.

Callan Cohen

A view over the Zambezi Valley

MOZAMBIQUE

Renewed access to Mozambique after years of isolation resulting from civil war has created tremendously exciting opportunities, and the central and southern parts of the country have, since the mid-1990s, become popular destinations for keen birders and travellers. In addition to many species localised in historically more accessible Zimbabwe and South Africa, the threatened lowland forests and miombo woodlands of central and southern Mozambique offer some of the best sites globally for such species as African Pitta, Green-headed Oriole (montane), East Coast Akalat, White-chested Alethe, Chestnut-fronted Helmet-Shrike, Olive-headed Weaver, Plain-backed Sunbird and Locustfinch, and are the non-breeding grounds of the localised Mascarene Martin (winter). Furthermore, the coast offers such tropical exotica as wintering Crab Plover and Madagascar Pond Heron.

The vast area of Mozambique north of the Zambezi has, ornithologically, remained virtually unexplored since expeditions carried out in the early 1930s and 1940s, which revealed numerous enigmatic and elusive montane forest specials such as Dappled Mountain Robin, Long-billed Forest Warbler, Thyolo Alethe, White-winged Apalis, and Mozambique's only true endemic, the beautiful Namuli Apalis. Recent expeditions have shown that these species continue to thrive, and their mountain strongholds are accessible to adventurous birders.

Birders travelling inland must be largely self-sufficient in terms of camping equipment, water and extra fuel, and should preferably travel in convoys of more than one vehicle, ideally including at least one 4WD, equipment such as towropes, spades, an axe for clearing fallen trees, mud channels and high-lift jack during the wet season (see also *Driving*, p.12). Mozambique, once deemed unsafe, is now much safer to traverse, as long as simple precautionary measures are followed: do not drive at night or camp near cities. Don't drive on old tracks or walk near railway lines or abandoned buildings, as landmines remain a concern. Locals can advise you about safe areas; Portuguese is essential and a phrase book is recommended (see box *Where are the Landmines?* p.10).

ROUTE 29

SOUTHERN MOZAMBIQUE

TOP 10 BIRDS

- Crab Plover
- Neergaard's Sunbird
- Plain-backed Sunbird
- Pink-throated Twinspot
- Madagascar Bee-eater
- Mangrove Kingfisher
- Black-rumped Buttonquail
- Pale Batis
- Brown Scrub-Robin
- Olive-headed Weaver

Johann Grobbelaar

Olive-headed Weaver

Mozambique south of the Save River consists primarily of a vast coastal plain cloaked in mixed woodlands. Much of the interior is difficult to access, and birding is concentrated along the more diverse and accessible coastline, creating a linear route along the EN1 from Maputo up the coast, ultimately heading inland just south of the Save River and thence to the montane and miombo birding of central Mozambique. Key coastal sites, specifically Inhaca Island, offer superb birding and are situated around the capital of Maputo (easily accessed by road from South Africa via Komatipoort/Ressano Garcia). Also near Maputo are a number of good sites easily visited on a half-day trip from the city.

Moving north, the EN1 passes many beautiful coastal lakes, but also cuts through apparently endless and depauperate coconut palm plantations extending as far as Massinga. North of Inhambane, the vegetation reverts to woodland, and the coastline is peppered with villages offering tourist facilities and good birding. Inland, in the vicinity of Panda (west of Inhambane), lies a relict patch of miombo, which hosts an isolated yet accessible population of Olive-headed Weaver, as well as several other miombo specials. The northernmost key coastal localities are Vilankulo and the Bazaruto archipelago, where numerous sought-after tropical coastal species occur. These can be explored on a trip out to sea.

Approaching the Save, one passes through some magnificent woodlands that offer superb birding, including a taste of the lowland forest specials of central Mozambique.

262 Maputo Special (Elephant) Reserve

4X4 IBA ✔✔

This beautiful coastal reserve south of Maputo offers excellent birding in its extensive areas of sand forest, grasslands and wetlands, including several Maputaland specials that also occur in far northern KwaZulu-Natal. However, access is not straightforward and visitors need to be equipped with 4WD and camping gear.

SPECIALS: African Pygmy Goose*, Southern Banded Snake-Eagle, Black-rumped Buttonquail, Senegal Lapwing, Lesser Jacana, Black Coucal, African Broadbill*, Rosy-breasted Longclaw*, Woodwards' Batis, Neergaard's Sunbird*, Pink-throated Twinspot*.

SEASON: Birding is good throughout the year.

HABITATS: Tall sand forest, mangroves, riverine woodland, grassland, freshwater and tidal wetlands, and seashore.

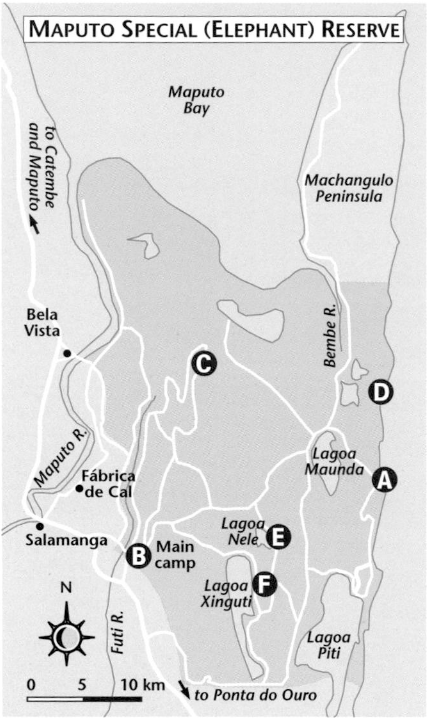

BIRDING: Birding at and around Ponta Milibangalala Ⓐ can be rewarding. **Brown Scrub-Robin** is common, and **White-starred Robin** is present in winter; other forest species include **Black-throated Wattle-eye**, **Blue-mantled Crested Flycatcher**, **Grey Sunbird** and **Dark-backed Weaver**. In the grasslands nearby, look for **Black Saw-wing** and **Grey-rumped Swallows**. **Black-chested Snake-Eagle**, **African Goshawk**, **Thick-billed Weaver** and **Klaas's Cuckoo** occur along the forest edge. **Spotted Ground-Thrush*** has been seen at Ponta Membene Ⓓ, north of Ponta Milibangalala, and is probably a regular visitor.

Good grassland birding is possible around the Mirador lookout point Ⓒ and around Lake Nele Ⓔ. Possible sightings include **African Marsh-Harrier**, **Shelley's Francolin**, **Denham's Bustard***, **Black Coucal** (summer), **Senegal Lapwing** and possibly **Black-rumped Buttonquail**. You may also wish to explore the road from the main camp northwards along

GETTING THERE

The shortest route to the reserve from Maputo involves taking the ferry across the bay to Catembe. Take the only road south of Catembe, and look out for the signposts to the reserve after about 60 km. The ferry crossing is slow and expensive, and the alternative route via Boane is preferable. The main tracks within the reserve are very sandy, making 4WD a necessity. Also, there are at present no accurate reserve maps available. Please beware of Elephant when birding in denser habitat, and of Crocodile and Hippo around the lakes.

The only official camp site in the reserve is at Ponta Milibangalala Ⓐ, situated on the coast, north-east of the entrance to the main camp Ⓑ. The main camp is currently not operational; therefore, to reach Ponta Milibangalala, you need to drive across the reserve; at the time of writing, the journey took about 3 hours. At Lake (Lagoa) Maunda, take the track that goes south-east around the lake, and look for the sign that indicates that Ponta Milibangalala is 8 km further on. The camp site is in a lovely location in a dune forest, near the beach. There are no facilities apart from a well, which only produces water suitable for washing. There are forest clearings in which you can pitch a tent.

Nigel J. Dennis

Crested Guineafowl

the Futi, which passes several water bodies and provides a good vantage point from which to search for a variety of storks and herons, **African Pygmy Goose*** (common), **Lesser Jacana**, and, in the riparian vegetation, **Pel's Fishing-Owl***, **Southern Brown-throated Weaver** and **Magpie Mannikin***.

If you manage to access the mangroves and tidal lagoons of the north, birding possibilities include **Sooty Falcon**, **Madagascar Bee-eater** and **Mangrove Kingfisher*** (the latter in winter; in summer it moves into the riverine forest elsewhere in the reserve to breed). Lagoon edges have, in roughly decreasing order of abundance, **Common Whimbrel**, **Eurasian Curlew** and **Terek Sandpiper**, **Common Greenshank**, **Grey Plover**, **Eurasian Curlew**, **Bar-tailed Godwit**, **Greater Sand Plover** and the occasional **Chestnut-banded Plover** and **Great White Pelican**. Look out for **Crab Plover***, which has not been recorded yet but probably occurs here.

The drive southwards to Lake Xinguti **F** and its surrounding forest offers **Southern Banded Snake-Eagle**, **Crested Guineafowl**, **Livingstone's Turaco**, **Green Malkoha**, **Narina Trogon***, **African Broadbill***, **Brown Scrub-Robin**, **Eastern Nicator**, **Black-throated Wattle eye**, **Woodwards' Batis**, **Rudd's Apalis**, **Olive** and **Gorgeous Bush-Shrikes**, **Neergaard's Sunbird***, **Pink-throated** and **Green Twinspots*** and, occasionally, **Palm-nut Vulture***.

OTHER ANIMALS: The park hosts about 150 Elephant; common mammals include Red Duiker and Samango Monkey.

NEARBY SITES: Ponta do Ouro and Ponta Malongane, just to the south of the reserve and close to the South African border, are very popular dive sites (Whale Shark may be found here). Great forest, woodland and wetland habitats offer **Palm-nut Vulture***, **Green Malkoha**, **Rudd's Apalis**, **Woodwards' Batis** and **Grey Waxbill**. The forest-fringed lakes adjacent to Ponta Malongane and Zitundo hold **African Pygmy Goose*** and **Lesser Jacana**, and **Senegal Lapwing**, **Shelley's Francolin**, **Swamp Nightjar***, **Broad-tailed Warbler**, **Pale-crowned Cisticola**, and **Rosy-breasted Longclaw*** have all been seen in the surrounding grassland. The dambos south of Ponta Malongane are well worth exploring when flooded; **Eurasian Bittern** has even been recorded nearby.

263 Inhaca Island ✔✔

This beach- and mangrove-fringed island, an hour's boat ride across Maputo Bay, is the site of some spectacular coral reefs, and offers good birding in its mangroves, freshwater swamps, mudflats and dune forest. Most notably, a selection of key tropical coast species are reliably found here, including **Sooty Falcon**, **Greater Sand Plover** and **Mangrove Kingfisher*** (the last mainly in winter).

SPECIALS: Green Malkoha, Olive Sunbird, Sooty Falcon, Greater Sand Plover, Osprey, Mangrove Kingfisher*.

SEASON: Most wader species are summer migrants, but there is good birding year-round.

HABITATS: Mangroves, freshwater swamps, mudflats and dune forests.

BIRDING: Birding is best in the undisturbed habitats around the Biological Research Station **C** on the map. **Sooty Falcon** occurs annually in reasonable numbers and hunts especially over the Saco **D**; scan taller, dead mangrove trees

GETTING THERE

A speedboat transfer to the island can easily be organised through any travel agent or hotel in Maputo. There are regular and relatively inexpensive daily flights from Maputo with TransAirways. There is one hotel on the island, Inhaca Lodge **A**. There is also a lovely camping site at Ponta Torres **B** in the dune forest – a good spot for forest species, but getting there is not easy if you don't have your own boat.

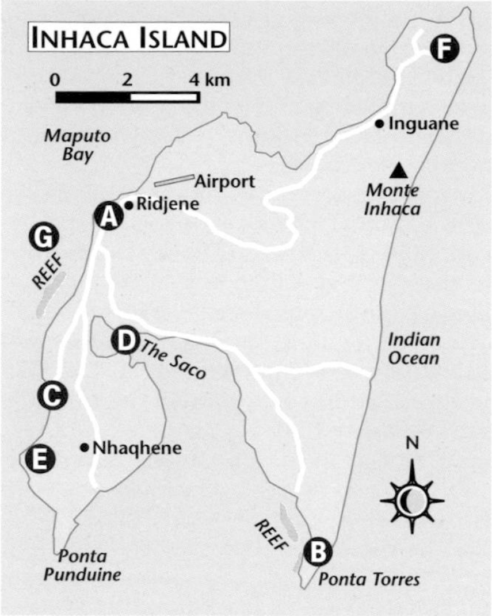

at the bay edges and around the Nhaqhene Swamp for perching birds. It has also been seen on the hill, near the lodge. **Crab Plover*** is occasionally seen in small groups during summer; most sightings have been recorded in the vicinity of Ponta Raza Ⓔ.

The thickets and forest patches on the southern outskirts of the lodge Ⓐ are worth exploring. The easiest way is to take the path going up to the *Posto Administrativo* on top of the hill. **Green Malkoha** occurs here, and **Spotted Ground-Thrush*** was seen here recently. At low tide the 5 km walk on the beach along the forest towards the Biological Research Station can be quite rewarding as far as both waders and forest species are concerned. **Osprey** is often seen flying in this area in summer, and **Black-throated Wattle-eye** may be seen in the forest. **Olive Sunbird** and **Mangrove Kingfisher*** occur in the mangroves north of the lodge and around the Saco. After storms, it is worth scanning for pelagics from the lighthouse area Ⓕ, or from any point along the island's east coast.

OTHER ANIMALS: Snorkelling and diving are excellent, particularly as the Inhaca reefs have been largely unaffected by the Indian Ocean coral bleaching events of the late 1990s. Deep-sea diving can also be outstanding, with frequent sightings of Whale Shark and other big pelagics. There is a well-equipped diving centre at the Inhaca Lodge. One can go snorkelling either at the Barreira Vermelha reef (Ⓖ, 3 km south of the lodge), or at Ponta Torres Ⓑ. The lodge provides boat transport to these sites.

264 Panda

IBA ✔✔✔

Panda is a short way inland from the southern Mozambique coast, close to a dwindling patch of miombo woodland, which is presently the only site south of the Zambezi where you will find the localised miombo specialist, **Olive-headed Weaver***. Since Clancey first reported its presence here in the early 1960s, none were seen until they were rediscovered by Vincent Parker during the course of his fieldwork for the Mozambique Atlas Project in 1996. A population of 100 breeding pairs is estimated to occur in the woodlands near the town of Panda, and a good selection of other miombo and thicket species occur here too.

GETTING THERE

Panda can be reached from the coast either via Maxixe or from nearby Homoine (48 km), if approaching from the north, or from Inharrime (60 km), if approaching from the south. Both roads are in good condition, although the Inharrime road offers the attraction of some good dambos along the way. To reach the **Olive-headed Weaver*** woodland from Panda, take the only road south-west out of Panda (recently upgraded), travel 13 km and take a track to the left which leads into the best woodland after 2 km. The tracks which lead into the woodland are very sandy and a 4WD is strongly recommended. Most birders camp in the woodland; however, there are also formal camp sites along the seafront at Maxixe.

SPECIALS: Mascarene Martin*, Southern Hyliota, Red-faced Crombec, Neergaard's Sunbird*, Olive-headed Weaver*, Black-eared Seed-eater.

SEASON: **Olive-headed Weaver*** is possible year-round.

HABITATS: Mosaic of tall miombo woodland and subsistence agriculture.

BIRDING: The best miombo woodland lies between 12 and 18 kilometres south-west of Panda. In winter, **Olive-headed Weaver*** is usually found among mixed bird parties, but in summer they are in isolated pairs. They are inconspicuous and somewhat sluggish birds, foraging along branches and dangling from clumps of old-man's-beard lichen, from which they also construct their solitary, pendulous nests. The bird's jizz is unmistakeable: rotund, compact, and short-tailed, with a small bill, rich yellow underparts and olive upper parts.

Other miombo species that occur here in bird parties are **Green-backed Honeybird**, **White-breasted Cuckooshrike**, **Southern Hyliota**, **Red-faced Crombec**, **Pale Batis** and **Black-eared Seed-eater**. **Racket-tailed Roller*** is relatively common but, as ever, inconspicuous. Both **Retz's** and (rarely) **Chestnut-fronted* Helmet-Shrikes** occur.

Claire Spottiswoode

Olive-headed Weaver breeds in this tree at Panda.

Other interesting broad-leaved woodland species are **Brown-headed Parrot**, **Böhm's Spinetail***, **Flappet Lark**, **Grey Penduline-Tit** and **Pallid Flycatcher**. Moving west out of the miombo into tall mixed woodlands, you may find species such as **Red-necked Spurfowl**, **Broad-billed Roller**, **Crowned Hornbill**, **Red-backed Mannikin** and **Neergaard's*** and **Purple-banded Sunbirds**. **Fawn-coloured Lark** is common. **Mascarene Martin*** has been seen feeding over the woodland in winter. In disturbed, cultivated areas along the road to Panda from Inharrime, look out for **Lemon-breasted Canary***.

NEARBY SITES: A large dambo crosses the Panda-Inharrime road 13.5 km south of the Panda T-junction (GPS 24°10.36'S, 34°46.09'E). When wet, this can provide **Dwarf Bittern**, **White-backed Duck**, **African Pygmy Goose***, **African Marsh-Harrier**, **Lesser Moorhen**, **Allen's Gallinule**, **Lesser Jacana** and **Black Coucal**. **Eurasian Bittern** has even been heard booming here. It is also worth taking a stroll here in winter, when **Black-rumped Buttonquail** and **Pale-crowned Cisticola** have been flushed, and **Grey-rumped Swallow** breeds. **Collared Palm-Thrush** and **Palm-nut Vulture*** have been seen, and **Shelley's Francolin** occurs in the surrounding grassland.

265 Inhambane Region IBA ✔

The coastline in the Inhambane region is dotted with seaside fishing villages and small holiday resorts, which also provide access to some wonderful beaches, mudflats, marshes and coastal forests, all offering good birding. These include, running south to north, Guinjata Bay, Ponta da Barra, Maxixe, Morrungulo and Pomene. The numerous roadside lakes and ponds (often with lilies) and flooded areas usually hold a good diversity of water birds; characteristic species include **African Pygmy Goose***, **White-backed Duck**, **African Rail**, **Rufous-winged Cisticola** and **Fan-tailed Widow**. Mudflats supply a reasonable variety of migrant waders, including **Mongolian**, **Greater Sand** and **Grey Plovers** and **Terek Sandpiper**, and terns, including **Caspian**, **Lesser Crested**, **Little** and **Swift Terns**. Productive mudflats lie in front of Maxixe, Barra Reef, Ilha do Barro, and along the mangroves lining the Inhambane lagoon. **Mangrove Kingfisher*** can be quite common around the lagoon, which can be reached by taking the path from immediately behind the Barra Lodge or behind the Barra Reef Hotel. **Crab Plover*** has been seen on the Maxixe mudflats, and flocks of up to several hundred birds have been seen in summer on the shore of Ilha do Barro. An isolated population of **White-fronted Bee-eater** occurs at Pomene. Interesting forest species reported are **Magpie Mannikin*** near Ponta da Barra, **Collared Palm-Thrush** in coconut palms at Ponta da Barra and Morrungulo, **Livingstone's Flycatcher** at Pomene and, further south, **Brown Scrub-Robin** at Xai-Xai, as well as more widespread forest and thicket species such as **Crested Guineafowl**, **Eastern Nicator**, **Black-throated Wattle-eye**, **Pale Batis**, **Gorgeous Bush-Shrike**, **Retz's Helmet-Shrike** and **Brimstone Canary**. Look out for **Lemon-breasted Canary*** and **African Hobby*** in the general area.

266 Vilankulo & Bazaruto Archipelago IBA ✔✔

Vilankulo village lies on the mainland Mozambique coast, opposite the famously beautiful Bazaruto archipelago, and offers good coastal and wetland birding in addition to providing a base for pelagic trips. The smaller and less touristy village of Inhassouro, 50 km north along the coast, is quieter and more picturesque than Vilankulo, and also worth a visit.

SPECIALS: Crab Plover*, Madagascar Bee-eater, Mascarene Martin*, Lemon-breasted Canary*.

SEASON: Most wader and tern species are summer migrants, but there is good birding year-round.

HABITATS: Lily-covered pans, sandy shoreline, mudflats, coastal forest, ocean.

BIRDING: In the vicinity of the turn-off to Vilankulo from the EN1 (and also along the Inhassouro access road, 58 km to the north), there is a network of pretty, lily-covered pans, and good habitat associated with the Govuro River (crossed by the Vilankulo access road). These areas are best known for the occasional **Madagascar Pond Heron** (note that **Squacco Heron** is common here, and juveniles have similar markings to Madagascar Pond Heron). From May to September, small flocks of **Mascarene Martin*** may be seen. Other interesting species include **African Pygmy Goose***, **White-backed Duck**, **African Openbill**, **Saddle-billed Stork**, **African Rail**, **Blue-cheeked Bee-eater**, **Croaking** and **Rufous-winged Cisticolas** and **Yellow Weaver**; more scarcely, **Mangrove Kingfisher*** and **Lemon-breasted Canary*** have been seen around the pan edges. **African Cuckoo Hawk** is common here and often perches on telephone lines. **Eleanora's Falcon** has been seen in this vicinity several times, and may be a regular summer visitor.

In Vilankulo town, **Madagascar Bee-eater** occurs year-round along the beachfront and in gardens, and breeds in the vicinity. The mudflats immediately in front of the main seafront in town may provide tern roosts, and waders such as **Common Whimbrel**, **Bar-tailed Godwit**, **Terek Sandpiper** and **Mongolian** and **Greater Sand Plovers**; also try the flats in front of the Blue Waters resort, 5 km beyond the airport.

The shores of the islands of the Bazaruto archipelago are excellent for terns and waders. Mostly famously, **Crab Plover*** regularly occurs during summer, usually in small groups. The best areas to search for **Crab Plover*** are the west coast of Benguerra Island (scan the extensive mudflats near Benguerra Lodge), and especially the sandy spit running north from the tip of the Saõ Sebastiaõ peninsula towards Marguruque Island. The latter is only accessible by boat; if approaching from Vilankulo, time your visit carefully to avoid being stranded in the bay at low tide. This is also an excellent site for large tern roosts; throughout the islands, species include **Common**, **Swift**, **Sandwich**, **Lesser Crested**, **Little**, and occasionally **Sooty** and **Roseate Terns**. **Madagascar Bee-eater** breeds in good numbers in the dune slacks of the eastern seaboard of all three islands of the archipelago. On Bazaruto Island, there is also good

GETTING THERE

Access to Vilankulo is by tar road, 21 km from the main EN1 (226 km north of Maxixe). Vilankulo is a busy holiday destination and there are many hotels and camping sites in the area. If you wish to visit the Bazaruto archipelago, transport (by helicopter, speedboat or dhow) can be arranged through any of the hotels in town.

Dominique Halleaux

Crab Plover migrates to the Mozambique coast in summer.

thicket, grassland and swamp-forest birding. Local specials include isolated populations of **Green Malkoha** and **Black-headed Apalis**, and **Pel's Fishing-Owl*** has also been seen here. The sandspit at the north of the island sometimes hosts thousands of **Bar-tailed Godwit**, and **Eurasian Oystercatcher** is a regular visitor. Vagrants to the archipelago have included **Red-footed Booby**, **Lesser Frigatebird** and **Brown Noddy**. See pp.20-23 for information on Pelagic Birding.

OTHER ANIMALS: Snorkelling and diving are excellent and can easily be arranged through one of the firms in Vilankulo town. Marine mammal sightings can also be exciting, and Sperm and Humpbacked Whales and, best of all, Dugong have all been reported on day trips out of Vilankulo.

NEARBY SITES: En route from Panda/Inhambane to Vilankulo, the EN1 passes two particularly impressive Baobab forests (interspersed with villages), where **Mottled** and especially **Böhm's*** **Spinetails** are abundant, and **Mosque Swallow** is common. These are respectively 47 and 57 km north of Massinga (or 110 and 100 km south of the Vilankulo turn-off).

Warwick Tarboton

Mozambique coast

267 Save Woodlands ✔✔

The roadside mixed woodland along the EN1 north and especially south of the Save River is magnificent and provides great coastal woodland and thicket birding. It is worth stopping and birding anywhere between Vilankulo and Inchope, but one site particularly worth investigating is Save Pan. To reach it, turn off to the south-west onto a small track 13 km south of the Save River bridge (GPS 21°12.45'S, 34°40.17'E), and continue for 1.5 km along this track to the edge of the picturesque pan, which can at times be largely obscured by reeds. **Madagascar Pond Heron** has been seen here in winter, in addition to the more common **Rufous-bellied Heron**, **African Pygmy Goose*** and **Lesser Jacana**.

The woodland between the pan and the tar road provides **Green Malkoha**, **Narina Trogon***, **Mangrove Kingfisher***, **Eastern Nicator**, **Bearded Scrub-Robin**, **Green-capped Eremomela**, **Red-faced Crombec**, **Pale Batis**, **Livingstone's Flycatcher**, **Gorgeous Bush-Shrike**, and **Plain-backed**, **Neergaard's*** and **Purple-banded Sunbirds**. **Grey-headed Parrot** overflies, shrilly calling at dawn and dusk. Both **Chestnut-fronted*** and **Retz's Helmet-Shrikes** occur commonly, and hence also **Thick-billed Cuckoo***, the latter's brood parasite. **African Cuckoo Hawk** and **Dickinson's Kestrel** are unusually plentiful between Vilankulo and Inchope; while driving also keep an eye out for **Racket-tailed Roller***.

268 Zinave National Park ✔

The beautiful and remote Zinave National Park is well worth a visit for those with the time to explore. It lies on the southern bank of the Save, and is reached by taking the road west from the EN1 (turn off at Maphinhane village, 32 km south of the Vilankulo turn-off) to the town of Mabote. Continue through Mabote and, for a further 50 km, through sand forest and miombo to Maculuve. The park gate is 10 km beyond Maculuve, and 30 km south of the Save River. There is a camp site with basic facilities. Habitats in the park include baobab forests, mopane and miombo woodland, riverine forest, and pans lined with fever trees. Big game only passes through, but antelope include Suni, Oribi and Impala. **White-crowned Lapwing**, **Collared Pratincole** and **African Skimmer*** grace the Save, along with the few remaining Hippo. Woodland birds around the camp site include **Double-banded Sandgrouse**, **Bronze-winged Courser**, **Racket-tailed Roller***, **Scaly-throated Honeyguide**, **Eastern Nicator**, **Green-capped Eremomela** and **Pale Batis**.

ROUTE 30

CENTRAL MOZAMBIQUE

Central Mozambique runs east to west from the highlands of the Zimbabwean border region to the Indian Ocean, and south to north from the Save to the Zambezi River. It is primarily flat, with the notable exceptions of the 1 863 m-high granite massif of Mount Gorongosa, which rises abruptly from the sprawling woodlands north of the Pungwe River, and the gentle incline of the miombo-cloaked Cheringoma Plateau south of the Zambezi. Between Gorongosa and the Indian Ocean lie superb tracts of miombo woodlands interspersed with forest patches, now sadly under intense pressure from charcoal burning and commercial logging.

TOP 10 BIRDS

- White-chested Alethe
- Green-headed Oriole
- East Coast Akalat
- Plain-backed Sunbird
- Chestnut-fronted Helmet-Shrike
- African Pitta
- Lesser Seedcracker
- Mascarene Martin
- Speckle-throated Woodpecker
- Blue Quail

Up to now, most birders have concentrated their efforts at three main sites: Mount Gorongosa for Green-headed Oriole*, the Chinizuia woodlands for miombo and lowland forest species, and Rio Savanne, near Beira, for grassland and coastal birding, and have until recently neglected the vast coastal forests of the readily accessible Zambezi Delta hunting concessions. Do not underestimate the time it takes to travel from one site to another; on small tracks or during the rainy season, average travelling speed is usually in the region of 20 km per hour.

Callan Cohen

Mount Gorongosa is home to an endemic subspecies of Green-headed Oriole.

269 Mount Gorongosa

4X4 IBA ✔✔✔

Mount Gorongosa is an extensively forested massif that rises abruptly from the plains of central Mozambique, and is legendary as the only site south of the Zambezi for **Green-headed Oriole*** (the distinctive *speculifer* subspecies is endemic). The rough drive and hike to the montane forest is also rewarded by great scenery and numerous other montane forest and tropical lowland specials. This tried-and-tested yet tiring undertaking requires a good two to three days from the main Beira road and back, a capable vehicle and a reasonable level of fitness.

SPECIALS: Green-headed Oriole*, Pallid Honeyguide, Swynnerton's Robin*, Chirinda Apalis*, Black-and-white Flycatcher*, Moustached Grass Warbler, Anchieta's Tchagra*, Magpie Mannikin*, and Lesser Seedcracker*.

SEASON: Forest birding is good year-round. However, access to Vinduzi, at the foot of the mountain, during the wet season is by 4WD only.

HABITATS: The lower slopes of the mountain are covered in a mixture of remnant thicket, moist woodland and subsistence agriculture, as well as rank undergrowth along the numerous perennial streams. On the eastern flank (the most accessible side) of the massif, forest cover is restricted to the higher valleys. Grassland and bracken occur between forest patches and on the summit ridge.

BIRDING: The mosaic of agricultural crops and remnant natural vegetation on the lower slopes offers excellent birding en route to the montane forest, including a good diversity of seed-eaters. Look carefully among the common species for **Magpie Mannikin***, **Orange-winged Pytilia**, **Grey Waxbill**, **Black-winged Bishop** and, with much luck, the shy and stocky **Lesser Seedcracker***. Patches of thicket support **Blue-Spotted Wood-Dove**, **Green-backed** and **Speckle-throated Woodpeckers**, **African Broadbill***, **Black-throated Wattle-eye**, **Pale Batis** and **Red-throated Twinspot** and, occasionally, **Black-and-white Flycatcher***. **African Cuckoo Hawk** is fairly common, and **Miombo Blue-eared Starling** occurs in the cultivated areas. **Moustached Grass Warbler**, **Red-winged Warbler** and **Croaking Cisticola** are all quite common in areas of long grass and especially along the numerous streams.

GETTING THERE

Take the tarred EN1 from Inchope to Gorongosa. Drive through Gorongosa town and continue over the bridge and along the Caia road for 1 km. Take the turn-off to the right onto a secondary road (GPS 18°40.21'S, 34°04.67'E) Ⓐ. This track leads through the villages of Muloza and Tazarunda for 28.2 km before reaching Vinduzi Ⓑ (GPS 18°28.88'S, 34°12.57'E). Although it seems that you are moving away from the mountain, do not despair; you actually aren't! Allow at least one and a half hours for this journey, and take great care with the several somewhat uneven river crossings (including one next to a destroyed bridge, 5.3 km before Vinduzi). If the river is swollen, you may wish to walk through first to check the depth and surface. Once you enter Vinduzi, you will probably be surrounded by a crowd of people, and herded off to the local police station, or the administrator, or the Gorongosa National Park office, where you must get permission to ascend the mountain and camp in the village. You will need to engage the services of a car guard and a guide. The mountain is sacred to the inhabitants, and visitors who do not follow the prescribed procedures will be met with hostility.

It is preferable to begin your climb up the mountain at dawn or even earlier. The start of the hike is relatively easy, along a flat stretch that runs through agricultural land, before it slowly climbs through small, low forest patches. After about an hour of walking, you may be bidden to stop at the house of the park ranger (or 'fiscal'). From the house, the path leads through a band of scrappy woodland and, at an altitude of about 800 m, into forest and grassland.

The walk takes anything from two to five hours, depending on your level of fitness, so carry sufficient water. If you go up only for the day, it is well worth walking the extra few hundred metres to the summit of this eastern flank of the mountain to admire the superb view over the ridge and into the broad, partly forested valley beyond. A very desirable alternative is to camp at the summit, which you can do for two days. This is easily arranged with the ranger and guide, who will descend at night and meet you again the next morning. Access will soon be possible to the closer western slopes (see www.birdingafrica.com for updates).

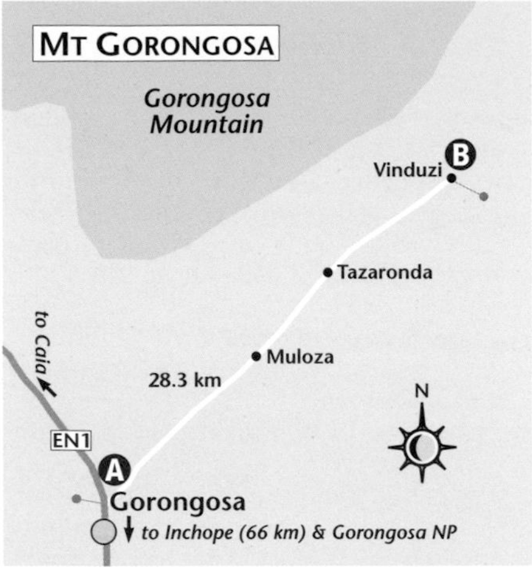

The forest understorey is, for the most part, fairly open, albeit boulder-strewn in places, and one can bird here with relative ease. Throughout the tall montane forest, **Green-headed Oriole*** is common year-round, and easy to locate by its calls (liquid notes very like Black-headed Oriole, and a harsh 'aaaeeergh' like African Golden Oriole), though patience may be needed to obtain good views as the birds remain in the forest canopy. The orioles readily venture to the forest edge and may be seen without entering the forest. Other birds of the forest canopy are **Narina Trogon***, **Livingstone's Turaco**, **Silvery-cheeked Hornbill**, **Pallid Honeyguide**, **Grey Cuckooshrike**, **Striped-cheeked Greenbul**, **Black-fronted Bush-Shrike*** and, if lucky, **Eastern Bronze-naped Pigeon***. Gorongosa also hosts two species otherwise mainly restricted to the Eastern Highlands of Zimbabwe: the noisy and conspicuous **Chirinda Apalis***, and inconspicuous **Swynnerton's Robin***. The latter is uncommonly seen here, and is much more accessible in the Eastern Highlands of Zimbabwe. Similarly, **White-chested Alethe*** has been heard just once since being collected here in the 1960s, but keep a look out for it anyway!

A vigil over the forest canopy is likely to yield a good diversity of raptors – possibilities include **Ayres' Hawk-Eagle***, **African Crowned Eagle**, **Palm-nut Vulture***, **African Cuckoo Hawk**, **African Goshawk** and **Peregrine Falcon**. Also look out for **Böhm's Spinetail*** and **Eastern Saw-wing**. **Singing Cisticola** occurs in the grassland in between forest patches. In the grassland, bracken and thicket mosaic on the summit, look out for an isolated population of **Miombo Double-collared Sunbird**; the sunbird has been collected here, but has not been seen for some years.

Also consider taking a walk along the river next to Vinduzi village, where **Anchieta's Tchagra*** and **Mountain Wagtail** are regularly seen, in addition to the species found on the lower slopes of the mountain.

270 Gorongosa National Park IBA ✔✔

The Parc Naçionale de Gorongosa was once one of the greatest big game areas in southern Africa. It remains a beautiful wilderness, effectively lying at the southern end of the Great Rift Valley between the Gorongosa-Barúe Highlands to the west and the Cheringoma Plateau to the east. Game is sparse, as a result of heavy culling during the war, and poaching and charcoal logging remain important threats. However, conservation efforts are afoot to restore the area to some of its former glory.

SPECIALS: Long-toed Lapwing, Senegal Lapwing, Pennant-winged Nightjar*, Thick-billed Cuckoo*, Black-and-white Flycatcher*, Magpie Mannikin*.

SEASON: The road to Chitengo becomes very muddy during the rains, but birding on the Urema flood plain is best during the late wet and early dry seasons.

HABITATS: Extensive dry woodlands, palm savannas and vast, seasonally flooded wetlands.

BIRDING: En route from the park gate to Chitengo Camp, check the numerous grass-lined streams for **Moustached Grass Warbler**, **Grey Waxbill** and **Magpie Mannikin***, and the good miombo woodland in between for **Pennant-winged Nightjar*** (unusually common here in summer), **Thick-billed Cuckoo***, **White-breasted Cuckooshrike**, **Arnot's Chat**, **Broad-tailed Paradise-Whydah**, **Black-eared Seed-eater** and **Cabanis's Bunting**. Good birding is possible in Chitengo Camp, but beyond it landmines are a possibility, so stick to the roads and the landing strip. **Black-and-white Flycatcher*** occurs at the camp, **Red-necked Falcon, Dickinson's Kestrel, Racket-tailed Roller*** and **Collared Palm-Thrush** in the surrounding palm savanna, and **Senegal Lapwing** and **Grey-rumped Swallow** on the adjoining landing strip.

In the northern section of the park, explore the beautiful Urema flood plain, which remains perennially moist (best during about Jan-Jul) and can provide magnificent waterbirding. Species may include **Great White** and **Pink-backed Pelicans, Dwarf Bittern, African Openbill, Saddle-billed Stork, Baillon's Crake, Allen's Gallinule, Lesser Moorhen, Long-toed Lapwing, Greater Painted Snipe** (in large numbers), **Wattled*** and **Grey Crowned Cranes, Montagu's Harrier, Collared Pratincole, Black-winged Bishop, Red-headed Quelea*** and waterfowl in their thousands, all against the stunning backdrop of Mount Gorongosa. **Madagascar Pond Heron** has also been seen here, among the numerous common **Squacco Heron**.

OTHER ANIMALS: Although big game is scarce, you may see a variety of antelope (including Lichtenstein's Hartebeest, Impala, Bushbuck, Waterbuck, Sable Antelope and Oribi) and perhaps some of the remaining Elephant, African Buffalo and Hippo.

GETTING THERE

The park can be reached via the EN1 from Inchope to Gorongosa. The turn-off to the park (marked by an impressive sign) (GPS 18°56.03'S, 34°07.58'E) is in productive miombo woodland about 5 km north of the Pungwe River bridge on the EN1. A good gravel road follows the southern boundary of the park for 11 km to the park gate (you can follow the track to the right for a few kilometres, down to the old Villa Machado and the Pungwe River). Chitengo Camp is 17 km beyond the gate, and has chalets and a shady camp site with basic facilities (including a water supply), maintained by Fauna e Floresta Moçambique.

271 Rio Savane ✔✔

The flood plains associated with the mouth of the Savane River, a mere hour's drive north of Beira, have produced very exciting birding over the last few years. This area also boasts a well-organised resort, where secure camping and chalet accommodation is available.

SPECIALS: Blue Quail*, Senegal Lapwing, Mangrove Kingfisher*, Short-tailed Pipit, Locustfinch*, Eurasian Bittern, Madagascar Pond Heron.

SEASON: The grasslands are productive year-round.

HABITATS: Wet coastal grassland, mangroves, estuarine mudflats and sandbanks, seashore.

BIRDING: The road from Beira passes flood plains associated with the Pungwe, where, among other water birds, **Wattled Crane*** and **Black Coucal** frequently occur. **Palm-nut Vulture*** is also regularly seen along this road. The road also passes through a small coastal forest patch, where **Green Malkoha, Slender Greenbul, Black-headed Apalis, Woodwards' Batis, Red-backed Mannikin** and even **East Coast Akalat** may be found.

After about 11 km, the road enters superb grassland areas with flooded meadows (opposite a road to a prawn factory on the right). There is more grassland and woodland beyond a chained side road here (GPS 19°39.52'E, 35°07.71'S). If you wish to drive through, the keys can be picked up at the resort, but you can park and walk in. **Locustfinch*** can be flushed here from flooded areas with grass up to 50 cm high. Other grassland and flood-plain species that have been flushed here include **Eurasian Bittern, Blue Quail*, Madagascar Pond Heron** (winter), **Great Snipe, Red-chested Flufftail, Black-rumped Buttonquail** and **Short-tailed Pipit***. Other possibilities are **Rufous-bellied Heron** (large

GETTING THERE

To reach Rio Savane, approach Beira on the EN6 dual carriageway and look out for the signposted turn-off to 'Savane' (GPS 19°46.56'S, 34°52.99'E). This sign is regularly stolen, and an alternative landmark is the blue airport sign 100 m east of the turn-off. If you reach a flyover to the airport/Beira industrial, you have overshot the turn-off and will need to turn full circle, as the traffic island blocks the easterly approach. The river is reached 34 km along this gravel road (allow at least an hour's drive, without birding stops). On the north bank of the river is the Rio Savane holiday resort (accessible via a small ferry, operational in daylight hours). Cars can be left securely on the south bank.

numbers), **African Marsh-Harrier**, **Collared Pratincole**, **Grey-rumped Swallow** and, in drier areas, **Senegal Lapwing** and **Temminck's Courser**. During winter, **Mascarene Martin*** has also been seen.

Mangrove Kingfisher* occurs fairly commonly year-round in the vicinity of the river ferry. Other birds of the riparian vegetation around the resort are **Green-backed Woodpecker**, **Grey**, **Purple-banded** and **Copper Sunbirds**, **Yellow Weaver** and **Magpie Mannikin***. **Blue-cheeked Bee-eater** is common in summer, and **Madagascar Bee-eater** is also occasionally seen. From the resort, take a walk down to the estuary and along the beach. The mudflats and estuarine sandbanks may hold large numbers of waders in summer, including **Grey Plover** and **Greater Sand Plover** (flocks), **Terek Sandpiper**, **Common Whimbrel**, and the occasional **Red Knot** or **Sanderling**. **Common**, **Little** and **Lesser Crested Terns** roost on the sandbanks and beach. Scan carefully for **Greater Frigatebird**, which occasionally passes offshore and has even been seen right over the estuary. Other rarities here include **Eurasian Oystercatcher** (seen several times) and **Black-naped Tern**. The area's more common raptors include **Osprey**, **African Fish-Eagle** and **Red-necked Falcon**, and **Ayres' Hawk-Eagle*** has occasionally been seen over the riverine woodland.

OTHER ANIMALS: The riparian vegetation holds Red and Blue Duiker, Bushpig and Hippo; also look out for the fascinating mudskippers when birding in the mangroves.

272 Chinizuia Forest 4X4 ✔✔✔

Chinizuia, an area of woodland along a small track from Muanza to the Chinizuia River, provides some of the best lowland miombo and forest birding in southern Africa. A host of lowland forest specials may be seen along the short stretch of track through riverine forest. However, this area is under intense threat from loggers (previously good forests further south, in the vicinity of Dondo, have already been virtually destroyed) and its days are probably numbered.

SPECIALS: Southern Banded Snake-Eagle, 'Kirk's' (a subspecies of Crested) Francolin, Barred Long-tailed Cuckoo*, Silvery-cheeked Hornbill, African Broadbill*, African Pitta*, Speckle-throated and Green-backed Woodpeckers, Mascarene Martin*, Slender Greenbul, White-chested Alethe*, East Coast Akalat*, Yellow-bellied Hyliota, Chestnut-fronted Helmet-Shrike*, Plain-backed Sunbird, and Lesser Seedcracker*.

SEASON: The forest can be relatively quiet during the dry season, but the roads are much easier to traverse at this time.

HABITATS: Tall miombo woodland, lowland riverine forest.

BIRDING: Woodland birding is very good along much of the road from Dondo to Muanza, so keep an eye out for foraging flocks and raptors as you negotiate the potholes, corrugations and wash-aways, and gawk at the hundreds of abandoned, bombed railway carriages lining the road on your drive north. Also keep alert for passing groups of **Mascarene Martin*** (Jun-Sept), especially over clearings, and for **European Honey-Buzzard*** in summer.

GETTING THERE

The turn-off to Muanza and Inhamitanga is 4 km west of Dondo, directly opposite a transmitting tower on the south side of the road. Muanza is 90 km north of this point, and the turn-off to Chinizuia forest (signposted 'Chenapamima') a further 11 km north of Muanza at Ⓐ. The Chinizuia forest track passes through prime miombo woodland Ⓑ. Continue along this road, driving past the turn-off to Chenapamima Ⓒ; after 35 km, take the turn-off to the left Ⓓ. Just 2 km from this junction you will reach the Chinizuia stream Ⓔ; this last section may be overgrown or obstructed by fallen trees or wash-aways, so you may need to camp some distance from the stream. It is a good idea to hire a local person to guard your camp when you are out birding, as theft is a problem. The condition of the road to Chinizuia is a perennial topic of conversation for birders, and at all times of year at least one 4WD is strongly advised and frequently essential. It is preferable to travel with more than one vehicle. Water is available from the stream, but if you do not wish to boil or filter it, you should bring your own. Also ensure that you have enough fuel for the 300 km round trip from Dondo, as it may not be available in the smaller towns. Chinizuia can also be reached from Catupu (p.304).

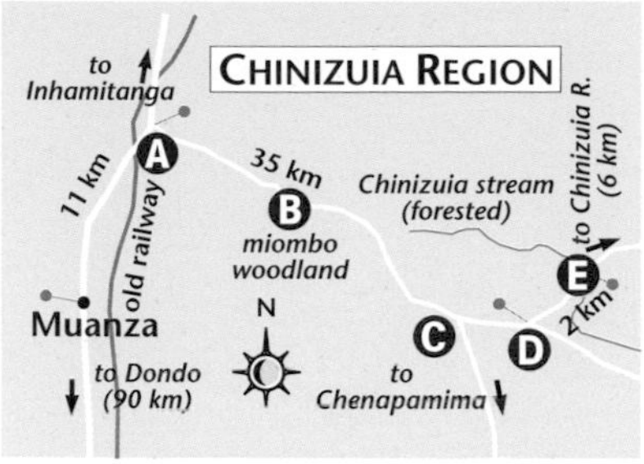

From the turn-off to Chinizuia (A), the road passes through superb, tall miombo woodland (B), and birding is excellent all the way to the forest. Stay alert for bird parties, and stop particularly around the edges of grassy clearings. More common miombo birds include **African Golden Oriole, White-breasted Cuckooshrike, Red-faced Crombec, Stierling's Wren-Warbler, Southern Hyliota** and **Pale Batis**, as well as **Mottled** and (more commonly) **Böhm's* Spinetails, Green-backed Honeybird, Flappet Lark, Grey Penduline-Tit, Green-capped Eremomela, Miombo Blue-eared Starling, Violet-backed Sunbird, Black-eared Seedeater** and **Cabanis's Bunting**. Numerous woodpecker species occur, and careful searching will turn up **Green-backed** and **Speckle-throated** (rare) **Woodpeckers**. A surprisingly high density of **Racket-tailed Roller*** and **Southern-Ground Hornbill*** occur along this road. **Yellow-bellied Hyliota** is scarce, but apparently resident. **Lesser Seedcracker*** is occasionally seen in areas of denser undergrowth. **Kirk's Francolin** (the *rovuma* subspecies of **Crested**) is usually heard calling in the mornings, but can be surprisingly tricky to find. **Madagascar Cuckoo** has been heard and seen only a few times. A couple of species that occur more characteristically at the forest edge often venture into the miombo: **Black-and-white Flycatcher*** and **Chestnut-fronted Helmet Shrike*** (beware confusion with the more common **Retz's Helmet-Shrike**). Raptors are common, and regular sightings of **White-headed Vulture, European Honey-Buzzard, Ayres' Hawk-Eagle*, Bateleur, Ovambo Sparrowhawk** and **Lizard Buzzard** have been reported. The miombo is interspersed with grassy, occasionally flooded glades. **Short-winged Cisticola** and **Red-winged Warbler** are both fairly common in these clearings (the latter also in degraded forest areas), and **Blue Quail*** and **Red-chested Flufftail** have also been flushed several times. From about June to September, small groups of **Mascarene Martin*** fly over these and forest clearings.

Most birders choose to camp in one of the cleared areas alongside the track, shortly before the forest edge on the approach to the Chinizuia stream (E). The track continues through the band of forest, across the river and ultimately through a cultivated area to the broad Chinizuia River. **White-chested Alethe*** is most vocal at dusk, and several pairs appear to occur in the vicinity of the bridge at (E) (they are seen mainly Oct-Jun). Note that the calls here differ from those in Malawi. **East Coast Akalat*** is common and very vocal at dawn and dusk. However, it is unobtrusive, even when singing, and a little patience is usually needed to locate the bird, often perched motionless in the understorey, less than 1 m above the ground. **Barred Long-tailed Cuckoo*** occurs annually, and several pairs can usually be heard within walking distance of the stream crossing during July-Jan. **Black-and-white Flycatcher*** and **Chesnut-fronted Helmet-Shrike*** especially favour forest clearings. More common specials of the forest are the **Blue-spotted Wood-Dove, Green-backed Woodpecker, Slender Greenbul, Pale** and **Woodwards' Batises, Black-headed Apalis** (very common), **Plain-backed Sunbird** (fairly common), and **Red-throated Twinspot**, along with more widespread species

Claire Spottiswoode

Miombo woodland along the main track at Chinizuia

Hugh Chittenden

White-chested Alethe

including **Crested Guineafowl, Green Malkoha, African Pygmy-Kingfisher, Eastern Saw-wing** and **Blue-mantled Crested Flycatcher. African Broadbill*** and **Narina Trogon*** are remarkably common, and the calls of the former are explosive at dawn. **Eastern Bronze-naped Pigeon*** and groups of **Silvery-cheeked Hornbill** flop through the canopy. **Pallid Honeyguide** is scarce. **African Pitta*** sometimes occurs, and is seen from late November to January. **Southern Banded Snake-Eagle** is heard regularly and seen occasionally. Check the forest edges for **Grey Waxbill, Magpie Mannikin***, and **Red-throated** and **Green* Twinspots**. The stream and scattered forest pools nearby frequently hold **Half-collared Kingfisher** and sometimes **African Finfoot*** and **Mangrove Kingfisher***, and a **Madagascar Pond Heron** has even been seen here. If you are able to cross the stream by car, continue for about another 6 km to the Chinizuia River, where you may have the chance to see some good tropical water birds, including **Dwarf Bittern, Saddle-billed Stork** and breeding **Mangrove Kingfisher***. Beyond the river lies a mosaic of grassland and woodland.

At night, you may be awoken by **Barred Long-tailed Cuckoo*** and '**Kirk's Francolin**', in addition to the more traditional chorus of Greater Bushbaby, **African Wood-Owl, Barred Owlet** and **Buff-spotted Flufftail. Pennant-winged Nightjar*** occurs in the miombo.

OTHER ANIMALS: Regularly seen forest mammals include Blue Duiker and Red Bush Squirrel and, in the miombo woodland, Mutable Sun Squirrel, Lichtenstein's Hartebeest (scarce) and Sharpe's Grysbok. Herping is excellent, and a night walk is likely to turn up many interesting snakes and frogs, and perhaps an African Civet or Greater Galago.

273 Zambezi Coutadas

IBA ✔✔

Coutadas (hunting concessions) 10, 11, 12 and 14 enclose a huge area of undisturbed coastal forest, interspersed with grassland and pans. The hunting concessions, which are not well known, are accessed by a tar road, and good dirt roads traverse the area. Chinizuia lies on the southern extremity of this region, and has become popular despite the fact that it is difficult to access.

SPECIALS: African Pitta*, White-chested Alethe*, East Coast Akalat*, Chestnut-fronted Helmet-Shrike*, Barred Long-tailed Cuckoo*, Madagascar Cuckoo, Short-tailed Pipit*, Wattled Crane*, Southern Banded Snake-Eagle, Plain-backed Sunbird, Black-headed Apalis, Mascarene Martin*, Slender Greenbul and Silvery-cheeked Hornbill.

SEASON: The camps and some of the roads are closed during the period December to March, but at that time you can still drive through Coutadas 11 and 12; the road comes out in Marromeu.

BIRDING: Follow the main roads and search any or all of the forest patches for the specials mentioned above. See the Chinizuia account (p.302) for general descriptions of birds and habitats.

OTHER ANIMALS: A great diversity of big game occurs, including Buffalo, Elephant, Lion, Leopard, Sable, Nyala and Red Duiker.

GETTING THERE

From Inchope take the tar highway through Gorongosa, around Gorongosa Mountain towards Caia. Be sure to stop several times along the way to bird in tall miombo or lowland forest. Look for **Green Sandpiper** from the river bridge about 70 km out of Gorongosa. Also stop at the flood plain of the Zangue River near the Inhamitanga turn-off. Continue for 11 km past this turn-off to Catupu, where there is a camp site and guest cottages, and up-to-date information about access to the coutadas can be obtained ☎.

274 Casa Msika ✔

Casa Msika is a camp on the northern shore of the Chicamba Real Dam, between Chimoio and Manica and near the EN6 to Beira. It is a popular place to overnight en route to Gorongosa or the coast, and also provides some good birding along the dam edges and in the woodland that lines the entrance road. To reach Casa Msika, take the signposted turn-off 45 km west of Chimoio (or 23 km east of Manica), and continue along this good gravel road for 4 km. There is a camp site, hutted accommodation and a restaurant.

275 Mount Tsetserra ✔✔

A site of unsurpassed scenic splendour, Mount Tsetserra forms part of the Chimanimani range that spans the border with Zimbabwe, and is remarkable for its extensive, undisturbed montane habitats (although the summit is spoilt by an old pine plantation). The slopes offer a complete succession of forest types, from tall miombo at the base to Afromontane forest near the top, with grassland in between.

To reach Mount Tsetserra, take the EN6 from Manica to Chimoio. After passing the turn-off to Casa Msika, take the right turn to Chicamba, 33 km east of Manica (or 35 km west of Chimoio). The road crosses a bridge immediately below the dam wall, and continues for about 60 km before winding its way up the mountain. The road is in good condition, but 4WD is recommended for the ascent because of loose gravel on the steep slopes. There's a camp site at the summit, maintained by the Wildlife Department, but stopping on the way up may be preferable.

Species are similar to those of the Eastern Highlands of Zimbabwe, and include **Orange Ground-Thrush**, **Red-faced Crimsonwing**, **White-starred Robin**, **Olive Bush-Shrike**, **Black-fronted Bush-Shrike**, **Bronzy Sunbird**, **Barratt's Warbler**, **Chirinda Apalis**, **Roberts' Warbler**, **Eastern Bronze-naped Pigeon*** and **Whyte's Barbet**. Several species more typical of the lowlands also occur, and include **Silvery-cheeked Hornbill** and **Chestnut fronted Helmet-Shrike***.

276 Furancungo IBA ✔✔

Furancungo is a remarkably rich and easily accessible miombo woodland birding destination in northern Tete Province, to date totally neglected by birders.

To get there, cross the Zambezi at Tete (**Peregrine Falcon** is sometimes seen perching on the bridge) and take the left turn after the BP service station onto the EN221 tar road to the Zambian border. There are two routes on good dirt roads to Furancungo. The first is to follow the EN221 for 33 km, then take the turn-off onto the EN222 and follow the Cazula route to Furancungo. This route is shorter (about 150 km from the turn-off) but more rugged, and offers more birding opportunities. However, beware of blind corners on steep slopes, and note that two of the drifts cannot be crossed after a downpour. Alternatively, stick to the EN221 for a further 106 km, before taking the turn-off, and follow the longer but easier Chidzolomondlo route. On reaching Furancungo, enquire at the Mozambique Leaf Tobacco office (on the left off the main road, past the big sheds) about access to the camp site that lies on the outskirts of town.

Although it's only a short distance north of the Zambezi, several species of bird that are unknown in the southern African region occur here. Around the town you can find **Red-capped Crombec** and **White-tailed Blue Flycatcher**. A high-pitched, piping call, like someone practising scales on a flute, emanates from **Southern Citril**. **Schalow's Turaco**, **Hildebrandt's Francolin**, **Ayres' Hawk-Eagle*** and **Palm-nut Vulture*** can be seen from the camp site and, in summer, flocks of **Eurasian Hobby** fill the evening sky. The best chance for **Olive-headed Weaver*** is on the wooded slopes immediately south of the tobacco company offices, but also look around the high points on the Cazula route. In the tall woodlands along the Cazula route, look for **Shelley's Sunbird***. **Anchieta's Sunbird** and **Bertrand's Weaver** were collected here in 1932, but have not been seen recently. In thickets around stream crossings, look for **Grey-olive Greenbul**. The tall woodland at the foot of the steep, uphill climb into town that terminates the Chidzolomondlo route offers **Stierling's Woodpecker**, **Souza's Shrike***, **Spotted Creeper*** and **Yellow-bellied Hyliota**.

277 Lake Cahora Bassa

IBA ✔

As you approach Tete from the south, take the turn-off to Songo and Ugezi Lodge (20 km before Tete) and continue for 150 km along a tar road. The lodge and camp site at Ugezi are convenient for exploring the spectacular Songo gorge (with **Barratt's Warbler**, surprisingly). A drive around the southern shore of the lake towards the upper reaches (beyond Chicoa) through tall mopane woods (**Meves's Starling** and **Red-billed Hornbill** are abundant) brings you into the range of **Lillian's Lovebird**, sometimes in flocks of hundreds in cleared lands. A boat trip from Songo to the mouth of the Siji River on the north bank takes you to the easternmost breeding colony of **Southern Carmine Bee-eater**. **White-crowned Lapwing** line the shore, and **Osprey** is frequently seen here.

MAKING A CONTRIBUTION

The country still offers much untapped potential to adventurous birders, and every trip turns up many exciting species from both a southern African and a global perspective. Please submit your records to the ongoing and extremely worthwhile Mozambique Atlas Project ☎; every record is valuable and will ultimately contribute to conservation in this troubled yet tremendously beautiful and exciting country. Most of Mozambique's key habitats are or will shortly be under enormous human pressure, and a second way in which you can contribute to their continued survival is to ensure that local people are not only aware of your interests, but even benefit from your visit by acting as guides, porters, interpreters or hosts.

Ian Michler/IOA

Much exploring still needs to be done in northern Mozambique, such as in the Niassa Province.

ROUTE 31

NORTHERN MOZAMBIQUE

Northern Mozambique, from the Zambezi to the Rovuma, is a vast and extraordinarily wild area. Where else can one crest a rise and see pristine, closed-canopy miombo woodland extend in an unbroken swathe across the horizon, then drive a short distance to a palm-fringed beach with a sixteenth-century Arab fortress? This is one of the most poorly known parts of the broader southern African region, and there undoubtedly remain many exciting discoveries to be made here. Until very recently, the only ornithological accounts from northern Mozambique were from a 1932 expedition to Mount Namuli, led by Colonel Jack Vincent, and observations on the birds at Serra Jeci (Njesi Plateau) in 1945 by Jali Makawa, a collector in the employ of CW Benson. Recent exploratory efforts reveal that the majority of the exciting birds and localities described by these pioneers are still to be found here.

TOP 10 BIRDS

- Namuli Apalis
- Thyolo Alethe
- Dapple-throat
- Long-billed Forest Warbler
- Red-capped Forest Warbler
- Green Barbet
- Olive-flanked Robin-Chat
- Bertrand's Weaver
- Blue Quail
- Crab Plover

Infrastructure in the northern parts of Mozambique is remarkably good, and birders despairing of the mangled roads of the central lowlands will find the usually excellent gravel and tar surfaces of the far north a great pleasure to travel on – fortunately, given the enormous distances involved. However, the most exciting places for birds are the massifs, and birding is very much an 'expedition'. You will need to be prepared to negotiate to engage the services of local porters and guides, carry water-filtering equipment, and hike some distance.

The sparsely populated Niassa Province in the far north-west still teems with big game, including Elephant, Lion and Buffalo.

One tremendously exciting site in northern Mozambique that remains ornithologically very poorly known is the enormous and stunningly beautiful Niassa Reserve, which lies between the Lugenda and Rovuma rivers, just south of the Tanzanian border. Efforts are afoot to improve the reserve's infrastructure and conservation status, and it may yet become a key birding site in the region.

Access from the south has been complicated by the fact that, although usually operational, the Zambezi River ferry crossing at Caia is unreliable. And while the Zambezi can be crossed by bridge further upstream at Sena, one cannot proceed into northern Mozambique from there as there is no bridge across the Shire River. The most reliable route is, therefore, via Tete and through Malawi, but you must have a multiple entry visa to re-enter Mozambique. Please note there are two extremely important sites of which we cannot currently give precise details, and which urgently need exploration. These are Mount Chiperone (where White-winged Apalis* occurs, among many other highland forest species) near the Malawi border town of Milange, and Moebase (where flocks of Madagascar Pond Heron and Zanzibar Red Bishop have been reported) on the coast between Quelimane and Angoche and, at the time of writing, accessible only via Pebane.

Callan Cohen

Namuli Apalis, Mozambique's only endemic

278 Northern Mozambican Dambos ✔

The extensive woodlands of Zambezia Province are peppered with grassy dambos that have enormous potential after rain. An exploratory stroll through a broad dambo a few kilometres from Corromana on the Molumbo road (GPS 15°42'S, 36°04'E) may produce, among others, **Dwarf Bittern, Harlequin** and numerous **Blue* Quail, Marsh Owl, African Grass-Owl*, Black Coucal, Croaking Cisticola, Moustached Grass Warbler** and **Black-winged Bishop**. Areas of tall grass at woodland edges or along streams in this region also appear reliably to provide **Red-winged Warbler**.

279 Mount Namuli 4X4 IBA ✔✔✔

The Namuli massif is possibly the most scenically spectacular and biologically exciting locality in Mozambique. It is a vast and rugged massif, capped by the sheer, 500 m high granite dome of Monte Namuli (at 2 412 m, the second highest peak in Mozambique) and supporting several substantial patches of montane forest and beautiful montane grassland, punctuated by tree ferns and orchids. Though the scenic beauty of the massif cannot be overstated, for birders its star attraction is a species that occurs nowhere else in the world – the attractive and locally common **Namuli Apalis***, rediscovered in 1998 after a gap of 66 years. **Dapple-throat** and **Thyolo Alethe*** respectively occur otherwise only in the Udzungwas of Tanzania and a few fragmented forest areas in southern Malawi. It is still possible that species unknown to science occur here.

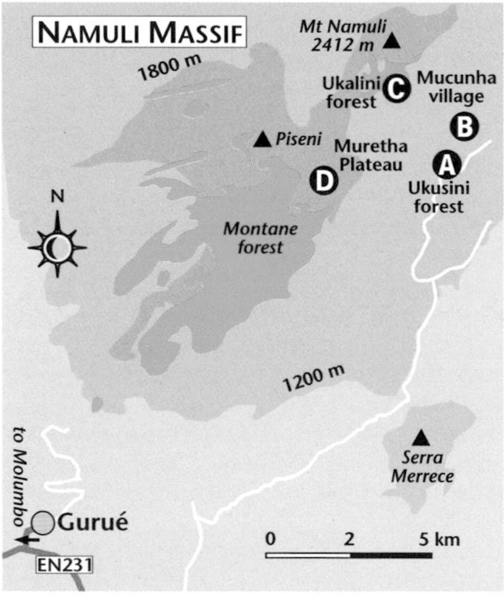

SPECIALS: Namuli Apalis*, Dapple-throat, Thyolo Alethe*, Bar-tailed Trogon*, Green Barbet*, Red-rumped Swallow, Olive-flanked Robin-Chat, Evergreen Forest Warbler, Forest Double-collared Sunbird, and Bertrand's Weaver.

SEASON: All the forest specials are resident year-round.

HABITATS: Afromontane forest, montane grassland, miombo woodland, cultivated land and tea plantations on the lower slopes.

BIRDING: Look out for **Red-rumped Swallow** while walking or driving up through the tea plantations above Gurué, and **Half-collared Kingfisher** and **Anchieta's Tchagra*** along the Malema River. **Namuli Apalis*** occurs from about 1 200 m altitude, and may even be seen in small patches of riparian forest, as well as within the montane forest 'proper'. It is fairly easily located once its call is known. The main forest birding is in the Ukalini Forest

GETTING THERE

At Namuli, you should be prepared to pay your respects to local authorities, engage the services of porters, hike some distance, and camp self-sufficiently for at least two nights. Reaching Gurué from the south is straightforward, as the gravel roads through Molumbo are in good condition. From Gurué, it is possible either to drive or hike to the base of Mount Namuli. It is possible to drive a 4WD to the Ukusini Forest Ⓐ, along the Malema valley, and beyond to Mucunha village Ⓑ. Permission must be obtained from the 'regulo', the spiritual leader of Namuli, at Mucunha. You would be best advised to contact the Pensão Gurué in the Gurué main street and ask the owner to make local arrangements, including transport to the top of the tea plantation. From the tea plantation, it is a long but relatively easy hike of about 11 hours to the main Ukalini Forest Ⓒ.

Ⓒ, around the base of the granite dome of Monte Namuli. **Dapple-throat** and **Thyolo Alethe*** are fairly common but very inconspicuous understorey skulkers, and being familiar with their calls (Dapple-throats usually only call at dawn and dusk) is essential to locate them.

Callan Cohen

Mount Namuli: looking over the remnants of Ukusini Forest, with Ukalini Forest at top left

Other common forest species are **Livingstone's Turaco**, **Stripe-cheeked** and **Yellow-streaked Greenbuls**, **White-starred Robin**, **White-tailed Crested Flycatcher**, **Malawi Batis**, and **Olive** and **Forest Double-collared Sunbirds**. **Green Barbet*** is scarcer, but can be located by its far-carrying, 'chopping' call. Other canopy species include **Bar-tailed Trogon***, **Scaly-throated Honeyguide**, and **Black-fronted Bush-Shrike***; the mid-strata hold **Placid Greenbul**, **Yellow-throated Woodland-Warbler** and **Black-headed Apalis**, while denser tangles and the lower strata are the habitat of **Olive-flanked Robin-Chat**, **Orange Ground-Thrush**, **Evergreen Forest Warbler** and **Red-faced Crimsonwing**. **Dark-capped Yellow Warbler** occurs in the bracken at the forest edge, and the adjacent montane grassland and protea woodland provide **Wailing Cisticola**, **Red-rumped Swallow**, and **Striped** and **African Pipits**.

Below the Ukalini Forest lie the remnants of the Ukusini Forest Ⓐ, flanked by subsistence agriculture and miombo woodland. The narrow strip of riparian forest provides a number of species rarer or absent from the prime forest higher up, such as **African Broadbill***, **Little Greenbul**, and **Eastern Nictator**. **Thyolo Alethe*** is remarkably common here, and pairs of these birds can be heard singing about every 150 m along the stream. The mix of rank growth and crops beyond the forest edge provides **Moustached Grass Warbler**, **Singing Cisticola**, **Red-winged Warbler**, **African Firefinch** and **Southern Citril**. The northern slope of the valley is host to some fine miombo, and holds a good selection of miombo specials, including **Cinnamon-breasted Tit**, **Pale Batis**, **Western Violet-backed Sunbird** and **Cabanis's Bunting**.

You may also wish to try to attain the Muretha Plateau Ⓓ, a stiff walk south of the peak. Here, forest patches fringed with tall orchids and tree ferns (which hold all the species found at Ukalini) mingle with montane meadows, where **Striped Flufftail*** has been flushed. **Bertrand's Weaver** has also been seen here.

Keep a lookout for **Scarce** and **Mottled Swifts** overhead, and for **African Wood-Owl** and **Cape Eagle-Owl*** at night.

The massif is spectacularly scenic. The view from Knife Edge Ridge above the Ukalini Forest over the valley lying to the west of the peak is particularly breathtaking, but take care on the steep scramble up the granite slopes.

OTHER ANIMALS: A new species of orchid and a chameleon previously known only from Mulanje were collected on the massif in 1998, and many more new species no doubt remain to be discovered. During Jack Vincent's travels to Namuli in 1932, twenty-one local people had been killed by lions in the preceding three weeks.

Peter Ginn

White-starred Robin

280 Njesi Plateau 4X4 IBA ✔✔

The Njesi Plateau, also known as Serra Jeci on some modern maps, is a low (1 600 m), rambling and patchily forested plateau north of Lichinga, capital of the remote Niassa Province. Though topographically less spectacular than the Namuli massif, Njesi Plateau is ornithologically nearly as exciting, being the only site outside of Tanzania where **Red-capped Forest Warbler** (African Tailorbird) and especially the endangered **Long-billed Forest Warbler** (Long-billed Tailorbird) occur. Collected here in 1945, the tailorbirds remained ignored until a 2001 expedition revisited the massif, and a visit to the plateau is almost guaranteed to turn up many other exciting finds.

SPECIALS: Red-capped and Long-billed Forest Warblers (or Tailorbirds), Stierling's Woodpecker, Orange Ground-Thrush, Evergreen Forest Warbler, White-tailed Blue Flycatcher, and Olive-headed* and Bertrand's Weavers.

SEASON: Vehicle access is limited throughout the year. Although both the above-mentioned expeditions took place in the dry season, the wet is probably better for birding.

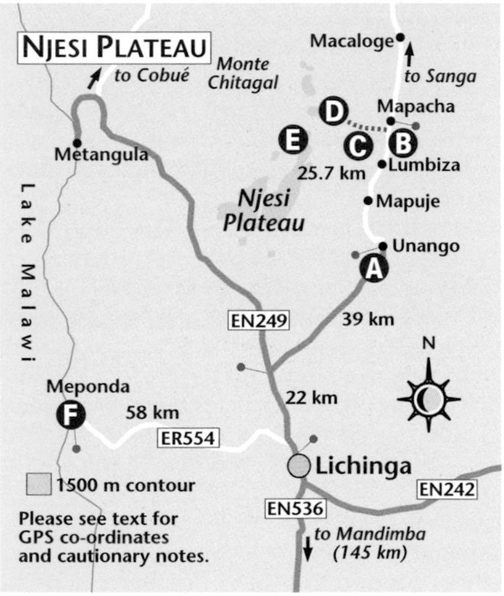

HABITATS: Afromontane forest, miombo woodland, montane grassland.

BIRDING: The pristine miombo woodland (C) along the track from Mapacha to the mountain should be searched for mixed-species foraging flocks holding, among others, **Olive-headed Weaver***, **Speckle-throated Woodpecker**, **Spotted Creeper*** and **Arnot's Chat**. A stream behind the farm at (D) is lined with a narrow strip of riparian forest, providing **Little Greenbul**, **Square-tailed Drongo**, **White-tailed Crested Flycatcher** and **Red-throated Twinspot**.

Foraging flocks occur in the tall miombo cloaking the base and steep sides of the mountain, through which you will hike to reach the montane forest, and these are well worth searching for **Stierling's Woodpecker** (otherwise a near-endemic to Malawi), **Spotted Creeper***, **Cinnamon-breasted Tit**, **Western Violet-backed Sunbird**, **Reichard's**

GETTING THERE

Birders proposing to visit the Njesi Plateau should be independent, well equipped, reasonably physically fit, and have some knowledge of Portuguese. To reach the base of the mountain, take the tarred EN249 north of Lichinga and travel for 22 km, then turn right onto the tarred road to Unango. Just before Unango village, 39 km further on, the road forks (A); turn left here onto the gravel road that runs north to Sanga. Just before reaching Mapacha village (B), look carefully for a track leading into the miombo woodland to the left of the road (GPS 12°40.01'S, 35°24.99'E and 200 m south of the 'Unango 25 km' milestone). This track leads through beautiful, tall miombo woodland (C) for about 15 km. Keep going straight; DO NOT take the left fork about 10 km further on, as it is reputedly mined. At the end of the main track, you will reach a small farm (D). Here, you must request permission from the owner to park your vehicle, and engage the services of porters and guides for the 4-hour hike to the nearest patch of montane forest (E). Ideally, spend at least one night on the mountain. Guides are essential to find your way, but some landmarks are reported on the map. The plateau grassland is dense and overgrown with tall and near-impenetrable thickets in many places; you may find it convenient to follow the broad and numerous elephant paths at your own risk. During the dry season, no water is available on the plateau, so ensure that you carry sufficient with you. Locals have made mention of landmines on certain parts of the plateau, so please take heed of the recommendations made by your porters and guides.

Seed-eater and other typical miombo species. As you emerge onto the plateau, grassland species such as **Singing** and **Wailing Cisticolas** make their appearance.

The forest patch Ⓔ investigated by the 2001 expedition is small and with a broken canopy, but provides an excellent array of forest species. Here, **Red-capped Forest Warbler** is fairly common in the undergrowth, and responds well to pishing. **Long-billed Forest Warbler** is apparently much scarcer, and occurs in the forest canopy. Common forest species are **Livingstone's Turaco**, **Little Greenbul**, **Black-headed Apalis**, and **Olive** and **Forest Double-collared Sunbirds**, and a number of species more characteristic of moist woodland, including **Green-backed Woodpecker** and **White-tailed Blue Flycatcher**, also penetrate the forest. **Orange Ground-Thrush** and **Red-capped Robin-Chat** feed in the leaf litter, and **Evergreen Forest Warbler** is commonly found in the denser understorey. **African Hill Babbler**, collected in 1945, has not been seen since. Forest edges provide **Yellow-bellied Waxbill** and, probably more scarcely, **Bertrand's Weaver**.

The larger forest that lies to the north, on the slopes of Njesi Peak, cannot be reached because local people are reluctant to take visitors up (it is reputedly inhabited by evil spirits).

OTHER ANIMALS: Elephants are common on the plateau as well as in the surrounding miombo. Sable Antelope, Lion and Leopard have been reported, while more common large mammals include Yellow Baboon and Klipspringer.

281 Meponda ✔

Meponda is the easiest place to gain access to the Mozambican shore of Lake Malawi. It is a picturesque, friendly fishing village with good snorkelling (especially in the vicinity of rocky outcrops along the shore); note that this area is free of bilharzia and crocodiles. The birding offers a mixture of riparian and miombo species, notably the superb **Böhm's Bee-eater***. To reach Meponda (Ⓕ on map opposite) take the tar road (EN249) north to Metangula from Lichinga, then turn left onto the gravel road (ER554), 5.7 km from the main Lichinga roundabout (at the government buildings). Meponda is 57 km further on along a reasonable gravel road, and it is also well worth stopping to bird the miombo, especially between 15 and 25 km from Meponda.

282 Far Northern Mozambique Coast ✔

The Segundas Archipelago, off the coast of Nampula Province near Angoche, hosts the only known nesting colony of **Sooty Tern** in Mozambique (Jul-Nov). Despite being periodically harvested by local fishermen, the colony (on Puga-Puga Island) hosts about 5 000 pairs. **Crab Plover*** also occurs here (also check the mudflats of the Angoche Estuary), as do small numbers of migrant **Eurasian Oystercatcher** and, after storms, **Brown Noddy**.

Puga-Puga lies approximately 3 km from the coast of Quelelene, and a boat trip of about 25 km from Angoche town.

Contact IDPPE (☎) in Bairro Muchelele, as they are involved in conservation efforts at the tern colony and may be able to assist with transport as well as with advice.

The coral reefs around the island are still pristine and the overall marine biodiversity is high. Four species of turtles occur and there may be a small population of Dugong around Ndjovo Island.

Between Ilha de Moçambique and the mouth of the Rovuma lies a vast, beautiful and historically intriguing stretch of coastline. Its sandy and coralline shore is dotted with a succession of ancient fortress towns – perhaps most famously Ilha de Moçambique, which is a World Heritage Site. Some of the best birding is around the beautiful island of Ibo in the Quirimba Archipelago, between the town of Pemba and the Rovuma River. Large numbers of **Crab Plover*** and Palearctic waders have been seen on the extensive mudflats around the island. Ibo can be reached from the mainland via dhow from Tanganhane village (just north of Quissanga) – a one- to six-hour journey, depending on wind and tide – or by fishing boat or chartered speedboat or plane from Pemba.

MALAWI

Malawi's topography is completely dominated by the Rift Valley, which forms the lake and its associated hot lowland areas, and by the numerous important highland regions that broadly constitute the southern extreme of the great Eastern Arc mountains of East Africa. Malawi is one of Africa's smallest countries, and yet it is packed with an extraordinary natural diversity, particularly along the 900 km-long western and southern shores of the Rift Valley's southernmost major lake. This diversity is reflected in its avifauna, and Malawi boasts over 650 bird species. Although the country has only one strict endemic, the Yellow-throated Apalis, Malawi's montane regions offer a number of species that are highly localised or difficult to find elsewhere. The relatively easily accessible and numerous range-restricted montane specials are complemented by a high diversity of tropical lowland species found along Lake Malawi and in the hot, dry lowlands of the southern Rift. This, along with the country's scenery and excellent game-viewing opportunities, relatively well-developed infrastructure and exceptionally friendly people, makes Malawi an excellent destination for birders looking for both high diversity and montane specials.

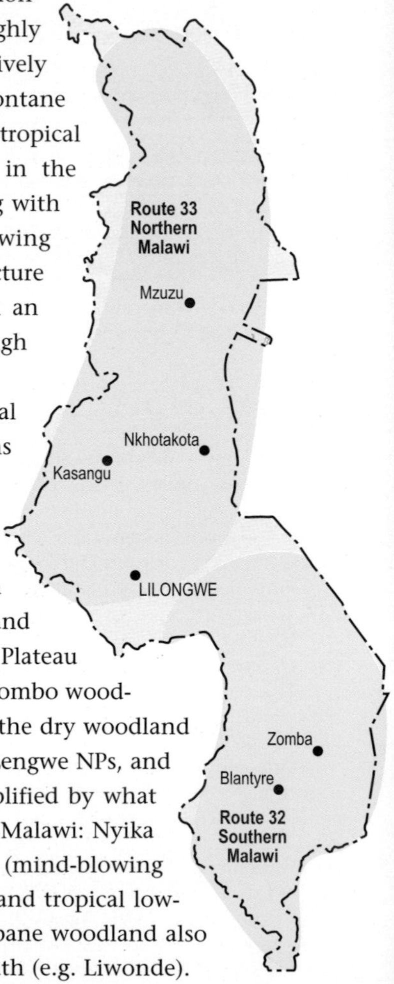

Malawi has a fast-growing and principally rural population, and little natural vegetation remains outside of protected areas. Hence, birding in Malawi is concentrated in the country's well-developed network of parks and reserves.

Three main habitat types should be covered in a birding trip to Malawi: montane grasslands and forests (especially Nyika NP in the north, Zomba Plateau and Mounts Thyolo and Mulanje in the south), miombo woodland (mainly Dzalanyama and Vwaza Marsh) and the dry woodland and thicket of the Rift Valley itself (Liwonde and Lengwe NPs, and the lake shore). These habitats are perhaps exemplified by what for many are the three key highlights of a visit to Malawi: Nyika NP (scenery and montane birding), Dzalanyama (mind-blowing miombo bird parties) and Liwonde NP (big game and tropical lowland birding). Small but important pockets of mopane woodland also exist in the north-west (e.g. Vwaza Marsh) and south (e.g. Liwonde).

ROUTE 32

SOUTHERN MALAWI

TOP 10 BIRDS

- White-winged Apalis
- Thyolo Alethe
- Green-headed Oriole
- Yellow-throated Apalis
- Southern Mountain Greenbul
- Bar-tailed Trogon
- Bertrand's Weaver
- Malawi Batis
- Brown-breasted Barbet
- Böhm's Bee-eater

Malawi south of the lake is a small region, making travelling very manageable. All the sites described in this route are within an hour's drive of the main M1, M2 and M3 highways that radiate from southern Malawi's principal town, Blantyre. None require rough camping or, at least during the dry season, 4WD transport. Two key forest sites (Mounts Soche and Thyolo) lie within a short driving distance from Blantyre, and can easily be tackled by those with private transport who have even a single day to spare. However, at least a week is needed to do justice to southern Malawi.

The two largest forested massifs east of the Rift are Mount Mulanje and the Zomba Plateau, respectively about 100 km east and 70 km north of Blantyre. At least two days should be spent at each, although those with more time available would undoubtedly continue to turn up more interesting species during a longer stay, and also have the opportunity better to explore some of their wonderful landscapes – especially on Mount Mulanje, the less accessible but more scenic of the two. The hot, game-filled woodland and flood plains of the Liwonde National Park, a short drive north of Zomba, contrast strikingly with the latter's mist-shrouded forests, as does the Lengwe National Park of the south-west.

Note that southern Malawi is also the easiest access point to the beautiful, sparsely populated and poorly known northern Mozambican interior. For example, the base of the Namuli Massif (see p.308) is a mere four hours' drive via Molumbo from the Malawi border at Muloza/Milange, and the base of the Njesi Plateau (see p.310) a similar distance, largely on a good tar road via Lichinga, from the Mandimba border post (best reached via Liwonde, not Mangochi – the escarpment road beyond the latter is extremely slow-going).

Claire Spottiswoode

Lake Malawi is the southernmost lake of the Rift Valley.

283 Mount Soche

IBA ✔✔

Mount Soche, a 1 530 m peak, is nominally protected by the Soche Forest Reserve, which lies to the south of Blantyre. Although the lower reaches are being rapidly deforested, several key species probably still occur in the remaining forest fragments, including **Spotted Ground-Thrush***, **Thyolo Alethe*** and **White-winged Apalis***. Information about their current status here is urgently needed. White-winged Apalis* preferred the lower-altitude forest galleries on the mountain's north-eastern slopes, and at the forest edge in the vicinity of the beacon. Other forest species included **Livingstone's Turaco, Bar-tailed Trogon*, Placid Greenbul, White-eared Barbet, Orange Ground-Thrush, Evergreen Forest Warbler, Black-headed Apalis, Malawi Batis** and **Black-fronted Bush-Shrike***.

To reach the forest, take the Limbe Road (Chipembere Highway) from the city centre and turn right onto Mahatma Gandhi Road near the Queen Elizabeth Central Hospital; turn left after 1.2 km, onto Kapeni Road. This leads up a hill towards a conspicuous satellite tower; turn right at the crossroads 4.5 km further on, and park at the village 800 m ahead. You may wish to make arrangements for your car to be guarded in your absence. From the village, walk past the PHC Church towards the mountain, following any of the numerous steep trails heading up through deforested slopes towards remaining forest patches just below the ridge of the flat-topped peak (about an hour's walk). Rocky areas in remnant miombo (such as around the quarry at the roadside, 400 m beyond the village) may provide **Lazy Cisticola, Mocking Cliff-Chat** and **Miombo Rock-Thrush**. **Spotted Creeper*** also occurs in the miombo.

284 Mount Thyolo

IBA ✔✔

Sadly, much of Mount Thyolo has been deforested, but patches of Afromontane and riparian forest remain on several of the tea estates on and around the mountain, and good forest birding is still possible, notably for **Green-headed Oriole*** and **White-winged Apalis***.

SPECIALS: Green-headed Oriole*, White-winged Apalis*, Green* and White-eared Barbets, Bar-tailed Trogon*, Grey Cuckooshrike, Grey-olive Greenbul, Thyolo Alethe*, Black-fronted Bush-Shrike*, Bertrand's Weaver, and Southern Citril.

SEASON: Birding is good year-round. **Green-headed Oriole*** is easiest to find during Sept-Oct, when it is particularly noisy; it quietens down during Nov.

HABITATS: Afromontane forest, riparian forest, tea plantations.

BIRDING: The list of specials includes range-restricted montane forest birds such as **Green-headed Oriole***, the near-endemic **Thyolo Alethe*, Bar-tailed Trogon*, Malawi Batis, White-winged Apalis*** and **Green Barbet***. In Malawi, the latter is found only here and in the Misuku Hills in the far north. The distribution of the particular Green Barbet* sub-species that occurs here is limited to Mount Thyolo and the Namuli Massif in Mozambique; it is easily located by its far-carrying, 'chopping' call. The forest abounds with greenbuls, and **Little, Placid, Grey-olive** (very localised in Malawi) and **Yellow-streaked Greenbuls** all vie for attention. Other forest birds include **Trumpeter** and, occasionally, **Silvery-cheeked Hornbills, Black-headed Apalis, Evergreen Forest Warbler, Grey Cuckoo-shrike** (localised in Malawi), **Yellow-throated Woodland-Warbler, White-tailed Crested Flycatcher, Black-fronted Bush-Shrike*, Bertrand's Weaver** (especially at the forest edge), **Red-faced Crimsonwing** and **Southern Citril**.

Most of these species are fairly easy to find by their calls, except skulking **Thyolo Alethe***.

GETTING THERE

From Blantyre city centre, head out on the Zomba/Mulanje highway and continue through Limbe. At Limbe's eastern outskirts, turn right onto the Thyolo/Mulanje road (M2). The entrances to Namingomba and Mwalantunzi tea estates are clearly signposted (opposite each other) about 25 km further on, and the entrances to Mikundi (left) and Satemwa (right) shortly thereafter. You must obtain permission from management (at each estate) before entering the forest. Satemwa offers self-catering accommodation not far from the montane forest ☎.

There is also good birding immediately around Chawani Bungalow at Satemwa and in riparian forest elsewhere; search for **African Broadbill*** in the forest below the dam, and for **White-eared Barbet** and **Red-throated Twinspot** in the garden.

285 Mount Mulanje

IBA ✔✔

At 3 001 m, Mulanje's Sapitwa Peak is the highest point between Kilimanjaro and the Drakensberg. The Mulanje Massif rises almost vertically on all sides from the 700 m-high surrounding plain to a plateau of about 2 000 m altitude. Mulanje, viewed from a distance, is breathtaking: sheer, mile-high rock faces emerge from the green girdle of tea plantations that circle its base, and the massif is topped by bare peaks and shrouds of cloud, which instantly explain its local name: 'the Island in the Sky'. Those who wish to combine a scenic trek with montane birding cannot miss out on Mount Mulanje.

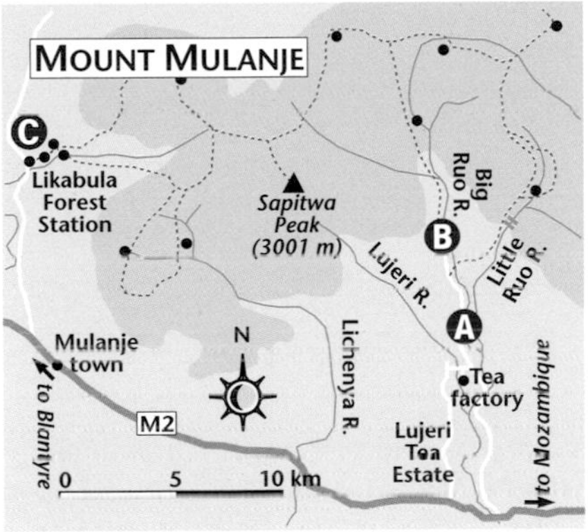

SPECIALS: Scarce Swift, Bar-tailed Trogon*, Silvery-cheeked Hornbill, Southern Mountain, Stripe-cheeked, Yellow-streaked, Little and Placid Greenbuls, Blue* and Red-rumped Swallows, Orange and Spotted* Ground-Thrushes, Thyolo Alethe*, Olive-flanked Robin-Chat, Cinnamon Bracken and Evergreen Forest Warblers, Yellow-throated, White-winged* (scarce) and Black-headed Apalis, Malawi Batis, White-tailed Crested Flycatcher, Black-fronted Bush-Shrike*, Bertrand's Weaver, Forest Double-collared Sunbird, Southern Citril.

SEASON: Between May and Aug, it may freeze at night. May-Jul is the season of the so-called 'Chiperoni', a drizzling mist that may envelop the mountains for days. The heaviest rains fall from Dec-Mar, and may make some stream crossings difficult. The intermittent months are probably the most pleasant, but access to the mountain is possible year-round.

HABITATS: The two main habitats on the plateau are grassland and forest. Interspersed are areas of bare rock and bracken slopes. The drier valleys (Likabula, for example) that cut into the plateau are clad with miombo and riverine forest. The wetter valleys (especially Ruo) support a gradual transition from lowland through submontane to montane forest.

Maggie Westrop/IOA

Mount Mulanje looms above tea plantations.

GETTING THERE

It is possible to visit the Ruo Gorge, where most of the forest specials occur, on a day trip via the Lujeri Tea Estate **A**, easily reached from the M2 that runs to the Mozambique border. Permission and directions for Ruo Gorge can be obtained at the Tea Estate office. Alternatively, if you have time to trek (trails start at Likabula or Ruo), book at Likabula Forest Station **C**. There is excellent birding on the mountain and accommodation can be found in eight huts along the way.

BIRDING: The spectacular Ruo Gorge Ⓑ, formed by the wild Ruo River that cuts deep into the massif, is the wettest place in Malawi. The roar of the river, the precipitous cliffs, lush jungle and fine forest birding make this a compelling place. An easy hike a few hundred metres up- and downstream of the small hydroelectric plant at the bottom of the gorge (just above the tea plantations of the Lujeri Estate) is likely to supply **African Goshawk, Silvery-cheeked Hornbill**, and **Yellow-streaked, Little** and **Placid Greenbuls, Square-tailed Drongo, Olive-flanked Robin** (only above altitudes of 1 000 m), **Spotted Ground-Thrush*, Evergreen Forest Warbler, Yellow-throated Woodland-Warbler, Black-headed** and **Yellow-throated Apalises, Black-fronted*** and the more common **Olive Bush-Shrike, Mountain Wagtail, Dark-backed Weaver**, and **Red-throated** and **Green* Twinspots**.

The Ruo Gorge is a good site to find **Thyolo Alethe***. An early morning walk over the huge water pipes that feed the power plant (along the path upstream from the plant) may produce several of these shy birds.

286 Lengwe National Park

IBA ✔

Lengwe is a hot, low-lying park on the Shire Plain, dominated by dense thickets (habitat of Nyala), and is particularly good for Palearctic and intra-African migrants, but road conditions during the rains can be unreliable. Specials include **Crested Guineafowl, Thick-billed Cuckoo*, Böhm's*** and **Mottled Spinetails, Narina Trogon*, Böhm's Bee-eater*, Livingstone's Flycatcher***, and **Grey Sunbird**. Some of the best riparian thicket birding is to be found by walking from the park gate and bridge along the Nkombedzi River; here **Böhm's Bee-eater*** can be seen hawking insects from vegetation, and **Black-and-white Flycatcher*** has recently been found to be resident and breeding here (also try the footpath to the river 100 m before North Hide). Shortly past the entrance gate, turn off to the right onto North Thicket Drive, a good road for other birds of dense thicket. The more open woodland on the southerly park roads may provide **Retz's Helmet-Shrike** and good numbers of its brood parasite, **Thick-billed Cuckoo***. **Rudd's Apalis** is very rare. Lengwe is about two hours' drive from Blantyre: the signposted turn-off west from the M1 to the park is 20 km south of the Shire Bridge at Chikwawa (43 km south of Blantyre), and the park gate lies 10 km further on through sugar cane plantations.
NEARBY SITES: Nyala Park (signposted from Nchalo village), situated on the Sucoma Sugar Estate, is good for **Lemon-breasted Canary***.

287 Zomba Plateau

✔✔✔

Zomba is a rolling, patchily forested plateau which rises above the eastern Rift. The plateau is heavily planted with pines, but several easily accessible montane forests still remain. The forest remnants that lie behind Zomba town, at the base of the escarpment, are a particularly convenient place in which to search for the highly localised, sought-after and beautiful **White-winged Apalis***.
SPECIALS: White-winged and Yellow-throated Apalises*, White-eared Barbet, Thyolo Alethe*, Southern Mountain and Placid Greenbuls, Evergreen Forest Warbler, Malawi Batis, Forest Double-collared Sunbird, and Southern Citril.
SEASON: The roads on the plateau can become extremely muddy during the rains, sometimes precluding 2WD vehicles.
HABITATS: Patches of Afromontane forest interspersed with grassland, pine plantations and, lower down, some fine miombo woodland.
BIRDING: White-winged Apalis* can be searched for on the outskirts of Zomba town: follow the signs marked 'University of Malawi Centre for Social Research' from the main road, east of the town centre, to Livingstone Road and then left onto Malemia Road Ⓐ, and listen carefully for its typically apalis-like 'plopping' call in the trees all along this road, but especially above the Herbarium. **White-eared Barbet** – a localised bird in Malawi – **Blue-spotted Wood Dove**,

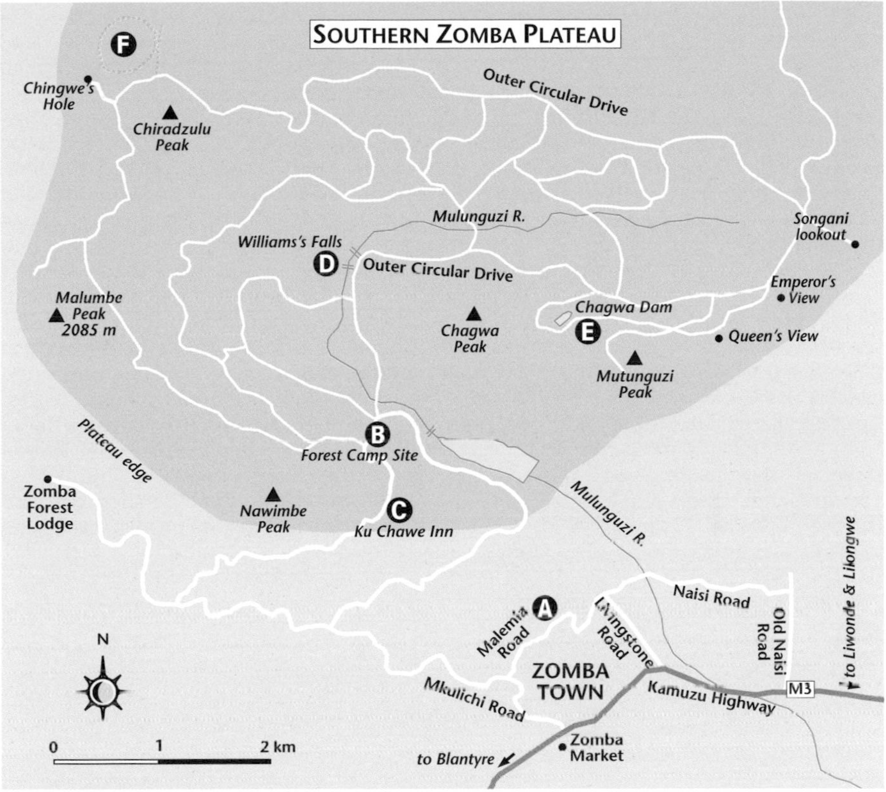

Pale Batis and **Red-throated Twinspot** can also be found here.

The lower slopes of the escarpment, between Zomba town and the forests around Chagwa Dam and Ku Chawe, are largely covered by pine plantations, and are of relatively little birding interest. However, any foraging flocks seen in the patches of miombo that line the roadside are worth searching for **Speckle-throated Woodpecker**.

Callan Cohen

Thyolo Alethe occurs in forest near Chagwa Dam.

GETTING THERE

Steep, narrow roads lead up and down the plateau's southern slope, above Zomba town. 4WD is not usually needed, but care should be taken during the rainy season, when the steep switchbacks may become slippery. To reach the plateau, turn north (left if coming from Blantyre) from the main road through town (Kamuzu Highway) onto Mkulichi Road, opposite the PTC Supermarket. Guesthouse accommodation is available in Zomba town; on the plateau itself, accommodation is available at the Zomba Forest Lodge (see Land & Lake Safaris, ☎), the very upmarket Ku Chawe Inn C, and two excellent camp sites.

Good forest patches for birding are around the Department of Forestry's Forest Camp Site **B**, around Ku Chawe Inn **C**, along the trail following the Mulunguzi River between the camp site and Williams's Falls **D**, at Chagwa Dam **E**, and on the slopes of Chiradzulu Peak **F**. Ku Chawe Inn and the Forest Camp Site are reached soon after cresting the edge of the plateau. Birds of the camp site and adjacent forest edge include **African Wood-Owl, Eastern Saw-wing, White-eared Barbet, White-starred Robin, Dark-capped Yellow Warbler, Black-headed** and **Yellow-throated Apalis, Malawi Batis, Forest Double-collared Sunbird, Southern Citril, Yellow-bellied Waxbill, Red-faced Crimsonwing, Green Twinspot*** and **Bertrand's Weaver**, while **Evergreen Forest Warbler** skulks and churrs in the thickets among the camp sites.

To reach Chagwa Dam from the Forest Camp Site, continue past the 'Down Road to Zomba' turn-off, ignoring all subsequent turn-offs until a right turn after 4.3 km, which leads 700 m on through forest to the dam. Bird from the road, or take a slow walk through the low forest. The forest canopy provides **Livingstone's Turaco, Southern Mountain** and **Olive-headed Greenbuls** (very common), **Black-headed Apalis, Yellow-throated Woodland-Warbler** and **Olive Bush-Shrike**. The mid-strata hold **Placid Greenbul, Forest Double-collared Sunbird, Red-faced Crimsonwing** and **Southern Citril**, and the forest edges provide **Red-backed Mannikin**. Search the leaf litter and listen carefully for **Lemon Dove** and **Orange Ground-Thrush** and, especially in the vicinity of ant trails, the difficult **Thyolo Alethe***. **Mountain Wagtail** occurs around Chagwa Dam. Also check river crossings (such as the one 600 m from the Forest Camp Site, en route to Chagwa) for this species and for **Half-collared Kingfisher**. The forest on the northern side of Chiradzulu Peak provides similar birding.

288 Liwonde National Park   IBA ✔✔

Liwonde is a low-lying, relatively arid park that stretches along the Shire River. Lying in the southern Rift, it is in many ways reminiscent of the Zambezi and Luangwa valleys of Zimbabwe and adjacent Zambia. As such, it offers excellent riverine and woodland birding, in addition to game-viewing and good tourism facilities. For birders, Liwonde's greatest attraction may well be one's most reliable chance of finding the localised **Brown-breasted Barbet**, followed closely by a host of other specials such as **Böhm's Bee-eater*** and **Lillian's Lovebird**.

SPECIALS: Brown-breasted Barbet, Böhm's Bee-eater*, Lillian's Lovebird, White-backed Night-Heron*, Western Banded Snake-Eagle, Racket-tailed Roller*, Collared Palm-Thrush, and Livingstone's Flycatcher*.

SEASON: Birding is good year-round; however, note that **Brown-breasted Barbet** may be absent or difficult to find during the dry season, when the riverine fig trees are not in fruit.

HABITATS: Mopane woodland, river banks and riverine thicket, flood plain, ilala (*Hyphaene*) palm savanna, miombo on the hill slopes.

BIRDING: From Mvuu, it is possible to explore on foot the riverine thicket along the Shire and its minor watercourses, which offers a great selection of tropical species, and to take boat trips along the Shire itself. The 28 km drive through the reserve from the main gate to Mvuu provides game-filled woodland, which supplies the limited selection of

GETTING THERE

Coming from Lilongwe, drive straight through the Liwonde town centre and over the Shire bridge. Continue for 1.3 km, and turn left at the turn-off signposted 'Ntaja'. Continue through this market area, and turn right after 300 m at the national park signpost. Follow this road for 2.9 km before turning left at a second national park sign. The park's main gate is 3.4 km further on, beyond the railway line. A complex network of roads (largely signposted) exists within the park, so it is best to pick up a map at the main gate. Mvuu Camp, operated by Central African Wilderness Safaris ☎, forms the focus of most birding in the park. Mvuu provides camping and hutted accommodation, and runs birding boat trips on the Shire. An alternative to staying at the camp is to drive or use public transport to reach Ulongwe, on the Liwonde-Mangochi road, then catch a ride on the back of a bicycle (easily arranged) for the 14 km to the banks of the Shire opposite Mvuu Camp. A ferry is available to transfer visitors across to Mvuu.

mopane specials. Early in the morning, small flocks of **Lillian's Lovebird** are regularly encountered, usually flying overhead en route to the water, and betraying their presence with shrill, metallic screeching. They may also be encountered at the outskirts of Mvuu Camp. Other characteristic species of the mopane include **Brown-headed Parrot**, **Crested Barbet**, **Red-billed Hornbill**, **Bennett's** and **Speckle-throated Woodpeckers**, **Mosque Swallow**, **Arnot's Chat**, **Retz's Helmet-Shrike** (and occasionally its parasite, **Thick-billed Cuckoo***), **Greater Blue-eared** and especially **Meves's Starlings**, **Red-headed Weaver** and **White-browed Sparrow-Weaver**. The surprisingly inconspicuous **Racket-tailed Roller*** usually perches quietly in mid-canopy. You may also encounter groups of **Southern Ground-Hornbill***. Carefully check any clearings with short grass for the **Senegal Lapwing**; also scan the airstrip, just north of Mvuu Camp, for this species.

There is superb birding at Mvuu Camp itself, both in the grounds and in adjacent riverine thicket. The thicket is punctuated by large fig trees, which should be carefully searched for **Brown-breasted Barbet**. Confiding **Böhm's Bee-eater*** and **Collared Palm-Thrush** are usually very much in evidence around the camp buildings. Also search the over-hanging riverine vegetation along the camp site for roosting **White-backed Night-Heron***. Other notable species found in the outskirts of the camp and in adjacent thicket to the north and east include **Red-necked Spurfowl**, **Green Malkoha**, **Grey-headed Parrot** (usually seen flying over, screeching, early in the morning), **Bearded Scrub-Robin**, **Livingstone's*** and **Fan-tailed Flycatchers**, and **Purple-banded Sunbird**. Carefully scan the crowns of the numerous palms for **Red-necked Falcon** and **Dickinson's Kestrel**.

If you'd like to take a longer walk into the riverine vegetation beyond the camp, you must be accompanied by a guide from Mvuu Camp. This is well worth the investment, as the guide may have stake-outs for **Brown-breasted Barbet** nests and daytime roosts of **Pel's Fishing-Owl*** and other species. **African Pitta*** has been recorded here. And, if there are no guests at the luxurious Mvuu Wilderness Lodge just to the north, you may be granted permission to have a look at the marshy inlet there, where **White-backed Night-Heron*** hunt at dusk and other marshland species occur. Also check any seasonal pools for **Dwarf Bittern** (Nov-Apr).

A number of good water and riverine species can be seen simply by relaxing at Mvuu and idly watching the Shire below. These include **Black**, **Goliath** and **Rufous-bellied Herons**, **African Openbill**, **Palm-nut Vulture***, **African Fish-Eagle**, **Osprey**, **Western Banded Snake-Eagle** (common), **Black Crake**, **Long-toed** and **African Wattled Lapwings**, **Water Thick-knee**, **African Skimmer***, **Giant Kingfisher**, **Southern Carmine Bee-eater** (Jan-Aug, or whenever breeding elsewhere on the river is complete), and, more rarely, **Gull-billed Tern** (mainly a scarce summer visitor, especially Sept-Dec, but sometimes also in winter). **Spur-winged Lapwing** has been resident in very small numbers since 1993, and has bred here, including in hybrid pairs with **Blacksmith Lapwing**. **Southern Brown-throated Weaver** breeds in the reeds lining the camp, as do three other weaver species (**Spectacled**, **Village** and **Lesser Masked Weavers**) in the trees nearby. Better still, take a boat trip upstream (easily arranged at Mvuu Camp; ask in advance for a special early departure), to cover more ground and obtain close-up views. Ideally, take this trip again in the late afternoon and return in the dark, spotlighting for **Pel's Fishing-Owl*** and **White-backed Night-Heron***.

Night drives can also be arranged at Mvuu, and these often produce interesting nocturnal mammals, as well as **Bronze-winged Courser**, **Square-tailed** and **Fiery-necked Nightjars**, **Verreaux's Eagle-Owl**, **African Scops-Owl** and, in the Chiunguni area, **Barred Owlet**.

Claire Spottiswoode

Böhm's Bee-eater

OTHER ANIMALS: Game-viewing is excellent. Hippopotamus are abundant at Mvuu (check them for **Red-billed Oxpecker**), and Elephant are also numerous. A variety of antelope occur, perhaps most notably a good population of Sable.
NEARBY SITES: Many of the flood-plain specials of the Mvuu area (including **African Skimmer***, if sandbanks are exposed, and **Böhm's Bee-eater***) occur around the lodges on the northern outskirts of Liwonde town, as do marshland species such as **Allen's Gallinule** and **Black Coucal**.

289 Chongoni Mountain ✔

When travelling from Blantyre (or Zomba, or Liwonde National Park) to Lilongwe, those with a limited budget may wish to break the journey at Chongoni Forestry Lodge. The Lodge (inexpensive, self-catering, all rooms with bath and toilet) is signposted on the right a few kilometres after Dedza, and is reached on a 5 km track (accessible all year). It is set in beautiful surroundings (miombo, rocky hills) with some good birds in the immediate vicinity, including **Miombo Tit** (very common), **Souza's Shrike** (fairly common), **Miombo Rock-Thrush**, **Spotted Creeper***, **Red-capped Crombec**, **Lazy Cisticola** (very high densities), and **Violet-backed** and **Miombo Double-collared Sunbirds**.

Small patches of forest on the slopes of Kangoli Hill (100 m from the lodge) hold **Schalow's Turaco**, **Hildebrandt's Spurfowl**, **Moustached Green Tinkerbird** and **Bar-throated Apalis** (*whitei*). There is also a chance of **Boulder Chat*** on the cliffs along Kangoli Hill, as well as **Striped Pipit** and **Mocking Cliff-Chat**. A little way further up the hill there are several large *Acacia abyssinica* trees, inhabited by **Brown Parisoma**; search here too for **Southern Citril**, **Bertrand's Weaver**, and **Black-eared** and **Reichard's Seed-eaters**. Check any dambos which you encounter in the Dedza and Lilongwe vicinities for **Locustfinch*** and **Rosy-breasted Longclaw***.

290 Southern Lake Malawi ✔

A number of 'resort' villages exist along the southern sections of Lake Malawi. Although they are worth visiting primarily for snorkelling and to observe the Lake's extraordinarily diverse, beautiful and evolutionarily intriguing cichlid fish, there are also a number of interesting birding possibilities. At Senga Bay, **Böhm's*** (resident) and **Madagascar** (mainly late Aug to early Oct) **Bee-eaters** and **Livingstone's Flycatcher*** occur in the lakeside thickets. Mpatsanjoka Dambo is a series of marshy areas just to the south of the village (turn off onto the track just east of the bridge on the Salima-Senga Bay road) and is well worth investigating, especially for **Rufous-bellied Heron**; other species occasionally seen here include **Dwarf Bittern** (Nov-Apr), **African Pygmy Goose***, **White-backed Duck**, **Lesser Jacana**, **Black Coucal**, **Blue-cheeked Bee-eater** and **Yellow Weaver**.

Cape Maclear National Park and adjacent Monkey Bay, at the lake's southern extreme, are particularly good for snorkelling. Along the lake shore, **African Fish-Eagle** is abundant, and the uncommon **Gull-billed Tern** may drift past during summer.

WHEN TO VISIT MALAWI

The rainy season in Malawi is from Nov-Apr, and this is when bird activity is at its peak. However, it can become quite hot in the lowlands during these months, and roads at many key sites have significantly deteriorated, necessitating the use of 4WD vehicles. The cool, dry season, from May-Aug, provides particularly pleasant daytime weather (very cold at night at Nyika!) and better road conditions, but migrant species are absent and forest species, in particular, may be significantly less vocal. The hot, dry season (Sept-Oct) is perhaps the least pleasant time to visit Malawi, although many resident birds are breeding during this period.

ROUTE 33

NORTHERN MALAWI

Malawi north of Lilongwe deserves at least 10 days' birding on a 'bare-bones' visit, but one could easily spend several weeks hiking and driving through its montane and lowland habitats. The Dzalanyama Forest Reserve is only a day trip from the capital, although this excellent miombo site really deserves at least two full days. Tranfers from Lilongwe are available for those without private transport, and birding is easy and even desirable on foot. North of Lilongwe, the M1 runs the length of the country and large distances can be covered quickly on this good tar road. More troublesome are the unsurfaced access roads to many key sites – notably the superb Nyika National Park – many of which become mudbaths during the rainy season, when 4WD is highly recommended and often essential. Nyika forms the focus of most trips to the region, and at least three days are needed to sample the key habitats even briefly. A week or more could be well spent here.

TOP 10 BIRDS

- White-winged Babbling Starling
- Olive-headed Weaver
- Spot-throat
- Sousa's Shrike
- Stierling's Woodpecker
- Scarlet-tufted Sunbird
- Rwenzori Nightjar
- Ludwig's Double-collared Sunbird
- Chapin's Apalis
- Olive-flanked Robin-Chat

A visit to Nyika is usually combined with game-viewing and lowland birding at the neighbouring Vwaza Marsh Wildlife Reserve. Other than Nyika, the two principal highland areas forming Malawi's northern spine are the Southern Viphya Plateau and Misuku Hills. The former is crossed en route north and provides pleasant montane forest birding. The Misukus are remote and accessible only to the more intrepid, but offer some superb forest birding. Most visitors add side trips to the lake shore in Nkhata Bay (notably for East Coast Akalat*) or to Senga Bay regions, and to Kasungu National Park.

Note that the Luangwa National Park of south-eastern Zambia (see p.354) is fairly easily accessible from Lilongwe, via the Mchinji border crossing. South Luangwa is justifiably famous for big game and easy tropical woodland birding, and a trip to this national park combines very well with highland forest birding in northern Malawi. The border crossing is usually without problems, and the park's Mfuwe Gate a 130 km drive beyond (allow three hours during the dry season, and typically double that during the wet).

Maggie Westrop/IOA

Miombo woodland in northern Malawi

291 Lilongwe Nature Sanctuary ✔

Despite its situation in central Lilongwe, this small (150 ha) sanctuary that lines the Lingadzi River provides good riverine forest birding (including, notably, **African Broadbill*** and **African Finfoot***). The entrance is on Kenyatta Road, at the junction with Youth Road just west of the modern city centre. The sanctuary is always accessible. Head left (south) from the entrance gate to join the signposted 'Riverside Trail' along the Lingadzi for access to riverine forest and species such as **Narina Trogon***, African Broadbill*, African Finfoot*, **Half-collared Kingfisher**, **White-backed Night-Heron***, **Schalow's Turaco**, **Black-throated Wattle-eye**, **Red-throated Twinspot**, **African Black Duck**, and **Mountain Wagtail**. Safety has been a concern in recent years, so enquire locally.

292 Dzalanyama Forest Reserve IBA ✔✔✔

Dzalanyama is undoubtedly one of Malawi's very best birding localities. Situated just 58 km from the capital, the 100 000 ha reserve protects a vast tract of largely pristine woodland along and to the east of a low range of hills along the Mozambican border. Miombo birding here is excellent, and the localised **Stierling's Woodpecker** is probably more accessible at Dzalanyama than anywhere. A number of miombo specials reach their southerly limit here, and the reserve also provides convenient access to many more widespread species of miombo woodland and riparian forest. Although it is just a couple of hours' drive from Lilongwe, it is preferable to overnight here and invest two to three days in exploring the woodland.

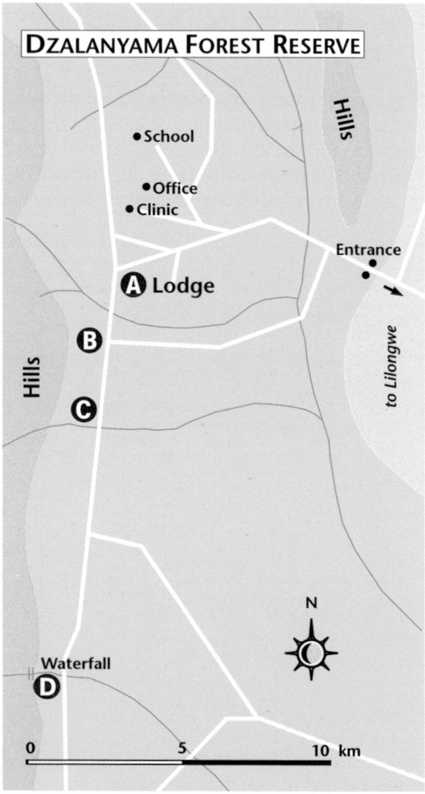

SPECIALS: Stierling's Woodpecker, Pale-billed Hornbill, Miombo Pied Barbet, Boulder Chat*, Miombo Scrub-Robin, Miombo Tit, Red-capped Crombec, Red-winged Warbler, Yellow-bellied Hyliota, Böhm's and White-tailed Blue Flycatchers, Souza's Shrike, Wood Pipit, Shelley's Sunbird*, Olive-headed Weaver*, Orange-winged Pytilia, and Black-eared Seed-eater.

SEASON: Miombo is good all year round, although foraging flocks are more frequent in winter, and many species are more vocal in Aug-Oct, just prior to the rainy season. The access road from Lilongwe is occasionally impassable during the rains.

HABITATS: Most of the reserve is cloaked in miombo woodland. There are also a number of specials associated with its rocky hills, numerous dambos and small patches of riparian forest.

BIRDING: Birding in miombo is critically dependent on finding foraging flocks, and long, very quiet patches are interspersed with occasional pandemonium, when a bird party bursting with mouth-watering species is encountered. A good strategy is to drive slowly through the woodland, looking out for activity, and to stop and follow on foot any parties encountered. Make sure that you take note of the direction in which you are walking, however, as miombo all looks very much the same (especially in overcast weather) and it is surprisingly easy to lose one's sense of direction! If you have a GPS, you may consider taking a waypoint before setting out from the road.

Some of the best birding at Dzalanyama is around the lodge Ⓐ and along the final 7 km of road that leads up to it. For most birders, the real prizes to be found at Dzalanyama are **Stierling's Woodpecker**, **Souza's Shrike**, **Olive-headed Weaver*** and **Shelley's Sunbird***. The first three of these often join mixed-species foraging flocks – the woodpeckers and weavers in pairs, and the shrikes often in trios, usually in the mid-stratum. The weavers favour areas where 'old-man's-beard' lichen drips from the branches, and are fairly often seen in the vicinity of the lodge, as are the shrikes. **Shelley's Sunbird*** is scarce, and best searched for by watching any flowering creepers (such as mistletoe) and trees; most of the lodge's trees flower during winter. Other species that may be seen here include **Violet-backed**, **Miombo Double-collared** and **Anchieta's Sunbirds**; the last favours areas of woodland with proteas.

Callan Cohen

Dambo and miombo at Dzalanyama

Sought-after miombo species that are present in many foraging flocks are **Whyte's** and **Miombo Pied Barbets**, **Green-backed Honeybird**, **Miombo Rock-Thrush** (not necessarily near rocks), **Rufous-bellied** and **Miombo Tits**, **Yellow-bellied** and **Southern Hyliotas**, **Böhm's** and **White-tailed Blue Flycatchers**, **Red-capped Crombec**, **Black-eared Seed-eater** and **Reichard's Seed-eater**. **Miombo Scrub-Robin** is often present in patches of slightly denser vegetation, such as on termite mounds. **Hildebrandt's Spurfowl** and **Wood Pipit** are usually seen at road edges or when flushed from the woodland floor. **Spotted Creeper*** should be looked for on trunks and larger branches. **Whyte's Barbet** is fairly inconspicuous, and often sits motionless in the canopy, whereas small groups of **Pale-billed Hornbill** flop noisily overhead. More widespread species of broad-leaved woodland include **Thick-billed Cuckoo***, **Green-backed Honeybird**, **White-breasted Cuckooshrike**, **African Golden Oriole**, **Arnot's Chat**, **Grey Penduline-Tit**, **Stierling's Wren-Warbler**, **Green-capped Eremomela** and **Red-headed Weaver**. **Orange-winged Pytilia** is fairly common, sometimes with its host, **Broad-tailed Paradise Whydah**, nearby. In summer, **Pennant-winged Nightjar*** is occasionally flushed from the woodland floor, and several other nightjar species (**Fiery-necked**, **Square-tailed** and **Freckled Nightjars**) can be seen along the roads at night. Raptors include **Wahlberg's Eagle**, **Bateleur** and, less commonly, **African Cuckoo Hawk** and **Western Banded Snake-Eagle**.

To reach the dambos and the rockier, miombo-clad hill slopes, walk or drive from the lodge back out along the entrance road

GETTING THERE

To reach Dzalanyama from central Lilongwe, take Glyn Jones Road south-west out of town, drive through the Likuni roundabout and past the golf course and Kibobo Camp. The road becomes unsurfaced and passes for 24 km through villages and agricultural lands to the gate of the reserve (check any wet dambos in this vicinity for **Rosy-breasted Longclaw***). The unsurfaced road is often in poor condition during the rainy season, so allow at least an hour and a half for the journey, or, preferably, check in advance with Land & Lake Safaris ☎ that it is passable. You are requested to sign a book at the gate, but there is no entrance charge. Dzalanyama Forest Lodge Ⓐ is where the best birding is, and where you will probably want to set up a base. It can be found signposted 20 km further along the miombo woodland-lined road. The lodge offers good, reasonably priced chalet accommodation. Transfers can be arranged from Lilongwe, conveniently allowing you to bird the area on foot or on a rented bicycle.

for about 2 km, and park close to the second wooden bridge near the grassy dambo Ⓒ; cross the dambo and search for **Boulder Chat*** on the hill on the right. The ridge is also fairly easily accessible from the T-junction Ⓑ. Other species of this habitat include **Striped Pipit**, **Mocking Cliff-Chat**, **Miombo Rock-Thrush** and **Cabanis's** and **Cinnamon-breasted Buntings**. Also search the dambo fringes near the bridge for specials such as **Red-winged Warbler**, **Broad-tailed Warbler**, **Yellow-mantled Widowbird** and perhaps even a **Lesser Seedcracker***. There is a single record of **Chestnut-headed Flufftail*** from a Dzalanyama dambo, although this species is easier to find in Zambia.

A good patch of riparian forest is present around the waterfall Ⓓ. Species here include **Schalow's Turaco**, **Broad-billed Roller** (summer), **Scaly-throated Honeyguide**, **Green-backed Woodpecker**, **African Broadbill*** and **Red-throated Twinspot**, as well as the tricky **Lesser Seedcracker***.

293 Viphya Plateau ✔

South Viphya is a large, sprawling plateau covered by a mosaic of grassland, pine plantations, granite hills and remnant patches of Afromontane forest. It is traversed by the main M1 highway from Lilongwe to Mzuzu (look out for passing **White-headed Saw-wing** during Oct-Apr), and in several places this road provides instant access to small forest patches that offer a good selection of highland species. Viphya's principal special is **Scaly Francolin**, a more typically East African species that occurs nowhere else in Malawi and is rarely seen by birders. It is easier to see this species in the understorey of neglected pine plantations than in its natural habitat, and it is best found if you wander along some of the forestry tracks east of Chikangawa.

Luwawa Forest Lodge provides a good base from which to explore the plateau. To reach it, head north on the M1 from Lilongwe for 234 km. Turn right onto a sand track at the 'Luwawa Forest Lodge' sign, and follow this track through stunted miombo woodland and pine plantations for 10.6 km to the lodge. Situated in a broad, grassy dambo (which yields **Yellow-mantled Widowbird**, **Southern Citril**, **Singing Cisticola**, **Broad-tailed Warbler** and **Anchieta's Tchagra***), the lodge is surrounded by low miombo woodland (**Trilling Cisticola**, **Red-capped Crombec**, **Bertrand's Weaver**, **Cabanis's Bunting**), forest (possibly **Scaly Francolin**, **Moustached Tinkerbird**, **Olive Woodpecker**, **Olive-flanked Robin-Chat**, **Fülleborn's Boubou**, **Southern Mountain Greenbul**, **White-eyed Slaty Flycatcher**, **Yellow-crowned Canary**) and adjacent grassland (**Blue Swallow***). The lodge gardens attract a variety of birds, including **Forest Double-collared**, **Bronze** and **Yellow-bellied Sunbirds**, **Red-necked Spurfowl** and **Evergreen Forest Warbler**. On the approach to Vipha from Lilongwe, consider stopping in the mossy miombo where the M1 crosses the Chimaliro Forest Reserve. There is good miombo birding here, including a decent chance of **Olive-headed Weaver***.

The Uzumara Forest Reserve protects an excellent forest on Uzumara Peak (1 920 m) in the North Viphya Mountains that lie between Lake Malawi and the Nyika Plateau. The peak can be reached by 4WD on a track leading to a radio-transmitting tower. Montane forest species are similar to those found on Nyika, but **Mountain Illadopsis** is quite common here, as is **Sharpe's Akalat**. **Oriole Finch** can also be quite common here.

294 Kasungu National Park ✔

This large national park which runs along the Zambian border consists primarily of flat or gently rolling miombo woodland, interspersed with a number of small dambos. A good diversity of big game occurs, and there is a pleasant mix of lowland and miombo birding. The most productive miombo is to be found in the hillier northern section of the park.

To reach the park, take the M1 to Kasungu town (244 km from Lilongwe), and turn off to the west onto the well-signposted D187. The park entrance is a further 38 km along this unsurfaced road.

295 Nyika National Park 4X4 IBA ✔✔✔

Red-winged Francolin

Extending into neighbouring Zambia, Nyika is perhaps the most famous birding site in Malawi, offering superb montane forest and grassland birding.This vast, high-altitude (about 2 000 m asl) plateau is mainly covered by rolling grasslands, dotted with forest patches that represent the southern range limit of numerous sought-after East African species. Furthermore, it is possible to drive to most sites, making Nyika almost uniquely accessible as a south-central African montane region. Once at each site, walking on foot is permitted, and, in fact, essential for finding forest species.

SPECIALS: Pallid Harrier*, Hildebrandt's Spurfowl, Red-winged Francolin, Wattled Crane*, Denham's Bustard*, Rwenzori Nightjar, Dusky Turtle-Dove, Black-backed Barbet, Moustached Tinkerbird, Bar-tailed Trogon*, Angola, Red-rumped and Blue* Swallows, White-headed Saw-wing, Sharpe's and Southern Mountain Greenbuls, Sharpe's Akalat, White-chested Alethe*, African Hill Babbler, Brown Parisoma, Mountain Yellow and Cinnamon Bracken Warblers, Chapin's and Brown-headed Apalises, Black-lored, Trilling and Churring Cisticolas, Fülleborn's Boubou, Waller's and Slender-billed Starlings, Scarlet-tufted, Bronzy, Anchieta's, Ludwig's Double-collared and Green-headed Sunbirds, Montane Widowbird, Bertrand's and Baglafecht Weavers, Red-faced Crimsonwing, Yellow-crowned Canary, Southern Citril.

SEASON: A number of species are absent or harder to find during the dry season, but roads are usually far easier to navigate at this time of year.

HABITATS: The plateau is dominated by rolling, montane grassland with areas of bracken, protea savanna, and bogs. The grassland is interrupted by small patches of low-canopy forest, and substantial Afromontane forests at Chowo, Zovo-Chipolo and Manyenjere. At the park's headquarters at Chelinda Camp Ⓗ (altitude 2 300 m), there is also a series of small dams, *Hagenia* woodland, and blocks of exotic plantations. The plateau is surrounded by miombo-clad foothills, most easily reached from the area in the vicinity of Thazima Gate.

BIRDING: There is good birding all over the park, but the best places to focus your attention are Chowo Forest Ⓖ for Afromontane forest specials (and Manyenjere Forest Ⓔ if you must see **Sharpe's Akalat**) and the area around Chelinda Camp Ⓗ for assorted grassland and marsh species. However, also allow for some birding in the miombo woodland around

GETTING THERE

Nyika is about eight hours' drive from Lilongwe. The road is tarred all the way to Rumphi. From here to the park entrance at Thazima Gate (53 km) the gravel road S85 is in reasonable condition, but for the 110 km road from Thazima Gate to Chelinda Camp a high-clearance vehicle is advisable. Although 2WDs regularly make the journey during the dry season, road conditions often deteriorate significantly during the wet season (Jan-Apr), when 4WD is usually essential and sections may become wholly impassable. There is an airstrip at Chelinda.

All park facilities are centred around Chelinda Camp, where there is a restaurant, fuel pump, and accommodation ranging from comfortable self-catering chalets to the newly built Chelinda Lodge, a battalion of luxurious log cabins. Chelinda Camp, run by Nyika Safari Company ☎, offers game drives (day and night), horseriding, fly-fishing, and the services of guides/porters for multi-day hiking trips.

For hikers, a well-equipped camp site is situated 2 km from Chelinda. There is unrestricted access to the Zambian section of Nyika, and camping is permitted (no facilities) alongside the Zambian Rest House – a somewhat derelict building next to the Zambian game scout camp near Chowo Forest – as well as at the Malawian game scout camp in prime miombo woodland near Thazima Gate. Winter nights at Nyika are cold, so come prepared, especially if planning to camp!

Miombo woodland on the drive up the plateau

Thazima Gate **A**, and for various spots along the 'border road' between Thazima Gate and Chowo Forest, bearing in mind that, even in dry conditions, it can take four hours to drive from Thazima to Chelinda. Zovo-Chipolo forest **D** is easily accessible from Chowo Forest, and also provides good forest birding, and is worth a stroll if you miss any specials at Chowo.

Thazima to Chowo: A band of the miombo woodland, confined to the park's lower altitude areas and most accessible here, is found just beyond the entrance gate into the park **A**. Look for foraging flocks at the roadside, and visit the valley below the park's administration camp. To reach it, turn off to the right just past the entrance gate, and follow the track past the staff village, through a tract of miombo woodland and down to the Kaswerere Stream. The latter is known as Malawi's best stake-out for **Black-backed Barbet** – look particularly in the larger trees along the river. Miombo species found in bird parties here and along the first approximately 18 km of road into the park include **Whyte's Barbet**, **White-breasted Cuckooshrike**, **Spotted Creeper***, **Arnot's Chat**, **Miombo Rock-Thrush**, **Rufous-bellied** and **Miombo Tits**, **Trilling Cisticola**, **White-tailed Blue Flycatcher**, **Yellow-bellied Hyliota**, **Green-headed**, **Miombo Double-collared** and **Anchieta's Sunbirds**, **Reichard's** and **Black-eared Seed-eaters**, **Cabanis's Bunting** and, rarely, **Collared Flycatcher** (summer). **White-winged Black Tit** occurs along the sparser woodland edges. If lucky, you may flush a **Pennant-winged Nightjar*** while walking here (Sept-Feb).

As the road rises in altitude, the miombo thins and is replaced by grassland and bracken. Look out for **White-headed Saw-wing** flitting over the road during Oct-Apr. At 20.3 km from Thazima Gate, stop at the band of beautiful *Acacia abyssinica* at **B**. This is a very reliable site for **Brown Parisoma**, an unassuming bird with a loud and distinctive song. Also look out for **White-tailed Blue Flycatcher**, **Reichard's** and **Yellow-browed Seed-eaters**, **Grey Waxbill** and in winter, when the creepers that drape the trees are flowering, **Green-headed**, **Miombo Double-collared**, **Anchieta's** and **Bronzy Sunbirds**. The small forest patch here, and the many others further along the road, provide a number of thicket and forest-edge species such as **Fülleborn's Boubou** and **Cinnamon Bracken Warbler**; these are also the best places to search for **Brown-headed Apalis**, which can be common between 1 900 and 2 050 m altitude. **Churring** and the huge and noisy **Black-lored Cisticolas** are common and conspicuous in the protea woodland and dense bracken at the roadside all the way from here to Chowo and Chelinda. Look out for **Hildebrandt's Spurfowl** and **Jackson's Pipit**, regularly disturbed at the roadside.

Forest birding: The first major forest one encounters is perhaps Nyika's prime birding locality, Chowo Forest **C** in Zambia. The entrance is clearly marked along the border road, 40 km from Thazima Gate. A footpath descends fairly steeply into the forest from the entrance. Walk slowly along the trail, scan the canopy for movement, and constantly keep an ear open for song. The most common species of the canopy and mid strata are **Schalow's Turaco**, **Southern Mountain** and **Sharpe's Greenbuls**, **Bar-throated Apalis**, **White-tailed Elminia (Crested Flycatcher)**, **Malawi Batis** and **Forest Double-collared Sunbird**, all of which are fairly noisy and easily seen. By investing several hours in the forest and following up calls, you will eventually start to pick off some of the scarcer or more elusive forest specials. Other canopy species include **Bar-tailed Trogon*** and **Moustached Tinkerbird** (both easily called up), **Black-fronted Bush-Shrike*** and **Waller's Starling**, while other birds of the middle and lower forest strata include **Olive Woodpecker** (distinctive *ruwenzori* subspecies), **Little Greenbul, African Hill Babbler, White-chested Alethe*, Olive-flanked Robin-Chat, White-starred Robin, Evergreen Forest Warbler, Chapin's** and **Brown-headed Apalis** (the latter is scarce), **Fülleborn's Boubou** and parties of **Red-faced Crimsonwing. Lemon Dove** is usually flushed from the forest floor or heard gently padding through the leaf litter.

It is also well worth investigating the impressive granite boulders ('Chowo Rocks') that lie above the entrance to the forest, not least as a vantage point to scan for **Scarce Swift** (Sep-Apr; most commonly Oct-Mar) overflying the forest canopy below. The *nyassae* form of **Long-billed Pipit** occurs here, as well as **Scarlet-tufted** (breeding during the early rainy season) and **Ludwig's Double-collared Sunbirds, Hildebrant's Spurfowl** and **Mocking Cliff-Chat**; you may even flush a **Striped Flufftail*** (especially Nov-Jun).

Although Chowo Forest provides excellent birding, **Sharpe's Akalat** is effectively absent here. To see this species, it is necessary to hike or drive well into the Zambian section of the park, to the beautiful Manyenjere Forest Ⓔ. The turn-off to the Zambian Rest House Ⓕ is just 2.5 km beyond Chowo Forest. A path leads from the Rest House into the forest, but is relatively rarely used and may be overgrown in places; you may consider hiring a guide from Chelinda Camp. Notably, there is a small, loose colony of **Angola Swallows** nesting on the Rest House buildings. The birds are present from about May and have bred Oct-Dec. When not breeding they are most conspicuous at dawn and dusk, when they return to roost in the building's eaves. Several pairs of **Blue Swallow*** also nest in the grassland around the Rest House. Look out too for **Slender-billed Starling**, as at least one pair breeds along the stream below the Rest House. The grassland and bracken in this vicinity are especially good for species of this habitat and forest edge. **Hildebrandt's Spurfowl** and **Black-lored Cisticola** are particularly plentiful; also look out for **Bertrand's Weaver, Ludwig's Double-collared Sunbird, Yellow-bellied Waxbill, Southern Citril** and **Yellow-browed Seed-eater**, and perhaps even a flushed **Striped Flufftail***.

The path to Manyenjere Forest is also good for **Scarlet-tufted Sunbird** and **Hildebrandt's Spurfowl**, and the scarce **Slender-billed Starling** occasionally flies overhead. An alternative to walking from the Rest House is to drive 7.6 km from the Chelinda/Chitipa junction towards

Maggie Westrop/IOA

Nyika Plateau supports rich Afromontane forest patches.

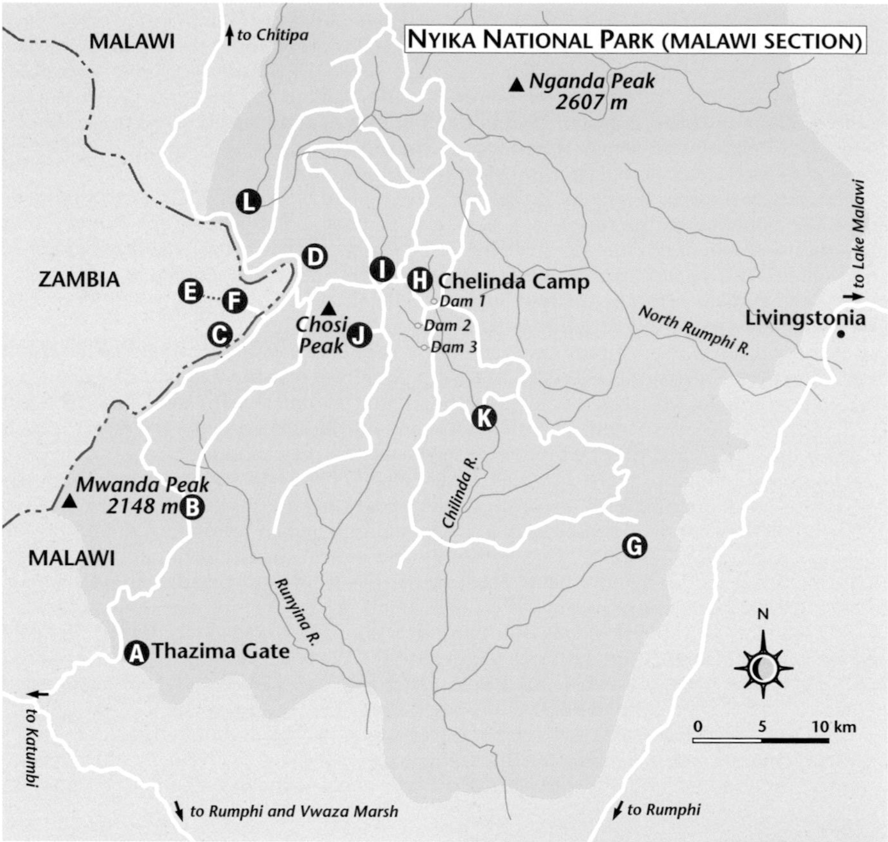

Chitipa; look for a grassy track on the left and follow this for 3.6 km into the hills. Apart from offering great views off the western escarpment into Zambia, the track takes you right to the very edge of the forest. Once inside the forest interior, it is easy to move around. **Sharpe's Akalat** is quite common but inconspicuous here, especially in dense shrubbery along streams. Carefully watch aggregrations of ants, which the akalat regularly attends together with **Olive-flanked Robin-Chat** and **White-chested Alethe***, among others. **Brown-headed Apalis** appears to be more common here than at Chowo, and is best located by its call.

Two sought-after forest species, **Mountain Illadopsis** and **Oriole Finch,** are restricted to the less accessible eastern escarpment forests. These include the steep Kasaramba Forest **G**, a frequently impass-

Warwick Tarboton

Malachite Sunbird: beware confusion with the similar Scarlet-tufted Sunbird

able 40 km drive from Chelinda, and the Mwenembwe block just to the north of it. The latter is reached on foot, through grassland, and is traversed by a traditional footpath to the villages below; it is particularly good for Mountain Illadopsis.

Around Chelinda Camp: The plantation edges around the buildings and camp site at Chelinda Ⓗ are good for **Dusky Turtle-Dove** and **African Olive-Pigeon**, and **Rwenzori Nightjar** and **Spotted Eagle-Owl** fly around the camps at night. Thickets around the camp site hold **Cinnamon Bracken Warbler, Malawi Batis** and **Fülleborn's Boubou**. For marshland species, follow the path alongside the stream that emerges below the wall of Chelinda Dam 1. **Blue Swallow*** may occur in good numbers in this area from mid Sept-Mar, as well as over marshy areas elsewhere in the park (300 pairs in total). **Angola Swallow** also feeds around the dams, but during the dry season (May-Oct) only. Small flocks of **Montane Widowbird** frequent the sedges and scrub here and at the dam edges, and are easily identifiable even out of the breeding season by their canary-yellow wing patches and pale blue (male) and pale pink (female) bills. **Mountain Yellow Warbler** occurs in the thickets between the stream and the path, and although moderately skulking is fairly easy to locate by its loud song, or rather sunbird-like 'tchak' contact call.

Callan Cohen

Rolling grasslands of the plateau

Black-lored and **Churring Cisticolas, Cape Robin-Chat, Baglafecht Weaver, Yellow-browed Seed-eater, Southern Citril**, and **Malachite, Scarlet-tufted** and **Ludwig's Double-collared Sunbirds** also occur in the riverine vegetation. This path also allows the opportunity to admire more closely some beautiful higher-altitude vegetation, such as the floppy-leaved *Hagenia* trees, tree ferns, and giant lobelias. Similar bird species can also be found around Lake Kaulime Ⓘ, a natural lake 8 km from Chelinda on the road to Chowo; also check here and on the airstrip for **Wattled Crane***.

Grassland drives: Scan the grassland that lines the numerous scenic roads radiating from Chelinda Camp for raptors and ground birds – when not distracted by the often excellent game-viewing. A good area close to the camp is Chosi Peak viewpoint Ⓙ; for a longer drive, try the Chelinda Valley circular route, stopping to bird on foot around Chelinda Bridge Ⓚ. In summer, the elegant **Pallid Harrier*** occurs in good numbers and can be seen quartering the grasslands throughout the park; more rarely, **Western Marsh** and **Montagu's Harriers** may also occur. Other grassland species include **Denham's Bustard*** (scan carefully for white blobs in the distance), **Red-winged Francolin** (Nyika-endemic subspecies), **Wattled Crane*** (near dambos or depressions), **Augur Buzzard, Common Quail, Rufous-naped Lark, Rufous-chested Sparrowhawk, Black-lored, Churring** and **Wing-snapping Cisticolas** and **Malachite** and **Scarlet-tufted Sunbirds**. The signposted road to Chisanga Waterfalls Ⓛ is also worth taking, as several pairs of **Slender-billed Starling** breed (Sep-Dec) in the area.

OTHER ANIMALS: The park boasts one of the highest densities of Roan Antelope anywhere; Burchell's Zebra, Reedbuck and Eland are also fairly common in the grasslands, and Bushbuck and Bushpig occur in the forest patches. The forests hold a number of interesting and highly localised small mammals, most notably Tanganyikan Mountain Squirrel and Chequered Elephant Shrew. Leopard are relatively numerous and occasionally seen. Nyika is also noted for its diverse orchid flora, which includes four endemic species.

296 Vwaza Marsh Wildlife Reserve IBA ✔✔

Vwaza is a lowland park that lies to the west of Nyika, along the Zambian border. Although there is good tropical birding throughout the park, most species here are widespread, and the main objective for most birders would be to search for the two localised specials of well-developed woodland, **White-winged Babbling Starling*** and **Chestnut-backed Sparrow-Weaver**.

SPECIALS: White-winged Babbling Starling* and Chestnut-backed Sparrow-Weaver.

SEASON: Year-round.

HABITATS: Along its eastern border lies a low range of miombo-clad hills, whereas the plains to the west have mopane woodland (here at its northernmost limit), thorny thickets and an extensive network of pans and marshes.

BIRDING: White-winged Babbling Starling* and **Chestnut-backed Sparrow-Weaver** occur in very tall miombo and mixed mopane-miombo. The starling especially favours hill slopes, and occurs in noisy (nasally calling), fast-moving flocks (sometimes large – flocks of 60 have been seen). By contrast, the sparrow-weaver is sluggish and inconspicuous, although it does offer a distinctly firefinch-like trilling call. It often perches in trees, with grass cover below. Both species are more likely to be found along the 33 km road that runs from the main camp at Kazuni to the scout camp at Kawiya, along the eastern edge of the reserve. Other good woodland species found in the reserve include **Grey-headed** and **Meyer's Parrots**, **Racket-tailed Roller***, **Miombo Pied Barbet**, **Arnot's Chat**, **Miombo Scrub-Robin**, **Böhm's Flycatcher**, **Miombo** and **Rufous-bellied Tits**, **Miombo Blue-eared Starling**, **Broad-tailed Paradise Whydah** and **Cabanis's Bunting**.

Kazuni Camp, just inside the main park entrance at Kazuni Gate, overlooks a pan with abundant game and a variety of birds, sometimes including **Grey Crowned Crane** and **Collared Pratincole**. **Senegal Coucal** and **Collared Palm-Thrush** occur around the camp. Raptors are numerous, and include **Dickinson's Kestrel**. For game-viewing, also try the road that runs parallel to the river along the southern edge of the park to Zoro Pools.

OTHER ANIMALS: Big game includes Elephant, Buffalo, Sable, Roan, Puku and Hippopotamus.

GETTING THERE

To reach the main entrance at Kazuni Camp at the reserve's south-eastern corner, follow the Nyika road (S85) and turn left 9 km after Rumphi onto the S49 (signposted 'Vwaza'); the reserve gate is a further 19 km along this road. The reserve can also be entered at its north-eastern corner, but the rough track (signposted 'Kawiya'), 44 km from Rumphi, is in poor condition. Kazuni Camp, including hutted accommodation and a camp site, is run by the Nyika Safari Company ☎.

297 Nkhata Bay ✔✔

Hugh Chittenden

East Coast Akalat

Nkhata Bay, at the lakeside 50 km east of Mzuzu, is best known among birders as the easiest place in Malawi to search for the lowland forest special, **East Coast Akalat***, which occurs in remnant forest patches near the town. One good site is Mkuwazi (also known as Nkwadzi, or variations of this) Forest Reserve, which lies on the Chinteche road, 13.2 km south of the Nkhata Bay/Mzuzu/Chinteche junction and just past Vizara Estate (the second rubber plantation). Also try Kalwe Forest Reserve, just 8 km from Nkhata Bay, on the southern side of the Mzuzu road, near the 'Department of Agriculture' sign. A road leads a few hundred metres into the forest. **East Coast Akalat*** is inconspicuous but not difficult to find with knowledge of its call. It calls predominantly at dawn and dusk. Other species in these forest patches include **Green Malkoha** (common), **Narina Trogon***, **Green-backed Woodpecker, Eastern Nicator, Terrestrial Brownbul, Blue-mantled Crested Flycatcher** (Kalwe) and excellent forest butterflies. There are a number of accommodation possibilities offered for tourists in Nkhata Bay; those further south, towards Chinteche, are quieter and more pleasant (**Yellow Weaver** here). **White-fronted Plover** occurs on the lake beaches.

The Mzuzu Wildlife Education Centre, reached on a track leading north of the Nkhata Bay road (3 km from the government Rest House in Mzuzu town), has some forest patches where **East Coast Akalat*** and **Grey-olive Greenbul** may be found.

298 Misuku Hills

IBA ✔✔

These hills are rarely visited by birders. Lying just south of the Tanzanian border, they are partially protected by two forest reserves, Mugesse and Wilindi-Matipa, which run along parallel ridges separated by a cultivated valley. Very good forest blocks remain, as the forests are well respected and conserved by the local people. The Afromontane forest birding is largely similar to that of the Nyika National Park, with the notable exception of three East African species that reach the southern limit of their distributions at the Misuku Hills and are found nowhere else in Malawi; these are **Shelley's Greenbul, Spot-throat*** and **Forest Batis**.

There are two ways of visiting the forests. Firstly, one can drive to Mugesse and from here drive right into the forest, as there is a farm track crossing it. One can camp at the forest edge (near Mugesse Mission), or inside the forest. Mugesse is best for **Green Barbet*** and **Silvery-cheeked Hornbill** (the largest breeding population in Malawi); **Forest Batis** and various bulbuls are all relatively easy.

Secondly, in order to search for **Spot-throat***, ideally one needs to drive right through to the other side, to reach Matipa Forest, where it is also safe to camp. The bird is common at Matipa: one should hear plenty, but of course it requires some patience to see. It also occurs in Wilindi Forest, but if this is approached from the Wilindi side one needs to walk some distance into the forest before reaching suitable altitude for the bird.

Other noteworthy forest species include **Mountain Buzzard, Scarce Swift, Dusky Turtle Dove, Bar-tailed Trogon*, Moustached Tinkerbird, Green Barbet*, Fülleborn's Boubou, Olive-headed Greenbul, White-chested Alethe*, Orange Ground-Thrush, White-eyed Slaty Flycatcher, Chapin's Apalis, Bertrand's Weaver, Oriole Finch, Southern Citril, Bronzy** and **Forest Double-collared Sunbirds** and **Waller's Starling**. Grassland birds such as **Blue Swallow*** and **Black-lored Cisticola** occur around both forests.

Maggie Westrop/IOA

Clearing a rockfall from the road in the Misuku Hills; be prepared for challenges

ZAMBIA

Zambia is surprisingly underestimated as a birding destination, given that it offers a high diversity of habitats and localised species. Apart from its reasonable infrastructure and stable political environment, it offers huge expanses of wilderness, abundant game and wonderfully friendly people.

Much of the country remains covered in miombo woodland interspersed with grassy dambos along the drainage lines (see boxes on p.267 and p.264). Over 750 bird species have been recorded in Zambia – including Shoebill, reliably found in lechwe-ridden swamps, and some uniquely accessible Congolese rainforest specials. Only one species is a true endemic: Chaplin's Barbet, the snowy-white fig specialist of the Kafue Flats. The mopane-dwelling Black-cheeked Lovebird is a near endemic to this country. Yet, to place undue emphasis on a paucity of endemics would do Zambia a great injustice, as it offers some of the most diverse and productive miombo woodland birding anywhere (offering all but one of the miombo specialists), as well as superb waterbirding at several sites (most notably Lochinvar National Park and the Bangweulu Swamps, where Shoebill lurks). There is excellent montane forest and grassland birding on the Zambian Nyika Plateau (the plateau straddles the border with Malawi; see p.325) and, in the Mwinilunga district of the far north-west, a host of species otherwise largely restricted to Congolese rainforest and forest edge (including Black-collared Bulbul) occur in a tongue of 'mushitu' forest that extends into Zambia from the inaccessible Democratic Republic of Congo.

A trip to Zambia can be planned in a number of ways. Birders with their own capable vehicles (a rugged 2WD vehicle with high-clearance is a minimum, and 4WD is essential during the rains) will find Zambia – a short hop across the Zambezi – a tractable and rewarding destination. Nearly all sites are accessible by road, and camping and park fees are not unreasonable, although fuel is relatively expensive here. On the other hand, organised tours offer a plethora of possibilities in the way of fly-in safaris, luxury camps and guided trips.

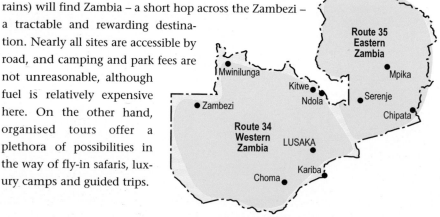

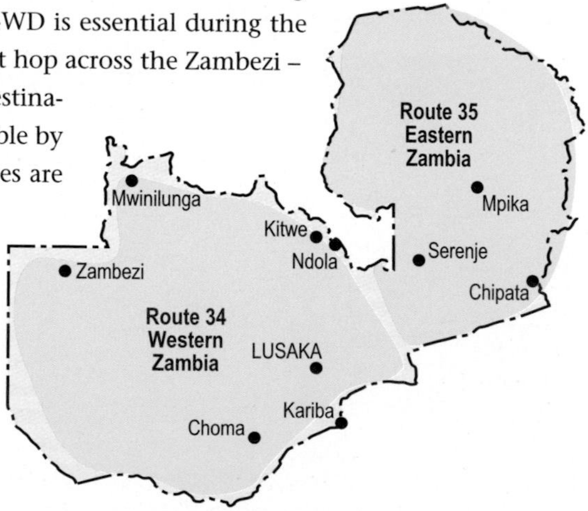

ROUTE 34

WESTERN ZAMBIA

Western Zambia is dominated by two great drainages, the Zambezi and Kafue rivers, which bring images to mind of some of the country's best-known attractions, among them that of the Zambezi river plunging over a hundred metres into the Batoka Gorge at Victoria Falls, and that of teeming game on the flood plains of Kafue National Park. Kafue, which is one of the largest national parks in Africa, is also one of the better sites for the near-endemic Black-cheeked Lovebird*.

TOP 10 BIRDS

- Black-cheeked Lovebird
- Chaplin's Barbet
- Black-collared Bulbul
- Angola Lark
- Bamboo Warbler
- Forbes's Plover
- Grimwood's Longclaw
- Black-and-rufous Swallow
- Laura's Woodland-Warbler
- Margaret's Batis

Not all of Zambia's birding sites are well developed for tourism, and many, if not most, require an element of adventure and self-sufficiency. Those who do make the effort to explore will be rewarded with some of the most spectacular birding to be found anywhere, especially around the far north-western town of Mwinilunga, which offers a host of more typically Congolese rainforest species. Birders visiting this region may harbour a secret ambition to rediscover the enigmatic White-chested Tinkerbird, described from a single specimen collected in 1964 in the towering Mavunda forests (p.344) and never seen again. To be fair, though, considerable dispute persists as to whether this distinctive-looking bird was not simply a colour abberation of Yellow-rumped Tinkerbird.

Many of Zambia's best birding sites are remote, and do not lie on any clearly demarcated route. However, there are a number of localities situated within striking distance of commonly used overland access points from Namibia (Mulobezi) and Zimbabwe (Livingstone).

Kafue, Liuwa Plain, Lochinvar and Blue Lagoon constitute Zambia's four western flood plain national parks. Kafue and Lochinvar can be reached by road from Lusaka. The Liuwa Plain and Blue Lagoon national parks, while very remote, can also be reached by road. The dense woodlands and rainforest outliers that make up the Mwinilunga district in the far north-west, arguably western Zambia's most exciting birding locality, are accessible almost entirely along tar roads (the T3 and T5) all the way from Lusaka.

A number of areas, including several private farms in the Lusaka and Choma districts (Zambia's only indisputable endemic, Chaplin's Barbet*, may be found here), and the lower Zambezi River Valley (Chirundu district), where African Pitta* and other lowland species occur, are accessible in excursions from the capital.

A good way to begin birding around Lusaka is to contact the Zambian Ornithological Society ☎ for guidance. Members may be available to accompany you, or may help with introductions to local landowners on whose properties you can bird, such as Lazy J Miombo Sanctuary, Kasisi Mission (Zambezi Indigobird) and a number of lodges.

Gerald Cubitt

Ross's Turaco

299 Livingstone

IBA ✔✔

Livingstone, situated on the Zambian bank of the Victoria Falls (see p.282) about 10 km from the falls proper, is formally protected by the Mosi-Oa-Tunya National Park (entrance at Ⓐ). Birding here is rewarding, and typical species of the forest in the falls' spray zone include **Schalow's Turaco, Trumpeter Hornbill, Yellow-bellied Greenbul, White-browed Robin-Chat** and **Bearded Scrub-Robin**. Above the falls, the Zambezi is accessible from several spots such as at Flood Memorial Ⓑ, and many tourist lodges along its banks as far as Kazungula. From about Aug-Jan, when rocks are exposed, look for **Rock Pratincole***, and in and around the riparian vegetation for **Western Banded Snake-Eagle, African Finfoot*, Giant** and **Half-**

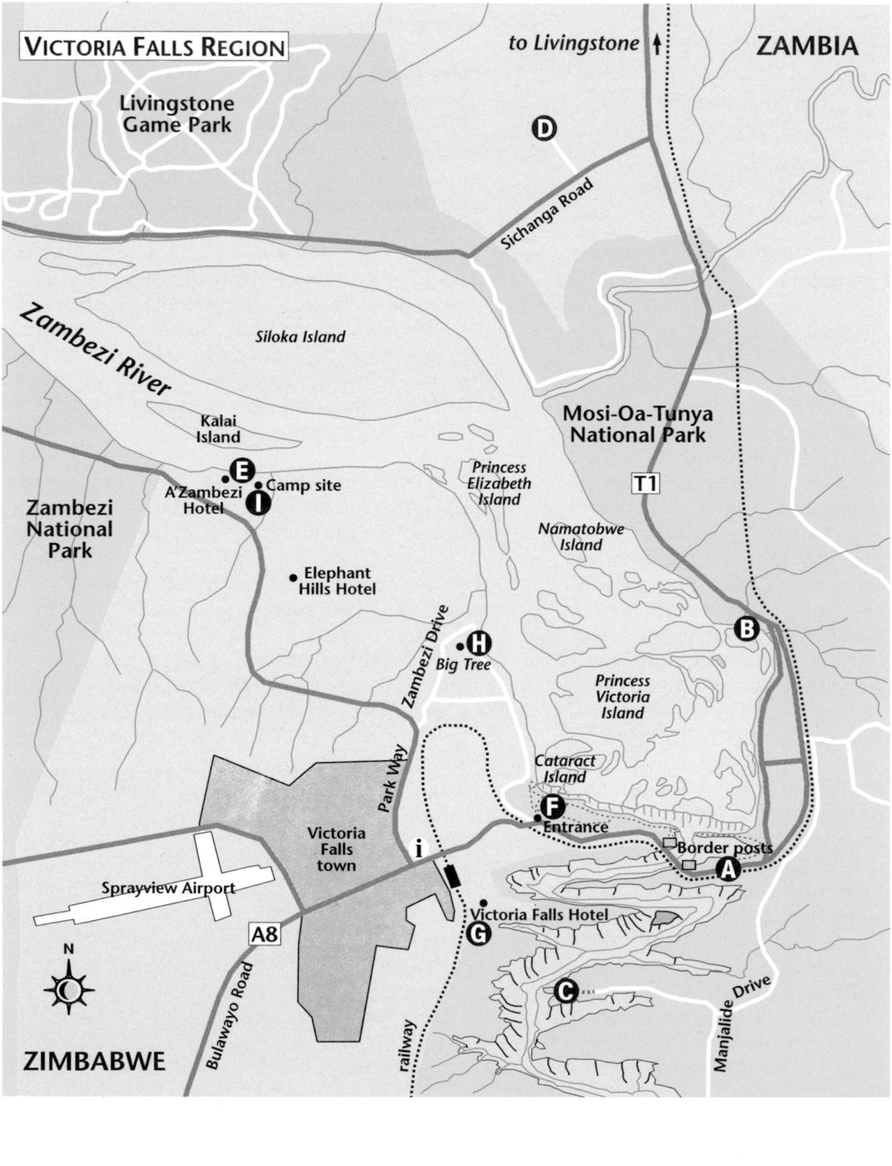

collared Kingfishers, and **Brown Firefinch**. At dawn and dusk, watch for **White-backed Night-Heron*** flying to or from its roost. Throughout the area, listen carefully for singing indigobirds; the enigmatic form of an undescribed species that parasitises (and imitates the song of) Brown Firefinches may be found here. But be warned: these look identical to **Village Indigobirds**, which are very common.

Take the track turning south through dry woodland to the viewpoint **C**, 600 m before the border post; not only is the view over the Batoka Gorge below the falls fantastic, but a vigil here should turn up **African Black Swift, Rock Martin, Red-winged Starling, Cinnamon-breasted Bunting,** the occasional **Black Stork**, and a wide variety of raptors (such as **Augur Buzzard, Peregrine** and **Lanner Falcons** and **Verreaux's** and **African Crowned Eagles**). **Taita Falcon*** is now extremely scarce and most 'possibles' turn out to be **Peregrine Falcon**.

Birders looking for a quick, but rewarding stop should visit the Livingstone Sewage Ponds **D**. These usually hold a very interesting array of water birds and many rarities have been found here. Take the road to the Mosi-Oa-Tunya National Park and turn right after Nyala Lodge. Continue to the end of the track and park and walk, or drive around the large ponds.

300 Mulobezi & Simungoma 4X4 IBA ✔

Two areas of interest are to be found west of Livingstone, along the newly tarred Livingstone-Sesheke road. At the small village of Simungoma (located on this road), turn off to the north towards Mulobezi and into mopane country to look for **Black-cheeked Lovebird***. Several tracks leading east from the Mulobezi road take you closer to the Machile River (ask for the road to Sibalabala and Magumwi). Patient sitting at Machile waterholes in the early morning or late afternoon can be productive.

Turn south at the Simungoma junction onto a rough sandy track, and you'll reach the broad Zambezi flood plain. A 4WD and a good sense of direction are useful as there is no established road network, but off-road driving is easy and there are many beautiful camping spots. Pools on the plain are worth searching for **Slaty Egret*, Kori Bustard, White-bellied** and **Red-crested Korhaans, Burchell's Sandgrouse, African Mourning Dove, Pearl-breasted Swallow, Hartlaub's Babbler** and **Burchell's Starling**, but note that the main river is not always accessible.

Back in the thorny thickets, even those that line the main road, you may find several species that have very limited distributions in Zambia, such as **Acacia Pied Barbet, Red-eyed Bulbul, Chestnut-vented Tit-Babbler, Marico Flycatcher, Marico Sunbird, Scaly-feathered Finch** and **Black-faced Waxbill.**

L. Warburton

Black-cheeked Lovebirds gather in trees around waterholes early in the morning.

301 Nkanga River

IBA ✔✔

Situated just north of Choma, Nkanga River Conservation Area is made up of a group of privately owned farms that have been protecting this section of the Southern Province's wildlife for several decades. This is one of the best places to see Zambia's only true endemic, **Chaplin's Barbet***. The conservation area can be reached from the Namwala road, which heads north from Choma's eastern fringe, but a more pleasant road to take is signposted (Masuku Lodge and 'Bruce-Miller') about 3 km east of the town. Follow the dirt road which runs from the tar for 19 km and then turn left at the next sign. After a further 1.5 km, stop and make enquiries at the Nansui farmhouse and school.

Chaplin's Barbet* occurs widely in open areas with scattered sycamore fig trees: carefully scan the tree tops for conspicuous white shapes. The easiest spot to search is on the track to Lake Meg. **Cuckoo Finch*** can be abundant from Oct-Dec in reedbed roosts near the dams, and **Streaky-breasted Flufftail** can be common in the dambos in good rainy seasons.

There is a beautiful camp site beside the Nkanga River, there are chalets at the main farmhouse, and in the north-east corner is Masuku Lodge. For more information and bookings, contact Nansai Farm ☎.

302 Kafue Flats: Lochinvar

4X4 IBA ✔✔

Lochinvar National Park offers some of the most exciting wetland birding anywhere, and over 400 species have been recorded there. The Kafue flood plain here stretches over a vast area some 70 km wide. The park is accessible for much of the year, though visits after heavy rain are strictly for the brave and well-equipped. The main focus is the Chunga Lake and adjacent flooded areas. As in many enormous wetlands, birds may not be numerous everywhere, but with some searching you'll usually find good concentrations somewhere.

It is well worth driving out to both the north-east and north-west sides of the lake to explore areas of either shallow, flooded grassland, or mudflats, depending on the season. If you are not confident about navigating these largely road-free areas, then ask at headquarters if a game scout can accompany you. And, if it looks wet – *don't drive further*! The flood plain is pure black-cotton clay, and it is very easy to get stuck.

Perhaps the most exciting time to visit is towards the end of the dry season (Sept-Oct), when the local birds are joined by vast numbers of migrant waders. Many species such as **Squacco** and **Black Herons**, **African Openbill**, **Glossy Ibis**, **Fulvous** and **White-faced Ducks**, **Egyptian** and **Spur-winged Geese**, **Red-billed Teal**, **Red-knobbed Coot**, **Collared Pratincole**, **Blacksmith Lapwing**, **Kittlitz's** and **Caspian Plovers**, and **Ruff** are regularly found in their thousands. Other specials include **Slaty Egret***, **Wattled Crane***, **Black-tailed Godwit**, **Long-toed Lapwing**, **Gull-billed Tern** and **African Skimmer***. To this heady mix are added many thousand endemic Kafue Lechwe (unique to the Kafue Flats) and hundreds of Plains Zebra.

Away from the water there are large areas of dry plains, where species include **Secretarybird**, **Denham's Bustard***, **Yellow-throated Sandgrouse**, **Chestnut-backed Sparrowlark** and **African Quailfinch**. Raptors abound, and the patches of thicket around Sebanzi Hill and the park headquarters can be productive.

Although you may find yourself grounded to the axles in the rains, you are often rewarded with birds such as **Dwarf Bittern**, **Pallid*** and **Montagu's Harriers**, **Amur Falcon**, **Streaky-breasted Flufftail**, **Corncrake**, **Great Snipe** and **Olive-tree Warbler***.

Roads are in very poor condition and high clearance is essential. There is a basic camp site, although camping is permitted anywhere. There is also a luxury tented camp on the shores of Chunga Lake NP. To reach the park, follow the signs marked 'Lochinvar' – turn west onto the dirt road just north of Monze town. After about 15 km, turn right, and after another 11 km, turn left. From here the road twists and turns for about 16 km until it reaches the park gate. There are more signs, but if in doubt, ask for directions from local residents.

303 Kafue Flats: Blue Lagoon

IBA ✓

Lochinvar's 'sister park' is situated on the north bank of the flats. Blue Lagoon National Park is poorly developed and the birding is unpredictable, although as the floodwaters recede, it can be fantastic. From Lusaka, take the Great West Road and turn left after about 23 km. Continue straight where the main road swings left (about 20 km further on). The park gate is about another 65 km from here. Ask for directions to the old farmhouse (where **Chaplin's Barbet*** occurs in the fig trees) and then on to the causeway that stretches out onto the flood plain. This will involve back-tracking a few kilometres from the park gate. During the rains, birding can be excellent on the approach road, where the flooded open woodlands may produce species such as **Dwarf Bittern**, **Streaky-breasted Flufftail** and **Striped Crake***.

304 Lower Zambezi

4X4 IBA ✓✓

One of the main reasons for visiting this area is to search for **African Pitta***. The best place to start is in the riparian thickets along the Mutulanganga and Mbendele rivers on the Siavonga Road, about 25 km and 35 km from the Chirundu road turn-off respectively. It is possible to camp at either site, but there are no facilities of any sort and you shouldn't leave vehicles unattended. It is possible to make day trips from Lusaka, and there is also accommodation in both Siavonga and Chirundu. The best time to visit is from mid-Nov-Mar.

Other species to look for include **Barred Long-tailed*** and **Emerald Cuckoos**, **Böhm's*** and **Mottled Spinetails**, **African Broadbill***, **Sombre Greenbul**, **Eastern Nicator**, **Red-capped Robin-Chat**, **Thrush Nightingale***, **River Warbler*** and **Livingstone's Flycatcher^**. The Lower Zambezi National Park also holds many of these species, but access in the rains is very limited, and exploring the thickets on foot is a risky business because of large mammals. However, it is a beautiful park with many places to stay, ranging from camp sites to luxury lodges. Some lodges arrange transfers by boat from Gwabi Lodge near Chirundu, but if you are driving in, cross the Kafue on the pontoon near Gwabi, and follow the dirt road beyond for about 50 km to reach the park gate. Many camps are situated along this stretch outside the park and the thickets here are easier to explore. It is a particularly good area for **Crested Guineafowl**. Within the park is a variety of other habitats to explore, including oxbow pools, mopane woodland, dense riparian woodland and plains.

Adriadne van Zandbergen/IOA

African Pitta occurs in thickets in the Zambezi Valley, an area also favoured by big game.

305 Kafue National Park 4X4 IBA ✔✔

Birding in the Kafue National Park is rich and varied, which is hardly surprising in a park that is the size of Belgium. The park is conveniently divided by the Great West Road (M9). The forest-lined Kafue River runs into and through the northern sector, and is flanked by miombo woodland and dambos, and feeds the beautiful Busanga Plains and associated wetlands found in the north-west of the park. The southern sector also has much miombo, but teak forest, savanna and mopane woodland occur in the far south, where **Black-cheeked Lovebird*** may be found.

SPECIALS: Black-cheeked Lovebird*, White-backed Night-Heron*, Saddle-billed Stork, Crested Guineafowl, Wattled Crane*, African Finfoot*, Rock Pratincole, Ross's Turaco*, Pel's Fishing-Owl*, Böhm's Bee-eater*, Racket-tailed Roller*, and Black-backed Barbet.

SEASON: Most of the park is inaccessible during the rains (Nov-Apr), although this varies depending on the season.

HABITATS: Mopane and miombo woodland, riparian and teak forest, thicket, savanna, dambos, flood plain.

BIRDING: The northern sector's dambos and oxbows hold various water birds such as **Saddle-billed Stork** and **Wattled Crane***. Its miombo woodland often produces bird parties, but don't forget about the presence of big game when you investigate these. In the miombo look out for birds such as **Pale-billed Hornbill**, **Miombo Scrub-Robin**, **Böhm's Flycatcher** and **Souza's Shrike***. The riparian forest along the major rivers is home to many interesting species, including **White-backed Night-Heron*, Ross's Turaco*, Pel's Fishing-Owl*, Black-backed Barbet**, **Olive** and **Green-backed Woodpeckers**, **Grey-olive Brownbul** and **Black-throated Wattle-eye**. Look for **African Finfoot*** in the shady water below and **Rock Pratincole*** (Aug-Jan) perched on rocks in the river. Where there are dry thickets near the river, look for the unobtrusive but charming **Böhm's Bee-eater***. The Busanga Plains hold large numbers of water birds at times, and the isolated trees provide refuge for many migrants in Oct-Nov. Lions are very common here, so be careful when on foot. Other interesting bird species include **Fülleborn's** and **Rosy-breasted* Longclaws**, and many raptors.

In the far south of the park, **Black-cheeked Lovebird*** occurs between Ndumdumwenze Gate Ⓐ and the Nanzhila River Ⓑ, usually in or near mopane woodland. Its piercing call often gives it away, and pools are worth watching for the lovebird in the early morning and late afternoon, when large flocks sometimes come to drink. Other typical mopane birds include **Three-banded Courser*, Red-billed Hornbill, Arnot's Chat, Meves's Starling** and **White-browed Sparrow-Weaver**. Watch for bird parties in the miombo in this area too, and for

GETTING THERE

The northern sector is only accessible in the dry months (about May-Nov), and can be reached from the Great West Road (M9) from Lusaka. Shortly after crossing the Kafue River turn onto a dirt road, which leads through the northern reaches of the park right up to the Busanga Plains. From this road, various loops and access tracks lead to several camps and lodges situated along the Kafue and Lufupa rivers. Chunga camp site, situated in the southern section of the park, is fairly close to the tar road (just below the M9) just beyond the Kafue bridge, and several other camps (both seasonal and permanent) are signed from the Great West Road.

The southern sector is best accessed in the dry season, although the 'cattle cordon' from Ndumdumwenze to Ngoma should be passable in the rains. The southernmost area of the park is reached via the town of Kalomo, 122 km north-east of Livingstone on the tarred T2. From the T2, turn west into Independence Avenue (opposite the water tower) and drive through the market. After 700 m, turn right at the T-junction on the edge of town, then left after 100 m. Cross the railway line, then turn left at the fork a further 3 km on. Ndumdumwenze Gate is another 69 km from here, and you should allow at least 2.5 hours for this drive.

Alternatively, enter the park at Itezhi-Tezhi (turn off from the Great West Road from Lusaka at the signpost). There are several camps and lodges around Itezhi-Tezhi Dam and one in the Nanzhila Plain area further south. If camping, ask game scouts at the park gates about suitable sites, and be aware of big game!

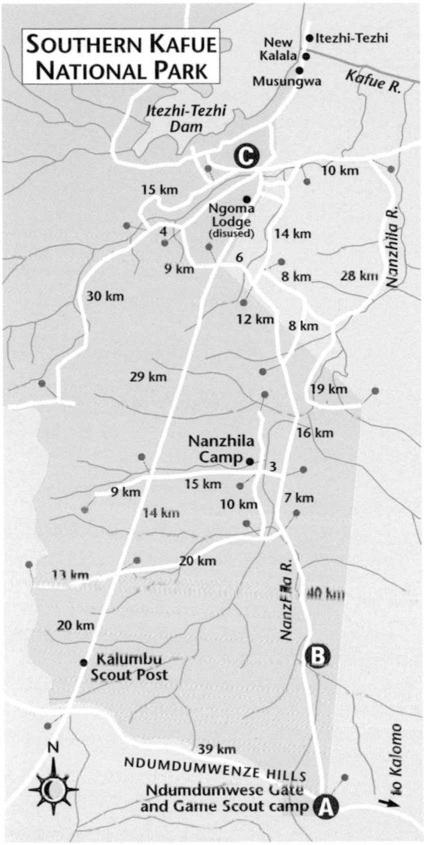

species such as **Miombo Pied Barbet**, **Red-capped Crombec**, **Yellow-bellied Hyliota** and **Shelley's Sunbird***.

The dense teak forest between Ngoma and Itezhi-Tezhi (Ngoma thickets) **C** has been degraded by fire, but **Crested Guineafowl** is still regular and can often be seen crossing the road.

OTHER ANIMALS: Despite intense poaching pressure, both the Nanzhila and Lufupa-Busanga areas still hold good concentrations of game, including the largest number of antelope species found in any African park.

Peter Pickford/IOA

Saddle-billed Stork

Claire Spottiswoode

Mopane woodland in the Kafue National Park

306 Liuwa Plain National Park 4X4 IBA ✔

This remote park, situated between the Luambimba and Luanginga rivers, is dominated by huge plains. Game-viewing can be spectacular, with good numbers of Lion, and Liuwa boasts the second largest Wildebeest migration in the world. The plains flood during the rains, and as the waters recede during the dry season, vast numbers of water birds congregate, including significant numbers of **Slaty Egret*** and **Wattled Crane***. **Collared Pratincole** can be very common, though they can be vastly outnumbered by **Black-winged Pratincole** during Oct-Nov. **Caspian Plover** may also be abundant on the drier parts of the plains, where other species include **Denham's*** and **White-bellied Bustards**, **Greater Kestrel**, **Black-rumped Buttonquail**, and isolated populations of **Eastern Clapper** and **Pink-billed Larks**. Visitors need to be self-sufficient and equipped with (preferably) two 4WD vehicles and, ideally, a GPS.

Daryl & Sharna Balfour/IOA
Keep a careful eye out for Lion.

The park is only accessible during the dry season (ca Jun-Nov). From Mongu, drive across the Zambezi flood plain, cross the Zambezi on the pontoon and head for Kalabo. Sometimes the road becomes vague, but there are always people to ask if you are unsure. It is worth visiting the park office in Kalabo before entering Liuwa; officials here often part with valuable advice, and game scouts are willing to accompany you into the park. Just outside Kalabo, you can cross the Luanginga on a pontoon, though when the water is very low, vehicles may have to ford the river. Fill up with fuel in Mongu, as supply in Kalabo is erratic.

307 Western Zambezi District 4X4 ✔✔

This remote corner of Zambia is sparsely populated and very beautiful. Visitors must be completely self-sufficient and armed with 4WD, maps and, ideally, a GPS. Pontoons cross the Zambezi at Chavuma, Zambezi town and Chinyingi. Next to the Chinyingi pontoon is the famous foot bridge that spans the river at a dramatic height. One of the main attractions in the area is the vast sandy plains on which **White-throated Francolin** occurs. Listen for calls that are similar to that of the Coqui Francolin in the early morning – these will guide you to the birds.

Also in this habitat are **Greater Kestrel**, **Black-rumped Buttonquail**, **White-bellied Bustard**, **Swamp Nightjar***, **Blue-breasted Bee-eater**, **Angola Lark**, **Cape Crow**, **Long-tailed Paradise-Whydah**, and a very isolated population of **Cloud Cisticola***. In the woodland, look out for **Black Scimitarbill**.

There are scattered patches of wet evergreen forest in the area, two of which are particularly rewarding. Mbulo Forest is just north of the Lukolwe-Luzu road (GPS 13°13.36'S, 22°50.57'E). Birds here include **Lemon Dove**, **Blue-breasted Kingfisher**, **Yellow-rumped Tinkerbird**, **Black-backed Barbet**, **Grey Apalis**, **Blue-mantled Crested Flycatcher**, **Bannerman's Sunbird**, **Many-coloured Bush-Shrike** and **Splendid Glossy Starling**. In addition, **Grimwood's Longclaw** occurs on the adjacent dambo.

At the point where the Chinyama Litapi-Zambezi road crosses the Southern Kashiji river, there is a small patch of forest at GPS 13°36'S, 22°47'E. Birds of interest here include **Pel's Fishing-Owl***, **Shining-blue** and **Blue-breasted Kingfishers**, **Black-backed Barbet** and **Black-bellied Seedcracker**.

308 Mwinilunga District

IBA ✔✔✔

The far north-western corner of Zambia stretches up between Angola and the Democratic Republic of Congo, and provides some of the best birding in Zambia. It is also the most accessible area for several exciting Central African specials, and the avifauna has a distinctly Congolese flavour. Most visitors base themselves at Hillwood, a private farm near Ikelenge, from which other sites (Chitunta Plain, the Source of the Zambezi, the Zambezi Rapids and the Jimbe Drainage area in the extreme north) can be reached fairly easily. One of the special habitat types here is known as 'mushitu' (pronounced moo-*shee*-too), which is a patch of moist evergreen forest, usually in the centre of dambos, that holds a characteristic set of birds more typical of Congo forests.

SPECIALS: Black-rumped Buttonquail, Forbes's Plover, Afep Pigeon, Western Bronze-naped Pigeon, Ross's Turaco*, Olive Long-tailed Cuckoo, Western and Pallid Honeyguides, Angola Lark, Black-and-rufous Swallow, Red-tailed Bristlebill, Honeyguide Greenbul, Black-collared Bulbul*, Fraser's Rufous Ant-Thrush, Grey-winged Robin-Chat, Bamboo Warbler, Laura's Woodland-Warbler, Dambo and Whistling Cisticolas, White-chinned Prinia, Buff-throated Apalis, Grimwood's Longclaw, Cassin's Flycatcher, Red-bellied Paradise-Flycatcher, Bates's and Bannerman's Sunbirds, Bocage's Weaver, and Black-bellied Seedcracker.

SEASON: Sept-Oct is ideal, when bird activity is high. Nov, Dec and even later in the rainy season can be interesting, but extremely wet. In the late rainy season (Mar-May), access to some sites is still limited, and in the cold, dry season (Jun-Jul) forest birds are very quiet.

HABITATS: Mushitu, miombo, bracken briar, dambo, plain, rivers with riparian forest and rapids.

BIRDING: *Luakera Forest Reserve* Ⓐ lies between Mwinilunga town and the Chitunta Plain. The reserve comprises rich miombo woodland; stop for bird parties and look for such widespread species as **Thick-billed Cuckoo*, Anchieta's Barbet, Black-necked Eremomela, Red-capped Crombec, White-tailed Blue Flycatcher, Souza's Shrike*** and **Bar-winged Weaver***.

Chitunta Plain Ⓑ is a broad dambo, drained by a perennial stream and traversed by the T5, about half-way between Mwinilunga and Hillwood. Look out for two wooden bridges, about 50 m apart, and explore from here (ideally, in gumboots). **Grimwood's Longclaw** inhabits the wet centre of the dambo, whereas **Rosy-breasted and Fülleborn's Longclaws** tend to be on slightly drier ground. Resident species include **Angola Lark, Sooty Chat, Stout, Wing-snapping, Levaillant's** and **Dambo Cisticolas, Locustfinch*** and **Black-chinned Quailfinch**. In the dry season, look for **Black-and-rufous** and **Angola Swallows**, and once the rains have started, for **Great Snipe, Blue Quail*** and **Short-tailed Pipit*. Bocage's Weavers** breed in bushes overhanging the Luakera River between about Aug-Oct. To reach this area, walk west along the north side of the dambo for about 3 km. East of the road, check stunted termitaria scrub on the south side of the dambo for **Red-throated Wryneck**

At *Hillwood* Ⓒ, most birding can be done on foot from the Nchila Camp, which is flanked by mushitu on one side, miombo on the other, and overlooks a beautiful plain. Check the

GETTING THERE

It is possible to drive from Lusaka to Mwinilunga in a day, but it is the best part of 1 000 km, and easier over two days with an overnight stop, perhaps at Chimfunshi (see p.344). It takes about four hours from Lusaka to Kitwe (in the Copperbelt), and a further 7-8 hours should be allowed to reach Hillwood. The road is tarred from Lusaka to Mwinilunga town (the only stretch in poor condition is between Mwinilunga and Solwezi). Navigation is not difficult, but note that there is an important right-hand turn about 30 km beyond Solwezi (it is marked, but can easily be missed). Continue straight through Mwinilunga town and out the other side towards Ikelenge. After a few kilometres, the tar ends, and after about 30 km, the road crosses the sprawling Chitunta Plain Ⓑ. After another 20 km you will see a sign and gate on the right to the Source of the Zambezi Ⓓ; a further 10 km on, the road forks. Turn right here for Hillwood Ⓒ, and follow the signs for a few kilometres until you reach the farm complex. Hillwood is a private ranch and includes a protected area and game ranch (Nchila Wildlife Reserve). Nchila offers accommodation and camping ☎.

edges of the plain for **Denham's Bustard*** and **Sooty Chat**. Out in the open grassland, watch for **Blue Quail***, **Black-rumped Buttonquail**, **Corncrake**, **African Crake**, **Great Snipe**, **Swamp Nightjar***, **Blue-breasted Bee-eater**, **Angola Lark**, **Black-and-rufous Swallow**, **Broad-tailed Warbler**, **Dambo**, **Wing-snapping** and **Stout Cisticolas**, **Short-tailed Pipit***, **Fülleborn's** and **Rosy-breasted* Longclaws**, **Marsh Widowbird**, **Red-headed Quelea**, **Locustfinch*** and **Black-chinned Quailfinch**.

The mushitu alongside the camp is one of the richest in avifauna, and species to look for include **Afep Pigeon**, **Ross's Turaco***, **Olive Long-tailed Cuckoo**, **Green Malkoha**, **Blue-breasted Kingfisher**, **Yellow-rumped Tinkerbird**, **African Broadbill***, **Little**, **Cabanis's** and **Honeyguide Greenbuls**, **Red-tailed Bristlebill**, **Fraser's Rufous Thrush**, **African Thrush**, **Grey-winged Robin-Chat**, **Laura's Woodland-Warbler**, **Bamboo** and **Evergreen Forest Warblers**, **Buff-throated Apalis**, **Red-bellied Paradise-Flycatcher**, **Bates's** and **Bannerman's Sunbirds** and **Splendid Glossy Starling**.

Needless to say, many of these species take some work to find and, as in all forest environments, careful listening is vital, so do learn calls, and exercise patience. There are several other mushitus on the farm and the forest along the Sakeji Stream is quite productive. Several species are less easily categorised.

Black-collared Bulbul* is not uncommon, but it is unobtrusive. Look for it in areas of scrub and regenerating vegetation. A good area to try is around Sakeji School and along the airstrip. **Whistling Cisticola** and **Moustached Grass Warbler** are typically found in bracken briar, scrub and long grass, and although **White-chinned Prinia** may be in such habitats it is rarely found far from the forest edge. Both **Anchieta's Tchagra*** and **Black-bellied Seedcracker** tend to be in rank, sometimes swampy undergrowth, the latter generally near forest. **Palm-nut Vulture*** is usually seen drifting up and down the Sakeji Valley.

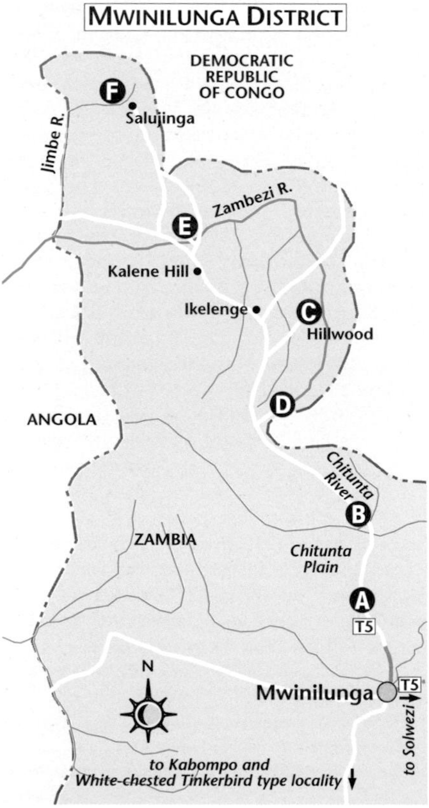

After signing the visitors' book at the entrance gate, and paying a small fee, drive about 5 km along a well-maintained track to a parking area, where you may camp, although there are no facilities. Both the miombo along the approach road to *Source of the Zambezi* **D** and the mushitu that constitutes the source are worth exploring. Birds are similar to those found at Hillwood.

A visit to the *Zambezi Rapids* **E** is worth the effort if only for the simple enjoyment of their beauty, but two species that are hard to find elsewhere occur here, making it even more worthwhile. **Forbes's Plovers** are not particularly common and may be seasonal, but they are usually present between at least Sept-Jan. If you do not find them along the rocky shores of the rapids themselves, try checking carefully on the large granite outcrops which can be found away from the river near the approach road. **Cassin's Flycatcher** is usually found above the rapids, along the forested stretch of river between the rapids and the road bridge.

To get to the rapids, drive approximately 20 km north of Ikelenge and past the left turn to Kalene Hill Hospital. Take a right turn soon after this and confirm directions with local residents. This track leads to the road bridge

LITTLE-KNOWN BIRDS OF NORTHERN ZAMBIA

Grey-winged Robin-Chat

Black-collared Bulbul

Bannerman's Sunbird

mentioned above. However, a little way before this, turn left at a small sign to the rapids, and drive down to the bottom of the waters. From here you can walk, wade and rock-hop up the rapids. If you are unsure of the way, there are usually people about who are keen to show you.

For the adventurous, determined, self-sufficient and tick-hungry birder, the exciting *Jimbe Drainage* Ⓕ area beckons. Sadly, many of the most impressive mushitus have been cleared, but there is still forest worth exploring. Follow either the road from the rapids or the track that leaves the main Jimbe road a little further on, and head for Salujinga. The roads are slow-going, making a day-trip from Hillwood unlikely; plan to camp at least one night and ideally more. Stop at the first river crossing past Salujinga (the Kachifwiru) to listen and look for **White spotted Flufftail** running about on the forest floor like a miniature bantam. Then head for the village 'at the end of the road', Kayuka. Either make arrangements to park and walk from here or try driving, via Mulundu, to a point on the Jimbe River known as Madman's Crossing (GPS 10°57.17'S, 24°04.97'), where some of the best forest is to be found.

Explore both up- and downstream along the Jimbe and its tributaries, looking not only for the more widespread Mwinilunga forest birds, but also for species such as **White-bellied Kingfisher**, **Brown-eared Woodpecker**, **Sooty Flycatcher**, **African Shrike-Flycatcher**, **Chestnut Wattle-eye**, **Spotted Thrush-Babbler*** and **Orange-tufted** and **Green-throated Sunbirds**. **Compact Weavers** are most common a few kilometres downstream, where the Jimbe is flanked by a dambo. East of Kayuka are several streams that constitute the headwaters of the Jimbe. These have been extensively cleared, but species such as **Black-collared Bulbul***, **Bamboo Warbler**, **White-chinned Prinia**, **Sooty Flycatcher** and **Black-bellied Seedcracker** are easier to find in such habitat. Beyond the headwaters is a large, dry watershed plain (the border with the Democratic Republic of Congo runs across it) and several interesting grassland species can be found here, including **White-bellied Bustard**.

NEARBY SITES: Between the Copperbelt and Mwinilunga, check all road bridges for breeding **Red-throated Cliff Swallows** (Apr-Nov). One of the most reliable sites is the Mutanda Bridge (30 km west of Solwezi). Birders seeking a challenge should search the area south of Mwinilunga for the enigmatic **White-chested Tinkerbird**, still known only from the type

WHEN BEST TO VISIT ZAMBIA

Climatically, Zambia is similar to most south-central African countries, in that the year can be broadly divided into a hot and rainy season (Nov-Apr), a cool and dry season (May-Aug) and a hot and dry season (Sept-Oct). There is good birding year-round, but the best birding can be had between August and November, in both miombo and forest. The rainy season brings the most species diversity, but road conditions over these months are not good, and several key sites (such as much of Mwinilunga and the South Luangwa and southern Kafue national parks) become wholly inaccessible. The cool, dry season lacks migrants, but weather conditions are exceptionally pleasant and the roads mercifully firm. The legendary **Shoebill***, obviously a critical target for most visits, is easiest to find in the early dry season (May-Jul).

specimen. Take the Kabompo road heading south from Mwinilunga town. After about 100 km, the landscape transforms into beautiful, tall and very dense mavunda forest. This is where the specimen tinkerbird was collected, and the habitat stretches for tens of kilometres. This dry, evergreen forest holds a fascinating combination of miombo and mushitu species, so you can be watching **Bar-winged Weaver*** and **Red-capped Crombec** forage in the canopy while **Purple-throated Cuckooshrike** and **Western Least Honeyguide** perch in the mid-stratum, and **Crested Guineafowl** trots about on the ground. Two other species worth searching for here are **Perrin's Bush-Shrike** and **Margaret's Batis**, both in the dense understorey. There are no facilities so if you plan to camp, ensure that you are self-sufficient.

309 Chimfunshi Wildlife Orphanage IBA ✔✔

Chimfunshi is a large, private farm on the banks of the Kafue River west of Chingola, best known for its collection of orphaned chimpanzees. There is good miombo and mushitu birding along the approach road, as well as throughout the farm itself. To reach Chimfunshi, drive through Chingola on the T5 and continue for 47.5 km (4 km past Munchinshi village) towards Solwezi. Turn right at the Chimfunshi signpost, then left at the second signpost 2 km later, marked 'Chimfunshi 15 km'. There is a camp site near the river, there are chalets at the main farmhouse and there is an education centre with two big dormitories on the far side of the property near the largest chimp enclosures. If possible, book in advance ☎.

There is good miombo throughout, and even the stretch between the camp site turn-off and the main farmhouse can be very productive in the early morning. Species include **Pale-billed Hornbill**, **Whyte's** and **Miombo Pied Barbets**, **Green-backed Woodpecker**, **Green-backed Honeybird**, **Miombo Scrub-Robin**, **Trilling Cisticola**, **Black-necked Eremomela**, **Red-capped Crombec**, **Souza's Shrike** and **Chestnut-backed Sparrow-Weaver**. It is also perhaps the easiest area in which to find **Sharp-tailed Starling***.

In the riparian forest fringing the Kafue, look for **Western Banded Snake-Eagle**, **Black-backed Barbet** and **Olive Woodpecker**. Some forest species, such as **Ross's Turaco***, **Yellow-rumped Tinkerbird**, **Purple-throated Cuckooshrike**, **Yellow-throated Leaf-love** and **Grey Apalis**, are regularly found around the farmhouse.

Next to the Education Centre is a strip of gallery mushitu, where you can find **Grey-olive Brownbul** and **Blue-mantled Crested Flycatcher**. If you follow this valley you reach a broad dambo with a large, very wet mushitu in its centre. This can be difficult to get into, but it is easiest to approach from the west side; gumboots are recommended. Once inside, it is not difficult to explore, and there is a wealth of birdlife. **Bocage's Akalat** and **Evergreen Forest Warbler** are particularly common, and other species include **Laura's Woodland-Warbler**, **White-chinned Prinia** and **Many-coloured Bush-Shrike**. **Moustached Grass Warbler**, **Anchieta's Tchagra*** and **Grey Waxbill** occur in the long grass at the mushitu edges and in other rank growth around the farm. In the dambo, look for **Fülleborn's** and **Rosy-breasted* Longclaws**, **Marsh Widowbird**, **Fawn-breasted Waxbill** and **Black-chinned Quailfinch**.

ROUTE 35

EASTERN ZAMBIA

Like Western Zambia, Eastern Zambia offers a number of well-established sites within reasonable striking distance of tarred roads, as well as limitless possibilities for adventurous birders with capable vehicles and the time and inclination to venture off the beaten track. A number of superb sites are readily accessible by 2WD vehicle, in the dry season at least, and only one site – the Bangweulu Swamps – cannot be reached by private vehicle, although the swamp edge at Chikuni village is accessible in the dry season.

TOP 10 BIRDS

- Shoebill
- Black-necked Eremomela
- Chestnut-headed Flufftail
- Bocage's Akalat
- Ross's Turaco
- Anchieta's Barbet
- Black-backed Barbet
- Bar-winged Weaver
- Anchieta's Sunbird
- Tanzania Masked Weaver

Broadly speaking, Eastern Zambia's three key habitats are miombo woodland (best site is probably Mutinondo Wilderness; also excellent at the Forest Inn, Kasanka National Park and Shiwa Ng'andu), which is often punctuated by exciting dambos, papyrus swamp (notably at Bangweulu, of Shoebill* renown, and along the lower Luapula River), and mushitu swamp forest (most accessibly at Kasanka National Park and Shiwa Ng'andu). For the more intrepid, there are some exciting opportunities in the vicinity of the far northern Congolese border, near Lake Mweru, and Zambia's three remote northern national parks, where such exotic specials as Bamboo Warbler and Spotted Thrush-Babbler* may be found.

Callan Cohen

Approaching a Shoebill by boat

The tarred T2 Great North Road to Tanzania provides quick and easy access to most sites. A notable exception is the very popular South Luangwa National Park, lying in the vast Luangwa Valley that falls away below the miombo woodlands of the Muchinga escarpment and Bangweulu Basin beyond. South Luangwa can be reached either by a long drive from Lusaka on the Great East Road or, more easily, from Lilongwe in Malawi. Indeed, South Luangwa is a popular big-game add-on to many Malawi tours but, because it is dominated by riparian and mopane woodland, offers none of the specials to be found further north and west. If approaching Zambia from northern Malawi or vice-versa, note that the most reliable crossing is via Tanzania.

310 The Forest Inn ✔✔✔

A good overnight stop en route north, the Forest Inn surrounds provide very productive miombo birding right next to the Great North Road. The inn itself is surrounded by 160 ha of protected miombo woodland.
SPECIALS: Miombo Pied Barbet, Spotted Creeper*, Miombo Scrub-Robin, Black-necked Eremomela, Red-capped Crombec, Yellow-bellied Hyliota, White-tailed Blue Flycatcher, Souza's Shrike*, Chestnut-backed Sparrow-Weaver, and Bar-winged Weaver*.
SEASON: Bird parties are more common from Jan-Jul, although most birds can be found all year-round.
HABITATS: Tall, closed-canopy miombo woodland.
BIRDING: A number of tracks radiate from the camp into the woodland outside of the fence. One of the best tracks runs off to the west, parallel to the T2; here, mixed-species foraging flocks yield a number of exciting species.

The much sought-after miombo special found in this area is the superb **Black-necked Eremomela**, which occurs in pairs or small groups, often joins bird parties, and may be detected by its trilling, slightly buzzy 'trrrr-trrrrr' call (not dissimilar to that of **Green-capped Eremomela**, which is also present). Similarly, the localised **Chestnut-backed Sparrow-Weaver** (look out for typical sparrow-weaver nests) is easiest to locate if you listen for its very high-pitched, penetrating trills, as it is otherwise remarkably inconspicuous, preferring to perch in mid-stratum. **Souza's Shrike*** is also found in the mid-stratum, and often perches quietly on smaller shrubs and trees. Both **Yellow-bellied** and **Southern Hyliotas** occur, giving an opportunity to compare the deep blue gloss and richer peachy-orange underparts of males of the former, with the matt black plumage and lemon-yellow of the latter. Bird parties may also include **Red-capped Crombec, Spotted Creeper*, White-tailed Blue Flycatcher and Rufous-bellied Tit. Miombo Pied Barbet, Green-backed Woodpecker** and **Scaly-throated Honeyguide** also occur. Denser vegetation, such as that found on termitaria, often holds **Miombo Scrub-Robin** (listen for the very long phrases of typical scrub-robin song). **Bar-winged Weaver*** is scarce and inconspicuous at this site, but feeds particularly along branches festooned with old-man's-beard lichen. As you walk, watch the path edges for feeding **Orange-winged Pytilia**, and **Cabanis's** and **Golden-breasted Buntings**. In summer, look out for migrant **Collared Flycatchers**. The camp site itself provides poorer birding, but **Miombo Scrub-Robin** is sometimes seen feeding on the lawns.
NEARBY SITES: Between Mkushi and Mpika, the road passes through more miombo, which holds similar birds. You also cross several dambos, which can be searched for species such as **Chestnut-headed Flufftail, Fülleborn's Longclaw, Stout Cisticola, Marsh Widowbird, Fawn-breasted Waxbill** and **Locustfinch***.

GETTING THERE
Forest Inn is clearly signposted on the southern side of the T2, 63 km from Kapiri Mposhi and 28 km from the Mkushi turn-off. A restaurant, a clean, spacious camp with rondavels and a well-maintained camp site and hutted accommodation are available ☎.

311 Kasanka National Park IBA ✔✔

Although just a small park, Kasanka neverthless provides a number of key specials in a great selection of miombo, swamp and mushitu habitats. This national park is situated on the southern edge of the Bangweulu Basin, and offers good game-viewing in a beautiful and accessible setting.
SPECIALS: Wattled Crane*, Pel's Fishing-Owl*, Ross's Turaco*, Böhm's Bee-eater*, Pale-billed Hornbill, Black-backed and Anchieta's Barbets, Purple-throated Cuckooshrike, Grey-olive Brownbul, Cabanis's Greenbul, Bocage's Akalat, Black-necked Eremomela, Grey Apalis, and Collared, Böhm's and White-tailed Blue Flycatchers.
SEASON: As with all Zambian sites, the going can be tough between Jan-Mar at the height of the rains, but many areas of the park are still accessible.

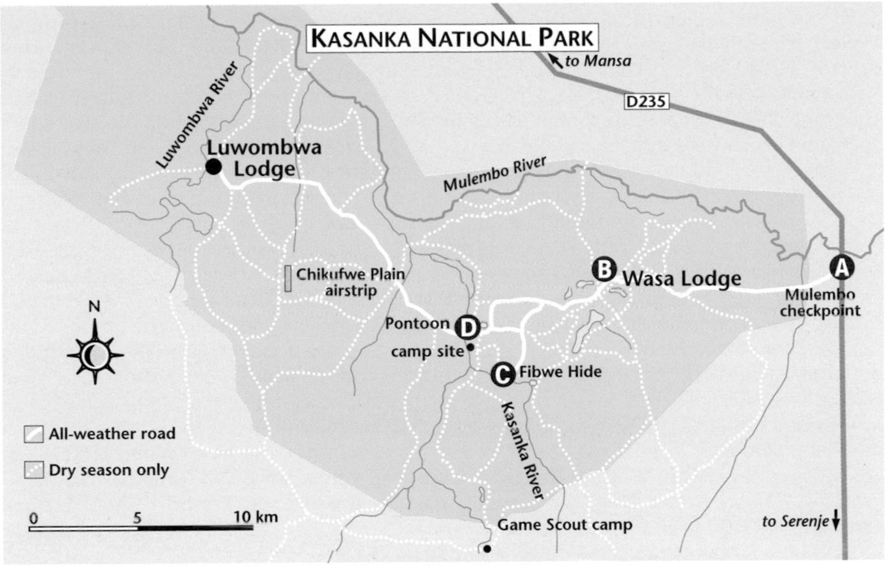

HABITATS: Miombo woodland, flood plain, pans, papyrus swamp, mushitu and riparian forest.

BIRDING: The road between the park gate Ⓐ and Wasa Lodge Ⓑ initially passes through low miombo, which is worth searching for bird parties. Among the miombo specials that occur here are **Racket-tailed Roller***, **Miombo Pied**, **Anchieta's** and **Whyte's Barbets**, **Spotted Creeper***, **Rufous-bellied** and **Miombo Tits**, **Miombo Rock-Thrush**, **Miombo Scrub-Robin**, **Black-necked Eremomela**, **White-tailed Blue** and **Böhm's Flycatchers**, **Yellow-bellied Hyliota**, **Red capped Crombec**, **Trilling Cisticola**, **Anchieta's Sunbird**, **Black-eared Seed-eater**, and **Cabanis's Bunting**. Other characteristic species of broad-leaved woodland, such as **Grey Penduline-Tit**, **Green-capped Eremomela**, **Bushveld Pipit** and, scarcely, **Thick-billed Cuckoo***, also occur.

Wasa Lodge is adjacent to two pans, and offers a convenient viewing tower. Scanning the emergent vegetation from here should reveal **White-backed Duck**, **African Pygmy Goose***, **Hottentot Teal**, and **African** and **Lesser Jacanas**. **Short-winged Cisticola** occurs around the flood-plain edges.

The prime birding area in the park is in the vicinity of the Fibwe Hide Ⓒ, built in a strip of mushitu fringing the Kapabi papyrus swamp. The hide itself, a small platform perched 18 m from the ground in a magnificent African Mahogany, offers a superb view over the extensive swamp and an extraordinary opportunity to observe large numbers of the notoriously elusive Sitatunga (commonly more than 20 at one time). The grassy surrounds of the small parking area provide **Moustached Grass Warbler**, **Short-winged Cisticola** and **Brown Firefinch**, and **Böhm's Bee-eater*** hawks from surrounding thickets.

To the right, beyond the picnic area, a small footpath leads through the mushitu, offering superb birding. Typical mushitu species include **Ross's Turaco***, **Black-backed Barbet**, **Purple-throated Cuckooshrike**, **Yellow-throated Leaf-love**, **Cabanis's Greenbul**, **Bocage's Akalat**, **African Thrush**, **Grey Apalis** and **Green-headed Sunbird**, as well

GETTING THERE

The park entrance is 55 km north of the T2, along the tarred D235 leading to Mansa and Samfya (turn north 36 km beyond Serenje, which is the last source of fuel). Wasa Lodge, the park headquarters, is 11 km beyond the entrance gate along a good gravel road. Self-catering rondavel accommodation is available here, and at Luwombwa Lodge. The latter lies at the park's western border and, because it can only be reached by pontoon across the Kasanka River, is closed during the rainy season. There is a camp site next to the pontoon ☎.

as various more widespread forest species such as **African Crowned Eagle**, **Yellow-rumped Tinkerbird**, **Scaly-throated Honeyguide**, **African Broadbill***, **Little Greenbul**, **Blue-mantled Crested Flycatcher** and **Dark-backed Weaver**. Carefully scan larger branches for roosting **Pel's Fishing-Owl***, and check areas of seeding grass at the forest edges for **Red-throated Twinspot**, **Red-backed Mannikin** and **Grey Waxbill**. While exploring the trail, be aware that you could encounter Elephant and Buffalo, and be prepared for mosquitoes and tsetse flies.

The Fibwe Hide also offers a good vantage point from which to scan the swamp for a variety of water birds, and **Coppery-tailed Coucal** can be seen sunning itself in the morning. Despite popular myth, **Shoebill*** is only a very rare vagrant here. A pathway or cutline through the reeds is maintained in order to provide access to the water's edge from the parking area, and hence also to reedbed species such as **African Rail**, **Red-chested Flufftail**, **Greater Swamp-Warbler**, **Chirping Cisticola** and **Anchieta's Tchagra***. **Black-faced Canary** is also sometimes found in the swamp, but more often along the forest edges nearby. Venturing west from Fibwe, the pontoon across the Kasanka River **D** offers a fine opportunity to search for riparian species such as **African Finfoot***, **Pel's Fishing-Owl*** and **Half-collared Kingfisher**.

On the whole, a variety of grasslands, including flood plains, dambos, and the fringes of the many pans and, in the west, the extensive Chikufwe Plain, can be explored at Kasanka. Resident species include **Wattled Crane***, **Fülleborn's Longclaw**, **Sooty Chat**, **Broad-tailed Warbler**, **Marsh Widowbird** and **Fawn-breasted Waxbill**. Dry-season visitors include **Temminck's Courser** and **Grey-rumped Swallow**; during the rains, look for species such as **Blue Quail***, **Streaky-breasted Flufftail** and **Black Coucal**.

OTHER ANIMALS: Kasanka is one of the best places anywhere to see Sitatunga (dawn or dusk at the Fibwe Hide is recommended), as well as other flood-plain antelope such as Puku. In Nov-Dec, Straw-coloured Fruit-bats roost in the mushitu that surrounds Fibwe Hide, and the sight of millions of bats as they congregate during the day and emerge to forage at dusk is an unforgettable wildlife spectacle.

NEARBY SITES: If you only have time for a taste of the Bangweulu Basin and its flood-plain species, such as **Tanzania Masked Weaver** (subspecies *katangae*, 'Katanga Masked Weaver'), **Blue-breasted Bee-eater** and an isolated population of **Long-tailed Widowbird**, drive to Mukuku Bridge, about 100 km past Kasanka along the tar road towards Mansa.

Claire Spottiswoode

The view from Fibwe Hide in the Kasanka National Park

312 Bangweulu Swamps

4X4 IBA ✔✔✔

This vast area of flood plain and swamp covers a considerable portion of northern Zambia. It is best known as a reliable site for the curious and localised central African swamp specialist, the **Shoebill***, perhaps one of the most sought-after birds in the world.

SPECIALS: Shoebill*, Eurasian Bittern, Denham's Bustard*, Wattled Crane*, African Skimmer*, Blue-breasted Bee-eater, Hartlaub's Babbler, Sooty Chat, Greater Swamp-Warbler, Swamp Flycatcher, and Tanzania Masked Weaver.

SEASON: Water levels are highest in Mar-Apr, and birding is best as the waters recede from

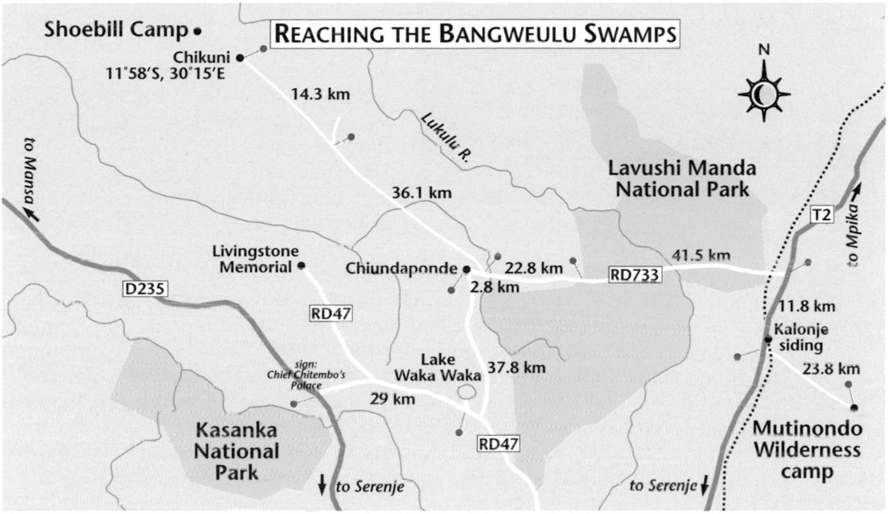

May-Jul, when **Shoebill*** is usually accessible by canoe. During the late dry season (Aug-Nov) you can search for the Shoebill* by foot or by vehicle from Shoebill Island Camp, but it can be difficult to find at this time of year.

HABITATS: Grassy flood plain, papyrus swamp, termitaria, miombo woodland and pockets of riparian forest.

BIRDING: If driving to Chikuni village, you will pass through lengthy stretches of superb, closed-canopy miombo woodland, providing excellent bird parties. As you get closer, the woodland changes to grassy, lightly wooded savanna, then abruptly to open flood plain. This transitional area is good for dambo and grassland species, such as **Sooty Chat**, **Capped Wheatear** and **Fülleborn's Longclaw**. The flood plain holds huge numbers of Black Lechwe, which mingle with large flocks (up to hundreds of birds) of **Wattled Crane***

GETTING THERE

Most visitors to Bangweulu use Shoebill Island Camp ☎ as a base. The island camp, situated at the southern end of the swamps, 2 km from the edge of the flood plain at Chikuni, offers hutted accommodation, camping and meals. Excellent and reasonably priced canoe trips led by skilled guides who keep track of the whereabouts of local **Shoebills*** can be embarked upon from here. The easiest way to reach Shoebill Island is by light aeroplane. It is possible to drive (4WD only) as far as the southern village of Chikuni and travel to the camp by canoe or, during Aug-Nov, to drive all the way to Shoebill Island.

The drive to Chikuni is a rough and lengthy one, and at least five hours should be allowed for the 120 km trip, either from the D235 and Kasanka National Park, or the T2 and the Lavushi Manda National Park. When you reach Chikuni village, contact the game scout office (on your right as you enter the village), where boat transport to Shoebill Island can be arranged if necessary (preferably, e-mail the Kasanka Trust ☎ in advance); the office will guard your vehicle in your absence. Predictably, mosquitoes are abundant, so take appropriate precautions.

Shoebill, the only member of its family

and **Denham's Bustard***. Characteristic species of the dry flood plain include **Grey-rumped Swallow, Banded Martin** and **African Quailfinch**. During summer **Montagu's** and **Pallid* Harriers** quarter, and Palearctic waders may congregate in huge flocks in the shallow flooded areas.

From Feb-Aug (more or less), Shoebill Island is surrounded by flood waters; in Mar-Apr, **Shoebill*** is sometimes visible from the island, and is sought by boat or dugout until about Jul, when the area remains flooded. From about Aug-Nov, the bird retreats to areas of permanent swamp deep within Bangweulu; at this time, you can walk or drive from Shoebill Camp to seek it out. Singletons or loose groups may be seen searching for their lungfish prey in pools, or perching on the dense, floating mats of water weeds, or on palm trees.

Great waterbirding is possible, especially when searching for Shoebills* by boat. Flocks of herons, storks and waterfowl are regularly flushed, including **Goliath Heron, Black Heron, Hottentot Teal, Saddle-billed** and **Yellow-billed Storks**, and the occasional **Slaty Egret***. Flooded grassland and mats of floating vegetation may produce **Great Snipe** (common in summer), **Long-toed Lapwing, Wattled Crane*** and **Rosy-breasted Longclaw***. The extensive patches of lilies provide **African** and (commonly) **Lesser Jacana**. **Swamp Flycatcher** is common, and hawks prey over the channels from the reedbed edges, while **Greater Swamp-Warbler** and **Chirping Cisticola** call from within the beds, and both **Cuckoo Finch*** and the *katangae* subspecies of **Tanzania Masked Weaver** are regular. **African Marsh-Harrier** and the occasional **Western Marsh-Harrier** (summer) quarter above.

The swamp islands, where shrubs provide cover for birds, are all productive. Migrants are often attracted to such areas, and residents include **Brown Firefinch, Coppery-tailed Coucal, Hartlaub's Babbler** and **Blue-breasted Bee-eater**. A wide variety of raptors occur, and **Bateleur**, and **Hooded** and **Lappet-faced Vultures** are regularly seen overhead.

OTHER ANIMALS: Game-viewing is excellent, especially during the dry season. The endemic Black Lechwe can be spectacularly abundant on the flood plain, and smaller herds are also encountered regularly in the swamps 'proper'. Other interesting antelope include Tsessebe, Oribi and Sitatunga. Big game is more scarce, but includes Elephant and Buffalo.

NEARBY SITES: Both overland routes to Chikuni pass through prime miombo woodland, that hold most of the associated specials. If you approach Chikuni from the west, the best woodland is around Lake Waka Waka, and the 10 km stretch to the west of it. If you enter from the east (turn west from the T2 at the signposted track 176 km north of Serenje, or 60 km south of Mpika), the Lavushi Manda National Park segment (no entrance fee is required for transit vehicles) is a good spot for **Anchieta's Barbet** and the woodland between Lavushi and Chiundaponde is especially productive.

Searching for Shoebill

313 Mutinondo Wilderness ✔✔✔

Mutinondo, a privately owned 10 000 ha reserve perched just above the Muchinga escarpment, is a prime site for miombo birding.

SPECIALS: Chestnut-headed Flufftail, Anchieta's Barbet, Souza's Shrike, Anchieta's Sunbird, and Bar-winged Weaver*.

SEASON: Accessible year-round.

HABITATS: Tall miombo woodland, dambos, riparian forest, streams, granite hills.

BIRDING: There is great miombo birding along the entrance road and in the vicinity of the camp. A number of tracks and paths lead away from the campsite, all of them providing good birding. Miombo species include **Thick-billed Cuckoo***, **Pale-billed Hornbill**, **Racket-tailed Roller***, **Green-backed Honeybird**, **Spotted Creeper***, **Rufous-bellied Tit**, **Miombo Rock-Thrush** (even away from rocks), **Miombo Scrub-Robin**, **Long-tailed Cisticola**, **Red-capped Crombec**, **Yellow-bellied Hyliota**, **Böhm's** and **White-tailed Blue Flycatchers**, **Souza's Shrike***, **Violet-backed Sunbird**, **Miombo Double-collared Sunbird** and **Cabanis's Bunting**. **Reichard's Seed-eater** is unusually common, while **Wood Pipit** flushes easily from the edges of the entrance road.

GETTING THERE

Turn off to Mutinondo from the T2, just south of the Kalonje railway siding, 72 km south of Mpika and 164 km north of Serenje (GPS 12°22.80'S, 31°05.90'E). The siding signpost is visible only when approaching from the south. A good track with a hard sand surface leads for 25 km through miombo woodland to the camp in the wilderness area (GPS 12°27.13'S, 31°17.44'E). There is a well-maintained camp site and chalet accommodation ☎.

Mutinondo is probably the best place in Zambia to search for the elusive **Bar-winged Weaver***, which favours miombo branches (along which it creeps like a crombec or Miombo Tit) festooned with old-man's-beard lichen. The weavers occur widely, but a good place to start looking is between the camp site and stables, and from there back along the entrance road. They are not uncommon, but it is remarkably easy to overlook them. Carefully check foraging flocks, listening for their tit-like calls, and your patience should be rewarded.

There are several large dambos, including one that can be reached by following the track below the camp compound for about 1 km. Even during the dry season, parts of the dambos remain moist, and **Chestnut-headed Flufftail** can be found here, particularly in the spongy, drying margins. Their hooting calls (similar to Red-chested Flufftail, but slower) offer a good clue to their whereabouts.

Other dambo species include **Blue Quail***, **Swamp Nightjar***, **Short-winged** and **Stout Cisticolas**, **Broad-tailed Warbler**, **Fülleborn's Longclaw**, **Marsh Widowbird**, **Locustfinch*** and **Fawn-breasted Waxbill**.

Several small rivers run through the area, including one just below the camp, where you can find **Half-collared Kingfisher**, **African Black Duck**, **African Finfoot*** and **Mountain Wagtail**. In the thin riparian forest, look for **Black-backed** and **Anchieta's Barbets**, **Grey-olive Brownbul** and **Bar-throated Apalis**. In well-developed forest, look for **Bocage's Akalat** and **White-tailed Crested Flycatcher**.

The granite hills harbour many species, such as **Mocking Cliff-Chat**, **Augur Buzzard**, **Rock-loving Cisticola**,

Claire Spottiswoode

Mutinondo offers excellent miombo birding.

Rock Martin and **Red-winged Starling**, that are typical of rocky habitats. In areas of thin scrub around the hills, look carefully for a hitherto-undescribed species of sunbird: Mutinondo is one of the best places in which to see the newly discovered form. It is sometimes seen along with **Miombo Double-collared Sunbird**, but the male of the former has a longer bill, broader red breastband, and a more strident song. Keep your eyes open for thieving **White-necked Raven** – those around the camp have learnt to raid tourists' belongings.

314 Shiwa Ng'andu

IBA ✔✔✔

The elaborate 1920s English manor house and its historical association with the Gore-Brown family have brought fame to Shiwa Ng'andu private estate. Situated about 70 km north of Mpika, Shiwa Ng'andu is also well known for its hot springs, from where one can watch mushitu specials in the forest canopy while luxuriously wallowing in Kapishya's warm waters.
SPECIALS: Palm-nut Vulture*, Chestnut-headed Flufftail, Ross's Turaco*, Black-backed Barbet, White-headed Saw-wing, Bocage's Akalat, Laura's Woodland-Warbler, Evergreen Forest Warbler, Long-tailed and Stout Cisticolas, Green-headed Sunbird, Splendid Glossy Starling, Bar-winged Weaver* and Black-chinned Quailfinch.
SEASON: Accessible throughout the year, although birding is best between Aug-Dec.
HABITATS: Miombo woodland, dambo, mushitu, freshwater lake, rivers, swamp, rocky hills.
BIRDING: Once you have passed through the gate, the road winds through a patch of good miombo, where a number of specials occur, including **Bar-winged Weaver***. Look out for bird parties along this road. Shiwa House is surrounded by plantations of gums and other exotic trees, as well as indigenous forest patches. Birding in and around the gardens is surprisingly productive, and some of the most rewarding mushitu is in the small drainage line below the main house.

In the valley, a network of paths on causeways make birding an extremely comfortable exercise. Common species include **Ross's Turaco***, **Black-backed Barbet**, **Bocage's Akalat**, **Evergreen Forest Warbler**, **Laura's Woodland-Warbler**, **Grey Apalis** and **Splendid Glossy Starling** (Aug-Nov). This drainage line leads to a picturesque lake, Ishiba Ng'andu, around which are more patches of mushitu, grasslands, scrub and, at the western end, swamp. The swamp can be accessed via a number of small tracks leading off the left-hand side of the road to Kapishya. A wide variety of water birds can be found here, particularly towards the end of the dry season, and the fringing grasslands are good for **Black-chinned Quailfinch**.

There are numerous broad dambos on the estate worth exploring on foot (gumboots are advisable). Possibilities here include **Long-toed Flufftail**, **African Grass-Owl***, **Blue-breasted Bee-eater**, **Stout Cisticola**, **Marsh Widowbird**, **Fawn-breasted Waxbill** and the occasional **Corncrake** and **Great Snipe** during the wet season.

The Kapishya Hot Springs lie 19 km beyond Shiwa House. The riparian mushitu around the hot springs holds quite a few specials. **Ross's Turaco*** occurs in sparser tree cover along the Manshya – listen for its deep, typically turaco-like call. Both **Half-collared Kingfisher** and **African Finfoot*** can be found along the Manshya River, which runs below the camp site, and **Palm-nut Vulture*** regularly visits the raffia palms in the area.
NEARBY SITES: Shiwa makes a good starting point for trips into North Luangwa National Park. Shiwa Safaris ☎ will offer helpful advice if you are self-sufficient. The Muchinga escarpment en route is clad in beautiful miombo where you can look for **Shelley's Sunbird***,

GETTING THERE

To reach Shiwa House and the Kapishya Hot Springs, turn off the T2 (onto the unsurfaced road) 90 km north of Mpika. Shiwa House is 13 km from the T2. The unsurfaced road is sometimes in poor condition, and a high clearance vehicle is recommended. Shortly after the T2 turn-off, there is a gate leading onto the estate. At the hot springs, Kapishya Lodge ☎, run by the family that established Shiwa House, offers chalet accommodation, camping and a restaurant in a superb setting. It is also possible to stay in considerable comfort in the main house. Shiwa House itself is open to the public, and a visit is historically fascinating and thoroughly recommended.

Johann Grobbelaar

A roosting male Pennant-winged Nightjar

Chestnut-backed Sparrow-Weaver and the charismatic **White-winged Babbling Starling***. Big game occurs on the valley floor, where the birding is similar to that at South Luangwa (see p.354).

Although perhaps not strictly 'nearby', there are many interesting birding areas in the north east of Zambia, and adventurous tourists will find numerous beautiful spots in which to camp. There are also rest houses in all the larger towns (Kasama, Mbala, Mpulungu, Isoka), from which birding excursions can be made. Species restricted to this segment of the country include **Bare-faced Go-away-bird** (open country), **Spot-flanked Barbet** (figs), **Oustalet's Sunbird** (scrub and degraded miombo), **Tanzania Masked Weaver** (Saise River) and **Southern Citril** (scrub and forest edge).

315 Luapula Province & Beyond IBA ✔✔

This area has a lot to offer the more adventurous tourist, with some fascinating birding and wonderful scenery, including many spectacular waterfalls. The main attractions include the papyrus swamps of the lower Luapula River, the province's Itigi thickets, and the area's remote national parks.

SPECIALS: Palm-nut Vulture*, Green Malkoha, Böhm's Bee-eater*, African Pitta*, Angola Swallow, White-winged Swamp-Warbler, Papyrus Yellow Warbler, Swamp and Cassin's Flycatchers, Spotted Thrush-Babbler*, White-winged Babbling Starling*, Black-headed, Slender-billed and Tanzania Masked Weavers (subspecies *katangae*), Orange-cheeked Waxbill, and Black-faced Canary.

SEASON: A few areas become difficult to reach at the height of the rains between Jan-Mar, yet the papyrus and thickets remain accessible and are often most interesting at this time.

HABITATS: Papyrus swamp, Itigi thicket, miombo, mushitu, dambos.

GETTING THERE

From the T2 near Serenje there are good tar roads all the way to Nchelenge (on the shores of Lake Mweru) via Samfya and Mansa. With the exception of the Mbereshi-Kawambwa road, all other roads are gravel or dirt. A few become difficult during the rains, and bridges are occasionally swept away, but a quick chat with local residents should establish which routes are passable. High clearance is often useful, although 4WD is rarely needed. There are rest houses in most towns and gazetted camp sites at some of the popular waterfalls. Sumbu National Park has several safari camps.

BIRDING: *Lower Luapula papyrus:* The T2 tar road crosses several long causeways south of Nchelenge; check these for papyrus birds and, in the dry season, **Angola Swallow**, which breeds in the culverts. Turn off at Chabilikila Primary School (about 20 km south of Nchelenge) and drive to the small harbour (boats leave from here for Chisenga Island). Around the harbour, one can explore the swamp edge on foot, or hire a boat and explore the interior.

Papyrus birds found here include **White-winged** and **Greater Swamp-Warblers**, **Papyrus Yellow Warbler**, **Chirping Cisticola**, **Swamp Flycatcher**, **Anchieta's Tchagra***, **Black-headed**, **Slender-billed** and **Tanzania** (*katangae*) **Masked Weavers**, **Brown Firefinch**, and **Black-faced Canary**.

Mweru north shore: There are areas of scrub and thicket that lie just beyond Chiengi, set back slightly from the shore. Here you will find **Böhm's Bee-eater*** and **Orange-cheeked Waxbill**. The very elusive **Spotted Thrush-Babbler*** occurs in the dense riparian undergrowth across the Luao River.

Lusenga Plain National Park and waterfalls: Lusenga Plain is very rarely visited and is difficult to traverse, but it is possible to enter the south-western corner via a track that leads from Tambatamba village. Take the D76 to Kawambwa to reach Tambatamba. The park is completely wild, and consists mainly of miombo with strips of rich gallery mushitu along the drainage lines. The Kalungwishi River marks Lusenga Plain's eastern boundary, and it tumbles over several spectacular waterfalls, notably Lumangwe, Kabweluma and Kundabwika. Search the riparian forest near the latter for **Cassin's Flycatcher**.

Mweru Wantipa National Park: The D37 cuts through the centre of Mweru Wantipa, but other than that the habitat is almost unbroken Itigi thicket. Interesting species of the thicket include **Green Malkoha**, **Black-fronted Bush-Shrike*** and **Dark-backed Weaver**. In the rains, look for **African Pitta***. On the western side of the park, the miombo just north of Nsama holds an isolated population of **White-winged Babbling Starling***.

Sumbu National Park: There are several camps and lodges along the shores of Lake Tanganyika that offer game-viewing and fishing. Much of the park is Itigi thicket that holds similar species to Mweru Wantipa.

Lambwe Chikwama: A good gravel road runs from Chiengi (on Lake Mweru) to Kaputa. It passes through some beautiful miombo, across several rivers lined with forest and past the Chipani Swamp. At Lambwe Chikwama village there is remnant forest in which **Joyful Bulbul** once occurred. **Anchieta's Barbet**, **Red-rumped Swallow**, **Grey-winged Robin-Chat** and **Bamboo Warbler** have all been found here recently.

Kalungwishi: On the D39 between Luwingu and Mporokoso is an abandoned state ranch at the headwaters of the Kalunwishi River. The miombo, dambo and mushitu birding is all excellent here, and good birds include **Chestnut-headed Flufftail**, **Black-rumped Buttonquail**, **Wattled Crane*** and **Black-and-rufous Swallow**.

316 South Luangwa National Park IBA ✔✔

The birding in this vast area is most enjoyable, with large numbers of water birds and raptors. Furthermore, when combined with its superb game-viewing, beautiful scenery and good tourism facilities, it becomes clear why South Luangwa remains popular with visiting birders.
SPECIALS: African Skimmer* and Lilian's Lovebird.
SEASON: The park is officially open year-round, but during the rains the rising waters of the Luangwa River render large parts of the park wholly inaccessible, and even the road from Chipata may become impassable. Most (but not all) camps and lodges are open May-Nov.
HABITATS: Dominated by the broad, tropical Luangwa River, with associated sandbars, oxbow lakes and seasonal marshes, flanked by riparian forest and predominantly mopane woodland beyond.
BIRDING: When water levels are low, sandbanks along the Luangwa River should be scanned for **African Skimmer***, **White-fronted Plover** and **White-crowned Lapwing**. In several places, enormous colonies of **Southern Carmine Bee-eater** exist in the river banks and are active from Sept-Oct, as are breeding **Horus Swift** and **White-fronted Bee-eater**. **Pel's**

Fishing-Owl* occurs in the riparian trees, as do **Red-necked Spurfowl** and **Black-backed Barbet**.

During the rains (Dec-Apr), oxbow lakes and flooded areas form along the river, attracting interesting water birds, in particular, good numbers of **African Crake, Allen's Gallinule** and **Dwarf Bittern.** Impressive concentrations of water birds form as the oxbow lakes dry up during the early dry season. Luangwa is also well known for its two sizeable colonies of **Yellow-billed Stork** in the Nsefu sector.

Luangwa's famed 'big' birds include **Lappet-faced, Hooded** and **White-headed Vultures**, various large eagles, **Grey Crowned Crane** and **Southern Ground-Hornbill***. The extensive areas of mopane woodland hold such typical mopane species as **Meves's Starling, Arnot's Chat, White-browed Sparrow-Weaver** and **Lilian's Lovebird** (the latter usually most easily found when it comes to drink at surface water). Other interesting species of the well-developed woodland include **Dickinson's Kestrel, Racket-tailed Roller*, Stierling's Wren-Warbler** and **Broad-tailed Paradise-Whydah**. The Mfuwe bridge is an excellent spot and nine species of swift have been recorded in this spot alone, including both **Böhm's*** and **Mottled Spinetails.** A resident birder based at Kapani Camp ☎ is able to offer birding advice and wet-season trips in search of **African Pitta***. Boat trips and night drives, offered by many of the camps, are highly recommended.

OTHER ANIMALS: A diversity of big game occurs, including some of the more uncommon mammal species, such as Puku and Wild Dog. Resident 'Thornicroft's' Giraffe and 'Cookson's' Wildebeest are both endemic to the Luangwa Valley. Luangwa is one of the best places in Africa to see Leopard.

NEARBY SITES: North Luangwa National Park is far more difficult to access, and is predominantly served by walking safaris (see Shiwa, p.352).

GETTING THERE

Access to South Luangwa is via Mfuwe village. Fuel is available at the village, which lies 130 km from Chipata town; allow three hours for travelling when dry, and up to a day (if at all) when wet. It is also possible to fly to Mfuwe from Lusaka, or from Lilongwe in Malawi. Accommodation options abound, both in and around the park. Uniformly up-market lodges dot the banks of the Luangwa River within the park, and the secluded bush camps used on walking safaris are also fairly luxurious. For the less extravagant, there are numerous camp sites and backpacker establishments in and around Mfuwe village, and you can enter the park as a day visitor in your own vehicle; day visitors can join one of the many organised game-drives departing from Mfuwe.

Adriadne van Zandbergen/IOA

South Luangwa combines game-watching with large numbers of birds.

ANGOLA

Angola is one of Africa's most diverse countries, with habitats ranging from the gravel plains of the Namib, one of the world's driest deserts, to the rainforests of Cabinda and the Congo Basin. As a result of the country's rich habitat diversity, it supports a wealth of birds, with a total list of at least 920 species. For most birders, however, the key attraction is the 14 endemic species, and several other near-endemics, that occur here.

Many of these endemics are restricted to fragments of scarp and Afromontane forest scattered in the highland area of western Angola. The concentration of restricted-range endemics led to the recognition of the Western Angola Endemic Bird Area by BirdLife International. Given the lack of recent information about the status of these species, 12 of the country's 14 endemics are listed as threatened.

For much of the last three decades, civil war has raged in Angola, virtually isolating the country since 1974. It is only recently that visitors have ventured into Angola for the purpose of birding, and thus far, only a few choice sites have been deemed safe for birding, these being in the extreme western reaches of the country.

Birding around Luanda is very unproductive, but in gardens and larger parks, both Rufous-tailed Palm Thrush and Red-backed Mousebird occur.

A visit to Kissama National Park, relatively close to Luanda, should yield a number of Angola's endemic birds, including White-fronted Wattle-eye and Grey-striped Spurfowl. But, for most birders, the main aim will be to explore the forested escarpment near Gabela, such as Kumbira Forest, where most of the endemics occur.

Angola brims with birding potential and is one of the most exciting birding destinations in Africa. Recent rediscoveries have included White-headed Robin-Chat, Braun's Bush-Shrike, and Black-tailed Cisticola. However, travel is expensive, and one has to be well prepared, self-sufficient and able to speak Portuguese. The best birding areas can be reached either by a gruelling drive in a 4x4 vehicle from Namibia in the south or, more conveniently, by flying into Luanda and joining an organised tour. Landmines pose a danger over large parts of the country and it is important to seek local advice on safe areas. Birding Africa ☎ organises both ornithological research and birding tours in Angola and is able to provide advice and updated birding information.

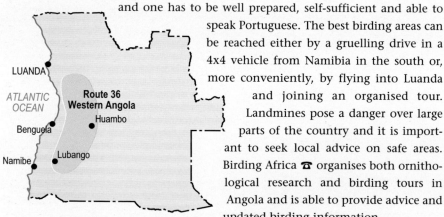

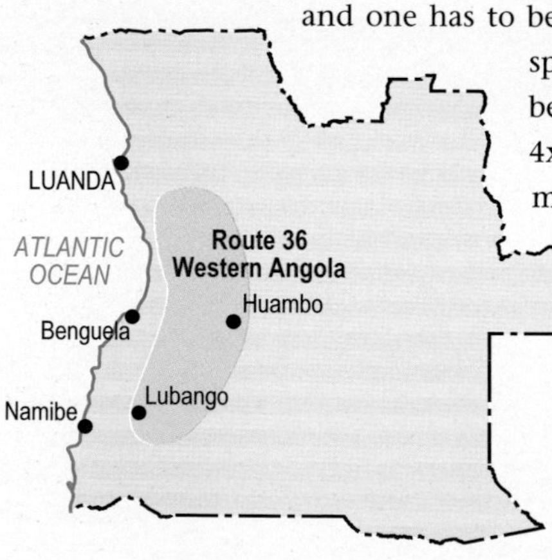

ROUTE 36

WESTERN ANGOLA

TOP 10 BIRDS

- Red-crested Turaco
- Gabela Akalat
- Angola Cave Chat
- Pulitzer's Longbill
- Monteiro's Bush-Shrike
- Gabela Bush-Shrike
- Angola Slaty Flycatcher
- White-fronted Wattle-eye
- Gabela Helmet-Shrike
- Grey-striped Spurfowl

The western highlands of Angola rise abruptly from a narrow coastal plain, and are isolated to the east by the vast, predominantly miombo-covered central plateau. They reach their highest point at Mount Moco, at 2 582 m, and are characterised by spectacular inselbergs. Dense forests cloak the lower slopes of the scarp, with a mosaic of grassland, open woodland and again forest on the higher peaks. In addition to the many endemics, the highland forests are of considerable biogeographic interest. They support populations of many species otherwise restricted to the Afromontane forests that extend along the highland chain from Eritrea and the Albertine Rift, through the Eastern Arc Mountains to the Cape Peninsula.

Many of the isolated Angolan subspecies are quite distinctive (e.g. the *bocagei* Yellow-bellied Waxbill, and the *gadowi* Bronzy Sunbird) and future research may well show them to be separate species, boosting the area's number of endemics.

The coastal lowlands are also well worth birding. The coastal plain grades from desert in the extreme south, through arid euphorbia scrub with dwarf baobabs, to mesic savanna and woodland in the north. The lowlands provide an intriguing array of birds, where species characteristic of the south-west arid zone intergrade with others more typical of the West African littoral. The entire mix is spiced up by a few species virtually restricted to Angola, notably Rufous-tailed Palm-Thrush*, White-fronted Wattle-eye, Golden-backed Bishop and Cinderella Waxbill*, although the wattle-eye and waxbill also occur higher up the scarp at some sites.

Callan Cohen

Kumbira Forest lies on the western front of Njelo Mountain.

317 Kissama National Park IBA ✔✔✔

Kissama (often spelled Quiçama) is situated 75 km south of Luanda, and has been open to tourists for the last few years. The park lies between the Kissama and Longa rivers, and is a good base to see most of the coastal plain species.

The best birding can probably be had in the riparian forest and thicket, which is home to several Angolan endemics, including **Red-backed Mousebird** and **White-fronted Wattle-eye**, as well as near-endemics such as the scarce **Pale-olive Greenbul**, and more abundant **Rufous-tailed Palm-Thrush***.

Bubbling Cisticola is common in a wide range of habitats throughout, whereas the scarce *toulsenii* subspecies of **Horus Swift**, known as 'Loanda' Swift, should be looked for along the rivers. Some of the larger gallery forests towards the interior of the park also support small numbers of **Red-crested Turaco***, but this species is much more easily found elsewhere. The real star of the show is the **Grey-striped Spurfowl**, which is locally common, albeit elusive. The best way to see it is to employ a local guide from the park's main camp; the guides imitate the francolin's whistling call, and either lure the bird into the open from the dense grass, or at least ensure a view as the bird flushes. **Gabela Helmet-Shrike** can be found in the remote south-east of the park.

Small flocks of the stunning **Golden-backed Bishop** occur in well-grassed savannas and in rank vegetation around the margins of wetlands, but they are easily overlooked if the males are not in breeding plumage.

Rio Longa Lodge ☎, situated on a small island in the mouth of the Longa River on the south border of Kissama National Park, offers good birding in a picturesque setting. **Rufous-tailed Palm-Thrush***, **Bubbling Cisticola** and **Palm-nut Vulture*** are all easily seen from the chalets, while the riverine vegetation, accessed via a short boat ride from the lodge, holds **White-fronted Wattle-eye**, **Angola Batis**, **Golden-backed Bishop** and **Swamp Boubou**.

If you drive south from Luanda towards Kissama, you will pass Luanda Bay, and the vast lagoon formed by the Mussulo Peninsula that extends 37 km south-west of the city. The peninsula plays host to many waders and other water birds, including **Royal Tern**.

Callan Cohen

Dry woodlands dominate the Kissama National Park.

318 Gabela & Kumbira Forest 4X4 IBA ✔✔✔

Three bird species take their names from the small yet famous town of Gabela: **Gabela Akalat***, **Gabela Bush-Shrike** and **Gabela Helmet-Shrike**. All are confined to a small area of western Cuanza Sul province and can be accessed at Kumbira Forest, which covers the western flank of Njelo Mountain – a long, rocky ridge running south-west from Conda. The forest ranges from 800-1 000 m asl, and the slopes above it are covered in grassland interspersed with rocky outcrops. Below the forest, the land is a mixture of subsistence agriculture and now-derelict shade coffee plantations. This site supports most of the Western Angolan endemics, with the notable exception of **Swierstra's Francolin**.

SPECIALS: Red-crested Turaco*, Gabela Akalat*, Angola Cave Chat*, Pulitzer's Longbill*, Monteiro's, Perrin's and Gabela Bush-Shrikes, Angola Slaty Flycatcher, White-fronted Wattle-eye.

SEASON: Kumbira is only reliably accessible during the dry season, from Apr to late Oct. During the rainy season, the road from Conda to Sumbe becomes a quagmire, limiting access to Kumbira to walking the 9 km of road to the forest from Conda.

HABITATS: Scarp forest, grassland with rocky outcrops, subsistence agriculture.

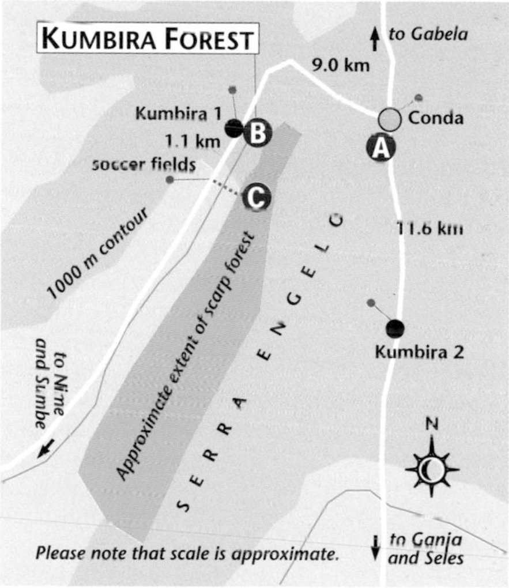

BIRDING: Gabela Bush-Shrike is common and usually easily located by its frog-like '*wor-worrrk*' call, superficially similar to the closely related Lühder's Bush-Shrike. It is just one of a suite of bush-shrikes in the area that includes **Perrin's Bush-Shrike** (common) and

Monteiro's Bush-Shrike

GETTING THERE

The town of Gabela is reached from the main coastal road via a rather indifferent tar road that runs inland from a point some 20 km north of Sumbe, and follows the Keve River. Shortly after crossing the spectacular Keve Falls, the road degenerates as it starts to ascend the escarpment. Turn south to Conda at Mile 17 on the Gabela road. Kumbira Forest is best accessed from Conda (A), along a track that leaves the town on its north-western side, and skirts the northern end of Njelo Mountain (if asking for directions in Conda, take care to specify Kumbira Primera, as there is a second Kumbira village that lies to the south). The track enters secondary forest and abdandoned coffee plantations after about 5 km, and the village of Kumbira Primera (B) (11°08'10.7"S 14°17'45.0"E) at 8 km from Conda. From Kumbira, continue towards Sumbe for 1.1 km, then turn left through a pair of old concrete gate posts and onto a track through an overgrown coffee plantation. At the fork 600 m further on, turn left. The track becomes heavily overgrown at a crossroads with a footpath, 800 m beyond the fork; this is a good spot to set up base (C) (11°08'48.2"S; 14°17'50.5"E). Here, it is advisable to hire a guide to navigate the intricate network of footpaths and old plantation tracks up through the forest. If you wish to camp in the forest, you should obtain permission from the local villagers.

The Angolan escarpment holds a high concentration of endemic birds.

surprisingly conspicuous **Monteiro's Bush-Shrike**. The latter species is thinly distributed, but several males have been heard calling in habitats ranging from near-pristine forest to quite degraded secondary scrub. However, the similar **Grey-headed Bush-Shrike** (pale lores, dark eye), which has been collected in the Gabela district, gives a virtually identical call, so check plumage differences carefully.

Gabela Akalat* occurs in small numbers among the forest and adjacent old coffee plantations. Like most akalats, it is easily overlooked if it is not calling, and is best searched for at dawn. **Pale-olive Greenbul**, a near-endemic to Angola, is also easily overlooked.

Red-crested Turaco* is much easier to see as it bounds through the remnant canopy. It is common, and the forest rings with its raucous choruses. The endemic *harterti* subspecies of **Grey-backed Camaroptera** is also common throughout the forest, whereas **Red-backed Mousebird** is confined to more open habitats.

The forest also supports several birds with localised ranges in western Central Africa. The handsome **Falkenstein's Greenbul** is abundant in secondary bush, and its nasal call is heard continuously. **Angola Batis** is quite common, often occurring in bird parties with **African Blue Flycatcher**, and **Southern Hyliota**. The diminutive **Yellow-throated Nicator** is arguably the most attractive of the nicators. At dusk and dawn, the impossibly deep call of **Gabon Coucal** emerges from the forest, sometimes calling well into the night, when it is joined by **Olive Long-tailed Cuckoo** and **African Wood-Owl**. There are also several subspecies endemic to the Angolan scarp, including isolated populations of **Dusky Tit** (*gabela*), **Forest Scrub-Robin** (*reichenowi*), **Naked-faced Barbet** (*vernayi*) and **Brown-chested Alethe** (*hallae*), while the local form of **Hairy-breasted Barbet** (*angolensis*) extends further to the north.

Other more widespread forest species that are present include **Blue Malkoha, Yellow-billed Barbet, Buff-spotted** and **Brown-eared Woodpeckers, African Broadbill*, Petit's Cuckoo-shrike, Brown Illadopsis, Rufous Flycatcher-Thrush, Buff-throated Apalis, Green Crombec, Green Hylia, Blue-headed Crested Flycatcher, Rufous-vented Paradise-Flycatcher, Yellow-bellied Wattle-eye*, Mackinnon's Fiscal, Pink-footed Puffback, Superb Sunbird** and **Grey-headed Nigrita**.

The uncommon **Pulitzer's Longbill*** is best located by its repetitive, three-note call. This rather drab warbler (if it can be clearly seen, its most striking feature is its powder-blue eye) is not particularly shy and can readily be seen moving through the mid-strata. Above about 1 000 m asl, the forest is largely confined to protected gullies. Search along the forest edge here for **Angola Slaty Flycatcher**, flitting among emergent forest trees and adjacent shrubs. **Ludwig's Double-collared Sunbird** also occurs at this elevation, replacing the **Olive-bellied Sunbird** found lower down. But the main reason for slogging up to above the forest is to find the enigmatic **Angola Cave Chat***, which perches on the lichen-encrusted rocks. Other species found at these elevations include **Rockrunner*** and **Oustalet's Sunbird**. The more open areas near Conda offer **Compact Weaver**, the entertaining **African Firefinch** (subspecies *landanae*, sometimes split as **Pale-billed Firefinch**), **Grey Waxbill** and **Black-and-white Mannikin**, as well as smaller numbers of **Red-faced Crimsonwing*** and **Red-headed Bluebill**. **Dusky Twinspot**, otherwise only known in the Albertine Rift in East Africa, also occurs in secondary habitats here.

319 Sumbe to Seles ✔✔

Many of the birds found at Kumbira also occur along the road from Sumbe to Seles, although road conditions are gruelling. Several unprepossessing patches of secondary bush around Bango (11°21.2'S; 14°13.3'E), a small village 14 km west of Seles, support a surprisingly good selection of birds, including large numbers of **Pulitzer's Longbill***, and at least a few **Gabela Akalat***, as well as **Red-crested Turaco*** and **White-fronted Wattle-eye**. Lower down, west of Bango, the road passes through some tall forest and dense woodland that probably contain **Gabela Helmet-Shrike**.

Bango can be reached directly from the coast at Sumbe. If you are travelling from Conda, it is best reached by travelling inland via Seles (formerly known as Oku). The road from Conda to Seles is a convoluted one, via the village of Ganja, and a local guide or interpreter is essential. Bango lies 14.3 km from Seles, and a particularly productive patch of bush lines the road 10.1-12.3 km from Seles. Doubtless the patches on the Sumbe side of Bango hold similar species.

320 Mount Moco 4X4 IBA ✔✔

Mount Moco, little explored over the past few decades, is best known as a reliable site for **Swierstra's Francolin**, which has recently been seen after a gap of 30 years. Huambo, which allows access to Mount Moco, can be reached from Lobito along a rather poor road. The turn-off from the main Huambo-Lobito road (1 km west of the turn-off to a small village, and at 12°19.5'S; 15°08.7'E) is easily overlooked.

You can drive to about 10 km north of the mountain peak (1 750 m asl), from where you need to explore the mountain on foot.

Above 1 900 m the miombo is gradually replaced by grasslands, with small patches of Afromontane forest. Some of the interesting birds that can be observed at higher elevations include **Angola Lark, Grimwood's Longclaw, Margaret's Batis** and **Red-crested Turaco***.

321 Tundavala IBA ✔✔

Although Tundavala may be beyond the range of most birders flying into Luanda (it is in the south of Angola), it is conveniently situated for birders driving into Angola from Namibia. **Angola Cave Chat*** is common on rocky outcrops, and **Angola Slaty Flycatcher** occurs along the margins of the few small forest patches in this area.

Tundavala lies approximately 16 km from Lubango on a good road (turn at 14°55.7'S; 13°28.3'E), and you can camp at the picnic site in the sole remaining area of miombo woodland in this reserve.

Rodney Cassidy

Angola Cave Chat

MADAGASCAR

Madagascar is world renowned for its unique diversity of flora and fauna, and this is well reflected in its bird species. Of the 280 birds known from the island, an incredible 111 are endemic, and a further 22 are near-endemics, their distribution shared only with neighbouring south-west Indian Ocean islands. Of greatest interest to itinerant birders are five endemic families: the mesites, asities, cuckoo-rollers, vangas and the incomparable ground-rollers, which make Madagascar an essential destination for anyone attempting to see all of the world's bird families. In addition to these avian attractions, this 'mini-continent' also boasts an extraordinary assemblage of endemic flora, reptiles (the island holds two-thirds of the world's chameleon species) and frogs, as well as mammals, not least of which are the lemurs.

Madagascar, which lies 400 km off the east coast of Africa, is the world's fourth largest island, extends almost 1 600 km from north to south and spans approximately 570 km at its widest point. A mountainous backbone runs the length of the island, roughly dividing the steeply sloping eastern escarpment and coastal lowlands from the more gently sloping plateaux and lowlands of the west. Few South Africans realise that Madagascar's southern tip lies off the east coast only marginally north of Gauteng!

Prevailing trade winds blow in from the Indian Ocean, and are forced to rise against these mountains, releasing moisture and resulting in a belt of evergreen forest in the east. In contrast, the western reaches of Madagascar lie in a rain-shadow, and here the dominant vegetation types comprise fairly arid scrubs and deciduous forests.

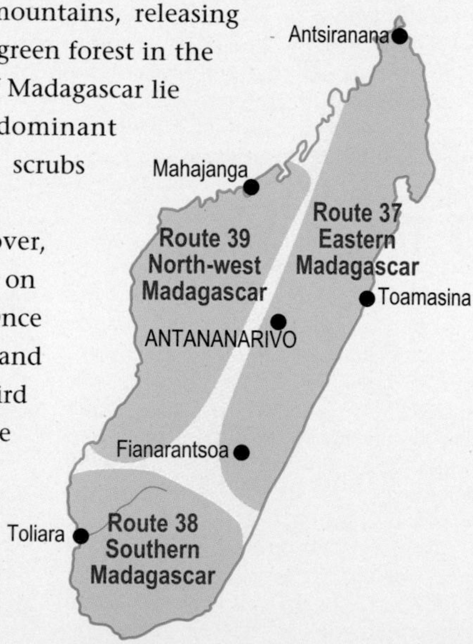

As has happened the world over, human expansion has impacted heavily on Madagascar for the past 2 000 years. Once an evolutionary wonderland, the island played host to the legendary Elephant Bird until the 16th century, and Alaotra Little Grebe and Madagascar Pochard have not been seen since the end of the 20th century; the future of such interesting creatures as today's Slender-billed Flufftail and Madagascar Serpent-Eagle remains uncertain.

ROUTE 37

EASTERN MADAGASCAR

TOP 10 BIRDS

- Scaly Ground-Roller
- Pitta-like Ground-Roller
- Rufous-headed Ground-Roller
- Short-legged Ground-Roller
- Nuthatch Vanga
- Helmet Vanga
- Madagascar Cuckoo-Roller
- Brown Mesite
- Crossley's Babbler
- Red-breasted Coua

The eastern evergreen forest is usually the priority habitat for first-time visitors to the island, boasting as it does the main share of Madagascar's endemic birds. Fortunately, a vast majority of these forest specials occur in the Analamazastra Special Reserve and Mantadia National Park, in the vicinity of the village of Andasibe (or Périnet, as it is more commonly known), easily accessible from Tana (Antananarivo).

However, in order to see the full suite of Madagascar's eastern forest endemics, birders should also visit Ranomafana National Park, 12 hours' drive south of the capital (particularly to see the Yellow-bellied Sunbird-Asity), the remote Masoala National Park near Maroansetra (for its specials like Helmet and Bernier's Vangas), as well as Montagne d'Ambre National Park in the far north-east (for Amber Mountain Rock Thrush).

Nick Garbutt/Indri Images

The secretive, Pitta-like Ground-Roller is endemic to Madagascar.

322 Antananarivo (Tana) ✔

Birders visiting Tana with time to spare should consider a trip to Lake Alarobia (Tsarasaotra) on the edge of town, known for its spectacular heronry (one of the best places to study **Madagascar Pond Heron** in its breeding plumage) and waterfowl (formerly **Meller's Duck**, but no recent records). Tsimbazaza Botanical and Zoological Garden offers **Madagascar Little Grebe, Torotoroka Scops-Owl, Hamerkop** and small passerines such as **Madagascar White-eye, Madagascar Mannikin** and **Madagascar Fody**.

323 Analamazaotra (Périnet) and Mantadia IBA ✔✔✔

These adjacent protected areas are the most accessible rainforest sites in Madagascar, boasting over 110 bird species, including more than 70 endemics. The village of Andasibe, often referred to as Périnet after the train station, and which lies in the foothills of the eastern escarpment at an altitude of 900 m asl, provides a perfect base from which to explore the world-famous Analamazaotra (Périnet) Special Reserve, and is close to the Mantadia National Park. Boasting almost all of the eastern rainforest endemics, and situated a mere 3-4 hours (by car) east of Tana, the national park is the logical first stop for birders visiting Madagascar.

SPECIALS: All the eastern rainforest endemics have been recorded here, with the exception of Bernier's Vanga (although Madagascar Serpent-Eagle, Helmet Vanga, Red-tailed Newtonia, Dusky Greenbul, Yellowbrowed Oxylabes, Yellow-bellied Sunbird-Asity and Brown Mesite are very rare here, and are best searched for at other sites). The national park is an especially good site for Madagascar Little Grebe, Madagascar Crested Ibis, Madagascar Rail, Madagascar Wood-Rail, Madagascar Long-eared Owl, Collared Nightjar, Nuthatch Vanga, and Scaly, Pitta-like, Rufous-headed and Short-legged Ground-Rollers.

SEASON: If it's the ground-rollers you are after, the best time to visit is during the Sept-Nov breeding season.

HABITATS: Mid-altitude rainforest (900-1 500 m asl) is the main birding habitat, with nearby montane marshes adding diversity.

BIRDING: The walk along the tarred road from Andasibe to the reserve entrance at Ⓐ offers an excellent introduction to forest birding in Madagascar, with good visibility and regular mixed-species foraging flocks of common forest passerines. **Common Newtonia, Madagascar White-eye, Madagascar Paradise-Flycatcher, Common Jery, Souimanga Sunbird**, and **Red-tailed Vanga** usually form the core of the flocks, with smaller numbers of **Ward's Flycatcher, Madagascar Cuckooshrike, Tylas, White-headed Vanga**, the exquisite **Blue Vanga** and **Nelicourvi Weaver** often present.

The real prize here, however, is the unusual **Nuthatch Vanga**, surely one of Madagascar's

GETTING THERE

Andasibe village and the nearby protected areas can be reached by road (the drive takes about 3-4 hours from Tana) and lies about 130 km east of Tana. Turn north off the RN2 and drive 2 km to the entrance. Visitors pay a fee at the Visitors' Centre at the park entrance. Local guides are compulsory and can be arranged at the entrance. There is an extensive trail system, and the excellent local guides assist with the location of lemurs, reptiles and birds. The turn-off to Andasibe is 1 km past the park entrance. Mantadia National Park lies 15 km beyond the village and is accessed by private vehicle or taxi. Permits must be obtained at the park office. Andasibe boasts a number of hotels to suit various budgets, and the Feon' ny ala, on the outskirts of the reserve, is most conveniently situated for birding. The upmarket Vakona Lodge is situated halfway between the village and Mantadia. There is no accommodation within the national park. The Association des Guides d'Andasibe is able to organise excellent naturalist guides.

best examples of convergent evolution, resembling in behaviour its unrelated northern hemisphere namesake. Groups of **Madagascar Blue Pigeon** sun themselves in the tree tops in the early morning, and these upper branches are also the favoured song perches of **Stripe-throated** and **Green Jerys, Rand's Warbler** and **Madagascar Green Sunbird**. Also, watch the canopy for **Hook-billed Vanga** and **Madagascar Starling**.

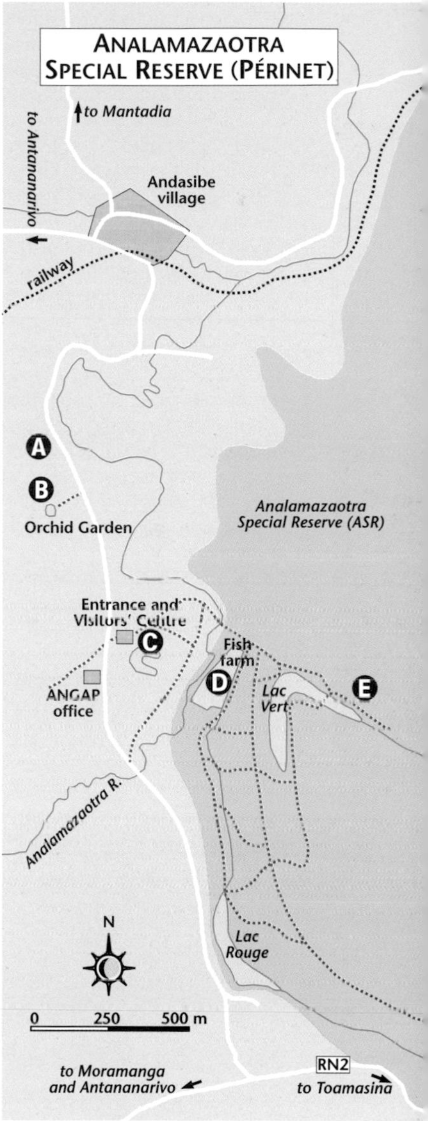

Wherever possible, scan the edges of the river as this provides one of the best opportunities for **White-throated Rail**. The forest trail holds the elusive **Madagascar Crested Ibis**. The ibises occasionally also feed in the open around the edge of the reservoir at the adjacent Orchid Garden **B**, especially at dusk, although they are far more frequently heard than seen. Many of the common forest birds may also be found around the Visitors' Centre **C**. The exotic pine trees to the south of the clearing have been a favourite roost site of **Madagascar Long-eared Owl** for the past few years; ask your guide for details.

Scrubby forest between the main entrance and the abandoned fish ponds **D** is favoured by **Spectacled Greenbul, Tylas** and **Hook-billed Vanga**, while a pair of **Pitta-like Ground-Roller** also holds fort here. The scrubby fringes of a former fish farm provide habitat for a variety of open country birds, such as **Madagascar Stonechat, Madagascar Brush Warbler, Madagascar Cisticola** and **Madagascar Mannikin**, and this area is also an excellent spot to scan for **Madagascar Buzzard, Madagascar Harrier Hawk, Malagasy Spine-tailed Swift, Madagascar Bee-eater**, and displaying **Madagascar Cuckoo-Roller**.

The picturesque Lac Vert **E** lies 100 m beyond the fish ponds, and forms the focal point of the reserve. A pair of **Madagascar Little Grebe** is sometimes present, while **Madagascar Kingfisher** feeds quietly along the margins of the lake.

In the morning and evening, the surrounding forests ring with the haunting songs of the reserve's most famous resident, the Indri. At this time of day, lakeside trails are also good areas to work for **Blue Coua, White-throated Oxylabes, Crossley's Babbler** and **Madagascar Wood-Rail**, although you will almost certainly require local guiding to find this area's most sought-after birds, the skulking **Red-breasted Coua** and the elusive **Collared Nightjar**.

Mantadia National Park protects a large tract of pristine forest, the most accessible patch of which lies at a slightly higher altitude than that in the Analamazoatra Special Reserve (ASR). This magnificent site was only opened to the public in 1995, and has already earned a reputation among birders. Indeed, it is possible to see all four species of rainforest ground-rollers in a day here: **Pitta-like** and **Scaly Ground-Rollers** in the level forest along the trails at the 'Km 14' post (both fairly common and recorded regularly), **Rufous-headed Ground-Roller** in the ravines or up the ridge at the 'Km 14' post and, with a measure of luck, **Short-legged Ground-Roller** at the roadside between the 'Km 11' and 'Km 14' posts. Locating these forest skulkers requires knowledge of their calls and considerable stalking skills.

All of the forest species found in the ASR are also present in Mantadia, but some, such as **Madagascar Flufftail, Grey-crowned Greenbul, Crossley's Babbler, Madagascar Starling** and **Forest Fody**, are easier to find here. Walk the trail across the footbridge at the 'Km 14' post into tall, level forest, listening for the two common ground-rollers and scanning good mixed-species foraging flocks for **Dark Newtonia** and **Nuthatch Vanga**. The trail meanders over the ridge into higher altitude forest, favoured by **Rufous-headed Ground-Roller**, **Forest Rock-Thrush** and **Brown Emutail**. Sift through the conspicuous **Lesser Vasa Parrots** for **Greater Vasa Parrot**, and listen for the scarce **Pollen's Vanga**, especially along the side road that leads to the graphite mine. **Madagascar Buzzard** is common at the roadside, but also keep a lookout for **Henst's Goshawk** (uncommon), as well as **Madagascar Serpent-Eagle**, which has been seen on a number of occasions in recent years. A night walk along the road is highly recommended, not only for nocturnal mammals and reptiles, but also for **Madagascar Long-eared Owl**, **White-browed Owl**, **Rainforest Scops-Owl**, and **Collared Nightjar**. The near-mythical **Madagascar Red Owl** is also recorded from this area.

NEARBY SITES: The higher altitude, ridge-top forest at Maromizaha has produced a few species that are difficult to see elsewhere in the Andasibe area. These include such elusive birds as **Brown Mesite** (rare), **Brown Emutail** and **Pollen's Vanga**. **Yellow-bellied Sunbird-Asity** is controversial here. **Rufous-headed Ground-Roller**, **Forest Rock-Thrush**, **White-throated Oxylabes** and **Cryptic Warbler** are other noteworthy species that are regularly recorded here.

The area is best explored by means of a footpath running eastwards along the ridge from just beyond the second quarry, at the top of a 1 km-long, heavily rutted 4WD track that climbs steeply southwards off the RN2 from a point about 3 km east of the turn-off to Andasibe.

Roadside marshes back along the B2 towards Moramanga hold a number of scarce birds that are endemic to eastern highland wetlands. These include the endangered **Meller's Duck**, **Madagascar Rail**, **Madagascar Snipe** and **Grey Emutail**. **Madagascar Flufftail** and **Madagascar Swamp-Warbler** are both relatively common, and can easily be located by means of their calls. Unfortunately, the most accessible sites change as the marshes come under pressure for conversion to rice paddies. Recently, the Ampasipotsy marsh (ca 0.5 km north of the B2 along a footpath that commences near the 'Km 122' post, i.e. ca 15 km west of the Andasibe junction) has been the site of choice, but try asking local guides for more up-to-date information.

Energetic birders should consider the long hike to Torotorofotsy Marsh, about 15 km west of Andasibe village along the railway line. One of the most pristine highland wetlands in all of Madagascar, Torotorofotsy is home to healthy populations of **Madagascar Rail**, **Madagascar Snipe** and **Grey Emutail**, and is also a relatively reliable site for the endangered **Meller's Duck**. **Slender-billed Flufftail** has also been reported with some regularity, and this is probably the best site in Madagascar for this exceptionally rare and elusive rallid.

OTHER ANIMALS: ASR is world famous for its resident Indri, although Brown Mouse Lemur, Greater Dwarf Lemur, Small-toothed Sportive Lemur, Eastern Avahi and Common Brown Lemur are also regularly seen here.

A visit to Mantadia National Park may reward the eager lemur-watcher with an additional two mega-mammals: the beautiful Diademed Sifaka and panda-like Black-and-White Ruffed Lemur. The bizarre Lowland Streaked Tenrec is also common here.

Nick Garbutt/Indri Images

Ranomafana National Park

324 Ranomafana National Park IBA ✔✔✔

Although it is a long day's drive south of Tana, the 41 500 ha Ranomafana National Park offers a superb selection of eastern rainforest specials, including some that are rare or absent from the Andasibe area, as well as montane specials.

SPECIALS: Almost all of Andasibe's specials are also present at Ranomafana, although Henst's Goshawk, Brown Mesite, Madagascar Yellowbrow, Brown Emutail, Yellow-bellied Sunbird-Asity and Pollen's Vanga are easier to find here.

SEASON: The best time for the ground-rollers is during Sept-Dec.

HABITATS: Rainforest ranging in altitude from 600-1 550 m asl, and adjacent high altitude marshes.

BIRDING: At Ranomafana, the place to start birding is at the mid-altitude forest around Belle Vue (C), which boasts **Pitta-like Ground-Roller**, **Velvet Asity**, **Common Sunbird-Asity**, **Yellowbrowed Oxylabes**, both **Spectacled** and **Grey-crowned Greenbuls** and **Wedge-tailed Jery**, as well as an almost full complement of the more widespread Madagascar forest passerines. Finding these specials requires knowledge of their calls, as most are very retiring by nature.

Another of Belle Vue's star avian attractions is **Brown Mesite**, and its rollicking morning duets are often heard from the steep valleys to the south. Some of the guides are adept at locating these forest phantoms; be sure to quiz your guide about this prior to hiring him.

The so-called Primary Forest lies a brisk hour's walk beyond Belle Vue, but the thrill of seeing **Henst's Goshawk** or **Short-legged Ground-Roller** will more than justify the required

GETTING THERE

The town of Ranomafana (A) lies about 50 km north-east of Fianarantsoa, effectively a 12 hour drive to the south of Tana. Fairly good accommodation is available in the village and at the park entrance (B) 2 km uphill to the west. Good trails allow access to mid-altitude forest near the main park entrance, and at a separate montane forest patch at Vohiparara, west of the main park entrance. As with Analamazaotra, local guides are mandatory (most are proficient general naturalists, although some birding specialists also possess in-depth knowledge of bird calls, territories, etc.). All permits can be arranged on arrival at the park.

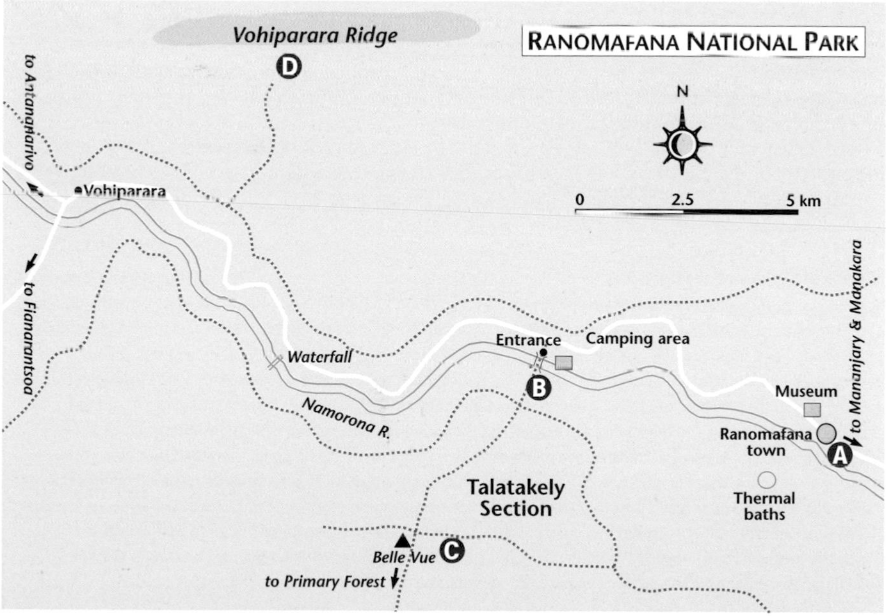

effort. However, finding these uncommon birds will definitely require the assistance of one of the specialist birding guides.

The higher altitude forest near Vohiparara village is the only relatively reliable and accessible site in Madagascar for the rare **Yellow-bellied Sunbird-Asity**, and is also an excellent place for **Rufous-headed Ground-Roller**, **Yellowbrowed Oxylabes**, **Brown Emutail**, **Cryptic Warbler** and **Pollen's Vanga**. A trail commences about 5 km uphill from the main park entrance, and runs through stunted forest favoured by **Yellowbrowed Oxylabes** and **White-throated Oxylabes**, before climbing up to a ridge Ⓓ. **Pollen's Vanga** often joins mixed vanga flocks working through the moss-encrusted trees here, while **Madagascar Flufftail** and **Rufous-headed Ground-Roller** call from the undergrowth. Thicker areas of bamboo along the ridge-top hold the skulking **Brown Emutail**, and this is where at least one pair of **Yellow-bellied Sunbird-Asities** is sometimes present. Waiting and listening for their high-pitched calls, either at known song posts or at nearby flowering trees, is the best way of locating these elusive birds. **Grey Emutail** and **Madagascar Swamp-Warbler** may be found in tiny patches of reeds among the rice paddies, about 2 km towards Vohiparara town from the trailhead, while **Madagascar Pratincole** is frequently encountered hawking over the Namorona River. Those with private transport should visit the 'Haunted House Marsh' north-west of Vohiparara (about 7 km off the RN7 and along the RN25), which holds good numbers of **Madagascar Flufftail**, **Madagascar Rail**, **Madagascar Snipe**, **Grey Emutail** and **Madagascar Swamp-Warbler**. A pair of **Réunion Harriers** is sometimes present over the wetland, and the increasingly scarce **Meller's Duck** is occasionally seen flying in at dusk. The marsh's rarest resident, however, is **Slender-billed Flufftail**, which is occasionally heard calling along the eastern edge of the wetland. Be sure not to disturb this endangered endemic. Both **Madagascar Buttonquail** and **Madagascar Partridge** may be flushed while traversing the surrounding scrubby grasslands.

OTHER ANIMALS: Ranomafana is a superb lemur site, with specials including three species of bamboo lemur (the only accessible site for Golden and Greater Bamboo Lemurs), and the handsome Milne-Edwards's Diademed Sifaka. Brown Mouse, Greater Dwarf and Red-bellied Lemurs are easily photographed at the Belle Vue picnic site at dusk, as are Fanaloka and the handsome Ring-tailed Mongoose.

325 Masoala Peninsula

IBA ✔✔✔

The magnificent lowland forest on the Masoala Peninsula, recently spared the logger's chainsaw through the creation of the Masoala National Park, provides the only reasonable opportunity to see a number of incredible birds.

SPECIALS: Madagascar Serpent-Eagle, Madagascar Red Owl, Bernier's Vanga, Short-legged Ground-Roller and the incomparable Helmet Vanga.

GETTING THERE

In order to visit this remote area, you first need to get to the sleepy town of Maroantsetra (direct flights from Tana and Toamasina, or an unpleasant two-day overland marathon), where boats can be hired for the approximately 30 km trip across the Baie d'Antongil to the Masoala Peninsula. The traditional base for birders is the village of Ambanizana, where basic food and thatched shelters are available, although accessing good habitat from here is becoming increasingly challenging. A trail heads directly back from the shelters through rice paddies and climbs through clove plantations, eventually reaching the forest near the top of the ridge. A maze of tracks here still allows access to reasonable forest. However, the best birding is around the Peregrine Fund Research Station at Andranobe, 7 km to the south-east, where a network of trails allows exploration of pristine forest boasting all the area's specials. It is important to obtain permission in advance. Hiring a fishing boat to get there by sea from Ambanizana eliminates the alternative and tiring 2-3 hour hike along the coast. The recent construction of a new camp site at Lohatrazona, only about 3 km from Andranobe, should make access even easier, but visitors to this site will need to be fully self-sufficient. The easiest way to organise everything, including national park permits and guides, is through the Relais du Masoala or Motel Coco Beach in Maroantsetra ☎, but enquire about new lodges in the area.

SEASON: Oct-Nov, before the heavy Dec-Feb rains.
HABITATS: Lowland rainforest.
BIRDING: Birding of the Masoala Peninsula can be both an uncomfortable and an incredibly exhilarating experience. Temperature and humidity are usually high, trails are steep and often slippery, leeches and mosquitoes may be plentiful, and the birding can be frustratingly slow at times. However, when you bring your binoculars into focus on the luminous blue bill of a **Helmet Vanga**, or hear the territorial call of a **Madagascar Serpent-Eagle** ringing across the valley, all discomfort is soon forgotten.

Nick Garbutt/Indri Images
Helmet Vanga on the Masoala Peninsula

Finding the avian specials means listening out for their distinctive calls and pounding the trails in search of mixed-species foraging flocks (both **Bernier's** and **Helmet Vangas** are regular attendants). Of the three main specials, the Helmet Vanga is the most regular and local guides often know the locality of a nest. Even if they don't, you are fairly likely to bump into one during the course of two days' birding. Bernier's Vanga, on the other hand, can be elusive and a considerable amount of luck is required to find this species.

Madagascar Serpent-Eagle can be equally difficult to find, as it usually perches motionless in the canopy. Listening for its far-carrying calls in the valleys around Andranobe provides the only real chance of locating this recently 'rediscovered' raptor.

Fortunately, an abundance of other birds should keep you entertained during your quest for the 'Masoala specials', and even reputed skulkers such as **Madagascar Wood-Rail**, **Brown Mesite**, **Scaly Ground-Roller** and **Red-breasted Coua** are unusually confiding. **Red-tailed Newtonia** has also been claimed, and it is worth checking mixed-species foraging flocks for this rare species. **Madagascar Red Owl** occurs, although seeing this bird requires considerable good fortune.

If the forest birding becomes too much, the beautiful waters and coral reef communities of the Baie d'Antongil provide a welcome diversion.
OTHER ANIMALS: The Masoala Peninsula supports a healthy mammal fauna, most conspicuous and glamorous of which is the exquisite Red Ruffed Lemur. An overnight stop on the island of Nosy Mangabe is recommended for those in search of the bizarre and wonderful Aye-Aye (released onto the island in 1967, when the species was suspected to be on the brink of extinction), and a visit here should also produce White-fronted Brown Lemur, Black-and-White Ruffed Lemur (also both introduced), and numerous Fimbriated Leaf-tailed Geckos.

326 Montagne d'Ambre NP

IBA ✔✔

The mid-altitude forest on Montagne d'Ambre is most famous among birders as the only site on earth where you will find the highly localised and appropriately named **Amber Mountain Rock-Thrush**. This beautiful bird is usually easily found at the camp site at Station des Roussettes, along the 200 m trail to the Petite Cascade, or along the road leading up to the crater lake of Lac Vert.

Pitta-like Ground-Roller, **Madagascar Cuckoo-Roller**, **Spectacled Greenbul** and **Hook-billed Vanga** are also all fairly common and easily found in the park, which lies about 30 km (an hour's drive in a taxi) south of Antsiranana (Diégo Suarez) in northern Madagascar.

ROUTE 38

SOUTHERN MADAGASCAR

A combination of spectacular landscapes, relatively open habitats, and a plethora of beautiful endemics, many of them fairly common and easily seen, makes birding southern Madagascar a delight. Comprehensive coverage of the south would involve a visit to Isalo National Park, the newly proclaimed Zombitse National Park, the coastal sites north and south of Toliara, and the gallery forest in the famous private lemur reserve at Berenty, although birders with limited time usually restrict their exploration to the spiny forest at Ifaty. The south is best accessed by road from Ranomafana National Park, which necessitates an overnight stop at Isalo National Park, a 6-8 hour drive to the south-west across the High Plateau.

Callan Cohen

Subdesert Mesite

TOP 10 BIRDS

- Appert's Greenbul
- Long-tailed Ground-Roller
- Subdesert Mesite
- Red-shouldered Vanga
- Littoral Rock-Thrush
- Madagascar Plover
- Giant Coua
- Verreaux's Coua
- Lafresnaye's Vanga
- Madagascar Sandgrouse

Nick Garbutt/Indri Images

Long-tailed Ground-Roller

BIRDING TRAVEL IN MADAGASCAR

Madagascar is a poorly developed country with an infrastructure that will challenge even the most independent of birders. One way to see the numerous avian endemics is on a commercial birding tour, and many visitors choose this hassle-free option, although the country can also be easily birded in well-prepared small groups if the logistics are arranged through a reputable local operator. Independent birders with sufficient time may also be able to cover most of the sites by using public transport, in the form of informal buses, known locally as 'taxi-brousses', from Antananarivo (the capital city, known also as Tana). An internal air network converts 12-24 hour marathon road journeys into pleasant 1 hour flights – highly recommended for those who are not on a tight budget. Malagasy and French are the official languages, although French is only widely spoken in urban areas, and most of the guides in the main tourist areas also speak English.

327 Isalo NP and Zombitse Forest IBA ✔✔

Tony Camacho

Giant Coua

Namaqua Dove, **Madagascar Bush Lark** and **Madagascar Cisticola** are regularly encountered on the High Plateau journey from Ranomafana, and **Madagascar Partridge**, **Harlequin Quail** and **Madagascar Buttonquail** may be flushed from areas of thicker cover at the roadside. Stop frequently to scan for the scarce **Réunion Harrier**, especially along the final 100 km stretch between Ihosy and Ranohira (the village at the edge of Isalo National Park).

The highly localised **Benson's Rock-Thrush** is fairly common throughout the Isalo Massif; check the rocks behind the park's Interpretation Centre about 10 km south-west of Ranohira, as well as the rocky cliffs around the nearby 'Oasis', and the roofs of the upmarket Relais de La Reine, about 3 km further west.

Leave Isalo very early in the morning (before the heat kills any bird activity) to reach Zombitse Forest, which straddles the RN7 about 90 km to the west. Local guides are available from the park office at the forest, where entrance fees should also be paid. Park officials sometimes insist that groups purchase permits prior to entering the reserve. The endangered **Appert's Greenbul** is fairly common here, and may be seen in roadside forest (follow the rough pathway created by the Zebu), along with **Madagascar Cuckoo-Roller, Giant, Crested** and **Coquerel's Couas**, and **Rufous Vanga. White-browed Owl** and 'Torotoroka Scops-Owl' are also numerous here, but camp in the vicinity if you wish to see these night birds.

328 Toliara Area ✔

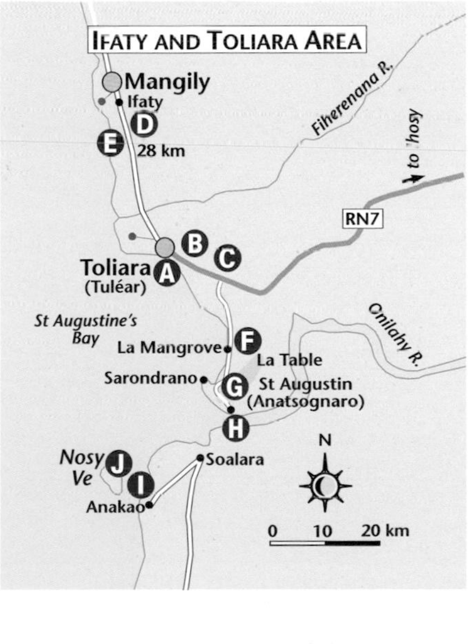

The mudflats around Toliara Harbour Ⓐ provide one of the most accessible sites for wader-watching in Madagascar and, in addition to terns (notably **Saunders' Tern**) and numerous Palearctic waders, often hold a few **Crab Plovers**. Check the saline ponds near the airport Ⓑ (about 7 km inland from Toliara) for the localised **Madagascar Plover**, although this may also be seen around Ifaty. Botanists and birders who do not have time to visit Berenty should consider a stop at the pleasant botanical gardens at the Arboretum d'Antsokay Ⓒ, signposted off the RN7, just north-east of the track to St Augustin. **Giant Coua** has been reported from here, and **Madagascar Buttonquail** and **Running Coua** are frequently encountered among the fine collection of succulents. Toliara has a variety of good hotels, and could be used as a base for birding the road to St Augustin, although having a base at either La Mangrove or Melody Beach Hotel is even more convenient.

329 Ifaty ✓✓✓

The surreal landscape inland of the fishing village of Ifaty hosts some of Madagascar's strangest, and most sought-after endemics, including **Subdesert Mesite** and **Long-tailed Ground-Roller**, and is the most convenient place to bird the spiny forest.

SPECIALS: Subdesert Mesite, Long-tailed Ground-Roller, Banded Kestrel, Madagascar Plover, Grey-headed Lovebird, Running Coua, Green-capped Coua, Archbold's Newtonia, Thamnornis Warbler, Subdesert Brush-Warbler, and Sickle-billed and Lafresnaye's Vangas.

SEASON: Specials are present year-round.

HABITATS: Spiny forest, consisting of strange, multi-stemmed 'Octopus trees' (Didieraceae and Alluaudiaceae) and other thorny shrubs, and bottle-shaped baobabs; marine coast and adjacent commercial saltpans.

BIRDING: Because daytime temperatures can be unbearably hot, a pre-dawn departure for the spiny forest is highly recommended; birding beyond about 10.30 in the morning is uncomfortable and usually unproductive. **Subdesert Mesite** and **Long-tailed Ground-Roller** are the main target species, but most of the other specials usually turn up during the search. Local guides often know the territories of these two endemics, following their calls or using teams of young boys to help locate them. It is absolutely essential to insist that Subdesert Mesites are NOT flushed into trees for ease of viewing, as this extreme predator-avoidance response is detrimental to these social, ground-dwelling birds.

Although both these skulkers are present in suitable habitat north of Ifaty, the spiny forest inland of the Mora Mora Hotel is the traditional viewing site Ⓓ, with numerous informal tracks allowing easy access to otherwise impenetrable thorn thickets. This area also supports **Thamnornis Warbler**, the uncommon **Archbold's Newtonia** and **Sickle-billed** and **Lafresnaye's Vangas**, all of which may be relatively easily located by their distinctive calls. Small flocks of **Grey-headed Lovebird** are frequent overhead, and an eye should be kept out for both **Banded Kestrel** and **Madagascar Cuckoo-Hawk**.

NEARBY SITES: Saltpans inland of the Lakana Vezo Hotel, south of Ifaty Ⓔ, hold small numbers of **Madagascar Plover**, which often feed on the mudflats in front of the hotel at low tide, as well as a variety of Palearctic waders. **Subdesert Brush-Warbler, Stripe-throated Jery, Souimanga Sunbird, Chabert's Vanga** and **Sakalava Weaver** are all conspicuous in the hotel gardens.

GETTING THERE

The beach resort commonly known as Ifaty lies 27 km north of Toliara in south-west Madagascar, along a sandy track best traversed in a 4WD vehicle (although taxi-brousses also regularly make the run up the coast from Toliara). Accommodation of varying standards is available in the adjacent village of Mangily. Local guides are not mandatory, but they do seem to know where to find the specials; ask at the Mora Mora Hotel reception desk, or in the village. Access to the fairly degraded spiny forest is by means of small tracks running inland behind the village. Birders in search of better quality spiny forest should continue to the village of Madiorano at PK34, 6 km further north, where bungalow-style accommodation is also available. Good quality habitat may also be found near Morombe.

A baobab in the spiny forest near Ifaty

330 St Augustin Road & Nosy Ve IBA ✔✔✔

The track that runs south along the coast for about 30 km from Toliara to the village of St Augustin (Anatsognaro) passes through unique coral rag scrub, which is home to a handful of highly localised endemics, most famous of which is the recently discovered **Red-shouldered Vanga**.

SPECIALS: Red-shouldered Vanga, Humblot's Heron, Red-tailed Tropicbird, Madagascar Sandgrouse, Verreaux's Coua, and Littoral Rock-Thrush.

SEASON: All year.

HABITATS: Euphorbia-dominated coral rag scrub, mangroves, extensive tidal mudflats, and freshwater wetlands at the Onilahy River estuary.

Callan Cohen

Red-shouldered Vanga habitat

BIRDING: Coral rag scrub specials occur in their ideal habitat near La Mangrove, and **Verreaux's Coua** is regularly seen in the vicinity of the hotel itself (F), as well as along the road, and **Red-shouldered Vanga** is present in the thick euphorbia scrub at the top of the plateau, a steep climb to the east of the road. **Humblot's Heron** is regularly seen on the extensive tidal mudflats in front of the hotel, and along the coast towards St Augustin, while **White-throated Rail** is common in the adjacent mangroves.

The easiest place to find **Red-shouldered Vanga**, however, is along the road across the plateau (sometimes called La Table), about 5 km south of La Mangrove (G). The track turns away from the coast and climbs steeply to the plateau, where a number of pairs of this bird occur, before dropping down to the Onilahy River. Listen for their far-carrying call in the area just beyond the third culvert (although they may occur anywhere on the plateau). **Verreaux's Coua** is also present, but may be confused with the handsome *pyropyga* subspecies of **Crested Coua**, which is numerous here. The Onilahy River (H) itself often holds a reasonable selection of water birds, including both **African Openbill** (rare) and **Humblot's Heron**, and is also an excellent site from which to observe **Madagascar Sandgrouse** as they come in to drink in the early morning.

Littoral Rock-Thrush occurs only in coastal euphorbia scrub south of the Onilahy River. The bird is common behind the hotel in the fishing village of Anakao (I), and is usually located within a few minutes of stepping ashore.

A boat excursion to Anakao is best combined with a visit to Nosy Ve, 4 km to the west (J). The island's main attractions are its superb snorkelling and its colony of **Red-tailed Tropicbirds**, which may be studied at close quarters on their nests. **Crab Plover** is sometimes present among **Saunders' Tern**, and **Lesser Crested Tern** roosts here, with small numbers of **Bridled Tern** frequently encountered offshore.

331 Berenty Private Reserve ✔✔

This island of gallery forest and spiny forest in a sea of sisal plantations is far more famous for its lemurs than it is for its birds. Nevertheless, Berenty is a fantastic stop on any tour of Madagascar, and a handful of its avian inhabitants are easier to find here than elsewhere on the island.

SPECIALS: Madagascar Buttonquail, Giant and Running Couas, Grey-headed Lovebird, Torotoroka Scops-Owl, White-browed Owl, Madagascar Green-Pigeon, Madagascar Sandgrouse, Madagascar Cuckoo Hawk, Madagascar Harrier Hawk, Madagascar Sparrowhawk, Banded Kestrel, and Lafresnaye's and Sickle-billed Vangas.

SEASON: Good year-round.

Callan Cohen

Verreaux's Sifaka

HABITATS: Tall gallery woodland along the Mandrare River, with adjacent strips of spiny forest.
BIRDING: The pheasant-like **Giant Coua** is usually the first avian speciality encountered when entering the gallery woodland. They make a huge noise, calling loudly and scratching nosily in the leaf litter, although at Berenty these stately birds are habituated, and often feed nonchalantly at the edge of the trails.

Berenty's target species are three rarely recorded raptors. Foremost on the list is the **Madagascar Sparrowhawk**, and the Ankoba Forest north-west of the bungalows is the best site on the island in which to find this rare (and frequently misidentified) endemic. In the woodland, listen for its distinctive 'squeaky-gate' call; don't confuse the Madagascar Sparrowhawk with the very similar and considerably more numerous **Frances's Sparrowhawk** (female Frances's is smaller, slimmer, shorter-tailed and browner above than Madagascar, and also lacks the latter's often prominent white undertail coverts and thighs).

A few pairs of the rarely seen **Madagascar Cuckoo Hawk** nest in tall trees along the Mandrare River. Listen for alarm calls from the lemurs and be careful not to immediately dismiss large brown raptors as **Madagascar Buzzard**.

Bat Hawk, also uncommon, is occasionally seen over riverside woodland east of the cattle corridor at dusk. The end of the cattle corridor is also the best spot from which to scan for **Comb Duck**, and to watch flocks of **Madagascar Sandgrouse** drinking at the Mandrare River (early to mid morning). The surrounding woodland should produce **Grey-headed Lovebird**, **Madagascar Harrier-Hawk**, and mixed-species foraging flocks that often include **Ashy Cuckoo-shrike**, and **Hook-billed** and **White-headed Vangas**. Flocks of **Sickle-billed Vangas**, emitting loud, wailing calls, are also occasionally seen here. The frugivorous **Madagascar Green-Pigeon** may be found in any fruiting fig tree in the woodland; groups of pigeons often sun themselves near the Madagascar Flying Fox roost. **White-browed Owl** is often and easily seen around the restaurant after dark, although **Torotoroka Scops-Owl** usually requires a spotlighting excursion into the woodland.
OTHER ANIMALS: Berenty's lemurs are nothing short of spectacular, with bands of Ring-tailed Lemur loitering around the cabins, ballerina-like Verreaux's Sifaka frequently seen bounding across the clearings, and the locally introduced Red-fronted Brown Lemur troops abundant in the gallery woodland. After dark, the woodland reverberates with the calls of White-footed Sportive Lemurs (which are also commonly found dozing in their tree-cavity day roosts). Spotlighting excursions through the spiny forest commonly bring to light the diminutive Grey Mouse Lemur.

332 Andohahela National Park ✔

This recently proclaimed national park that straddles the road between Tolagnaro and Berenty protects a range of habitats, from eastern rainforest to *Alluadia*-rich 'spiny desert'. While most of its birds are more easily seen elsewhere, Andohahela has recently been recognised as a reliable and accessible site for the scarce and localised **Red-tailed Newtonia**. Enquire at the park headquarters on the main road for directions to the forest, which lies at the foot of the mountains to the north.

ROUTE 39

NORTH-WEST MADAGASCAR

Although not as well developed for birding as the traditional sites in the east and south, the north-west is home to some of Madagascar's most exciting endemics, including White-breasted Mesite and the jewel-like Schlegel's Asity, the rare Bernier's Teal, and the critically endangered Madagascar Fish-Eagle. Fortunately for birders, almost all of the specials may be seen between the port of Mahajanga, which has regular air connections with Tana, and the forest station at Ampijoroa, two hours' drive to the south-east.

TOP 10 BIRDS

- Bernier's Teal
- Humblot's Heron
- White-breasted Mesite
- Schlegel's Asity
- Madagascar Fish-Eagle
- Van Dam's Vanga
- Sickle-billed Vanga
- Grey-headed Lovebird
- Madagascar Sacred Ibis
- Madagascar Jacana

Dominique Halleux

Sickle-billed Vanga

Nick Garbutt/Indri Images

Western dry forests in Ankarafantsika National Park

333 Ankarafantsika NP (Ampijoroa) IBA ✔✔✔

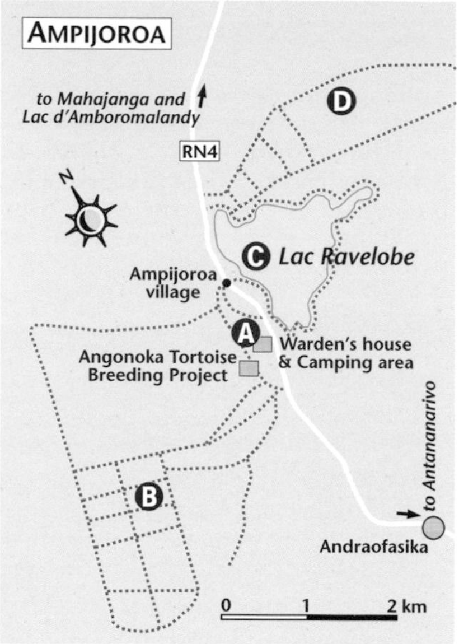

The deciduous woodland that surrounds the Ampijoroa Forestry Station in Ankarafantsika National Park is host to the full complement of spectacular north-west Madagascar forest endemics.

SPECIALS: White-breasted Mesite, Schlegel's Asity, Madagascar Fish-Eagle, Madagascar Buttonquail, Red-capped Coua, Grey-headed Lovebird, Madagascar Sandgrouse, Madagascar Pond Heron, Madagascar Crested Ibis, and Van Dam's Vanga.

SEASON: Specials present year-round, although temperatures are considerably higher from Nov-Feb.

HABITATS: Western deciduous forest surrounding a small lake, with more extensive wetlands around the nearby Lac d'Amboromalandy.

BIRDING: Ampijoroa's camp site Ⓐ provides an excellent starting point for birding, as **Madagascar Hoopoe**, **Crested Coua**, **Lesser Vasa Parrot**, **Grey-headed Lovebird**, **Madagascar Turtle-Dove**, and **Hook-billed** and **Chabert's Vangas** are usually readily seen here. A walk along any of the trails in the immediate vicinity often turns up **Red-capped Coua**, **Frances's Sparrowhawk** and parties of the superb **White-breasted Mesite**; the latter's distinctive choruses are conspicuous at dawn and dusk.

As good as the birding may be around the camp site, the real challenge starts with a hike south to the low plateau at Ⓑ, where the bulk of Ampijoroa's population of **Van Dam's**

GETTING THERE

Most visitors to Ankarafantsika fly to Mahajanga and hire transport for the 120 km (about 2 hours') drive to Ampijoroa. Although the journey can be made from Tana by car, it involves an 8-10 hour drive. One can either stay overnight in the new bungalows, or camp. The camp site has basic ablution facilities and meals are usually available (take back-up supplies in case not). Hiring a skilled bird/lemur guide is not mandatory, but it is highly recommended.

Gerald Cubitt

Forest trail in Ankarafantsika National Park

Vanga may be found. The rarest and most endangered of all vangas, Van Dam's Vanga is known from only one other forest. Fortunately, it is fairly vocal and conspicuous, and so very easy to locate; simply wander around the forest station, listening for its 'cracking whip' call. The woodland on the plateau also supports **Coquerel's Coua**, and the magnificent **Madagascar Crested Ibis**, easier to see here than anywhere else in Madagascar (ask the local guides about possible nests).

With a global population of just over 200 birds, the **Madagascar Fish-Eagle** is even more critically endangered than **Van Dam's Vanga**. Fortunately, a breeding pair nests on Lac Ravelobe at Ⓒ, and is usually conspicuous at the forest edge, and may even be seen soaring overhead. Pairs of **White-throated Rail** are often heard calling from adjacent swampy areas, but birds are otherwise scarce on the lake, although look out for **Madagascar Jacana**.

Madagascar Paradise-Flycatcher

A few pairs of **Schlegel's Asity** breed in taller woodland north of the lake at Ⓓ, accessible by means of a good trail network. Although you may stumble upon this bird while hiking the trails, knowledge of its call (or local guidance) definitely increases your chance of finding this scarce species. **Madagascar Crested Ibis**, **White-breasted Mesite**, **Red-capped Coua** and **Hook-billed Vanga** are other birds to watch for in this area.

OTHER ANIMALS: A variety of Ampijoroa's lemurs are largely restricted to this part of the island, most exciting of which include Coquerel's Sifaka, Mongoose Lemur, and the recently discovered Golden-brown Mouse Lemur.

NEARBY SITES: Lac d'Amboromalandy and its surrounding wetlands merit a few hours' birding on the way back to Mahajanga. The lake provides the most accessible and reliable site in Madagascar for **African Pygmy Goose**, **Humblot's Heron**, **African Openbill**, **Allen's Gallinule** and **Madagascar Jacana**. Stop and scan from the earthen wall (about 15 minutes' drive on the road to Mahajanga), or follow the 2WD track around its north-western edge to the more shallow northern shores.

334 Betsiboka Delta ✔✔

The Betsiboka Delta near Mahajanga is home to another two rare endemics, **Bernier's Teal** and **Madagascar Sacred Ibis**. Charter a motor launch through one of the tourist operators in Mahajanga, and time your visit to coincide with an incoming tide (when the boat can easily negotiate the sand bars in the estuary, and the teals concentrate on remaining areas of exposed mud). Trips in the early morning, before the wind and sea pick up, are more comfortable. Numerous other water birds, including large roosts of terns (notably **Saunders' Tern**), are commonly seen here. **Greater** and **Lesser Flamingos** are both erratic visitors.

335 Kirindy IBA ✔

Although isolated from the main tourist areas, this beautiful dry-forest site, 65 km north-east of Morondava, offers excellent birding and is worthy of further exploration. In addition to being one of the better areas to see **White-breasted Mesite**, **Giant Coua** and **Henst's Goshawk**, it boasts Giant Jumping Rat as one of its mammal attractions. Basic accommodation is available. You can also see **Bernier's Teal** on the salt flats at nearby Bedo. At the village of Beroboka, just north of the Kirindy camp, you can find a guide to take you to Bedo, just to the west.

THE REGION'S TOP 150 BIRDS

This selection of birds for the greater southern African region and the Top 20 for Madagascar (out of 1 400 within the region covered!) represents species that are highly sought-after and which can be difficult to locate without some extra guidance. The list encapsulates a balance between desirability and elusiveness. Each entry discusses the most reliable sites and the most fruitful techniques for finding these birds, and is intended to complement the main text. Birds featured in this list are cross-referenced to it in other parts of the book by means of an asterisk (*).

Wandering Albatross

With the longest wingspan of any bird (in excess of 3.5 metres in some cases), these majestic ocean travellers are able to spend many months on the open sea, effortlessly exploiting updrafts from the waves to stay aloft. They are perhaps best known for their pair bonding display, during which the two birds face each other with wings outstretched and bills pointing skywards. Birds remain paired for life. However, this albatross is under threat, and it is believed that up to 10% of the world population may be lost to longlining each year. As pairs can only raise, at most, one chick every two years, and because it takes 11 years before the offspring is ready to breed, urgent steps must be taken to avert the imminent extinction of this graceful seafarer. Pelagic trips off Cape Town in winter and spring offer the best chance of seeing this species.

Spectacled Petrel

The 'Ringeye', as it is more affectionately known, was only recently recognised as a full species, split from White-chinned Petrel. This taxonomic decision, based largely on the breeding calls, bestows upon it the dubious distinction of being one of the world's most threatened seabirds. Only about 10 000 individuals exist, breeding only on Inaccessible Island in the South Atlantic Ocean. Alarmingly, it is believed that as much as 5% of the population is killed annually by longline fishing off Brazil. The diagnostic white facial crescent separates it from White-chinned Petrel only at close range, and care must thus be taken not to confuse it with occasional White-chinned Petrels that show white patches on the head.

Bank Cormorant

This Benguela coast endemic has suffered a massive population decrease in recent years (only 4 000 breeding pairs remain). It is the only cormorant to build its nest from fresh kelp (seaweed), which it plasters to seaside boulders with its own droppings. Moreover, it is unique among birds in that its extraordinary turquoise eyes change to yellow from top to bottom as it matures, so that some individuals have bizarrely two-toned eyes. Reliable Atlantic Ocean coastal sites include Kommetjie, Bakoven, Stony Point, and up the West Coast.

Kahl/FitzPatrick Inst.

Numbers of Wandering Albatross have declined as a result of long-line fishing.

White-backed Night-Heron
Seeing this uncommon, nocturnal and secretive heron is not made any easier by the fact that it generally lives along remote and inaccessible tropical rivers. It is most often seen during boat cruises along the Okavango River (Namibia), near lodges in the Shakawe area (Botswana) or along the Zambezi River above Victoria Falls. In South Africa, the Keurbooms River (Western Cape), Nahoon River (Eastern Cape), Shongweni Dam (KwaZulu-Natal) and the Kruger National Park (Mpumalanga) have provided regular sightings.

Thomas P. Peschak

Bank Cormorant

Shoebill
Undoubtedly one of the world's most unusual birds, the Shoebill is variously considered a member of the stork, the pelican or its own monotypic family. It has a fragmented distribution, with the bulk of its estimated global total of 10 000 inhabiting Sudan's enormous Sudd Swamps. Smaller populations are restricted to extensive areas of papyrus further south in Uganda, the eastern DRC, Rwanda and northern Zambia. The Bangweulu Swamps provide the only real chance of seeing this mega-bird in southern Africa.

Southern Bald Ibis
Although not as rare as the critically endangered Northern Bald Ibis, this attractive South African endemic still ranks high on most birders' 'global wish list'. The species breeds during the winter, and there are accessible and traditional colonies at Malolotja National Park (Swaziland) and at Golden Gate National Park (Free State). The best sites to see it are Sani Pass in KwaZulu-Natal, around Wakkerstroom in Mpumalanga and Memel in the Free State.

African Pygmy Goose
Arguably the most handsome of the world's three species of 'pygmy goose', this diminutive water bird prefers shallow, often ephemeral, subtropical and tropical wetlands, where small groups blend cryptically into their lily-covered environment. Visitors to Botswana's Okavango Delta are sure to see this bird, with the eastern shores of Lake St Lucia, Mkhuze Game Reserve and, especially, wetlands between Ndumo Game Reserve and Kosi Bay being traditional sites on the South African birding circuit. Good numbers may also be found at Lake Amboromalandy, near Ampijoroa, in Madagascar.

Lammergeier
The Lammergeier is famous for its habit of dropping the bones of dead animals to break them open, exposing the marrow. Although the species is widespread across mountainous regions of Africa and Eurasia, during the 1900s it underwent a catastrophic population decrease due to changing agricultural practices and the poisoning of carcasses. The highly isolated southern African population currently numbers approximately 200 birds, all of which inhabit the rugged Drakensberg area spanning the northern Eastern Cape, western KwaZulu-Natal, Lesotho and the eastern Free State. The Vulture hide at Giant's Castle Game Reserve in KwaZulu-Natal is probably the best-known site, with other reliable sites including Naudesnek (Eastern Cape), Witsieshoek (Free State), the Mafika Lisiu Pass (Lesotho), and Sani Pass (KwaZulu-Natal).

Cape Vulture
Birders touring South Africa would find it worth their while to attempt to see this species at De Hoop NR, despite only about a hundred birds remaining here. It is a common fallacy that this bird is easy to see in the game reserves in the east of the country. In fact, it is difficult to find except in the Drakensberg mountains, in the far Eastern Cape, and in the vicinity of breeding colonies in Limpopo Province. Populations of this species have decreased drastically in South Africa in the past few decades, mainly because of poisoning from stock carcasses laid out by farmers to eradicate 'vermin'.

Bat Hawk
Bizarre, crepuscular and nowhere common, the Bat Hawk is one of the most sought-after raptors in southern Africa. Most twitchers have ticked the species at traditional nesting or feeding sites, e.g. the Pongola River near Ndumo Game Reserve, KwaZulu-Natal, and Magoebaskloof in Mpumalanga. However, birders should be alert for it feeding over any open areas, especially rivers, from Zululand northwards (e.g. at Omaruru and Ruacana, Namibia; Mutare and Mana Pools National Park, Zimbabwe; Liwonde National Park, Malawi; Berenty Private Reserve, Madagascar).

European Honey-Buzzard
Every year, almost a million honey-buzzards pour into Africa from the Palearctic – and seemingly disappear. In recent years, there has been a marked increase in the number of sightings in southern Africa, with good numbers annually at many forest and broad-leaved woodland sites, e.g. Cape Peninsula, Kruger National Park, Caprivi Strip (Namibia) and the Eastern Highlands of Zimbabwe. In the Western Cape, birds have been seen both displaying and in apparent family groups, raising the tantalising possibility of local breeding. Birders searching for the species should familiarise themselves with its subtle identification characteristics.

Ayres' Hawk-Eagle
An uncommon and inconspicuous eagle in southern Africa, where it is usually found soaring above moist woodland north of the Limpopo River (although it is recorded regularly in Pretoria). No dependable sites exist for this rare bird. The best chance of a sighting is while traversing Namibia's Caprivi Strip and adjacent Botswana, and especially miombo woodland in Zimbabwe.

Palm-nut Vulture
Abundant further north in the Afrotropics, this enigmatic, fruit-eating vulture is scarce in South Africa. It is easy to find in KwaZulu-Natal, near Mtunzini village and at Kosi Bay. From Mozambique northwards (e.g. in the Zambezi Delta area), it becomes increasingly common, and around Lake Malawi it is becoming a familiar sight. The species is very common along the Angolan coastline.

Forest Buzzard
Sometimes considered a subspecies of the Mountain Buzzard *Buteo oreophilus*, the Forest Buzzard has recently been treated as a full species, endemic to the Afromontane forests of South Africa. It has adapted well to exotic plantantions and is easily seen in coastal parts of the Western and Eastern Cape, e.g. around Cape Town, Knysna, and the Tsitsikamma area. In the east of the country, the Weza-Ngele Forest, Karkloof and Magoebaskloof areas are productive, especially in winter.

Rufous-chested Sparrowhawk
A scarce bird in the Afromontane forests further north in Africa, the Rufous-chested Sparrowhawk is easy to see around the extensive plantations of alien pines on the Cape Peninsula. A few hours spent in the Tokai or Newlands plantations on the Cape Peninsula should virtually guarantee a sighting of this handsome *Accipiter*. Also look out for this species on the Highlands Route.

Pallid Harrier
Numbers of this Palearctic-breeding migrant raptor have undoubtedly decreased in the last few decades; this elegant species is now an uncommon to rare visitor to open areas in the northern parts of southern

HPH Photography/Photo Access

Palm-nut Vulture

Africa. It may turn up anywhere on migration, although the northern Kruger National Park (Limpopo Province), Makgadikgadi Pans and Chobe National Park (Botswana), and wetlands around Harare (Zimbabwe) have proved productive in recent years.

Black Harrier

This striking harrier is one of five raptor species endemic to southern Africa, the others being Jackal and Forest Buzzards, Cape Vulture and Pale Chanting Goshawk. It ranges widely over scrub and grassland in western South Africa, and is fairly easy to see in the West Coast National Park, near Langebaan, Western Cape. With a population of only 1 500 pairs, Black Harrier is one of the world's rarest raptors and is the subject of a research programme examining its breeding habitat. The Black Harrier is the emblem of the Percy FitzPatrick Institute of African Ornithology, an organisation of international repute based at the University of Cape Town and involved in research on the ecology, evolution and conservation of Africa's birds.

African Hobby

The African Hobby is an uncommon raptor of moist woodlands in the northern part of the region. Breeding records are scattered throughout this range and it is most often seen in summer. Most recent sightings have been in and around the Caprivi Strip, e.g. around Rundu, Mahango Game Reserve, Katima Mulilo (Namibia), western parts of the Okavango Delta, Chobe Game Reserve, and Kasane (Botswana), as well as in Hwange National Park (especially around Main Camp) and near Victoria Falls (Zimbabwe).

Taita Falcon

This stocky falcon, one of Africa's rarest raptors, is restricted to areas of rocky gorges and escarpments from Mpumalanga to southern Ethiopia. It takes its name from the Taita Hills of southern Kenya. The famous and well-watched pairs near Victoria Falls in Zimbabwe have abandoned their traditional nesting area, probably as a result of disturbance from light aircraft, and the most accessible site is now the recently discovered nest at the Strijdom Tunnel in Mpumalanga, South Africa. Visitors to Zimbabwe's eastern

Rufous-chested Sparrowhawk

districts, especially the Haroni area, and south-eastern lowveld, especially near Birchenough Bridge and in Gonarezhou National Park, may also be lucky.

Hartlaub's Spurfowl

This peculiar gamebird, endemic to northern Namibia and southern Angola, favours rocky and scrubby areas along the arid Namibian escarpment. Coveys can occasionally be flushed from the jumbled boulders at the base of granite inselbergs, but the birds are best located at dawn, when pairs duet from prominent outcrops. A pre-dawn clamber up to a high vantage point in the Erongo Mountains near Omaruru or along the escarpment near Ruacana will give you the best chance of a sighting.

Blue Quail

The occurrence of this Afrotropical migrant in southern Africa appears to correlate with years of good summer rainfall, when small numbers may be found in damp grassland and along the edges of wetlands in northern Zimbabwe, e.g. in dambos around Harare and Marondera. Occasionally, birds remain well into the dry season, and recent birding expeditions to the coastal plain of central Mozambique have turned up Blue Quail at wetland edges throughout winter, e.g. at dambos near Rio Savanne and Chiniziua, and *coutadas* at the southern edge of the Zambezi Delta (where fairly common).

Hottentot Buttonquail

Hottentot Buttonquail is a poorly known, yet distinctive species, previously lumped with Black-rumped Buttonquail. It is restricted to fynbos, and occurs only from Cape Town (Western Cape) to Port Elizabeth (Eastern Cape) in South Africa. Previously thought to be very rare, Hottentot Buttonquail has now been found to be quite widespread in mountain fynbos. The Cape of Good Hope Nature Reserve is estimated to hold approximately 300-500 individuals. It is, however, difficult to observe, because most sightings are of birds flushing just in front of one's feet! The males (with streaky, straw-coloured upperparts) are best distinguished from Common Quail by their much smaller size and more fluttering flight, without the short glides often made by the latter. The more richly coloured females are further distinguished by their buffy-orange upperwing coverts. Fynbos adjacent to Arabella Country Estate near Kleinmond and Buchu Bush Camp (p.67) are proving very reliable sites, and it is also occasionally seen at Potberg in the nearby De Hoop Nature Reserve, and on Sir Lowry's Pass. Pictured is the only known photograph of a Hottentot Buttonquail, here on its nest near Cape Town.

Derek Longrigg

Hottentot Buttonquail

Wattled Crane

Not only is the Wattled Crane one of the most spectacular representatives of its family, it is also the rarest of the three southern African crane species. Once widespread in South Africa's mistbelt wetlands, this stately bird's decrease is attributed to a combination of habitat loss, disturbance, winter burning of its nesting sites, and poisoning. It is now one of South Africa's most endangered birds. The best sites for this bird include Namibia's Mahango Game Reserve, Botswana's Okavango Delta and Zambia's Bangweulu Swamps. However, small numbers may be seen around Karkloof and Creighton in KwaZulu-Natal, around Memel in the Free State, and Dullstroom in Mpumalanga.

Striped Crake

Owing to its incredibly skulking nature and irruptive movements, this rallid is certainly overlooked in southern Africa, and may not be as rare as records indicate. It prefers flooded grassy areas on the edge of small, temporary wetlands, and it arrives in the northern parts of our region with the rain, breeds and moves on. The best places to see it are probably Monavale and Marlborough vleis in Harare. It is found ever-increasingly in parts of northern South Africa, northern Namibia and Botswana in small, temporary wetlands with emergent grasses.

Striped Flufftail

The genus *Sarothrura* is represented by nine species of flufftail endemic to the Afrotropics and Madagascar. The far-carrying calls of these skulking 'pygmy-crakes', arguably the most difficult of all birds to see, are frequently heard, often in a tone that seems to add insult to injury! Striped Flufftail is a species of moist fynbos and montane grassland from the Western Cape (particularly at the top of Sir Lowry's Pass) northwards, and is one of the most challenging flufftails of all. Other good sites include Mount Currie (KwaZulu-Natal) and Kaapsehoop (Mpumalanga).

White-winged Flufftail

First collected by the famous naturalist Thomas Ayres at Potchefstroom, South Africa, in 1876, this charismatic bird was not seen in southern Africa for almost 100 years and was presumed to be locally extinct. Following its rediscovery in 1975, populations have been found in highland marshes in KwaZulu-Natal, Free State, Mpumalanga and Ethiopia. The species is still considered endangered, with a global population perhaps as small as 500 birds. The best option for finding a White-winged Flufftail is to join an organised outing by the Middelpunt Wetland Trust near Dullstroom.

It is imperative to keep disturbance of this rarity to a minimum and to respect sites where entering the marsh is strictly forbidden, e.g. at Dullstroom and Wakkerstroom, Mpumalanga.

African Finfoot

Largest of the three finfoot species, the African Finfoot is an uncommon bird of quiet backwaters, and is all the more elusive because of its shy and retiring nature. Although it may be seen by waiting patiently at suitable river bridges in Kruger National Park, e.g. bridges over the Sabie and Crocodile rivers, or walking quietly through known haunts, e.g. KwaZulu-Natal's Enseleni Nature Reserve and Ndumo Game Reserve (North Pongola Walk), the most reliable method of finding it is by boat, e.g. at Albasini Dam in Limpopo, Lake Phobane in KwaZulu-Natal, or along the Zambezi River upstream of Victoria Falls.

Denham's Bustard

The moist grasslands and lowland fynbos of South Africa should be searched for the *stanleyi* subspecies of Denham's Bustard. Particularly reliable sites are the Overberg farmland loops, particularly those east of Bredasdorp and the Bontebok National Park in the Western Cape. The grasslands of KwaZulu-Natal (e.g. Underberg area) and Mpumalanga (Dullstroom) can also be good, as can the Nyika Plateau in Malawi. In spring, displaying males strut around with their heads retracted and white throat pouches inflated.

Peter Pickford/IOA

African Black Oystercatcher

Ludwig's Bustard

This large, endemic bustard is restricted to arid areas, and undertakes seasonal movements, moving into the Succulent Karoo in winter. The best regions to search for the birds are Namaqualand (winter and spring), Bushmanland, anywhere across the Karoo, and the Sesriem and Spitzkoppe areas of Namibia. The birds are most often spotted in the morning or evening, flying to and from their roosts. Many die in collisions with electricity pylons.

Barrow's Korhaan

Unlike its congener, the Blue Korhaan, which frequently strolls about in the open, Barrow's Korhaan prefers areas of taller grass, from which it rarely emerges. Groups often give their position away by their croaking calls, but even then can be very difficult to see, especially during the summer breeding season. The species is most plentiful in the eastern escarpment area between KwaZulu-Natal, north-eastern Free State and south-eastern Mpumalanga, with grasslands around Winterton, in Chelmsford Dam Nature Reserve, Ithala Game Reserve, and near Wakkerstrom being most productive. Northern White-bellied Korhaan, recorded from Angola, Zambia and as a rarity in far northern Namibia, is now regarded as a separate species.

African Black Oystercatcher

Endemic to the Namibian and South African coast, this is one of the world's rarest oystercatchers. In recent years, however, numbers have increased due to better coastal protection and invasion of the shore by an alien mussel, which has improved the birds' food supply. Many of the juveniles born in South Africa migrate north to nursery areas in central and northern Namibia, returning 2-3 years later to where they were born (and never migrating again). It can be readily seen along most of the South African coastline from Lambert's Bay east to East London.

Crab Plover
A bizarre and striking wader, this colonial burrow-nester's mystique is heightened by its rarity on southern African shores. Richards Bay in KwaZulu-Natal is the most reliable South African site for this tropical vagrant, with at least one individual turning up most years. Summer visitors to the Mozambique coast – especially Inhaca and Benguerua islands – are more likely to find the bird. Mangrove swamps and estuaries around Inhambane and Maxixe sometimes support flocks of 200 birds.

Burchell's Courser
This endemic is undoubtedly the most frequently missed special in the Karoo, and its elusiveness is attributable to its nomadic behaviour and low population density; both its numbers and range have decreased dramatically in the last 50 years. In the non-breeding season, large nomadic groups may be seen in almost any open area. While today it is very much associated with arid areas from the Namib to the Karoo, the bird wanders widely, and small numbers move in winter into the higher-rainfall wheatlands of the south-western Cape, especially on the Vredenburg Peninsula, and into the grasslands of eastern South Africa. For the best chance of success, scan grassy plains along the road between Sesriem and Sossusvlei in Namibia, where this species may be found throughout the year.

Three-banded Courser
Despite being locally common, the Three-banded Courser is entirely nocturnal, and is probably the most difficult of the region's coursers to see. It is particularly common in the Middle Zambezi River Valley of Zimbabwe, e.g. around Kariba village, or near Chirundu, where many may be seen on the roads after dark. It is also regular in Zimbabwe's south-eastern lowveld, and in Hwange National Park, where park guards often locate roosting birds while guiding walks around Main Camp.

Rock Pratincole
A bird of the rocky rapids of tropical rivers, Rock Pratincoles are site-faithful, with pairs regularly using the same midstream rocks for nesting during the low water period. A visit to Namibia's Popa Falls National Park, Kasane (Botswana) or Zimbabwe's Victoria Falls between Sept and Feb should give sightings of these swallow-like waders, with noisy groups drawing attention to themselves as they hawk insects above the spray.

Callan Cohen

Antarctic Tern in non-breeding plumage

Greater Sheathbill
This bantam-like bird is a presumed ship-assisted vagrant from southern South America and Antarctica, with most records coming from the vicinity of Cape Town. An average of one bird per year is present each winter on the Cape Peninsula, where it forages along the rocky shoreline. One bird spent the season at the African Penguin colony at Boulders, reminiscent of its typical seabird-colony foraging habits in its natural polar habitat.

The best way to find out if this species is present in Cape Town is to join the e-mail network SA Rare Bird Alert, which will report on any current sightings. To join, you can simply send a blank email to 'sararebirdalert-subscribe'@yahoogroups.com. The only other species of sheathbill in the world, the Lesser Sheathbill, is found on the Prince Edward Islands.

Antarctic Tern
Unlike most of our migrants which are present in summer, this species migrates north to our shores in winter (Apr-Oct) to escape the more severe conditions further south. Day roosts, often mixed with other species of tern, occur at Kommetjie on the Cape Peninsula, Tsaarsbank in the West Coast National Park, rocks south of Paternoster village on the West Coast, and Cape Recife. It may also be seen foraging near the coast

on Cape pelagic trips in winter. While it is not always easy to distinguish at a glance from Common Tern in mixed roosts, the pot-bellied bulky jizz is one reliable character.

Damara Tern

This diminutive breeding endemic's largest colony is at Caution Reef, which lies between Swakopmund and Walvis Bay, Namibia. The Walvis Bay area is undoubtedly the easiest place to see it, although it is uncommon between May and Aug, when most birds migrate north out of the region. The best site in South Africa is the remote De Mond Estuary, near De Hoop Nature Reserve in the Western Cape. One excellent way to spot this bird is to listen for its characteristic call.

African Skimmer

One of three species of skimmers worldwide, the distribution of this Afrotropical migrant along the Zambezi, Okavango and Chobe rivers is largely determined by the presence of suitable sandbars for roosting and nesting. Visitors to these rivers between May and Nov should be rewarded with sightings of these elegant piscivores, though flooding may result in their early departure northwards, with some birds 'oversummering' during drought years. It is readily seen near Mahango (Namibia), Shakawe (Botswana), on boat trips from Kasane (Botswana), and above Victoria Falls (Zimbabwe).

Burchell's Sandgrouse

This near-endemic can be elusive, and is best seen in the Kgalagadi Transfrontier Park. It is only found on red Kalahari sands. The best way to see a Burchell's Sandgrouse is to wait near a waterhole, especially between two and four hours after sunrise. The male soaks his absorbent, water-retaining belly feathers, which will provide moisture for thirsty chicks when he returns to the nest. This species is most reliably found during the dry winter season, when it is more reliant on waterholes.

Eastern Bronze-naped Pigeon

Reasonably common in some evergreen forests, this beautiful pigeon is usually very difficult to see well, its presence most often being revealed by its distinctive hooting call. KwaZulu-Natal's Dhlinza Forest, where there is a canopy walkway, offers the best chance to see birds perched, although scanning over Ngoye and Ntumeni forests at dawn is more reliable for flight views. Zimbabwe's Bvumba and Haroni-Rusitu forests offer reasonable northern alternatives.

Hugh Chittenden

Eastern Bronze-naped Pigeon (female)

Cape Parrot

The Cape Parrot was once widespread throughout the Afromontane forest belt of the Eastern Cape and KwaZulu-Natal. However, a tragic combination of disease, illegal trapping and destruction of its mistbelt forest habitat has brought this handsome South African endemic to the verge of extinction. Now the country's rarest and most endangered endemic, with only about 1 000 remaining, it maintains a precarious foothold in a handful of forests, and is most easily seen in the Hogsback (Eastern Cape), Xumeni Forest (KwaZulu-Natal) and Magoebaskloof (Limpopo) areas. It has been treated as the same species as the Grey-headed Parrot, which occurs in woodland areas in the eastern Limpopo Province.

Rüppell's Parrot
This attractive parrot is an uncommon resident of arid woodland between central Namibia and extreme southern Angola. Although its numbers have undoubtedly decreased due to illegal trapping, this species was probably never very common, even in protected areas. The Waterberg National Park, where a few pairs nest around the Bernabé de la Bat rest camp, is the best site, although the species is also regular at Hobatere and along the Kunene River west of Ruacana.

Black-cheeked Lovebird
This endangered lovebird, with a distribution almost completely restricted to Zambia, is best found in mopane woodland in the Kafue National Park, especially between Dundumwese Gate and the Nanzhila River. Shrill calls draw attention to small flocks of this eye-catching species, especially in the early morning and evening when they fly to water to drink. It was once considered a subspecies of the more widespread Lilian's Lovebird, which does not have a black face, and which occurs in mopane woodland in the Zambezi Valley (such as around Chirundu in Zimbabwe) as well as in Malawi (Liwonde National Park).

Red-crested Turaco
This is the most highly sought-after of Africa's 23 turaco species due to its striking colours and the fact that only a handful of birders have ever seen it. It is only found in forests along the western escarpment of Angola. It is relatively common in forest patches within its range and, like all turacos, may be located by its raucous call, although it can remain remarkably well-concealed in the forest canopy. Red-crested Turaco is the closest relative of Bannerman's Turaco, an endangered species that clings to small forest patches in Cameroon to the north, and is an icon of West African bird conservation.

Ross's Turaco
This gaudily coloured species, with its bright yellow face and bill and red crest, is right on the southern edge of its range in our region. It is best searched for in Zambia, in the Kafue National Park. It is a species of riparian woodland, and the furthest south it has been recorded is the Okavango Delta in Botswana. Despite numerous searches, it hasn't been seen here again, although there are rumours that this tropical species has been seen regularly on islands in the Zambezi River at Kazangula. Birders hoping to find it should be especially alert to its loud calls.

Barred Long-tailed Cuckoo
Another species with appeal enhanced by the inaccessibility of its range, Barred Long-tailed Cuckoo could, for years, be found only in Zimbabwe's Haroni-Rusitu and Middle Zambezi areas. Even here, the species was extremely difficult to see well, calling incessantly from concealed perches high in the canopy. The opening up of the Central Mozambique coastal plain, however, has increased the species' accessibility in southern Africa, with the woodlands around Dondo and Chiniziua being especially reliable.

Slaty Egret
Although localised, the Slaty Egret is fairly common, favouring the shallow margins of well-vegetated tropical wetlands. Mahango Game Reserve (Namibia), almost any wetland area in the Okavango Delta, and the Chobe flood plain near Kasane (Botswana) are the best sites in southern Africa, with the Bangweulu Swamps (Zambia) being a reliable spot north of the Zambezi River. Birds are also regular at Marievale and Nylsvley in South Africa.

Richard du Toit

Rüppell's Parrot

Thick-billed Cuckoo

This uncommon cuckoo is usually only encountered by chance, when flying *Accipiter*-like through broad-leaved woodland. The best way to see this species is to listen for the distinctive calls given by males in early summer, then scan for them in display flight high above the canopy. In South Africa, this species, which parasitises Retz's Helmet-Shrike, is best encountered in riparian woodland along the Limpopo (such as the new Mapungubwe National Park) or Levuvhu (such as at Pafuri in the Kruger National Park, or even further south on the Sabie River) rivers. Woodland near the Lion and Elephant Motel and in Lake Mutirikwe National Park, both near Masvingo, are the best sites in Zimbabwe, while in Mozambique they are regularly seen along the road between Dondo and the Zambezi River.

African Grass-Owl

Although probably fairly common in certain parts of South Africa, African Grass-Owl is not often seen because it roosts in dense vegetation and rarely ventures out until long after dark. Night birding around vleis in Gauteng (such as Elandsvlei) and southern KwaZulu-Natal are the birder's best chance, although the species may also be seen at dusk around marshes anywhere in the eastern half of South Africa.

Cape Eagle-Owl

This large owl is infrequently seen, not only because it is uncommon, but also because it occurs in largely inaccessible mountainous terrain. It is restricted to very rocky areas, where it remains well concealed during the day, and is seldom flushed. Its bark-like hooting calls during the winter breeding season are often the only indication of its presence, and only the fortunate will observe this species on a visit to the region. Its western strongholds are in the Namaqualand mountains, the Cederberg, and Dullstroom in Mpumalanga, while the Drakensberg foothills area in KwaZulu-Natal (e.g. Creighton, Umgeni Valley) can be a most reliable area for it. Populations from Zimbabwe northwards (such as the Matopos Hills) are of the larger *mackinderi* subspecies.

L. Warburton

Black-cheeked Lovebird

Pel's Fishing-Owl

Undoubtedly one of the most charismatic of African birds, Pel's Fishing-Owl ranks high on most birders' 'Global Wish List'. Fortunately, several sites offer opportunities to see this piscivorous 'phantom', notably lodges in Botswana's Okavango Delta (especially the Shakawe area, where the success rate is very high). Other reliable sites include Zimbabwe's Haroni-Rusitu area, Malawi's Liwonde National Park, riparian forests in South Africa's Ndumo Game Reserve, and the lower Mkhuze/Muzi Pans area and northern Kruger National Park. In particular, Ndumo Game Reserve and the Mkhuze/Muzi Pans areas, which have excellent bird guides, offer a high 'hit rate' on this species.

Swamp Nightjar

Although common and widespread further north in Africa, Swamp Nightjar is uncommon and localised in southern Africa. Good sites in KwaZulu-Natal include the coastal grassland between Cape Vidal and St Lucia village – where small numbers of displaying birds may be found on the road at dusk, the Amatikulu Nature Reserve, and the KwaNganase grasslands west of Kosi Bay. In Zimbabwe and Zambia, the Zambezi flood plain west of Victoria Falls and the Bangweulu Swamps respectively are alternative localities.

Pennant-winged Nightjar

Perhaps the world's most spectacular night-bird, the extraordinary Pennant-winged Nightjar is a breeding summer visitor (Oct-Mar) to the north of the southern African subregion. Time spent around the Kruger National Park's Punda Maria camp may reward the birder with sightings of males in spectacular breeding plumage, but better sites exist further north. These include Zimbabwe's south-eastern lowveld, around Harare (especially Mukuvisi Woodlands, where males are often found at their day roosts) and in the Middle Zambezi River Valley. In Namibia, they are fairly common in the eastern Caprivi Strip, and are often plentiful in southern Zambia in broad-leaved woodland.

Böhm's Spinetail

Böhm's Spinetail boasts one of the most unusual silhouettes of any bird, with a strange, erratic flight style reminiscent of a bat, hence its more evocative alternative name of Bat-like Spinetail. Colonies of these almost tailless birds inhabit tree cavities in broad-leaved woodland (favouring baobabs) northwards from Punda Maria in the Kruger National Park, where they are fairly easy to see along the Pafuri River. They are especially numerous in Central Mozambique.

Narina Trogon

The brilliantly coloured Narina Trogon was reputedly named by the French explorer Francois Levaillant in honour of his Khoikhoi consort. It is the most widespread member of a highly sought-after bird family that is poorly represented in Africa. As with most forest-dwelling birds, it is far more often heard than seen; the trogon swoops in quietly to perch in the canopy, usually facing away from the birder, thus turning a cryptic green against the forest canopy. Fortunately, however, it is readily attracted by imitation of its hooting call. Narina Trogon occurs in any sizeable forest patch from Grootvadersbosch in the Western Cape northwards.

Bar-tailed Trogon

One of only three trogons in Africa, this species prefers montane forest and is found in the north of the region. As with many forest dwellers, it is a brightly coloured species that is best located by its call. It has a mewing call that is similar to the Narina Trogon, but the song is quite different: a series of high-pitched hooting notes that get progressively louder. Forests on the Nyika Plateau in Malawi are the best place to see this species.

Mangrove Kingfisher

Owing to its seasonal movements, this handsome bird is rarely encountered on commercial bird tours. The small South African population breeds during the summer in coastal forests along the Eastern Cape's remote Wild Coast, moving north-eastwards between Apr and Sept to overwinter in mangroves along the coasts of KwaZulu-Natal and southern Mozambique. In winter, it can be found without too much difficulty at Durban Bayhead, Mtunzini and St Lucia Estuary. Early morning, just prior to their departure in Sept, is when these birds are especially vocal and conspicuous. It is also common on Inhaca Island, Mozambique, year-round.

Böhm's Bee-eater

A localised endemic to eastern Africa, Böhm's Bee-eater has special significance to southern African birders as one of the marginal mega-rarities that remained tantalisingly out of reach during Mozambique's long civil war. Despite numerous searches since the advent of peace, however, this dashing bird has eluded rediscovery in the southern African subregion, although it has been seen on the north bank of the Zambezi River in Mozambique. The easiest place to find it is definitely along the Shire River at Liwonde National Park in Malawi.

Racket-tailed Roller

Although fairly large and brightly coloured, the Racket-tailed Roller is a surprisingly inconspicuous inhabitant of the broad-leaved woodlands of south-central Africa. Unlike its congeners, the Racket-tailed Roller favours perches below the canopy, so listen carefully for its call. Although small numbers frequent mopane woodland near the Kruger National Park's Punda Maria camp, this attractive species' stronghold lies further north, and the best place to search is in the miombo woodland of the central areas of Mozambique, and in Zambia. The road from Victoria Falls to Kazangulu, in Zimbabwe, is an excellent spot for this bird.

Warwick Tarboton

Ground Woodpecker

Southern Ground-Hornbill

The Southern Ground-Hornbill is one of only two species of this African-endemic family. Its northern counterpart, the Abyssinian Ground-Hornbill, replaces it in the Sahelian savannas. It is an increasingly scarce sight in the woodlands and savannas of eastern and southern Africa. Because of a combination of habitat destruction (it requires large tree cavities for nesting), the use of insecticides, and direct persecution (it is frequently used in traditional African medicine), the species is now rare except in protected areas, although it still occurs in some remote rural regions. South Africa's Kruger National Park and Zimbabwe's Hwange National Park are excellent sites for this stately bird.

Chaplin's Barbet

Zambia's only true endemic, this localised barbet is best searched for by scanning large fig trees. Strikingly white, it is relatively easy to pick out against the foliage. The best area to search for this species is in the Sycamore Fig trees of the Nkanga River Conservation Area in the vicinity of Choma, where it is fairly common.

Green Barbet

The local race of Green Barbet (*woodwardi*) is found only in South Africa's Ngoye Forest and 2 000 km further north on the Ronde Plateau of coastal Tanzania. Its taxonomy has long been debated, but most authorities now consider it conspecific with the nominate race that occupies Afromontane forests of the Eastern Arc Mountains, from southern Malawi northwards through Tanzania. The bird is common in Ngoye Forest, especially the western parts, and is easily located by its frequent and far-carrying call.

Ground Woodpecker

Found in rocky areas, this South African endemic is one of only three ground-dwelling woodpeckers in the world. It breeds in burrows, and feeds almost exclusively on ants. It is found in small groups, which are best located by their harsh, far-carrying calls. The best places to see the Ground Woodpecker in the western half of the country are the Cape Peninsula, Namaqualand, Sir Lowry's Pass, Rooiels, Karoo National Park and Kransvleipoort; in the eastern half of the country, search at Sani Pass, Memel, Lesotho highlands and Wakkerstroom.

Knysna Woodpecker

The world range of this unobtrusive and little-known species is confined to the narrow southern coastal strip of South Africa, extending as far north as southern KwaZulu-Natal. It is fairly common in dense coastal thicket and Afromontane forest, but is challenging to see, because it calls infrequently. The call is a short scream, likened by many to *'Skead!'* in honour of one of the Eastern Cape's great natural historians, CJ Skead. Close to Cape Town, it can be found in the thickets of the De Hoop Nature Reserve and the forests of Grootvadersbosch Nature Reserve and the Garden Route area, but it is most common in the coastal forests of the Eastern Cape (especially the Wild Coast). Oribi Gorge in KwaZulu-Natal is also reliable.

African Pitta

Ask almost any serious birder which bird in southern Africa they would like to see the most, and the answer is invariably African Pitta. Indeed, this dazzling inhabitant of gloomy riverine thickets is displayed on the covers of three southern African field guides!

One of only two African representatives of the pitta family, the African Pitta is rare, secretive, migratory and unpredictable to boot. For years, the only records came from chance encounters in lowland forest along the Zimbabwe/Mozambique border, occasional migrants disorientated by city lights, or overshot vagrants to South Africa. New, relatively predictable sites have been discovered in the middle Zambezi Valley (such as Masoka Camp) in Zimbabwe and Zambia, as well as in central Mozambique, e.g. coutadas (hunting concessions) south of the Zambezi Delta. A visit in mid- to late summer is most likely to be rewarded, although it far from guarantees a sighting, because (unpredictable) rainfall patterns determine its breeding and movements.

African Broadbill

This tiny bird, with its strange circular display flight, is a fairly common but elusive resident of lowland forest from southern KwaZulu-Natal northwards. The fairly open sand forests of Zululand, e.g. at Bonamanzi, Mkhuze and Ndumo game reserves, are the best and most accessible places to see this bird. It may also be seen at Roodewal (Limpopo), in the Haroni-Rusitu area in Zimbabwe, and in the lowland forests of central Mozambique, e.g. Chiniziua.

Melodious Lark

An inhabitant of medium-altitude, fairly arid grasslands, this accomplished songster is best located during early summer, when males give their rich mimicry from perches, or high overhead in a display flight. The best place to find Melodious Lark is in the southern Free State, e.g. along the N1 highway south of Bloemfontein, with other reliable sites including the Bapsfontein routes and Suikerbosrand Nature Reserve in Gauteng, and along the R74 south-east of Winterton and on Ladysmith airfield in KwaZulu-Natal. An isolated population in Zimbabwe is found 30 km south of Chivu on the road to Gutu.

Cape Clapper Lark

This endemic is named for its rapid, wing-clapping display (performed mainly in spring and summer) when the wings are beaten together a remarkable 26 times per second. Birds in the south-western Cape have darker brown upper parts that contrast more with the orange underparts than their eastern grassland counterparts, now split as Eastern Clapper Lark. Recent genetic and vocal work has shown that three species may exist in this complex, i.e. Cape, Agulhas and Eastern Clapper Larks. Cape Clapper Lark is best found on the West Coast, from Silverstroomstrand northwards. An excellent area is the Darling Hills road, and just south of Port Nolloth.

Rudd's Lark

This critically endangered South African endemic has a highly fragmented range in the high-rainfall, high-altitude grasslands of the eastern parts of the country. The core population is situated in eastern Mpumalanga, near Wakkerstroom and Volksrust, although the species may also be found near the top of Matatiele in southern KwaZulu-Natal, and near Memel in the Free State. Summer, especially Oct to Jan, is when males are at their most vocal.

Benguela Long-billed Lark

This is one of the five splits of the Long-billed Lark, and has a descending whistle call, similar to that of the other splits. This species is restricted to north-western Namibia (extending to southern Angola) and there has been some debate about its exact distribution, as it can be confused with the northern subspecies of Karoo Long-billed Lark that also occurs in Namibia. It is best found on the open plains north of the Brandberg, where it is the only species of long-billed lark present. The B35 that runs north of Uis is a good place for this bird.

Johann Grobbelaar

Dusky Lark

During the heat of the day, scan for larks sheltering under small shrubs.

Cape Long-billed Lark
This species is a recent split of Long-billed Lark, with the longest scimitar-like bill of the assemblage. It is restricted to the West Coast, and occurs from Langebaan to Port Nolloth in the Western Cape. It is especially easy to locate in spring, when males regularly perform their looping display flights, launched from roadside fence posts or tall bushes, accompanied by a descending whistle. When not calling, feeding birds can usually be found in stubble fields, often near roadside patches of indigenous scrub. The best places to search for this species are the road from Vredenburg to Paternoster, and the Port Nolloth area.

Short-clawed Lark
This little-known endemic of low acacia savanna has two very isolated populations: one centred in south-eastern Botswana, and the other around the town of Polokwane in Limpopo.

Be sure not to confuse this species with the very similar Sabota Lark, which co-occurs in the same localities. Its aerial display flights, launched from a perch atop a low bush, are accompanied by a whistled call. The most accessible place to find it is the Polokwane Game Reserve, but it may also be reliably found near Pitsane in Botswana (where it prefers heavily overgrazed areas), or just across the border in South Africa in the Botsalano Nature Reserve.

Red Lark
The nest of this little-known bird was only found for the first time as recently as 1986, and it is the only species whose global range is totally restricted to Bushmanland. It is reasonably common in its localised sandy habitat. It occurs in both a red and a brown colour form. However, recent research has shown that these are not sufficiently different from each other to warrant species status. Generally speaking, the rich reddish-backed 'dunes form' occurs on the red dunes in the north-west of the region near Aggenys, while the browner-backed 'plains form' is found in the east of its range (around Brandvlei, for instance). Males engage in conspicuous aerial displays, during which they call frequently.

Dusky Lark
The Dusky Lark is an Afrotropical summer migrant to the northern parts of southern Africa and, although widespread, it is neither common nor predictable in its occurrence. It favours barren ground within arid woodlands, especially mopane, and should be watched for in any open areas in the north. Regular sites include the central part of the Kruger National Park (South Africa), the Halali area in Etosha National Park, the Ruacana area, Mahango Game Reserve, and woodlands around Katima Mulilo in Namibia, and Hwange Game Reserve and the Victoria Falls area in Zimbabwe.

Botha's Lark
Also an endangered endemic lark of the high-altitude grassland in the eastern highveld of South Africa, Botha's Lark is often more challenging to locate than Rudd's Lark, because of its nomadic movements. It favours highly overgrazed areas, e.g. around cattle kraals. Over 90% of all sightings of this species come from roadsides north of Wakkerstroom, although the species can also be seen near Amersfoort in Mpumalanga, and Memel in the Free State.

Sclater's Lark
Largely restricted to Bushmanland and southern Namibia, Sclater's Lark is one of the region's most enigmatic specials. It is unique among local larks in that it lays only one egg. Adults experience huge thermal stress while sitting on the nest, which is sited on exposed rocky plains. Once the egg has hatched, small stones are placed in the nest to camouflage the chick's shape. Although still locally nomadic, artificial stock-watering points on farms must have benefited this species as, conveniently for birders, it needs to drink regularly. The best area to search is Bushmanland in the Northern Cape, such as around the town of Brandvlei, and between Kenhardt and Pofadder.

Gray's Lark
Due to its nomadic nature and cryptic coloration, this fairly common lark can be frustratingly difficult to locate on the Namib Desert's seemingly endless gravel plains. The trick is repeatedly and carefully to scan suitable areas of thinly vegetated desert, as many a birder has turned away in despair,

only to have a cluster of 'pale stones' take off at his feet. The inland race is often plentiful along roads through the Namib-Naukluft Park, and on the plains west of the Spitzkoppe, while the coastal race may often be found along the road south to Rooibank from Walvis Bay, around the Welwitschia Loop in the Namib-Naukluft Park, and along the Trekkopje railway siding, 70 km inland of Swakopmund.

Black-eared Sparrowlark

This is a highly nomadic species that moves around in large numbers in response to rain, often irrupting into areas where grass is seeding. Breeding takes place when conditions are favourable, and males hover, butterfly-like, in display flights. The nest cup, lined with grass and distinctively surrounded by a mix of earth and spider web, is usually built at the base of a small shrub. This species has one of the shortest incubation periods of any bird in the world and, unusually for a lark, sometimes nests in loose colonies. This species occurs widely in the Karoo, and the best areas to check include the Tanqua Karoo National Park, Bushmanland and the southern part of the road between Upington and the Kgalagadi Transfrontier Park.

Blue Swallow

The Blue Swallow has the dubious distinction of being one of South Africa's rarest breeding birds, with a total population of less than 150 individuals, confined to highland grasslands in the KwaZulu-Natal Midlands and Mpumalanga escarpment. A summer visit to any one of the known breeding sites, such as Hella-Hella Pass or Impendle Nature Reserve, KwaZulu-Natal, Kaapsehoop Pass or Mountain Mist, Mpumalanga, or Malalotja National Park, Swaziland, should guarantee sightings of these fast-flying birds. The grasslands around Nyanga in eastern Zimbabwe are also excellent for this species.

Mascarene Martin

Formerly known in the subregion from records near Inhaminga, Mozambique, in 1968, recent ornithological exploration of the Mozambique coastal plain between Beira and the Zambezi Delta has found the Mascarene Martin to be a common winter migrant. While it usually forages low over grasslands or wetlands, e.g. along the Zambezi Delta, flocks also often keep high over woodland areas, e.g. north of Dondo or Chiniziua, when the streaked underparts can be difficult to discern.

Green-headed Oriole

During the long years of civil war in Mozambique, none of the avian specials of the coastal plain were quite as tantalising as the Green-headed Oriole. Peace in the country brought with it the chance to visit Mount Gorongosa, the bird's only haunt south of the Zambezi. Although the trail up the mountain is fairly steep, the species is fairly easy to find once the forest is reached. Mounts Soche and Thyolo provide alternatives beyond in Malawi.

Spotted Creeper

This peculiar bird has an equally unusual global range, with two, widely disjunct populations in broad-leaved woodland in Africa and India. In southern Africa, the Spotted Creeper is most numerous in the northern parts of Zimbabwe's Mashonaland Plateau, e.g. in Mukuvisi Woodland or Lake Chivero, where it favours miombo woodland. Although quick to scramble behind a tree trunk when disturbed, its presence in a mixed-species foraging flock is usually betrayed by its distinctive, wispy call notes.

Spotted Thrush-Babbler

Currently, no well-supported research has revealed the closest relatives of this rather enigmatic species. It resembles a mix between a thrush and an illadopsis (a group of Central African forest babblers), and has beautiful orange-brown spotting on white underparts. Although highly secretive, pairs give a strikingly loud and liquid duet in the understorey, and this draws attention to them. In the region, it can only be found in riparian forests at Mwinilunga in north-western Zambia.

Bare-cheeked Babbler

This group-living bird has a range centred on the arid north-western Namibian escarpment, extending into southern Angola. It is regularly encountered on birding trips through Namibia on account of its predictability at many well-known sites, such as at Etosha National Park's Halali Camp, and the Hobatere and Ruacana areas, where noisy parties favour dry riverbeds and rocky areas in mopane woodland.

Black-faced Babbler

The Black-faced is the most difficult to find of the five species of southern Africa babbler. Preferring dense woodland, it is also scarce, secretive and quiet (for a babbler). Places where it is seen regularly include eastern parts of Etosha National Park, e.g. Dik-Dik Loop near Namutoni, Mokuti Lodge at the edge of Etosha at Namutoni Gate, and the road from Popa Falls (Namibia) to Shakawe (Botswana), but the most reliable site must be Roy's Camp near Grootfontein, Namibia (see p.232).

Bush Blackcap

The Bush Blackcap is a distinctive, taxonomically confusing frugivore, endemic to the eastern escarpment of South Africa and Swaziland, where it is most often found in montane *Leucosidea* (Ouhout) woodland and along the edges of Afromontane forest patches. Traditional sites on regular birding routes include the lower Sani Pass and Giant's Castle Game Reserve in KwaZulu-Natal, although the species can also be found at many other sites between Wakkerstroom (Mpumalanga) and Hogsback in the Eastern Cape.

Black-collared Bulbul

This unusual bird, currently thought to be related to bulbuls but previously allied with shrikes, has for years baffled scientists as to its taxonomic placement. Its most striking feature is its black breast band, reminiscent of a bush-shrike. It has a rather localised distribution in Central Africa, and prefers open woodland habitats. It is best searched for in north-western Zambia at Mwinilunga, especially the Hillwood area.

Spotted Ground-Thrush

The Spotted Ground-Thrush has a patchy distribution through eastern Africa, with many populations undertaking poorly understood altitudinal and latitudinal migrations. The bird can be seen fairly easily at several sites in KwaZulu-Natal, notably Pigeon Valley in Durban (winter only), Mtunzini (winter only) and Dhlinza Forest (year-round, most common in summer). Forests along the Wild Coast (Eastern Cape) are also good for this species. Scratching noises among the leaf litter usually reveal its presence.

Spot-throat

The affinities of this secretive forest species, formerly known as the Spot-throated Modulatrix, have been a source of much debate. It is allied to the Dappled Mountain Robin, and new research suggests that together they may constitute an ancient African endemic family. The Spot-throat has a beautiful call, and is a rather chunky, thrush-like species with a patch of bare skin around the eye. It occurs in the Misuku Hills in far northern Malawi and in the Eastern Arc Mountains of Tanzania.

Dappled Mountain Robin

This is one of Africa's legendary skulkers, resisting all attempts at a clear view in the forest understorey. It is best located by patiently following the distinctive whistled call. In the region, it only occurs on Mount Namuli in northern Mozambique. Resembling a mix between a bulbul and a thrush, the taxonomic affinities are a source of much debate, although it seems allied with the Spot-throat. It is also known as Dapple-throat. Further north, it occurs in just a few forests in Tanzania.

Warwick Tarboton

Bush Blackcap

Angola Cave Chat
This strange bird is the sole member of the genus *Xenocopsychus*, and resembles a mix between a White-throated Robin-chat and a Buff-streaked Chat. It is only known from four sites on the western escarpment of Angola, and pairs may be found on rocky outcrops in grassland above the forest. The rapid and tremulous call resembles that of a robin. Tundevala in the south of Angola is the best site for this bird, but it may also be found above Kumbira Forest near Conda.

Rufous-tailed Palm-Thrush
Rufous-tailed Palm-Thrush is a noisy and common species, found around *Borassus* palms and riparian thickets along the Kunene River in Namibia, from Ruacana westwards. It is also common along the coastal plain in Angola, and occurs in the grounds of Rio Longa Lodge, south of Kissama. A fairly shy bird, it is usually first located by its far-carrying and melodious song.

White-chested Alethe
Reaching the southern limit of its range in central Mozambique, this thrush skulks in the darkest recesses of the forest, and is one of the most difficult of all southern African birds to see well. Currently, it is known from only a handful of sites in Mozambique: Chiniziua, Mount Gorongosa, and *coutadas* south of the Zambezi Delta (the latter is the most reliable site). The Nyika Plateau in Malawi is also a good site for this species.

Thyolo Alethe
This skulking understorey thrush is restricted to just a handful of forests in Malawi and northern Mozambique. Relatively few people have seen this localised species, which is best distinguished from White-chested Alethe by its white-tipped tail. Like many other alethe species, Thyolo Alethe often feeds in association with army ant swarms, catching insects that the ants disturb. The best places to search for this species, initially described from the now-degraded Thyolo Forest near Blantyre, are the Zomba Plateau to the north, and Mount Namuli in Mozambique.

Swynnerton's Robin
Outside the southern African subregion, this forest understorey robin is known from only two disjunct forest areas in Tanzania. There are two local populations, one on Mount Gorongosa, Mozambique, and the other in the Eastern Highlands of Zimbabwe. It is particularly numerous and easily seen around Bvumba in Zimbabwe, e.g. at Seldomseen and the Bvumba Botanical Gardens. The best strategy is to listen for its diagnostic whistle, and patiently scan the forest understorey.

East Coast Akalat
The East Coast Akalat, formerly known as Gunning's Robin, is a locally numerous inhabitant of the understorey of lowland forest from central Mozambique northwards to Kenya. If you wait patiently in suitable habitat, and are alert to its tremulous whistle, you are bound to be rewarded. Well-known sites to see this bird on the Mozambique coastal plain include Chiniziua and Dondo, though it is also numerous on several Zambezi Delta *coutadas*. The forest on the western shore of Lake Malawi near Nkhata Bay is equally productive.

Gabela Akalat
This forest robin's peculiar shape and rictal bristles (around the mouth) led it to be first described, in 1957, as a flycatcher. Very few people have ever seen this akalat, which is only found deep within a few forests along the Angolan escarpment. Not only is it admittedly rather drab and skulking, but its calls are poorly known, making it tricky to locate. The best site is Kumbira Forest near Conda.

Callan Cohen

The little-known Gabela Akalat

Thrush Nightingale
This Palaearctic-breeding migrant is a skulking, uncommon visitor to southern Africa, where it occupies dense thickets, especially along watercourses. Usually present only from mid- to late-summer, these birds are best located by their rich songs. Suitable habitat in the far northern Kruger National Park (near Pafuri), eastern Botswana, e.g. along the Chobe River, and Zimbabwe, e.g. along the Runde, Save and middle Zambezi rivers, usually holds good numbers.

Boulder Chat
Although numerous in some parts of Zimbabwe's central plateau, e.g. Matobo National Park, and Gosho Park in Marondera, the Boulder Chat's retiring nature and specialised habitat of granite outcrops in broad-leaved woodland sometimes frustrate impatient birders. However, territorial groups are fairly easily located when they give their far-carrying, 'squeaky gate' calls. Boulder Chats also occur reliably in Botswana on the road between Francistown and Plumtree, and in Malawi at the Dzalanyama Forest Reserve.

Cape Rock-jumper
This species is endemic to rocky areas in the fynbos-covered Western Cape mountains, primarily at higher altitudes. Although fairly widespread, it is most easily seen at Sir Lowry's Pass, Rooiels, Bain's Kloof Pass, Middelberg Pass east of Citrusdal or, further east, on the Swartberg Pass. The presence of a group is often first revealed by the piping alarm call of the sentinel bird. As you approach the outcrop where they are feeding, you will see the group members disappear between the rocks or move onto the next outcrop in low, gliding flight. The Cape Rock-jumper breeds cooperatively, with helpers (probably related birds) assisting the breeding pair in feeding the young.

Herero Chat
Its scarcity, sombre plumage and inconspicuous behaviour combine to make Herero Chat the least frequently encountered of the Namibian escarpment passerine endemics. Even at well-known sites, such as Spreetshoogte Pass and the Spitzkoppe, the species seems to vary in numbers and visibility, sometimes almost common, at other times highly elusive. Searching at dawn, when its warbling song is most likely to be heard, is the key to finding this rather shrike-like chat.

Olive-tree Warbler
A loud, grating call emanating from dense acacia trees is the first indication of the presence of this summer migrant. It breeds in olive groves in south-east Europe, and migrates south to Africa where the bulk of the wintering range lies in the central parts of southern Africa. It is regularly overlooked and although once believed to be rare, improved knowledge of the call has seen this species regularly recorded across the northern part of South Africa, from the Kruger National Park to Mkhuze in KwaZulu-Natal. It is especially common in Botswana, and Zaagkuildrift in Gauteng is a reliable spot.

River Warbler
Exceptionally shy and elusive in Africa, the River Warbler rarely emerges from dense thickets in moist acacia or broad-leaved woodland. The only real opportunity to see this Palearctic migrant is just prior to its northward migration in Feb and Mar, when males give their scratchy, insect-like songs from thickets at dawn, before falling silent and disappearing for the remainder of the day. Most recent sightings have been from woodland, often with a grassy understorey, across the northern parts of South Africa, from Pretoria to the Kruger National Park. It has also been recorded in eastern Botswana, e.g. at Kasane Forest Reserve, and western Zimbabwe, e.g. along the road between Victoria Falls and Kazungulu. Numbers seem to vary hugely between years.

Knysna Warbler
This localised endemic, which occurs along the south coast of South Africa from Cape Town to the Eastern Cape, is best searched for in the riverine undergrowth of forests and thickets of the eastern slopes of Table Mountain (e.g the Constantia Greenbelts). Other good sites in the Western Cape include Grootvadersbosch Nature Reserve, and the Garden Route. Knysna Warbler is extremely skulking, although its penetrating, descending song makes up for its drab plumage and secretive habits. Its low, rattling contact calls are less obvious, but are useful in locating it. Stealthy and mouse-like,

it spends much of its time feeding on the ground, flicking its wings and tail to disturb arthropods from the leaf litter. Despite occurring in city suburbs, its nest was only discovered as recently as 1960, in the Kirstenbosch National Botanical Garden.

Victorin's Scrub-Warbler

This fynbos endemic is locally common in dense, moist mountain fynbos. The call is reminiscent of that of the Cape Grassbird, but is more repetitive, and, predictably, is the key to seeing the bird. It can be frustratingly skulking, approaching to within a metre or two, but remaining well concealed in streamside thicket. The trick is to look for it in slightly sparser vegetation and to keep very alert to birds darting between denser patches and pausing momentarily before weaving into cover. Often, birds will pop up into clear view once, and then disappear to skulk obstinately thereafter, while continuing to call. Accessible Western Cape sites are Sir Lowry's Pass, Bain's Kloof Pass, Harold Porter Botanical Garden, Grootvadersbosch Nature Reserve, and the Swartberg Pass.

Namuli Apalis

This striking bird is Mozambique's only endemic, restricted to a single mountain in the north of the country. Described from Mount Namuli in 1933, it wasn't seen again for a further 66 years, until its recent rediscovery by a team from the Percy FitzPatrick Institute of African Ornithology at the University of Cape Town. This species is common in remaining forest patches on the mountain, and is best located at the forest edge by the species' typical duetting call.

Chirinda Apalis

Chirinda Apalis is another special of the Eastern Highlands of Zimbabwe, where it inhabits the canopy of mid-altitude and Afromontane forest, favouring vine tangles. Fairly common at many traditional birding sites, including Bvumba Botanical Gardens, it is best located by its frequent song. It may also be encountered on Mount Gorongosa in central Mozambique.

White-winged Apalis

Beauty and rarity combine to make the White-winged Apalis an exceptional bird. Restricted to a handful of remote forests dotted along the mountains of the southern Great Rift Valley, this species is high on many people's 'most wanted' list. Even in their known haunts they are never common. Fortunately, a few pairs survive in the arboretum at the base of Malawi's Zomba Plateau – as accessible a site as one would want for a bird that evokes so much of the excitement of birding in the Afrotropics. It is also found on Thyolo Mountain.

Pulitzer's Longbill

This warbler has the longest bill of the four African members of the genus *Macrosphenus*. It has recently been found at two sites in Angola, after not having been recorded for over 30 years. This species usually forages in pairs in the forest canopy and thickets, and is best located by its distinctive call. The best place to search for it is in secondary forest on the escarpment near the Bango, but it also occurs in the upper reaches of Kumbira Forest near Conda.

Karoo Eremomela

This is a fairly common inhabitant of the Karoo, but can be surprisingly difficult to find. A cooperative breeder, it occurs in small flocks that remain constantly on the move, gleaning rapidly from low bushes before the group moves on. It calls often, and this is the best means of locating this species. The common call, not available on commercial recordings, is a rapid *krrr-krrr-krrr*, rather reminiscent of Spike-heeled Lark. The classic site for these birds is around Eierkop in the Tanqua Karoo, but there are also good sites close to the towns of Brandvlei and Springbok, Northern Cape, and in the Karoo National Park.

Cinnamon-breasted Warbler

A shy and little-known inhabitant of arid, rocky hill slopes, the Cinnamon-breasted Warbler is distinctive enough to have been accorded its own genus. Its behaviour most closely resembles that of a shy and diminutive rock-jumper, bounding across sun-baked boulders and calling loudly, before disappearing for long periods. Skitterykloof in the Tanqua Karoo is undoubtedly the best-known site for this species, but it is reasonably accessible over the whole of Namaqualand, in the Karoo National Park, Augrabies Falls National Park, as well as in the Akkerendam Nature Reserve.

Rockrunner
Despite being rather skulking and cryptically coloured, this Namibian escarpment and southern Angolan endemic is fairly easy to find because of its loud, melodious voice, and habit of sunning itself on exposed rocks. In Namibia, various rocky grassland sites around Windhoek, e.g. Avis Dam and Daan Viljoen Game Reserve, hold good numbers, although the species is perhaps most easily found further north, e.g. the Erongo Mountains near Omaruru, or along the self-guided trails up to the plateau at Waterberg National Park.

Cloud Cisticola
The Cloud Cisticola is best detected in spring when the calling males are visible as distant, almost imperceptible specks fluttering high in the air during their undulating display flight. Good views can often be obtained by waiting patiently until they eventually drop sharply to land in the grass. The southern Cape subspecies is distinct from others further north in South Africa and Zambia, both vocally and by its conspicuously streaked breast, which is an excellent field character to separate it from the otherwise similar Fan-tailed Cisticola. There are several indications that this distinctive subspecies may be a full species. In the Western Cape, it is best found in grassy

Callan Cohen

Pulitzer's Longbill, an Angolan endemic

and agricultural lands, especially the Tienie Versveld and Oudepos Wildflower Reserves and the Overberg wheatlands of the south coast. In the central part of the country it can be found on the N1 south of Bloemfontein and in Gauteng grasslands.

Tinkling Cisticola
Although widely distributed in the subregion, Tinkling Cisticola frequently slips through the international visitor's 'birding net'. It favours the scrubby understorey of broad-leaved woodland, especially on Kalahari sands, being most common in remote parts of southern Botswana. Accessible sites on regular birding routes include Seringveld (Gauteng), Nylsvley (Limpopo Province), Mahango Game Reserve and Caprivi Strip woodlands in Namibia, the western Okavango and woodlands south of Kasane, Botswana, and Hwange Game Reserve, Zimbabwe.

Roberts' Warbler
One of the last species of southern African birds to be described to science (in 1946), Roberts' Warbler is a localised endemic of Zimbabwe's Eastern Highlands and adjacent Mozambique. Small parties are noisy and conspicuous among rank, scrubby vegetation along forest edges, including edges of pine plantations. It is most readily seen around Bvumba and Nyanga in eastern Zimbabwe.

Namaqua Warbler
Formerly classified as a prinia, this species has recently been assigned its own genus, *Phragmacia*, appropriately named after its habitat of mixed *Phragmites* reeds and acacia thicket. It is a much more secretive bird than the similar Karoo Prinia, but every bit as noisy. The closest place to Cape Town to see Namaqua Warbler is Karoopoort. It is also abundant along the Orange River reedbeds (such as those at Upington), in Augrabies Falls National Park, in the camp site at the Karoo National Park, at the Shell service station in Calvinia, and in thickets around Leeu-Gamka and Three Sisters on the N1 between Cape Town and Johannesburg.

Black-and-white Flycatcher
The Black-and-white Flycatcher is fairly widespread on the Mozambique coastal

plain, its range extending into eastern Zimbabwe at the Haroni-Rusitu confluence. Locating this vanga-like bird means listening for its far-carrying call or watching for it bouncing high above the canopy of lowland forest, near the Vimba Forest along the Haroni River, around the base of Mount Gorongosa, near Chiniziua, or on the Zambezi Delta *coutadas*.

Yellow-bellied Wattle-eye

The sight of this species' bright yellow and orange plumage in the gloomy forest understorey always comes as a surprise to birders. It is most famous for occurring in Kenya's Kakamega Forest, and few birders realise that this gem may be found in the southern third of Africa, where it is relatively common at Kumbira Forest in Angola. Listen out for its high-pitched song and buzzy alarm calls, and scan the understorey at about eye level for the best chance of this species.

Livingstone's Flycatcher

Livingstone's Flycatcher is found in lowland areas between southern Mozambique and southern Tanzania, extending westwards along the Zambezi River to Victoria Falls. Small parties forage actively in a variety of woodland habitats, primarily in the canopy, and are easily located by their frequent calls. It is fairly common at many sites in the Middle Zambezi River Valley, e.g. Masoka Camp, Zimbabwe, on the Mozambique coastal plain south of the Zambezi Delta, as well as in southern Malawi in Liwonde National Park.

African Rock Pipit

This poorly known endemic is confined to South Africa's mountainous interior. It is an inconspicuous species, best detected by its call, a descending whistle quite different from that of other pipits. The greenish-yellow edging on the bird's folded wing, optimistically exaggerated in some field guides, is not a good field character. Rather concentrate on its very distinctive call, largely unstreaked plumage, and conspicuous supercilium to distinguish it from the Long-billed Pipit, which favours similarly rocky habitats. Good places to search for it are the Karoo National Park, Sani Pass and Wakkerstroom.

Short-tailed Pipit

An elusive and nomadic bird of medium-altitude, moist grassland in the eastern parts of southern Africa, the Short-tailed Pipit's movements are poorly understood. Undoubtedly it is frequently overlooked due to its cryptic plumage and habits: it flushes late and usually flies far, looking like a cross between a female widowbird and a medium-sized cisticola, before landing abruptly and darting into dense cover. The Short-tailed Pipit is most often encountered on its presumed wintering grounds in short coastal grasslands, e.g. Hluhluwe airstrip, and grasslands south of Sodwana Bay, in KwaZulu-Natal. It has also been found to be common in winter in grasslands north of Beira in Mozambique, e.g. around Savane and near the Zambezi Delta, and is an irregular breeder in Vernon Crookes Nature Reserve and Giant's Castle Game Reserve in KwaZulu-Natal, and in Doornkop, Mpumalanga.

Yellow-breasted Pipit

This uncommon, localised endemic of South Africa's eastern escarpment areas favours lush, sub-montane grasslands for breeding, descending to lower-altitude, drier grasslands during winter. Most birders find the Yellow-breasted Pipit near Wakkerstroom or Dullstroom in Mpumalanga, although it can also be seen on Naudesnek Pass (in the Eastern Cape), Matatiele Mountain (where

Callan Cohen

Yellow-bellied Wattle-eye

common) and Giant's Castle Game Reserve in KwaZulu-Natal, and around Memel in the Free State.

Rosy-breasted Longclaw

The Rosy-breasted Longclaw is a bird of damp grasslands and flooded margins of tropical wetlands. In South Africa, such habitat is only found on the Zululand coastal plain in KwaZulu-Natal, where accessible sites include the Greater St Lucia Wetland Park (especially the Hluhluwe River flood plain and Nibela Peninsula), Baya Camp at Lake Sibaya, and the KwaNgwanase grasslands west of Manguzi village. The species is considerably more numerous in parts of Zimbabwe's Mashonaland Plateau, e.g Marlborough grasslands in Harare, and on the Mozambique coastal plain.

Souza's Shrike

The global range of this enigmatic shrike is centred on the broad-leaved woodlands of south-central Africa, although it has been recorded in Namibia's Caprivi Strip, around Rundu, and near the Omega settlement east of Bagani Bridge. Malawi and Zambia are the most reliable countries in which to see it. Dzalanyama Forest Reserve, west of Lilongwe, is the most accessible and reliable site in Malawi, although even here the bird is elusive, spending much of the time perched quietly in the sub-canopy.

Southern Tchagra

This endemic, skulking member of the bush-shrike family is conspicuous in spring, when the males perform aerial displays accompanied by a descending call. Also, listen out for harsh alarm calls in its dense thicket habitats. The best place to see this species is De Hoop Nature Reserve in the Western Cape, and at any coastal sites in the Eastern Cape, although it may also be found in localised patches northwards to Mpumalanga.

Anchieta's Tchagra

Recently split from the Marsh Tchagra of Central Africa, Anchieta's Tchagra is restricted to rank, marshy vegetation from central Mozambique north to southern Tanzania. The most accessible site in southern Africa is at Wamba Marsh near Aberfoyle Tea Estate in Zimbabwe's Honde Valley, where the tiny

Johann Grobbelaar

Anchieta's Tchagra

remaining population is threatened by habitat destruction. There are also small numbers on the coastal plain of central Mozambique, e.g. near Dondo, and at the base of Mount Gorongosa.

Black-fronted Bush-Shrike

The Black-fronted Bush-Shrike inhabits the canopies of highland forests from Kenya south to northern Limpopo. Like most bush-shrikes, it is usually first located by its ringing call. The forests around Magoebaskloof in Mpumalanga provide the most accessible South African site, although the species is more common in the Eastern Highlands of Zimbabwe, e.g. the Bvumba area.

Chestnut-fronted Helmet-Shrike

Formerly accessible and reliable only near the Haroni-Rusitu confluence in Zimbabwe, with political change the Chestnut-fronted Helmet-Shrike has become much easier to see in southern Africa. It is the most common of the three helmet-shrike species on the lowland plain of central Mozambique, and is conspicuous around Dondo, at Chiniziua, and on the *coutadas* south of the Zambezi Delta. Vagrants occur south as far as Ndumo Game Reserve in KwaZulu-Natal.

White-winged Babbling Starling

Family groups of this species are best searched for in miombo woodland in northern Malawi, where they forage on the ground, only flying up into the trees and calling when alarmed. The closest relatives of this unique species, which are presumed to be starlings, are not known, and in fact they even superficially resemble helmet-shrikes as they move quickly through the trees. Vwaza Marsh Nature Reserve is the best place to search for this social species, and it can also be seen in miombo along the access road to Nyika from Rumphi.

Sharp-tailed Starling

Few birders have seen this south-central African woodland endemic at the same site twice, a reflection of its scarcity and apparent nomadism. Time spent in broad-leaved woodland along Namibia's 'Golden Highway' between Rundu and Katima Mulilo, especially between Bagani and Kongola, should yield sightings of small parties, although they are never guaranteed. The remote Kaudom Nature Reserve in northern Namibia is the best site, but visitors need to be in a convoy of at least two 4WD vehicles.

Cape Sugarbird

There are just two species of sugarbird, together constituting one of southern Africa's two endemic bird families. Their puzzling evolutionary relationships continue to perplex scientists, with conflicting evidence variously suggesting relationships with the starlings, the sunbirds, Australian honey-eaters, and most recently even the Dappled Mountain Robin and Spot-throat! The Cape Sugarbird is easily seen, conspicuous in distinctive silhouette, as it perches on the flower heads of the protea bushes that are a major element of fynbos vegetation. Local sugarbird populations fluctuate markedly over the years, with birds ranging up to 150 km in search of flowering protea bushes. Nonetheless, sugarbird-bedecked flowering proteas are found year-round in the Kirstenbosch National Botanical Garden. Other good sites are the Cape of Good Hope Nature Reserve, Sir Lowry's Pass and the Swartberg Pass, all in the Western Cape.

Gurney's Sugarbird

Gurney's Sugarbird favours highland areas between the Eastern Cape and eastern Zimbabwe, feeding primarily in stands of proteas and aloes (both wild and cultivated). Like its southern congener, it is

Nico Myburgh

Cape Sugarbird

often conspicuous, with males surveying their territories from exposed perches. Despite local movements in response to flowering of food plants, Gurney's Sugarbird can be reliably found year-round at sites on traditional birding routes, including Sani Pass and Giant's Castle Game Reserve in KwaZulu-Natal, and in the Bvumba area in Zimbabwe.

Shelley's Sunbird

This elusive sunbird is nowhere common, and relatively few southern African birders have ever seen it. For many years, it was included on the southern African list on the basis of a single nineteenth-century specimen taken 'along the Zambezi River'. A century later, regular sightings in the Mana Pools National Park have confirmed the species' occurrence in Zimbabwe. It is also regularly seen at Kalizo Lodge in the Caprivi Strip near Katima Mulilo. Shelley's Sunbird may also be found in miombo woodland in Malawi, e.g. at Dzalanyama, and in Zambia.

Neergaard's Sunbird

This small sunbird has an extremely restricted world range, being confined to southern Africa's eastern coastal plain between about Richards Bay, Zululand (KwaZulu-Natal), and Inhambane, southern Mozambique. Even within this range, it is confined to patches of fairly dry forest. The sand forest areas within False Bay Park (Greater St Lucia Wetland Park), Mkhuze Game Reserve (especially near Kubube hide) and, especially, Ndumo and Tembe game reserves, are the best places to search for this scarce endemic.

Olive-headed Weaver

This canopy-foraging weaver frequently joins mixed-species flocks in miombo woodland. The nest, constructed from old-man's-beard lichens, is one of the most camouflaged of any bird species. Formerly recorded from central Mozambique, the only recent records of this unusual woodland weaver south of the Zambezi are from near Panda, in southern Mozambique. Dzalanyama Forest Reserve in Malawi is also a reliable site.

Bar winged Weaver

This unique weaver more closely resembles a nuthatch as it clambers on the mossy branches of *Brachystegia trees*. It is endemic to Zambia and Angola, and is best found in mixed-species foraging flocks in miombo woodland. The typical hanging weaver nest is constructed from old man's-beard lichens, like that of the Olive-headed Weaver. The best place to search for this species is the Mutinondo Wilderness Area in Zambia, but it can also be found in the Mwinilunga district.

Cuckoo Finch

Although widely distributed throughout the moist grasslands of eastern southern Africa, the Cuckoo Finch is rarely encountered due to its scarcity and highly nomadic nature. Primarily an unpredictable summer visitor to South Africa, it should be watched for around Gauteng, e.g. wetlands near Pretoria, Suikerbosrand Nature Reserve, around Dullstroom (Mpumalanga), and at Nylsvley (Limpopo Province). In Zimbabwe, however, the species is more readily found, especially in vleis around Harare, where flocks sometimes number tens of hundreds.

Red-headed Quelea

In South Africa, this quelea is an uncommon, localised breeding migrant to KwaZulu-Natal, with males in breeding plumage present at traditional sites from late Sept through to early Feb. The easiest place to find the species is Darvill Resources Park in Pietermaritzburg, where good numbers have bred annually since 1983, although small colonies are present at numerous other wetlands in the KwaZulu-Natal Midlands, including Cedara Agricultural College. Flocks are also regular at Umvoti River Mouth, Richards Bay, and Ndumo Game Reserve, KwaZulu-Natal. It may also be seen at Kasane in Botswana.

Green Twinspot

Despite being common in eastern parts of southern Africa, the Green Twinspot has been the 'bogey bird' of many a birder. An inhabitant of coastal and Afromontane forest, dense bushveld, secondary growth and exotic plantations (seemingly favouring *Casuarina* groves), this bird is, however, relatively easily found once one is familiar with its exceptionally high-pitched calls. Good sites include Oribi Gorge Nature Reserve, Dhlinza Forest, Richards Bay and Cape Vidal (KwaZulu-Natal), Magoebaskloof and the Soutpansberg (Limpopo Province), and the Haroni Forest in Zimbabwe.

Tony Camacho

Gurney's Sugarbird

Red-faced Crimsonwing

A flash of crimson is often all that one sees of these tiny seed-eaters as they dart through the gloomy undergrowth of Afromontane forests. An ear for their high-pitched calls and patient stalking are usually required for even a half-decent view. South of the Zambezi, this southernmost of the world's four crimsonwings is restricted to Mozambique's Mount Gorongosa and the adjacent Eastern Highlands of Zimbabwe. Nowhere easy to find, they are best sought around Seldomseen and in the Bvumba Botanical Gardens. In Malawi, the species seems easier to see, e.g. at the forest edge around the camp site on top of the Zomba Plateau.

Lesser Seedcracker

The Lesser Seedcracker is confined to secondary growth (including overgrown cultivation) and rank vegetation at forest edges on the central Mozambique coastal plain, (e.g. Dondo and the Zambezi Delta area), extending marginally into extreme south-eastern Zimbabwe (e.g. the Haroni-Rusitu area and Honde Valley), and northwards through Malawi (e.g. Chinteche area) to southern Tanzania. Wamba Marsh, near Aberfoyle in the Honde Valley, Zimbabwe, is the most reliable site.

Pink-throated Twinspot

The Pink-throated Twinspot is endemic to the coastal plain of northern Zululand and southern Mozambique. It is relatively common and easily located at several accessible birding locales, especially once its quiet, tinkling calls are recognised. Parties are plentiful in Ndumo Game Reserve and frequent in thickets around Mantuma Camp and along entrance tracks to the sand forest hides in Mkhuze Game Reserve in KwaZulu-Natal.

Callan Cohen

Cape Siskin

Cinderella Waxbill

This elegant waxbill is the 'special' most frequently missed by birders visiting Ruacana in Namibia. Small parties are best searched for in the vegetated watercourses that lead off the escarpment above the Hippo Pools camp site in Ruacana, or further west near the Kunene River Lodge. However, this species is never common, and is usually only tracked down after hot and lengthy hikes along mostly dry watercourses in the hills adjoining the Kunene River. The 4-note call is surprisingly far-carrying.

Locustfinch

The uncommon and elusive Locustfinch has its distribution centred on the wetlands and damp dambo grasslands of the miombo belt of Zambia and Malawi, extending into southern Africa in northern Zimbabwe and central Mozambique. Although small numbers can usually be found at sites around Harare, the species seems more numerous at sites on the Mozambique coastal plain, such as Rio Savane.

Magpie Mannikin

Magpie Mannikin is a rare and localised species restricted to the eastern parts of southern Africa, from southern KwaZulu-Natal northwards. It is nomadic in response to food supply, and in most areas its occurrence is highly erratic, although small numbers are resident near Southport in southern KwaZulu-Natal, and in the Harare area in Zimbabwe. It is also widespread on the Mozambique coastal plain, e.g. around the base of Mount Gorongosa and the Zambezi Delta, and even on the outskirts of Maputo, as well as in eastern Zimbabwe, e.g. the Haroni-Rusitu area and the Honde Valley.

Zambezi Indigobird

This recently described species, formerly lumped with Black Indigobird, is the brood parasite of Red-throated Twinspot. It is fairly common in the range of its host, especially in central Mozambique and the Middle Zambezi River Valley of Zimbabwe, and the Burma Valley road near Bvumba. It is best identified by a combination of its call (which mimics the twinspot's) and the obvious green gloss of the male when seen in direct sunlight.

Lemon-breasted Canary

One of the last South African birds to be described to science, the Lemon-breasted Canary was discovered as recently as 1960. It is found in low-lying areas from northern KwaZulu-Natal to Gonarezhou National Park in Zimbabwe. Perhaps the best area to search for it is Bonamanzi Game Reserve near Hluhluwe, KwaZulu-Natal. Check the vicinity of all lala palms in this area, as well as beside the drive along the railway line from Hluhluwe. The bird occurs across the northern areas of Zululand, such as on the Nibela Peninsula in the Greater St Lucia Wetland Park. Another good area for this species is Crooks' Corner at Pafuri in the far northern Kruger National Park. Beware of confusion with the very similar Yellow-fronted Canary, which occurs in the same areas.

Cape Siskin

One of the more tricky fynbos endemics to find during a short visit, the Cape Siskin is nonetheless often a common bird of open, rocky fynbos, usually wind-blown and not conducive to good views of a small, mobile seed eater. They are usually detected as they give their distinctive trisyllabic flight call before disappearing over a ridge in small, nervous flocks. The male's white-tipped wings and tail are good field characters. Some of the best sites for this bird include the Cape of Good Hope Nature Reserve, Jonkersdam and Silvermine on the Cape Peninsula, Harold Porter Botanical Garden, and Swartberg Pass.

Black-headed Canary

This highly nomadic, often gregarious canary, endemic to the western parts of southern Africa, can be surprisingly difficult to find. Although widespread in arid regions, it is most common in rocky areas, especially where there are seeding grasses. It is best picked up by its high-pitched flight call, similar to that of Cape Canary, or by waiting near suitable drinking points.

Protea Seed-eater

The Protea Seed-eater is regarded as one of the most elusive of the fynbos endemics. It is, however, quite common in several of the more remote mountainous areas of the Western Cape, such as the Cederberg Wilderness Area. For visitors without the time to venture too far off the beaten track, the best areas to search for it are Kransvlei-poort, Paarl Mountain, and the Swartberg Pass. Although inconspicuous, it draws attention to itself by its distinctive song. Despite its name, it is by no means restricted to protea stands; in fact, in many areas it appears to be more common in tall, non-protea vegetation along streamsides.

Nico Myburgh

Protea Seed-eater can be remarkably elusive.

MADAGASCAR'S TOP 20 BIRDS

Madagascar Crested Ibis
With perseverance and the help of local guides, this strikingly handsome terrestrial ibis can usually be located at the traditional rainforest sites in Ranomafana National Park and, especially, around Andasibe. The key to seeing this bird is to scan the forest edges along streams and clearings, although all too often birders are rewarded with nothing more than a flash of rufous and white as the birds flush from the gloomy forest floor. The more open deciduous forest at Ampijoroa provides an even better chance, with small groups often seen on the wide paths at dawn and dusk.

Bernier's Teal
The endangered Bernier's Teal is known from remote freshwater and brackish lakes, and mangrove-fringed mudflats in the western reaches of Madagascar, where it undergoes poorly understood seasonal movements. This small duck had been seen by only a handful of ornithologists prior to November 1999, when some 120 birds were seen feeding on exposed mudflats in the Betsiboka Delta. A visit by motorboat takes about three hours, and can be arranged with tour operators in Mahajanga.

Madagascar Serpent-Eagle
Large, spectacular, rare, secretive, endemic, and 'lost for 50 years', the Madagascar Serpent-Eagle is one of Madagascar's most difficult 'ticks'. Lowland forest on the Masoala Peninsula, especially around the Peregrine Fund's camp at Andranobe, offers the best chance of seeing this fantastic raptor (even here it can be very difficult to locate), although recently there have also been a number of sightings in Mantadia, Analamazoatra and Ranomafana National Parks. The trumpeting call is often the only indication of the species' presence.

Nick Garbutt/Indri Images

Subdesert Mesite

Sakalava Rail
Although not the most prepossessing of Malagasy rallids, this Black Crake lookalike is certainly the least recorded. Until recently known from just three, widely separated western wetlands, Sakalava Rail is currently considered critically endangered. This seldom-encountered bird has been seen regularly at the remote Lake Kinkony on the north-west coast, where it is recorded on floating vegetation at the edge of reedbeds.

Slender-billed Flufftail
Flufftails are reputedly among the most difficult of all birds to see, and Slender-billed Flufftail is no exception. The species is currently known only from a few, scattered highland marshes in eastern Madagascar, the most accessible of which is the so-called 'Haunted House Marsh' near Vohiparara (though this is under extreme pressure from drainage for rice paddies and may no longer exist). Torotorofotsy Marsh, a 15 km walk along the railway line from Andasibe, is probably the best site to look for this critically endangered rallid.

Madagascar Wood Rail
Forest rails are generally a skulking bunch and this handsome bird is no exception. It may be seen, but is far more commonly heard, at all the main rainforest birding sites. Birds in Analamazoatra and Ranomafana seem especially retiring (possibly due to over-use of tape playback), while rails in Mantadia National Park and, particularly, Masoala National Park are more easily seen. Unlike all other rails in southern Africa, this species does not occur in wetlands, but forages on the forest floor, often near small streams.

Subdesert Mesite

Another of Madagascar's taxonomic enigmas, the Subdesert Mesite – one of three species that comprise the endemic mesite family – looks like a cross between a rail and a thrasher. The Subdesert Mesite is probably the most endangered of the three threatened species, owing to the rapid, ongoing degradation of its spiny forest habitat. The bird is traditionally seen at Itafy with local guides using their skills to track them through the thorny thickets. Elsewhere in the spiny forest, birders should also be able to locate groups by means of their rollicking dawn choruses.

Madagascar Red Owl

Recently rediscovered and undoubtedly rare, this owl is probably often overlooked, as it usually roosts in dense vegetation during the day and only emerges under cover of night to feed. It has been spotted on the Masoala Peninsula, and local guides at Ambanizana may just know of a day roost. The only other known locality is Mantadia National Park (ask local guides about sightings), although recent reports of a cave-roosting individual in the remote Ankarana Massif and one observation in Station des Roussettes in the Montagne d'Ambre National Park should prompt birders to watch for this species everywhere on the island.

Collared Nightjar

Most night birds are located by their calls, but Collared Nightjar is an exception, being one of only a handful of the world's nightjars for which the call is undescribed. Fortunately for birders, local guides at Andasibe are excellent at locating this handsome endemic at its nest or day roost, usually near the bases of Pandanus palms around Lac Vert in Analamazoatra. The species is also regularly encountered on night walks along the road in Mantadia National Park, and near Vohiparara in Ranomafana National Park.

Short-legged Ground-Roller

The largest, least terrestrial and most stout of the five ground-roller species, Short-legged Ground-Roller is usually found perched motionless in the sub-canopy of mid-altitude eastern rainforest. Like other members of this secretive family, its strange, frog-like breeding call is invariably the first indication of its presence. Small numbers occur along the road in Mantadia National Park, in remote parts of Analamazaotra Special Reserve, and in the primary forest at Ranomafana National Park, though even here considerable patience and effort is required to track it down. November is the best month to search for this species.

Nick Garbutt/Indri Images

The cryptic Collared Nightjar roosting on the forest floor

Scaly Ground-Roller

This skulking forest-dweller is often erroneously believed to be confined to lowland forest in eastern Madagascar. In fact, while this bird is definitely most numerous at lower altitudes, for example on the Masoala Peninsula, it is also present in mid-altitude forest, such as that found at Ranomafana and Mantadia national parks. Indeed, all four of Madagascar's rainforest ground-rollers can be found at Mantadia, which has become the traditional site for bird tours to find this secretive bird – a few pairs may be found in the vicinity of 'Km 14'.

Rufous-headed Ground-Roller

The smallest member of the family, Rufous-headed Ground-Roller is a predominantly terrestrial species that prefers the deep, damp leaf litter of montane forests. Though never numerous, it may be reliably found at a number of sites on the traditional birding route, such as Analamazoatra Special Reserve (uncommon), Mantadia National Park and Maromizaha in the Andasibe area, and near Vohiparara in Ranomafana National Park, where it seems especially common. As with other ground-rollers, this species is secretive and is only likely to be located by its territorial calls.

Long-tailed Ground-Roller

The only ground-roller to occur outside of eastern rainforests, this globally endangered species is restricted to taller deciduous dry forest in the extreme south-western corner of Madagascar. Although this species may be found throughout the narrow belt of spiny forest north of Toliara, almost every birder's first sighting of Long-tailed Ground-Roller is near the beach resort of Ifaty, where local guides have become adept at locating this species. The guides even follow the birds' tracks in the sand (!), and without their assistance many a birder has spent long, hot hours scouring the sandy tracks in vain.

Madagascar Cuckoo-Roller

Although fairly common and widespread, occupying habitats ranging from montane rainforest to spiny desert, this is undoubtedly one of Madagascar's most sought-after avian residents. The noisy aerial display flights of the males often attract attention at rainforests throughout the east, although the best chance of locating a perched bird is in the more open western deciduous forests, especially Zombitse National Park and Ampijoroa Forest Station.

Schlegel's Asity

The jewel-like Schlegel's Asity is often considered the most attractive of the marvellous endemic sub-family of asities. Seen in good light, the combination of the male's brilliant yellow underparts and apple-green and turquoise eye caruncles is indeed a magnificent sight. Although fairly widespread in the evergreen forest of the Sambirano (north-west Madagascar), most birders tend to see it at the more accessible Ampijoroa Forest

Nick Garbutt/Indri Images

Rufous-headed Ground-Roller is the smallest member of its family.

Station, specifically in the tall forest to the north of Lake Ravelobe.

Yellow-bellied Sunbird-Asity

Although Schlegel's may arguably be the more beautiful asity, Yellow-bellied is certainly the rarest of the four asity species. Restricted to montane forest in the east, this diminutive bird seems to favour the fairly short, stunted forest that grows along exposed ridges. The only reliable accessible site is at Vohiparara in Ranomafana National Park, although it is also known from the remote Marojejy Reserve (records from Maromizaha near Andasibe require confirmation).

Dusky Greenbul

This enigmatic greenbul is one of the least recorded of all the eastern forest endemics. It inhabits the understorey of lowland and mid-altitude forest between Marojejy Reserve in the north and Ranomafana National Park in the south. Dusky Greenbul may thus be found at any rainforest site below 1 000 m, but beware of confusion with both Spectacled Greenbul and the extremely similar juvenile White-throated Oxylabes. It has also been recorded from Analamazaoatra and the Masoala Peninsula.

Brown Emutail

The Brown Emutail is a peculiar denizen of mid-altitude and montane forest in the east, especially favouring dense vegetation along ridge tops. Although fairly common in places, for example, Maromizaha near Andasibe, and Vohiparara in Ranomafana National Park, it can be devilishly difficult to see, even though it is often heard singing from a concealed perch deep in the foliage. The trick is to creep inside the thicket and coax the singer closer with discriminate use of tape playback.

Red-tailed Newtonia

Essentially restricted to lowland forest, the uncommon Red-tailed Newtonia is only recorded with any regularity in the newly proclaimed Andohahela National Park near Tolagnaro. Like other members of its genus, it is vocal and is best located, and identified, by its distinctive call. Although also reported from the Masoala Peninsula and in lower altitude forest around Andasibe, the species seems rare here.

Nick Garbutt/Indri Images

Helmet Vanga

Bernier's Vanga

Bernier's Vanga appears to be one of the few Malagasy birds almost restricted to lowland forest. All recent records are from the northern part of the eastern rainforest belt, although even here the species is uncommon and local. Lowland forest on the Masoala Peninsula is the only site where this vanga is found with any regularity, usually in mixed-species flocks, although a visit to the remote Mananara National Park or Marojejy Reserve may well also yield sightings. Also seen recently in Mantadia and Analamazaotra

Helmet Vanga

Surely one of the most fabulous of all Madagascar's avian treasures, the Helmet Vanga is a bird unlike any other on Earth. Although recorded (very rarely) from Mantadia National Park, the only realistic chance of seeing this magnificent creature is on the Masoala Peninsula. Fairly common near Ambanizana, especially around Andranobe, where birders are likely to stumble upon it during the course of two days' birding. Its calls are virtually indistinguishable from those of Rufous Vanga, with which it sometimes associates in mixed-species foraging flocks.

Nuthatch Vanga

Surely one of the most remarkable examples of convergent evolution seen among birds, the Nuthatch Vanga (or Coral-billed Nuthatch, as it's sometimes known) has a wide distribution in the eastern rainforest belt. However, it is only numerous in the north, and is best sought among mixed flocks of vangas around Andasibe (Analamazoatra, and Mantadia National Park) and on the Masoala Peninsula.

USEFUL CONTACTS

Symbols for useful contacts ☎ within the text are cross-referenced to this list. Numbers on the left of each column refer to page numbers in the book.

INTRODUCTION

13 BirdLife South Africa: Tel: +27 (0) 11 794 1122; www.birdlife.org.za

13 Avian Demography Unit and SAFRING: www.aviandemography.org

13 Birding Africa: www.birdingafrica.com

14 African bird taxonomy: www.birdingafrica.com

23 Cape Town Pelagics: Cell:+27 (0) 83 256 0491; www.capetownpelagics.com

25 Extra maps: sabfmap@birdingafrica.com

ROUTES 1-7: WESTERN SOUTH AFRICA

27 Cape Birding Route: Tel: +27 (0) 21 685 4081; Cell: +27 (0) 83 256 0491; sabf@capebirdingroute.org; www.capebirdingroute.org

31 CBR raptor: raptors@capebirdingroute.org

38 Rondevlei boat trips: www.imvubu.co.za

39 Sir Lowry's Pass: permits@capebirdingroute.org

40 Dick Dent, John Carter: carts@iafrica.com

42 See **27** above

51 Cerebos: permits@capebirdingroute.org

55-67 Cape Birding Route: info@capebirdingroute.org

69 Honeywood Guest Farm: www.honeywoodfarm.co.za

73 Keurboom River Ferries: www.ferry.co.za

82 Diepvlei Guest Farm: info@capebirdingroute.org

93 Kimberley Bird Guides Association: info@capebirdingroute.org

93 Marrick Game Farm: www.marrick-safari.com

97 Vendutiekop Guest Farm: Tel: +27 051732, ask for 1412

ROUTES 8-17 EASTERN SOUTH AFRICA

105 Gonubie key, BirdLife Eastern Cape: www.birdlife.org.za

110 Cremorne Estate: Tel: +27 (0) 47 501 2812; clodge@wildcoast.biz

110 Barred Owlet: callan@birdingafrica.com

113 Magpie Mannikins, Tony at Turaco Concrete Products: Tel: +27 (0) 39 681 3363

115 Matatiele, Mr Whittell: Tel: +27 (0) 39 737 3170; www.mehloding.co.za

117 Malcolm Gemmel: Tel: +27 (0) 39 833 1029 (H); 118 Impendle Nature Reserve; Tel: +27 (0) 33 996 9613; Hbuttonbirding@futurenet.co.za

124 Jex Estate: Tel: +27 (0) 32 559 9562

126 KZN Wildlife, Midmar office: Tel: +27 (0) 33 330 2067

129 Benvie, John & Jenny Robinson: Tel: +27 (0) 33 502 9090

129 Highover: Tel: +27 (0) 11 442 7262; hella@mweb.co.za

130, 134, 135 Zululand Birding Route: Tel: +27 (0) 35 753 5644; richardsbay@birdlife.org.za; www.zbr.co.za

131 Eshowe B&B: Tel: +27 (0) 35 474 2276; chits@intekom.co.za

140 Bonamanzi: www.bonamanzi.co.za

141 Hluhluwe River Lodge: www.hluhluwe.co.za

144 See **130** above

147 Tembe Elephant Lodge: www.tembe.co.za

154 BLSA Wakkerstroom office: www.birdlife.org.za

156 Mahem Country House: Tel: +27 (0) 58 924 0400; info@memelgetaways.co.za; www.memelgetaways.co.za

159 Bearded Vulture hide: www.kznwildlife.com

164 Elandsvlei, Pretoria branch of BirdLife South Africa: Tel: +27 (0) 11 789 1122; Peter Barnes, BirdLife Northern Gauteng: Tel: +27 (0) 11 733 1086

165 Marietjie Wolmarans: Tel: +27 (0) 12 545 0055/6 (O/H)

167 Buffelsdrift birding: Cell: +27 (0) 82 393 8870

167 Birding information in Dinokeng and Seringveld, Etienne Marais: Cell: +27 (0) 82 898 6998 or Pete Irons: Tel: +27 (0) 12 808 5432

169 Wolfhuiskraal or to stay at the bushcamp, Danie and Rinette Opperman: Tel: +27 (0) 12 722 0212

171 Middelpunt Wetland Trust: PO Box 78908, Sandton, 2146; Tel: +27 (0) 11 884 2739 or Malcolm Drummond: Cell: +27 (0) 82 551 2919; malcolmd@metroweb.co.za

172 Mount Sheba: www.mountsheba.co.za

175 Edward Themba: Cell: +27 (0) 72 340 5588

176 Misty Mountains: www.mistymountain.co.za

177 Chrissiesmeer, Ané Steinberg: Cell: +27 (0) 82 804 1771 or Aretha Strijdom: Cell: +27 (0) 82 821 3081

177 Doornkop Reserve manager: Tel: +27 (0) 17 843 2444

178 Mahushe Shongwe Nature Reserve: Tel: +27 (0) 13 759 5432

180 Waterberg Birding & Raptor Group: Tel: +27 (0) 14 755 4062

180 Sericea, Warwick Tarboton: Tel: +27 (0) 14 743 1438

183 Blouberg: Tel: +27 (0) 15 593 0702

183 Langjan: Tel: +27 (0) 15 593 0129

185 Dave Letsoala for up-to-date information: Cell: +27 (0) 83 568 4678

186 Kurisa Moya, Ben or Lisa: Tel: +27 (0) 15 276 1131; Cell: +27 (0) 82 200 4596; info@krm.co.za

188 Soutpansberg, Limpopo birding route: www.limpopobirding.com/

188 Shiluvan Lakeside Lodge: Tel: +27 (0) 15 556 3406

189 Soutpansberg, Limpopo birding route: Cell: +27 (0) 82 785 0305; http://www.limpopobirding.com/

189 http://www.pafuri.co.za/

190 Soutpansberg, Limpopo birding route: http://www.limpopobirding.com/

190 Mopane Bush Lodge: http://www.mopanebushlodge.co.za/inleft.htm
190 Ratho Bush Camp: Tel: +27 (0) 15 575 1362 www.parks-sa.co.za
200 Vaalkop Dam Nature Reserve: Cell: +27 (0) 83 316 4445
201 For all these reserves, back-up contact is the North-west Parks Board: www.parksnorthwest.co.za
207 Molopo: Tel: +27 053922, ask for Vorstershoop 1722; Cell: +27 (0) 82 873 8780

ROUTES 18-21 NAMIBIA

216 Walvis, Keith Wearne: Tel: +264 (0) 64 205 057
217 Sandwich Harbour, Turnstone Tours: Tel: +264 (0) 64 403 290; turn@iafrica.com.na
220 Erongo Wilderness Lodge: eronwild@iafrica.com.na
224 Hobatere Lodge: hobatere@mweb.co.na
225 Ruacana Lodge: Tel: +264 (0) 65 270 031
226 Kunene River Lodge (5 km east of Swartbooi's Drift): Tel: +264 (0) 65 274 300; Fax: +264 (0) 65 274 301; kunener1@mweb.com.na
230 Tandala Ridge: http://www.tandalaridge.com/
232 Roy's Camp: Tel/Fax: +264 (0)67 240 302; royscamp@iway.na
233 Mark Paxton: Tel: +264 (0)66 256 179; Fax: +264 (0)66 258 297; shamvura@iway.na
238 Shakawe: PO Box 12, Shakawe, Botswana; Tel: +267 660 822/3; Fax: +267 660 493; t.wild@info.bw
238 Drotsky's: drotskys@info.bw
241 Kalizo Lodge: http://namplaces.com/kalizo/index.htm

ROUTES 22-24 BOTSWANA

BirdLife Botswana: www.birdlifebotswana.org.bw

ROUTES 25-28 ZIMBABWE

264 Crake Cottage, Dorothy Wakeling: piumosso@zol.co.zw
266 270 BirdLife Zimbabwe: birds@zol.co.zw
274 Katiyo Tea Estate (Aberfoyle Club): Tel: +263 28 384/5/7; Fax: +263 28 240
274 Aberfoyle Lodge: aberfoyle@aloe.co.zw
275 Kiledo Lodge: Kelly@orbit-travel.co.zw
275 Seldomseen, David or Angela: Tel: +263 20 68482; mhumhe@zol.co.zw
275 Ndundu: info@ndundu.com
277 Campfire (Haroni-Rusitu) CAMPFIRE Association: campfire@ecoweb.co.zw
282 Twitchers Lodge, Darryl Tiran: ecolynx@zol.co.zw
288 MASOKA, Charl Grobelar: cgsafari@samara.co.zw; see also **277** above

ROUTES 29-31 MOZAMBIQUE

304 P Gibsob B&B: bridgetg@senasugar.com
306 Mozambique Atlas Project: http://web.uct.ac.za/depts/stats/adu/p_mozat.htm
311 IDPPF, Vincent Parker: vinparker@yahoo.com

ROUTES 32-33 MALAWI

314 Satemwa, Thyolo: Satemwa Estate, PO Box 15, Thyolo; Tel: +265 (0)1 472 256; Fax: +265 (0)1 473 368; www.satemwa.com
317 Zomba Forest Lodge, Land & Lake Safaris: Tel: +265 (0)1 757 120 or +265; (0)1 754 393; Fax: +265 (0)1 754 560; landlake@africa-online.net; www.landlake.net
318 Liwonde, Central African Wilderness Safaris: Tel: +265 (0)1 771 393; Fax: +265 (0)1 771 397; info@wilderness.mw; www.wilderness-safaris-malawi.com
323 Lake & Land Safaris: Tel: +265 (0)1 757 120 or +265 (0)1 754 303; Fax: +265 (0)1 754 560; landlake@africa-online.net
325, 330 (Vwaza) Nyika Safari Company: www.nyika.com

ROUTES 34-35 ZAMBIA

333 Zambian Ornithological Society: PO Box 33944, Lusaka 10101; zos@zamnet.zm; http://www.wattledcrane.com/
336 Nansai Farm/Nkanga River Conservation Area: Tel: +260 (0) 32 20592; nansai@zamnet.zm
341 Nchila Wildlife Reserve: nchila@nchila-wildlife-reserve.com
344 Chimfunshi Wildlife Orphanage: www.chimfunshi.org.za
346 Forest Inn: www.forestinn-zambia.com
347 Kasanka Campsite: park@kasanka.com
349 Shoebill Island Camp, Kasanka: park@kasanka.com
349 Kasanka Trust: park@kasanka.com
351 Mutinondo: 2mwl@bushmail.net
352 Kapishya Lodge: 2mark@bushmail.net
352 Shiwa Safaris: http://www.shiwasafaris.com/
355 Kapani Camp, Norman Carr Safaris: kapani@super-hub.com

ROUTE 36 ANGOLA

356 Birding Africa: info@birdingafrica.com; www.birdingafrica.com;
358 Rio Longa: riolonga@iway.na

ROUTES 37-39 MADAGASCAR

368 Relais du Masoala/Motel Coco Beach: Tel: + 261 (0) 57 72006; relais@simicro.mg

CHECKLIST

This checklist to birds is arranged in traditional order and is based largely on the taxonomy and bird names used in *Birds of Africa south of the Sahara* (Struik, 2002) and *Birds of the Indian Ocean Islands* (Struik, 2003). Birds are grouped by family (identified by the blue bars); **families** endemic to any part of the region covered in this book are printed in white text within the blue bar.

A tick box is followed by the bird's common name (where relevant, old and alternate names appear in brackets), its scientific name, and the page numbers on which you will find it. Three further columns provide key information on distribution, endemism and status as follows:

In column headed Reg (for regularity):
blank = bird occurs in the traditional southern African region
B = bird occurs within the greater southern African region (cf p.8) but not in the traditional region
M = bird occurs in Madagascar only

In column headed End (for endemism):
E = species is endemic to region in which it occurs
NE = species is near-endemic to region in which it occurs

In the column headed Vag (for Vagrancy status):
blank = nothing special about bird's status
1 = rare vagrant to the region
2 = considered extinct
3 = introduced
M = vagrant to Madagascar

Further information is provided as follows:
Birds' names in red text denote Madagascan birds
Birds' names in green text indicate occurrence in the greater southern African region (cf page 8) but not in the traditional SA region
Birds' names in bolded text denote endemic or near endemic birds.

NOTE: This list is comprehensive for the traditional southern African region and largely for the greater southern African region; Angolan birds only appear in the table if they are mentioned in the book.

	Common Name	Scientific name	Page numbers	Reg	End	Vag
	Struthionidae	**Ostrich**				
❑	Common Ostrich	Struthio camelus	34, 48, 66, 84, 195, 211, 212, 227, 228			
	Spheniscidae	**Penguins**				
❑	King Penguin	Aptenodytes patagonicus				1
❑	Gentoo Penguin	Pygoscelis papua				1
❑	Little Penguin	Eudyptula minor				1
❑	**African (Jackass) Penguin**	**Spheniscus demersus**	18, 26, 27, 35, 38, 41, 53, 94, 104, 217		E	
❑	Magellanic Penguin	Spheniscus magellanicus				1
❑	Rockhopper Penguin	Eudyptes chrysocome				1
❑	Macaroni Penguin	Eudyptes chrysolophus				1

	Common Name	Scientific name	Page numbers	Reg	End	Vag
	Podicipedidae	**Grebes**				
❑	Great Crested Grebe	Podiceps cristatus	33, 37, 54, 66, 153, 162, 217, 218, 248			
❑	Black-necked (Eared) Grebe	Podiceps nigricollis	35, 36, 37, 51, 77, 93, 104, 105, 153, 164, 205, 214, 217, 229, 248, 254, 285			
❑	Little Grebe (Dabchick)	Tachybaptus ruficollis	45, 153			
❑	**Madagascar Little Grebe**	**Tachybaptus pelzelnii**	364, 365	M	E	
❑	**Alaotra Little Grebe**	**Tachybaptus rufolavatus**	19, 362	M	E	2
	Diomedeidae	**Albatrosses**				
❑	Southern Royal Albatross	Diomedea epomophora	23			1
❑	Northern Royal Albatross	Diomedea sanfordi	20, 21			1
❑	Wandering Albatross	Diomedea exulans	20, 21, 22, 378			
❑	Tristan (Wandering) Albatross	Diomedea dabbenena				1
❑	Shy Albatross	Thalassarche cauta	20, 21, 22			
❑	Salvin's (Shy) Albatross	Thalassarche salvini				1
❑	Chatham Albatross	Thalassarche eremita				1
❑	Laysan Albatross	Phoebastria immutabilis	23			1
❑	Black-browed Albatross	Thalassarche melanophris	20, 21, 22			
❑	Grey-headed Albatross	Thalassarche chrysostoma	20, 21, 22			1
❑	Atlantic Yellow-nosed Albatross	Thalassarche chlororhynchos	20, 21, 22			
❑	Indian Yellow-nosed Albatross	Thalassarche carteri	20			
❑	Buller's Albatross	Thalassarche bulleri	23			1
❑	Dark-mantled Sooty Albatross	Phoebetria fusca	23			1
❑	Light-mantled Sooty Albatross	Phoebetria palpebrata	23			1
	Procellariidae	**Shearwaters and Petrels**				
❑	Southern Giant-Petrel	Macronectes giganteus	20, 21, 22			
❑	Northern Giant-Petrel	Macronectes halli	20, 21, 22			
❑	Southern (Antarctic) Fulmar	Fulmarus glacialoides	20, 21			
❑	Antarctic Petrel	Thalassoica antarctica	23			1
❑	Pintado (Cape) Petrel	Daption capense	20, 21, 23			
❑	Bulwer's Petrel	Bulweria bulwerii				1
❑	Jouanin's Petrel	Bulweria fallax				1
❑	Great-winged Petrel	Pterodroma macroptera	20, 21			
❑	Barau's Petrel	Pterodroma baraui		M		M
❑	Soft-plumaged Petrel	Pterodroma mollis	20, 21, 22			
❑	White-headed Petrel	Pterodroma lessonii	22, 23			1
❑	Atlantic Petrel	Pterodroma incerta	23			1
❑	Kerguelen Petrel	Aphodroma brevirostris	23			1
❑	Blue Petrel	Halobaena caerulea	23			1
❑	Broad-billed Prion	Pachyptila vittata				1

	Common Name	Scientific name	Page numbers	Reg	End	Vag
❑	Antarctic Prion	Pachyptila desolata	20, 21, 22			
❑	Salvin's Prion	Pachyptila salvini				1
❑	Slender-billed Prion	Pachyptila belcheri	23			
❑	Fairy Prion	Pachyptila turtur	23			1
❑	White-chinned Petrel	Procellaria aequinoctialis	20, 21, 22, 23, 50, 217			
❑	Spectacled Petrel	Procellaria conspicillata	20, 21, 378			
❑	Grey Petrel	Procellaria cinerea	23			1
❑	Cory's Shearwater	Calonectris diomedea	21, 22			
❑	Streaked Shearwater	Calonectris leucomelas	22			1
❑	Great Shearwater	Puffinus gravis	20, 21, 22			
❑	Flesh-footed Shearwater	Puffinus carneipes	20, 21, 22			
❑	Sooty Shearwater	Puffinus griseus	20, 21, 22, 217			
❑	Manx Shearwater	Puffinus puffinus	20, 21			
❑	Balearic Shearwater	Puffinus mauretanicus				1
❑	Little Shearwater	Puffinus assimilis	23			
❑	Audubon's Shearwater	Puffinus lherminieri	22			
❑	Wedge-tailed Shearwater	Puffinus pacificus	22			
	Hydrobatidae	**Storm-Petrels**				
❑	European (British) Storm-Petrel	Hydrobates pelagicus	20, 21			
❑	Leach's Storm-Petrel	Oceanodroma leucorhoa	20, 21			
❑	Matsudaira's Storm-Petrel	Oceanodroma matsudairae	22			1
❑	Wilson's Storm-Petrel	Oceanites oceanicus	20, 21, 22, 23			
❑	White-faced Storm-Petrel	Pelagodroma marina				1
❑	White-bellied Storm-Petrel	Fregetta grallaria	22, 23			1
❑	Black-bellied Storm-Petrel	Fregetta tropica	20, 21, 22			
	Phaethontidae	**Tropicbirds**				
❑	Red-billed Tropicbird	Phaethon aethereus				1
❑	Red-tailed Tropicbird	Phaethon rubricauda	22, 23, 373			
❑	White-tailed Tropicbird	Phaethon lepturus				1
	Pelecanidae	**Pelicans**				
❑	Great White Pelican	Pelecanus onocrotalus	35, 37, 45, 51, 52, 54, 95, 121, 136, 137,141, 142, 216, 249, 254, 293, 301			
❑	Pink-backed Pelican	Pelecanus rufescens	121, 135, 136, 137, 142, 144, 248, 249, 301			
	Sulidae	**Gannets and Boobies**				
❑	Red-footed Booby	Sula sula	23, 297			
❑	Brown Booby	Sula leucogaster	22			1
❑	Masked Booby	Sula dactylatra		M		1
❑	**Cape Gannet**	**Morus capensis**	18, 20, 21, 22, 44, 50, 53, 54, 104, 217		NE	
❑	Australian Gannet	Morus serrator	54			1

	Common Name	Scientific name	Page numbers	Reg	End	Vag
	Phalacrocoracidae	**Cormorants**				
☐	White-breasted Cormorant	Phalacrocorax lucidus	32, 34, 37, 41, 50			
☐	**Cape Cormorant**	**Phalacrocorax capensis**	18, 22, 32, 34, 35, 37, 38, 41, 50, 53, 217, 218		E	
☐	**Bank Cormorant**	**Phalacrocorax neglectus**	18, 27, 32, 38, 41, 47, 85, 217, 378		E	
☐	Reed (Long-tailed) Cormorant	Phalacrocorax africanus				
☐	**Crowned Cormorant**	**Phalacrocorax coronatus**	18, 32, 34, 35, 38, 41, 47, 50, 53, 85, 217		E	
	Anhingidae	**Darters**				
☐	African Darter	Anhinga rufa	38, 45, 81, 166			
	Fregatidae	**Frigatebirds**				
☐	Greater Frigatebird	Fregata minor	22, 121, 137, 302			
☐	Lesser Frigatebird	Fregata ariel	297			1
	Ardeidae	**Herons, Egrets and Bitterns**				
☐	Grey Heron	Ardea cinerea	121			
☐	Black-headed Heron	Ardea melanocephala				
☐	**Humblot's (Madagascar) Heron**	**Ardea humbloti**	19, 373, 375, 377	M	E	
☐	Goliath Heron	Ardea goliath	54, 104, 121, 131, 135, 137, 141, 142, 144, 146, 162, 166, 168, 193, 200, 206, 237, 254, 289, 319, 350			
☐	Purple Heron	Ardea purpurea	38, 52, 54, 72, 121, 154, 184, 214, 217			
☐	Great (White) Egret	Egretta alba	169			
☐	Little Blue Heron	Egretta caerulea	34, 51			1
☐	Snowy Egret	Egretta thula				1
☐	Little Egret	Egretta garzetta	34, 45, 52			
☐	Western Reef Heron	Egretta gularis				1
☐	Dimorphic (Mascarene) Egret	Egretta dimorpha		M		
☐	Yellow-billed (Intermediate) Egret	Egretta intermedia	33, 45, 72, 154, 232			
☐	Black Heron (Egret)	Egretta ardesiaca	144, 146, 162, 163, 168, 180, 237, 239, 254, 260, 289, 319, 336, 350			
☐	**Slaty Egret**	**Egretta vinaceigula**	18, 146, 161, 162, 163, 164, 179, 180, 181, 231, 232, 233, 236, 237, 238, 239, 240, 241, 242, 243, 256, 257, 258, 259, 260, 269, 283, 335, 336, 340, 350, 386		E	
☐	Cattle Egret	Bubulcus ibis				
☐	Squacco Heron	Ardeola ralloides	147, 169, 226, 236, 260, 296, 301, 336			
☐	Madagascar Pond (Squacco) Heron	Ardeola idae	296, 297, 301, 304, 307, 364, 376			1
☐	Green-backed (Striated) Heron	Butorides striatus	193, 196, 200, 201			
☐	Rufous-bellied Heron	Ardeola rufiventris	146, 147, 180, 181, 190, 233, 238, 239, 240, 241, 242, 257, 258, 259, 260, 282, 287, 297, 302, 319, 320			
☐	Black-crowned Night-Heron	Nycticorax nycticorax	38, 43			
☐	White-backed Night-Heron	Gorsachius leuconotus	18, 73, 103, 124, 132, 136, 138, 178, 187, 188, 190, 195, 198, 199, 201, 203, 231, 235, 236, 237, 238, 239, 240, 241, 242, 256, 259, 260, 280, 281, 282, 318, 319, 322, 335, 338, 379			
☐	Little Bittern	Ixobrychus minutus	38, 42, 43, 54, 99, 102, 106, 135, 149, 154, 157, 162, 232			
☐	Dwarf Bittern	Ixobrychus sturmii	142, 168, 179, 180, 181, 184, 202, 233, 234, 236, 239, 240, 243, 295, 301, 304, 308, 319, 320, 336, 337, 355			
☐	Eurasian Bittern	Botaurus stellaris	115, 147, 149, 169, 181, 293, 295, 301, 349			

	Common Name	Scientific name	Page numbers	Reg	End	Vag
	Scopidae	**Hamerkop**				
❑	Hamerkop	Scopus umbretta	364			
	Ciconiidae	**Storks**				
❑	White Stork	Ciconia ciconia	65, 95, 126, 261			
❑	Black Stork	Ciconia nigra	91, 117, 123, 124, 129, 139, 151, 157, 158, 159, 160, 177, 178, 247, 335			
❑	Abdim's Stork	Ciconia abdimii	91, 261			
❑	Woolly-necked Stork	Ciconia episcopus	121, 131, 133, 135, 137, 142, 143, 146, 188, 260			
❑	African Openbill (Open-billed Stork)	Anastomus lamelligerus	143, 144, 146, 190, 197, 237, 241, 254, 260, 289, 296, 301, 319, 336, 373, 377			
❑	Saddle-billed Stork	Ephippiorhynchus senegalensis	137, 146, 190, 191, 197, 237, 254, 260, 296, 301, 304, 338, 350			
❑	Marabou Stork	Leptoptilos crumeniferus	254, 258, 260			
❑	Yellow-billed Stork	Mycteria ibis	137, 141, 142, 143, 146, 169, 190, 229, 254, 260, 350, 355			
	Balaenicipididae	**Shoebill**				
❑	Shoebill	Balaeniceps rex	332, 344, 345, 348, 349, 350, 379	B		
	Threskiornithidae	**Ibises and Spoonbills**				
❑	African Sacred Ibis	Threskiornis aethiopicus	121			
❑	**Madagascar Sacred Ibis**	**Threskiornis bernieri**	375, 377	M	NE	
❑	**Southern Bald Ibis**	**Geronticus calvus**	18, 111, 116, 117, 128, 132, 138, 148, 149, 150, 151, 152, 155, 156, 157, 158, 159, 160, 170, 171, 176, 177, 184, 379		E	
❑	**Madagascar Crested Ibis**	**Lophotibis cristata**	364, 365, 376, 377, 404	M	E	
❑	Glossy Ibis	Plegadis falcinellus	45, 146, 156, 336			
❑	Hadeda Ibis	Bostrychia hagedash				
❑	African Spoonbill	Platalea alba	38, 50, 52, 95, 121			
	Phoenicopteridae	**Flamingoes**				
❑	Greater Flamingo	Phoenicopterus ruber	37, 51, 52, 53, 54, 56, 77, 85, 93, 105, 161, 190, 216, 229, 232, 248, 254, 377			
❑	Lesser Flamingo	Phoenicopterus minor	51, 52, 54, 93, 190, 216, 229, 232, 248, 254, 377			
	Anatidae	**Ducks and Geese**				
❑	White-faced Duck	Dendrocygna viduata	43, 121, 180, 336			
❑	Fulvous Duck	Dendrocygna bicolor	137, 146, 240, 248, 260, 336			
❑	White-backed Duck	Thalassornis leuconotus	45, 69, 128, 135, 137, 144, 147, 164, 166, 168, 177, 180, 190, 236, 240, 248, 258, 259, 268, 295, 296, 320, 347			
❑	Egyptian Goose	Alopochen aegyptiacus	121, 336			
❑	**South African Shelduck**	**Tadorna cana**	37, 49, 51, 53, 54, 56, 58, 62, 63, 77, 85, 95, 105, 121, 128, 149, 154, 164, 205, 214, 215, 229		E	
❑	Mallard	Anas platyrhynchos				3
❑	Yellow-billed Duck	Anas undulata	36, 45, 121			
❑	**Meller's Duck**	**Anas melleri**	19, 364, 366, 368	M	E	
❑	African Black Duck	Anas sparsa	41, 42, 43, 68, 92, 96, 114, 123, 124, 129, 156, 157, 160, 166, 169, 176, 248, 322, 351			
❑	Cape Teal	Anas capensis	36, 37, 51, 53, 105, 162, 164, 248, 254			
❑	**Bernier's (Madagascar) Teal**	**Anas bernieri**	19, 375, 377, 404	M	E	
❑	Hottentot Teal	Anas hottentota	37, 38, 102, 162, 236, 240, 248, 254, 258, 347, 350			
❑	Red-billed Teal	Anas erythrorhyncha	36, 53, 214, 229, 232, 248, 254, 258, 336			

	Common Name	Scientific name	Page numbers	Reg	End	Vag
❑	Northern Pintail	Anas acuta				1
❑	Garganey	Anas querquedula				1
❑	Northern Shoveler	Anas clypeata				1
❑	**Cape Shoveler**	**Anas smithii**	36, 45, 128, 162, 164, 217, 229, 254		E	
❑	Southern Pochard	Netta erythrophthalma	36, 43, 153, 162, 166, 232, 248, 258			
❑	Tufted Duck	Aythya fuligula		B		1
❑	**Madagascar Pochard**	**Aythya innotata**	19, 362	M	E	2
❑	African Pygmy-Goose	Nettapus auritus	134, 135, 137, 140, 141, 143, 144, 146, 147, 168, 180, 190, 233, 236, 238, 241, 242, 257, 258, 259, 268, 292, 293, 295, 296, 297, 320, 347, 377, 379			
❑	Comb (Knob-billed) Duck	Sarkidiornis melanotos	144, 146, 166, 168, 206, 258, 260, 374			
❑	Spur-winged Goose	Plectropterus gambensis	121, 336			
❑	Maccoa Duck	Oxyura maccoa	35, 36, 37, 42, 43, 85, 127, 128, 153, 215, 217, 245, 248, 285			
	Sagittariidae	**Secretarybird**				
❑	Secretarybird	Sagittarius serpentarius	47, 65, 66, 68, 88, 89, 98, 109, 117, 126, 128, 139, 149, 158, 166, 168, 172, 173, 184, 195, 198, 203, 228, 230, 253, 255, 336			
	Accipitridae	**Hawks, Eagles and Kites**				
❑	Lammergeier (Bearded Vulture)	Gypaetus barbatus	107, 111, 116, 117, 150, 157, 158, 159, 160, 379			
❑	Egyptian Vulture	Neophron percnopterus	101, 110, 183, 229			1
❑	Hooded Vulture	Necrosyrtes monachus	191, 260, 280, 350, 355			
❑	**Cape Vulture**	**Gyps coprotheres**	64, 65, 66, 101, 107, 110, 114, 116, 117, 157, 158, 159, 160, 169, 178, 180, 182, 184, 190, 202, 203, 223, 245, 246, 247, 379		E	
❑	Ruppell's Vulture	Gyps rueppellii	179, 182			1
❑	White-backed Vulture	Gyps africanus	89, 93, 139, 184, 191, 203,205, 223, 229, 240, 251, 253, 255, 258, 280			
❑	Lappet-faced Vulture	Torgos tracheliotus	88, 91, 138, 139, 144, 149, 182, 184, 191, 203, 210, 223, 229, 246, 252, 253, 255, 260, 280, 350, 355			
❑	White-headed Vulture	Trigonoceps occipitalis	89, 139, 144, 191, 229, 252, 253, 255, 260, 280, 303, 355			
❑	Black Kite	Milvus migrans				
❑	Yellow-billed Kite	Milvus aegyptius	46, 234, 260			
❑	Black-shouldered (Black-winged) Kite	Elanus caeruleus	46, 48, 252			
❑	African Cuckoo Hawk (African Baza)	Aviceda cuculoides	70, 140, 141, 144, 146, 151, 166, 167, 173, 234, 235, 239, 241, 243, 268, 296, 297, 299, 300, 323			
❑	**Madagascar Cuckoo Hawk**	**Aviceda madagascariensis**	372, 373, 374	M	E	
❑	Bat Hawk	Macheiramphus alcinus	179, 185, 186, 187, 188, 221, 225, 234, 240, 241, 242, 257, 259, 260, 280, 380			
❑	European Honey Buzzard	Pernis apivorus	28, 31, 234, 303, 380			
❑	Verreaux's (Black) Eagle	Aquila verreauxii	30, 31, 32, 40, 41, 50, 54, 60, 63, 75, 77, 83, 84, 91, 96, 97, 99, 103, 108, 110, 117, 124, 129, 157, 158, 159, 169, 182, 202, 210, 221, 223, 247, 285, 335			
❑	Tawny Eagle	Aquila rapax	88, 139, 183, 191, 229, 234, 246, 251, 255, 260			
❑	Steppe Eagle	Aquila nipalensis	88, 179, 183, 195, 234, 253, 255, 260			
❑	Lesser Spotted Eagle	Aquila pomarina	89, 179, 195, 234, 253, 255, 260			
❑	Greater Spotted Eagle	Aquila clanga				1
❑	Wahlberg's Eagle	Aquila wahlbergi	181, 234, 253, 255, 260, 323			
❑	Booted Eagle	Hieraaetus pennatus	54, 60, 75, 77, 83, 84, 95, 97, 103, 109, 110, 184, 219, 223, 247			
❑	African Hawk-Eagle	Hieraaetus spilogaster	99, 148, 182, 184, 200, 223, 225, 228, 239, 247, 260			
❑	Ayres' Hawk-Eagle	Hieraaetus ayresii	165, 234, 239, 243, 257, 274, 275, 284, 287, 300, 302, 303, 305, 380			

	Common Name	Scientific name	Page numbers	Reg	End	Vag
❑	Long-crested Eagle	Lophaetus occipitalis	107, 108, 109, 114, 128, 166, 175, 186, 187, 275			
❑	Martial Eagle	Polemaetus bellicosus	40, 61, 65, 68, 78, 88, 99, 108, 109, 144, 149, 183, 191, 236, 252, 253, 255, 260			
❑	African Crowned Eagle	Stephanoaetus coronatus	18, 69, 72, 75, 101, 103, 107, 108, 109, 112, 113, 114, 119, 123, 124, 128, 129, 131, 132, 134, 149, 151, 174, 185, 196, 273, 278, 300, 335, 348			
❑	Brown Snake-Eagle	Circaetus cinereus	88, 182, 236, 260			
❑	Black-chested Snake-Eagle	Circaetus pectoralis	61, 78, 88, 184, 228, 254, 292			
❑	Southern Banded Snake-Eagle	Circaetus fasciolatus	18, 130, 136, 137, 138, 140, 141, 143, 144, 145, 146, 277, 278, 280, 292, 293, 302, 304			
❑	Western Banded Snake-Eagle	Circaetus cinerascens	231, 236, 237, 238, 239, 240, 241, 243, 256, 259, 260, 282, 287, 318, 319, 323, 334, 344			
❑	**Madagascar Serpent Eagle**	**Eutriorchis astur**	364, 366, 368, 369, 404	M	E	
❑	Bateleur	Terathopius ecaudatus	87,88, 138, 139, 144, 146, 149, 191, 228, 229, 234, 252, 253, 257, 260, 303, 323, 350			
❑	Palm-nut Vulture	Gypohierax angolensis	51, 133, 274, 293, 295, 300, 301, 305, 319, 342, 352, 353, 358, 380			
❑	African Fish-Eagle	Haliaeetus vocifer	35, 43, 54, 72, 73, 81, 85, 120, 135, 142, 188, 194, 201, 203, 242, 257, 260, 302, 319, 320			
❑	**Madagascar Fish-Eagle**	**Haliaeetus vociferoides**	19, 362, 375, 376, 377	M	E	
❑	Steppe Buzzard	Buteo vulpinus	31, 46, 72			
❑	Mountain Buzzard	Buteo oreophilus	331	B		
❑	**Forest Buzzard**	**Buteo trizonatus**	18, 31, 64, 69, 70, 72, 101, 109, 114, 118, 127, 128, 129, 159, 174, 187, 380		E	
❑	**Madagascar Buzzard**	**Buteo brachypterus**	365, 366, 374	M	E	
❑	Long-legged Buzzard	Buteo rufinus				1
❑	**Jackal Buzzard**	**Buteo rufofuscus**	31, 34, 40, 41, 47, 51, 75, 77, 83, 84, 109, 110, 114, 117, 129, 151, 157, 159, 160, 163, 174, 175, 187, 202		E	
❑	Augur Buzzard	Buteo augur	219, 220, 223, 225, 273, 275, 279, 329, 335, 351			
❑	Lizard Buzzard	Kaupifalco monogrammicus	144, 188, 195, 303			
❑	Rufous-chested (Red-breasted) Sparrowhawk	Accipiter rufiventris	27, 28, 31, 40, 116, 129, 171, 173, 273, 329, 380			
❑	**Madagascar Sparrowhawk**	**Accipiter madagascariensis**	373, 374	M	E	
❑	Ovambo Sparrowhawk	Accipiter ovampensis	161, 165, 172, 184, 221, 224, 303			
❑	Little Sparrowhawk	Accipiter minullus	75, 182, 201, 202 224, 228, 237, 241, 249			
❑	Black (Great) Sparrowhawk	Accipiter melanoleucus	28, 31, 66, 70, 122, 126, 128, 165, 169, 173, 175			
❑	**Henst's Goshawk**	**Accipiter henstii**	366, 367, 377	M	E	
❑	Shikra (Little Banded Goshawk)	Accipiter badius	92, 202, 224, 228, 252			
❑	**Frances' Goshawk**	**Accipiter francesii**	374, 376	M	NE	
❑	African Goshawk	Accipiter tachiro	28, 31, 66, 70, 72, 110, 118, 129, 132, 174, 176, 185, 187, 235, 276, 292, 300, 316			
❑	Gabar Goshawk	Melierax gabar	88, 146, 168, 182, 184, 224, 227, 252			
❑	**Pale Chanting Goshawk**	**Melierax canorus**	56, 58, 61, 78, 88, 95, 109, 182, 199, 200, 203, 228, 251, 284		E	
❑	Dark Chanting Goshawk	Melierax metabates	148, 234, 236, 260			
❑	Western (Eurasian) Marsh-Harrier	Circus aeruginosus	161, 162, 164, 165, 169, 190, 248, 254, 264, 266, 285, 329, 350			
❑	African Marsh-Harrier	Circus ranivorus	35, 37, 45, 49, 54, 72, 85, 144, 157, 162, 181, 237, 292, 295, 302, 350			
❑	**Reunion Harrier**	**Circus maillardi**	19, 368, 371	M	NE	
❑	Montagu's Harrier	Circus pygargus	89, 98, 147, 149, 162, 164, 165, 169, 179, 184, 195, 197, 198, 232, 245, 246, 252, 253, 261, 266, 279, 301, 329, 336, 350			

	Common Name	Scientific name	Page numbers	Reg	End	Vag
☐	Pallid Harrier	Circus macrourus	98, 165, 179, 195, 197, 198, 232, 246, 250, 251, 252, 253, 261, 266, 279, 325, 329, 336, 350, 380			
☐	**Black Harrier**	**Circus maurus**	26, 40, 44, 48, 49, 63, 65, 66, 68, 77, 89, 98, 103, 115, 154, 156, 381		E	
☐	African Harrier-Hawk (Gymnogene)	Polyboroides typus	31, 66, 108, 110			
☐	**Madagascar Harrier-Hawk**	**Polyboroides radiatus**	365, 373, 374	M	E	
	Pandionidae	**Osprey**				
☐	Osprey	Pandion haliaetus	49, 72, 73, 120, 121, 135, 188, 190, 200, 205, 293, 294, 302, 306, 319			
	Falconidae	**Falcons and Kestrels**				
☐	Peregrine Falcon	Falco peregrinus	31, 32, 33, 40, 49, 91, 103, 132, 157, 165, 220, 221, 223, 300, 305, 335			
☐	Lanner Falcon	Falco biarmicus	31, 51, 78, 84, 88, 114, 124, 128, 132, 138, 157, 159, 160, 165, 246, 247, 252, 335			
☐	Eurasian Hobby	Falco subbuteo	102, 186, 234, 240, 252, 255, 305			
☐	African Hobby	Falco cuvierii	232, 233, 234, 236, 239, 241, 242, 281, 283, 381			
☐	Sooty Falcon	Falco concolor	121, 136, 138, 143, 145, 146, 197, 293			
☐	Taita Falcon	Falco fasciinucha	170, 177, 278, 279, 282, 284, 287, 335, 381			
☐	Eleonora's Falcon	Falco eleonorae	296			
☐	Red-necked Falcon	Falco chicquera	87, 88, 89, 227, 228, 230, 252, 252, 254, 255, 257, 260, 287, 288, 301, 302, 319			
☐	(Western) Red-footed Falcon	Falco vespertinus	165, 166, 197, 234, 250, 252, 253, 255, 261			
☐	Amur (Eastern Red-footed) Falcon	Falco amurensis	98, 152, 163, 165, 166, 197, 234, 261, 267, 269, 336			
☐	Rock Kestrel	Falco rupicoloides	31, 32, 40, 50, 60, 61, 75, 110, 157, 160, 247			
☐	**Madagascar Kestrel**	**Falco newtoni**		M	E	
☐	Greater Kestrel	Falco rupicoloides	58, 61, 77, 78, 88, 184, 228, 246, 252, 340			
☐	Lesser Kestrel	Falco naumanni	65, 94, 98, 109, 152, 246, 252, 253, 255			
☐	Grey Kestrel	Falco ardosiaceus	222, 225, 226			
☐	**Dickinson's Kestrel**	**Falco dickinsoni**	99, 179, 109, 197, 232, 233, 234, 236, 239, 240, 255, 257, 260, 280, 281, 282, 283, 284, 286, 287, 297, 301, 319, 330, 355		NE	
☐	**Banded Kestrel**	**Falco zoniventris**	372, 373	M	E	
☐	African Pygmy Falcon	Polihierax semitorquatus	80, 87, 88, 90, 199, 207, 210, 211, 227			
	Phasianidae	**Francolins and Quails**				
☐	Chukar Partridge	Alectoris chukar	38			3
☐	Coqui Francolin	Peliperdix coqui	119, 126, 147, 165, 167, 168, 193, 202, 239, 243, 268			
☐	White-throated Francolin	Peliperdix albogularis	340	B		
☐	Crested Francolin (incl. Kirk's)	Peliperdix sephaena	144, 302, 303, 304			
☐	**Grey-winged Francolin**	**Scleroptila africanus**	34, 44, 48, 49, 56, 63, 65, 68, 77, 98, 107, 108, 115, 116, 117, 156, 157, 159, 160, 163, 164, 177		E	
☐	Shelley's Francolin	Scleroptila shelleyi	131, 147, 148, 149, 165, 166, 168, 172, 182, 188, 271, 273, 292, 293, 295			
☐	Red-winged Francolin	Scleroptila levaillantii	70, 116, 128, 151, 152, 154, 155, 156, 157, 159, 163, 164, 165, 171, 175, 202, 325, 329			
☐	**Orange River Francolin**	**Scleroptila levaillantoides**	93, 94, 95, 97, 98, 99, 161, 163, 164, 165, 199, 204, 206, 214, 215, 224, 230, 250, 253		E	
☐	**Red-billed Spurfowl**	**Pternistis adspersus**	215, 223, 230, 254, 257, 283		E	
☐	**Cape Spurfowl**	**Pternistis capensis**	28, 29, 37, 48, 49		E	
☐	**Natal Spurfowl**	**Pternistis natalensis**	99, 247		E	

	Common Name	Scientific name	Page numbers	Reg	End	Vag
❑	**Hartlaub's Spurfowl**	**Pternistis hartlaubi**	17, 208, 213, 220, 222, 223, 224, 225, 226, 230, 381		E	
❑	Hildebrandt's Spurfowl	Pternistis hildebrandti	305, 320, 323, 325, 326, 327	B		
❑	**Swierstra's Spurfowl**	**Pternistis swierstrai**	359, 361	B	E	
❑	Scaly Spurfowl	Pternistis squamatus	324	B		
❑	Red-necked Spurfowl	Pternistis afer	70, 71, 107, 109, 128, 159, 172, 173, 175, 225, 273, 280, 295, 319, 324, 355			
❑	**Grey-striped Spurfowl**	**Pternistis griseostriatus**	357, 358	B	E	
❑	**Swainson's Spurfowl**	**Pternistis swainsonii**	99, 128		E	
❑	**Madagascar Partridge**	**Margaroperdix madagascarensis**	19, 368, 371	M	E	
❑	Common Quail	Coturnix coturnix	47, 109, 126, 162, 329			
❑	Harlequin Quail	Coturnix delegorguei	126, 178, 184, 195, 197, 198, 251, 253, 269, 308, 371			
❑	Blue Quail	Coturnix adansonii	264, 298, 301, 303, 307, 308, 341, 342, 348, 351, 381			
❑	Common Peacock	Pavo cristatus	38			3
	Numididae	**Guineafowl**				
❑	Helmeted Guineafowl	Numida meleagris	29			
❑	Crested Guineafowl	Guttera pucherani	136, 139, 141, 145, 178, 187, 196, 293, 295, 304, 316, 337, 338, 339, 344			
	Turnicidae	**Buttonquails**				
❑	Kurrichane (Small) Buttonquail	Turnix sylvatica	88, 113, 141, 181, 195, 246, 261, 292			
❑	**Hottentot Buttonquail**	**Turnix hottentotta**	17, 27, 33, 39, 42, 65, 66, 67, 382		E	
❑	Black-rumped Buttonquail	Turnix nana	107, 111, 112, 117, 118, 127, 129, 134, 141, 147, 157, 158, 175, 177, 264, 291, 292, 295, 340, 341, 342, 354			
❑	**Madagascar Buttonquail**	**Turnix nigricollis**	19, 368, 371, 373, 376	M	E	
	Gruidae	**Cranes**				
❑	Wattled Crane	Grus carunculatus	18, 127, 128, 150, 155, 156, 170, 171, 177, 232, 236, 243, 259, 260, 261, 301, 304, 325, 329, 336, 338, 340, 346, 348, 349, 350, 354, 382			
❑	**Blue Crane**	**Anthropoides paradisea**	18, 26, 46, 47, 64, 65, 77, 102, 109, 126, 127, 128, 129, 149, 150, 152, 155, 156, 157, 158, 165, 170, 171, 172, 177, 227, 230		E	
❑	Grey Crowned Crane	Balearica regulorum	18, 106, 107, 109, 110, 112, 113, 117, 127, 128, 149, 150, 152, 154, 155, 156, 165, 172, 190, 253, 254, 301, 330, 355			
	Rallidae	**Rails and Coots**				
❑	African Rail	Rallus caerulescens	43, 48, 49, 50, 54, 69, 72, 102, 104, 106, 115, 124, 125, 149, 152, 154, 155, 156, 157, 162, 165, 172, 180, 181, 233, 240, 260, 265, 285, 295, 296, 348			
❑	**Madagascar Rail**	**Rallus madagascariensis**	19, 364, 366, 368	M	E	
❑	Corncrake	Crex crex	149, 177, 181, 197, 264, 336, 342, 352			
❑	**White-throated Rail**	**Dryolimnas cuvieri**	365, 373, 377	M	E	
❑	African Crake	Crecopsis egregia	141, 162, 168, 169, 178, 180, 181, 184, 232, 233, 236, 239, 240, 258, 260, 264, 342, 355			
❑	Black Crake	Amaurornis flavirostra	43, 50, 104, 106, 109, 125, 248, 258, 319			
❑	**Sakalava Rail**	**Amaurornis olivieri**	19, 404	M	E	
❑	Spotted Crake	Porzana porzana	125, 161, 162, 163, 181, 229, 233, 236, 240, 248, 285			
❑	Little Crake	Porzana parva		B		1
❑	Baillon's Crake	Porzana pusilla	72, 102, 106, 119, 125, 135, 149, 154, 161, 162, 181, 214, 232, 236, 240, 285, 301			
❑	Striped Crake	Aenigmatolimnas marginalis	149, 179, 181, 236, 240, 258, 263, 264, 265, 266, 284, 285, 337, 382			
❑	White-spotted Flufftail	Sarothrura pulchra	343	B		

	Common Name	Scientific name	Page numbers	Reg	End	Vag
❑	Red-chested Flufftail	Sarothrura rufa	54, 72, 109, 115, 124, 149, 154, 156, 161, 162, 165, 166, 172, 233, 260, 264, 265, 302, 303, 348, 351			
❑	Chestnut-headed (Long-toed) Flufftail	Sarothrura lugens	345, 346, 351, 352, 354	B		
❑	Buff-spotted Flufftail	Sarothrura elegans	30, 32, 72, 75, 101, 105, 107, 122, 127, 129, 131, 136, 137, 139, 141, 172, 173, 174, 185, 186, 252, 275, 276, 304			
❑	Streaky-breasted Flufftail	Sarothrura boehmi	181, 262, 263, 264, 266, 336, 337, 348			
❑	Striped Flufftail	Sarothrura affinis	30, 39, 40, 66, 111, 115, 151, 159, 170, 172, 175, 176, 177, 273, 309, 327, 380, 382			
❑	**White-winged Flufftail**	**Sarothrura ayresi**	11 5, 150, 154, 155, 157, 170, 171, 382		NE	
❑	**Slender-billed Flufftail**	**Sarothrura watersi**	19, 362, 366, 368, 404	M	E	
❑	**Madagascar Flufftail**	**Sarothrura insularis**	366, 368	M	E	
❑	**Madagascar Wood Rail**	**Canirallus kioloides**	364, 365, 369, 404	M	E	
❑	African Purple Swamphen	Porphyrio madagascariensis	36, 38, 43, 45, 54, 104, 106, 142, 154, 164, 217, 248			
❑	Allen's (Lesser) Gallinule	Porphyrula alleni	125, 142, 143, 144, 147, 168, 169, 179, 180, 190, 232, 233, 236, 237, 240, 241, 242, 258, 260, 268, 280, 282, 285, 295, 301, 320, 355, 377			
❑	American Purple Gallinule	Porphyrula martinicus				1
❑	Common Moorhen	Gallinula chloropus	45, 50			
❑	Lesser Moorhen	Gallinula angulata	125, 142, 144, 146, 147, 168, 189, 179, 180, 182, 190, 197, 202, 229, 232, 233, 240, 242, 248, 258, 260, 264, 265, 280, 295, 301			
❑	Red-knobbed (Crested) Coot	Fulica cristata	45, 336			
	Heliornithidae	**Finfoots**				
❑	African Finfoot	Podica senegalensis	71, 73, 74, 105, 106, 114, 132, 133, 136, 138, 145, 166, 170, 179, 187, 188, 189, 191, 192, 193, 194, 195, 196, 199, 201, 202, 240, 241, 242, 280, 281, 282, 304, 322, 334, 338, 348, 351, 352, 383			
	Mesitornithidae	**Mesites**				
❑	**White-breasted Mesite**	**Mesitornis variegata**	19, 375, 376, 377	M	E	
❑	**Brown Mesite**	**Mesitornis unicolor**	363, 364, 366, 367, 369	M	E	
❑	**Subdesert Mesite**	**Monias benschi**	19, 370, 372, 405	M	E	
	Otididae	**Bustards**				
❑	Kori Bustard	Ardeotis kori	78, 80, 87, 88, 108, 183, 190, 191, 194, 195, 198, 222, 227, 228, 230, 243, 252, 253, 255, 284, 335			
❑	Denham's (Stanley) Bustard	Neotis denhami	18, 64, 65, 68, 101, 103, 109, 115, 117, 126, 127, 128, 148, 149, 151, 152, 155, 159, 165, 166, 171, 172, 173, 177, 292, 325, 329, 336, 340, 342, 349, 350, 383			
❑	**Ludwig's Bustard**	**Neotis ludwigii**	16, 55, 61, 76, 77, 78, 80, 84, 91, 94, 97, 98, 101, 108, 209, 210, 211, 212, 218, 220, 228, 383		E	
❑	(Northern) White-bellied Bustard	Eupodotis senegalensis	340, 343	B		
❑	**Barrow's (Southern White-bellied) Korhaan**	**Eupodotis barrowii**	18, 101, 102, 148, 149, 154, 158, 165, 166, 172, 177, 199, 200, 335, 383		E	
❑	**Blue Korhaan**	**Eupodotis caerulescens**	18, 94, 97, 98, 150, 152, 154, 155, 156, 157, 158, 177		E	
❑	**Karoo Korhaan**	**Eupodotis vigorsii**	16, 58, 61, 65, 78, 79, 80, 81, 82, 83, 97, 101, 108, 209, 210		E	
❑	**Ruppell's Korhaan**	**Eupodotis rueppellii**	17, 208, 209, 211, 212, 213, 218, 219, 220		E	
❑	**Red-crested Korhaan**	**Eupodotis ruficrista**	92, 168, 198, 203, 206, 230, 255, 335		E	
❑	Black-bellied Bustard	Eupodotis melanogaster	139, 144, 155, 178, 194, 198, 260			
❑	**Southern Black Korhaan**	**Eupodotis afra**	44, 46, 47, 48, 49, 56, 66, 68, 77, 95, 109		E	
❑	**Northern Black Korhaan**	**Eupodotis afraoides**	83, 90, 92, 93, 99, 108, 168, 183, 199, 203, 204, 206, 228, 246, 250, 253, 255		E	

	Common Name	Scientific name	Page numbers	Reg	End	Vag
	Jacanidae	**Jacanas**				
❑	African Jacana	Actophilornis africanus	102, 142, 146, 164, 169, 236, 258, 259, 347, 350			
❑	**Madagascar Jacana**	**Actophilornis albinucha**	375, 377	M	E	
❑	Lesser Jacana	Microparra capensis	134, 135, 137, 144, 146, 147, 233, 236, 238, 240, 242, 256, 258, 259, 280, 285, 292, 293, 295, 297, 320, 347, 350			
	Rostratulidae	**Painted-snipes**				
❑	Greater Painted Snipe	Rostratula benghalensis	38, 141, 144, 146, 161, 162, 168, 169, 202, 229, 232, 233, 236, 238, 239, 240, 258, 260, 301			
	Haematopodidae	**Oystercatchers**				
❑	Eurasian Oystercatcher	Haematopus ostralegus	101, 102, 105, 137, 216, 217, 297, 302, 311			1
❑	**African Black Oystercatcher**	**Haematopus moquini**	18, 27, 32, 34, 37, 38, 47, 50, 53, 67, 85, 99, 103, 104, 105, 121, 217, 218, 383		E	
	Charadriidae	**Plovers and Lapwings**				
❑	Common Ringed Plover	Charadrius hiaticula	32, 49, 51, 52, 120, 121, 135, 216			
❑	Little Ringed Plover	Charadrius dubius				1
❑	**Madagascar Plover**	**Charadrius thoracicus**	370, 371, 372	M	E	
❑	Kentish Plover	Charadrius alexandrinus				1
❑	White-fronted Plover	Charadrius marginatus	32, 34, 49, 67, 85, 120, 197, 216, 233, 249, 254, 261, 331, 354			
❑	Chestnut-banded Plover	Charadrius pallidus	44, 47, 49, 51, 93, 164, 177, 216, 217, 218, 229, 253, 254, 293			
❑	Kittlitz's Plover	Charadrius pecuarius	49, 51, 169, 198, 200, 254, 336			
❑	Three-banded Plover	Charadrius tricollaris	45, 46, 50, 60			
❑	Forbes's Plover	Charadrius forbesi	341, 342	B		
❑	Mongolian (Lesser Sand) Plover	Charadrius mongolus	49, 67, 102, 121, 135, 295, 296			
❑	Greater Sand Plover	Charadrius leschenaultii	49, 67,102, 104, 119, 120, 121, 134, 135, 216, 293, 295, 296, 302			
❑	Caspian Plover	Charadrius asiaticus	49, 169, 190, 204, 227, 228, 232, 233, 250, 251, 252, 261, 336, 340			
❑	Pacific Golden Plover	Pluvialis fulva	102, 121, 135, 162			1
❑	American Golden Plover	Pluvialis dominica	34			1
❑	Grey (Black-bellied) Plover	Pluvialis squatarola	49, 52, 73, 85, 120, 121, 135, 137, 205, 254, 293, 295, 302			
❑	Crowned Lapwing (Plover)	Vanellus coronatus	193			
❑	Senegal (Lesser Black-winged) Lapwing	Vanellus lugubris	140, 141, 144, 145, 146, 147, 191, 193, 194, 280, 292, 293, 300, 301, 302, 319			
❑	Black-winged Lapwing (Plover)	Vanellus melanopterus	75, 106, 107, 110, 115, 119, 126, 127, 129, 147, 148, 151, 152, 155, 170, 171, 173, 175			
❑	Spur-winged Lapwing (Plover)	Vanellus spinosus	319			1
❑	Blacksmith Lapwing (Plover)	Vanellus armatus	49, 260, 319, 336			
❑	Brown-chested Lapwing (Plover)	Vanellus superciliosus		B		
❑	White-headed (White-crowned) Lapwing (Plover)	Vanellus albiceps	18, 190, 191, 194, 196, 198, 240, 241, 242, 281, 282, 288, 297, 306, 354			
❑	African Wattled Lapwing (Plover)	Vanellus senegallus	126, 127, 142, 147, 236, 237, 319			
❑	Long-toed Lapwing (Plover)	Vanellus crassirostris	144, 236, 237, 238, 242, 256, 257, 258, 260, 287, 288, 289, 300, 301, 319, 336, 350			

	Common Name	Scientific name	Page numbers	Reg	End	Vag
	Scolopacidae	**Sandpipers and allies**				
❑	Ruddy Turnstone	Arenaria interpres	32, 34, 49, 52, 67, 85, 137, 205			
❑	Terek Sandpiper	Xenus cinereus	49, 67, 102, 104, 105, 119, 120, 121, 124, 134, 135, 216, 293, 295, 296, 302			
❑	Common Sandpiper	Actitis hypoleucos	32, 43, 248			
❑	Green Sandpiper	Tringa ochropus	126, 205, 231, 233, 271, 304			
❑	Solitary Sandpiper	Tringa solitaria		B		1
❑	Wood Sandpiper	Tringa glareola	45, 232, 248			
❑	Spotted Redshank	Tringa erythropus				1
❑	Common Redshank	Tringa totanus	49, 135, 216, 232			1
❑	Lesser Yellowlegs	Tringa flavipes				1
❑	Marsh Sandpiper	Tringa stagnatilis	49, 52, 232, 248			
❑	Common Greenshank	Tringa nebularia	49, 52, 73, 120, 135, 232, 248, 254, 293			
❑	Greater Yellowlegs	Tringa melanoleuca				1
❑	Red Knot	Calidris canutus	49, 216, 302			
❑	Great Knot	Calidris tenuirostris				1
❑	Curlew Sandpiper	Calidris ferruginea	49, 51, 52, 73, 120, 121, 135, 162, 216, 232, 254			
❑	Dunlin	Calidris alpina				1
❑	Little Stint	Calidris minuta	37, 45, 49, 51, 52, 121, 135, 162, 248, 254			
❑	Long-toed Stint	Calidris subminuta				1
❑	Red-necked Stint	Calidris ruficollis	121			1
❑	White-rumped Sandpiper	Calidris fuscicollis	34, 49			1
❑	Baird's Sandpiper	Calidris bairdii	34, 161, 162			1
❑	Pectoral Sandpiper	Calidris melanotos	34, 49, 161, 162, 164			1
❑	Temminck's Stint	Calidris temminckii				1
❑	Sanderling	Calidris alba	34, 49, 52, 67, 85, 121, 216, 254, 302			
❑	Buff-breasted Sandpiper	Tryngites subruficollis	162, 205			1
❑	Broad-billed Sandpiper	Limicola falcinellus	49, 121, 135, 216			1
❑	Ruff	Philomachus pugnax	45, 51, 137, 162, 232, 248, 336			
❑	Great Snipe	Gallinago media	232, 236, 269, 302, 336, 341, 342, 350, 352			
❑	Common Snipe	Gallinago gallinago				1
❑	African (Ethiopian) Snipe	Gallinago nigripennis	38, 43, 45, 47, 125, 154, 156, 162, 164, 236, 240, 260			
❑	**Madagascar Snipe**	**Gallinago macrodactyla**	19, 366, 368	M	E	
❑	Jack Snipe	Lymnocryptes minimus		B		1
❑	Black-tailed Godwit	Limosa limosa	93, 161, 162, 205, 216, 232, 248, 254, 336			
❑	Hudsonian Godwit	Limosa haemastica	49, 104			1
❑	Bar-tailed Godwit	Limosa lapponica	49, 50, 52, 67, 73, 102, 104, 205, 216, 293, 296, 297			
❑	Asiatic Dowitcher	Limnodromus semipalmatus				1
❑	Eurasian Curlew	Numenius arquata	49, 52, 67, 102, 104, 217, 254, 293			
❑	Common Whimbrel	Numenius phaeopus	32, 34, 49, 52, 73, 104, 105, 120, 135, 293, 296, 302			
❑	Red (Grey) Phalarope	Phalaropus fulicaria	20, 162			
❑	Red-necked (Northern) Phalarope	Phalaropus lobatus	51, 216, 217, 218			

	Common Name	Scientific name	Page numbers	Reg	End	Vag
❑	Wilson's Phalarope	Steganopus tricolor				1
	Recurcirostridae	**Avocets and Stilts**				
❑	Pied Avocet	Recurvirostra avosetta	37, 51, 62, 77, 85, 137, 162, 164, 254			
❑	Black-winged Stilt	Himantopus himantopus	45, 49, 51, 164, 254			
	Dromadidae	**Crab Plover**				
❑	Crab Plover	Dromas ardeola	18, 101, 105, 121, 135, 290, 291, 293, 294, 295, 296, 307, 311, 371, 373, 384			
	Burhinidae	**Thick-knees**				
❑	Spotted Thick-knee (Dikkop)	Burhinus capensis	124, 126, 139, 198			
❑	Water Thick-knee (Dikkop)	Burhinus vermiculatus	42, 43, 105, 121, 139, 142, 146, 194, 196, 198, 200, 236, 319			
	Glareolidae	**Pratincoles and Coursers**				
❑	**Burchell's Courser**	**Cursorius rufus**	55, 61, 62, 76, 78, 79, 80, 81, 90, 91, 93, 156, 199, 208, 209, 210, 211, 212, 220, 228, 384		E	
❑	Temminck's Courser	Cursorius temminckii	90, 169, 194, 200, 204, 233, 236, 252, 261, 302, 348			
❑	Double-banded Courser	Rhinoptilus africanus	62, 79, 90, 91, 93, 97, 98, 183, 184, 204, 206, 207, 212, 218, 228, 233, 252, 253			
❑	Three-banded Courser	Rhinoptilus cinctus	179, 190, 241, 243, 280, 283, 284, 338, 384			
❑	Bronze-winged (Violet-tipped) Courser	Rhinoptilus chalcopterus	138, 139, 144, 167, 178, 182, 184, 190, 198, 224, 234, 243, 252, 284, 297, 319			
❑	Collared (Red-winged) Pratincole	Glareola pratincola	124, 141, 143, 144, 147, 198, 237, 238, 241, 242, 249, 260, 261, 288, 289, 297, 301, 302, 330, 336, 340			
❑	Black-winged Pratincole	Glareola nordmanni	98, 161, 162, 164, 232, 248, 253, 261, 340			
❑	**Madagascar Pratincole**	**Glareola ocularis**	368	M	NE	
❑	Rock Pratincole	Glareola nuchalis	18, 231, 235, 240, 241, 242, 281, 282, 334, 338, 384			
	Chionididae	**Sheathbills**				
❑	Greater (Snowy) Sheathbill	Chionis alba	384			1
	Stercorariidae	**Jaegers and Skuas**				
❑	Parasitic Jaeger (Arctic Skua)	Stercorarius parasiticus	20, 21, 22, 38, 53, 216			
❑	Long-tailed Jaeger (Skua)	Stercorarius longicaudus	20, 21, 22			
❑	Pomarine Jaeger (Skua)	Stercorarius pomarinus	20, 21, 22, 38, 216			
❑	Subantarctic (Brown) Skua	Catharacta antarctica	20, 21, 22, 38, 121			
❑	South Polar Skua	Catharacta maccormicki	23			1
	Laridae	**Gulls and Terns**				
❑	Sooty (Hemprich's) Gull	Larus hemprichii		B		1
❑	Kelp Gull	Larus dominicanus				1
❑	**Cape Gull**	**Larus vetula**	18		NE	
❑	Lesser Black-backed Gull	Larus fuscus	93, 119, 120, 121, 205, 254			
❑	Heuglin's Gull	Larus heuglini				1
❑	Grey-headed Gull	Larus cirrocephalus	43, 53, 254			
❑	**Hartlaub's Gull**	**Larus hartlaubii**	18, 38, 120		E	
❑	Franklin's Gull	Larus pipixcan	120, 121, 217			1

	Common Name	Scientific name	Page numbers	Reg	End	Vag
❑	Sabine's Gull	Xema sabini	20, 21, 38			
❑	Common Black-headed Gull	Larus ridibundus	120, 121, 217			1
❑	Slender-billed Gull	Larus genei	120			1
❑	Black-legged Kittiwake	Rissa tridactyla	23			1
❑	Gull-billed Tern	Sterna nilotica	135, 319, 320, 336			1
❑	Caspian Tern	Sterna caspia	38, 45, 51, 52, 54, 67, 73, 85, 104, 121, 124, 135, 137, 166, 205, 206, 216, 254, 295			
❑	Royal Tern	Sterna maxima	358			
❑	Swift (Greater crested) Tern	Sterna bergii	22, 32, 34, 37, 38, 45, 53, 121, 124, 135, 295, 296			
❑	Lesser Crested Tern	Sterna bengalensis	120, 121, 124, 134, 135, 137, 295, 296, 302, 373			
❑	Sandwich Tern	Sterna sandvicensis	34, 37, 121, 124, 135, 296			
❑	Common Tern	Sterna hirundo	32, 34, 120, 121, 124, 135, 296, 302			
❑	Arctic Tern	Sterna paradisaea	21, 22			
❑	Antarctic Tern	Sterna vittata	20, 21, 27, 32, 50, 103, 384			
❑	Roseate Tern	Sterna dougallii	101, 103, 121, 124, 296			
❑	Black-naped Tern	Sterna sumatrana	23, 121, 124, 302			1
❑	Sooty Tern	Sterna fuscata	22, 23, 121, 124, 137, 296, 311			
❑	Bridled Tern	Sterna anaethetus	22, 23, 104, 121, 373			1
❑	**Damara Tern**	**Sterna balaenarum**	18, 84, 87, 84, 85, 103, 209, 212, 216, 217, 218, 306		NE	
❑	Little Tern	Sterna albifrons	50, 52, 102, 104, 105, 121, 124, 135, 137, 295, 296, 302			
❑	Saunders' Tern	Sterna saundersi	371, 373, 377	M		
❑	White-cheeked Tern	Sterna repressa	124, 135			I
❑	Black Tern	Chlidonias niger	51, 121, 124, 216, 217			
❑	Whiskered Tern	Chlidonias hybridus	142, 146, 147, 153, 156, 157, 164, 254			
❑	White-winged Tern	Chlidonias leucopterus	43, 45, 121, 124, 135, 142, 146, 200, 254			
❑	Brown (Common) Noddy	Anous stolidus	121, 137, 297, 311			1
❑	Lesser Noddy	Anous tenuirostris				1
	Rynchopidae	**Skimmers**				
❑	African Skimmer	Rynchops flavirostris	18, 231, 235, 236, 237, 238, 240, 241, 242, 259, 260, 261, 281, 282, 286, 387, 288, 297, 319, 320, 336, 349, 354, 385			
	Pteroclididae	**Sandgrouse**				
❑	**Namaqua Sandgrouse**	**Pterocles namaqua**	51, 56, 58, 61, 79, 82, 88, 91, 199, 212, 218, 220, 228		E	
❑	**Burchell's Sandgrouse**	**Pterocles burchelli**	87, 88, 90, 91, 199, 204, 207, 230, 233, 236, 237, 249, 250, 253, 258, 261, 335, 385		E	
❑	Yellow-throated Sandgrouse	Pterocles gutturalis	199, 203, 204, 233, 243, 250, 253, 261, 336			
❑	**Double-banded Sandgrouse**	**Pterocles bicinctus**	91, 200, 202, 227, 228, 289, 297		E	
❑	**Madagascar Sandgrouse**	**Pterocles personatus**	19, 370, 373, 374, 376	M	E	
	Columbidae	**Pigeons and Doves**				
❑	Rock Dove (Feral Pigeon)	Columba livia				3
❑	Speckled Pigeon	Columba guinea	32, 175			
❑	African Olive-Pigeon (Rameron Pigeon)	Columba arquatrix	28, 32, 129, 173, 187, 329			

	Common Name	Scientific name	Page numbers	Reg	End	Vag
❑	Western Bronze-naped Pigeon	Columba iriditorques	341	B		
❑	Eastern Bronze-naped (Delegorgue's) Pigeon	Columba delegorguei	122, 131, 132, 134, 272, 274, 277, 300, 304, 305, 385			
❑	**Madagascar Turtle-Dove**	**Streptopelia picturata**	376	M	NE	
❑	European Turtle-Dove	Streptopelia turtur				1
❑	Dusky (Pink-breasted) Turtle-Dove	Streptopelia lugens	325, 329, 331	B		
❑	Red-eyed Dove	Streptopelia semitorquata				
❑	African Mourning Dove	Streptopelia decipiens	195, 197, 225, 235, 242, 257, 260, 280, 335			
❑	Cape Turtle (Ring-necked) Dove	Streptopelia capicola				
❑	Laughing (Palm) Dove	Streptopelia senegalensis				
❑	Namaqua Dove	Oena capensis	47, 50, 95, 371			
❑	Blue-spotted Wood-Dove	Turtur afer	179, 187, 189, 274, 275, 276, 277, 278, 299, 303, 316, 317			
❑	Emerald-spotted Wood-Dove	Turtur chalcospilos	109, 203			
❑	Tambourine Dove	Turtur tympanistria	68, 72, 96, 103, 12, 176, 196, 280			
❑	Afep Pigeon	Columba unicincta	341, 342	B		
❑	Lemon (Cinnamon) Dove	Aplopelia larvata	28, 30, 72, 103, 112, 114, 122, 129, 131, 134, 139, 173, 174, 187, 276, 318, 327, 340			
❑	African Green Pigeon	Treron calva	128, 138, 143, 145, 148, 176, 189, 193, 235, 257, 260			
❑	**Madagascar Blue Pigeon**	**Alectroenas madagascariensis**	365	M	E	
❑	**Madagascar Green Pigeon**	**Treron australis**	365, 373, 374	M	E	
	Psittacidae	**Parrots**				
❑	**Lesser Vasa Parrot**	**Coracopsis nigra**	366, 376	M	NE	
❑	**Greater Vasa Parrot**	**Coracopsis vasa**	366	M	NE	
❑	**Cape Parrot**	**Poicephalus robustus**	101, 108, 109, 111, 114, 117, 118, 127, 129, 185, 385		E	
❑	Grey-headed Parrot	Poicephalus suahelicus	179, 189, 197, 233, 239, 240, 241, 280, 283, 287, 288, 297, 319, 330			
❑	Brown-headed Parrot	Poicephalus cryptoxanthus	143, 144, 178, 191, 194, 195, 201, 280, 295, 319			
❑	Meyer's (Brown) Parrot	Poicephalus meyeri	99, 190, 201, 228, 243, 254, 257, 260, 280, 330			
❑	**Ruppell's Parrot**	**Poicephalus rueppellii**	208, 220, 221, 222, 223, 224, 225, 227, 230, 386		E	
❑	Rose-ringed Parakeet	Psittacula krameri	122			3
❑	**Grey-headed Lovebird**	**Agapornis cana**	372, 373, 374, 375, 376	M	NE	
❑	**Rosy-faced Lovebird**	**Agapornis roseicollis**	80, 81, 90, 208, 209, 210, 219, 221, 223, 224, 225, 283		E	
❑	**Lilian's (Nyasa) Lovebird**	**Agapornis lilianae**	286, 287, 288, 289, 306, 318, 319, 354, 355		E	
❑	**Black-cheeked Lovebird**	**Agapornis lilianae nigrigenis**	241, 332, 333, 335, 338, 386		E	
	Musophagidae	**Turacos**				
❑	**Knysna Turaco**	**Tauraco corythaix**	18, 26, 64, 71, 73, 74, 101, 103, 106, 109, 112, 113, 114, 117, 118, 127, 128, 129, 173, 174, 175, 185, 187		E	
❑	**Livingstone's Turaco**	**Tauraco livingstonii**	136, 137, 275, 276, 278, 293, 300, 309, 311, 314, 318		NE	
❑	Schalow's Turaco	Tauraco schalowi	240, 281, 282, 305, 320, 322, 324, 326, 334			
❑	**Red-crested Turaco**	**Tauraco erythrolophus**	357, 358, 359, 360, 361, 386	B	E	
❑	Purple-crested Turaco	Musophaga porphyreolopha	112, 122, 123, 133, 137, 138, 143, 145, 148, 176, 178, 187, 194, 196			

	Common Name	Scientific name	Page numbers	Reg	End	Vag
❑	Ross's Turaco	Musophaga rossae	231, 338, 341, 342, 344, 345, 346, 347, 352, 386			
❑	Bare-faced Go-away-bird	Corythaixoides personatus	353	B		
❑	**Grey Go-away-bird**	**Corythaixoides concolor**			NE	
	Cuculidae	**Old World Cuckoos and Couas**				
❑	Common (Eurasian) Cuckoo	Cuculus canorus	228			
❑	African Cuckoo	Cuculus gularis	193, 201, 221, 228, 267			
❑	Madagascar Cuckoo	Cuculus rochii	303, 304			
❑	Lesser Cuckoo	Cuculus poliocephalus	278			1
❑	Red-chested Cuckoo	Cuculus solitarius	28, 29, 32, 156			
❑	Black Cuckoo	Cuculus clamosus	108, 168, 248			
❑	Olive Long-tailed Cuckoo	Cercococcyx olivinus	341, 342, 360	B		
❑	Barred Long-tailed Cuckoo	Cercococcyx montanus	277, 289, 302, 303, 304, 337, 386			
❑	Great Spotted Cuckoo	Clamator glandarius	89, 215, 216, 221, 223, 227, 240			
❑	Levaillant's (Striped) Cuckoo	Oxylophus levaillantii	168, 193, 201			
❑	Jacobin (Black and white) Cuckoo	Oxylophus jacobinus	126, 168, 193, 223, 227, 240, 248			
❑	Thick-billed Cuckoo	Pachycoccyx audeberti	178, 179, 186, 189, 190, 191, 193, 241, 278, 280, 286, 287, 288, 289, 297, 300, 316, 319, 323, 341, 347, 351, 387			
❑	African Emerald Cuckoo	Chrysococcyx cupreus	75, 107, 108, 118, 129, 131, 144, 173, 174, 185, 235, 240, 288, 337			
❑	Klaas's Cuckoo	Chrysococcyx klaas	46, 66, 170, 292			
❑	Diderick Cuckoo	Chrysococcyx caprius	46, 267			
❑	Green Malkoha (Coucal/Yellowbill)	Ceuthmochares australis	112, 113, 122, 124, 131, 134, 136, 137, 139, 140, 141, 144, 146, 275, 277, 280, 293, 294, 297, 301, 304, 319, 331, 342, 353, 354			
❑	Blue Malkoha (Coucal/Yellowbill)	Ceuthmochares aereus	360	D		
❑	**Green-capped Coua**	**Coua olivaceiceps**	372	M	E	
❑	**Red-capped Coua**	**Coua ruficeps**	369, 376, 377	M	E	
❑	**Running Coua**	**Coua cursor**	19, 371, 372, 373	M	E	
❑	**Giant Coua**	**Coua gigas**	30, 370, 371, 373, 374, 377	M	E	
❑	**Coquerel's Coua**	**Coua coquereli**	19, 371, 377	M	E	
❑	**Red-breasted Coua**	**Coua serriana**	19, 363, 365, 369	M	E	
❑	**Red-fronted Coua**	**Coua reynaudii**	376	M	E	
❑	**Blue Coua**	**Coua caerulea**	365	M	E	
❑	**Crested Coua**	**Coua cristata**	371, 373, 376	M	E	
❑	**Verreaux's Coua**	**Coua verreauxi**	19, 370, 373	M	E	
❑	Gabon Coucal	Centropus anselli	360	B		
❑	Black Coucal	Centropus grillii	131, 138, 144, 146, 162, 178, 181, 194, 197, 236, 239, 240, 243, 260, 263, 264, 266, 287, 292, 295, 301, 308, 320, 348			
❑	**Madagascar Coucal**	**Centropus toulou**		M	E	
❑	**Coppery-tailed Coucal**	**Centropus cupreicaudus**	18, 231, 233, 236, 238, 239, 240, 241, 242, 256, 258, 259, 283, 348, 350		NE	
❑	Senegal Coucal	Centropus senegalensis	190, 196, 233, 257, 330			
❑	**Burchell's Coucal**	**Centropus burchelli**			NE	
❑	White-browed Coucal	Centropus superciliosus	225, 233, 235, 242, 287, 289			

	Common Name	Scientific name	Page numbers	Reg	End	Vag
	Tytonidae	**Barn-Owls**				
❑	Barn Owl	Tyto alba	88, 198, 228, 257			
❑	**Madagascar Red Owl**	**Tyto soumagnei**	366, 368, 369, 405	M	E	
❑	African Grass-Owl	Tyto capensis	127, 149, 154, 161, 164, 165, 182, 205, 266, 308, 352, 387			
	Strigidae	**Owls**				
❑	African Wood-Owl	Strix woodfordii	30, 32, 68, 71, 108, 109, 137, 139, 144, 173, 176, 178, 235, 238, 241, 304, 309, 318, 360			
❑	**Madagascar Long-eared Owl**	**Asio madagascariensis**	364, 365, 366	M	E	
❑	**White-browed Owl**	**Ninox superciliaris**	366, 371, 373, 374	M	E	
❑	Marsh Owl	Asio capensis	98, 127, 149, 161, 162, 163, 165, 198, 206, 252, 266, 308			
❑	African Scops-Owl	Otus senegalensis	88, 139, 144, 182, 195, 196, 198, 202, 221, 224, 228, 234, 241, 252, 257, 319			
❑	**Malagasy Scops-Owl**	**Otus rutilus**	364, 366, 371, 373, 374	M	NE	
❑	Southern White-faced Scops-Owl	Ptilopsus granti	88, 90, 139, 167, 182, 220, 223, 224, 228, 234, 252			
❑	Pearl-spotted Owlet	Glaucidium perlatum	88, 91, 144, 182, 195, 198, 215, 221, 224, 227, 228, 252, 257			
❑	Cape Eagle-Owl	Bubo capensis	41, 60, 63, 76, 77, 81, 82, 84, 86, 96, 108, 109, 110, 115, 116, 117, 127, 128, 156, 157, 159, 160, 171, 172, 173, 202, 210, 270, 281, 285, 309, 387			
❑	(African) Barred Owlet	Glaucidium capense	101, 110, 141, 144, 146, 178, 198, 225, 235, 237, 238, 241, 257, 260, 270, 304, 320			
❑	Spotted Eagle-Owl	Bubo africanus	30, 32, 60, 88, 139, 144, 198, 228, 329			
❑	Verreaux's (Giant / Milky) Eagle-Owl	Bubo lacteus	87, 88, 90, 139, 146, 198, 221, 224, 225, 228, 243, 254, 260, 319			
❑	Pel's Fishing-Owl	Scotopelia peli	18, 25, 94, 99, 130, 141, 143, 144, 145, 146, 178, 179, 190, 191, 196, 208, 231, 237, 238, 239, 240, 241, 256, 259, 260, 277, 278, 280, 287, 293, 297, 319, 338, 340, 346, 348, 354, 355, 387			
	Caprimulgidae	**Nightjars**				
❑	European Nightjar	Caprimulgus europaeus	198, 234			
❑	**Madagascar Nightjar**	**Caprimulgus madagascariensis**		M	E	
❑	Fiery-necked Nightjar	Caprimulgus pectoralis	68, 139, 144, 182, 198, 234, 319, 323			
❑	Rufous-cheeked Nightjar	Caprimulgus rufigena	81, 182, 224, 227, 228, 234			
❑	Rwenzori (Montane) Nightjar	Caprimulgus ruwenzorii	321, 325, 329	B		
❑	Swamp (Natal) Nightjar	Caprimulgus natalensis	110, 130, 131, 136, 137, 138, 140, 147, 260, 283, 293, 340, 342, 351, 387			
❑	Freckled Nightjar	Caprimulgus tristigma	86, 114, 148, 190, 195, 198, 202, 210, 220, 221, 223, 225, 285, 323			
❑	**Collared Nightjar**	**Caprimulgus enarratus**	364, 365, 366, 405	M	E	
❑	Square-tailed (Mozambique) Nightjar	Caprimulgus fossii	147, 198, 234, 319, 323			
❑	Long-tailed Nightjar	Caprimulgus climacurus		B		1
❑	Pennant-winged Nightjar	Macrodipteryx vexillarius	179, 190, 197, 198, 234, 239, 240, 243, 266, 268, 270, 271, 284, 288, 289, 300, 304, 323, 326, 388			
	Apodidae	**Swifts**				
❑	Common (European) Swift	Apus apus	89, 246			
❑	African (Black) Swift	Apus barbatus	30, 32, 33, 41, 50, 124, 157, 165, 175, 202, 335			
❑	**Bradfield's Swift**	**Apus bradfieldi**	82, 87, 92, 214, 219, 223		E	
❑	**Madagascar Black Swift**	**Apus balstoni**		M	NE	
❑	Pallid Swift	Apus pallidus				1

	Common Name	Scientific name	Page numbers	Reg	End	Vag
❑	White-rumped Swift	Apus caffer	154			
❑	Horus Swift	Apus horus	66, 162, 165, 196, 200, 354, 358			
❑	Little Swift	Apus affinis	154			
❑	Alpine Swift	Tachymarptis melba	32, 41, 157, 165, 175			
❑	Mottled Swift	Tachymarptis aequatorialis	270, 273, 285, 309			
❑	Scarce Swift	Schoutedenapus myoptilus	273, 274, 279, 309, 315, 327, 331			
❑	African Palm Swift	Cypsiurus parvus	81, 229, 260			
❑	**Madagascar Spine-tailed Swift**	**Zoonavena grandidieri**	365	M	NE	
❑	Mottled Spinetail	Telacanthura ussheri	94, 99, 179, 189, 190, 191, 196, 278, 280, 286, 287, 288, 289, 297, 303, 316, 337, 355			
❑	Bohm's (Bat-like) Spinetail	Neafrapus boehmi	179, 196, 278, 280, 286, 287, 288, 289, 295, 297, 300, 303, 316, 337, 355, 388			
	Coliidae	**Mousebirds**				
❑	Speckled Mousebird	Colius striatus	29, 30, 34, 96			
❑	**Red-backed Mousebird**	**Colius castanotus**	356, 358, 360	B	E	
❑	**White-backed Mousebird**	**Colius colius**	35, 46, 48, 56, 60, 61, 77, 84, 95, 96, 167, 199, 210, 214		E	
❑	**Red-faced Mousebird**	**Urocolius indicus**	53, 96		NE	
	Trogonidae	**Trogons**				
❑	Narina Trogon	Apaloderma narina	18, 64, 69, 70, 71, 73, 74, 105, 106, 107, 109, 112, 113, 114, 123, 124, 127, 128, 131, 132, 133, 136, 137, 138, 139, 140, 141, 143, 145, 172, 174, 175, 176, 185, 187, 189, 196, 197, 238, 240, 278, 280, 293, 297, 300, 304, 316, 322, 331, 388			
❑	Bar-tailed Trogon	Apaloderma vittatum	308, 309, 313, 314, 315, 325, 327, 331, 388	B		
	Alcedinidae	**Kingfishers**				
❑	Pied Kingfisher	Ceryle rudis	46, 88, 121, 183, 260			
❑	Giant Kingfisher	Megaceryle maxima	68, 69, 92, 99, 106, 121, 166, 188, 193, 201, 259, 319, 334			
❑	**Madagascar Kingfisher**	**Corythornis vintsioides**	365	M	NE	
❑	Half-collared Kingfisher	Alcedo semitorquata	73, 74, 103, 114, 132, 148, 149, 159, 166, 177, 188, 201, 202, 242, 269, 278, 282, 304, 308, 318, 322, 334, 335, 348, 351, 352			
❑	Malachite Kingfisher	Alcedo cristata	38, 42, 54, 72, 99, 106, 121, 154, 259			
❑	Shining-blue Kingfisher	Alcedo quadribrachys	340	B		
❑	White-bellied Kingfisher	Alcedo leucogaster	343	B		1
❑	African Pygmy-Kingfisher	Ispidina picta	123, 124, 126, 241, 304			
❑	**Madagascar Pygmy-Kingfisher**	**Ispidina madagascariensis**		M	E	
❑	Woodland Kingfisher	Halcyon senegalensis	145, 189, 193, 202, 248, 249			
❑	Mangrove Kingfisher	Halcyon senegaloides	18, 101, 110, 119, 120, 133, 135, 136, 291, 293, 294, 295, 296, 297, 301, 302, 304, 388			
❑	Blue-breasted Kingfisher	Halcyon malimbica	340, 342	B		
❑	Brown-hooded Kingfisher	Halcyon albiventris	68			
❑	Grey-headed (Chestnut-bellied) Kingfisher	Halcyon leucocephala	201, 202, 225, 241			
❑	Striped Kingfisher	Halcyon chelicuti	166, 167, 195, 248, 252			
	Meropidae	**Bee-eaters**				
❑	European Bee-eater	Merops apiaster	47, 78, 234			

	Common Name	Scientific name	Page numbers	Reg	End	Vag
❑	Madagascar (Olive) Bee-eater	Merops superciliosus	222, 224, 225, 291, 293, 296, 302, 320, 365			
❑	Blue-cheeked Bee-eater	Merops persicus	134, 135, 136, 141, 143, 144, 168, 169, 196, 200, 234, 236, 254, 259, 296, 302, 320			
❑	Southern Carmine Bee-eater	Merops nubicoides	168, 234, 236, 238, 242, 254, 257, 259, 261, 288, 289, 306, 319, 354			
❑	Northern Carmine Bee-eater	Merops nubicus		B		1
❑	White-throated Bee-eater	Merops albicollis				1
❑	**Bohm's Bee-eater**	**Merops boehmi**	311, 313, 316, 318, 319, 320, 338, 346, 347, 353, 354, 388		NE	
❑	White-fronted Bee-eater	Merops bullockoides	92, 99, 131, 139, 144, 145, 165, 189, 234, 261, 289, 295, 354			
❑	Little Bee-eater	Merops pusillus	120, 176, 189, 234, 248			
❑	Blue-breasted (White-cheeked) Bee-eater	Merops variegatus	340, 342, 348, 349, 350, 352	B		
❑	Swallow-tailed Bee-eater	Merops hirundineus	81, 88, 91, 199, 205, 207, 212, 215, 220, 221, 248, 258			
	Coraciidae	**Rollers**				
❑	European Roller	Coracias garrulus	255			
❑	Lilac-breasted Roller	Coracias caudata	90, 193, 203, 255			
❑	Racket-tailed Roller	Coracias spatulata	189, 197, 234, 239, 241, 243, 280, 281, 283, 286, 287, 288, 289, 295, 297, 301, 303, 318, 319, 330, 338, 347, 351, 355, 388			
❑	Purple (Rufous-crowned) Roller	Coracias naevia	201, 202, 215, 228			
❑	Broad-billed Roller	Eurystomus glaucurus	99, 141, 144, 145, 189, 196, 197, 243, 269, 288, 295, 324			
	Brachypteraciidae	**Ground-Rollers**				
❑	**Short-legged Ground-Roller**	**Brachypteracias leptosomus**	363, 364, 366, 367, 368, 405	M	E	
❑	**Scaly Ground-Roller**	**Brachypteracias squamigera**	19, 363, 364, 365, 369, 406	M	E	
❑	**Pitta-like Ground-Roller**	**Atelornis pittoides**	363, 364, 365, 367, 369	M	E	
❑	**Rufous-headed Ground-Roller**	**Atelornis crossleyi**	19, 363, 364, 365, 366, 368, 406	M	E	
❑	**Long-tailed Ground-Roller**	**Uratelornis chimaera**	19, 370, 372, 406	M	E	
	Leptosomatidae	**Cuckoo-Roller**				
❑	**Madagascar Cuckoo-Roller**	**Leptosomus discolor**	363, 365, 369, 371, 406	M	NE	
	Upupidae	**Hoopoes**				
❑	African Hoopoe	Upupa africana	46, 93, 267			
❑	**Madagascar Hoopoe**	**Upupa marginata**	376	M	E	
	Phoeniculidae	**Wood-Hoopoes**				
❑	Green (Red-billed) Wood-Hoopoe	Phoeniculus purpureus	71, 74, 107, 223, 228			
❑	**Violet Wood-Hoopoe**	**Phoeniculus damarensis**	208, 221, 222, 223, 224, 227, 228		E	
❑	Common Scimitarbill	Rhinopomastus cyanomelas	88, 93, 98, 126, 164, 168, 196, 251			
❑	Black Scimitarbill	Rhinopomastus aterrimus	340	B		
	Bucerotidae	**Hornbills**				
❑	Trumpeter Hornbill	Bycanistes bucinator	106, 107, 109, 113, 124, 128, 131, 133, 138, 143, 148, 178, 193, 243, 314, 334			
❑	Silvery-cheeked Hornbill	Bycanistes brevis	274, 275, 276, 277, 300, 302, 304, 305, 314, 315, 316, 331			

	Common Name	Scientific name	Page numbers	Reg	End	Vag
❑	African Grey Hornbill	Tockus nasutus	251			
❑	**Southern Red-billed Hornbill**	**Tockus rufirostris**	186, 193, 202, 223, 230, 258, 306, 319, 338		E	
❑	**Damara Red-billed Hornbill**	**Tockus damarensis**	208, 220, 221, 224, 228, 230		E	
❑	**Southern Yellow-billed Hornbill**	**Tockus leucomelas**	90, 91, 168, 186, 193, 199, 203		E	
❑	Crowned Hornbill	Tockus alboterminatus	106, 107, 109, 124, 128, 129, 131, 138, 143, 178, 295			
❑	**Bradfield's Hornbill**	**Tockus bradfieldi**	223, 232, 233, 234, 239, 243, 257, 261, 281, 283		E	
❑	**Monteiro's Hornbill**	**Tockus monteiri**	17, 208, 211, 213, 214, 215, 219, 220, 221, 223, 224, 225, 230		E	
❑	**Pale-billed Hornbill**	**Tockus pallidirostris**	322, 323, 338, 344, 346, 351	B	NE	
	Bucorvidae	**Ground-Hornbills**				
❑	Southern Ground-Hornbill	Bucorvus leadbeateri	110, 129, 134, 138, 139, 148, 191, 195, 243, 261, 288, 289, 303, 319, 355, 389			
	Lybiidae	**African Barbets and Tinkerbirds**				
❑	Naked-faced Barbet	Gymnobucco calvus	360	B		
❑	Black-collared Barbet	Lybius torquatus	138, 193			
❑	**Chaplin's Barbet**	**Lybius chaplini**	332, 333, 336, 337, 389	B	E	
❑	Brown-breasted Barbet	Lybius melanopterus	313, 318, 319	B		
❑	**Black-backed Barbet**	**Lybius minor**	325, 326, 338, 340, 344, 345, 346, 347, 351, 352, 355	B	NE	
❑	**Streaky-throated Barbet**	**Tricholaema flavipunctata**	360	B		
❑	Spot-flanked Barbet	Tricholaema lacrymosa	353	B		
❑	**Acacia Pied Barbet**	**Tricholaema leucomelas**	46, 49, 50, 53, 60, 67, 80, 81, 83, 84, 91, 93, 95, 96, 98, 99, 164, 199, 252, 335		E	
❑	**Miombo (~ Pied) Barbet**	**Tricholaema frontata**	322, 323, 330, 339, 344, 346, 347	B	NE	
❑	White-eared Barbet	Stactolaema leucotis	122, 131, 133, 136, 138, 143, 144, 145, 274, 314, 315, 316, 318			
❑	Whyte's Barbet	Stactolaema whytii	263, 266, 267, 268, 269, 271, 273, 276, 305, 323, 326, 344, 347			
❑	**Green Barbet**	**Stactolaema olivacea**	18, 130, 134, 307, 308, 309, 314, 331, 389		NE	
❑	**Anchieta's Barbet**	**Stactolaema anchietae**	341, 345, 346, 347, 350, 351, 354	B	NE	
❑	Red-fronted Tinkerbird	Pogoniulus pusillus	109, 110, 146			
❑	Yellow-fronted Tinkerbird	Pogoniulus chrysoconus	167, 176, 194, 200, 202, 235, 266			
❑	Yellow-rumped Tinkerbird	Pogoniulus bilineatus	133, 138, 176, 276, 333, 340, 342, 344, 348			
❑	Moustached (Green-) Tinkerbird	Pogoniulus leucomystax	320, 324, 325, 327, 331	B		
❑	Green Tinkerbird	Pogoniulus simplex				
❑	**White-chested Tinkerbird**	**Pogoniulus makawai**	333, 343	B	E	2
❑	Yellow-billed Barbet	Trachyphonus purpuratus	360	B		
❑	Crested Barbet	Trachyphonus vaillantii	92, 99, 126, 319			
	Indicatoridae	**Honeyguides**				
❑	Greater Honeyguide	Indicator indicator	47, 66, 128, 167			
❑	Scaly-throated Honeyguide	Indicator variegatus	71, 74, 75, 112, 131, 136, 143, 144, 145, 173, 174, 178, 185, 187, 297, 309, 324, 346, 348			
❑	(Western) Least Honeyguide	Indicator exilis	341, 344	B		
❑	Lesser Honeyguide	Indicator minor	66, 68, 93, 167, 201, 221, 278			

	Common Name	Scientific name	Page numbers	Reg	End	Vag
❑	Pallid (Eastern Least) Honeyguide	Indicator meliphilus	274, 277, 278, 299, 300, 304, 341			
❑	Brown-backed (Sharp-billed) Honeybird	Prodotiscus regulus	41, 66, 116, 119, 126, 127, 128, 129, 148, 149, 164, 167, 184, 268, 269, 270			
❑	Green-backed (Slender-billed) Honeybird	Prodotiscus zambesiae	233, 234, 243, 267, 268, 269, 270, 273, 279, 295, 303, 323, 344, 351			
	Picidae	**Woodpeckers**				
❑	**Ground Woodpecker**	**Geocolaptes olivaceus**	30, 32, 34, 39, 41, 54, 59, 60, 75, 83, 84, 95, 97, 101, 107, 109, 110, 114, 115, 116, 127, 151, 152, 153, 154, 155, 156, 157, 158, 159, 160, 170, 171, 389		E	
❑	**Bennett's Woodpecker**	**Campethera bennettii**	146, 148, 178, 186, 193, 195, 197, 202, 225, 239, 319		NE	
❑	Speckle-throated (Reichenow's) Woodpecker	Campethera scriptoricauda	298, 299, 302, 303, 310, 317			
❑	Golden-tailed Woodpecker	Campethera abingoni	90, 91, 194			
❑	Brown-eared Woodpecker	Campethera caroli	343, 360	B		
❑	Buff-spotted Woodpecker	Campethera nivosa	360	B		
❑	**Knysna Woodpecker**	**Campethera notata**	18, 64, 65, 66, 69, 70, 72, 75, 101, 103, 105, 106, 107, 108, 109, 110, 111, 113, 114, 389		E	
❑	Green-backed (Little Spotted) Woodpecker	Campethera cailliautii	274, 276, 277, 299, 302, 303, 311, 324, 331, 338, 344, 346			
❑	Cardinal Woodpecker	Dendropicos fuscescens	46, 49, 68, 96, 99, 193, 266			
❑	**Stierling's Woodpecker**	**Dendropicos stierlingi**	186, 306, 310, 321, 322, 323	B	NE	
❑	Bearded Woodpecker	Dendropicos namaquus	139, 144, 146, 193, 215			
❑	Olive Woodpecker	Dendropicos griseocephalus	40, 41, 68, 70, 71, 74, 96, 106, 107, 109, 118, 127, 128, 129, 131, 132, 134, 159, 173, 174, 187, 243, 324, 327, 338, 344			
❑	Red-throated Wryneck	Jynx ruficollis	123, 124, 126, 128, 164, 175, 177, 342			
	Eurylaimidae	**Broadbills**				
❑	African Broadbill	Smithornis capensis	99, 113, 114, 124, 130, 136, 137, 140, 141, 142, 145, 146, 147, 178, 179, 187, 188, 275, 277, 280, 284, 288, 292, 293, 299, 302, 304, 309, 315, 322, 324, 337, 342, 348, 360, 390			
	Philepittidae	**Asities**				
❑	**Velvet Asity**	**Philepitta castanea**	367	M	E	
❑	**Schlegel's Asity**	**Philepitta schlegeli**	19, 375, 376, 377, 406	M	E	
❑	**Common Sunbird-Asity**	**Neodrepanis coruscans**	19, 367	M	E	
❑	**Yellow-bellied Sunbird-Asity**	**Neodrepanis hypoxantha**	19, 363, 364, 366, 367, 368, 407	M	E	
	Pittidae	**Pittas**				
❑	African Pitta	Pitta angolensis	25, 262, 277, 284, 286, 288, 290, 298, 302, 304, 319, 333, 337, 353, 354, 355, 389			
	Alaudidae	**Larks**				
❑	**Melodious Lark**	**Mirafra cheniana**	18, 94, 97, 98, 99, 149, 161, 163, 164, 165, 166, 199, 246, 390		E	
❑	**Madagascar Lark**	**Mirafra hova**	19, 371	M	E	
❑	**Angola Lark**	**Mirafra angolensis**	333, 340, 341, 342, 361	B	NE	
❑	**Monotonous Lark**	**Mirafra passerina**	87, 88, 91, 190, 191, 197, 207, 215, 228, 246, 255		E	
❑	Rufous-naped Lark	Mirafra africana	92, 168, 183, 203, 206, 236, 246, 329			
❑	**Cape Clapper Lark**	**Mirafra apiata**	34, 44, 46, 47, 53, 63, 77, 390		E	
❑	**Agulhas Clapper Lark**	**Mirafra marjoriae**	17, 65, 67, 68		E	

	Common Name	Scientific name	Page numbers	Reg	End	Vag
❑	**Eastern Clapper Lark**	**Mirafra fasciolata**	88, 90, 92, 93, 97, 98, 99, 110, 163, 165, 199, 204, 206, 207, 228, 230, 246, 250, 252, 253, 340		E	
❑	Flappet Lark	Mirafra rufocinnamomea	139, 144, 146, 166, 167, 168, 182, 195, 203, 236, 295, 303			
❑	**Rudd's Lark**	**Heteromirafra ruddi**	18, 115, 150, 152, 153, 154, 155, 156, 390		E	
❑	**Fawn-coloured Lark**	**Calendulauda africanoides**	81, 83, 88, 90, 165, 166, 167, 199, 206, 236, 246, 252, 295		E	
❑	**Sabota Lark (incl. Bradfield's)**	**Calendulauda sabota**	81, 82, 93, 139, 144, 146, 183, 193, 195, 215, 220, 246, 248		E	
❑	**Karoo Lark**	**Calendulauda albescens**	14, 16, 46, 48, 50, 53, 56, 58, 61, 77, 78, 83, 84, 85		E	
❑	**Dune Lark**	**Calendulauda erythrochlamys**	17, 209, 211, 212, 213, 216, 217		E	
❑	**Barlow's Lark**	**Calendulauda barlowi**	14, 16, 76, 84, 85, 209, 210		E	
❑	**Red Lark**	**Calendulauda burra**	16, 76, 77, 78, 79, 82, 391		E	
❑	**Dusky Lark**	**Pinarocorys nigricans**	179, 183, 228, 236, 260, 261, 283, 284, 287, 391		NE	
❑	**Gray's Lark**	**Ammomanopsis grayi**	17, 208, 209, 212, 213, 216, 218, 220, 391		E	
❑	**Spike-heeled Lark**	**Chersomanes albofasciata**	58, 61, 79, 90, 91, 92, 93, 97, 98, 109, 110, 152, 165, 166, 199, 204, 207, 228, 252		E	
❑	**Benguela Long-billed Lark**	**Certhilauda benguelensis**	17, 208, 213, 218, 225, 390		E	
❑	**Karoo Long-billed Lark**	**Certhilauda subcoronata**	16, 62, 78, 81, 82, 83, 91, 95, 210		E	
❑	**Cape Long-billed Lark**	**Certhilauda curvirostris**	44, 51, 53, 84, 85, 391		E	
❑	**Agulhas Long-billed Lark**	**Certhilauda brevirostris**	14, 17, 64, 65		E	
❑	**Eastern Long-billed Lark**	**Certhilauda semitorquata**	18, 97, 109, 127, 128, 152, 153, 154, 155, 156, 163, 164, 165, 171		E	
❑	**Short-clawed Lark**	**Certhilauda chuana**	17, 92, 94, 99, 179, 182, 183, 184, 199, 204, 245, 246, 248, 391		E	
❑	Chestnut-backed Sparrowlark	Eremopterix leucotis	169, 195, 198, 200, 204, 228, 246, 250, 261, 280, 336			
❑	**Grey-backed Sparrowlark**	**Eremopterix verticalis**	51, 82, 90, 199, 207, 210, 228, 252, 261		E	
❑	Fischer's Sparrowlark	Eremopterix leucopareia		B		
❑	**Black-eared Sparrowlark**	**Eremopterix australis**	16, 55, 61, 76, 77, 79, 90, 91, 210, 392		E	
❑	Red-capped Lark	Calandrella cinerea	46, 47, 51, 68, 61, 65, 77, 93.98, 152, 163, 169, 200, 228, 238, 252			
❑	**Pink-billed Lark**	**Spizocorys conirostris**	79, 87, 88, 90, 93, 95, 98, 149, 152, 155, 156, 166, 199, 205, 210, 228, 227, 228, 246, 250, 251, 252, 340		E	
❑	**Botha's Lark**	**Spizocorys fringillaris**	18, 90, 150, 152, 153, 155, 156, 391		E	
❑	**Sclater's Lark**	**Spizocorys sclateri**	16, 25, 76, 78, 79, 80, 81, 82, 83, 210, 391		E	
❑	**Stark's Lark**	**Spizocorys starki**	79, 80, 81, 82, 83, 91, 210, 212, 218, 220		E	
❑	**Large-billed Lark**	**Galerida magnirostris**	47, 49, 51, 58, 65, 77, 83, 84, 95, 97, 98, 99, 109, 110, 117, 160		E	
	Hirundinidae	**Swallows**				
❑	Barn (European) Swallow	Hirundo rustica	36, 46, 48, 154, 166			
❑	Angola Swallow	Hirundo angolensis	226, 231, 325, 327, 329, 341, 353, 354			
❑	**White-throated Swallow**	**Hirundo albigularis**	36, 43, 45, 46, 66, 154, 214		NE	
❑	**Blue Swallow**	**Hirundo atrocaerulea**	18, 111, 118, 129, 150, 151, 170, 175, 176, 185, 186, 272, 273, 279, 315, 324, 325, 327, 329, 331, 392		NE	
❑	Wire-tailed Swallow	Hirundo smithii	136, 178, 193, 237			
❑	**Black-and-rufous Swallow**	**Hirundo nigrorufa**	333, 341, 342, 354	B	NE	
❑	**Pearl-breasted Swallow**	**Hirundo dimidiata**	46, 48, 53, 66, 68, 69, 109, 167, 335		NE	
❑	Red-breasted Swallow	Hirundo semirufa	92, 133, 246			
❑	Mosque Swallow	Hirundo senegalensis	99, 197, 280, 283, 297, 319			

	Common Name	Scientific name	Page numbers	Reg	End	Vag
❑	Red-rumped Swallow	Hirundo daurica	308, 309, 315, 325, 354			
❑	Red-throated (Angolan) Cliff Swallow	Hirundo rufigula	343	B	NE	
❑	**Greater Striped Swallow**	**Hirundo cucullata**	46, 154, 266		NE	
❑	Lesser Striped Swallow	Hirundo abyssinica				
❑	**South African Cliff-Swallow**	**Hirundo spilodera**	77, 93, 94, 97, 99, 154, 163, 245, 246		NE	
❑	Rock Martin	Hirundo fuligula	32, 41, 335, 352			
❑	Common House Martin	Delichon urbica	154			
❑	Grey-rumped Swallow	Pseudhirundo griseopyga	137, 141, 144, 147, 198, 226, 237, 260, 261, 264, 266, 292, 295, 301, 302, 348, 350			
❑	Sand Martin (Bank Swallow)	Riparia riparia	164, 166, 246			
❑	Brown-throated (Plain) Martin	Riparia paludicola	36, 45, 50, 66, 154			
❑	Banded Martin	Riparia cincta	46, 152, 237, 246, 260, 350			
❑	**Mascarene Martin**	**Phedina borbonica**	290, 294, 295, 296, 298, 302, 303, 304, 392		NE	
❑	White-headed Saw-wing	Psalidoprocne albiceps	324, 325, 326, 352			
❑	Black Saw-wing	Psalidoprocne pristoptera	29, 41, 42, 69, 173, 279, 292			
❑	**Eastern Saw-wing**	**Psalidoprocne orientalis**	109, 146, 274, 275, 276, 278, 300, 304, 318		NE	
	Motacillidae	**Wagtails and Pipits**				
❑	African Pied Wagtail	Motacilla aguimp	193			
❑	Mountain (Long-tailed) Wagtail	Motacilla clara	105, 114, 123, 124, 129, 159, 176, 185, 186, 300, 316, 318, 322, 351			
❑	Cape Wagtail	Motacilla capensis	49			
❑	**Madagascar Wagtail**	**Motacilla flaviventris**		M	E	
❑	Yellow Wagtail	Motacilla flava	124, 125, 162, 165, 248, 260, 285			
❑	Grey Wagtail	Motacilla cinerea	186, 279			1
❑	Citrine Wagtail	Motacilla citreola	102			1
❑	White Wagtail	Motacilla alba		B		1
❑	African (Grassveld) Pipit	Anthus cinnamomeus	46, 47, 93, 107, 115, 152, 236, 309			
❑	**Mountain Pipit**	**Anthus hoeschi**	18, 101, 107, 111, 115, 116, 117, 150, 157, 158, 159, 160		E	
❑	Jackson's Pipit	Anthus latistriatus	326	B		
❑	Long-billed Pipit	Anthus similis	14, 65, 97, 98, 171, 175, 214, 215, 327			
❑	**Kimberley Pipit**	**Anthus pseudosimils**	92, 93, 97		E	
❑	**Woodland (Wood) Pipit**	**Anthus nyassae**	232, 233, 234, 236, 237, 241, 243, 266, 268, 269, 271, 322, 323, 351			
❑	Plain-backed Pipit	Anthus leucophrys	33, 34, 93, 134, 148, 236			
❑	**Buffy Pipit**	**Anthus vaalensis**	92, 93, 98, 166		NE	
❑	**Long-tailed Pipit**	**Anthus longicaudatus**	87, 92, 93		E	
❑	Striped Pipit	Anthus lineiventris	114, 115, 123, 128, 129, 132, 134, 139, 144, 148, 165, 167, 169, 182, 193, 195, 200, 202, 247, 309, 320, 324			
❑	**African Rock (Yellow-tufted) Pipit**	**Anthus crenatus**	63, 92, 94, 95, 96, 97, 98, 101, 107, 109, 110, 115, 154, 156, 157, 160, 163, 164, 398		E	
❑	Tree Pipit	Anthus trivialis	276			
❑	Red-throated Pipit	Anthus cervinus				1
❑	Bushveld (Bush) Pipit	Anthus caffer	138, 139, 141, 144, 145, 14, 166, 167, 182, 183, 184, 193, 195, 202, 347			
❑	Short-tailed Pipit	Anthus brachyurus	112, 115, 118, 138, 151, 159, 170, 177, 301, 302, 304, 341, 342, 398			

	Common Name	Scientific name	Page numbers	Reg	End	Vag
❑	**Yellow-breasted Pipit**	**Anthus chloris**	18, 107, 115, 150, 152, 154, 155, 156, 157, 159, 164, 170, 171, 398		E	
❑	Golden Pipit	Tmetothylacus tenellus				1
❑	**Cape (Orange-throated) Longclaw**	**Macronyx capensis**	34, 47, 65, 109, 141, 152, 166, 175, 265		E	
❑	Yellow-throated Longclaw	Macronyx croceus	133, 141, 188, 194, 195, 265			
❑	**Fülleborn's Longclaw**	**Macronyx fuellebornii**	338, 341, 342, 344, 346, 348, 349, 351	B	NE	
❑	Rosy-breasted (Pink-throated) Longclaw	Macronyx ameliae	136, 137, 138, 141, 147, 236, 237, 243, 260, 264, 265, 292, 293, 320, 338, 341, 342, 344, 350, 399			
❑	**Grimwood's Longclaw**	**Macronyx grimwoodi**	333, 340, 341, 361	B	E	
	Campephagidae	**Cuckoo-shrikes**				
❑	Black Cuckooshrike	Campephaga flava	66, 124, 126, 167, 193, 202			
❑	Petit's Cuckooshrike	Campephaga petiti	360	B		
❑	Purple-throated Cuckooshrike	Campephaga quiscalina	344, 346, 347	B		
❑	White-breasted Cuckooshrike	Coracina pectoralis	179, 189, 197, 232, 233, 234, 237, 239, 266, 268, 271, 279, 295, 300, 303, 323, 326			
❑	Grey Cuckooshrike	Coracina caesia	70, 71, 74, 109, 112, 114, 118, 129, 131, 173, 174, 176, 185, 187, 278, 300, 314			
❑	**Madagascar Cuckooshrike**	**Coracina cinerea**	364, 374	M	E	
	Dicruridae	**Drongos**				
❑	Fork-tailed Drongo	Dicrurus adsimilis				
❑	Square-tailed Drongo	Dicrurus ludwigii	112, 137, 140, 141, 143, 145, 174, 185, 274, 277, 280, 310, 316			
❑	**Crested Drongo**	**Dicrurus forficatus**		M	NE	
	Oriolidae	**Orioles**				
❑	Eurasian Golden Oriole	Oriolus oriolus	99, 182, 197, 202			
❑	African Golden Oriole	Oriolus auratus	99, 179, 189, 225, 234, 257, 267, 303, 323			
❑	(Eastern) Black-headed Oriole	Oriolus larvatus	71, 74, 192			
❑	Green-headed Oriole	Oriolus chlorocephalus	18, 290, 298, 299, 300, 313, 314, 392		NE	
	Corvidae	**Crows**				
❑	Cape (Black) Crow	Corvus capensis	65, 84, 246, 340			
❑	Pied Crow	Corvus albus	46			
❑	House Crow	Corvus splendens	40, 121			3
❑	White-necked Raven	Corvus albicollis	32, 63, 157, 159, 160, 273, 352			
	Paridae	**Tits**				
❑	White-winged Black Tit	Parus leucomelas	326	B		
❑	**Grey Tit**	**Parus afer**	50, 51, 54, 58, 59, 60, 83, 84, 85, 98, 117, 143		E	
❑	**Ashy Tit**	**Parus cinerascens**	17, 88, 91, 93, 98, 99, 164, 168, 180, 181, 184, 199, 200, 201, 202, 203, 207, 214, 215, 219, 252, 284		E	
❑	**Miombo Tit**	**Parus griseiventris**	266, 268, 271, 275, 276, 287, 320, 322, 323, 326, 330, 347		E	
❑	**Southern Black Tit**	**Parus niger**	192, 202, 268		E	
❑	**Carp's Tit**	**Parus carpi**	208, 214, 215, 221, 222, 223, 224, 225, 228, 230		E	
❑	**Rufous-bellied Tit**	**Parus rufiventris**	232, 233, 234, 236, 237, 323, 326, 330, 346, 347, 351		NE	
❑	**Cinnamon-breasted Tit**	**Parus pallidiventris**	263, 267, 270, 271, 272, 275, 309, 310		NE	
❑	Dusky Tit	Parus funereus	360	B		

	Common Name	Scientific name	Page numbers	Reg	End	Vag
	Remizidae	**Penduline-Tits**				
❑	**Cape (Southern) Penduline-Tit**	**Anthoscopus minutus**	44, 46, 48, 49, 50, 51, 53, 58, 61, 77, 78, 84, 85, 95, 168, 181, 199, 200, 210, 214, 215, 284		E	
❑	Grey (African) Penduline-Tit	Anthoscopus caroli	144, 146, 193, 194, 266, 295, 303, 323, 347			
	Certhiidae	**Creepers**				
❑	(African) Spotted Creeper	Salpornis spilonotus	263, 266, 267, 268, 269, 270, 275, 276, 287, 306, 310, 314, 320, 323, 326, 346, 347, 351, 392			
	Timaliidae	**Babblers**				
❑	Mountain Illadopsis	Illadopsis pyrrhoptera	324, 328, 329	B		
❑	Brown Illadopsis	Illadopsis fulvescens	360	B		
❑	African (Abyssinian) Hill Babbler	Pseudoalcippe abyssinica	311, 325, 327	B		
❑	Arrow-marked Babbler	Turdoides jardineii	257, 260			
❑	**Black-faced Babbler**	**Turdoides melanops**	91, 227, 230, 232, 233, 236, 237, 393		E	
❑	**Hartlaub's Babbler**	**Turdoides hartlaubii**	18, 231, 233, 234, 235, 236, 237, 238, 239, 240, 241, 242, 256, 257, 260, 283, 335, 349, 350		NE	
❑	**Southern Pied Babbler**	**Turdoides bicolor**	17, 92, 168, 180, 181, 183, 199, 200, 201, 202, 203, 207, 221, 223, 227, 229, 230, 233, 252, 253, 254, 258, 283		E	
❑	**Bare-cheeked Babbler**	**Turdoides gymnogenys**	208, 222, 224, 225, 227, 228, 230, 393		E	
❑	(Spotted) Thrush Babbler	Ptyrticus turdinus	333, 343, 345, 353, 354, 392	B		
❑	**Bush Blackcap**	**Lioptilus nigricapillus**	18, 101, 108, 109, 111, 114, 116, 117, 118, 127, 129, 149, 150, 152, 154, 155, 156, 157, 158, 159, 170, 173, 174, 175, 393		E	
❑	**Stripe-throated Jery**	**Neomixis striatigula**	365, 372	M	E	
❑	**Common Jery**	**Neomixis tenella**	364	M	E	
❑	**Green Jery**	**Neomixis viridis**	365	M	E	
❑	**Wedge-tailed Jery**	**Hartertula flavoviridis**	367	M	E	
	Pycnonotidae	**Bulbuls**				
❑	**Cape Bulbul**	**Pycnonotus capensis**	34, 37, 41, 42, 46, 66, 68, 75, 109		E	
❑	**African Red-eyed Bulbul**	**Pycnonotus nigricans**	80, 91, 96, 109, 164, 199, 335		E	
❑	Dark-capped (Black-eyed) Bulbul	Pycnonotus tricolor	109			
❑	Terrestrial Brownbul	Phyllastrephus terrestris	69, 70, 71, 74, 103, 122, 133, 145, 173, 189, 192, 235, 240, 242, 257, 260, 331			
❑	Grey-olive Greenbul	Phyllastrephus cerviniventris	306, 314, 331, 338, 344, 346, 351	B		
❑	**Pale-olive Greenbul**	**Phyllastrephus fulviventris**	358, 360	B	E	
❑	Cabanis's Greenbul	Phyllastrephus cabanisi	342, 346, 348	B		
❑	Placid Greenbul	Phyllastrephus placidus	309, 314, 315, 316, 318	B		
❑	Fischer's Greenbul	Phyllastrephus fischeri		B		
❑	Tiny (Slender) Greenbul	Phyllastrephus debilis	18, 277, 278, 301, 302, 303, 304			
❑	Yellow-streaked Greenbul	Phyllastrephus flavostriatus	131, 132, 134, 172, 173, 174, 175, 185, 187, 276, 277, 309, 314, 315, 316			
❑	**Sharpe's Greenbul**	**Phyllastrephus alfredi**	326	B	NE	
❑	Slender-billed Greenbul	Andropadus gracilirostris	360	B		
❑	Little Greenbul	Andropadus virens	309, 310, 311, 314, 315, 316, 327, 342, 348			
❑	Shelley's Greenbul	Andropadus masukuensis	331			
❑	Sombre Greenbul	Andropadus importunus	28, 32, 66, 70, 71, 74, 140, 141, 173, 188, 337			

	Common Name	Scientific name	Page numbers	Reg	End	Vag
☐	**Southern (Olive-breasted) Mountain Greenbul**	**Andropadus fusciceps**	313, 315, 316, 318, 324, 325, 326	B	NE	
☐	Stripe-cheeked Greenbul	Andropadus milanjensis	273, 275, 276, 278, 279, 300, 309, 315, 318		E	
☐	**Olive-headed Greenbul**	**Andropadus olivaceiceps**	331	B	NE	
☐	Yellow-throated Greenbul (Leaf-love)	Chlorocichla flavicollis	344, 347, 348	B		
☐	Falkenstein's Greenbul	Chlorocichla falkensteini	360	B		
☐	Yellow-bellied Greenbul	Chlorocichla flaviventris	133, 140, 141, 145, 188, 189, 196, 235, 240, 242, 260, 334			
☐	Joyful Greenbul	Chlorocichla laetissima	354	B		
☐	Red-tailed (Common) Bristlebill	Bleda syndactyla	341, 342	B		
☐	Honeyguide Greenbul	Baeopogon indicator	341, 342	B		
☐	Eastern (Yellow-spotted) Nicator	Nicator gularis	136, 137, 140, 141, 143, 144, 145, 178, 187, 189, 196, 197, 278, 280, 284, 288, 293, 295, 297, 309, 331, 337			
☐	Western Nicator	Nicator chloris		B		
☐	Yellow-throated Nicator	Nicator vireo	360	B		
☐	Black-collared Bulbul (Greenbul)	Neolestes torquatus	332, 333, 341, 342, 343, 393	B		
☐	**Madagascar Bulbul**	**Hypsipetes madagascariensis**		M	NE	
☐	**White-throated Oxylabes**	**Oxylabes madagascariensis**	365, 366, 368	M	E	
☐	**Yellow-browed Oxylabes**	**Crossleyia xanthophrys**	19, 364, 367, 368	M	E	
☐	**Crossley's Babbler**	**Mystacornis crossleyi**	363, 365, 366	M	E	
☐	**Long-billed Greenbul**	**Bernieria madagascariensis**		M	E	
☐	**Spectacled Greenbul**	**Bernieria zosterops**	365, 367, 369	M	E	
☐	**Appert's Greenbul**	**Bernieria apperti**	19, 370, 371	M	E	
☐	**Dusky Greenbul**	**Bernieria tenebrosa**	264, 407	M	E	
☐	**Grey-crowned Greenbul**	**Bernieria cinereiceps**	366, 367	M	E	
	Spot-throat and Dapple-throat	**Spot-throat and Dapple-throat**				
☐	Spot-throat (Modulatrix)	Modulatrix stictigula	18, 321, 331, 393	B		
☐	**Dappled Mountain Robin (Dapple-throat)**	**Arcanator (Modulatrix) orostruthus**	18, 290, 307, 308, 309, 394	B	NE	
	Rock-jumpers	**Rock-jumpers**				
☐	**Cape Rock-jumper**	**Chaetops frenatus**	17, 26, 27, 39, 40, 63, 66, 75, 395		E	
☐	**Drakensberg (Orange-breasted) Rock-jumper**	**Chaetops aurantius**	18, 107, 109, 111, 116, 116, 117, 150, 157, 158, 159, 160		E	
	Turdidae	**Thrushes**				
☐	**Boulder Chat**	**Pinarornis plumosus**	245, 249, 262, 263, 269, 270, 271, 281, 285, 320, 322, 324, 395		E	
☐	Kurrichane Thrush	Turdus libonyanus	192, 219, 230			
☐	**Olive Thrush**	**Turdus olivaceus**	28, 173, 185, 276		E	
☐	Mountain Thrush	Turdus abyssinicus		B		
☐	**Karoo Thrush**	**Turdus smithii**	91, 199		E	
☐	African Thrush	Turdus pelios	342, 348	B		
☐	Spotted Ground-Thrush	Zoothera guttata	101, 110, 112, 113, 114, 119, 122, 123, 131, 132, 133, 134, 292, 294, 314, 315, 316, 393			

	Common Name	Scientific name	Page numbers	Reg	End	Vag
❑	Orange Ground-Thrush	Zoothera gurneyi	95, 101, 108, 109, 114, 117, 118, 127, 129, 170, 172, 173, 174, 185, 186, 187, 276, 305, 309, 310, 311, 314, 315, 318, 331			
❑	Groundscraper Thrush	Psophocichla litsipsirupa	90, 194, 195, 201, 228			
❑	**Amber Mountain Rock-Thrush**	**Monticola erythronotus**	363, 369	M	E	
❑	**Littoral Rock-Thrush**	**Monticola imerinus**	19, 370, 373	M	E	
❑	**Forest Rock-Thrush**	**Monticola sharpei**	19, 366, 372	M	E	
❑	**Cape Rock-Thrush**	**Monticola rupestris**	33, 34, 39, 41, 63, 75, 110, 114, 116, 123, 127, 151, 159, 163, 164, 169, 172, 173, 175		E	
❑	**Sentinel Rock-Thrush**	**Monticola explorator**	34, 39, 75, 107, 109, 110, 116, 117, 151, 152, 153, 154, 155, 157, 158, 159, 160, 163, 164, 170, 171, 172, 202		E	
❑	**Short-toed Rock-Thrush (incl. Transvaal)**	**Monticola brevipes**	91, 96, 97, 98, 161, 166, 167, 180, 199, 200, 201, 203, 210, 214, 215, 220, 221, 223, 224, 225, 247		E	
❑	**Miombo Rock-Thrush**	**Monticola angolensis**	243, 263, 266, 267, 268, 270, 271, 273, 279, 287, 314, 320, 323, 324, 326, 347, 351		NE	
❑	Rufous-tailed (Mountain/ European) Rock-Thrush	Monticola saxatilis	107	B		1
❑	Northern (European) Wheatear	Oenanthe oenanthe				
❑	Isabelline Wheatear	Oenanthe isabellina				1
❑	Pied Wheatear	Oenanthe pleschanka				1
❑	**Mountain Wheatear**	**Oenanthe monticola**	56, 60, 77, 83, 84, 96, 109, 110, 115, 153, 154, 156, 158, 164, 171, 210, 211, 215, 219		E	
❑	Capped Wheatear	Oenanthe pileata	46, 47, 51, 65, 66, 169, 252, 349			
❑	**Buff-streaked Chat**	**Oenanthe bifasciata**	18, 108, 109, 110, 114, 115, 116, 117, 127, 129, 148, 151, 152, 153, 154, 155, 156, 157, 158, 159, 170, 171, 172, 173, 174, 175, 180		E	
❑	Fraser's Rufous Thrush (Rufous Flycatcher-Thrush)	Neocossyphus fraseri	341, 342, 360	B		
❑	Familiar Chat	Cercomela familiaris	34, 39, 46, 78, 127, 201			
❑	**Tractrac Chat**	**Cercomela tractrac**	16, 58, 61, 78, 210, 212, 218, 220		E	
❑	**Sickle-winged Chat**	**Cercomela sinuata**	44, 63, 78, 97, 98, 108, 109, 110, 117, 160		E	
❑	**Karoo Chat**	**Cercomela schlegelii**	16, 56, 58, 78, 81, 95, 98, 218		E	
❑	Mocking Cliff-Chat	Thamnolaea cinnamomeiventris	99, 114, 123, 127, 132, 139, 144, 148, 151, 158, 164, 165, 166, 175, 193, 194, 195, 198, 247, 249, 279, 314, 320, 324, 327, 351			
❑	Sooty Chat	Myrmecocichla nigra	341, 342, 348, 349	B		
❑	Arnot's (White-headed Black) Chat	Myrmecocichla arnotti	179, 186, 189, 196, 197, 233, 234, 239, 241, 243, 259, 260, 280, 283, 284, 286, 288, 289, 300, 310, 319, 323, 326, 330, 338, 355			
❑	**(Southern) Ant-eating Chat**	**Myrmecocichla formicivora**	51, 52, 57, 78, 83, 90, 92, 93, 99, 183, 204, 206, 228, 246		E	
❑	Common Stonechat	Saxicola torquata	49, 51, 365			
❑	Whinchat	Saxicola rubetra				1
❑	**Chorister Robin-Chat**	**Cossypha dichroa**	18, 71, 74, 103, 105, 106, 107, 108, 109, 117, 118, 127, 129, 131, 134, 139, 173, 174, 185, 187		E	
❑	**White-headed Robin-Chat**	**Cossypha heinrichi**	356	B	NE	
❑	White-browed (Heuglin's) Robin-Chat	Cossypha heuglini	144, 176, 192, 235, 241, 242, 257, 260			
❑	Grey-winged Robin-Chat	Cossypha polioptera	341, 342, 354	B		
❑	Red-capped (Natal) Robin-Chat	Cossypha natalensis	105, 106, 122, 133, 176, 187, 192, 195, 198, 241, 278, 311, 337			
❑	Cape Robin-Chat	Cossypha caffra	29, 33, 46, 48, 173, 329			
❑	**Olive-flanked Robin-Chat**	**Cossypha anomala**	307, 308, 309, 315, 316, 321, 324, 327, 328	B	NE	
❑	**White-throated Robin-Chat**	**Cossypha humeralis**	143, 144, 149, 167, 168, 176, 188, 192, 193, 195, 196, 199, 201, 245, 247, 334		E	

	Common Name	Scientific name	Page numbers	Reg	End	Vag
❑	Angola Cave Chat	Xenocopsychus ansorgei	357, 359, 360, 394	B	E	
❑	Collared Palm-Thrush	Cichladusa arquata	197, 237, 241, 242, 274, 278, 280, 281, 282, 287, 288, 295, 301, 318, 319, 330			
❑	**Rufous-tailed Palm-Thrush**	**Cichladusa ruficauda**	222, 225, 226, 356, 357, 358, 394		NE	
❑	Common Redstart	Phoenicurus phoenicurus				1
❑	**White-chested Alethe**	**Pseudalethe fuelleborni**	290, 298, 300, 302, 303, 304, 325, 327, 328, 331, 394		NE	
❑	Thyolo (Cholo) Alethe	Pseudalethe choloensis	290, 307, 308, 309, 313, 314, 315, 316, 318, 394	B	E	
❑	Brown-chested Alethe	Alethe poliocephala	360	B		
❑	White-starred Robin	Pogonocichla stellata	72, 75, 103, 107, 108, 109, 118, 129, 172, 173, 174, 185, 292, 305, 309, 318, 327			
❑	**Swynnerton's Robin**	**Swynnertonia swynnertoni**	18, 262, 272, 273, 275, 276, 299, 300, 394		NE	
❑	Sharpe's Akalat	Sheppardia sharpei	18, 324, 325, 327, 328	B	NE	
❑	Gabela Akalat	Sheppardia gabela	357, 359, 360, 361, 395	B	E	
❑	**East Coast (Gunning's) Akalat**	**Sheppardia gunningi**	290, 298, 302, 303, 304, 321, 330, 331, 394		NE	
❑	Bocage's Akalat (Robin)	Sheppardia bocagei	344, 345, 346, 348, 351, 352	B		
❑	Thrush Nightingale	Luscinia luscinia	190, 191, 196, 197, 240, 241, 242, 249, 254, 270, 280, 285, 337, 395			
❑	White-browed Scrub-Robin	Cercotrichas leucophrys	106, 126, 188, 192, 193, 196, 200, 203			
❑	**Karoo Scrub-Robin**	**Cercotrichas coryphaeus**	46, 48, 77, 98, 99		E	
❑	Rufous-tailed Scrub-Robin (Rufous Bush Chat)	Cercotrichas galactotes		B		1
❑	**Kalahari Scrub-Robin**	**Cercotrichas paena**	17, 88, 93, 99, 104, 108, 180, 104, 199, 200, 203, 204, 206, 233, 250, 252, 258, 283, 284		E	
❑	**Brown Scrub-Robin**	**Cercotrichas signata**	18, 101, 103, 105, 106, 107, 108, 109, 110, 112, 113, 114, 132, 134, 136, 137, 147, 174, 105, 291, 292, 293, 295		E	
❑	Bearded Scrub-Robin	Cercotrichas quadrivirgata	136, 137, 140, 141, 144, 145, 178, 188, 189, 191, 192, 196, 241, 242, 288, 297, 319, 334			
❑	Miombo (Central Bearded) Scrub-Robin	Cercotrichas barbata	322, 323, 330, 338, 344, 346, 347, 351	B	NE	
❑	Forest (Northern Bearded) Scrub-Robin	Cercotrichas leucosticta	360	B		
❑	**Herero Chat**	**Namibornis herero**	17, 208, 209, 211, 213, 218, 219, 225, 395		E	
❑	**Madagascar Magpie-Robin**	**Copsychus albospecularis**		M	E	
	Sylviidae	**Old World Warblers**				
❑	Garden Warbler	Sylvia borin	39, 129, 247, 249, 254			
❑	Common (Greater) Whitethroat	Sylvia communis	168, 169, 181, 184, 196, 200, 243			
❑	(European) Blackcap	Sylvia atricapilla				
❑	(European) Barred Warbler	Sylvia nisoria		B		1
❑	Brown Parisoma (Warbler)	Parisoma lugens	320, 325, 326	B		
❑	**Chestnut-vented Tit-Babbler**	**Parisoma subcaeruleum**	17, 46, 48, 49, 56, 61, 79, 95, 96, 164, 172, 181, 203, 252, 258, 335		E	
❑	**Layard's Tit-Babbler**	**Parisoma layardi**	46, 48, 54, 55, 58, 59, 60, 75, 77, 83, 84, 95, 97, 98, 103, 108, 109, 110, 117, 160, 219		E	
❑	Yellow-bellied Hyliota	Hyliota flavigaster	267, 302, 303, 306, 322, 323, 326, 339, 346, 347, 351,			
❑	Southern (Mashona) Hyliota	Hyliota australis	179, 188, 197, 267, 268, 269, 271, 279, 294, 295, 303, 323, 346, 351, 360			
❑	Icterine Warbler	Hippolais icterina	149, 168, 169, 215, 223, 227, 254			

	Common Name	Scientific name	Page numbers	Reg	End	Vag
❑	Olivaceous Warbler	Hippolais pallida		B		1
❑	Olive-tree Warbler	Hippolais olivetorum	141, 144, 148, 168, 169, 184, 196, 199, 200, 243, 245, 246, 248, 250, 254, 257, 258, 261, 336, 395			
❑	River Warbler	Locustella fluviatilis	168, 194, 197, 241, 243, 249, 282, 283, 337, 395			
❑	Great Reed-Warbler	Acrocephalus arundinaceus	72, 106, 125,136, 181, 248			
❑	Basra Reed-Warbler	Acrocephalus griseldis	248			
❑	Eurasian Reed-Warbler	Acrocephalus scirpaceus	234, 245, 248			
❑	African (Marsh-) Reed-Warbler	Acrocephalus baeticatus	37, 43, 60, 77, 81, 95, 125, 136, 163, 165, 234, 248			
❑	(European) Marsh-Warbler	Acrocephalus palustris	106, 181			
❑	(European) Sedge-Warbler	Acrocephalus schoenobaenus	125, 136, 163, 248			
❑	Lesser (Cape Reed-) Swamp-Warbler	Acrocephalus gracilirostris	27, 49, 50, 60, 72, 81, 106, 125, 163, 165, 217, 235, 248			
❑	Greater Swamp-Warbler	Acrocephalus rufescens	235, 236, 237, 238, 241, 242, 259, 348, 349, 350, 354			
❑	**Madagascar Swamp-Warbler**	**Acrocephalus newtoni**	366, 368	M	E	
❑	Dark-capped Yellow Warbler	Chloropeta natalensis	109, 119, 125, 128, 133, 165, 166, 172, 275, 309, 318			
❑	Mountain Yellow Warbler	Chloropeta similis	325, 329	B		
❑	Papyrus Yellow Warbler	Chloropeta gracilirostris	353, 354	B		
❑	Little Rush (African Sedge-) Warbler	Bradypterus baboecala	37, 45, 49, 50, 54, 72, 106, 125, 154, 165, 248, 267			
❑	White-winged Swamp-Warbler	Bradypterus carpalis	353, 354	B		
❑	Bamboo (Scrub-) Warbler	Bradypterus alfredi	333, 341, 342, 343, 345, 354	B		
❑	Evergreen Forest Warbler	Bradypterus lopezi	308, 309, 310, 311, 314, 315, 316, 318, 324, 327, 342, 344, 352	B		
❑	**Barratt's Warbler**	**Bradypterus barratti**	18, 105, 106, 107, 109, 114, 116, 117, 118, 150, 156, 157, 159, 172, 173, 174, 175, 185, 273, 276, 305, 306		E	
❑	**Knysna Warbler**	**Bradypterus sylvaticus**	18, 27, 28, 30, 32, 69, 70, 72, 73, 101, 105, 114, 396		E	
❑	**Victorin's Scrub-Warbler**	**Bradypterus victorini**	17, 27, 39, 40, 41, 63, 69, 70, 73, 75, 96, 103, 396		E	
❑	Cinnamon Bracken Warbler	Bradypterus cinnamomeus	315, 325, 326, 329	B		
❑	**Brown Emu-tail**	**Dromaeocercus brunneus**	19, 366, 367, 368, 407	M	E	
❑	**Grey Emu-tail**	**Amphilais seebohmi**	19, 366, 368	M	E	
❑	**Subdesert Brush-Warbler**	**Nesillas lantzii**	19, 372	M	E	
❑	**Madagascar Brush-Warbler**	**Nesillas typica**	365	M	NE	
❑	**Thamnornis Warbler**	**Thamnornis chloropetoides**	372	M	E	
❑	Broad-tailed (Fan-tailed) Warbler	Schoenicola brevirostris	107, 110, 112, 117, 118, 128, 129, 134, 149, 151, 159, 174, 175, 177, 264, 266, 273, 293, 324, 342, 348, 351			
❑	Willow Warbler	Phylloscopus trochilus				
❑	Yellow-throated Woodland-Warbler	Phylloscopus ruficapillus	69, 70, 71, 74, 106, 109, 114, 118, 129, 132, 173, 175, 187, 276, 309, 314, 316, 318		NE	
❑	**Laura's Woodland-Warbler**	**Phylloscopus laurae**	333, 341, 342, 344, 352	B	NE	
❑	Bar-throated Apalis	Apalis thoracica	32, 41, 42, 46, 48, 66, 68, 70, 71, 74, 118, 173, 175, 188, 200, 247, 276, 320, 326, 351			
❑	Yellow-throated Apalis	Apalis flavigularis	312, 313, 315, 316, 318	B	E	

	Common Name	Scientific name	Page numbers	Reg	End	Vag
☐	Namuli Apalis	Apalis lynesi	290, 307, 308, 396	B	E	
☐	Chapin's (Chestnut-headed) Apalis	Apalis chapini	321, 325, 327, 331	B	NE	
☐	Chirinda Apalis	Apalis chirindensis	18, 262, 272, 273, 275, 277, 299, 300, 305, 396		E	
☐	Grey Apalis	Apalis cinerea	340, 344, 346, 348, 352	B		
☐	Brown-headed Apalis	Apalis alticola	325, 326, 327, 328	B	NE	
☐	Black-headed Apalis	Apalis melanocephala	277, 295, 297, 301, 303, 304, 309, 311, 314, 315, 316, 318			
☐	White-winged Apalis	Apalis chariessa	18, 290, 307, 313, 314, 315, 316, 396	B	NE	
☐	Yellow-breasted Apalis	Apalis flavida	137, 144, 176, 188, 192, 268, 277			
☐	Rudd's Apalis	Apalis ruddi	18, 130, 134, 136, 137, 140, 141, 143, 144, 145, 293, 316		E	
☐	Buff-throated Apalis	Apalis rufogularis	341, 342, 360	B		
☐	Red-faced Crombec	Sylvietta whytii	269, 279, 287, 294, 295, 297, 303			
☐	Long-billed Crombec	Sylvietta rufescens	46, 48, 54, 60, 203		NE	
☐	Red-capped Crombec	Sylvietta ruficapilla	267, 305, 320, 322, 323, 324, 339, 341, 344, 346, 347, 351		NE	
☐	Green Crombec	Sylvietta virens	360	B		
☐	Green Hylia	Hylia prasina	360	B		
☐	Kretschmer's Longbill	Macrosphenus kretschmeri		B		
☐	Pulitzer's Longbill	Macrosphenus pulitzeri	357, 359, 360, 361, 396	B	E	
☐	Salvadori's Eremomela	Eremomela salvadorii		B	NE	
☐	Yellow-bellied Eremomela	Eremomela icteropygialis	51, 53, 78, 181, 184, 193, 194			
☐	Karoo Eremomela	Eremomela gregalis	16, 55, 58, 61, 76, 78, 83, 84, 210, 396		E	
☐	Green-capped Eremomela	Eremomela scotops	145, 166, 167, 178, 181, 182, 194, 196, 198, 232, 233, 234, 236, 237, 266, 267, 271, 297, 303, 323, 346, 347			
☐	Black-necked Eremomela	Eremomela atricollis	267, 341, 344, 345, 346, 347	B	NE	
☐	Burnt-necked Eremomela	Eremomela usticollis	17, 144, 146, 181, 184, 192, 193, 204, 216, 228, 229, 268, 284		E	
☐	Rand's Warbler	Randia pseudozosterops	365	M	E	
☐	Dark Newtonia	Newtonia amphichroa	366	M	E	
☐	Archbold's Newtonia	Newtonia archboldi	19, 372	M	E	
☐	Common Newtonia	Newtonia brunneicauda	364	M	E	
☐	Red-tailed Newtonia	Newtonia fanovanae	19, 364, 369, 374, 407	M	E	
☐	Red-capped Forest Warbler (African Tailorbird)	Orthotomus (Artisornis) metopias	307, 310, 311	B		
☐	Long-billed Forest Warbler (Moreau's Tailorbird)	Orthotomus (Artisornis) moreaui	290, 307, 310, 311	B	NE	
☐	Green-backed Camaroptera	Camaroptera brachyura	71, 74, 109, 173, 192			
☐	Grey-backed Camaroptera	Camaroptera brevicaudata	168, 195, 200, 201, 257, 360			
☐	Barred Wren-Warbler	Calamonastes fasciolatus	168, 169, 180, 181, 183, 184, 199, 200, 201, 203, 204, 206, 214, 215, 221, 223, 227, 228, 230		E	
☐	Stierling's Wren-Warbler	Calamonastes stierlingi	146, 186, 191, 193, 232, 234, 236, 237, 239, 243, 266, 267, 303, 323, 355		NE	
☐	Pale (Miombo) Wren-Warbler	Calamonastes undosus		B		
☐	Cinnamon-breasted Warbler	Euryptila subcinnamomea	16, 55, 56, 59, 76, 77, 81, 82, 83, 84, 86, 91, 96, 97, 211, 397		E	

	Common Name	Scientific name	Page numbers	Reg	End	Vag
❑	**Cape Grassbird**	**Sphenoeacus afer**	30, 32, 34, 39, 40, 41, 46, 48, 75, 116, 151, 158, 164, 173, 273, 275		E	
❑	**Rockrunner (Damara Rock-jumper)**	**Achaetops pycnopygius**	17, 208, 213, 214, 215, 220, 221, 223, 224, 361, 397		E	
❑	Moustached Grass-Warbler	Melocichla mentalis	274, 299, 300, 308, 309, 342, 344, 347			
❑	**Cryptic Warbler**	**Cryptosylvicola randrianasoloi**	19, 366, 368	M	E	
❑	Zitting (Fan-tailed) Cisticola	Cisticola juncidis	81, 113, 126, 149, 151, 162, 265			
❑	Desert Cisticola	Cisticola aridulus	88, 149, 168, 203, 228, 230, 246, 252, 253			
❑	**Cloud Cisticola**	**Cisticola textrix**	34, 44, 47, 65, 97, 149, 151, 162, 340, 397		E	
❑	**Madagascar Cisticola**	**Cisticola cherina**	19, 365, 371	M	E	
❑	Wing-snapping (Ayres') Cisticola	Cisticola ayresii	109, 126, 127, 129, 149, 151, 152, 164, 171, 172, 173, 175, 202, 265, 329, 341, 342			
❑	**Dambo (Cloud-scraping) Cisticola**	**Cisticola dambo**	341, 342	B	NE	
❑	**Pale-crowned Cisticola**	**Cisticola cinnamomeus**	112, 113, 119, 126, 127, 129, 137, 152, 156, 171, 172, 264, 265, 293, 295		NE	
❑	**Grey-backed Cisticola**	**Cisticola subruficapillus**	33, 34, 46, 48, 49, 58, 60, 98, 105, 214		E	
❑	**Wailing Cisticola**	**Cisticola lais**	107, 109, 117, 129, 151, 156, 158, 159, 173, 175, 309, 311		NE	
❑	**Tinkling (Grey) Cisticola**	**Cisticola rufilatus**	161, 166, 167, 179, 180, 181, 182, 183, 206, 232, 233, 234, 236, 237, 239, 240, 283, 284, 392		E	
❑	Rattling Cisticola	Cisticola chinianus	120			
❑	Singing Cisticola	Cisticola cantans	274, 275, 277, 278, 300, 309, 311, 324			
❑	Whistling Cisticola	Cisticola lateralis	341, 342	B		
❑	Trilling Cisticola	Cisticola woosnami	324, 325, 326, 344, 347	B		
❑	Bubbling Cisticola	Cisticola bulliens	358	B		
❑	**Black-lored Cisticola**	**Cisticola nigriloris**	325, 326, 327, 329, 331	B	NE	
❑	Red-faced Cisticola	Cisticola erythrops	121, 124, 144, 176, 193, 194, 242			
❑	**Churring Cisticola**	**Cisticola njombe**	325, 326, 329	B	NE	
❑	**Luapula (Black-backed) Cisticola**	**Cisticola luapula**	231, 237, 238, 241, 242, 259, 283, 341		E	
❑	**Rufous-winged (Black-backed) Cisticola**	**Cisticola galactotes**	121, 124, 133, 136, 144, 198, 280, 295, 296		E	
❑	Winding (Black-backed) Cisticola	Cisticola marginatus		B		
❑	**Chirping Cisticola**	**Cisticola pipiens**	18, 231, 236, 237, 238, 239, 241, 242, 256, 259, 283, 348, 350, 354		NE	
❑	Levaillant's Cisticola	Cisticola tinniens	30, 36, 45, 49, 50, 52, 60, 109, 151, 154, 173			
❑	Stout Cisticola	Cisticola robustus	341, 342, 346, 351, 352	B		
❑	Croaking Cisticola	Cisticola natalensis	107, 113, 126, 132, 149, 151, 188, 194, 195, 265, 296, 299, 308			
❑	**Lazy Cisticola**	**Cisticola aberrans**	74, 128, 129, 132, 151, 158, 159, 172, 195, 247, 271, 314, 320		NE	
❑	Rock-loving Cisticola	Cisticola emini	351, 352	B		
❑	Short-winged (Siffling) Cisticola	Cisticola brachypterus	274, 278, 303, 347, 351			
❑	**Black-tailed (Slender-tailed) Cisticola**	**Cisticola melanurus**	356	B	NE	
❑	Long-tailed (Tabora) Cisticola	Cisticola angusticauda	351, 352	B		
❑	**Neddicky (Piping Cisticola)**	**Cisticola fulvicapillus**	32, 39, 41, 75, 151, 234		NE	
❑	Red-winged Warbler	Heliolais erythroptera	274, 277, 278, 299, 303, 308, 309, 322, 324			
❑	Tawny-flanked Prinia	Prinia subflava	193			

	Common Name	Scientific name	Page numbers	Reg	End	Vag
❑	**Roberts' (Briar) Warbler (Prinia)**	**Oreophilais robertsi**	18, 262, 272, 273, 275, 276, 305, 397		E	
❑	White-chinned Prinia	Prinia (Schistolais) leucopogon	341, 342, 343, 344	B		
❑	**Black-chested Prinia**	**Prinia flavicans**	17, 78, 91, 199, 212, 219		E	
❑	**Karoo (Spotted) Prinia**	**Prinia maculosa**	29, 33, 39, 41, 77, 98, 109, 117		E	
❑	**Drakensberg (Spotted) Prinia**	**Prinia hypoxantha**	18, 117, 132, 152, 155, 159, 173, 174, 175		E	
❑	**Namaqua Warbler**	**Phragmacia substriata**	16, 55, 56, 62, 75, 77, 81, 91, 95, 96, 98, 99, 103, 108, 109, 110, 210, 397		E	
❑	**Rufous-eared Warbler**	**Malcorus pectoralis**	16, 53, 55, 58, 61, 78, 95, 98, 103, 108, 110, 199, 205, 206, 207, 210, 228, 251, 252		E	
	Muscicapidae	**Old World Flycatchers**				
❑	Spotted Flycatcher	Muscicapa striata				
❑	Sooty Flycatcher	Muscicapa infuscata	343	B		
❑	**Boehm's Flycatcher**	**Muscicapa boehmi**	322, 323, 330, 338, 346, 347, 351	B	NE	
❑	Swamp Flycatcher (Alseonax)	Muscicapa aquatica	349, 350, 353, 354	B		
❑	African Dusky Flycatcher	Muscicapa adusta	28, 32, 41, 70, 71, 74, 106, 173, 174			
❑	Cassin's (Grey) Flycatcher (Alseonax)	Muscicapa cassini	341, 342, 353, 354	B		
❑	Ashy (Bluegrey) Flycatcher	Muscicapa caerulescens	106, 124, 138, 189, 194, 196, 241, 260			
❑	Collared Flycatcher	Ficedula albicollis	271, 279, 326, 346			
❑	Grey (Fantailed/Lead-coloured) Tit-Flycatcher	Myioparus plumbeus	138, 142, 182, 192, 193, 194, 196, 201, 235, 241, 247, 319			
❑	Southern Black Flycatcher	Melaenornis pammelaina	108, 167, 192, 200, 202			
❑	White-eyed Slaty-Flycatcher	Dioptrornis fischeri	324, 331	B		
❑	**Angolan Slaty-Flycatcher**	**Dioptrornis brunneus**	357, 360, 360, 361	B	E	
❑	**Marico Flycatcher**	**Bradornis mariquensis**	17, 88, 184, 188, 199, 203, 206, 223, 248, 250, 252, 258, 335		E	
❑	Pale (Mouse-coloured/Pallid) Flycatcher	Bradornis pallidus	137, 166, 187, 181, 182, 193, 195, 202, 285			
❑	**Chat Flycatcher**	**Bradornis infuscatus**	53, 78, 90, 91, 97, 108, 199		E	
❑	**Fiscal Flycatcher**	**Sigelus silens**	34, 40, 42, 46, 63, 67, 68, 93, 103, 139		E	
❑	African Shrike-Flycatcher	Megabyas flammulatus	343	B		
	Batises and allies	**Platysteiridae**				
❑	Black-and-white (Vanga) Flycatcher	Bias musicus	272, 277, 278, 299, 300, 301, 303, 316, 397			
❑	**Ward's Flycatcher**	**Pseudobias wardi**	364	M	E	
❑	**Margaret's Batis**	**Batis margaritae**	333, 344, 361	B	NE	
❑	Forest Batis	Batis mixta	331	B		
❑	**Cape Batis**	**Batis capensis**	18, 28, 30, 32, 41, 42, 70, 71, 74, 96, 106, 108, 118, 128, 129, 131, 139, 155, 156, 173, 176, 185, 188, 285		E	
❑	**Malawi Batis**	**Batis dimorpha**	309, 313, 314, 315, 316, 318, 326, 329	B	NE	
❑	Chinspot Batis	Batis molitor	106, 126, 188, 230, 267, 285			
❑	**Pale (Mozambique/East Coast) Batis**	**Batis soror**	274, 291, 295, 297, 298, 303, 309, 317			
❑	**Pririt Batis**	**Batis pririt**	56, 59, 60, 61, 75, 78, 79, 81, 83, 91, 92, 96, 99, 108, 199, 206, 207, 210, 212, 215, 221, 227, 252		E	
❑	**Angola Batis**	**Batis minulla**	358, 360	B	NE	

	Common Name	Scientific name	Page numbers	Reg	End	Vag
❑	**Woodwards' Batis**	**Batis fratrum**	18, 130, 136, 137, 147, 278, 280, 292, 293, 301, 303		E	
❑	**White-tailed Shrike**	**Lanioturdus torquatus**	17, 208, 213, 215, 219, 220, 221, 224, 225, 230		E	
❑	Black-throated Wattle-eye (Wattle-eyed Flycatcher)	Platysteira peltata	120, 124, 131, 133, 134, 136, 143, 145, 146, 189, 196, 267, 275, 277, 287, 288, 292, 293, 294, 295, 299, 322, 338			
❑	**White-fronted Wattle-eye**	**Platysteira albifrons**	357, 358, 359, 361	B	E	
❑	Yellow-bellied Wattle-eye	Dyaphorophyia concreta	360, 398	B		
❑	Chestnut Wattle-eye	Dyaphorophyia castanea	343	B		
	Unrelated Flycatchers					
❑	**Fairy Flycatcher**	**Stenostira scita**	54, 55, 56, 58, 59, 60, 75, 77, 79, 83, 95, 96, 116, 117, 158, 159, 160, 164, 168, 169, 210		E	
❑	**Livingstone's Flycatcher**	**Erythrocercus livingstonei**	284, 286, 287, 288, 295, 297, 316, 318, 319, 320, 337, 398		NE	
❑	African Blue Flycatcher	Elminia longicauda	360	B		
❑	White-tailed Blue Flycatcher	Elminia albicauda	305, 310, 311, 322, 323, 326, 341, 346, 347, 351	B		
❑	White-tailed Elminia (Crested Flycatcher)	Elminia albonotata	275, 278, 309, 310, 314, 315, 326, 351			
❑	Blue-mantled Crested Flycatcher	Trochocercus cyanomelas	41, 69, 70, 71, 74, 106, 118, 129, 131, 137, 139, 143, 173, 174, 175, 185, 187, 292, 304, 331, 340, 344, 348			
❑	Blue-headed Crested Flycatcher	Trochocercus nitens	360	B		
❑	Red-bellied (Black-headed) Paradise-Flycatcher	Terpsiphone rufiventer	341, 342	B		
❑	Rufous-vented Paradise-Flycatcher	Terpsiphone rufocinerea	360	B		
❑	African Paradise-Flycatcher	Terpsiphone viridis	28, 32, 41, 43, 70, 173, 267			
❑	**Madagascar Paradise-Flycatcher**	**Terpsiphone mutata**	364	M	NE	
	Laniidae	**Shrikes**				
❑	Lesser Grey Shrike	Lanius minor	89, 195			
❑	Common Fiscal (Fiscal Shrike)	Lanius collaris	30, 46			
❑	MacKinnon's Fiscal	Lanius mackinnoni	360	B		
❑	Red-backed Shrike	Lanius collurio	126, 139			
❑	Red-tailed (Isabelline) Shrike	Lanius isabellinus		B		1
❑	**Souza's Shrike**	**Lanius souzae**	231, 234, 306, 320, 321, 322, 323, 338, 341, 344, 346, 351, 399		NE	
❑	Magpie (Long-tailed) Shrike	Corvinella melanoleuca	148, 193, 200, 203, 233			
❑	**Southern White-crowned Shrike**	**Eurocephalus anguitimens**	99, 193, 228, 236, 240, 248, 251		E	
	Malaconotidae	**Bush-shrikes and Allies**				
❑	**Southern Boubou**	**Laniarius ferrugineus**	29, 33, 34, 35, 41, 66, 68, 110, 156, 176, 195		E	
❑	Tropical Boubou	Laniarius aethiopicus	189, 190, 196, 241, 249			
❑	Swamp Boubou	Laniarius bicolor	18, 225, 233, 234, 235, 236, 237, 238, 239, 240, 241, 242, 257, 260, 358			
❑	**Crimson-breasted Shrike**	**Laniarius atrococcineus**	17, 88, 92, 93, 168, 181, 183, 184, 199, 202, 203, 204, 206, 207, 215, 221, 223, 227, 243, 250, 252, 283		E	
❑	Fuelleborn's (Black) Boubou	Laniarius fuelleborni	324, 325, 326, 327, 329, 331	B	NE	

	Common Name	Scientific name	Page numbers	Reg	End	Vag
❑	Braun's Bush-Shrike	Laniarius brauni	356	B	E	
❑	Lühder's Bush-Shrike	Laniarius leuhderi	359	B		
❑	**Gabela Bush-Shrike**	**Laniarius amboimensis**	357, 359	B	E	
❑	Black-backed Puffback	Dryoscopus cubla				
❑	Pink-footed Puffback	Dryoscopus angolensis	360	B		
❑	Brubru	Nilaus afer	91, 92, 126, 182, 192, 252			
❑	**Southern Tchagra**	**Tchagra tchagra**	64, 65, 66, 67, 68, 75, 96, 101, 102, 103, 104, 105, 106, 108, 109, 110, 123, 124, 126, 128, 172, 173, 399		E	
❑	Brown-crowned (Three-streaked) Tchagra	Tchagra australis	98, 139			
❑	Black-crowned Tchagra	Tchagra senegala				
❑	**Anchieta's Tchagra**	**Tchagra anchietae**	272, 274, 299, 300, 308, 324, 342, 344, 348, 354, 399		NE	
❑	**Bokmakierie**	**Telophorus zeylonus**	46, 48, 78, 164, 169, 175, 217, 246, 279		E	
❑	**Perrin's Bushshrike**	**Telophorus viridis**	344, 359	B	NE	
❑	Gorgeous Bush-Shrike	Telophorus quadricolor	18, 124, 133, 138, 140, 141, 144, 145, 176, 178, 187, 188, 189, 194, 196, 276, 280, 293, 295, 297			
❑	Many-coloured Bush-shrike	Telephorus multicolor	340, 344	B		
❑	Orange-breasted Bush-Shrike	Telophorus sulfureopectus	106, 126, 176, 192, 193, 198			
❑	Black-fronted Bush-Shrike	Telophorus nigrifrons	179, 185, 186, 187, 274, 275, 276, 277, 300, 305, 309, 314, 315, 316, 327, 354, 399			
❑	**Olive Bush-Shrike**	**Telophorus olivaceus**	18, 69, 70, 71, 74, 106, 114, 127, 128, 129, 139, 173, 175, 176, 185, 188, 293, 305, 316, 318		E	
❑	Grey-headed Bush-Shrike	Malaconotus blanchoti	129, 144, 146, 176, 192, 194, 198, 240, 249, 360			
❑	**Monteiro's Bush-Shrike**	**Malaconotus monteiri**	357, 359, 360	B	NE	
	Prionopidae	**Helmet-Shrikes**				
❑	White (-crested) Helmet-Shrike	Prionops plumatus	139, 193, 197, 202, 203, 228, 260			
❑	Retz's (Red-billed) Helmet-Shrike	Prionops retzii	145, 147, 178, 189, 191, 193, 196, 237, 238, 240, 241, 243, 258, 279, 280, 295, 297, 303, 316, 319			
❑	Chestnut-fronted Helmet-Shrike	Prionops scopifrons	18, 277, 278, 290, 295, 297, 298, 302, 303, 304, 305, 399			
❑	**Gabela Helmet-Shrike**	**Prionops gabela**	357, 358, 359, 360, 361	B	E	
	Vangidae	**Vangas**				
❑	**Red-tailed Vanga**	**Calicalius madagascariensis**	364	M	E	
❑	**Red-shouldered Vanga**	**Calicalius rufocarpalis**	19, 370, 373	M	E	
❑	**Rufous Vanga**	**Shetba rufa**	371	M	E	
❑	**Hook-billed Vanga**	**Vanga curvirostris**	365, 369, 374, 376, 377	M	E	
❑	**Lafresnaye's Vanga**	**Xenopirostris xenopirostris**	19, 370, 372, 373	M	E	
❑	**Van Dam's Vanga**	**Xenopirostris damii**	19, 375, 376, 377	M	E	
❑	**Pollen's Vanga**	**Xenopirostris polleni**	19, 366, 367, 368	M	E	
❑	**Sickle-billed Vanga**	**Falculea palliata**	372, 373, 374, 375	M	E	
❑	**White-headed Vanga**	**Leptopterus viridis**	364, 374	M	E	
❑	**Chabert Vanga**	**Leptopterus chabert**	372, 376	M	E	
❑	**Madagascar Blue Vanga**	**Cyanolanius madagascarinus**	364	M	E	
❑	**Bernier's Vanga**	**Oriolia bernieri**	19, 363, 368, 369, 407	M	E	

	Common Name	Scientific name	Page numbers	Reg	End	Vag
❑	**Helmet Vanga**	**Euryceros prevostii**	19, 363, 364, 369, 407	M	E	
❑	**Tylas**	**Tylas eduardi**	364, 365	M	E	
❑	**Nuthatch Vanga**	**Hypositta corallirostris**	363, 364, 366, 407	M	E	
	Sturnidae	**Starlings**				
❑	Common Starling	Sturnus vulgaris				2
❑	Common Myna	Acridotheres tristis				2
❑	**(White-winged) Babbling Starling**	**Neocichla gutturalis**	267, 321, 330, 353, 354, 399	B	NE	
❑	**African Pied Starling**	**Spreo bicolor**	46, 48, 65		E	
❑	**Madagascar Starling**	**Hartlaubius aurata**	365, 366	M	E	
❑	Wattled Starling	Creatophora cinerea	48, 50			
❑	Violet-backed (Plum-coloured/Amethyst) Starling	Cinnyricinclus leucogaster	126, 192, 247			
❑	**Burchell's Starling**	**Lamprotornis australis**	148, 193, 195, 199, 202, 236, 240, 252, 258, 335		NE	
❑	**Meves's Starling**	**Lamprotornis mevesii**	179, 190, 191, 196, 224, 225, 236, 253, 258, 260, 280, 287, 288, 289, 306, 319, 338, 355		E	
❑	**Cape Glossy Starling**	**Lamprotornis nitens**	83, 84, 192		NE	
❑	Greater Blue-eared Starling	Lamprotornis chalybaeus	186, 191, 192, 228, 319			
❑	Miombo Blue-eared Starling	Lamprotornis elisabeth	266, 267, 270, 299, 303, 330			
❑	**Sharp-tailed Starling**	**Lamprotornis acuticaudus**	231, 232, 233, 234, 237, 239, 344, 400		NE	
❑	Splendid Glossy-Starling	Lamprotornis splendidus	340, 342, 352	B		
❑	Black-bellied Starling	Lamprotornis corruscus	18, 71, 74, 103, 112, 124, 133, 136, 137, 138, 143			
❑	Waller's Starling	Onychognathus walleri	325, 327, 331	B		
❑	Red-winged Starling	Onychognathus morio	32, 33, 56, 335, 352			
❑	**Pale-winged Starling**	**Onychognathus nabouroup**	16, 56, 60, 63, 75, 80, 81, 83, 91, 97, 108, 110, 215, 219, 221		E	
❑	Slender-billed Starling	Onychognathus tenuirostris	325, 327, 329	B		
	Buphagidae	**Oxpeckers**				
❑	Yellow-billed Oxpecker	Buphagus africanus	191, 197, 226, 280, 281, 283, 284, 289			
❑	Red-billed Oxpecker	Buphagus erythrorhynchus	109, 255, 280, 289, 320			
	Promeropidae	**Sugarbirds**				
❑	**Cape Sugarbird**	**Promerops cafer**	17, 26, 27, 28, 34, 39, 40, 41, 42, 73, 75, 95, 96, 103, 109, 400		E	
❑	**Gurney's Sugarbird**	**Promerops gurneyi**	18, 109, 114, 115, 116, 117, 150, 151, 157, 158, 159, 170, 171, 172, 173, 174, 175, 180, 273, 276, 279, 400		E	
	Nectariniidae	**Sunbirds**				
❑	**Orange-breasted Sunbird**	**Anthobaphes violacea**	17, 28, 32, 34, 39, 41, 42, 66, 73, 75, 96, 103		E	
❑	Malachite Sunbird	Nectarinia famosa	34, 41, 42, 46, 48, 58, 68, 75, 85, 103, 115, 116, 158, 159, 164, 169, 171, 173, 174, 175, 276, 329			
❑	Scarlet-tufted Sunbird	Nectarinia johnstoni	321, 325, 327, 329	B		
❑	Bronzy (Bronze) Sunbird	Nectarinia kilimensis	273, 275, 276, 305, 324, 325, 326, 331, 357			
❑	**Bocage's Sunbird**	**Nectarinia bocagei**		B	NE	
❑	Plain-backed (Blue-throated) Sunbird	Anthreptes reichenowi	18, 147, 280, 290, 291, 297, 298, 302, 303, 304			

	Common Name	Scientific name	Page numbers	Reg	End	Vag
❑	**Anchieta's (Red-and-Blue) Sunbird**	**Anthreptes anchietae**	267, 306, 323, 325, 326, 345, 347, 351	B	NE	
❑	Western Violet-backed Sunbird	Anthreptes longuemarei	270, 271, 303, 309, 310, 320, 323			
❑	Uluguru Violet-backed Sunbird	Anthreptes neglectus		B		
❑	Copper (Coppery) Sunbird	Cinnyris cupreus	239, 240, 241, 242, 267, 270, 302			
❑	Marico Sunbird	Cinnyris mariquensis	146, 168, 192, 258, 335			
❑	Purple-banded Sunbird	Cinnyris bifasciatus	120, 121, 133, 140, 141, 241, 270, 287, 295, 297, 302, 319			
❑	**Shelley's Sunbird**	**Cinnyris shelleyi**	240, 241, 286, 287, 306, 322, 323, 339, 353, 400		NE	
❑	**Neergaard's Sunbird**	**Cinnyris neergaardi**	18, 130, 140, 141, 145, 147, 291, 292, 293, 294, 295, 297, 400		E	
❑	**Southern (Lesser) Double-collared Sunbird**	**Cinnyris chalybea**	29, 32, 34, 41, 46, 48, 85, 103, 156, 158, 175, 187		E	
❑	**Miombo Double-collared Sunbird**	**Cinnyris manoensis**	267, 269, 270, 271, 276, 300, 320, 323, 326, 351, 352		NE	
❑	Olive-bellied Sunbird	Cinnyris chloropygius	360	B		
❑	**Greater Double-collared Sunbird**	**Cinnyris afra**	35, 69, 70, 72, 96, 103, 117, 155, 157, 158, 159, 169, 174, 175		E	
❑	**Ludwig's (Montane) Double-collared Sunbird**	**Cinnyris ludovicensis**	321, 325, 327, 329, 360	B	E	
❑	**Forest (Eastern) Double-collared Sunbird**	**Cinnyris fuelleborni**	308, 309, 311, 315, 316, 318, 324, 326, 331	B	NE	
❑	Variable (Yellow-bellied) Sunbird	Cinnyris venustus	267, 276, 324			
❑	**White-bellied Sunbird**	**Cinnyris talatala**	182, 270		NE	
❑	**Oustalet's (~ White-bellied) Sunbird**	**Cinnyris oustaleti**	353, 361	B	NE	
❑	Orange-tufted Sunbird	Cinnyris bouvieri	343	B		
❑	**Dusky Sunbird**	**Cinnyris fusca**	60, 62, 78, 81, 83, 84, 91, 96, 110, 199, 212, 219		E	
❑	Bates's Sunbird	Cinnyris batesi	341, 342	B		
❑	Superb Sunbird	Cinnyris superbus	360	B		
❑	Olive Sunbird	Cyanomitra olivacea	131, 133, 174, 276, 278, 293, 294, 309, 311			
❑	Green-headed Sunbird	Cyanomitra verticalis	325, 326, 348, 352	B		
❑	**Bannerman's Sunbird**	**Cyanomitra bannermani**	340, 341, 342	B	NE	
❑	Grey (Mouse-coloured) Sunbird	Cyanomitra veroxii	18, 103, 112, 123, 133, 137, 144, 292, 302, 316			
❑	Green-throated Sunbird	Chalcomitra rubescens	343	B		
❑	Amethyst (Black) Sunbird	Chalcomitra amethystina	31, 40, 69, 96, 103, 175, 270, 276			
❑	Scarlet-chested Sunbird	Chalcomitra senegalensis	188, 192, 270			
❑	Collared Sunbird	Hedydipna collaris	103, 123, 144, 176, 192, 276, 278			
❑	**Madagascar Green Sunbird**	**Nectarinia notata**	365	M	NE	
❑	**Souimanga Sunbird**	**Nectarinia souimanga**	364, 372	M	NE	
	Zosteropidae	White-eyes				
❑	**Madagascar White-eye**	**Zosterops maderaspatanus**	364	M	NE	
❑	**Cape White-eye**	**Zosterops capensis**			E	
❑	**Orange River White-eye**	**Zosterops pallidus**	14, 81, 85, 91, 93, 199, 206, 207, 217		E	
❑	African Yellow White-eye	Zosterops senegalensis	144, 189, 266			

	Common Name	Scientific name	Page numbers	Reg	End	Vag
	Passeridae	**Old World Sparrows**				
❑	House Sparrow	Passer domesticus				3
❑	**Great Sparrow**	**Passer motitensis**	168, 169, 200, 203, 212, 215, 250		E	
❑	**Cape Sparrow**	**Passer melanurus**	46, 49		NE	
❑	**Southern Grey-headed Sparrow**	**Passer diffusus**	68		NE	
❑	Northern Grey-headed Sparrow	Passer griseus	282			
❑	Swahili Sparrow	Passer suahelicus		B		
❑	**Yellow-throated Petronia**	**Petronia superciliaris**	103, 168, 182, 193, 195, 202		NE	
	Ploceidae	**Weavers and Allies**				
❑	Red-billed Buffalo-Weaver	Bubalornis niger	99, 148, 195, 200, 202, 229			
❑	White-browed Sparrow-Weaver	Plocepasser mahali	88, 202, 215, 319, 338, 355			
❑	**Chestnut-backed Sparrow-Weaver**	**Plocepasser rufoscapulatus**	330, 344, 346, 352, 353	B	NE	
❑	**Sociable Weaver**	**Philetairus socius**	80, 89, 90, 199, 206, 211, 227, 245, 246		E	
❑	**Scaly-feathered Finch**	**Sporopipes squamifrons**	82, 89, 169, 181, 206, 212, 215, 246, 335		E	
❑	Thick-billed (Grosbeak) Weaver	Amblyospiza albifrons	106, 142, 176, 193, 267, 292			
❑	Dark-backed (Forest) Weaver	Ploceus bicolor	106, 276, 277, 292, 316, 348, 354			
❑	**Olive-headed Weaver**	**Ploceus olivaceiceps**	267, 290, 291, 294, 295, 305, 310, 321, 322, 323, 324, 401		NE	
❑	**Bar-winged Weaver**	**Ploceus angolensis**	341, 344, 345, 346, 351, 352, 401	B	NE	
❑	Spectacled Weaver	Ploceus ocularis	176, 257, 319			
❑	Village (Spotted-backed) Weaver	Ploceus cucullatus	319			
❑	Black-headed (Yellow-backed) Weaver	Ploceus melanocephalus	353, 354	B		
❑	Chestnut Weaver	Ploceus rubiginosus	210, 220, 221, 224, 225, 230			
❑	**Nelicourvi Weaver**	**Ploceus nelicourvi**	364	M	E	
❑	**Sakalava Weaver**	**Ploceus sakalava**	372	M	E	
❑	**Bocage's Weaver**	**Ploceus temporalis**	341	B	NE	
❑	**Cape Weaver**	**Ploceus capensis**	46, 48, 49, 106, 164, 165, 175		E	
❑	Southern (Vitelline) Masked-Weaver	Ploceus velatus	46, 165			
❑	**Tanzania Masked (Lake Lufira) Weaver**	**Ploceus reichardi**	345, 348, 349, 350, 353, 354	B	NE	
❑	Baglafecht Weaver	Ploceus baglafecht	325, 329	B		
❑	**Bertrand's (Bertram's) Weaver**	**Ploceus bertrandi**	306, 307, 308, 309, 310, 311, 313, 314, 315, 318, 320, 324, 325, 327, 331	B	NE	
❑	Slender-billed Weaver	Ploceus pelzelni	353, 354	B		
❑	Lesser Masked-Weaver	Ploceus intermedius	142, 229, 319			
❑	(Holub's) Golden Weaver	Ploceus xanthops	141, 176, 225, 235, 236, 237, 238, 257, 260			
❑	Yellow (African Golden) Weaver	Ploceus subaureus	106, 124, 133, 296, 302, 320, 331			
❑	**Southern Brown-throated Weaver**	**Ploceus xanthopterus**	124, 125, 134, 136, 141, 146, 236, 237, 238, 242, 260, 293, 319		NE	
❑	Compact Weaver	Pachyphantes superciliosus	343, 361	B		

	Common Name	Scientific name	Page numbers	Reg	End	Vag
❑	Red-headed Weaver	Anaplectes rubriceps	178, 186, 189, 194, 197, 198, 201, 260, 266, 319, 323			
❑	Cuckoo Finch (Parasitic Weaver)	Anomalospiza imberbis	124, 127, 149, 161, 162, 177, 237, 263, 264, 266, 283, 336, 350, 401			
❑	Red-billed Quelea	Quelea quelea	81, 195, 224, 227, 254			
❑	Red-headed Quelea	Quelea erythrops	119, 124, 125, 136, 138, 141, 146, 239, 242, 301, 342, 401			
❑	Cardinal Quelea	Quelea cardinalis				
❑	**Madagascar Fody**	**Foudia madagascariensis**	364	M	NE	
❑	**Forest Fody**	**Foudia omissa**	366	M	E	
❑	Southern Red Bishop	Euplectes orix	43, 81, 106, 109, 163, 165			
❑	Black-winged (Fire-crowned) Bishop	Euplectes hordeaceus	274, 277, 278, 299, 301, 308			
❑	Zanzibar Red Bishop	Euplectes nigroventis	307	B		
❑	Yellow-crowned (Golden) Bishop	Euplectes afer	93, 109, 127, 152, 158			
❑	Yellow Bishop (Yellow-rumped Widow)	Euplectes capensis	39, 41, 54, 128, 163, 171, 173, 175			
❑	**Golden-backed Bishop**	**Euplectes aureus**	357, 358	B	E	
❑	Fan-tailed (Red-shouldered) Widowbird	Euplectes axillaris	106, 162, 295			
❑	White-winged Widowbird	Euplectes albonotatus	126			
❑	Yellow-mantled (Yellow-backed) Widowbird	Euplectes macrourus	264, 265, 324			
❑	Red-collared Widowbird	Euplectes ardens	176, 267			
❑	(Hartlaub's) Marsh Widowbird	Euplectes hartlaubi	342, 344, 346, 348, 351, 352	B		
❑	**Montane (Mountain Marsh) Widowbird**	**Euplectes psammocromius**	325, 329	B	NE	
❑	**Long-tailed Widowbird**	**Euplectes progne**	18, 94, 98, 161, 163, 246, 348		NE	
	Estrildidae	**Waxbills and Allies**				
❑	Grey-headed Nigrita (Negrofinch)	Nirgrita canicapillus	360	B		
❑	Orange-winged (Golden-backed) Pytilia	Pytilia afra	195, 243, 270, 282, 283, 289, 299, 322, 323, 346			
❑	Green-winged Pytilia (Melba Finch)	Pytilia melba	91, 139, 164, 200, 236			
❑	Green Twinspot	Mandingoa nitidula	112, 113, 114, 122, 123, 124, 131, 133, 134, 136, 137, 139, 141, 142, 174, 176, 185, 186, 187, 274, 280, 293, 30 , 316, 318, 401			
❑	Red-faced Crimsonwing	Cryptospiza reichenovii	272, 273, 275, 276, 305, 309, 314, 318, 325, 327, 361, 402			
❑	**Lesser Seedcracker**	**Pyrenestes minor**	272, 274, 278, 298, 299, 302, 303, 324, 402		NE	
❑	Red-headed Bluebill	Spermophaga ruficapilla	361	B		
❑	Black-bellied Seedcracker	Pyrenestes ostrinus	340, 341, 342, 343	B		
❑	**Pink-throated Twinspot**	**Hypargos margaritatus**	18, 129, 130, 136, 137, 140, 141, 143, 144, 145, 147, 178, 189, 291, 292, 293, 402		E	
❑	Red-throated (Peters's) Twinspot	Hypargos niveoguttatus	189, 269, 274, 276, 278, 284, 287, 299, 303, 304, 310, 315, 316, 317, 322, 324, 348			
❑	**Dusky Twinspot**	**Euschitospiza cinereovinacea**	361	B	NE	
❑	African (Blue-billed) Firefinch	Lagonosticta rubricata	103, 167, 168, 188, 193, 309, 361			
❑	Jameson's Firefinch	Lagonosticta rhodopareia	144, 188, 193, 196, 226, 235, 260			
❑	Red-billed Firefinch	Lagonosticta senegala	75, 95, 188, 193, 196, 202, 226, 235, 258, 260, 282			
❑	**Brown Firefinch**	**Lagonosticta nitidula**	231, 233, 234, 235, 236, 237, 238, 239, 241, 242, 256, 259, 260, 281, 282, 335, 347, 350, 354		NE	

	Common Name	Scientific name	Page numbers	Reg	End	Vag
❑	Red-cheeked Cordonbleu	Uraeginthus bengalus		B		
❑	Blue Waxbill (Southern Cordonbleu)	Uraeginthus angolensis	202, 282			
❑	**Violet-eared Waxbill (Common Grenadier)**	**Granatina granatina**	89, 91, 169, 200, 203, 204, 206, 215, 221, 227, 229, 233, 236, 243, 252		NE	
❑	Common Waxbill	Estrilda astrild	30, 45, 165			
❑	Black-faced (Black-cheeked) Waxbill	Estrilda erythronotos	17, 164, 167, 168, 180, 181, 183, 184, 199, 200, 203, 206, 214, 215, 221, 224, 236, 252, 258, 335			
❑	**Grey (Black-tailed) Waxbill**	**Estrilda perreini**	112, 114, 123, 124, 131, 133, 136, 137, 140, 141, 142, 145, 274, 277, 278, 293, 299, 300, 304, 326, 344, 348, 360		NE	
❑	**Cinderella Waxbill**	**Estrilda thomensis**	17, 222, 225, 226, 357, 402		E	
❑	**Swee Waxbill**	**Estrilda melanotis**	31, 32, 41, 66, 68, 69, 72, 96, 114, 116, 117, 118, 124, 129, 159, 173, 174, 175, 187, 279		E	
❑	Yellow-bellied Waxbill (East African Swee)	Estrilda quartinia	273, 274, 275, 276, 311, 318, 327, 357			
❑	Fawn-breasted Waxbill	Estrilda paludicola	344, 346, 348, 351, 352	B		
❑	Crimson-rumped Waxbill	Estrilda rhodopyga		B		
❑	Orange-cheeked Waxbill	Estrilda melpoda	353, 354	B		
❑	African Quailfinch	Ortygospiza atricollis	68, 126, 127, 129, 169, 204, 246, 336, 350			
❑	Red-billed (Black-chinned) Quailfinch	Ortygospiza gabonensis	341, 342, 344, 352	B		
❑	Locustfinch	Ortygospiza locustella	263, 264, 268, 269, 290, 301, 320, 341, 342, 346, 351, 402			
❑	Orange-breasted (Zebra) Waxbill	Amandava subflava	125, 126, 127, 161, 162, 164, 165			
❑	Cut-throat Finch	Amadina fasciata	169, 197			
❑	**Red-headed Finch**	**Amadina erythrocephala**	89, 154, 169, 199, 204, 224, 252		E	
❑	**Madagascar Mannikin**	**Lonchura nana**	264, 364, 365	M	E	
❑	Bronze Mannikin	Lonchura cucullata	176, 193, 270			
❑	Black-and-white Mannikin	Spermestes bicolor	361	B		
❑	Red-backed Mannikin	Lonchura nigriceps	112, 114, 129, 137, 176, 186, 193, 270, 295, 301, 318, 348			
❑	Magpie (Pied) Mannikin	Lonchura fringilloides	111, 112, 267, 270, 293, 295, 299, 300, 302, 304, 402			
❑	Pin-tailed Whydah	Vidua macroura	46, 65			
❑	**Shaft-tailed Whydah**	**Vidua regia**	89, 92, 168, 169, 199, 200, 201, 203, 214, 215, 221, 223, 227, 233, 251		E	
❑	Long-tailed (Eastern) Paradise-Whydah	Vidua paradisaea	146, 164, 200, 340			
❑	Broad-tailed Paradise-Whydah	Vidua obtusa	241, 243, 281, 282, 283, 287, 300, 323, 330, 355			
❑	Variable Indigobird ( )	Vidua funerea	188			
❑	Purple Indigobird (Purple Widowfinch)	Vidua purpurascens	188, 196			
❑	**Zambezi Indigobird**	**Vidua codringtoni**	276, 277, 333, 402		NE	
❑	Village Indigobird (Steel-blue Widowfinch)	Vidua chalybeata	188, 196, 226, 335			
	Fringillidae	**Canaries and Finches**				
❑	Common Chaffinch	Fringilla coelebs	31, 32			3
❑	Yellow-fronted (Yellow-eyed) Canary	Serinus mozambicus	109, 140, 280			
❑	Black-throated Canary	Serinus atrogularis	81, 93, 214, 224, 227			
❑	**Lemon-breasted Canary**	**Serinus citrinipectus**	130, 140, 144, 189, 190, 196, 280, 295, 296, 316, 403		E	
❑	**Cape Canary**	**Serinus canicollis**	54, 108, 158		E	

	Common Name	Scientific name	Page numbers	Reg	End	Vag
❑	Yellow-crowned Canary	Serinus flavicollis	324, 325	B		
❑	Southern Citril	Serinus hypostictus	305, 309, 314, 315, 316, 318, 320, 324, 325, 327, 329, 331, 353	B		
❑	Black-faced Canary	Serinus capistratus	348, 353, 354	B		
❑	**Forest Canary**	**Serinus scotops**	18, 28, 30, 69, 72, 103, 108, 117, 129, 173, 174, 175		E	
❑	**Cape Siskin**	**Pseudochloroptila totta**	17, 27, 30, 31, 32, 33, 34, 39, 41, 60, 63, 66, 73, 75, 96, 102, 103, 403		E	
❑	**Drakensberg Siskin**	**Pseudochloroptila symonsi**	18, 107, 111, 116, 117, 150, 157, 158, 159, 160		E	
❑	**Black-headed Canary**	**Alario alario**	16, 55, 58, 59, 60, 61, 76, 77, 78, 80, 81, 82, 83, 86, 110, 140, 403		E	
❑	**Damara Canary**	**Alario leucolaema**	83, 86, 209, 210		E	
❑	Brimstone (Bully) Canary	Serinus sulphuratus	30, 35, 41, 54, 120, 176, 295			
❑	**Yellow Canary**	**Serinus flaviventris**	46, 47, 48, 50, 51, 56, 61, 65, 117, 162, 164, 167, 204, 207		E	
❑	**White-throated Canary**	**Serinus albogularis**	46, 48, 50, 54, 56, 58, 60, 83, 84, 95, 98, 109, 110		E	
❑	Reichard's (Stripe-breasted) Seedeater	Serinus reichardi	310, 311, 320, 323, 326, 351	B		
❑	Yellow-browed Seedeater	Serinus whytii	326, 327, 329	B		
❑	**Protea Seedeater**	**Serinus leucopterus**	17, 42, 44, 54, 60, 63, 75,95, 96, 103, 403		E	
❑	**Streaky-headed Seedeater**	**Serinus gularis**	42, 54, 68, 96, 109, 128		E	
❑	**Black-eared Seedeater**	**Serinus mennelli**	110, 269, 271, 279, 294, 295, 300, 303, 320, 322, 323, 326, 347		NE	
❑	Oriole Finch	Linurgus olivaceus	324, 328, 331	B		
	Emberizidae	**Buntings**				
❑	Cabanis's Bunting	Emberiza cabanisi	270, 271, 275, 276, 279, 287, 300, 303, 309, 324, 326, 330, 346, 347, 351			
❑	Golden-breasted Bunting	Emberiza flaviventris	92, 126, 193, 346			
❑	**Cape Bunting**	**Emberiza capensis**	33, 46, 48, 50, 60, 77, 96, 110, 156, 158, 160, 173, 215, 279		NE	
❑	Cinnamon-breasted Bunting	Emberiza tahapisi	110, 158, 173, 194, 203, 215, 224, 228, 247, 324, 335			
❑	**Lark-like Bunting**	**Emberiza impetuani**	58, 61, 79, 82, 89, 98, 210, 224		E	

GENERAL INDEX

MAMMALS INDEX